Economic Policy in the International Economy

This book contains fifteen major essays on international economics. The authors investigate five principal themes: theory and empirics of financial issues in open economies; economic growth; public economies; and political economy. Written to honor Professor Assaf Razin of Tel Aviv and Cornell Universities on the occasion of his sixtieth birthday, the essays pay close attention to policy issues as well as formal analysis. The contributors include renowned specialists in international economics based in North America, Europe, Israel, and China. This volume of cutting-edge research will be of interest to scholars, policy makers, and advanced students alike.

Elhanan Helpman is Professor of Economics at Harvard University, Archie Sherman Professor of International Economic Relations at Tel Aviv University, and Fellow of the Canadian Institute for Advanced Research. A cofounder of the "new trade theory" and "new growth theory," he is coauthor of four major works in international economics: *Market Structure and Foreign Trade* and *Trade Policy and Market Structure*, both with Paul Krugman, and *Innovation and Growth in the Global Economy* and *Special Interest Politics*, both with Gene Grossman. Professor Helpman has served as President of the Econometric Society, of which he is also a Fellow, as Editor of the *European Economic Review*, and as Coeditor of the *Journal of International Economics*. He is Member of the Israeli Academy of Sciences and Humanities, a Foreign Honorary Member of the American Academy of Arts and Sciences, and an Honorary Member of the American Economic Association. He received the Israel Prize in 1991, among other awards.

Efraim Sadka is Henry Kaufman Professor of International Capital Markets at Tel Aviv University and Research Fellow at CESifo, Munich. From 1982 to 1985 he served as Chairman of the Eitan Berglas School of Economics, Tel Aviv University, and from 1987 to 1989 he served as the Director of the Sapir Center for Economic Development there. He is the author or coauthor of seven books, including *Population Economics*, *The Economy of Modern Israel*, and *Labor, Capital and Finance*, all with Assaf Razin. Professor Sadka has published articles in the *American Economic Review*, the *Quarterly Journal of Economics*, the *Review of Economic Studies*, *Econometrica*, the *Journal of Political Economy*, the *Journal of Public Economics*, and the *Journal of International Economics*. He is Associate Editor of the journals *International Tax and Public Finance* and *Finanz Archiv*, and Coeditor of CESifo *Economic Studies*.

T0323569

Economic Policy in the International Economy

Essays in Honor of Assaf Razin

Edited by

ELHANAN HELPMAN

Harvard and Tel Aviv Universities

EFRAIM SADKA

Tel Aviv University

CAMBRIDGE
UNIVERSITY PRESS

CAMBRIDGE UNIVERSITY PRESS
Cambridge, New York, Melbourne, Madrid, Cape Town,
Singapore, São Paulo, Delhi, Tokyo, Mexico City

Cambridge University Press
The Edinburgh Building, Cambridge CB2 8RU, UK

Published in the United States of America by Cambridge University Press, New York

www.cambridge.org
Information on this title: www.cambridge.org/9780521178426

First published 2003
First paperback edition 2011

A catalogue record for this publication is available from the British Library

Library of Congress Cataloguing in Publication data
Economic policy in the international economy : essays in honor of Assaf Razin.
488 p. 228 cm.
Papers presented at a conference in honor of Assaf Razin's 60th birthday at the Tel Aviv
University, Mar. 25–26, 2001.
Includes bibliographical references and index.
ISBN 0-521-81519-3
1. Economic policy – Congresses.   2. Economic development – Congresses.
3. International finance – Congresses.   4. International economic relations – Congresses.
I. Razin, Assaf.   II. Helpman, Elhanan.   III. Sadka, Efraim.

HD87 .E26135   2002
337 – dc21   2002024456

ISBN 978-0-521-81519-2 Hardback
ISBN 978-0-521-17842-6 Paperback

Contents

List of Contributors

David Altig
Federal Reserve Bank
Cleveland, Ohio, USA

Carlos Arteta
Department of Economics
University of California
Berkeley, California, USA

Alan J. Auerbach
Department of Economics
University of California
Berkeley, California, USA

Gadi Barlevy
Department of Economics
Northwestern University
Evanston, Illinois, USA

Barry Eichengreen
Department of Economics
University of California
Berkeley, California, USA

Robert P. Flood
Research Department
International Monetary Fund
Washington, D.C., USA

Vitor Gaspar
European Central Bank
Frankfurt, Germany

Roger H. Gordon
Department of Economics
University of California
La Jolla, California, USA

Sebnem Kalemli-Ozcan
Department of Economics
University of Houston
Houston, Texas, USA

Laurence J. Kotlikoff
Boston University
Boston, Massachusetts, USA

Paul Krugman
Department of Economics
Princeton University
Princeton, New Jersey, USA

Prakash Loungani
Research Department
International Monetary Fund
Washington, D.C., USA

Enrique G. Mendoza
Department of Economics
Duke University and NBER
Durham, North Carolina, USA

Yair Mundlak
Faculty of Agriculture
The Hebrew University
Rehovoth, Israel

Maurice Obstfeld
Department of Economics
University of California
Berkeley, California, USA

Torsten Persson
Institute for International Economic Studies
Stockholm University
Stockholm, Sweden

Kenneth S. Rogoff
Research Department
International Monetary Fund
Washington, D.C., USA

Andrew K. Rose
Haas School of Business Administration
University of California
Berkeley, California, USA

Hans-Werner Sinn
Center for Economic Studies
University of Munich
Munich, Germany

Kent A. Smetters
Wharton School
University of Pennsylvania
Philadelphia, Pennsylvania, USA

Bent E. Sørensen
Department of Economics
SUNY-Binghamton
Binghamton, New York, USA

Phillip Swagel
Research Department
International Monetary Fund
Washington, D.C., USA

Aaron Tornell
Department of Economics
University of California
Los Angeles, California, USA

Jan Walliser
International Monetary Fund
Washington, D.C., USA

Charles Wyplosz
Graduate Institute
of International Studies and ICMB
Geneva, Switzerland

Oved Yosha
The Eitan Berglas School of Economics
Tel Aviv University
Tel Aviv, Israel

Chi-Wa Yuen
University of Hong Kong,
Peking University,
and Wuhan University
People's Republic of China

Preface

Assaf Razin is a distinguished economist who has made major contributions to a number of fields. He is particularly known for his work on human capital and growth, the economics of the family, public economics, and international economics. In international economics he played a major role in the application of modern analytical tools to the study of the balance of payments and exchange rates. He is one of the founders of the intertemporal approach to the balance of payments and his book with Jacob Frenkel established a standard for all future work in this area.

But Assaf Razin is not only a great scholar. He is also one of the founders of the Department of Economics at Tel Aviv University, where he has spent most of his adult life. And he is a great friend. For all these reasons it was indeed a pleasure and a privilege for us to organize a conference in honor of his 60th birthday. The organization proved to be an easy task, because Assaf's many friends happily flocked from all over the globe to celebrate his birthday. As a result we were able to bring together the most distinguished members of our profession to discuss international economic issues. This volume contains the papers from that conference, which took place at the Eitan Berglas School of Economics at Tel Aviv University, March 25–26, 2001.

The conference was organized and funded by the Sapir Center for Development Studies. We thank the Center for its contribution to what turned out to be a magnificent event.

Introduction

This volume brings together fifteen essays from various fields of economics to which Assaf Razin has made major contributions in the last thirty years – international economics, economic growth, public economics, and political economy. They all share a common feature: close relevance to economic policy, something which is at the essence of all of Assaf's contributions.

In "Crises: The Next Generation?" Paul Krugman reviews the evolution of the literature on currency and financial crises and suggests a direction to which this literature will turn in the future. The first-generation models were tailored to address a simple scenario. A government maintains a fixed exchange rate while running a budget deficit. The budget deficit is monetized, leading to a loss of foreign exchange reserves. As the level of reserves reaches a lower bound there is a run on the central bank that wipes out the remaining reserves. Unable to support the exchange rate, the government floats the currency. Under these circumstances the timing of the crisis is predictable, as are its consequences. It is an inevitable outcome of a set of inconsistent policies.

This description suited various episodes during the operation of the Bretton Woods system. With the advent of floating exchange rates, however, the nature of crises changed. This is particularly true of the 1992 episodes in Europe, which triggered the development of second-generation models. In these models the government is endowed with a reaction function; namely, its policy reacts to the economic environment. In particular, it is expected to abandon the defense of an exchange rate target in the face of a major speculative attack. As a result, a major speculative attack leads to a crisis, and the crisis is consistent with self-fulfilling

1

expectations. Importantly, now a crisis can occur for no evident economic reason.

Third-generation models were developed after the Asian crisis of the late 1990s. These models paid particular attention to balance sheet effects and, in some cases, to the banking sector. Unlike the previous models, they allowed for a decline in output as part of a crisis.

The balance sheet effect operates when capital markets are imperfect. In such economies poor balance sheet positions restrict the borrowing opportunities of enterprises and limit their investment levels. Companies that are exposed to foreign currency risks as a result of past foreign-currency–denominated borrowing suffer a deterioration of their net worth as a result of a currency depreciation. In response they cut back investment projects, bringing about a decline in aggregate demand. As a result there can be multiple self-fulfilling expectations equilibria, some with a strong currency and a high level of economic activity, others with a weak currency and a low level of economic activity. Under these circumstances an economy that operates in a good equilibrium – with a strong currency and a high level of economic activity – can suddenly shift to a bad equilibrium – with a weak currency and a low level of economic activity – because traders change their expectations about the value of the currency.

While the balance sheet effect that works through the liability side has been emphasized by third-generation models, Krugman suggests that one can take a broader view of such effects. In particular, on the asset side of the balance sheet the value of the assets depends on asset prices and those are related to expectations. As a result, a decline in confidence can lead to a decline in asset prices which leads in turn to a decline in investment that validates the decline in asset prices. This channel produces a positive feedback that allows pessimism to feed on itself.

Importantly, the policy implications depend on the mechanism that has caused a crisis and whether the economy is in a liquidity trap. These ideas are examined with the help of simple models that illustrate their explanatory potential.

Chi-Wa Yuen examines alternative ways to defend a fixed exchange rate. In "Solutions (?) to the 'Devaluation Bias': Some Preventive Measures to Defend Fixed Exchange Rates against Self-Fulfilling Attacks" he draws an analogy between a "devaluation bias" and an "inflation bias." He then shows how the conclusions from the "inflation bias" literature can be used to shed light on the design of policies for the defense of an exchange rate. This defense is designed to prevent an expectations-based self-fulfilling currency crisis of the second-generation type.

As in the literature on monetary policy and central banking, in this case too an exit penalty helps. Namely, the likelihood of a crisis is reduced when the policymaker pays a price for abandoning the fixed exchange rate. And if this price is high enough no speculative attack takes place. The appointment of a conservative central banker, who places high weight on the exchange rate target, is also helpful. But such a central banker cannot secure a first best outcome as long as his weight on the exchange rate target is not infinite. On the other hand, there exists a contract that induces the central banker to credibly defend the exchange rate.

After discussing how practical these solutions may be, Yuen compares a fixed exchange rate that is defended by monetary policy with a fixed exchange rate that is defended by a currency board. Drawing on the experience of Hong Kong around the times of the Asian financial crisis, he argues why these solutions may not work to exclude the speculative attacks of the "double market play" type and discusses the usefulness of "convertibility insurance" as an alternative defensive measure.

Aaron Tornell argues in "Growth-Enhancing Effects of Bailout Guarantees" that the fact that such guarantees can lead to a financial crisis does not make them necessarily undesirable, and moreover, that a crisis of this sort is not intimately linked to a fixed exchange rate regime. In economies with severe credit constraints, financial liberalization often leads to faster growth. This is because financial liberalization eases borrowing constraints and thereby encourages investment. At the same time financial liberalization may generate political pressure to extend bailout guarantees, at least on the transition path. Clearly not every bailout guarantee works equally well. For example, unconditional bailouts introduce well-known moral hazard problems that can cause severe damage of their own. But systemic bailouts, argues Tornell, can in fact play a useful role. In this context a systemic bailout is a bailout that takes place in case of broad-based failures only. Namely, a company cannot count on being saved from its own action or an idiosyncratic shock. It can expect to be saved, however, when many other companies fail.

To make these points Tornell develops a model economy with traded and nontraded goods in which firms face borrowing constraints in the nontraded sector. The introduction of bailout guarantees into such an economy provides an implicit subsidy that eases borrowing constraints and might lead to higher growth. However, the guarantees induce firms to borrow in foreign currency. This makes the financial system vulnerable to a self-fulfilling crisis in which balance sheet effects play an important role. Such sunspot equilibria exist only if crisis is a rare event. Importantly, a crisis is more likely to happen toward the end of an economic boom. This feature is in line with the evidence that crises of the new kind are preceded by lending booms, as well as by the evidence that many lending booms have not ended in a crisis.

Maurice Obstfeld and Kenneth Rogoff founded the "new open economy macroeconomics." This school of thought uses monopolistic competition to describe product markets and some form of nominal staggering in prices or wages. Importantly, consumer demand is derived from well-specified utility functions, which are then used to evaluate alternative policies and exchange rate regimes.

In "Risk and Exchange Rates" Obstfeld and Rogoff develop a detailed model of international macroeconomic fluctuations in which wages are flexible, while monopolistically competitive firms set prices while facing uncertainty about the state of the economy. These prices are frequently adjusted, but always before the resolution of uncertainty about the demand level. As a result shifts in demand affect output.

Using assumptions about the distributions of the underlying shocks, they solve explicitly for the equilibrium first and second moments of key variables. This enables them to shed light on a host of important issues. They show, for example, that home-currency denominated assets can serve as a useful hedge against consumption risk whenever home monetary volatility is an important source of uncertainty. They also show circumstances in which, in a two-country world, the two countries rank similarly alternative exchange rate regimes. And they show how their model can be used to calculate the value of reduced volatility that results from the adoption of a fixed exchange rate. Evidently, the model is suitable for addressing major macroeconomic questions.

Economic integration has many facets, and debates about the desirability of integration have proceeded along several lines. An important set of arguments concerns the comovement of output levels. Output can fluctuate for various reasons, and the framework developed in "Economic Integration, Industrial Specialization, and the Asymmetry of Macroeconomic Fluctuations" is suitable for dealing with most of them.

Sebnem Kalemli-Ozcan, Bent Sørensen, and Oved Yosha propose a two-way decomposition of output fluctuations: One component – which depends on the sectoral composition of the economy – is sensitive to sector-specific shocks, while the other component is sensitive to economy-wide shocks. Unlike previous studies, which have focused on the latter component, the authors examine the importance of the sectoral composition. Countries or regions that differ in sectoral structure will experience different output fluctuations. In particular, countries or regions that are more specialized at the sectoral level are expected to experience larger output volatility.

Rather than using simple measures of volatility, as is common in much of the literature, the authors develop a novel measure that is based on the theory of risk bearing. This measure equals the percentage increase in base consumption that provides the same gain in the expected present value of utility as the substitution from consuming one's own GDP to consuming a fixed fraction of the aggregate GDP that will obtain under perfect risk sharing (here aggregate output refers to the aggregation across all countries or regions). With the help of standard assumptions about the stochastic properties of the economies, they derive a closed-form solution for this measure.

After developing indexes of sectoral specialization patterns, they show with the aid of data from OECD countries and the United States that regions with more specialized sectoral structures experience more asymmetric output fluctuations. This central result is robust to estimation methods (IV versus OLS) and alternative specifications. The instrumental variables estimation also lends support to the hypothesis that the effect runs from sectoral specialization to asymmetry of output fluctuations. The authors then discuss the implications of this finding for debates about the desirability of economic integration.

Uncovered interest parity plays a prominent role in the theory of international finance. As an example, the use of an interest rate policy in defence of currency values is effective only in the absence of uncovered interest parity. In various periods preceding the 1990s the uncovered interest parity hypothesis was rejected, however. In "Uncovered Interest Parity in Crisis: The Interest Rate Defense in the 1990s" Robert Flood and Andrew Rose suggest that the 1990s may provide a better testing ground for this relationship, because during that decade a number of countries experienced financial crises as a result of which those data exhibit large cross-country variations.

After explaining the basic theory, Flood and Rose test for uncovered interest parity in a sample of twenty-three countries. The sample includes developed and developing countries. In every group some countries experienced a financial crises in the 1990s and others did not. Unlike previous studies, they find some support for the uncovered interest parity hypothesis. But one of the most striking results is the large heterogeneity of the estimated coefficients across countries.

In the last part of the chapter they examine the efficacy of an interest rate policy in defending an exchange rate. The results are mixed. Although the data do not reject the efficacy of such policies outright, they also do not support it.

The gains-from-trade literature suggests that the "invisible hand" is present also in the international arena. Trade openness and international capital flows are conducive to growth and well-being. However, whereas there are ample empirical studies to support the hypothesis of a positive effect of trade in goods and especially inward foreign direct investment on economic growth, the empirical evidence on the effect of financial capital flows (that is, capital account liberalization) is less convincing. Carlos Arteta, Barry Eichengreen, and Charles Wyplosz provide a fresh look and new interpretations on the latter evidence. They allude to the second-best theory: When there are many imperfections and distortions in the domestic financial markets and macroeconomic imbalances (such as persistent large public deficits), capital account liberalization may actually depress rather than enhance economic growth and well-being. Thus, high-income countries which are usually characterized by more efficient financial markets and institutions and by the absence of macroeconomic imbalances may benefit from capital market liberalization more than low-income countries with less-developed financial systems and often with macroeconomic imbalances. Arteta, Eichengreen, and Wyplosz emphasize the importance of the sequencing of economic reforms: First, an efficient financial system should be developed, trade openness promoted, black-market foreign exchange premia (reflecting macroeconomic imbalances) eliminated and only then the capital account liberalized.

Not surprisingly, Prakash Loungani and Phillip Swagel find macroeconomic imbalances to be significant in "Sources of Inflation in Developing Countries." In fact, the fiscal deficit is the key source of inflation in "large deficit" (over five percent of GDP) countries. But "small deficits" were found to have little impact on inflation. The sources of inflation are also found to vary from fixed exchange rate regimes (as in most of the countries in Africa and Asia) to floating exchange rate regimes (as in most of the countries in South America). In the first group of countries, past realizations of inflation and inertial forces play a dominant role; oil and non-oil commodity prices have also a statistically significant effect on inflation in these countries; money growth plays a lesser though statistically significant role. In the second group of countries, the dominant role is played by macroeconomic variables such as money growth and exchange rate shocks.

Like Kalemli-Ozcan et al., Gadi Barlevy also deals with the importance of fluctuations, but from a very different perspective. Robert Lucas in his book on business cycles presented an important argument about the welfare costs of consumption fluctuations. Fitting a model of consumption growth to data from the United States economy, he estimated the average rate of growth of aggregate consumption as well as its volatility around this trend. He then estimated the fraction of initial consumption that the consumer would be willing to sacrifice in order to eliminate the volatility of consumption around its growth path. This fraction turned out to be extremely small, less than one-tenth of one percent. It has been interpreted as a measure of gains from the elimination of business cycles, the implication being that business cycles are not very costly. At the same time, Lucas argued, a one percentage point increase in the rate of growth of consumption would be valued at 20% of its initial level, suggesting that growth is much more important than fluctuations.

In "Growth Effects and the Cost of Business Cycles" Barlevy revisits this issue, suggesting that the cost of business cycles can be much larger if fluctuations affect the average rate of growth. In order to demonstrate a link between fluctuations and growth, he develops a neoclassical model of economic growth in which capital accumulation does not depress the marginal productivity of capital. As a result, capital accumulation can sustain long-run growth.

In Barlevy's economy the rate of growth depends on the level of investment, which depends in turn on the level of economic activity. Under the circumstances the stabilization of output shocks around their mean affects the rate of growth through two distinct channels. First, it changes the average rate of investment and higher investment stimulates faster growth. Second, it changes the *volatility* of investment, which affects average growth.

Using estimates of the link between average growth and the volatility of output or investment, Barlevy suggests that the effect of investment volatility has a substantial influence on the rate of growth; its elimination would increase the rate of growth by one-half of one percent. Based on Lucas' estimate of the value of growth rates, this is valued at 10% of initial consumption. Evidently, this is much larger than the less than one-tenth of one percent value of the reduction in consumption fluctuations.

Barlevy's estimates assume a constant average investment level. Therefore they provide a lower bound on welfare gains, because the optimal response to the elimination of shocks includes a change in average investment. He then goes on to examine a variety of other issues that need to be addressed in order to obtain a reliable estimate of such welfare gains. The bottom line is, however, that once growth rates are linked to volatility, the elimination of fluctuations can produce large welfare gains.

Yair Mundlak examines economic growth from a different perspective in his chapter "Explaining Economic Growth." Recognizing the importance of technological change, he proposes to distinguish between *available technology* and *implemented technology*. Evidently, as knowledge accumulates in the world economy it improves the available technology, but not every country benefits from these improvements to the same degree. Some countries are able to implement larger fractions of the available technology than others. As a result income per capita differs between countries not only because of differences in, say, capital–labor ratios, but also as a result of differences in implemented technology. The fraction of the available technology that is implemented depends in turn on a country's economic environment, which consists of resource constraints, restrictions on their mobility, and incentives. This approach can be used to interpret the evidence in a somewhat different way and it has implications for the empirical methodology.

After reviewing the evidence on the sources of economic growth, Mundlak illustrates an empirical application of these ideas to agricultural production functions, using a sample of 37 countries over the period 1970–91. The pooled data are used to fit regressions between countries, based on country means; between time, based on annual means; and within time–country, based on deviations of the observations from country means and annual means. Under the neoclassical framework of growth analysis, the estimates obtained from these alternative regressions should be the same, but they are not. Importantly, the elasticity of output with respect to capital differs across these regressions, and in particular, the elasticity of the between-time regression is about three times as large as the other two. Mundlak discusses the interpretation of the findings in the context of growth analysis that aims at explaining the diversity in the growth experience across countries and over time.

David Altig, Alan Auerbach, Laurence Kotlikoff, Kent Smetters, and Jan Walliser simulate tax reform in "Simulating Fundamental Tax Reform in the United States." They employ a detailed general equilibrium microeconomic model with perfect foresight and with intragenerational heterogeneity with respect to earnings ability, bequest preferences, and other features. Output is produced by capital and labor according to a

Cobb–Douglas or some other constant-elasticity-of-substitution production function. The stock of physical capital adjusts slowly, because there are Tobin-type adjustment costs. Altig et al. study five tax reforms that are all fundamental in the sense that they eliminate all specific tax preferences and tax all sources of capital and labor income at the same flat rate, with very few exceptions, such as personal exemptions, full capital expensing, and a higher tax rate on high-wage earners. The reforms are a proportional income tax, a proportional consumption tax, a flat tax, a flat tax with transition relief, and the X tax. A flat tax differs from a proportional consumption tax mainly by allowing a standard deduction. The X tax is essentially a flat tax with a surcharge on high-wage income. All reforms are revenue neutral. The simulations clearly illustrate the uneasy trade-offs among the various tax reforms that policymakers face. The higher the long-run output gain of a reform, the heavier usually is the burden imposed on the initial middle-aged and the elderly or the poorest members of society. As an example, the proportional consumption tax raises long-run output by over nine percent, the highest gain among all five reforms. But it inflicts losses on the initial middle-aged and elderly, and the poorest members of society. In contrast, a flat tax with transition relief that alleviates these losses raises long-run output by less than two percent.

In contrast to the closed-economy model of Altig et al., Enrique Mendoza simulates tax reform in an open economy in "The International Macroeconomics of Taxation and the Case against European Tax Harmonization." Unlike Altig et al., Mendoza's agents are infinitely-lived and identical in all respects (age, preferences, initial endowments, earnings ability). There are two countries (the United Kingdom and Continental Europe, which consists of France, Germany and Italy); one immobile factor (labor) and one mobile factor (capital) that can accumulate only gradually because of adjustment costs; international lending and borrowing, but no cross-border ownership of firms (or physical capital); time-invariant taxes on labor income, on consumption, and on income from physical capital; and balanced fiscal budgets (in present value terms). Mendoza emphasizes three channels through which a tax reform in any one country affects welfare. A change in the capital income tax in one country affects factor prices in both countries (wages and interest rates), the total stock of capital and its distribution between the two countries, and the tax base in every country. It therefore necessitates a revenue-compensating change in some other taxes (specifically, the labor income tax, but not the consumption tax, by assumption). Mendoza simulates the effects of harmonizing the capital income tax in Continental Europe and the United Kingdom. Currently, the effective capital income tax is 47% in the United Kingdom, but only 28% in continental Europe. If these rates were harmonized at their average level of 37.5%, then capital would flow from Continental Europe to the United Kingdom, enlarging the capital income tax base in the latter and shrinking it in the former. This would enable the United Kingdom to lower its labor income tax by 1.8 percentage points. Revenues from the capital income tax in Continental Europe would not rise as a result of the tax hike (because capital would flow out), and therefore the labor tax rate would remain unchanged. All in all, the United Kingdom would record a welfare gain equivalent to a 2% permanent increase in consumption, whereas Continental Europe would suffer a 2.7% welfare loss.

Taxation of capital income in the integrated world economy is the primary focus of Roger Gordon and Vitor Gaspar in "Home Bias in Portfolio and Taxation of Asset Income." Empirical evidence suggests that there is a strong home bias in equity investment. This is often used to explain the so-called Feldstein–Horioka puzzle: The strong positive correlation between national saving and domestic investment, despite the fact that an open economy can channel its national saving into foreign investment. Gordon and Gaspar begin by constructing a simple model of the world economy with price and exchange rate fluctuations in which investors can hedge against random domestic prices by purchasing domestic stocks. Therefore, when the monetary policy focuses on stabilizing the exchange rate and leaves domestic prices to fluctuate randomly, a home bias in equity investment arises. On the other hand, when the monetary policy stabilizes domestic prices the home bias disappears. Nevertheless, Gordon and Gaspar find that under both monetary policy regimes domestic investment responds strongly and positively to an increase in national saving.

They then proceed to examine the implications of their model to the taxation of risky capital income. The existing literature on international taxation often argues that the case for capital income taxation in the open economy is significantly weakened, because of either enforcement or efficiency considerations. Yet Gordon and Gaspar conclude that it is efficient to levy a tax on capital income when the monetary policy stabilizes domestic prices and the home bias vanishes. And the case for taxing capital income becomes particularly weak when monetary policy stabilizes the exchange rate, allowing domestic prices to fluctuate.

Hans-Werner Sinn examines in "Social Dumping in the Transition Process" the normative and positive aspects of labor market regulations along the transformation path of an (initially) less developed economy that joins a well-developed economic union. These regulations may include a weekly maximum working time, minimum safety standards, minimum time for maternity leaves, and various other workers' rights that raise labor costs. At the normative level, Sinn examines the question whether the national government fails to establish "adequate" regulations. He constructs a simple analytical model in which physical capital can freely flow from the developed economies in an economic union to the underdeveloped newcomer, allowing for a Tobin-type adjustment cost of investment. Workers can migrate in the opposite direction, but with an increasing cost of living abroad. Sinn refutes the complaint often raised by business representatives and union leaders in the developed economies that governments in the less developed economies are engaged in social dumping. He shows that there are no externalities between the underdeveloped economies and the developed ones. Thus, when the national government in an underdeveloped economy designs a system of labor standards so as to maximize the welfare of its citizens, then the welfare of the union is maximized too. Therefore, there is no need for a supranational government to design a uniform set of labor standards.

At the positive level, Sinn describes the transition path of the less developed country that joins a developed economic union. At first, capital flows from the capital-abundant developed countries to the labor-abundant underdeveloped country, but not all at once, because there are adjustment costs of investment. Labor flows in the opposite direction. The flow of capital dissipates gradually over time and migrants return home until the capital–labor ratio in the (initially) less developed economy rises to the level that exists in the developed economies.

"Do Political Institutions Shape Economic Policy?" This question is addressed by Torsten Persson. The answer is naturally in the affirmative. However, the more difficult question is how. Together with Guido Tabellini, Persson has made some of the more important contributions to this subject. In this chapter he reviews the implications of various theoretical models for the impact of political institutions on the conduct of fiscal policy. These predictions are then examined with data from a large panel of countries.

Persson focuses on electoral rules and political regimes. Electoral rules are classified according to the size of districts and the electoral formula. The latter determines how votes translate into seats in a legislative body. Some systems combine small voting districts with plurality rules. Others combine large districts with proportional representation. Some countries have presidential regimes, others have parliamentary regimes.

Some theoretical models predict that the size of government and spending on broad programs should be smaller in presidential regimes. They also predict smaller political rents in presidential regimes. And spending on broad programs should be smaller in systems with proportional representation.

The empirical findings support the prediction that presidential regimes have smaller governments and countries with majoritarian election rules have smaller welfare-state–type programs. But the data also raise a number of interesting puzzles that are carefully discussed by the author, suggesting directions for future research.

PART ONE

FINANCIAL ISSUES IN OPEN ECONOMIES: THEORY

## ONE

Crises: The Next Generation?

Paul Krugman

When I first began working on the theory of currency crises in 1977, I imagined that it was a subject mainly of historical interest. The motivating events were the speculative attacks that brought down the Bretton Woods system in 1971 and the Smithsonian system in 1973. Given the end of fixed rates for major economies, it seemed unlikely that such events would recur.

Of course, that's not how it turned out. The fixed rates of Latin American nations offered a target for large speculative attacks in the runup to the debt crisis of the 1980s; the fixed rates of the European Monetary System offered targets for a wave of speculative attacks in 1992–93; and the more or less fixed rates of Asian and other developing nations offered targets for yet another round of attacks in 1997–98.

Yet while the continuing relevance of the general idea of speculative attacks has justified the original theoretical interest in the subject, the actual models have not fared as well. When Eichengreen, Rose, and Wyplosz (1995) introduced the terminology of "first-generation" and "second-generation" crisis models, they also highlighted the somewhat disheartening fact that each wave of crises seems to elicit a new style of model, one that makes sense of the crisis *after the fact*. And sure enough, the Asian crisis led to a proliferation of "third-generation" models, quite different from either the first or the second generation. (Like third-generation mobile phone service, the third generation of crisis models has not yet quite lived up to its billing. Producers have not been able to agree on a common set of standards, and with the fading of the Asian financial crisis there is also question about whether we have a "killer ap." But with recent financial news in Japan and the United States, things may be looking up.)

This paper represents a very rough effort to get ahead of the curve, by asking what a "fourth-generation" crisis model might look like. The main insight, if there is one, is that third-generation currency crisis models are actually not very specific to *currency* crises: the mechanisms for speculative attack and self-fulfilling pessimism that these models identify, while they do make room for an Asian-style crisis in which capital flight leads to plunging currencies that validate the initial loss of confidence, also allow with small modification for other types of financial crisis. In particular, some third-generation crisis models are very close in spirit to the closed-economy "financial fragility" models of Bernanke and Gertler (1989). What this suggests is that a fourth-generation crisis model may not be a currency crisis model at all; it may be a more general financial crisis model in which other asset prices play the starring role.

Moreover, I will argue that even the open-economy aspects of third-generation models may not be all that crucial. It's true that a simple story of financial collapse is easier to tell if one assumes that capital has someplace else to run to; otherwise, a loss of confidence leads to a fall in the price of capital, which at first sight seems to rule out the kind of self-fulfilling loop that plays so central a role in many models. However, this need not always be the case. In particular, I will argue for a tie-in between the possibility of financial crisis and another one of my obsessions, the possibility of Japanese-style liquidity traps.

This paper is in four parts. The first part briefly summarizes the evolution of currency crisis models, from first generation to third. The second part focuses on third-generation models, and in particular on what they say about policy during a crisis. The third part then offers a highly stylized open-economy fourth-generation model. The fourth part offers a loose translation of that model into closed-economy IS-LM-type macroeconomics, which allows a discussion of policy options during a fourth-generation crisis.

1. A Brief History of Currency Crisis Modeling

The history of currency crisis modeling is presumably familiar to all economists working in international macroeconomics. The only value that can be added in this brief recapitulation is an effort to identify several trends that seem to be present in the moves between successive generations.

First-generation crisis models, exemplified by Krugman (1979) and Flood and Garber (1984) essentially viewed a central bank's efforts to peg an exchange rate using reserves as being similar to a commodity agency's efforts to peg a resource price using its stockpile. In each case, if there is a long-run upward trend in the "shadow price" – the resource price or exchange rate that would prevail if the stock of resources or foreign exchange were all to be sold – the stabilization policy is ultimately doomed. And in fact in each case it can be shown that rational, fully informed speculators will abruptly clean out the stock the instant the shadow price exceeds the peg. The reason is backward induction: Any delay would offer an opportunity for capital gains, so individual speculators have an incentive to purchase the stock ahead of the expected crisis date; and in so doing they advance that crisis date, until it occurs at the earliest possible moment.

From the perspective of what has happened since, there are three things worth noting about this analysis.

First, the root cause of the crisis is poor government policy. In these models, the source of the upward trend in the shadow exchange rate is the government's need for seignorage; solve the fiscal problem and there would be no crisis. And the speculative target is provided by the government's pursuit of inconsistent policies: persistent deficits together with an exchange rate peg. So the models basically imply that governments get the crisis they deserve.

Second, the crisis, though sudden, is deterministic: A crisis is inevitable given the policies, and the timing is in principle predictable (though a look at the models suggests that it would be very hard to predict that timing in practice.)

Finally, the credibility of the finance minister aside, first-generation crises seem to do no harm. They only reveal an economic problem that was there in any case. The simple models, by construction, cannot exhibit a postcrisis recession; but even if one tries to introduce realistic features like nontraded goods and even price stickiness, it is more or less impossible to generate a real-economy slump in the aftermath of a first-generation currency crisis.

In self-defense, I might note that the currency crises of the early 1970s, which were the inspiration for the original model, did in retrospect seem inevitable; and also that they were not followed by real-side punishment. So all of this did not seem as off-base then as it does now, several major waves of crisis later. The Latin American crisis of 1982 *was* followed by a real-side slump; but while currency runs were part of the story there, the main event seemed to be a sovereign debt crisis, which plausibly could explain the nasty output and employment consequences.

On to the second generation. The inspiration for second-generation modeling was the series of speculative attacks on EMS currencies in 1992–93; the seminal papers were by Obstfeld (1994a,b).

There were several obvious divergences in the EMS crisis from the assumptions of first-generation models. Seignorage was not an issue: the governments involved retained access to capital markets throughout, and the activities of their printing presses were dictated by macroeconomic policy considerations, not budget needs. Indeed, it's hard to see much evidence of irresponsible policies in any of the countries involved. Also, there was not an obvious long-run trend in equilibrium exchange rates – a point that has gained even more force as the years have passed, and the pound sterling has actually appreciated to well above its precrisis level against continental currencies. Finally, the connection between capital flight and abandonment of the peg was not the mechanical linkage envisioned in the early models – you run out of reserves, and that's it. Instead, it was a matter of policy choice: In 1992 British officials chose not to pay the price for defending the pound with higher interest rates, while French officials made the opposite decision.

So the second-generation models gave a quite different version of what a crisis was all about. In truth Obstfeld (1994a) offers several variants, and one of them is a budget-driven story that, while not about seignorage per se, is still about fiscal imperatives. But the main story that has stuck focuses on macroeconomic tradeoffs and decisions.

In the canonical version, more or less based on Britain in September 1992, a country's government has imperfectly committed itself to a currency peg at an uncomfortable level. That is, the level of the currency is one that constrains monetary policy, forcing the government to accept a lower level of employment in the short run than it would otherwise have wanted to have. Nonetheless, as long as the peg is credible, this is a price that the government is willing to pay, presumably because there are political and/or long-run economic goals served by maintaining the peg.

However, if the peg ceases to be credible, investors will demand higher interest rates in order to hold assets denominated in the country's currency. And if the government defends the peg by providing those higher interest rates, it will worsen employment, increase financial distress (the prevalence of floating-rate mortgages in Britain was a key political consideration in 1992), or both. So even a government that would be willing to pay the price of sustaining its peg in the absence of speculative attack might be unwilling to stand up to such an attack. And so speculators who believe that other speculators are about to attack are themselves encouraged to do so. The result is the possibility of self-fulfilling crises of confidence.

Two points of difference between this story and the previous one: First, crises are no longer the result of obviously irresponsible policy. Perhaps one can argue that a government should not try to peg unless it is unalterably committed to the peg – the "bipolar" hypothesis, aka the law of the excluded middle. But much of the stigma is removed from government actions.

Second, the determinacy of the crisis is removed. There is a question about whether second-generation models necessarily imply that crises are self-fulfilling, or for that matter whether self-fulfilling crises can occur for first-generation reasons. However, the general thrust of the second-generation models is toward the idea that crises may occur suddenly in situations where no crisis seemed inevitable.

One point from the earlier models remains, however: If a speculative attack drives a currency off its peg, this does not imply a negative shock to employment and output. Indeed, in this case the contrary should be true: because the policy constraint of a peg is removed, the result is actually positive for short-run macroeconomics. (Other costs may lie down the road, assuming that the government had some good reason for adopting the peg, but that is a different question.)

Again, this result seemed broadly plausible after the EMS crisis, since Britain at least did quite well after its ejection from the Exchange Rate Mechanism. (I used to joke that they should put up a statue of George Soros in Trafalgar Square.) But obviously this implication raises eyebrows when one comes to the Asian crisis. Admittedly one crisis country, Brazil, discovered that it was more like Britain than like Thailand: Its devaluation, when it came, turned out to be expansionary rather than contractionary (and this good news, arguably, marked the end of the crisis.) But the general rule was that currency crises led to severe short-term real output declines.

At this point there are three main variants of the third-generation crisis story; I bear some of the blame for two of them. One version involves moral-hazard-driven investment, which leads to an excessive buildup of external debt and then to a collapse. This story has its origins in work by McKinnon and Pill (1996), was picked up in Krugman (1998), and was extensively developed in papers by Corsetti, Pesenti, and Roubini (1998). A second version, largely associated with Chang and Velasco (1998a,b) is built around open-economy versions of the Diamond–Dybvig bank-run model.

Finally, a third story stresses the balance-sheet implications of currency depreciation. A crude formal version of this type of third-generation model was in Krugman (1999a), and an even cruder but easier to understand informal version in Krugman (1999b). A number of more sophisticated models have since been developed, including efforts like that of Schneider and Tornell (2000) to combine a moral-hazard-driven bubble with a balance-sheet driven crisis when the bubble bursts.

It is this third variant that I will focus on, and will review in the next part of the paper. But let me now say something about the direction in which the literature seems to have trended.

In the original crisis models a currency crisis was something that was deserved, predictable, and harmless. That is, it was caused by the government's pursuit of contradictory and unsustainable policies; given this, it had to happen, and indeed had to happen at a particular time; and since it only made the economic fundamentals visible, the crisis did not actually damage the economy. With the second generation models it becomes much less clear that the crisis is deserved, and it becomes unpredictable, though it is still mostly harmless. With the third-generation models, crises become a clearly bad thing – largely because they are no longer mainly about monetary policy. Indeed, as we'll see shortly, the depreciation of the nominal exchange rate becomes more a symptom than a fundamental aspect of these crises.

2. The Balance-Sheet View of Crises

The third-generation model that I introduced in Krugman (1999a) was in a sense similar in spirit to the Chang–Velasco bank-run models: It attempted to explain crises in terms of a flight of capital from an economy that was not fundamentally unsound. However, I was concerned that what seemed to me to be the most striking aspect of the Asian crisis, the dramatic reversal in the current account balances as a share of GDP, did not seem crucial – and also therefore that the dilemmas of economic policy in a crisis were not fully captured. Quoting myself: "Despite the evident centrality of the transfer problem to what actually happened to Asia, this issue has been remarkably absent from formal models. Perhaps because the modelers have been mainly concerned with the behavior of investors rather than with the real economy per se, all of the major models so far have been one-good models in which domestic goods can be freely converted into foreign and vice versa without any movement in the terms of trade or the real exchange rate."

How could the transfer problem be placed at the center of the story? The balance-sheet problems that clearly afflicted Asian economies (and still afflict them, years later) offered a natural link. Start with highly leveraged firms with lots of foreign-currency-denominated debt, and imagine a large outflow of capital for whatever reason. This would lead to currency depreciation, which would greatly reduce if not eliminate the net worth of firms. And if one supposes, in the fashion of Bernanke and Gertler (1989) that an imperfect capital market means that firms with poor balance sheets cannot invest, the result can be a real investment collapse that validates the capital flight.

Let me not do a restatement of the original model, but instead focus on the "cartoon" version offered in Krugman (1999b). This version "translates" the more formal version, which is actually a real model with no monetary variables, into a modified version of the Mundell–Fleming model. The simplest version of Mundell–Fleming involves three equations. First is an aggregate demand equation relating domestic spending to real income and the interest rate, together with net exports that depend on the real exchange rate:

$$y = D(y, i) + NX(eP^*/P, y), \qquad (1)$$

where D is domestic demand, y real output, i the numeral interest rate, NX net exports, e the exchange rate, and P and P^* the domestic and foreign price levels.

Second is a money-demand equation:

$$M/P = L(y, i), \qquad (2)$$

where M is the money supply.

Finally, in the simplest version, investors are supposed to be risk-neutral and have static expectations about the exchange rate, implying an interest-arbitrage equation

$$i = i^*. \qquad (3)$$

In practice, this model is too simple for even the most basic uses; in particular, nobody believes in static expectations about e. Even if one is prepared to dismiss rational intertemporal modeling, almost everyone would prefer a version of (3) in which markets expect e to return to some "normal" value, possibly one determined by purchasing power parity. But let us stick with the simplest version.

This setup can be regarded as simultaneously determining output y and the exchange rate e. Figure 1.1 shows how this works. The curve AA shows

Price of foreign exchange, *e*

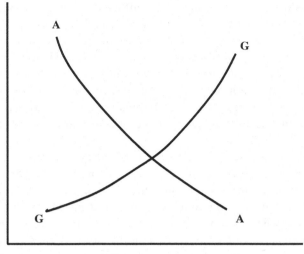

Figure 1.1. Macroeconomic equilibrium in an open economy: the normal case

all the points at which, given (2), the domestic and foreign interest rates are equal. Meanwhile, the curve GG shows how output is determined given the exchange rate; it is upward-sloping because depreciation increases net exports and therefore stimulates the economy.

To turn this into a model that can yield crises, all we need to do is add a strong balance sheet effect from currency depreciation. Suppose, then, that many firms are highly leveraged, that a substantial part of their debt is denominated in foreign currency, and that under some circumstances their investment will be constrained by their balance sheets. Then the aggregate demand equation will have to include a direct dependence of domestic demand on the real exchange rate:

$$y = D(y, i, eP^*/P) + NX(eP^*/P, y). \tag{1'}$$

Let's also, for the sake of a slight improvement in realism, suppose that "fear of floating" leads the central bank to lean against the exchange rate, so that we replace the AA curve with one that includes a monetary response:

$$M(e)/P = L(y, i) \text{ with } M \text{ decreasing in } e.$$

This gives an AA curve that is backward-bending; as we'll see in a second, this helps us tell a story about output effects.

The importance of the balance-sheet effect would depend on the level of the exchange rate. At very favorable exchange rates, few firms would be balance-sheet constrained; so at low $eP*/P$ the direct effect of the exchange rate on aggregate demand would be minor. At very *unfavorable* real exchange rates, firms with foreign-currency debt would be unable to invest at all, and therefore the direct exchange-rate effect on demand would be trivial at the margin. But in an intermediate range, the effect might be large enough to outweigh the direct effect on export competitiveness, so that over that range depreciation of the currency would be contractionary rather than expansionary.

So, as suggested by Aghion, Bacchetta, and Banerjee (1999), we might expect the GG curve to have a backward-bending segment, as in Fig. 1.2; and hence there could be multiple stable equilibria, one with a "normal" exchange rate, one with a hyperdepreciated exchange rate and a bankrupt corporate sector; given that monetary policy becomes more contractionary, we also get a fall in output.

And so we have the possibility of a third-generation currency crisis. Something – it could be anything – causes a sudden large currency depreciation; this depreciation creates havoc with balance sheets; and the economy plunges into the crisis equilibrium.

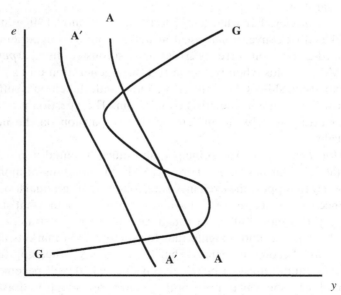

Figure 1.2. Balance-sheet effects and multiple equilibria

It's all very crude and ad hoc; but it does seem to get at some of the issues that arise in real crises. In particular, this approach helps suggest why policy during a crisis is so difficult. In Krugman (1999b) I ran through the usual answers and found each one wanting:

1. *IMF financial support*: This provides a country with additional funds to intervene in the exchange market – more dollars to support the baht, won, whatever. Leaving aside monetary policy, however, this is a *sterilized* intervention; so it is an attempt to use sterilized intervention to move the exchange rate away from the crisis equilibrium. Calling the IMF the international lender of last resort sounds impressive; calling it, more accurately, the "sterilized intervenor of last resort" probably more accurately conveys the limits of what it can accomplish.

2. *Rollovers and standstills*: Anything that induces investors who would otherwise have tried to convert domestic currency into dollars not to do so is in effect a sterilized intervention on behalf of the currency. And if there is a very large pool of mobile capital, a standstill that freezes only bank loans (or even one that also freezes bondholders) will alter the composition of capital flight but not its volume; the economy can still be plunged into the bad equilibrium regardless.

3. *Fiscal policy*: For what it worth, this kind of model suggests that instead of conventional fiscal austerity, countries experiencing a third-generation currency crisis ought to consider fiscal *expansion*. (More on this when we come to fourth-generation crises.) Fiscal expansion shifts GG to the right, and if undertaken on a sufficient scale can rule out the crisis equilibrium. The question is whether countries are able to undertake such expansion on the needed scale.

4. *Monetary policy*: The principal, and much-disputed, tool in IMF stabilizations has been a temporary sharp tightening of monetary policy to support the exchange rate, following by gradual loosening once confidence seems to have been restored. Somewhat surprisingly, this model allows a rough rationale for this strategy. Consider Fig. 1.2, and imagine that for some reason markets appear to have become convinced that the economy is heading for the crisis equilibrium – a belief that, if unchecked, will become self-fulfilling. One way to prevent this from happening is to drastically tighten monetary policy, shifting the AA curve so far to the left that it becomes like A'A' – that is, far enough to rule out the crisis

equilibrium. Once investors have become convinced that the exchange rate is not going to depreciate massively, this monetary contraction can be relaxed. The problem, of course, is that along the way the economy faces a sharp contraction in real output, with all the social and perhaps political disruption that causes. And in any case, the exchange rate is not the only potential source of balance-sheet problems – which will become apparent when we come to the fourth-generation model.

5. *Structural reform*: When crises occur, governments are invariably urged to announce and implement major structural reforms such as privatization, cleanup of bad banks, and so forth. In the context of our model, it is hard to see why this is an effective crisis policy. That is not to say that structural reform is a bad thing: many crisis countries had (and still have) very unsound economic systems. But if you believe that the crisis itself is mainly a matter of self-fulfilling pessimism, it is hard to see why structural reform should be helpful – unless, the all-purpose answer, it somehow leads to increased confidence.

The kind of reasoning described above is what led me to endorse the idea of ruling out the bad equilibrium by *force majeure*, imposing capital controls as a temporary emergency measure during a crisis. Nothing that has happened since suggests that this was a silly position: Malaysia clearly got away with controls, and recent analysis by Kaplan and Rodrik (2001) makes a plausible case that the controls did a lot of short-term good. However, let me not dwell on this point, because my fourth-generation approach will lead in a quite different direction.

Instead, let me emphasize a funny thing about this type of model. If one grants that the effects of asset prices like the exchange rate are a key linkage in financial crisis, why emphasize the exchange rate above other alternatives? The main answer is experience: Exchange rate movements seem to have played a key role in the most recent major bout of financial crises. But if we want to get ahead of the curve, to do models not of the last wave of crises but of possible future crises, we should look for what is possible given our general approach rather than what has already happened.

So here's my proposal for a fourth-generation crisis model: It looks a lot like a third-generation model, except that it considers asset prices other than the exchange rate.

Having said that, one quickly realizes that to a large extent the model already exists, in the Bernanke et al. analysis of balance-sheet effects and financial fragility in domestic macro. But in the remainder of this paper I will try to take that analysis to a few new places, and stress the continuity with the currency crisis modeling.

3. Asset Prices and Crises

The starting point for the particular variant of third-generation crisis model I have described is the observation, stressed by Bernanke and Gertler (1989) in a domestic-macro context, that balance sheets matter – that in an imperfect capital market the ability of firms to exploit even profitable investment opportunities may depend on their ability to provide sufficient collateral to let them borrow the needed funds. The potential havoc wrought by currency depreciation then operates through the liability side of that balance sheet: If the price of foreign exchange rises, and firms have foreign currency debt, their net worth falls.

But why not also talk about the asset side of the balance sheet? The natural, and not at all original, story is one in which a decline in confidence leads to declining asset prices, which leads to a fall in investment that validates both the decline in asset prices and the fall in confidence.

The point I want to make in this section is how easily such considerations can turn a negative-feedback story with a unique equilibrium into a positive-feedback story where pessimism can feed on itself.

Consider, then, a setup similar to the illustrative model in Bernanke and Gertler (1989), but even more artificial. We imagine a small open economy, producing a single tradable good. The economy lasts for only two periods. In period 0 investors may or may not borrow "seed money" to get themselves into business; there are N such investors, and each must borrow B in terms of the single good to get started. The real interest rate on this borrowing is r, and we may take it as given.

Each investor is also endowed with an equal share of a productive resource, with the total quantity of that resource equal to K. In period 1 an investor who has made the initial investment of B can choose to produce according to a production function $F(k)$, where k is the amount of the resource he uses. He may use either more or less than he owns, selling any surplus for a price q. The price of the resource will be determined in a competitive market in which those potential investors who borrowed the necessary seed money are the buyers, and the potential investors who did not borrow are the sellers.

Suppose that $n < N$ potential investors actually went ahead. Then it is immediately apparent that the price of the resource will be

$$q = F'(K/n), \qquad (4)$$

which is increasing in n. It is also immediately apparent that an investor who does borrow will earn an economic profit of

$$EP = S(q)/(1+r) - B, \qquad (5)$$

where $S(q)$ is the "surplus" earned in period 1 over and above the cost – either market cost or opportunity cost – of the resources used in production. $S(q)$ will be decreasing in q; so from (4) and (5) we see that the profitability of investing is decreasing in the number of actual investors.

If capital markets were perfect, then, there would be a unique equilibrium value of n – perhaps 0 or N, but also possibly an interior solution.

But now suppose that there are problems with monitoring. Again following Bernanke and Gertler (1989), let me suppose that these are extreme: that the lender in period 0 has no way of knowing what the borrower has done with the loan. The lender's only recourse in the case of nonpayment is the ability to seize the borrower's marketable resource in period 1. So the lender will not lend more than the borrower's collateral:

$$B \le (qK/N)/(1+r). \qquad (6)$$

Suppose that (6) is always binding – that is, that investing is always profitable, *if* the seed money can be borrowed. But q is increasing in n. So we now have the result that each investor will invest – will be *able* to invest – only if enough other investors are also expected to invest, so that his collateral is worth enough to persuade lenders to give him the necessary seed money.

And we therefore have multiple equilibria. One equilibrium is with all N potential investors investing; this leads to a high q, which allows each investor to offer sufficient collateral to raise the necessary seed money. The other equilibrium is with no investment, and hence in this hard-edged model a zero q, so that nobody has collateral – and hence nobody can invest.

"Stylized" doesn't do justice to the unrealism of this model, but it makes the point: Balance-sheet considerations can turn what would otherwise be a model with a unique equilibrium into one in which self-fulfilling pessimism can cause investment to collapse, not because of the exchange rate and transfer problems stressed in the third-generation crisis models, but because of the effects of confidence on domestic asset prices. The basic story line is pretty much the same, but the asset price is different.

With some tweaking it would clearly be possible to soften the result in this model, making self-fulfilling financial crisis something that is possible under certain conditions, rather than always. It would also clearly be possible to put the usual suspects into the list of factors creating vulnerability: excessive past investment, high leverage, and so on. However, let me leave this model with the observation that we have now seen that the basic story of the latest wave of currency crisis models is basically a story about financial crises in general, and that the exchange rate need not play the starring (or any) role in that story. And with that let me move to the translation into IS-LM–type modeling.

4. Financial Crisis in a Closed Economy

Let's now see how the story described above could lead to a crisis scenario that is a close cousin of the Asian-style crisis modeled earlier, but this time in a closed economy. (We need not really mean that the economy is closed, only that domestic asset markets rather than the currency market become central.) To do this we make the jump already implicit in the symbols used above, namely that the q we are talking about is indeed Tobin's q.

We start by assuming a demand-side driven economy, which implicitly means assuming some kind of nominal stickiness, in which q determines investment and hence through a multiplier the level of output:

$$y = y(q). \tag{7}$$

What determines q? Having done a rigorous if silly model, we can now allow ourselves some serious ad hockery; so let's simply suppose that q is increasing in y, which determines profits, and decreasing in i. (This is pretty much how the models of market gurus like Abby Joseph Cohen work! Is that a positive or negative indicator?)

$$q = q(y, i). \tag{8}$$

Rather than have a money demand function, let me last follow the suggestion of Romer (2000) and go directly to a monetary reaction function, which in this stripped-down exposition is simply a matter of the central bank raising interest rates if y is high, reducing them if y is low.

$$i = i(y). \tag{9}$$

Equation (7) will define a goods-market equilibrium schedule; Equations (8) and (9) together an asset-market equilibrium schedule. So we can think about this cartoon model in y, q space.

Drawing on the old tradition of nonlinear business cycle theory (e.g., Tobin 1955), we can suppose that the impact of q on y is nonlinear. Below some level reducing q has little effect, because gross investment is near

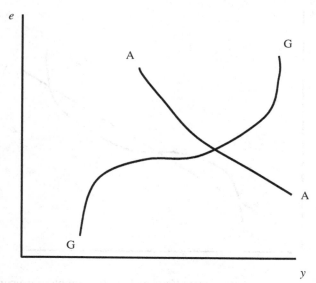

Figure 1.3. Macroeconomic equilibrium in a closed economy

zero and cannot go any lower; above some level raising q also has little effect, because capacity constraints or something prevent further expansion. (My vagueness is deliberate.) So we get a goods-market equilibrium schedule that looks like the curve GG in Fig. 1.3. The family resemblance to GG in the previous figures is not accidental.

What about asset-market equilibrium? This depends both on the private-sector response (8) and on the monetary reaction function (9). Clearly, the schedule can slope either way.

If the monetary authority is sufficiently responsive to output levels, the schedule AA is downward-sloping, as in Fig. 1.4. In that case there is a unique equilibrium, and nothing that looks like a financial crisis.

If the monetary authority is not sufficiently responsive, we can have an upward-sloping AA schedule, and therefore the possibility of multiple equilibria as in Fig. 1.4. So one could envision a version of financial crisis in which the economy suddenly jumps to the bad equilibrium here, and that monetary policy simply is not responsive enough to prevent it from doing so. However, that is a pretty unconvincing story, or at any rate one that calls simply for better policy at the central bank.

If one wants a really scary story, one has to imagine that for some reason the central bank *cannot* cut the interest rate enough to make the AA curve slope downward. And of course there is such a scenario: What

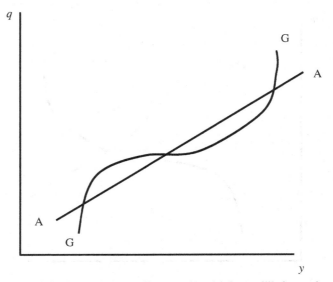

Figure 1.4. Balance sheet effects and multiple equilibria, again

if the interest rate is already at zero? Then we have the zero-bound or liquidity trap story, which becomes a very serious one if one is depending on monetary policy to avert financial crisis. The picture would look like Fig. 1.5: as y declines the monetary authority would cut i enough to make AA downward-sloping, but once the interest rate is zero there is nothing more it can do, and the AA curve becomes upward-sloping. In that case monetary policy cannot rule out the bad equilibrium, if it exists.

Now we have our domestic financial-market counterpart to the currency crisis story. Something happens to confidence: a technology bubble bursts, or a hapless Prime Minister refuses to resign, or a president talks down the economy in an effort to build support for his tax cut, or something. The result is a drop in asset prices that, because of its effects on investment, deflates the economy, validating that price decline; and the central bank is unable to stop the collapse into the bad equilibrium even by cutting rates all the way to zero.

At this point the policy options become limited. I have argued at length, in the case of Japan, that zero is not necessarily a lower bound for inflation – that promises to pursue an inflation target should in principle be able to reduce the real interest rate below zero and hence regain traction for monetary policy. Work by Svensson (2000), in particular, has refined that idea, suggesting that price level and/or exchange rate targets might serve the purpose better than an inflation target. However, in all

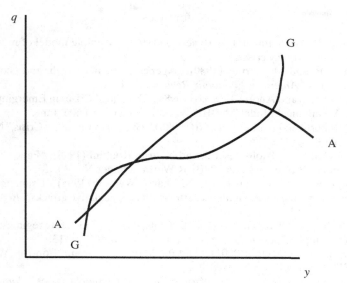

Figure 1.5. The zero bound and multiple equilibria

cases such policies would be hard to make credible – and credibility is all-important.

This is also the kind of situation in which "pump-priming" fiscal expansion could live up to its name: a sufficiently large temporary fiscal expansion could rule out the bad equilibrium and put the economy back into a favorable equilibrium. Again, the key words are "sufficiently large": half-hearted fiscal expansion, Japanese-style, would not be enough to achieve self-sustaining recovery.

In the event of such a crisis one could also be sure to hear calls for structural reform. As in the case of currency crisis, however, it is hard to see why such reform would actually help in dealing with the crisis as opposed to raising general efficiency.

The general point is that intellectually consistent solutions to a domestic financial crisis of this type, like solutions to a third-generation currency crisis, are likely to seem too radical to be implemented in practice. And partial measures are likely to fail.

So that is my proposal for a fourth-generation crisis approach – one that could certainly be refined and made far more rigorous. Have I succeeded in the goal of getting ahead of the curve, of sketching out a model of crisis *before* the events actually occur? Only time will tell. Intellectually, I hope so. But as someone who actually has to live in the world economy, I hope this modeling approach is irrelevant.

References

Aghion, P., P. Bacchetta, and A. Banerjee (1999), "A simple model of monetary policy and currency crises."

Bernanke, B. and M. Gertler (1989), "Agency costs, net worth, and economic fluctuations," *American Economic Review* 79: 14–31.

Chang, Roberto and Andres Velasco (1998a), "Financial Crises in Emerging Markets: A Canonical Model," NBER Working Paper No. 6606, June.

Chang, Roberto and Andres Velasco (1998b) "The Asian Liquidity Crisis," NBER Working Paper No. W6796.

Corsetti, Giancarlo, Paolo Pesenti, and Nouriel Roubini (1998), "Paper Tigers? A Model of the Asian Crisis," NBER Working Paper No. W6783.

Eichengreen, Barry, Andrew Rose, and Charles Wyplosz (1995), "Exchange market mayhem: The antecedents and aftermath of speculative attacks," *Economic Policy*, 251–312.

Flood, Robert and Peter Garber (1984), "Collapsing exchange rate regimes: Some linear examples," *Journal of International Economics* 17: 1–13.

Kaplan, E. and D. Rodrik (2001), "Did the Malaysian Capital Controls Work?" NBER Working Paper No. W8142.

Krugman, Paul (1979), "A model of balance-of-payments crises," *Journal of Money, Credit, and Banking* 11: 311–25.

Krugman, Paul (1998), "What happened to Asia?"

Krugman, Paul (1999a), "Balance sheets, the transfer problem, and financial crises," in Peter Isard, Assaf Razin, and Andrew K. Rose, eds. *International Finance and Financial Crises: Essays in Honor of Robert P. Flood, Jr.*. Boston, Dordrecht and London: Kluwer Academic; Washington, D.C.: International Monetary Fund, pp. 31–44.

Krugman, Paul (1999b) "Analytical afterthoughts on the Asian crisis."

McKinnon, Ronald and Huw Pill (1996), "Credible liberalizations and international capital flows: The 'overborrowing syndrome,' " in T. Ito, and A. Krueger, (eds.), *Financial Deregulation and Integration in East Asia*, Chicago: University of Chicago Press.

Obstfeld, Maurice (1994a), "The logic of currency crises," *Cahiers economique et monetaires* 43:189–212.

Obstfeld, Maurice (1994b).

Schneider, M, and A. Tornell (2000), "Balance Sheet Effects, Bailout Guarantees and Financial Crises," NBER Working Paper No. W8060.

Svensson, L. (2000), "The Zero Bound in an Open Economy: A Foolproof Way of Escaping from a Liquidity Trap," NBER Working Paper No. W7957.

Tobin, J. (1955), "A dynamic aggregative model," *Journal of Political Economy*, 103–15.

Romer, Paul (2000) "Keynesian macroeconomics without the LM curve," NBER working paper No. 7641.

TWO

Solutions (?) to the "Devaluation Bias": Some Preventive Measures to Defend Fixed Exchange Rates against Self-Fulfilling Attacks*

Chi-Wa Yuen

1. Introduction

Research on currency crises has largely been focused on their economic causes – in particular, the role of fundamentals versus self-fulfilling expectations. [See, e.g., Krugman (1979, 1998, 1999, 2001) and Obstfeld (1986, 1994, 1996).] Some attention has recently been directed to the defense of fixed exchange rates against speculative attacks in particular and the prevention of financial crises in general. [See, e.g., Ozkan and Sutherland (1995), Drazen (1999), Flood and Jeanne (2000), and Lahiri and Végh (2000).] Attacks arising from "wrong" fundamentals such as the policy inconsistency in first-generation crisis models of Krugman (1979) and Flood and Garber (1984) are simply unavoidable. The only way to prevent them is to "correct" such fundamentals through, say, better and more consistent coordination of policy actions among different branches of the government. On the other hand, attacks arising from self-fulfilling expectations as in second-generation models of Obstfeld (1996) and in third- and fourth-generation models of Krugman (1999, 2001) are in principle

* Prepared for the conference on "*Economic Policy in the International Economy*" in honor of Assaf Razin's 60th birthday, organized by Elhanan Helpman and Efraim Sadka, at the Pinhas Sapir Center for Development, Tel Aviv University, March 25–26, 2001. I would like to thank Alex Chan, Nai-fu Chen, Leonard Cheng, Alex Cukierman, Sebnem Kalemli-Ozcan, and participants at the Razin conference for useful suggestions and comments. Most of all, I would like to thank Assaf Razin for his fruitful collaboration and unfailing support and encouragement over the years. Though not drawn on any of my joint work with Assaf, this paper belongs to the area of currency crisis, to which he has also made contributions [see, e.g., Milesi-Ferretti and Razin (2001)]. Financial support from the HK Research Grant Council is gratefully acknowledged. The usual disclaimer applies.

avoidable – if, somehow, such expectations can be altered or eliminated by appropriate preventive measures. As Krugman (2001) makes clear, younger (third and fourth) generation models of financial crises based on, say, financial fragility and balance sheet effects – where asset prices other than exchange rates have a more prominent role to play – need not have much to do with currency crisis per se. In this paper, we shall focus on the analysis of the prevention of self-fulfilling currency attacks of the kind examined in second-generation models, and ignore other types of self-fulfilling crises.[1]

Most papers in this currency crisis literature treat standard pegs and currency boards – alternative fixed exchange rate arrangements – as one and the same thing. [Chang and Velasco (2000) is an obvious exception.] Differences between their institutional features (see Appendix (Section 6) for details), however, imply that their adjustment mechanisms in face of currency attacks can be quite different. Specifically, central banks can resort to either foreign exchange intervention or (active) interest rate defense under standard pegs, whereas (passive) interest rate adjustment through bank arbitrage has to be relied upon under currency boards. Between them, would the nature of attacks and thus the desired preventive measures be very different? We shall provide some discussion about this issue.

The objective of this paper is to provide an analysis of alternative preventive measures that can be introduced to defend these two alternative forms of fixed exchange rates against possible attacks. The organization of the paper is as follows. Section 2 reviews the self-fulfilling crisis model of Obstfeld (1996), which we shall use as the theoretical framework throughout. Some solutions familiar from the inflation bias literature – namely, imposition of a reputational constraint, appointment of a conservative central banker, design of an incentive contract for the central banker, and inflation targeting – are examined as possible measures to prevent self-fulfilling attacks in Section 3. These measures can be commonly applied to both regular pegs and currency boards. Section 4 discusses possible differences in forces behind attacks on currency boards rather than standard pegs, and considers convertibility insurance as an alternative defensive measure. Concluding remarks are contained in Section 5.

---

[1] Given the observational equivalence between first- and second-generation models found by Eichengreen, Rose, and Wyplosz (1995), one could mistake a 1G attack for a 2G attack and wrongly apply 2G preventive measures to defend the fixed rate. It is of interest to investigate whether collapse, though inevitable, can be delayed by such measures. By focusing only on 2G attacks, we shall ignore this issue in the current paper.

2. The Self-Fulfilling Crisis Model of Obstfeld (1996)

Suppose, as in Obstfeld (1996), that

* the country in question has adopted a fixed exchange rate regime;
* purchasing power parity holds, so that the rate of change of exchange rate (ε) equals the domestic inflation rate (g_p), given a constant foreign price level ($g_p^* = 0$);
* the government cares about both output stability and exchange rate (hence, inflation) stability, so that its loss function is given by $\mathcal{L} = E[(y - \tilde{y})^2 + \beta\varepsilon^2]$, where y and $\tilde{y}$ are respectively the actual and socially optimal levels of output, and $\beta \in [0, \infty)$ the weight attached to the exchange rate objective;
* the government faces a Lucas-type supply function (mirror image of the expectations-augmented Phillips curve), viz., $y = \bar{y} + \alpha(\varepsilon - \varepsilon^e) - u$, where $\bar{y}$ is the natural level of output (which falls short of the social optimum due to some distortions in the economy, i.e., $\bar{y} = \tilde{y} - d < \tilde{y}$), ε^e the expected rate of devaluation (or inflation), u an adverse supply shock, and $\alpha > 0$ the effectiveness of surprise devaluation (or inflation) in stimulating output; and
* the government enjoys an informational advantage, observing the true value of the supply shock *before* making its decision whether to adhere to the fixed rate regime; while the public observes the realized value of u only *after* (and thus has to form expectations about the equilibrium exchange rate ε^e *before*) the government makes its policy choice.

If the government sticks to the fixed rate regime, then $\varepsilon = 0$ so that $y = \bar{y} - (\alpha\varepsilon^e + u) = \tilde{y} - (\alpha\varepsilon^e + u + d)$ and, given ε^e and the realization of u, its *ex post* policy loss is

$$\mathcal{L}^{\text{fix}} = (y - \tilde{y})^2 = (\alpha\varepsilon^e + u + d)^2. \tag{1}$$

If the government chooses to switch to a floating rate regime either through a devaluation ($\varepsilon > 0$) or a revaluation ($\varepsilon < 0$), its discretionary choice of the rate of change of exchange rate will be determined by solution to the following problem:

$$\text{Min}_{\{\varepsilon\}} E[(y - \tilde{y})^2 + \beta\varepsilon^2 \mid \varepsilon^e, u]$$
$$\text{s.t. } y = \bar{y} + \alpha(\varepsilon - \varepsilon^e) - u \quad \text{and} \quad \tilde{y} = \bar{y} + d.$$

The optimal devaluation rate is given by

$$\varepsilon = \left(\frac{\alpha}{\alpha^2 + \beta}\right)(\alpha\varepsilon^e + u + d), \tag{2}$$

which implies an actual output level of $y = \tilde{y} - (\frac{\beta}{\alpha^2+\beta})(\alpha\varepsilon^e + u + d)$. Hence, the government's *ex post* loss is

$$\mathcal{L}^{\text{flex}} = [(y - \tilde{y})^2 + \beta\varepsilon^2] = \left(\frac{\beta}{\alpha^2 + \beta}\right)(\alpha\varepsilon^e + u + d)^2. \qquad (3)$$

Comparing (1) and (3), we see that $\mathcal{L}^{\text{fix}} \geq \mathcal{L}^{\text{flex}}$ for all possible values of ε^e and u (where the equality holds iff $\alpha\varepsilon^e + u + d = 0$).[2] In other words, in the absence of some preventive measures, the government always has the temptation to voluntarily abandon the peg irrespective of its ability (say, in terms of its reserve position) to maintain it. Understanding this, the public will rationally expect such outcome and choose to attack the regime before it is abandoned. In other words, the fixed rate regime is not sustainable.

This "devaluation bias" is in many ways akin to the "inflation bias" in monetary policy analysis.[3] [See, e.g., Cukierman (1992, Chapter 5), and Walsh (1998, Chapter 8).] For this reason, we examine in the next section whether three "solutions" that have been proposed to reduce or eliminate the latter bias will also work for the former.

3. Some Measures to Prevent Self-Fulfilling Attacks

3.1. Imposing an Exit Penalty or Reputational Constraint (á la *Barro–Gordon (1983)*)

Suppose, in breaking the peg, the government has to incur a fixed exit cost, C, due to, say, loss of reputation and credibility. Given this reputational constraint, the cost C has to be incorporated into $\mathcal{L}^{\text{flex}}$ in (3). Direct comparison of $\mathcal{L}^{\text{fix}}$ in (1) with this modified $\mathcal{L}^{\text{flex}}$ indicates that the government will choose to give up the peg if the supply shock is too large in absolute values. Define the critical shock values as follows:

$$u^0 \equiv \sqrt{\left(\frac{\alpha^2 + \beta}{\alpha^2}\right)C} - (\alpha\varepsilon^e + d) \leq \mu \quad \text{and}$$

$$u_0 \equiv -\sqrt{\left(\frac{\alpha^2 + \beta}{\alpha^2}\right)C} - (\alpha\varepsilon^e + d) \geq -\mu. \qquad (4)$$

---

[2] *Ex ante*, the government's policy losses are respectively $\mathcal{L}^{\text{fix}} = \sigma_u^2 + d^2$ and $\mathcal{L}^{\text{flex}} = (\frac{\beta}{\alpha^2+\beta})\sigma_u^2 + (\frac{\alpha^2+\beta}{\beta})d^2$ (assuming that u has zero mean and constant variance σ_u^2). Hence, $\mathcal{L}^{\text{fix}} \gtreqless \mathcal{L}^{\text{flex}}$ as $\sigma_u^2 \gtreqless (\frac{\alpha^2+\beta}{\beta})d^2$. In other words, σ_u^2 must have been estimated to be smaller than $(\frac{\alpha^2+\beta}{\beta})d^2$ for the fixed rate regime to be chosen in the first place.

[3] This analogy is not surprising, given the purchasing power parity assumption (which implies $\varepsilon = g_p$).

Then, the peg will be kept intact (i.e., $\varepsilon = 0$) if $u_0 \leq u \leq u^0$. There will be a devaluation ($\varepsilon > 0$), however, when $u > u^0$, and a revaluation ($\varepsilon < 0$) when $u < u_0$.

It is not difficult to see that, by setting the punishment at a high enough level, the government can be induced not to switch to the floating rate under all circumstances. Specifically, the society should set C at a level such that $\mathcal{L}^{\text{fix}} \leq \mathcal{L}^{\text{flex}} + C$ at all possible levels of ε^e and for all possible realizations of u, i.e.,

$$C \geq \left(\frac{\alpha^2}{\alpha^2 + \beta}\right)(\alpha\varepsilon^e + u + d)^2 \qquad \text{for all } \varepsilon^e, u. \tag{5}$$

One can easily verify that setting C this way will ensure that the supply shock will always fall within the no-attack zone $[u_0, u^0]$.

Under rational expectations, we have

$$\varepsilon^e = E(\varepsilon) = \Pr(u > u^0) \cdot E(\varepsilon \mid u > u^0) + \Pr(u < u_0) \cdot E(\varepsilon \mid u < u_0), \tag{6}$$

where $E(\varepsilon \mid u > u^0) = (\frac{\alpha}{\alpha^2 + \beta})[(\alpha\varepsilon^e + d) + E(u \mid u > u^0)]$ and $E(\varepsilon \mid u < u_0) = (\frac{\alpha}{\alpha^2 + \beta})[(\alpha\varepsilon^e + d) + E(u \mid u < u_0)]$.[4] As an example, suppose that u is uniformly distributed on $[-\mu, \mu]$, $\mu \in \Re_+$.[5] Then, $\Pr(u > u^0) = \frac{\mu - u^0}{2\mu}$ and $\Pr(u < u_0) = \frac{\mu + u_0}{2\mu}$ whereas $E(u \mid u > u^0) = \frac{\mu + u^0}{2}$ and $E(u \mid u < u_0) = \frac{u_0 - \mu}{2}$. Together with (4), these expressions suggest that (6) is a quadratic equation in ε^e. As Obstfeld (1996) shows, in addition to the two roots corresponding to this quadratic equation, ε^e can assume an even higher value of $\varepsilon^e_{\max} = \alpha d/\beta$ corresponding to the depreciation expectation under a completely flexible exchange rate[6] – as when the devaluation threshold u^0 is stuck at its lower bound $-\mu$.

Despite the possibility of multiple equilibria, the government can fully eliminate self-fulfilling currency crises (i.e., the "bad" equilibria) if it is constrained by a reputational cost of

$$\overline{C} \equiv \left(\frac{\alpha^2}{\alpha^2 + \beta}\right)(\alpha\varepsilon^e_{\max} + u_{\max} + d)^2 = \left(\frac{\alpha^2}{\alpha^2 + \beta}\right)\left[\left(\frac{\alpha^2 + \beta}{\beta}\right)d + \mu\right]^2. \tag{5'}$$

Note that $\overline{C}$ is defined for the worst case scenario, namely, maximum possible levels of ε^e (i.e., $\varepsilon^e_{\max} = \alpha d/\beta$) and u (i.e., $u_{\max} = \mu$). Consequently,

---

[4] We omit the term $\Pr(u_0 \leq u \leq u^0) \cdot E(\varepsilon \mid u_0 \leq u \leq u^0)$ because $\varepsilon = 0$ for $u \in [u_0, u^0]$.

[5] In this case, the definitions of the threshold values of u given in (4) have to be modified as $u^0 \equiv \max\{\min[\sqrt{(\frac{\alpha^2 + \beta}{\alpha^2})}C - (\alpha\varepsilon^e + d), \mu], -\mu\}$ and $u_0 \equiv \min\{\max[-\sqrt{(\frac{\alpha^2 + \beta}{\alpha^2})}C - (\alpha\varepsilon^e + d), -\mu], \mu\}$.

[6] Under a floating rate regime, the (rationally) expected rate or depreciation satisfies $\varepsilon^e = E(\varepsilon) = E[(\frac{\alpha}{\alpha^2 + \beta})(\alpha\varepsilon^e + u + d)] = (\frac{\alpha}{\alpha^2 + \beta})(\alpha\varepsilon^e + d)$, which implies $\varepsilon^e = \frac{\alpha d}{\beta}$.

a sufficient condition for the government to strictly adhere to the fixed rate is to set the exit penalty C at the level $\overline{C}$.[7]

3.2. Appointing a Conservative Central Banker (à la *Rogoff (1985)*)

An alternative way to prevent the government from shifting to a float is to assign the duty of maintaining the peg to a "conservative" central banker, that is, one with a higher weight (say, $\beta + \delta$) attached to the exchange rate objective than the society at large. As a result, the central banker's loss function becomes:

$$\mathcal{L} = E\{[\alpha(\varepsilon - \varepsilon^e) - (u + d)]^2 + (\beta + \delta)\varepsilon^2 \mid \varepsilon^e, u\}, \qquad (7)$$

which implies $\varepsilon = [\frac{\alpha}{\alpha^2 + (\beta + \delta)}](\alpha\varepsilon^e + u + d)$, $y = \tilde{y} - [\frac{\beta}{\alpha^2 + (\beta + \delta)}](\alpha\varepsilon^e + u + d)$, and

$$\mathcal{L}^{\text{flex}} = \left[\frac{\beta + \delta}{\alpha^2 + (\beta + \delta)}\right](\alpha\varepsilon^e + u + d)^2. \qquad (3')$$

How weight-conservative do we want this central banker to be? From (3'), we require $\delta \to \infty$ for $\mathcal{L}^{\text{flex}} \to (\alpha\varepsilon^e + u + d)^2 = \mathcal{L}^{\text{fix}}$ – unless $u = -(\alpha\varepsilon^e + d)$, in which case the conservative banker has no role to play anyway. This means that, in the absence of the exit penalty, the difficult task of eliminating self-fulfilling attacks should be assigned to a die-hard conservative – one with $\beta + \delta \simeq \infty$.[8]

It is straightforward to show, however, that the socially optimal level of δ – obtained from minimizing the (indirect) social loss function with respect to δ – is finite.[9] In other words, although this conservative central banker solution is feasible, it is by no means socially efficient.

3.3. Designing an Incentive Contract for the Central Banker (à la *Walsh (1995)*)

Instead of punishing a noncredible central banker or appointing an ultra-conservative one, we can design a compensation package for the banker to give her/him the proper incentive to adhere strictly to the peg.

---

[7] Morris and Shin (1998) have shown how introducing some noise in speculators' observations of the fundamentals may help eliminate the multiple equilibria.

[8] In the presence of the exit penalty, we require $\delta \geq (\frac{\alpha^2}{C})(\alpha\varepsilon^e + u + d)^2 - (\alpha^2 + \beta)$ for all ε^e and u, which implies that setting δ at $\bar{\delta} = (\frac{\alpha^2}{C})(\alpha\varepsilon^e_{\max} + u_{\max} + d)^2 - (\alpha^2 + \beta)$ will do. This suggests that a combination of reputational constraint and conservativeness would work better than pure (ultra) conservativeness.

[9] This is because, from the society's perspective, an increase in δ will induce a higher variability in output while containing the variability in exchange rates.

Suppose the incentive contract takes the simple linear form:

$$W(\varepsilon) = W_0 + \omega\varepsilon. \tag{8}$$

In the presence of this contract, the wage compensation W has to be deducted from the government's objective function to obtain the relevant (net) policy losses.

Under the fixed rate regime, $\varepsilon = 0$ so that $W(\varepsilon) = W_0$ and the central banker's *ex post* policy loss is

$$\mathcal{L}^{\text{fix}} = (\alpha\varepsilon^e + u + d)^2 - W_0. \tag{1'}$$

Under the alternative floating rate regime, the optimal choice of ε is determined by minimization of the loss function:

$$\mathcal{L} = E\{[\alpha(\varepsilon - \varepsilon^e) - (u + d)]^2 + \beta\varepsilon^2 - W(\varepsilon) \mid \varepsilon^e, u\}. \tag{7'}$$

The optimal devaluation rate becomes

$$\varepsilon = \left(\frac{1}{\alpha^2 + \beta}\right)\left[\alpha(\alpha\varepsilon^e + u + d) + \frac{\omega}{2}\right], \tag{2'}$$

which implies an actual output level of $y = \bar{y} - (\frac{1}{\alpha^2+\beta})[\beta(\alpha\varepsilon^e + u + d) - \frac{\alpha\omega}{2}]$. Hence, the banker's *ex post* loss is

$$\mathcal{L}^{\text{flex}} = \left(\frac{1}{\alpha^2 + \beta}\right)\left\{\beta(\alpha\varepsilon^e + u + d)^2 + \left(\frac{\omega}{2}\right)^2 \right.$$
$$\left. -\omega\left[\alpha(\alpha\varepsilon^e + u + d) + \frac{\omega}{2}\right]\right\} - W_0. \tag{3''}$$

In designing the incentive contract, we would like to choose W_0 and ω in such a way that $\mathcal{L}^{\text{fix}} \leq \mathcal{L}^{\text{flex}}$ for all possible values of ε^e and u. Subtracting (3'') from (1'), we have

$$\mathcal{L}^{\text{fix}} - \mathcal{L}^{\text{flex}} = \left(\frac{1}{\alpha^2 + \beta}\right)\left[\alpha(\alpha\varepsilon^e + u + d) + \frac{\omega}{2}\right]^2 \geq 0.$$

The best we can do in order to maintain the peg is thus to set the *proportional* payment at a rate (contingent on devaluation expectations and realizations of the supply shock[10]):

$$\omega = -2\alpha(\alpha\varepsilon^e + u + d), \tag{8a}$$

[10] In this "state-contingency" or *ex post* sense, the incentive contract we consider here is not the same as the non-state-contingent, *ex ante* contract examined by Walsh (1995).

proportional to ε, so as to keep $\mathcal{L}^{\text{fix}} = \mathcal{L}^{\text{flex}}$. The *lump-sum* component W_0 can be freely set, though, at any finite level. Under such contract, a central banker that chooses to devalue (as expected under large, adverse supply shocks), say, will have to suffer a salary cut proportional to the devaluation rate she/he chooses.[11]

Substituting (8a) into (2'), we get $\varepsilon = 0$ – i.e., under this incentive scheme, the central banker will willingly stick to the peg even though she/he has the option to shift to the float.

3.4. An Assessment of the Practicality of the Three Solutions (and Their Equivalents)

All three solutions considered above hinge upon an independent central bank and the negative correlation between inflation (exchange rate devaluation) and central bank independence. Basically, they all yield the same outcomes in terms of the actual and expected rates of change of exchange rate and the equilibrium level of output.[12] In particular, complete exchange rate stability is achieved, but only at the expense of output volatility.

It is difficult, however, to conceive how these solutions can actually be implemented in practice. Independent central bankers are especially hard to come by in developing countries where corrupt governments are entrusted to oversee everything including monetary and exchange affairs. The second (conservative central banker) solution is even harder to implement due to (a) its social suboptimality as argued above and (b) the difficulty in reality in identifying the true preferences of potential candidates for the central banker. If one is willing to ignore (a), then the problem in (b) can somehow be dodged by assigning to the central banker – whatever her/his degree of conservativeness – a flexible *exchange rate devaluation* (or inflation) *target* of $\bar{\varepsilon} = 0$ and imposing on

---

[11] In the presence of an exit penalty, $\omega = \pm 2\sqrt{(\alpha^2 + \beta)C} - 2\alpha(\alpha\varepsilon^e + u + d)$, where C can be interpreted as the reduction in base salary for the central banker under the flexible rate regime due to, say, the lessened responsibility to manage the exchange rate through intervention in the foreign exchange market.

[12] This implied equivalence between incentive contracts and conservative central banker as solutions to the devaluation bias stands in stark contrast to the superiority of the former to the latter as solutions to the inflation bias. This is because in the case of inflation bias, the monetary policy rule (which allows money supply to respond to the output shock) entails an output-stabilizing effect that is stronger under the former than the latter; whereas in the case of devaluation bias, the fixed exchange rate rule precludes its dependence on the output shock altogether.

her/him a penalty related to deviations from the target devaluation rate of $\mathcal{P} = \rho E(\varepsilon - \bar{\varepsilon})^2$.

Adding this penalty term $\mathcal{P}$ to the central banker's loss function, given $\bar{\varepsilon} = 0$, yields

$$\mathcal{L} = E\{[\alpha(\varepsilon - \varepsilon^e) - (u + d)]^2 + (\beta + \rho)\varepsilon^2 \mid \varepsilon^e, u\}. \qquad (7'')$$

Observe that $(7'')$ is equivalent to the conservative central banker's loss function (7) for $\rho = \delta$. Again, $\mathcal{L}^{\text{flex}} \to \alpha(\varepsilon^e + u + d)^2 = \mathcal{L}^{\text{fix}}$ for $\rho \to \infty$. This means that the penalty for failing to achieve the devaluation target ($\bar{\varepsilon} = 0$) has to be prohibitively high in order to ensure that a central banker with arbitrary weight-conservativeness will try to hit such target. Though plausible, this alternative targeting solution is no more realistic than the original conservative central banker solution.

Turning to the first (reputational constraint) and third (incentive contract) solutions, they are very similar to one another in nature. Both are alternative forms of punishment schemes to deter the central banker from breaking the peg. Due to its simple lump-sum form, the former is nonetheless more easily implementable than the latter.

Once more, the problem is the rarity we actually see them used in practice. Even when adopted, they probably would not assume the exact same forms as these two solutions would dictate. We show below, however, that the incentive contract solution is replicable by a more commonly adopted targeting rule [cf. Svensson (1997)].

Suppose the central banker has been assigned an *exchange rate devaluation target* of $\bar{\varepsilon}$ (possibly different from zero), but the penalty for failing to hit the target is negligibly small (i.e., $\rho \simeq 0$). Then her/his objective function will be altered as follows:

$$\mathcal{L} = E\{[\alpha(\varepsilon - \varepsilon^e) - (u + d)]^2 + \beta(\varepsilon - \bar{\varepsilon})^2 \mid \varepsilon^e, u\}.$$

Upon rearranging terms, we can express it as

$$\mathcal{L} = E\{[\alpha(\varepsilon - \varepsilon^e) - (u + d)]^2 + \beta\varepsilon^2 - V(\bar{\varepsilon}, \varepsilon) \mid \varepsilon^e, u\}, \qquad (7''')$$

where

$$V(\bar{\varepsilon}, \varepsilon) = -\beta\bar{\varepsilon}^2 + (2\beta\bar{\varepsilon})\varepsilon. \qquad (8')$$

Observe that $(7''')$ assumes the same form as $(7')$, and $(8')$ the same form as (8). Consequently, we can equate the slope term in $(8')$ to the ω term in (8a), implying that a devaluation (revaluation if $\alpha\varepsilon^e + u + d < 0$) target of $\bar{\varepsilon} = -\alpha(\alpha\varepsilon^e + u + d)/\beta$ will replicate the incentive contract solution.[13] In this sense, one can view the solution as being more popularly used in this disguised (targeting) form in practice.

4. Are Currency Boards Different from Regular Pegs?

The solutions we have examined thus far do not permit even the slightest adjustment in the exchange rate one way or the other from the fixed parity rate. This is obviously too stringent a restriction to impose on the monetary authority. In reality, most fixed exchange rate regimes around the world are better characterized as "currency bands" and/or "adjustable pegs," where some room for exchange rate movement and/or realignment is allowed. Incorporation of these possibilities will complicate the analysis without affecting the essence of the solutions.[14]

On the other hand, there do exist in the real world exchange rate regimes that are literally "fixed" and have strict rules governing their operations – viz., currency boards. [See Appendix (Section 6) for a brief description of their salient features.] In fact, under this rule-based monetary system, such operational (e.g., reserve backing and exchange rate parity) rules are like laws written in stone.[15] Although there is no explicit statement as to how the monetary authority will be penalized if it fails to abide by the rules, the perceivable costs involved in altering these rules are by no means minor. The deterring effects of these costs are comparable to those of the reputational constraint considered in Section 3.1.

---

[13] In addition, we should set the intercept term $W_0 = -\beta\bar{\varepsilon}^2 = -[\alpha(\alpha\varepsilon^e + u + d)]^2/\beta < 0$. It may not make sense to pay the central banker a negative lump-sum while penalizing her/him for deviations from the peg. But since the lump-sum component does not really affect the central banker's marginal choice between sticking to the peg and switching to the float, we can add an arbitrary constant to convert it into a positive sum without affecting the results.

[14] Currency bands can be modeled by modifying the exit penalty term as follows:

$$C = \begin{cases} 0 & \text{if } \varepsilon \in [\varepsilon^-, \varepsilon^+] \\ \bar{C} & \text{otherwise} \end{cases},$$

where, given the fixed parity at $\bar{e}$, the lower band is $e^- = \bar{e}(1 + \varepsilon^-)$ and the upper band is $e^+ = \bar{e}(1 + \varepsilon^+)$.

[15] For instance, Article 111 of the *Basic Law of the Hong Kong Special Administrative Region of the People's Republic of China* states that "... *[T]he authority to issue the Hong Kong currency shall be vested in the Government of the Hong Kong Special Administrative Region. The issue of the Hong Kong currency must be backed by a 100% reserve fund. The system regarding the issue of the Hong Kong currency and the reserve fund system shall be prescribed by law....*"

Does it mean then that self-fulfilling attacks on currency boards can never occur? Under the *classical* currency board, the monetary base (M_0) is fully backed by foreign reserves so that its convertibility is guaranteed. Coupled with a fractional reserve banking system with a money multiplier larger than unity, however, convertibility of the money supply (M_1 and M_2) is not similarly assured. This suggests that if a currency crisis should ever occur due to internal drains (rather than or in addition to external attacks), it will be accompanied by bank runs. Under our theoretical framework where the public knows for sure the determination and ability of the central banker in maintaining the fixed parity, fortunately, such attacks can be ruled out by the same three solutions examined in the previous section.[16]

Could we thus conclude that, with a credible and strong (in terms of reserves and other economic fundamentals) government and with either one of these preventive measures in place, currency boards will be free from attacks? A glimpse at the recent history of Hong Kong at the height of the Asian financial crisis suggests, unfortunately, that the answer is negative. In October 1997 and again in August 1998, even with its high reserves and sound banking system, the Hong Kong dollar (HKD) was attacked by foreign speculators. In retrospect, these market players might not have expected their actions to result in any sizable depreciation at all. What then motivated them to attack the HKD in the first place? The answer probably lies in their perfect understanding of the operation of the currency board system. Under the system, any attack on the HKD would reduce liquidity in the banking system and thus drive up the interest rate through an automatic adjustment mechanism. Given the negative correlation between the interest rate and stock prices, this would lead to a drop in the prices of Hong Kong stocks. Seeing through such market interrelations, speculators could therefore engineer a "double market play" to make profits by attacking the HKD in the foreign exchange market on the one hand and short-selling Hong Kong stocks in the market for stock futures on the other – without actually causing a collapse in the HKD.[17]

---

[16] If the government views a bank run as inflicting extra costs on the society, then such costs will appear as an extra term in its loss function, thus making it less likely to abandon the fixed parity. In formulating its policy, it will have to be more cautious and to take into account the possibility of triggering bank runs. See Kaminsky and Reinhart (1999) for an analysis of the coexistence of financial and banking crises in general, and Ho (1999) for such analysis in the context of a currency board.

[17] These speculators were ultimately fended off by the Hong Kong Monetary Authority through an intervention in the spot market for Hong Kong stocks.

[See Chakravorti and Lall (2000) for a theoretical analysis of this double play.] These episodes suggest that depreciation expectations is not a necessary condition for a currency attack.[18] What is necessary instead is the existence of some sort of expected profits that the attack could generate.

Obviously, the preventive measures analyzed in Section 3 above do not work here. Two questions immediately come to mind. First, could regular pegs also encounter the "double play" type of attack? Second, what other measure(s) could prevent such attacks?

Regarding the first question, the answer is "yes, but not absolutely necessary." The difference with regular pegs is that the government could choose to use (sterilized) foreign exchange intervention rather than (active) increase in interest rate as a defensive device – so that the expected sharp rise (drop) in interest rates (stock prices) may not materialize to generate profits for the speculators. If the government choose to rely on active interest rate defense instead, however, speculators would still have room to manipulate a double play.[19] Our argument here thus strengthens Flood and Jeanne's (2000) conclusion that raising the interest rate could hasten the speculative attack.[20]

Regarding the second question, it has been noticed that the sharp rise in interest rates in Hong Kong when its currency was attacked in 1997 and 1998 was not merely a natural consequence of auto-piloting, but also a reflection of a confidence problem – that is, depreciation expectations – arising from the discretionary intervention of the Hong Kong Monetary Authority (HKMA) in the currency market in 1997 and in the stock market in 1998. Instead of demonstrating its determination and ability to defend the HKD-USD link, the interventions raised suspicion among the local people about the HKMA's confidence in the currency board system

---

[18] The existence of large players such as Soroi are also not necessary. In principle, such attacks could be initiated either internally or from outside and either by unconcerted efforts among a large group of small players or by large players. It is debatable whether to classify them as "fundamental" or "self-fulfilling" – as one could argue that they arise from a fundamental problem built into the system through its over-reliance on interest rate arbitrage as the sole adjustment mechanism.

[19] The same would be true under foreign exchange interventions if such actions fail to lower depreciation expectations so that the risk premium associated with domestic currency holding will also jack up the domestic interest rate.

[20] Their analysis is conducted in a Krugman–Flood–Garber type first-generation model, where it is shown that while increasing domestic interest rate can make domestic assets more attractive, it will at the same time weaken the domestic currency by increasing the government's fiscal liabilities and thus induce speculative attacks when the economy is fiscally fragile.

itself (which is supposed to be rule-bound and discretion-free). As a costly signal to show its commitment to the public, the HKMA could issue an HKD put option, originally proposed by Chan and Chen (1999) and later endorsed and renamed as structured notes by Miller (1998), at an exercise price equal to the official HKD/USD exchange rate of 7.8 with a 3-month to 6-month maturity (to be reissued upon expiration). They (Chan and Chen 2000) also show in a theoretical model how the government could use such a signaling device to convince the public of its determination to keep the link. In particular, the currency option will help induce a separating equilibrium and rule out self-fulfilling attacks on currencies with relatively good fundamentals. In a nutshell, issuing such options is like providing "convertibility insurance" to lower the public's devaluation expectations.[21] This proposal has been subject to heated debate among academics and policy makers in Hong Kong. Lui, Cheng, and Kwan (2001) argue forcefully that it turns out to be the ultimate winner.[22]

But so far as the convertibility insurance proposal is related to the solution of the devaluation bias, the infamous time inconsistency problem remains. In particular, how can the government, however benevolent and well-intentioned, guarantee that it will never renege on such insurance just as it always has the temptation to default on public debt in its optimal fiscal policy design?[23] We therefore surmise that a combination of the solutions we consider in Section 3 and this insurance proposal will enhance the workability of the latter. The issues here involve the explicit role of foreign reserves and asymmetric information between the government and the public about the former's preferences and constraints, which the

---

[21] Adapting the idea of catastrophe insurance, Chu (2000) has also proposed an introduction of the Soros bonds that pay an interest higher than the market alternatives in ease of an unsuccessful attack, but will be defaulted in case the attack is successful. These bonds play both an insurance role and a strategic role that transforms Soros-followers into domestic-currency defenders. Their workability depends on the public's confidence in the government's determination to defend the peg, which, nonetheless, is usually lacking in times of crisis.

[22] They view that, in addition to strengthening the interest rate arbitrage mechanism, the so-called "technical" measures introduced by the HKMA in September 1998 are functionally equivalent to such convertibility insurance. Using credibility measures extracted from financial market data, they show how the implementation of this proposal has put the HKMA back on a rule-bound track and made the auto-piloting mechanism effective again.

[23] To dodge this problem, Chan and Chen (1999) have also proposed a reserve currency liquidity adjustment facility that allows banks to borrow reserve currency from the monetary authority and to repay either in the same currency with interest or the domestic currency equivalent at the fixed parity rate.

simple theoretical framework of this paper has failed to capture. We shall leave these complications for future research.

5. Conclusion

Drawing on the similarity between the "devaluation bias" and the "inflation bias," we have examined a few solutions familiar from the latter literature as possible preventive measures against self-fulfilling attacks. In some sense, all of them can be thought of as different forms of punishment schemes to penalize the central banker for abandoning the fixed rate. A relevant question that comes to mind is whether, as the psychologists would believe, rewards would be better than punishment? It is straightforward to see that if the reward/penalty is lump-sum (as in the case of a fixed cost of reputation), then rewarding a central banker for doing the right thing is equivalent to punishing a banker for doing the wrong thing. If the reward/penalty is made some function of the exchange rate deviation ε (as in the case of an incentive contract for the central banker), however, then the reward scheme will not work because the reward base is zero when the central banker is adhering to the peg.[24]

One obvious limitation of this analogy between the twin biases lies in its reliance on the PPP assumption. But since PPP is a long-run implication, whereas speculative attacks and currency crises are short-run problems, it is important to examine the robustness of our results in the absence of PPP – as when $g_p = \varepsilon + \nu$, where ν is a random disturbance. [See Yuen (2001).]

Besides our proposed measures, are there alternative solutions that others have proposed but we have somehow overlooked? Among others, the most prominent one is capital controls. [See, e.g., Krugman (1999) and Kaplan and Rodrik (2001).] Such controls are designed to fend off external attacks (say, by giant players like Soros), but will be useless when attacks are initiated by *internal* drains or a confidence crisis from within such as in the framework we have been using.

In addition to capital controls, Ozkan and Sutherland (1995) have also considered other solutions to increase the life expectancy of a fixed exchange rate. Their second solution – raising the costs of leaving the fixed rate – is essentially the same as our exit penalty. However, their third and fourth solutions – increasing the average maturity of private debt

---

[24] When the reward/penalty is infinitely large (as in the case of a conservative central banker), it is again immaterial which scheme is adopted in practice.

and altering the policy-maker's discount rate – can only be examined by dynamizing our theoretical framework.

Obviously, our analysis conducted in such a simple static framework has limited our ability to address many interesting questions. The supply shock is assumed to have been observed by the central banker before it makes its policy choice. How would the absence of knowledge about the shock affect its policy decisions and the usefulness of the preventive measures considered in this paper? Could asymmetric information between the public and the monetary authority about the latter's determination and ability to commit as well as its degree of conservativeness give rise to self-fulfilling attacks on fixed exchange rates? [See, e.g., Cukierman (1992, Chapter 16) and Drazen (1999).] If so, what preventive measures are needed? What other preventive measures are required to rule out self-fulfilling attacks of the type induced by financial fragility, balance sheet effects, and liquidity traps as emphasized by third- and fourth-generation models of financial crises *à la* Krugman (1999, 2001)? [See also Kaminsky and Reinhart (1999).] These issues are left for future research.

6. Appendix: Salient Features of Currency Boards

Fixed exchange rates are seldom "fixed" literally. Instead, they typically have explicit finite bands (sometimes called "currency bands" or "target zones") within which exchange rates are allowed to fluctuate without any central bank interventions. For instance, the bands were ±1% around dollar parities under the Bretton Woods System and ±2.25% around bilateral central rates against member currencies under the European Monetary System. On the other hand, there does exist in reality an extreme form of "fixed" rate regime where the rate is rigidly fixed at some level without any bands around it. One such example is the linked exchange rate regime under the currency board system as currently adopted by Hong Kong, Argentina, and some East European countries.

Under pure currency boards, there are rigid reserve backing rules that govern the issuance of currency and legal restrictions on revisions of exchange rates and on the discretionary use of other policy tools. In this sense, a currency board can be interpreted as a rule-based monetary system that serves to establish credibility in exchange rate stability. In outlook, however, the "standard pegs" and the "linked rate" are so similar that many people fail to make the distinction and simply think of them as one and the same system, thus leading to a lot of confusions in the debate about the merits of the latter *vis à vis* the floating rate regime. [See, e.g., Roubini (1998).]

One major difference between currency boards and currency bands lies in the adjustment mechanism that will be triggered whenever the otherwise market equilibrium exchange rate deviates from the target rate in the former case and from the (upper and lower) bands in the latter. In the former case, the disequilibrium (over- or undervaluation of the domestic currency) will be eliminated through an automatic adjustment in the domestic interest rate – that is, through market forces.[25] In the latter case, the disequilibrium has to be corrected through central bank interventions in the foreign exchange market and/or active use of interest rate policy as a defensive device – that is, through artificial forces. One implication of this difference is that a country adopting an orthodox currency board need not have a central bank. As a consequence, there is no room for monetary policies and there is no lender of last resort under a classical currency board system.

In summary, the distinct features of a *pure* or *classical* currency board include:

- *reserve backing rule:* 100% backing of the monetary base by foreign exchange reserves, hence full convertibility of M_0, which implies restrictions on currency issuance and credit creation;
- *commitment to exchange rate parity:* an explicit legislative commitment to exchange domestic currency for a specified foreign (reserve) currency at a fixed exchange rate (the "linked" rate), which implies a legal barrier to exchange rate realignments;[26]
- *legal restrictions on the use of other policy tools:* restrictions on discretionary monetary policy (esp. monetary financing of fiscal deficits), which also imply fiscal discipline and
- *absence of traditional central bank functions* such as monetary operations, banking supervision, and lender of last resort;

---

[25] Under devaluation pressure as when there is a fall in private demand for domestic currency in the FX market, for instance, there exists arbitrage opportunities for those who care to buy up the domestic currency "cheaply" at the prevailing ER from the FX market and turn around and sell it "dearly" at the official ER to the monetary authority issuing the currency. These arbitrage activities will set in motion a fall in the supply of domestic currency, which will induce in turn a rise in the domestic interest rate, making it more attractive to hold the domestic currency (i.e., releasing the pressure of devaluation). The reverse argument holds when there is pressure for revaluation.

[26] Excess reserves must be used in a way that subordinates concerns over monetary and banking sector developments to the objective of preserving the exchange rate parity.

- *adjustment mechanism when the market rate deviates from the linked rate:* through automatic adjustments in domestic interest rates induced by foreign exchange arbitrage rather than through central bank intervention in the foreign exchange market and/or active interest rate defense.

In practice, instead of being bound rigidly by the above features, *modern* currency boards that exist today may diverge in one way or another from this pure or classical benchmark. In particular, they may differ with respect to their detailed arrangements:

- *exchange rate rule:* choice of reserve currency, target level of the linked rate, extent of access to convertibility at the monetary authorities, and degree of foreign exchange control;
- *backing rule:* coverage of backing, set of assets eligible for backing, and the power of the monetary authority to change the exchange rate rule and the backing rule; and
- *profit transfer rule* for seigniorage revenue earned from the foreign reserves.

In addition, modern day currency boards may vary by the details of their central banking operations in terms of the set of monetary instruments (such as reserve requirements, liquidity requirements, rediscounts and advances, Treasury bills, etc.), the payments system, as well as Treasury operations (including operations in relation to government deposits and credit to government by the monetary authorities). Last but not least, they may differ according to their prudential arrangements (i.e., the existence of a supervising/regulatory agency for banks and of deposit insurance and other prudential measures) and the availability of lender-of-last-resort facilities. In other words, while preserving the benefits of credibility offered by the essentially rule-based system, some flexibility is built into the working of these "*quasi* currency boards" of today. [See Baliño et al. (1997) and Schwartz (1993) for further details.]

References

Baliño, Tomás J. T. et al. (1997), "Currency board arrangements: Issues and experiences," *IMF Occasional Paper No. 151,* August (1983).

Barro, Robert J., and David B. Gordon (1983). "Rules, discretion, and reputation in a model of monetary policy," *Journal of Monetary Economics* 12, 101–21.

Chakravorti, Sujit, and Subir Lall (2000). "The double play: simultaneous speculative attacks on currency and equity markets," working paper, Federal Reserve
Bank of Chicago, December.

Chan, Alex, and Nai-fu Chen (1999). "An intertemporal currency board," *Pacific
Economic Review* 4, 215–32.

Chan, Alex, and Nai-fu Chen (2000). "A theory of currency board with commit-
ments," working paper, University of Hong Kong, December.

Chang, Roberto, and Andres Velasco (2000). "Financial fragility and the exchange
rate regime," *Journal of Economic Theory* 92, 1–34.

Chu, C. Y. Cyrus (2000). "Introducing the Soros bond: Insuring against self-
fulfilling financial crises," working paper, Institute of Economics, Academia
Sinica, July.

Cukierman, Alex (1992). *Central Bank Strategy, Credibility, and Independence:
Theory and Evidence,* MIT Press.

Drazen, Allan (1999). "Interest rate defense against speculative attack under
asymmetric information," paper prepared for the NBER IFM program meeting,
March 19.

Eichengreen, Barry, Andrew K. Rose, and Charles Wyplosz (1995). "Exchange
market mayhem: the antecedents and aftermath of speculative attacks," *Economic Policy,* 251–312.

Flood, Robert P., and Peter M. Garber (1984). "Collapsing exchange-rate regimes:
Some linear examples," *Journal of International Economics* 17, 1–13.

Flood, Robert P., and Olivier Jeanne (2000). "An interest rate defense of a fixed
exchange rate," *IMF Working Paper No. WP/00/159,* October.

Ho, Corrinne M. (1999). "To kill a currency board: Soroi not necessary," working
paper, Princeton University, November.

Kaminsky, Graciela, and Carmen Reinhart (1999). "The twin crises: The causes
of banking and balance of payments problems," *American Economic Review*
89, 473–500.

Kaplan, Ethan, and Dani Rodrik (2000). "Did the Malaysian capital controls work?" paper prepared for an NBER conference on Currency Crises,
December.

Krugman, Paul (1979). "A model of balance of payments crises," *Journal of Money,
Credit, and Banking* 11, 311–25.

Krugman, Paul (1998). "Bubble, boom, crash: Theoretical notes on Asia's crisis,"
January.

Krugman, Paul (1999). "Balance sheets, the transfer problem, and financial crises,"
International Tax and Public Finance 6, 459–72.

Krugman, Paul (2001). "Crises: The next generation," paper presented at a conference on *"Economic Policy in the International Economy"* in honor of Assaf
Razin's 60th birthday, March; Chapter 1 herein.

Lahiri, Amartya, and Carlos A. Végh (2000). "Fighting currency depreciation:
Intervention or higher interest rates?" paper prepared for NBER conference
on Currency Crises Prevention, December.

Lui, Francis T., Leonard K. Cheng, and Yum K. Kwan (2001). "Currency board,
Asian financial crisis, and the case for put options," working paper, Hong Kong
University of Science and Technology, March.

Milesi-Ferretti, Gian-Maria, and Assaf Razin (2001). "Current account reversals and currency crisis: empirical regularities," in Paul Krugman (ed.), *Currency Crises,* University of Chicago Press.

Miller, Merton H. (1998). "The current Southeast Asia financial crisis," *Pacific Basin Finance Journal* 6, 225–33.

Morris, Stephen, and Hyun Song Shin (1998). "Unique equilibrium in a model of self-fulfilling currency attacks," *American Economic Review* 88, 587–97.

Obstfeld, Maurice (1986). "Rational and self-fulfilling balance-of-payments crises," *American Economic Review* 76, 72–81.

Obstfeld, Maurice (1994). "The logic of currency crises," *Cahiers Economique et Monetaires* 43, 189–212.

Obstfeld, Maurice (1996). "Models of currency crises with self-fulfilling features," *European Economic Review* 40, 1037–48.

Ozkan, F. Gulcin, and Alan Sutherland (1995). "Policy measures to avoid a currency crisis," *Economic Journal* 105, 510–19.

Rogoff, Kenneth (1985). "The optimal commitment to an intermediate monetary target," *Quarterly Journal of Economics* 100, 1169–89.

Roubini, Nouriel (1998). "The case against currency boards: Debunking 10 myths about the benefits of currency boards," New York University, February.

Schwartz, Anna J. (1993). "Currency boards: Their past, present, and possible future role," *Carnegie-Rochester Conference Series on Public Policy* 39, 147–87.

Svensson, Lars E. O. (1997). "Optimal inflation targets, 'conservative' central banks, and linear inflation contracts," *American Economic Review* 87, 98–114.

Walsh, Carl E. (1995). "Optimal contracts for central bankers," *American Economic Review* 85, 150–67.

Walsh, Carl E. (1998). *Monetary Theory and Policy,* MIT Press.

Yuen, Chi-Wa (2001). "The devaluation bias vs. the inflation bias: How alike are the twins?" work in progress, University of Hong Kong, October.

## THREE

Growth-Enhancing Effects of Bailout Guarantees

Aaron Tornell

1. Introduction

During recent balance of payments crises dramatic currency deprecia-
tions have coincided with meltdowns of the banking system. Because
such crises have typically been preceded by lending booms, not by large
fiscal deficits, it has been suggested that financial liberalization programs
have been ill-conceived. These programs have often been implemented
in an environment characterized by bailout guarantees. As a result, financial liberalization programs have often been followed by excessive risk
taking and lending booms that have rendered economies prone to crisis.
Moreover, in some policy circles it has been suggested that the adoption
of fixed exchange rates has exacerbated the problem by inducing agents
to denominate their debt in foreign currency on an unhedged basis.

The central theme of this paper is that, given the distortions faced by
emerging markets, the financial liberalization policies of the late 1980s and
the early 1990s can be considered as growth-enhancing, even if we accept
that bailout guarantees were the inevitable consequence of such policies.
Furthermore, we will argue that, conceptually, the boom–bust cycles experienced by emerging economies are independent of the exchange rate
regime.

Several of the emerging economies that implemented financial liberalization had gone through decades of statism. Thus, at the time of
reform the private sector was too small and financial markets were not
well developed. In fact, bank credit was practically the only source of
external finance for most firms in the nascent private sector. In this environment many profitable investment projects could not be undertaken

because agents were credit-constrained. We will argue that in such a credit-constrained world bailout guarantees can be turned into a growth enhancing vehicle, provided they are accompanied by the right set of policies. Furthermore, we will argue that crises were not the inevitable consequence of bad policy but simply bad draws that did not have to happen. They were the price that had to be paid in order to attain faster long-run growth.[1]

Bailout guarantees may promote long-run growth because under some conditions they promote investment by easing borrowing constraints and by providing an implicit subsidy to constrained firms. Clearly, it is not just any bailout policy that induces higher growth. We identify three conditions which are necessary for this to occur: bailout guarantees must be systemic, there must be an efficient regulatory framework in place, and the environment must be "risky" (but not too risky). We consider each in turn.

In order to have growth enhancing effects, bailout guarantees must be systemic, as opposed to unconditional. The latter are granted whenever there is an individual default, as in a deposit insurance scheme. In contrast, the former are granted only if a critical mass of agents defaults. That is, it is essential that authorities can commit not to grant bailout guarantees on an idiosyncratic basis, but only in case of systemic crisis.

An efficient regulatory framework is needed because in the presence of bailout guarantees it is essential to limit the extent of connected loans and to prevent fraudulent activities on the part of banks. When these conditions are satisfied systemic bailout guarantees have the advantage of using the screening and monitoring role of banks. This ensures that the implicit subsidy will be directed to those firms with profitable projects. More generally, to the extent that there is an efficient regulatory framework, systemic bailout guarantees will not generate the incentive problems that plague direct transfer schemes.

A risky environment is necessary because the subsidy implicit in systemic bailout guarantees can be cashed in only if there exist some states of the world in which there is a systemic crisis. In the absence of exogenous shocks that bankrupt many agents, there must be *endogenous volatility*. Lending booms and risky dollar debt can generate this endogenous volatility by making the economy susceptible to self-fulfilling crises. In fact, as a way of allowing risk into the system dollar debt has the

---

[1] We would like to emphasize that we will not defend some policy measures that simply mask corruption.

wonderful feature of being a good coordinating device, as it can be observed by others. It follows that if prudential regulation is introduced with the goal of minimizing risk in the banking system, for instance by forbidding nontradable sector firms to borrow in dollars, then the investment enhancing effect of systemic bailout guarantees might be blocked.

However, having a risky environment does not mean that a crisis is inevitable along the transition path. In fact, the likelihood of crisis must be small, or otherwise systemic bailout guarantees might have the unintended effect of drastically reducing productive investment. If the environment is too risky, firms would not find it profitable to invest in the first place.

Now we turn to the second point of the paper. In some policy circles it has been maintained that fixed exchange rate regimes make economies more susceptible to crises, among other things because they provide fewer incentives for agents to hedge their debts. In this paper we argue that systemic bailout guarantees can induce the adoption of risky debt structures in flexible as well fixed exchange rate regimes. Guarantees may appear under different guises and need not be explicit. The precise form the bailout takes will depend on the regime. For instance, under fixed rates the bailout rate is mostly determined by the amount of reserves authorities are willing to use in order to defend the currency. In contrast, in a pure floating regime the bailout may take the form of direct transfers to agents.

In order to substantiate our claims we will use a simplified version of the model in Schneider and Tornell (2000), which we present in Section 2. Then, in Section 3 we address the policy issues raised above.

2. Conceptual Framework

The conceptual framework that one uses to evaluate the role of bailout guarantees must take into account the imperfections of the economies in which financial liberalization policies were designed, and must be able to explain the basic features of the boom–bust cycles that characterize emerging economies. In this paper we will use the model developed by Schneider and Tornell (2000) to make such a policy evaluation.

The most salient facts of the boom–bust cycle experienced by countries afflicted by crises are the following. During the boom phase there is a real exchange rate appreciation and a lending boom in which debts are often denominated in foreign currency. As a result, any incipient capital account reversal leads to widespread bankruptcies due to the existence of balance sheet effects. A crisis is typically followed by a short-lived drop in aggregate GDP, and a long-lived credit crunch that affects especially the nontradable sector.

To explain some of the stylized facts third-generation crises models have looked to financial market imperfections as key fundamentals. The models are typically based on one of two distortions: either bad policy, in the form of bailout guarantees, or bad markets, in the form of an imperfection that induces balance sheet effects, such as asymmetric information, or the imperfect enforceability of contracts.[2]

Schneider and Tornell (2000) consider an economy that is simultaneously subject to these two distortions: systemic bailout guarantees and the imperfect enforceability of contracts. They also stress the role of the nontradables sector, which is often overlooked in the debate about the causes of recent crises. They show that the interaction of the two distortions generates a coherent account of a complete boom-bust episode. The setup is a small open economy which exists for T periods. There are two goods: an internationally tradable (T) good, which is the numeraire, and a nontradeable (N) good. We will denote the inverse of the real exchange rate by $p_t = \frac{p_{N,t}}{p_{T,t}}$. In this economy the only source of uncertainty is a sunspot variable σ_t, which is i.i.d. and takes values in $\{good, bad\}$ with α probability of the "good" state. We will denote by $\overline{p}_{t+1}$ and $\underline{p}_{t+1}$ the values that the price of nontradables is expected to take on in period $t+1$ in the good and bad state, respectively. Thus, the expected price of nontradables is: $p_{t+1}^e := \alpha \overline{p}_{t+1} + (1-\alpha)\underline{p}_{t+1}$.[3]

To ensure the existence of complete markets it is assumed that two bonds with no default risk are traded: an N-bond and a T-bond. The T-bond pays one unit of tradables next period and trades today at a price $\beta := \frac{1}{1+r}$, where r is the constant world interest rate. Meanwhile, the N-bond pays p_{t+1} units of tradables next period, and trades today at a price $\frac{1}{1+r_t^n}$.

---

[2] See Aghion, Bachetta, and Banerjee (2000), Bernanke, Gertler, and Gilchrist (1999), Burnside, Eichenbaum, and Rebelo (2000), Caballero and Krishnamurthy (1999), Calvo (1998), Chang and Velasco (1998), Corsetti, Pesenti, and Roubini (1998), Krugman (1998), and McKinnon and Pill (1998).

[3] Considering a two-sector economy is essential because the transfer of resources from the N- to the T-sector has played a leading role in recent crises, and because two sectors are needed to analyze the real exchange rate appreciation observed prior to the onset of crises and the asymmetric recovery in the aftermath of crises. Considering an economy with no fundamental uncertainty rules out explanations of crises based on the premise that emerging markets suffer from more and bigger exogenous shocks than developed countries.

There are three types of agents: managers of N-sector firms, consumers, and foreign investors. We describe each in turn. Where q_{t+1} is the amount of N-goods produced, I_t represents physical investment, and θ is a techno-logical parameter, managers produce N-goods with nontradables as the only input using a linear production technology

$$q_{t+1} = \theta I_t. \tag{1}$$

We can think of a manager as a banker who lends to the N-sector. A manager of the period t cohort is a risk neutral agent who cares for con-sumption of tradables in period $t+1$ only. Each "generation" consists of a continuum of firms of measure one. Since we will impose symmetry throughout, we state everything in terms of a representative firm. The manager in period t begins with internal funds w_t. He raises an amount b_t by issuing one-period bonds that pay off in T-goods, and an amount b_t^n by issuing one-period bonds that pay off in N-goods. Since the promised in-terest rates on these bonds are ρ_t and ρ_t^n, respectively, the total repayment promised by the entrepreneur is $p_{t+1}(1 + \rho_t^n)b_t^n + (1 + \rho_t)b_t$.[4]

Since b_t and b_t^n are measured in T-goods, the budget constraint is

$$p_t I_t + s_t + s_t^n = w_t + b_t + b_t^n, \tag{2}$$

where s_t and s_t^n are the amounts invested in riskless bonds that pay off in tradables and nontradables, respectively. Here I_t, b_t, b_t^n, s_t and s_t^n must be non-negative. In the following period, a manager sells the output of N-goods. He then pays out a fixed fraction c of the profits as dividends to himself and passes on the remainder to the next manager. The goal of every manager is to maximize expected profits in the following period.

We have allowed the manager to choose between T-debt and N-debt in order to address the question of when is it that agents in an economy will issue risky debt.

The representative consumer consumes tradable (c_t^{tr}) and nontrad-ables goods (c_t^{nt}), and can issue riskless bonds. His utility is

$$\sum_{t=0}^{T} \beta^t \left[c_t^{tr} + d_t \log \left(c_t^{nt} \right) \right]. \tag{3}$$

Consumers are endowed with ε units of the T-good in every period. Since there are complete markets, their budget constraint is

$$E\left[\sum_{t=0}^{T} \beta^t \left(c_t^{tr} + p_t c_t^{nt} - \varepsilon \right) \right] \leq 0.$$

---

[4] The actual repayment may differ from the promised repayment. This is described below.

As long as ε is large enough (which we assume is the case), consumers' demand for N-goods will be

$$D_t(p_t) = \frac{d_t}{p_t}. \tag{4}$$

Reform (such as trade liberalization) or discovery of a natural resource (oil) induces a future outward shift in the demand for N-goods by the T-sector (offices, services, etc.). Typically, the expectation of future good times is what drives lending booms. We capture this fact through a shift in the preference parameter d_t:

$$d_t = \begin{cases} d & \text{if } t < T \\ \hat{d} \geq d & \text{if } t = T. \end{cases} \tag{5}$$

2.1. Distortions

The financing decision is subject to two distortions: an enforceability problem and systemic bailout guarantees. We consider each in turn.

ENFORCEABILITY OF CONTRACTS. A firm is called *insolvent* if cash flow, defined by

$$\hat{\pi}(p_{t+1}) := p_{t+1}\theta I_t - (1 + \rho_t^n)p_{t+1}b_t^n - (1 + \rho_t)b_t$$
$$+(1+r)s_t + (1+r^n)p_{t+1}s_t^n \tag{6}$$

is negative. We will use the random variable ζ_{t+1} to indicate solvency. A *solvent* entrepreneur ($\zeta_{t+1} = 1$) can default strategically even though he would in principle be able to repay. We assume that he can divert all returns from investment to himself at time $t + 1$, provided that he has incurred a nonpecuniary diversion cost $hp_t I_t$ at time t. In this case, lenders are left with nothing. "Diversion" can be interpreted as an activity that reflects "crony capitalism."

In case of insolvency ($\zeta_{t+1} = 0$), the manager's payoff is zero. In addition, the gross returns from investment are dissipated in bargaining among the large number of creditors (so creditors also get a zero payoff).

It follows that there is *no diversion* if and only if the expected repayment is less than the diversion cost:

$$(1 + \rho_t^n)E_t[\zeta_{t+1}p_{t+1}]b_t^n + (1 + \rho_t)E_t[\zeta_{t+1}]b_t \leq hp_t I_t. \tag{7}$$

We will refer to this condition as the firm's *borrowing constraint*.

The parameter h can be interpreted as a measure of the severity of the enforceability problem. If h increases beyond $1 + r := \beta^{-1}$, it is always cheaper to repay debt rather than to divert, so that there is no enforceability problem. Since we are interested in firms that face financing constraints, we make the following assumption

$$\beta h < 1. \tag{8}$$

BAILOUT GUARANTEES. In a *bailout* lenders receive a fraction F of the outstanding debts of all defaulting entrepreneurs, regardless of debt denomination (N- or T-goods). The bailout policy is contingent on the number of defaults, in that the agency grants bailouts only if it faces a critical mass of defaults. For concreteness we assume that a bailout occurs if and only if more than 50% of firms default in a given period. The bailout is granted by an international organization.[5]

The contingent rule for bailouts captures the fact that bailouts typically occur when a large number of banks get in trouble. It is also crucial for financing constraints to bite: If there was a basic deposit insurance scheme (i.e., if a bailout was granted whenever a single entrepreneur defaulted), then guarantees would neutralize the enforceability problem.

This completes the description of the economy. We have considered a minimal setup in which we have assumed neither borrowing constraints nor risky debt denomination. Furthermore, since the production function is linear, the gradual character of the dynamics and the vulnerability to meltdowns that will emerge in equilibrium will derive from the interaction of the two distortions we emphasize in this paper.

2.2. Investment and Debt Denomination
In order to rationalize the facts mentioned in the Introduction it is essential that borrowing constraints arise in equilibrium, and that entrepreneurs find it profitable to invest in the production technology, and to issue T-debt. In order to determine the circumstance under which this occurs it is useful to classify plans according to whether they might lead to insolvency and/or diversion of funds.

In this part we discuss the investment and financing decisions of an individual firm at a given point in time. Taking as given current prices (p) and expected future prices ($\overline{p}$, $\underline{p}$), the representative manager chooses a plan ($I, s^n, s, b^n, b, \rho^n, \rho, \zeta$) that maximizes expected profit subject to the

---

[5] It thus represents a windfall gain for the country. Alternatively, one could assume that a lump sum tax is levied on consumers. Since consumers are not subject to wealth effects, this does not affect the rest of the equilibrium as long as their endowment is large enough.

budget constraint (2) and the interest rates that foreign lenders are willing to accept (ρ, ρ^n).

In order for borrowing constraints to be binding in equilibrium and all debt to be denominated in T-goods there must be sufficient real exchange rate risk. As we shall see, returns must satisfy the following condition:

$$\frac{\overline{p}^{\theta}}{p} > 1 + r > h > \frac{\underline{p}^{\theta}}{p}. \tag{9}$$

In this subsection we will assume (9) holds. Then, in the next subsection we will determine the circumstances under which it holds along the equilibrium path. The first inequality ensures that if crises are rare events (α close or equal to one), investment in N-goods is a positive NPV activity. This must clearly hold in any interesting equilibrium of the model. The third inequality says the crisis return is lower than the opportunity cost of diversion. It implies that firms will go bankrupt in a crisis state. Since in the model price risk is present if and only if bankruptcy risk is present, this must be true in any equilibrium in which $\alpha < 1$. The second inequality follows from assumption (8). In the next subsection we will derive the conditions under which (9) holds along the equilibrium path.

One can show that if (9) holds and α is large, then plans that lead to diversion are not funded by lenders. Since lenders are risk neutral, the interest rates that managers must pay depend on whether the investment plan is risky (i.e., it leads to bankruptcy if the low price realizes next period), or it is safe (i.e., it never leads to bankruptcy). In the good state the debt is repaid in full and there is no bailout, while in the bad state there is bankruptcy and each lender receives a proportion F of what he was promised. Since the probability of a good state is α, interest rates satisfy

$$(1 + \rho_t)[\alpha + (1 - \alpha)F] = 1 + r,$$
$$(1 + \rho_t^n)[\alpha \overline{p}_{t+1} + (1 - \alpha)\underline{p}_{t+1} F] = 1 + r. \tag{10}$$

If the managers chooses a safe plan, he will always be able to repay. Thus, interest rates satisfy

$$\rho_t = r,$$
$$(1 + \rho_t^n)[\alpha \overline{p}_{t+1} + (1 - \alpha)\underline{p}_{t+1}] = 1 + r. \tag{11}$$

Since $\overline{p}_{t+1} > \underline{p}_{t+1}$, we can see from (10) that if a risky plan is chosen, T-debt is cheaper than N-debt. Under a risky plan the expected repayments per unit debt are $\frac{\alpha[1+r]}{\alpha+(1-\alpha)F}$ for T-debt and $\frac{\alpha[1+r]}{\alpha+(1-\alpha)F\frac{p}{\bar{p}}}$ for N-debt, where F is the share of the promised debt repayment that the lender receives from the bailout agency in the case of a systemic crisis and p and $\bar{p}$ are the values that the relative price of nontradables takes in the bad and good states, respectively. Since $\bar{p} > p$, T-debt is strictly cheaper than N-debt for all $F > 0$.

One can show that if (9) holds and α is large, then when there are no guarantees ($F = 0$) it is optimal to choose a safe plan, while if F is large, it is optimal to choose a risky plan. Undertaking risky plans goes hand in hand with a preference for T-debt. If there is enough exchange rate risk there will be bankruptcy in the bad state. Furthermore, if $F > 0$, the bailout agency will pay part of the promise in the bad state. It is thus desirable for the firm to shift as much of the payment as possible into the bad state. This is achieved precisely by denominating all debt in tradables. Since lenders must break even, switching from nontradable to tradable debt always shifts some of the debt burden from the good to the bad state, making the firm better off.

In order to derive the equilibria, recall that bailouts are granted only during a systemic crisis. Thus, as long as nobody expects a bailout, everybody hedges, and a crisis – and hence a bailout – cannot occur. In other words, a safe symmetric equilibrium of the credit market game always exists. In this equilibrium firms' borrowing constraints bind, it is optimal to denominate all debt in nontradables, defaults do not occur, and the value of investment is

$$_pI^s = m^s w := \frac{1}{1 - \beta h} w. \tag{12}$$

If systemic bailout guarantees are sufficiently generous and crises are rare events (α large but less than one), there are also risky symmetric equilibria where each manager believes that all other managers will undertake risky plans. He will conclude that a bailout will occur in the bad state. Thus, he will refrain from hedging and take on real exchange rate risk. As a result he will go bankrupt in the bad state, along with all the other managers, triggering a bailout. In this equilibrium firms' borrowing constraints bind, and the value of investment is

$$_pI^r = m^r w =: \frac{1}{1 - \beta h \left[1 + \dfrac{1-\alpha}{\alpha} F\right]} w. \tag{13}$$

The debt burden, in terms of tradables, during the following period is $L = \alpha^{-1} h p I = \alpha^{-1} h m^r w$.

We can see that systemic bailout guarantees need not neutralize the effect of the enforceability problem. Under the condition on returns (9), lenders do not finance diversion plans. This gives rise (via (7)) to a borrowing constraint which, in turn, generates the familiar *credit multiplier* result: The amount of credit is proportional to the borrower's internal funds. Furthermore, if the production technology has positive NPV ($\frac{p^0}{p} > 1 + r$), firms prefer investment to speculation in bonds and the credit multiplier m^r translates into an investment multiplier.

2.3. Real Exchange Rate Risk

In this part we investigate under which circumstances there will be enough real exchange rate variability so that condition (9) is satisfied. Recall that this condition is necessary for managers to have incentives to denominate their debt in T-goods.

We determine the real exchange rate by characterizing a temporary equilibrium. Suppose incumbent managers enter the current period with a supply of nontradables q_t, no bond holdings, and a debt burden $L_t + p_t L_t^n$, where $L_t = \alpha^{-1} h m_t w_t$ and $L_t^n = (p_{t+1}^e)^{-1} p_{t+1} h m_t w_t$. The new cohort chooses its plans taking as given future prices and the value of the internal funds they get from incumbents' sales.

In order to characterize equilibria we need to specify the market clearing condition for nontradables:

$$\frac{d_t}{p_t} + I_t = \theta I_{t-1}, \tag{14}$$

where consumers' demand for nontradables is equal to d/p_t and the supply of nontradables is given by $q_t = \theta I_{t-1}$. As we saw earlier a firm will invest in the production technology if the expected return $(\theta p_{t+1}^e / p_t)$ is greater than the return on bonds. If this is the case, investment expenditure will simply be proportional to internal funds as stated in (12) and (13): $p_t I_t = m_t w_t$. The evolution of internal funds is given by: $w_0 = e_0$, and for $t \geq 1$,

$$w_t = \begin{cases} [1 - c]\hat{\pi}(p_t) & \text{if } \hat{\pi}(p_t) > 0 \\ e & \text{otherwise.} \end{cases} \tag{15}$$

As long as incumbents are solvent, internal funds are $w_t = (1 - c)\hat{\pi}_t$, where $\hat{\pi}_t = p_t \theta I_t - L_t - p_t L_t^n$. In contrast, if the bad state is realized, firms become insolvent and the new cohort starts out with an endowment of T goods e.[6] Investment expenditure is thus

$$
p_t I_t = \begin{cases} \eta_t \left[p_t q_t - L_t - p_t L_t^n \right] & \text{if } p_t q_t \geq L_t + p_t L_t^n \\ m_t e & \text{otherwise,} \end{cases} \tag{16}
$$

where the cash flow multiplier η_t is defined by $\eta_t := (1 - c)m_t$. The size of the investment multiplier in period t, m_t, depends on whether safe ($m_t = m^s$) or risky ($m_t = m^r$) plans are undertaken.

The real exchange rate equalizes aggregate demand and the (predetermined) supply of nontradables: $D(p_t) = q_t$. Combining the preceding equations we have that $q_t = \theta I_{t-1}$ and

$$
D(p_t) = \begin{cases} \dfrac{d}{p_t} + \eta_t \left[q_t - \dfrac{L_t}{p_t} - L_t^n \right] & \text{if } p_t q_t > L_t + p_t L_t^n \\ \dfrac{d + m_t e}{p_t} & \text{otherwise.} \end{cases} \tag{17}
$$

Since supply is given, the key to having multiple equilibria is a backward bending aggregate demand curve. This is impossible if incumbent managers have only nontradables debt ($L_t = 0$). In this case $q_t > L_t^n$, aggregate demand slopes downward and there is a unique equilibrium price.

However, multiple equilibria are possible if $L_t > 0$ and $L_t^n = 0$. In this case price movements affect revenues, but keep the debt burden unchanged. It thus becomes important to distinguish between insolvent and solvent firms. For prices below the cutoff price $p_t^c = L_t / q_t$, all N-firms go bankrupt because revenues do not cover the debt burden. As a result, internal funds are only e. Total demand in this range is downward sloping. In contrast, for prices above p_t^c, an increase in the price is accompanied by a more than proportional increase in internal funds. The reason is that revenues increase while the debt burden remains the same. Equivalently, part of the debt burden measured in terms of nontradables is inflated away. Consequently, investment demand is increasing in price.

It is apparent that if the balance sheet effect is strong enough to make aggregate demand bend backward, as in Fig. 3.1, multiple market clearing prices, and hence self-fulfilling "twin crises" can exist. From (17), multiple market clearing prices arise if and only if

$$
L_t > d + m_t e \qquad \text{and} \qquad \eta_t > 1. \tag{18}
$$

---

[6] We assume that whenever there is default, new managers in cohort t receive an "aid payment" e to jump start their firms. In period 0, there is both a cohort of initial incumbent managers who have an amount q_0 of nontradables to sell and a cohort of new managers who have an endowment e in terms of tradables.

Equilibrium in the Nontradables' Market

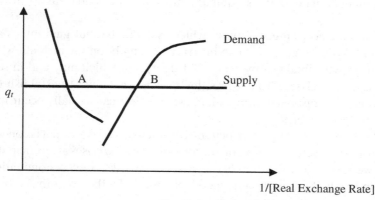

Figure 3.1.

With identical fundamentals, in terms of supply and debt, the market may clear in one of two equilibria. In a "solvent" equilibrium (point B in Fig. 3.1), the price is high, inflating away enough of firms' debt (measured in nontradables) to allow them to bid away a large share of output from consumers. In contrast, in the "crisis" equilibrium of point A, the price is low to allow consumers and bankrupt firms with little in the way of internal funds to absorb the supply of nontradables.

Which of these two points is reached depends on expectations. Fundamentals determine only whether the environment is fragile enough to allow two equilibria. In view of (18), the relevant factors are a strong balance sheet effect and a high enough level of *tradables* debt. The former is facilitated by a low dividend payout rate and easy enforceability of contracts. The latter has been taken as given in this part.

In the next subsection we will show that anticipated endogenous price risk can induce managers to take on enough T-debt for such risk to actually arise. For this to happen, bailout guarantees have to be generous. To carry out this analysis, however, we must turn to an explicitly dynamic analysis.

2.4. Equilibrium Dynamics

We have seen that, in the absence of bailout guarantees, managers will not be inclined to issue T-debt. In the model, the only source of uncertainty is the sunspot. Furthermore, multiple market clearing prices, which are crucial for a sunspot to matter, exist only if debt is denominated in tradables.

It follows that, in the absence of bailout guarantees, there cannot be an equilibrium in which prices depend on the sunspot. Instead, in economies without bailout guarantees, equilibria must be "safe" and firms are always solvent.

Consider now an economy in which systemic bailout guarantees are present. Will the economy exhibit risky lending booms, which allow for faster growth (financed by "cheap" T-debt), but which may end in self-fulfilling twin crises? To address this question we need to establish the existence of *sunspot equilibria* along which crises can actually occur with positive probability.

It is technically simpler to focus on unanticipated crises, but it is conceptually unsatisfactory for several reasons. First, only if crises are anticipated can we rationalize this fragility as a result of risky debt denomination. Second, only if crises are anticipated can we make the point that growth is faster with bailout guarantees.

In order to construct a sunspot equilibrium recall that under exchange rate risk and bailout guarantees, managers may create credit risk from real exchange rate risk by financing investment with T-debt. They will do so in particular if they expect (i) a sufficiently high return on investment in the absence of a depreciation; (ii) a sufficiently low return after a depreciation, so that it is possible to claim the bailout subsidy by defaulting; and (iii) a sufficiently low probability of a crisis, which ensures that the ex-ante expected return is high enough and borrowing constraints bind. Recall also that if there is enough T-debt, there are two possible market clearing prices, where the lower price bankrupts firms, and hence triggers a bailout. The question is whether these two mechanisms can be elements of one consistent story.

Formally, can we construct an equilibrium price process by making the sunspot variable σ_t select among market clearing prices, such that the resulting return distribution encourages firms to issue enough T debt to validate the price process? In other words, we need to construct *a set of beliefs about future prices* that is consistent with a rationally anticipated self-fulfilling crisis. We thus need to find a range of probabilities α for the sunspot process, so that the sunspot matters over a number of periods before the next to last one.

One can prove that if (i) crises are rare events (i.e., α close to one); (ii) parameters are such that the N-sector can grow over time:

$$c < \beta h; \tag{19}$$

(iii) the demand shift at terminal time T (i.e., $\hat{d}$) is large enough to ensure that the N-sector can repay its accumulated deficits; (iv) the initial endowment e is large enough; and (v) the N-sector has enough time to grow (large enough T), then the sunspot can eventually matter and self-fulfilling crises can be anticipated on a time interval $[\tau, T - 1]$. During this time interval a crisis occurs with conditional probability $1 - \alpha$.

Along the lucky path on which no crisis occurs, the value of output $(p_t q_t)$ follows an increasing path. The technology parameter θ determines how this rise in value translates into changes in prices and quantities. If θ is very high, supply would outpace demand. As a result the price would fall over time, while investment would rise. At the other extreme, if θ is small, we could have an equilibrium along which nontradables become more and more scarce while firms chase the returns offered by rising prices but can afford to invest less and less. To match the observations that N-sector growth coincides with a real appreciation, we fix θ at an intermediate value:

$$\theta \in \left(1, \frac{\eta^s h}{\eta^s - 1}\right). \tag{20}$$

If assumption (20) holds, then (i) the output of nontradables increases over time from τ on, and (ii) the real exchange rate appreciates between τ and $T - 1$.

It should be emphasized that the *likelihood of self-fulfilling crises is not a free parameter*. First, sunspot equilibria exist only if crises are relatively rare events. If the probability of a crisis was too high, low ex-ante returns would discourage managers from investing in the first place. We take this feature of the model as a check of the plausibility of our particular sunspot story. Second, crises are more likely to happen toward the end of a boom, as the anticipated event that triggered the boom draws near. Note that even though prosperity is near for the N-sector, fragility and the size of a possible downturn become more severe.

To highlight the fact that systemic bailout guarantees might induce faster economic growth by easing borrowing constraints, but increase the likelihood of a crisis, consider two economies A and B. The only difference between these economies is that A has systemic bailout guarantees. Then, there is a sunspot equilibrium where A and B behave identically up to a certain time, after which the N-sector in economy A grows faster and exhibits higher leverage along the lucky path, as long as a crisis does not occur. However, A experiences a crisis and subsequent recession with positive probability while B does not.

NECESSARY INGREDIENTS FOR BOOM–BUST CYCLES. A key point of Schneider and Tornell (2000) is that the interaction of contract enforceability problems and bailout guarantees creates the fragility required for self-fulfilling crises. If there were no guarantees, firms would not be willing to take on price risk to claim a subsidy. Costly enforceability of contracts alone would still imply that the N-sector can only grow gradually and balance sheet effects would play a role during the lending boom. However, there would be no force to make the boom end in a crisis. Alternatively, if there were only guarantees but no enforceability problems, then there would not be any balance sheet effects that make demand backward-bending, a necessary condition for a sunspot to matter.

Lending booms that feature fragility cannot occur in just any economy with bailout guarantees and enforceability problems. It is also necessary to have a future increase in the demand of the T-sector for nontradables. Otherwise, the N-sector would not be able to repay the accumulated deficits it runs during the lending boom. Backward induction then indicates that the sequence of returns that supports the lending boom would collapse. This suggests that the boom–bust episodes are more likely to occur during a transition period (for instance, following a far-reaching reform or a natural resource discovery).

Even during a transitional period the likelihood of a self-fulling crisis is not a free parameter. If crises were not rare events, either borrowing constraints would not arise, or would not be binding in equilibrium if they did arise. In either case, credit would not be constrained by internal funds and balance sheet effects would not exist in equilibrium. Clearly, if this was the case, crises could not occur. If the probability of crises is not small enough, enforceability problems do not generate borrowing constraints.

3. Policy Evaluation

An emerging economy is one where the future is much brighter than the present, but where profitable investment projects cannot be undertaken because (i) the private sector is small (i.e., entrepreneurial wealth is low), and (ii) the amount of external financing is severely limited, specially for firms in the nontradable sector. The reforms of the late 1980s liberalized trade and financial markets in many emerging markets. These reforms also brought a significant reduction in the role of the state in the economy. Suddenly, the future looked much brighter than before, and the private sector much smaller than what was desirable. Unfortunately legal and judicial reform could not be implemented as easily as the other reforms. As a result, many of the institutions that support the provision of external finance in developed economies did not flourish in emerging markets.

Firms in the tradable sector could finance themselves in international markets. However, this option was not open to N-sector firms.

The policy problem then became how to better promote the fast development of the private sector in an environment where external finance to the nontradable sector is constrained by internal funds of firms, and where N-sector investment is too low relative to investment opportunities (e.g., infrastructure, services, etc.). One is tempted to say that if a government had the appropriate information and correct incentives, the optimal policy would have been to transfer resources to those in the population with better entrepreneurial skills, and to let them make the investment decisions. Of course, we now know that this is wishful thinking. After many failed experiments of this sort carried out during the last century, we now know that either governments do not posess the appropriate information, or are too inclined to crony capitalism and rampant corruption.

Since direct made-to-measure government transfers are not feasible, during the 1990s governments had to design second-best policies to foster the development of the private economy, especially in the N-sector. In many countries the decision was made to privatize the banks and allow them to be the means through which resources would be channeled to the nascent private sector. The issues described in the Introduction should be analyzed from this perspective.

We will analyze these issues by using the framework described in Section 2. Since this model explains many of the stylized facts that characterize the boom–bust cycles experienced by emerging markets during the 1990s, it is an appropriate framework to evaluate the policies implemented by emerging markets. We will argue that when taking into consideration the distortions that exist in emerging markets, there is a sense in which these policies are second-best-optimal instruments to foster the nontradable sector's growth. We would like to distinguish between these policies and those which are designed to mask corruption. The latter are clearly undefendable.

3.1. Policies During a Boom

Consider the two-sector economy described in Section 2 in which firms in the T-sector can easily obtain financing in international capital markets, while firms in the N-sector must rely more heavily on domestic bank credit. Furthermore, since emerging markets face acute enforceability problems, firms in the N-sector face severe borrowing constraints that limit their ability to undertake profitable projects. As a result, the growth rate of the N-sector is kept below its potential. It follows that a policymaker, whose

objective is to maximize social welfare, must design second-best policies that will ease borrowing constraints and increase investment in the
N-sector. Because the N-sector and the T-sector compete for productive resources and any policies to support the N-sector have implicit fiscal
costs, the optimal support level for the N-sector cannot be arbitrarily large.

We have seen that in the presence of severe enforceability problems
in financial markets credit is constrained by internal funds. As a result,
profitable investment projects will not be undertaken, especially in the
N-sector. Thus, over the medium-run growth will be significantly lower
than its potential. This indicates that systemic bailout guarantees might
actually play a socially beneficial role. Systemic bailout guarantees provide an implicit subsidy that reduces the cost at which firms can fund
themselves, and increases the credit multiplier. This increases investment
and growth at each level of internal funds. In the absence of better instruments to promote investment and growth of the N-sector, systemic bailout
guarantees are a second-best instrument to make transfers to this sector.
We would like to emphasize that this mechanism uses the information
and monitoring capacity of banks.

Although there are several ways systemic bailouts can be implemented,
for simplicity consider the generosity of bailout guarantees (F) as the
policy instrument. An increase in F induces an increase in the investment
multiplier in (13), which in turn leads to a higher growth rate of the
N-sector. Therefore, in an emerging economy it is optimal to set F higher
than zero in order to reduce the underinvestment problem. However,
there are trade-offs: first, the greater F the greater the contingent fiscal
cost; second, the greater F, the greater the share of resources allocated
to the N-sector at the expense of the T-sector. Therefore, the level of F
should not be set too high. There is an interior optimum.

We would like to emphasize three points. First, systemic bailout guarantees do not curtail the discipline faced by either individual banks or
firms because they are granted only if a critical mass of agents defaults.
At the same time, systemic bailout guarantees generate an investment
subsidy only if the banks' portfolios are risky, that is, only if there exist
states of nature in which there are systemic crises. In the absence of large
exogenous shocks, guarantees will be effective in promoting investment
only if the banking system generates risk endogenously (we address this
issue below). Second, systemic bailout guarantees imply that the government can credibly commit not to bailout individual agents in the case of
idiosyncratic default. Third, if in a given country banks play no monitoring role and are prone to fraud, systemic bailout guarantees will not be
socially beneficial.

The experience of Mexico during the 1990s illustrates, in a rather sharp manner, the policy dilemma faced by reformers. Several critics have pointed to the false rosy expectations generated by the government, and the promises of bailout guarantees, as the culprits for the Tequila crisis. Certainly, in hindsight this is true, a policymaker would say. However, at that time it seemed a sensible policy. It was a way to avoid low growth and bottlenecks in the N-sector that would otherwise limit the overall future growth of the economy. Plus, from a political standpoint the development of the private sector encouraged by the policy had the added virtue of creating new power bases that would block attempts by statist groups to go back to the old ways. It was a way to ensure the continuity of the reforms.

An important issue that we have not discussed yet is unconditional bailout guarantees, which are granted whenever an individual debtor defaults. Deposit insurance is a prime example. If all guarantees were unconditional, the discipline in the banking system would disappear and guarantees would not play the investment promoting role we described above.

However, if unconditional bailout guarantees are granted to small bank depositors, they might play a socially beneficial role. This policy avoids bank runs generated by cascading rumors, but does not impinge negatively on the market discipline faced by an individual bank because small depositors have typically very little information regarding the bank's portfolio. As it is the case in the United States, market discipline should be imposed by noninsured bank debt, the interest rate of which should serve as an indicator of a bank's health.

THE ROLE OF RISKY DOLLAR DEBT. As mentioned above, systemic bailout guarantees have investment-enhancing effects only in the presence of risk. In the absence of large exogenous shocks, some endogenous volatility must be present if the policy is to be effective. Therefore outlawing risky dollar debt could undo the investment-enhancing effects of systemic bailout guarantees. Thus, if the conditions of a country call for bailouts as a second-best policy to promote the growth of the private sector, then risky debt (or another way to generate endogenous volatility) must also be allowed. Of course, this does not mean that banks should be allowed to have outrageously risky portfolios. It just means that a naive policy of outlawing risky dollar debt is not correct from a normative perspective.

Since systemic bailout guarantees can be cashed in states of the world only where there is a systemic crisis, systemic bailout guarantees are effective in increasing investment only if a significant part of the economy is vulnerable to systemic crises. It is only during a systemic meltdown that the bailout agency makes payments to lenders. Thus, the expected value of the subsidy is determined by the likelihood of a crisis and by the generosity of the bailout. The greater the expected value of the subsidy, the lower interest rates that lenders are willing to accept. Clearly, banks' portfolios cannot be outrageously risky, as the likelihood of crisis must be quite small in order for the mechanism identified in this paper to be operative. Otherwise, firms would not find it profitable to borrow and invest in the first place. Note however, that small is not the same as zero. In the absence of major exogenous shocks, the fragility must come from within the system. This is precisely the role of risky debt denomination. As we explained above, if a majority of borrowers have unhedged debt, the economy as a whole can become vulnerable to self-fulfilling crises.

As a way of allowing risk into the economy, dollar debt has the wonderful feature of being a coordinating device, as it can be observed by others. It plays the same role as the real-estate buildup on an uninsured basis in catastrophe-prone areas. The principle that "if everyone else does it, then I am safe" reigns.

From a positive perspective it is impossible to outlaw short-term dollar debt. Many firms need such debt in order to carry out their international transactions. Since it is impossible to distinguish what part of dollar debt is used by a given firm to finance international transactions, it is not feasible to enforce a law that forbids dollar debt for uses other than international trade. This lesson has been painfully learned by many countries that have tried to implement dual exchange rates, and then were faced with rampant misinvoicing of imports and exports.

In conclusion, the degree of banks' and firms' portfolio riskiness should be strictly regulated. However, risky debt should not be outlawed altogether. It is neither socially optimal nor practically implementable.

THE ROLE OF LENDING BOOMS AND ASSET PRICE INFLATION. During a lending boom credit grows unusually fast and, as many observers have pointed out, monitoring effectiveness declines. Thus, it is less likely that unprofitable and white elephant projects will be detected and stopped. At the same time, firms in emerging markets have a very low level of external finance, especially in the N-sector. Thus, a lending boom is a mechanism by which faster growth can be attained. In fact, the lending boom is a transitional phase that is ignited by deep economic reforms that make the future much brighter than the present.

Stopping a lending boom, for example by increasing reserve requirements, would interrupt the policy of promoting the growth of the private sector. However, allowing the lending boom to continue unchecked increases the debt burden of the economy which makes it more vulnerable to crises. Hence, it is not clear ex-ante at which point should a lending boom be stopped.

It is interesting to note that although crises typically are preceded by lending booms (Tornell (1999)), the converse is not true. Gourinchas et al. (2001) find that for a large panel of countries the probability that a lending boom ends in a crisis is quite small. That is, in the majority of cases, lending booms end with soft landings. Furthermore, theoretically lending booms can only develop if the probability of crisis is small, and they are expected to end with a soft landing if they last long enough (see Schneider and Tornell (1999)).

Clearly, India has not experienced lending booms of such magnitude as the ones experienced by Korea. Moreover, India has not suffered currency crises as deep as those endured by Korea. Certainly, this does not mean that over the last half century the Indian economy has performed better than Korea's. Of course, with hindsight Korean performance could have been improved on the margin. However, we should beware of fine-tuning policies designed (ex-post) to look great ex-post.

Prior to several crises it has been observed that some assets, such as real estate, experience a steep price inflation which is followed by a price collapse at the time of crisis. Since real estate is used as collateral, there is a close link between lending and asset price inflation during a boom. Thus, implementing policies that would stop asset price inflation will also reduce the growth of credit. Clearly, it might be dangerous to leave asset price inflation unchecked. However, some degree of inflation might be desirable as a tool to ease borrowing constraints.[7]

BAILOUT GUARANTEES AND THE EXCHANGE RATE REGIME. There are several ways in which systemic bailout guarantees can be implemented. The particulars will of course depend on the exchange rate regime. A nice feature of Schneider and Tornell's framework is that the effects of guarantees and the forces that generate boom–bust cycles are independent of the exchange rate regime or monetary policy rule. This permits us to study how guarantees affect the economy under different regimes.

With fully flexible exchange rates the mechanism is literally the same as the one we consider in Section 2. If agents are highly leveraged and have risky dollar debt, the economy is vulnerable to self-fulfilling crises in

---

[7] Schneider and Tornell (1999) study the interplay between asset prices and lending along a boom.

which there is a severe real depreciation and several agents in the N-sector suffer from balance sheet effects and are unable to repay their debts. As a result, creditors get paid a proportion F of the contracted payment. This bailout payment can be financed by an international organization and/or by an increase in future taxes to the rest of the economy. The real depreciation can arise by either a nominal depreciation, a change in nominal prices or a combination of both.

Consider the other extreme of a fixed exchange rate regime. In the case of an attack the central bank can defend the currency by either running down reserves or increasing the interest rate. If the attack is successful, the reduction in reserves constitutes a bailout payment to bank creditors that withdraw their funds and convert them into foreign currency. Thus, any defense policy has associated with it a bailout rate F. Clearly, the bailout rate need not be 100%, as reserves might not suffice to cover all the liabilities of the banking system. We should add that the bailout can be complemented by an explicit transfer, as in Mexico during the Tequila crisis. Again, the real depreciation can come about through a combination of a nominal depreciation and a change in nominal prices.

In the real world we observe a mixture of both regimes. However, it should be clear that the underlying forces are essentially the same in both cases.

4. Conclusions

Bailout guarantees seem to be an inevitable consequence of financial liberalization. Does this mean that financial liberalization will inevitably lead to crisis and lower long-run growth? In this paper we have argued that, in a credit-constrained world, financial liberalization may induce higher long-run growth provided authorities can commit not to grant bailouts on an idiosyncratic basis, but only in case of systemic crisis. Furthermore, an efficient regulatory framework must be in place in order to limit the extent of connected loans and to ensure that banks perform their monitoring and screening roles effectively.

Higher long-run growth comes at the cost of a higher vulnerability to crises. This, however, does not mean that a crisis must happen along the transition path. In fact, the likelihood of crisis must be small. Otherwise, systemic bailout guarantees might have the unintended effect of drastically reducing productive investment.

Finally, we have argued that in a credit-constrained economy with bailout guarantees the forces that generate higher growth and vulnerability to crises are independent of the exchange rate regime. Thus, fixed exchange rates are not necessary for the boom–bust cycles that emerging economies have experienced during the recent past.

References

Aghion, Philippe, Philippe Bachetta, and Abhijit Banerjee (2000), "Capital Markets and the Instability of Open Economies," mimeo, Study Center Gerzensee.

Bernanke, Ben, Mark Gertler and Simon Gilchrist (1999), "The Financial Accelerator in a Quantitative Business Cycle Framework," in *Handbook of Macroeconomics*, North Holland.

Burnside, Craig, Martin Eichenbaum and Sergio Rebelo, (2000), "Prospective Deficits and the Asian Currency Crisis," *Journal of Political Economy*, 109(6), December 2001, pp. 1155–97.

Caballero, Ricardo and Arvind Krishnamurthy (1999), "International and Domestic Collateral Constraints in a Model of Emerging Market Crises," *Journal of Monetary Economics*, 48(3), December 2001, pp. 513–48.

Calvo, Guillermo (1998), "Capital Flows and Capital Market Crises: The Simple Economics of Sudden Stops," *Journal of Applied Economics*, pp. 35–54.

Chang Roberto and Andres Velasco (1998), "Financial Crises in Emerging Markets: A Canonical Model," NBER working paper 6606.

Corsetti, Giancarlo, Paolo Pesenti, and Nouriel Roubini (1998). "Paper Tigers: A Model of Asian Crisis" *European Economic Review* 43(7), 1211–1236.

Gourinchas, Pierre Olivier, Oscar Landerretche, and Rodrigo Valdes (2001), "Lending Booms: Latin America and the World," NBER working paper 8249.

Krugman, Paul (1998), "Bubble, Boom, Crash: Theoretical Notes on Asia's Crisis," working paper, MIT.

McKinnon, Ronald and Huw Pill (1998), "Exchange-Rate Regimes for Emerging Markets: Moral Hazard and International Overborrowing," *Oxford Review of Economic Policy* 15(3), Autumn 1999, 19–38.

Schneider, Martin and Aaron Tornell (1999), "Lending Booms and Asset Price Inflation," working paper, UCLA.

Schneider, Martin and Aaron Tornell (2000), "Balance Sheet Effects, Bailout Guarantees and Financial Crises," NBER working paper 8060.

Tornell, Aaron (1999), "Common Fundamentals in the Tequila and Asian Crises," NBER working paper 7193.

FOUR

Risk and Exchange Rates*

Maurice Obstfeld and Kenneth S. Rogoff

Nominal exchange risk is a ubiquitous factor in international economic policy analysis. For example, sudden appreciations of the dollar following financial crises outside the United States often are ascribed to "safe haven" portfolio shifts. The elimination of national currencies in Europe has been rationalized in part by the claim that uncertain exchange rates discourage trade, and thereby hamper the full realization of the gains from removing other obstacles to commodity and asset-market integration.

Unfortunately, the analytical underpinnings of such widely discussed phenomena have received scant attention. In analyzing the properties of stochastic general-equilibrium monetary models, researchers typically rely on a certainty equivalence assumption to approximate exact equilibrium relationships. This practice, as Kimball (1995, p. 1243) remarks, "precludes a serious welfare analysis of changes that affect the variance of output." In the relatively rare cases in which higher moments are considered theoretically, tractability usually has required the assumption of

* Prepared for the conference in honor of Assaf Razin, Tel-Aviv University, March 2001. Earlier drafts of this paper were presented in 1998 at Harvard, Wharton, MIT, Stanford, LSE, and at the 1998 National Bureau of Economic Research Summer Institute. Following our initial presentations of this paper, its approach has furnished the workhorse framework for an important subsequent literature that has made substantial advances. See, for example, Bacchetta and van Wincoop (2000), Devereux and Engel (2000), Engel (1999), and Obstfeld and Rogoff (2000, 2002). We do not attempt to survey that literature here; see Obstfeld (2001, 2002) for more recent discussions. This version of our original paper adds only slight revisions and corrections to National Bureau of Economic Research Working Paper 6694 (August 1998). We have benefited from helpful comments from Paolo Pesenti, Alan Stockman, and Cedric Tille. Remaining errors are ours alone. Support from a National Science Foundation grant to the NBER is acknowledged with thanks.

instantaneously flexible commodity prices and wages.[1] That modeling choice not only assumes away much of the real effect of nominal exchange rate uncertainty. It simultaneously precludes discussion of the feedback from monetary nonneutralities to market risks, and instead imposes exogenously the covariances between monetary shocks and consumption levels. And it is unrealistic. There is strong, indeed overwhelming, empirical evidence that the nominal prices of domestically produced goods tend to adjust far more sluggishly than exchange rates.[2] But the implications of product price setting in general-equilibrium models with uncertainty remain largely unexplored, despite being at the core of the debate over the impact of exchange-rate volatility.

The model we propose in this paper extends the "new open-economy macroeconomics" framework of Obstfeld and Rogoff (1995, 1996), Corsetti and Pesenti (2001), and others to an explicitly stochastic environment.[3] We analyze a sticky-price monetary model in which risk has an impact not only on asset prices and short-term interest rates, but also on the price-setting decisions of individual producers, and thus on expected output and international trade flows.

Our approach allows one to quantify explicitly the welfare tradeoff between alternative exchange-rate regimes, and to relate that tradeoff to country size. In its emphasis on the exact welfare analysis of alternative exchange-rate regimes, this paper follows in the pioneering footsteps of Assaf Razin and his coauthor Elhanan Helpman (see, for example, Helpman and Razin 1979). Interestingly, we find in this paper's model that even in cases where uncertainty induces substantial heterogeneity across countries both ex ante and ex post, there may be a strong, even perfect, convergence of interests in choosing a global monetary system.

---

[1] General-equilibrium models of exchange-rate risk typically follow Lucas (1982) in assuming that all prices are fully flexible. See Svensson (1985), Hodrick (1989), Engel (1992), and Obstfeld and Rogoff (1996, Chapter 8) for relevant extensions.

[2] See, for example, Mussa (1986), Baxter and Stockman (1989), Flood and Rose (1995), and Obstfeld (1998).

[3] Rankin (1998) develops a very interesting analysis of a small open economy with complete asset markets and competitive production, in which monopolistic labor suppliers preset money wages. While (like us) he examines the positive effects of monetary uncertainty, he does not systematically explore the welfare effects of policies. An earlier complete-markets model with nominal rigidities is that of Svensson and van Wijnbergen (1989), who, building on Svensson's (1986) closed-economy model, provide an early discussion of price-setting in advance by maximizing firms facing uncertainty. The appendix to Svensson (1986) briefly discusses the welfare impact of an infinitesimal degree of money-supply variability, but such higher moment effects are not the main focus of his paper.

Although the main thrust of our approach is normative, the model also yields some potentially important positive results. For example, we show how exchange risk affects the *level* of the exchange rate, and not just the predictable return to forward speculation that has been studied extensively in earlier literature. While these two effects of exchange risk turn out to be proportional, the multiplier linking them can be quite large. Indeed, our analysis suggests that fluctuations in the level risk premium may be a very significant source of exchange-rate volatility, one that is missing or inadequately captured in standard empirical exchange rate equations (e.g., Meese and Rogoff, 1983).[4]

Finally, under specified conditions, we can solve the model explicitly for equilibrium second as well as first moments. The solution yields novel insights about the exchange risk premium in a sticky-price setting within which the covariance between monetary shocks and consumption is endogenous, unlike models such as Lucas's (1982). For example, we find that when home monetary volatility is an important source of uncertainty, home-currency assets actually may serve as a hedge against consumption risk. The reason is that under price stickiness, positive home monetary surprises lead home output and consumption to covary positively with the home-currency price of foreign exchange. If so, domestic nominal interest rates are *lower* than would be the case under risk neutrality. We show, however, that greater domestic monetary variability, despite causing lower home nominal interest rates and an appreciation of the home currency (all else equal), must reduce expected welfare both at home and abroad.

Section 1 of the paper presents a basic model with monetary and productivity shocks, while Section 2 employs a key simplifying feature which turns out to imply that current accounts are always zero in equilibrium. Section 3 shows how the presetting of nominal goods prices can be analyzed without a certainty-equivalence assumption, and discusses some implications. In Section 4 we complete the derivation of the model's equilibrium, and in Section 5 we show how to calculate the exchange risk

---

[4] A large effect of risk factors on exchange rate levels was suggested by Frankel and Meese (1987), based on partial-equilibrium intuition. Hodrick (1989), using a version of Svensson's (1985) cash-in-advance model with a variable velocity of money, showed the effect of higher moment fundamentals on exchange rates in a flexible-price, general equilibrium setting, but his restrictive money-demand specification implied a generally moderate effect of monetary risk factors. In our setup, in which the interest semielasticity of money demand may be any negative number, the exchange-rate level effect of exchange risk can plausibly be an order of magnitude higher than in Hodrick's.

premium explicitly as a function of underlying money-supply shocks. Except for the money demand function (which we generally must log–linearize), the model is naturally log–linear provided the underlying monetary and productivity shocks are lognormally distributed. Section 6 offers a guide to quantifying the "amplification effect" linking the level exchange rate risk premium to the standard forward risk premium that characterizes excess returns to currency speculation.

Section 7 discusses the link between policy uncertainty and ex ante welfare, taking up results on country size (which can be surprising) and developing a quantitative example illustrating that the costs of exchange volatility can be big. Importantly, we find that by explicitly treating price setting under uncertainty, we obtain much more general and elegant welfare results than would be possible under the usual assumption of certainty equivalence. It is important to note that many of the key welfare results derived in this section do not depend on the ancillary linearization of the money-demand function needed to get a closed-form solution in Sections 4 and 5. Finally, Section 8 summarizes; a variety of extensions and technical derivations are relegated to appendices.

1. A Stochastic Two-Country Model

The model is a stochastic version of the one in Obstfeld and Rogoff (1995, 1996), modified along lines proposed by Corsetti and Pesenti (2001), who present a model in which current account imbalances are always zero *in equilibrium*. The general issue of current accounts is quite important to any complete model of international policy transmission, but allowing for imbalances here would pose some very subtle and difficult technical issues, issues that we prefer to abstract from in a first pass at a stochastic sticky-price model.

1.1. Preferences and Technology

There are two countries, Home and Foreign. Home agents are indexed by numbers in the interval $[0, n]$, while Foreign agents reside on $(n, 1]$. Every individual is a "yeoman farmer" and is presumed to have a monopoly in producing a single good, also indexed by n. Preferences of the representative Home agent are given by

$$U_t = \mathrm{E}_t \left\{ \sum_{s=t}^{\infty} \left(\frac{1}{1+\delta} \right)^{s-t} \left[\frac{C_s^{1-\rho}}{1-\rho} + \frac{\chi}{1-\varepsilon} \left(\frac{M_s}{P_s} \right)^{1-\varepsilon} - \frac{\kappa_s}{2} Y_s^2 \right] \right\}, \quad (1)$$

where C is an index of per capita consumptions of Home and Foreign commodity bundles,

$$C = \frac{C_H^n C_F^{1-n}}{n^n (1-n)^{1-n}}, \tag{2}$$

with

$$C_H = \left[\left(\frac{1}{n} \right)^{\frac{1}{\theta}} \int_0^n C(z)^{\frac{\theta-1}{\theta}} \, dz \right]^{\frac{\theta}{\theta-1}},$$

$$C_F = \left[\left(\frac{1}{1-n} \right)^{\frac{1}{\theta}} \int_n^1 C(z)^{\frac{\theta-1}{\theta}} \, dz \right]^{\frac{\theta}{\theta-1}}, \qquad \theta > 1. \tag{3}$$

Thus, across goods produced within a country the elasticity of substitution is θ, while the elasticity of substitution between the composite Home and Foreign goods is 1. Utility depends negatively on individual output, Y, because production requires irksome labor effort. Utility depends positively on individual domestic real money balances, M/P, because of the role of money in reducing transaction costs. Foreign agents have identical preferences except that κ^* may differ from κ, Y^* may differ from Y, and Foreign agents hold their own national currency M^*, which is deflated in their utility function by the Foreign general consumer price index P^*.

The coefficient κ – which multiplies Y^2 in the utility function (1) and can be viewed as inversely related to productivity – may be a random variable. All random shocks in the model are assumed to be lognormally distributed.

1.2. Prices, Demand, and Budget Constraints
The overall Home-currency consumption-based price index is given by

$$P = P_H^n P_F^{1-n} \tag{4}$$

where the subindexes for Home and Foreign products are, respectively,

$$P_H = \left[\frac{1}{n} \int_0^n P(z)^{1-\theta} dz \right]^{\frac{1}{1-\theta}}, \qquad P_F = \left[\frac{1}{1-n} \int_n^1 P(z)^{1-\theta} dz \right]^{\frac{1}{1-\theta}}.$$

The law of one price is assumed to hold across all individual goods, so that $P(z) = \mathcal{E} P^*(z)$, $\forall z \in [0, 1]$, where asterisks denote Foreign values of the corresponding Home variables, and $\mathcal{E}$ is the nominal exchange rate (the Home price of Foreign currency). Because Home and Foreign agents have identical preferences, the law of one price implies that purchasing power parity must hold for overall consumer price indexes:

$$P = \mathcal{E} P^*.$$ (5)

Under the subutility functions in (3), the allocation of a representative individual's demand across each of the goods produced within a country is given by

$$C(h) = \frac{1}{n} \left[\frac{P(h)}{P_H} \right]^{-\theta} C_H, \qquad C(f) = \frac{1}{1-n} \left[\frac{P(f)}{P_F} \right]^{-\theta} C_F,$$ (6)

(where h denotes the representative Home good and f the representative Foreign good). The Cobb–Douglas *total* consumption index, Equation (2), implies that demands for the composite Home and Foreign goods, C_H and C_F, are given by

$$C_H = n \left(\frac{P_H}{P} \right)^{-1} C, \qquad C_F = (1-n) \left(\frac{P_F}{P} \right)^{-1} C.$$ (7)

Define world consumption as

$$C^w \equiv nC + (1-n)C^*,$$ (8)

where C is the total consumption of a representative Home resident and C^* that of a representative Foreign resident. (Since world population is 1, C^w is per capita as well as total world consumption.) Then, combining Equations (6) and (7), and aggregating the result with the identical Foreign demand functions, we see that the global demand for individual goods is given by

$$C(h) = \left[\frac{P(h)}{P_H} \right]^{-\theta} \left(\frac{P_H}{P} \right)^{-1} C^w, \qquad C(f) = \left[\frac{P(f)}{P_F} \right]^{-\theta} \left(\frac{P_F}{P} \right)^{-1} C^w.$$ (9)

Home and Foreign agents can trade riskless real bonds that are indexed to total consumption C. Let r_t denote the consumption-based real interest rate between dates $t-1$ and t (the own-rate of interest on the total consumption basket). Written in terms of Home money, the intertemporal budget constraint for the representative Home agent is

$$P_t B_{t+1} + M_t = P_t(1+r_t) B_t + M_{t-1} + P_t(h) Y_t(h) - P_t C_t - P_t \tau_t,$$ (10)

where τ denotes lump-sum taxes and B_{t+1} denotes end of period t bond holdings. [In contrast, our assumption on money holdings is that M_t denotes the end of period t stock; recall also Equation (1).] It is important

to note that although we do not explicitly allow for international trade in
equity in this model, such trade will turn out to be redundant. In equilibrium (as we will show), each country's share of world income is constant
due to the assumption of a unit elasticity of intratemporal demand across
the Home and Foreign composite goods.

We simplify by setting government spending equal to zero throughout,
so that the Home government budget constraint, for example, is given by

$$0 = \tau_t + \frac{M_t - M_{t-1}}{P_t}. \tag{11}$$

Appendix A indicates how government spending shocks could be introduced. The (gross) rate of growth of the money supply is assumed to be
a lognormally distributed random variable.

We also assume that initial net international asset holdings $B = 0$.

2. Goods Market Clearing and the Redundancy
of Securities Markets

Whether flexible or preset prices prevail, the goods market clears. Even
before examining the first-order optimality conditions of consumer/pro-
ducers, we can infer the key relationships linking national to global consumption levels, and global consumption to national outputs. We explore
these relationships first because they imply a key (though special) property of the model: Securities markets are redundant and, as a result, current accounts always balance exactly in equilibrium.

Taking account of the differing populations in the two countries, total
output supplies equal demands when

$$n[nPC + (1-n)PC^*] = nP_H Y,$$
$$(1-n)[nPC + (1-n)PC^*] = (1-n)P_F Y^*.$$

These equations imply that

$$\frac{P_H}{P_F} = \frac{Y^*}{Y}. \tag{12}$$

As in Corsetti–Pesenti (2001), this relation, together with our assumption that initial net international asset holdings $B = 0$, implies that current accounts always are zero. The intuition for this result, of course,
is that Equation (12) gives countries constant (indeed equal) shares of
per capita world real income, regardless of the pattern of shocks. Given

constant real income shares (and our assumption of isoelastic preferences over total consumption C), countries always consume exactly their real incomes:

$$C = \frac{P_H Y}{P}, \qquad C^* = \frac{P_F^* Y^*}{P^*}. \tag{13}$$

As Cole and Obstfeld (1991) point out, price responses can make international trade in securities redundant with Cobb–Douglas preferences.[5]

An immediate corollary of Equations (12) and (13) is that

$$C^w = C = C^*. \tag{14}$$

Per capita consumption shares for Home and Foreign are not only constant, but equal.[6,7]

3. Producer Behavior under Preset Prices

We now look at how monopolistic producers plan output and prices when commodity prices are set a period in advance in producers' currency and cannot be revised until the following period.[8] Thus, we assume that $P_t(h)$

---

[5] More formally, notice that for the allocation in Eq. (13), Home and Foreign intertemporal marginal rates of consumption substitution are equal for every future state of nature. Since leisure is a nontraded good, there are no unexploited gains from trade and international trade in securities therefore is redundant. Without the assumption that initially $B = 0$, this would not necessarily be the case. Shocks that led to temporary changes in the real interest rate could then induce current account movements. [See Eq. (26) on p. 78 of Obstfeld and Rogoff (1996).]

[6] One reason for this equality, of course, is that we have chosen the utility function so that expenditure shares are the same as population shares. That assumption is plausible and convenient but easily relaxed.

[7] Recall from (5) that $P = \mathcal{E} P^*$ always holds. Note then, by Eqs. (4), (8), (12), and (13), that

$$C^w = n \frac{P_H Y}{P} + (1 - n) \frac{P_F^* Y^*}{P^*}$$

$$= n \left(\frac{P_H}{P_F} \right)^{1-n} Y + (1 - n) \left(\frac{P_F^*}{P_H^*} \right)^n Y^*$$

$$= Y^n (Y^*)^{1-n}.$$

[8] While this paper assumes the law of one price and pricing in producers' currencies, extensions such as Devereux and Engel (2000) model the failure of the law of one price at the consumer level as well as the apparent rigidity of all consumer prices (even those of imported retail goods) in local currency terms. A debate has arisen over the importance

and $P_t^*(f)$ are set at the end of period $t-1$ and cannot be changed during period t.[9] With preset prices, supply is no longer determined by the leisure–consumption tradeoff that governs behavior under flexible prices. (Appendix A describes the flexible-price solution.) Instead, because price initially exceeds marginal cost, supply moves to accommodate any unanticipated shock to demand (provided the shock is not so large that full accommodation of demand would raise marginal cost above price).[10]

In a certainty-equivalence setup, equilibria with preset prices differ from ones with flexible prices only because of the effects of unanticipated shocks. But that is not the case in an explicitly stochastic version of the model. When $P_t(h)$ and $P_t^*(f)$ are set at the end of period $t-1$, they are not generally set at their certainty-equivalent values. Prices are set with a view toward hedging the risks the producer faces. This nuance is quite important, both in understanding the effects of risk on the exchange rate and other macro variables and in using the model to ascertain the welfare effects of alternative macroeconomic policies.

3.1. The Price Setting Problem

Consider the pricing decision of the representative Home agent. On date $t-1$, $P_t(h)$ is set to maximize the objective function (1), but with the expected value conditional on date $t-1$, instead of date t, information. Using the individual's intertemporal budget constraint (10) to substitute out for C_t in the utility function (1), then using the demand function (9) to substitute out for $Y_t(h)$, and finally taking $t-1$ expectations over both sides, we obtain the maximand $E_{t-1}U_t$ as the infinite sum (starting with

---

of distinguishing between actual import prices and the retail prices consumers pay for goods that originate abroad. Obstfeld (2001) offers a more detailed discussion, and argues that failure of the law of one price at the consumer level is consistent with expenditure-switching effects of exchange rate changes such as those we analyze below.

[9] More realistic dynamics would result from the assumption of Calvo-style multiperiod staggered price setting; see Kimball (1995), for example. We forgo that realism here to obtain simpler and more accessible results, and leave the inclusion of Calvo contracts for future research.

[10] One must be careful in interpreting a stochastic version of the model if one assumes that supply always accommodates demand under sticky prices. For large enough shocks the voluntary participation constraint will be violated, as Corsetti and Pesenti (2001) stress. Thus, the results of our stochastic model under sticky prices should be viewed as approximate. The approximation can be made arbitrarily precise by looking at ever-smaller variances for the exogenous shocks.

$s = t$) of terms of the form

$$
E_{t-1}\left(\frac{1}{1+\delta}\right)^{s-t}\left\{\frac{1}{1-\rho}\left[\left(\frac{P_s(h)}{P_{H,s}}\right)^{1-\theta}C_s^w+(1+r_s)B_s-B_{s+1}\right.\right.
$$

$$
+\frac{M_{s-1}-M_s}{P_s}-\tau_s\bigg]^{1-\rho}+\frac{\chi}{1-\varepsilon}\left(\frac{M_s}{P_s}\right)^{1-\varepsilon}
$$

$$
-\frac{\kappa}{2}\left[\left(\frac{P_s(h)}{P_{H,s}}\right)^{-\theta}\left(\frac{P_{H,s}}{P_s}\right)^{-1}C_s^w\right]^2\bigg\}.
$$
(15)

Optimal price setting in period $t-1$ reflects minimization of the *expected* discrepancy between the marginal utility of marginal revenue and the marginal disutility of effort.

Differentiating the above expression with respect to $P_t(h)$ yields

$$
E\{C^{-\rho}(\theta-1)P(h)^{-\theta}P_H^{\theta-1}C^w\}
$$

$$
= E\left\{\kappa\theta[P(h)^{-\theta-1}P_H^{\theta-1}PC^w]\left[\left(\frac{P(h)}{P_H}\right)^{-\theta}\left(\frac{P_H}{P}\right)^{-1}C^w\right]\right\},
$$

where we suppress $t-1$ subscript on the expectations operator and t subscripts on all variables when there is no risk of confusion. Noting that $P(h) = P_H$ (in a symmetric equilibrium), that P_H is known in advance, and finally that $C = C^w$ – Equation (14) applies – we can rewrite this expression as

$$
E\{C^{1-\rho}\} = E\left\{\kappa\left(\frac{\theta}{\theta-1}\right)\left(\frac{PC}{P_H}\right)^2\right\}.
$$
(16)

The parallel Foreign relation is

$$
E\{C^{1-\rho}\} = E\left\{\kappa^*\left(\frac{\theta}{\theta-1}\right)\left(\frac{P^*C}{P_F^*}\right)^2\right\},
$$
(17)

where $C = C^*$ has been used.

Notice that the (flexible) nominal Home wage implicit in this model is given by

$$
\frac{W}{P} = \kappa\frac{Y}{C^{-\rho}}.
$$

Since $PC/P_H = Y$ in equilibrium (the national budget constraint), Equation (16) would reduce to the constant-elasticity markup equation

$P_H = (\frac{\theta}{\theta-1})W$ under certainty (with the corresponding equation for P_F^*).[11]
Equation (16) and its Foreign analog modify those familiar relationships
to account for uncertainty subsequent to the setting of nominal product
prices.

3.2. Implications for Ex Ante Terms of Trade

Assuming that C and $\mathcal{E}$ are jointly lognormally distributed, we can express
the solution for the ex ante terms of trade and ex ante consumption in
natural logarithms. (We shall show later that C and $\mathcal{E}$ indeed have lognormal distributions in equilibrium if the exogenous shocks hitting the world
economy are lognormal as well.) The solution procedure is not especially
illuminating, so it is relegated to Appendix B.

To gain some preliminary intuition about the solution described by
Equations (16) and (17), we simplify and adopt the convenient assumptions that κ and κ^* have identical lognormal distributions and are serially uncorrelated, so that $E_{t-1} \log \kappa_t = E_{t-1} \log \kappa_t^*$. Notice that if these
shocks to "productivity" are purely temporary, then they have no effect
on consumption or on the exchange rate, ceteris paribus (since output is
demand-determined in the short run).[12] If monetary policy reacts systematically to productivity shocks, however, productivity shocks *may* affect
consumption and exchange rates through the induced effects on money
supplies, so the ceteris paribus caveat in the last sentence is essential.

As Appendix B shows, the ex ante terms of trade are given by

$$p_H - p_F^* - Ee = (1 - 2n)\sigma_e^2 + 2\sigma_{ce} + (1 - n)\sigma_{\kappa e} + n\sigma_{\kappa^* e} + \sigma_{\kappa c} - \sigma_{\kappa^* c},$$
(18)

where we use lower-case letters to denote natural logarithms (except
for interest rates and the country-size parameter n). Here, σ_e^2 stands
for the date $t - 1$ conditional variance $\sigma_{e,t-1}^2 \equiv \text{Var}_{t-1}\{e_t\}$, σ_{ce} stands for
$\sigma_{ce,t-1} \equiv \text{Cov}_{t-1}\{c_t, e_t\}$, and so on. If consumption is unexpectedly high
when the domestic currency is unexpectedly weak, meaning that $\sigma_{ce} > 0$,
Home producers will find themselves with a highly variable marginal disutility of effort because exchange-rate and world-consumption effects on

---

[11] Obstfeld and Rogoff (2000) and Obstfeld (2001, 2002) explore related models with sticky
nominal wages.

[12] While under sticky prices the output effect of a purely temporary positive productivity
shock (a fall in κ *or* κ^*) is nil, the disutility from the previously planned level of labor
effort falls. If instead the shock were somewhat persistent, consumption would rise, raising
demand and with it, current output. See Obstfeld and Rogoff (1995) for similar results.

demand will tend to reinforce each other. Foreign producers will be in the opposite situation. Accordingly, Home producers will set relatively high prices ex ante, and Foreign producers relatively low prices. If Home is relatively small ($n < \frac{1}{2}$), greater currency variability σ_e^2 will raise its ex ante terms of trade. In this case, exchange-rate fluctuations have a bigger effect on the Home than on the Foreign demand curves, making world demand for Home goods relatively more variable and making Home's expected disutility of effort higher at internationally equal ex ante production levels. This asymmetry causes a relative preference of Home producers for leisure, improving Home's ex ante terms of trade. If $n = \frac{1}{2}$, σ_e^2 naturally does not affect the ex ante terms of trade. Note, finally, that if, for example, Home's disutility-of-effort parameter κ tends to be unexpectedly high when the exchange rate e is unexpectedly high and Home's products therefore are cheap relative to Foreign's, Home producers will on average be in the position of supplying extra labor when it is most painful to do so. Accordingly, they will set higher product prices ex ante, lowering their planned labor supply, and Foreign producers will adjust their own prices downward when σ_{κ^*e} rises.

3.3. Implications for Ex Ante Consumption

Appendix B also shows that the expected value of the log of (world) consumption is

$$
\begin{aligned}
Ec = \frac{1}{1+\rho} \Bigg\{ &\log\left(\frac{\theta-1}{\theta}\right) - E\log\kappa - \frac{1}{2}\sigma_\kappa^2 - 2n(1-n)\sigma_e^2 \\
&- \left[2 - \frac{1}{2}(1-\rho)^2\right]\sigma_c^2 - 2n(1-n)(\sigma_{\kappa e} - \sigma_{\kappa^*e}) \\
&- 2[n\sigma_{\kappa c} + (1-n)\sigma_{\kappa^* c}] \Bigg\}.
\end{aligned}
\tag{19}
$$

Certainty-equivalent expected log consumption is $Ec = \frac{1}{1+\rho}[\log(\frac{\theta-1}{\theta}) - E\log\kappa]$ (see Appendix A). However, uncertainty plainly affects expected log (world) consumption, and, hence, pricing and ex ante log output levels. The relationship between consumption variability, as measured by σ_c^2, and expected log consumption is ambiguous. According to Equation (19), $\partial Ec/\partial\sigma_c^2$ is negative for $\rho < 3$, and nonnegative otherwise.

What do Equations (18) and (19) imply for producers' date $t-1$ decisions about date t prices? Observe that the expectation of the logarithm of the individual monopolist's demand curve (9) is

$$
Ey(h) = -\theta p(h) + (\theta-1)p_H + Ep + Ec^w
$$

when domestic-currency prices are preset [in which case $Ep(h) = p(h)$ and $Ep_H = p_H$]. A change in σ_c^2 affects Home and Foreign producers symmetrically, and hence has identical effects on $Ey(h)$, $Ey(f)$, and Ec^w. The last equation therefore shows (because the individual producer takes p_H, Ep, and Ec^w as given) that if a rise in σ_c^2 depresses Ec^w in equilibrium, for example, it must induce every producer in the world to raise price and thereby lower the expected log of his output. Accordingly, higher σ_c^2 is associated with higher nominal product prices when $\rho < 3$ and with lower prices when producers are so risk averse that $\rho > 3$.[13]

What explains the ambiguity? It results from the opposition of two effects. Greater consumption variability implies greater demand variability in equilibrium, which in itself induces producers to raise prices so as to limit the ex post variability in labor supply. Roughly speaking, the elasticity of this effect is given by the coefficient on labor supply in the utility function (1), namely, 2.

On the other hand, an increase in σ_c^2 alters the expectation of $C^{-\rho} \times C = C^{1-\rho}$, which is proportional to the equilibrium marginal utility value of sales; see Equation (16). Because

$$EC^{1-\rho} = \exp\left[(1-\rho)Ec + \frac{(1-\rho)^2}{2}\sigma_c^2\right],$$

an increase in σ_c^2 raises the expected marginal utility value of sales at given prices (i.e., given Ec) with elasticity $\frac{1}{2}(1-\rho)^2$. Plainly the second effect will dominate the first, inducing lower producer prices ex ante, only when $\rho > 3$. One can view this second case as reflecting a sufficiently strong precautionary saving motive, under which higher future consumption variability leads producers to choose a higher mean

---

[13] Because $\log EC = Ec + \frac{1}{2}\sigma_c^2$, a rise in σ_c^2 raises the expected *level* of consumption EC mechanically, with Ec and producer prices held constant, simply because $C = \exp c$ is a convex function of c. We can compute the sign of the relation between σ_c^2 and EC by using Eq. (19) and calculating

$$\frac{\partial \log EC}{\partial \sigma_c^2} = \frac{-[2 - \frac{1}{2}(1-\rho)^2]}{1+\rho} + \frac{1}{2} = \frac{\rho - 2}{2}.$$

According to the last expression, the expected consumption level rises with σ_c^2 when $\rho > 2$ (but, as noted, for $2 < \rho < 3$, EC rises due to a convexity effect even though producers raise their prices and lower the expected *log* of consumption). Notice also that the variance of the level of consumption, σ_C^2 is given by

$$\sigma_C^2 = \exp\left(2Ec + \sigma_c^2\right)\left[\exp\left(\sigma_c^2\right) - 1\right]$$

(due to lognormality of C), so an increase in σ_c^2, holding producer prices (i.e., Ec) constant, implies an increase in σ_C^2.

level of future (log) consumption despite higher expected disutility from effort.

Equation (19) also shows that greater exchange volatility, other things equal, unambiguously lowers expected consumption. Exchange rate volatility operates through its effect on the volatility of demand for a country's good, which alters the expected marginal disutility of work. Productivity volatility, σ_κ^2, works the same way.[14] The covariance terms in this equation are intuitive as well. If, for example, the covariance between the real disutility shocks and world consumption is high, individuals expect that world demand and hence labor supply will be unexpectedly high on average precisely when effort is unexpectedly costly, so they will curtail their planned labor supply. That reduces planned output and planned consumption worldwide.

Of course, the relationships in Equation (19) between expected consumption and the displayed variances and covariances are relationships between endogenous variables. While suggestive, they do not reveal how exogenous changes will affect the economy. To determine that, we must fully solve for the model's equilibrium.

4. Equilibrium

An equilibrium is a path for consumption, output, and prices that satisfies the conditions for individual optimality, given the preset producer prices of the last section. We compute the equilibrium in steps.

4.1. First-Order Conditions for Consumption and Money

The first step is to add consumers' first-order conditions with respect to the dynamic consumption path and money holdings. Since these relationships are standard (see, for example, Obstfeld and Rogoff, 1996), we do not include detailed derivations. The following individual optimality conditions hold regardless of whether nominal domestic goods prices are flexible or sticky.

The intertemporal Euler equation for total real consumption is

$$C_t^{-\rho} = \frac{1 + r_{t+1}}{1 + \delta} \mathrm{E}_t \left\{ C_{t+1}^{-\rho} \right\}, \tag{20}$$

[14] Interestingly, for equally sized countries, higher exchange rate variability will, ceteris paribus, reduce expected output in both countries, and therefore will also reduce the volume of trade (though not trade's output share in GDP). Trade could fall as a share of total GDP in a model with nontraded goods (other than leisure). Bacchetta and van Wincoop (2000) model the impact of exchange rate variability on trade, but in their model the sign of the effect is theoretically ambiguous.

while the intertemporal Euler equation for money is

$$1 - \frac{\chi P_t^\varepsilon (C_t)^\rho}{M_t^\varepsilon} = \frac{1}{1+\delta} \mathrm{E}_t \left\{ \frac{P_t}{P_{t+1}} \left(\frac{C_t}{C_{t+1}} \right)^\rho \right\}. \tag{21}$$

The nominal interest rate is (easily shown to be) given by the consumption-based Fisher equation

$$1 + r_{t+1} = \frac{P_t (1 + i_{t+1}) \mathrm{E}_t \left\{ \frac{C_{t+1}^{-\rho}}{P_{t+1}} \right\}}{\mathrm{E}_t \left\{ C_{t+1}^{-\rho} \right\}}. \tag{22}$$

Combining the three equations immediately above, we can write the money demand equation as

$$\left(\frac{M_t}{P_t} \right)^\varepsilon = \chi \left(\frac{1 + i_{t+1}}{i_{t+1}} \right) C_t^\rho. \tag{23}$$

4.2. Log-Linearization and the Exchange-Rate Risk Premium

As noted in the last section, we are going to assume that all the shocks to the model are lognormally distributed. That assumption, as we shall see later in this section, will turn out to imply that consumption is lognormally distributed as well. In that case, one can write Equation (20) for Home as

$$-\rho c_t = \log \left(\frac{1 + r_{t+1}}{1+\delta} \right) - \rho \mathrm{E}_t c_{t+1} + \frac{\rho^2}{2} \sigma_{c,t}^2 \tag{24}$$

[where $\sigma_{c,t}^2 \equiv \mathrm{Var}_t(c_{t+1})$], with a parallel relation for Foreign. Of course $\sigma_{c,t}^2 = \sigma_{c^*,t}^2$ [recall Equation (14)]. We allow for a time-varying variance to capture the possibility of changes in the distributions of the exogenous shocks hitting the economy. We will illustrate later how to compute σ_c^2 and other second moments in terms of the variance–covariance structure of the underlying exogenous economic disturbances.

Taking logs of Equation (22) yields

$$\log(1 + i_{t+1}) = \log(1 + r_{t+1}) - \log \mathrm{E}_t \left\{ \frac{C_{t+1}^{-\rho}}{P_{t+1}} \right\} - p_t + \log \mathrm{E}_t \left\{ C_{t+1}^{-\rho} \right\}.$$

Lognormality of C and P allows us to write the preceding equation as

$$\log(1 + i_{t+1}) = \log(1 + r_{t+1}) + \mathrm{E}_t p_{t+1} - p_t + v_t, \tag{25}$$

with v_t given by

$$v_t = -\frac{1}{2} \sigma_{p,t}^2 - \rho \sigma_{cp,t} \tag{26}$$

[where $\sigma_{p,t}^2 \equiv \text{Var}_t(p_{t+1})$, and $\sigma_{cp,t} \equiv \text{Cov}_t(c_{t+1}, p_{t+1})$]. Note that the first component of v_t, involving the variance of prices, comes entirely from Jensen's inequality and therefore does not depend on any characteristics of the individual's utility function. It reflects that a mean-preserving rise in expected future price-level variability mechanically raises the expected future real value of money (which is a convex function of the price level). The nominal interest rate falls as a result, other things equal.

Now consider the money market equilibrium condition. It is at this point that we need to resort to an approximation, since the left-hand side of the money Euler equation (21) is not log-linear.[15] We approximate it in the neighborhood of a nonstochastic steady state with a constant rate of growth in consumption and in the money supply. In the steady state, the left-hand side of (21) is

$$1 - \frac{\chi \overline{P}_t^\varepsilon (\overline{C}_t)^\rho}{\overline{M}_t^\varepsilon} = 1 - \frac{\overline{i}}{1 + \overline{i}} = \frac{1}{1 + \overline{i}},$$

where overbars denote the nonstochastic steady state. Log linearizing the left-hand side of (21) therefore gives

$$\overline{i}\varepsilon(m_t - \overline{m}_t) - \overline{i}\varepsilon(p_t - \overline{p}_t) - \rho\overline{i}(c_t - \overline{c}_t) - \log(1 + \overline{i})$$

$$= \overline{i}\varepsilon(m_t - p_t) - \rho\overline{i}c_t - \overline{i}\log\left[\frac{\chi(1 + \overline{i})}{\overline{i}}\right] - \log(1 + \overline{i}).$$

The log of the right-hand side of (21) follows with no approximation from properties of the lognormal distribution:

$$-\log(1 + \delta) - \text{E}_t\{p_{t+1} - p_t\} - \rho\text{E}_t\{c_{t+1} - c_t\} + \frac{1}{2}\text{Var}_t\{p_{t+1} + \rho c_{t+1}\}.$$

Thus, Equation (21) can be approximated as

$$\varepsilon(m_t - p_t) = \log\left[\frac{\chi(1 + \overline{i})^{\frac{1+\overline{i}}{\overline{i}}}}{\overline{i}(1 + \delta)^{\frac{1}{\overline{i}}}}\right] - \frac{1}{\overline{i}}\text{E}_t\{p_{t+1} - p_t + v_t\}$$

$$- \frac{\rho}{\overline{i}}\text{E}_t\left\{c_{t+1} - c_t - \frac{\rho}{2}\sigma_{c,t}^2\right\} + \rho c_t, \tag{27}$$

where the substitution $\text{Var}_t\{p_{t+1} + \rho c_{t+1}\} = \rho^2\sigma_{c,t}^2 - 2v_t$ follows from Equation (26).

---

[15] As we illustrate in Appendix C, no approximation is needed for the special case in which $\varepsilon = 1$ and money supplies (but not necessarily other exogenous shocks) follow a random walk. The approximation we use below may not be a close one outside a neighborhood of $\varepsilon = 1$.

4.3. Equilibrium Exchange Rates and the "Level" Risk Premium

Assume that Home and Foreign have equal trend inflation rates, and therefore (in this model) equal long-run nominal interest rates in the non-stochastic steady state. Notice that, following the discussion of Equation (24), the term $E_t\{c_{t+1} - c_t - \frac{\rho}{2}\sigma_{c,t}^2\}$ is identical for Home and Foreign. Taking Equation (27), subtracting its foreign counterpart, and making use of the logarithmic PPP relation $e = p - p^*$ implied by (5), we therefore obtain

$$\varepsilon(m_t - m_t^* - e_t) = -\frac{1}{\bar{\imath}}(E_t e_{t+1} - e_t + v_t - v_t^*) + \rho(c_t - c_t^*).$$

Except for the risk premium term,

$$v_t - v_t^* = \frac{1}{2}\left(\sigma_{p*,t}^2 - \sigma_{p,t}^2\right) + \rho(\sigma_{cp*,t} - \sigma_{cp,t}), \tag{28}$$

this exchange rate equation is the same as in the certainty-equivalence model of Obstfeld and Rogoff (1995).[16] Here, however, because $c_t - c_t^* = 0$, it simplifies to

$$\varepsilon(m_t - m_t^* - e_t) = -\frac{1}{\bar{\imath}}(E_t e_{t+1} - e_t + v_t - v_t^*). \tag{29}$$

Equations (27) and (29) can both be solved in the usual way (assuming there are no speculative bubbles). The solution to (29) is

$$e_t = \frac{\bar{\imath}\varepsilon}{1 + \bar{\imath}\varepsilon} \sum_{s=t}^{\infty} \left(\frac{1}{1 + \bar{\imath}\varepsilon}\right)^{s-t} E_t \left\{ m_s - m_s^* + \frac{v_s - v_s^*}{\bar{\imath}\varepsilon} \right\}. \tag{30}$$

---

[16] Equation (28) is derived from Eq. (26) and its Foreign counterpart, recalling that $c = c^*$ in equilibrium.

As we were careful to point out immediately after Eq. (26), the term

$$\frac{1}{2}(\sigma_{p*,t}^2 - \sigma_{p,t}^2)$$

arises entirely from Jensen's inequality, whereas it is the term

$$\rho(\sigma_{cp*,t} - \sigma_{cp,t})$$

alone that depends on risk aversion (given the covariances in parentheses). Thus, it is the latter term that is more properly labeled "risk premium." A section of Engel (1999) is devoted to discussion of this point. As is often done in the literature, however, we will sometimes abuse language and refer to the sum of the two preceding terms as a risk premium, since that is the term examined in many empirical studies of foreign exchange market excess returns. See Engel (1992) for a theoretical context within which the distinction is important.

The term involving $\{v_s - v_s^*\}_{s=t}^{\infty}$ contributes a *level* risk premium to the exchange rate. This term is not precisely equal to the conventional forward exchange rate risk premium, which relates the forward rate to the expected future spot rate, but only because it is multiplied by the (possibly large) number $1/\bar{i}\varepsilon$.[17]

Hodrick (1989) showed the presence of related variability effects in the closed-form solution to a flexible-price exchange rate model. However, the cash-in-advance specification he employed to model money demand, while allowing a variable velocity of money, still implies a fairly low elasticity of the exchange rate level with respect to *monetary* risk factors such as those in Equation (28). And it is the conditional variance of monetary factors that is likely to be most volatile, and thus likely to have the best chance of explaining exchange-rate fluctuations. In contrast, the monetary specification we have used allows for an unrestricted Cagan semielasticity of money demand $1/\bar{i}\varepsilon$, which – see Equation (29) – determines the response of the spot exchange rate to expectations and risk premia. Equation (30) thus raises the possibility that higher moments of economic variables, not just first moments, could have significant exchange-rate impacts.[18]

By Equation (25), a fall in v (the result, e.g., of a rise in the covariance of c and p) is associated with a lower Home nominal interest rate and, by Equation (30), with an appreciation of Home's currency (a fall in e,

---

[17] The exchange rate risk premium is conventionally defined as the difference between the log forward exchange rate and the expected future log spot exchange rate (although we have already noted Engel's 1992 correction to the conventional definition). Covered interest parity ensures that the forward exchange rate level $\mathcal{F}t$ obeys the arbitrage relation

$$1 + i_{t+1} = \frac{\mathcal{F}_t}{\mathcal{E}_t}(1 + i_{t+1}^*).$$

Taking logs of both sides of the covered interest parity relation, substituting Eq. (25) and its Foreign counterpart, and making use of the PPP relationship (5) yields the logarithmic risk premium as

$$f_t - \mathrm{E}_t(e_{t+1}) = v_t - v_t^*, \tag{31}$$

where $v_t - v_t^*$ is given by Eq. (28). Note that this is exactly the same term that enters into the exchange rate *level* risk premium in Eq. (30), except that the term's effect on the exchange rate level is multiplied by a factor of $1/\bar{i}\varepsilon$. We argue later that this multiplicative factor is likely to be significantly greater than 1. While Eqs. (28), (30), (31), and (32) all hold whether output prices are sticky or flexible, the value of the risk premium may, of course, depend on the degree of price flexibility.

[18] Hodrick (1989) found little support in the data for a model in which exchange rate levels depend on the conditional variances of money supply and industrial output, modeled as generalised ARCH processes. However, his tests comprise only a small subset of the possible risk factors that could be at work.

resulting from higher Home money demand as i falls). Thus, the reduced relative riskiness of investments in the Home currency leads simultaneously to a fall in its nominal interest rate and an appreciation in the foreign exchange market. This experiment captures the idea of a portfolio shift toward the Home currency or, equivalently, of a "safe haven" effect on the Home currency.

One may similarly solve Equation (27) forward for the price level. Ignoring the fixed constant term (which is irrelevant for calculating the effects of unanticipated shocks), the result is[19]

$$
p_t = \frac{\bar{\imath}\varepsilon}{1 + \bar{\imath}\varepsilon} \sum_{s=t}^{\infty} \left(\frac{1}{1 + \bar{\imath}\varepsilon}\right)^{s-t} E_t \left\{ m_s + \frac{v_s - \frac{\rho^2}{2}\sigma_{c,s}^2}{\bar{\imath}\varepsilon} \right\}
$$
$$
+ \frac{\bar{\imath}\varepsilon}{1 + \bar{\imath}\varepsilon} \sum_{s=t+1}^{\infty} \left(\frac{1}{1 + \bar{\imath}\varepsilon}\right)^{s-t} \left(1 - \frac{1}{\varepsilon}\right)\rho E_t\{c_s\} - \left[\frac{\rho(1 + \bar{\imath})}{1 + \bar{\imath}\varepsilon}\right] c_t.
$$
(32)

4.4. The Short-Run Effects of Monetary Shocks

We next proceed to solve for current consumption. The easiest way to proceed is by multiplying Equation (27) by n and its Foreign equivalent by $1 - n$, and then adding the two equations. The result is

$$
\varepsilon(m_t^w - p_t^w) = \log\left[\frac{\chi(1 + \bar{\imath})^{\frac{1+\bar{\imath}}{\bar{\imath}}}}{\bar{\imath}(1 + \delta)^{\frac{1}{\bar{\imath}}}}\right] - \frac{1}{\bar{\imath}}E_t\left\{p_{t+1}^w - p_t^w + v_t^w\right\}
$$
$$
- \frac{\rho}{\bar{\imath}}E_t\left\{c_{t+1} - c_t - \frac{\rho}{2}\sigma_{c,t}^2\right\} + \rho c_t,
$$

where $m^w \equiv nm + (1 - n)m^*$, $p^w \equiv np_H + (1 - n)p_F^*$, and $v^w \equiv nv + (1 - n)v^*$. (Recall again that $c = c^w$ is the same at home and abroad.) Solving

[19] The ambiguously signed terms $(1 - \frac{1}{\varepsilon})\rho E_t\{c_s\}$ in this equation deserve comment. Higher expected future (log) consumption has two countervailing effects on the equilibrium price level, other things equal. By reducing desired saving and thereby increasing the real (and nominal) interest rate, it reduces money demand and puts upward pressure on the current price level. On the other hand, higher expected future consumption raises expected future money demand and hence lowers expected inflation, incipiently reducing the current nominal interest rate and putting downward pressure on the current price level. If $\varepsilon > 1$ – implying a relatively inelastic response of money demand to the nominal interest rate – the first effect is dominant.

forward yields an equation isomorphic to Equation (32) for the domestic price level (where again we ignore the uninstructive constant). Rearranging it in the form of an equation for world consumption, gives

$$\left[\frac{\rho(1+\bar{i})}{1+\bar{i}\varepsilon}\right]c_t = -p_t^w + \frac{\bar{i}\varepsilon}{1+\bar{i}\varepsilon}\sum_{s=t}^{\infty}\left(\frac{1}{1+\bar{i}\varepsilon}\right)^{s-t}E_t\left\{m_s^w + \frac{v_s^w - \frac{\rho^2}{2}\sigma_{c,s}^2}{\bar{i}\varepsilon}\right\}$$

$$+ \frac{\bar{i}\varepsilon}{1+\bar{i}\varepsilon}\sum_{s=t+1}^{\infty}\left(\frac{1}{1+\bar{i}\varepsilon}\right)^{s-t}\left(1-\frac{1}{\varepsilon}\right)\rho E_t\{c_s\}. \qquad (33)$$

One derives the full solution by substituting into the final right-hand side term above the earlier formula for expected future consumption, Equation (19). Because p_t^w is a predetermined variable as of date t, Equation (33) shows that, other things equal, higher than expected (as of date $t-1$) current/expected future money raises current consumption.

While the consumption effects of innovations in current or expected future money are the same internationally regardless of where in the world the shock originates, other effects do depend on which country generates the monetary impulse. By Equation (30), a positive innovation in Home money depreciates its currency, worsening its terms of trade and inducing a demand shift toward Home products.

Because of the Home currency depreciation, Home producers work harder than they would absent the exchange-rate change, Foreign producers enjoy more leisure. Because the short-run Home and Foreign consumption responses necessarily are equal, we know that the surprise Home monetary expansion benefits Foreign more than Home.[20] We examine these ex post welfare effects formally in Appendix D.

While the preceding discussion is suggestive, it is also possibly misleading for thinking about general-equilibrium effects. Equation (33) is not a reduced-form expression, of course, because the consumption and exchange variances it includes are endogenous variables that depend on the interaction among the model's exogenous shocks. We now illustrate how to solve explicitly for the model's covariance structure, focusing on implications for the foreign exchange risk premium.

---

[20] The money shock has no real effects beyond the period it occurs, in contrast to the model of Obstfeld and Rogoff (1995), because the current account is zero in equilibrium in this model. For the same reason as in the model of Obstfeld and Rogoff (1995), there is no exchange-rate overshooting in response to monetary shocks.

5. Solving for Exchange Risk Premia

Suppose, for example, that the Foreign money supply is constant and the Home money supply follows a random walk,

$$m_t = m_{t-1} + \mu_t,$$

where $\mu_t \sim \mathcal{N}(0, \sigma_\mu^2)$ for *every* date t. Because the distribution from which money shocks are drawn is time-invariant and lognormal, all of the variances and covariances in the model also will be constant over time.[21] Consider the Home nominal interest rate risk premium in Equation (26), which can be written as $v_t = -\frac{1}{2}\text{Var}_t(p_{t+1}) - \rho\text{Cov}_t(c_{t+1}^w, p_{t+1})$. Because p_H and p_F^* are preset,

$$\text{Var}_t(p_{t+1}) = (1-n)^2\text{Var}_t(e_{t+1}).$$

Also, we can compute the innovation in e_{t+1} easily from (30) because v and v^* are constants.[22] The innovation in e_{t+1} is

$$\left(\frac{\bar{i}\varepsilon}{1+\bar{i}\varepsilon}\right)\sum_{s=t+1}^{\infty}\left(\frac{1}{1+\bar{i}\varepsilon}\right)^{s-t-1}\mu_{t+1} = \mu_{t+1},$$

implying that

$$\text{Var}_t(p_{t+1}) = (1-n)^2\sigma_\mu^2.$$

By (33) the innovation in c_{t+1}^w is

$$\left[\frac{1+\bar{i}\varepsilon}{\rho(1+\bar{i})}\right]\left(\frac{\bar{i}\varepsilon}{1+\bar{i}\varepsilon}\right)\text{E}_t\left\{\sum_{s=t+1}^{\infty}\left(\frac{1}{1+\bar{i}\varepsilon}\right)^{s-t-1}n\mu_{t+1}\right\}$$

$$= \left[\frac{n(1+\bar{i}\varepsilon)}{\rho(1+\bar{i})}\right]\mu_{t+1}, \tag{34}$$

---

[21] Under the assumptions made in Section 3, productivity shocks are correlated with exchange rates and consumption only to the extent that monetary policy reacts systematically to them. Given that the money-supply process assumed in this section allows no feedback from productivity shocks to policy, we therefore need no further assumptions regarding the shocks κ and κ^*: they do not influence risk premia, expected consumption, or the expected terms of trade.

[22] The analysis becomes more complicated when the covariances, rather than being constants, can evolve stochastically over time. In that case innovations in second moments influence the exchange rate and consumption. Closed-form solutions for dynamic models with time-varying second moments are offered by Abel (1988) and Hodrick (1989).

and so

$$\text{Cov}_t\left(c_{t+1}^w, p_{t+1}\right) = \text{Cov}_t\left\{\left[\frac{n(1+\bar{i}\varepsilon)}{\rho(1+\bar{i})}\right]\mu_{t+1}, (1-n)\mu_{t+1}\right\}$$

$$= \left[\frac{(1-n)n(1+\bar{i}\varepsilon)}{\rho(1+\bar{i})}\right]\sigma_\mu^2. \tag{35}$$

Collecting terms, we see that the Home currency's risk premium (including the convexity term) is

$$v = -\sigma_\mu^2\left\{\frac{1}{2}(1-n)^2 + \left[\frac{(1-n)n(1+\bar{i}\varepsilon)}{1+\bar{i}}\right]\right\}.$$

If the only uncertainty is Home money-supply uncertainty, then the Home nominal interest rate will be below the level suggested by Fisher nominal–real parity because world consumption rises when the Home currency depreciates. Note also that the degree of risk aversion ρ drops out of the expression because ρ enters the consumption response to a fall in world interest rates as well as the calculation of the marginal utility of consumption.[23]

We can similarly calculate v^*. With sticky prices, the innovation to p_t^* is given by $-n\mu_{t+1}$, so that

$$\text{Var}_t(p_{t+1}^*) = n^2\sigma_\mu^2.$$

At the same time,

$$\text{Cov}_t\left(c_{t+1}^w, p_{t+1}^*\right) = \text{Cov}_t\left\{\left[\frac{n(1+\bar{i}\varepsilon)}{\rho(1+\bar{i})}\right]\mu_{t+1}, -n\mu_{t+1}\right\}$$

$$= -n^2\sigma_\mu^2\left[\frac{1+\bar{i}\varepsilon}{\rho(1+\bar{i})}\right].$$

---

[23] With more general preferences, both the degree of risk aversion and the elasticity of intertemporal substitution would appear separately in the solution for v. A cateris paribus rise in risk aversion would raise the absolute value of v. A rise in intertemporal substitutability, by magnifying the current consumption response to a fall in the world real interest rate, would also raise the absolute value of v.

Note that for a closed economy ($n = 1$), the price level is fully predictable with sticky prices and therefore $v = 0$.

Thus (again adding in the convexity term),

$$v^* = -n^2\sigma_\mu^2\left[\frac{1}{2} - \left(\frac{1 + \bar{i}\varepsilon}{1 + \bar{i}}\right)\right],$$

and

$$v - v^* = -\sigma_\mu^2\left[\frac{1 - 2n}{2} + \frac{n(1 + \bar{i}\varepsilon)}{1 + \bar{i}}\right].$$

is the risk premium.[24]

Thus, recalling Equation (30), we see that for empirically reasonable nominal interest rates (and in all cases for $n = \frac{1}{2}$), a rise in the level of Home monetary variability leads to both a *fall* in the "level" exchange-rate risk premium for the Home currency and a *fall* in its forward exchange rate risk premium. For plausible values of $\bar{i}$ and ε, the former effect is potentially much larger than the latter effect [because the coefficient $1/\bar{i}\varepsilon$ multiplying the risk premium in Equation (30) can be large].

Interestingly, our analysis contradicts the common casual presumption that financial markets will attach a positive risk premium to the currency of a country with high monetary volatility. Controlling for expected trend inflation differentials, that presumption is by no means necessarily borne out in a sticky-price world. Ceteris paribus, a rise in Home monetary volatility may lead to a fall in the forward premium, even holding expected exchange rate changes constant. Why? If positive domestic monetary shocks lead to increases in global consumption, then domestic money can be a hedge, in real terms, against shocks to consumption. (The real value of Home money will tend to be unexpectedly high in states of nature where the marginal utility of consumption is high.) Furthermore – and this effect also operates in a flexible-price model – higher monetary variability raises the expectation of the future real value of money, other things equal (the convexity term).[25]

---

[24] Excluding convexity terms (as arguably is more appropriate for a theoretical examination of the effects of risk), the risk premium would instead be

$$\rho\left[\text{Cov}_t\left(c_{t+1}^w, p_{t+1}^*\right) - \text{Cov}_t\left(c_{t+1}^w, p_{t+1}\right)\right] = -\sigma_\mu^2\left[\frac{n(1 + \bar{i}\varepsilon)}{1 + \bar{i}}\right].$$

The distinction is irrelevant here for $n = \frac{1}{2}$ as the convexity terms cancel out.

[25] These effects offer a possible insight into the "forward premium puzzle." The puzzle is the empirical regularity that (across the major currencies with floating exchange rates), high interest rates do not seem to be associated with expected depreciation. (If anything, the opposite is true.) Suppose that countries with higher trend inflation tend to experience

By the same logic that we have applied to a currency's excess return, we also see that higher domestic monetary policy volatility can lead to an appreciation of the domestic currency's *level* in the foreign exchange market. This effect would result from a *decline* in the "level" risk premium. Indeed, for plausible parameters, this effect can be big, as we have noted.

Although high Home monetary policy volatility may tend to strengthen the nominal value of the Home currency (since a fall in e is an appreciation), it does not necessarily improve Home's terms of trade. By the same logic we used to derive Equation (35), we infer that

$$\sigma_{ce} = \left[\frac{n(1+\bar{i}\varepsilon)}{\rho(1+\bar{i})}\right]\sigma_\mu^2.$$

Then, using Equation (18), we find that

$$E\{p_H - p_F^* - e\} = \left\{(1 - 2n) + \left[\frac{2n(1+\bar{i}\varepsilon)}{\rho(1+\bar{i})}\right]\right\}\sigma_\mu^2,$$

so that the effect of σ_μ^2 is theoretically ambiguous. The intuition is straightforward. First, consider the case where $n = 1/2$, so that the first term on the right-hand side above drops out. Then, a rise in Home monetary volatility strengthens Home's expected terms of trade, because Home producers contract planned output in the hope of limiting the rise in their labor-supply volatility (and Foreign producers do the reverse). On the other hand, if n and ρ are relatively large, a rise in σ_μ^2 may worsen Home's ex ante terms of trade. If the Home country is larger, exchange rate variability creates relatively greater demand variability for Foreign agents, leading them to substitute into leisure by setting prices higher.

Finally, our discussion has suggested that some of the results on the sign of risk premia carry over to the case of flexible prices. Plainly the results involving the expected terms of trade do not, since these were derived from price-setting behavior under risk. But the qualitative results concerning monetary variability and the nominal exchange rate risk premium do carry over. In fact, in the case $\varepsilon = 1$ (log utility for real balances),

---

greater volatility in monetary policy (a fairly well-documented fact; see, e.g., Alesina and Summers 1993). Then, across countries with relatively similar inflation rates (e.g., the main industrialized countries), it is at least theoretically possible that the forward premium is opposite in sign to the expected rate of depreciation of the exchange rate. Empirically, measured money-supply variability probably is too small to explain forward-rate bias based on a model like ours. In reality, however, monetary shocks also result from hard-to-measure money-demand factors, such as unpredictable shifts in the transactions technology.

both the forward exchange rate risk premium and the level exchange rate risk premium are identical for sticky- or flexible-price models (provided all shocks are monetary); see Appendix C. There are two offsetting factors involved in the result. Under flexible prices, the covariance between consumption and prices is zero (rather than a negative number) when all shocks are monetary. However, the overall price level is more volatile when it is flexible, and this makes the Jensen's inequality component of the risk premium larger. In the $\varepsilon = 1$ case, these two changes in moving from sticky to flexible prices offset each other exactly. Of course, under more general assumptions ($\varepsilon \neq 1$, nonmonetary shocks, and so on), the attributes of risk premia can depend on whether the model has flexible or sticky goods prices.

6. The Magnitude of the "Level" Exchange Rate Risk Premium

Is the level exchange rate risk premium potentially very large and volatile? Its magnitude depends on that of the forward risk premium and of model parameters. Little is known empirically about the magnitude of the forward risk premium. Fama (1984) has argued that the small coefficients one usually gets in forward premia regressions are a strong indication that the forward risk premium must be highly volatile, and probably more volatile than the expected rate of change of the exchange rate itself. Magnitudes of 0.5 to 1 percent for the mean absolute value of the one-year forward exchange rate risk premium seem conservative, given the evidence surveyed in Lewis (1995).[26]

The *level* exchange rate risk premium is larger than the forward exchange rate risk premium by a factor of $1/\bar{i}\varepsilon$ in our model [recall Equation (30)]. Assuming time is measured in years (on the same scale as the risk premium number we have just discussed), then a value between 0.04 and 0.08 seems plausible for $\bar{i}$. It is usually thought that ε is higher than one, though not necessarily by a large margin. Thus, based on a priori reasoning, it is not implausible to assume that $1/\bar{i}\varepsilon = 15$, suggesting that even a 0.5% risk premium in the forward rate could translate into an effect of 7.5% on the level of the exchange rate. One can also try to quantify $1/\bar{i}\varepsilon$ by noticing the interpretation of $1/\varepsilon$ as the interest elasticity

---

[26] Engel (1999) shows that when import prices are set in domestic-currency terms under pricing to market, and a cash-in-advance constraint makes money demand completely interest inelastic, a model of the type set out here can easily generate (realistically) large forward risk premia. In the model Engel describes, however, risk factors do not contribute to the conditional volatility of exchange rates.

of money demand, and then drawing on the theoretical and empirical literature on that topic. Both the Miller–Orr (1966) and Whalen (1966) models of money demand predict an interest elasticity of -0.33, which, with an average interest rate of 5% suggests a value for $1/\bar{i}\varepsilon$ of more than 5. Goldfeld's (1973) estimates of the interest elasticity of money demand are lower, on the order of -0.1 to -0.2, so an estimate of -0.33 may be on the high side. Nevertheless, it remains plausible that exchange risk can have a significantly larger effect on the level of the exchange rate than on the forward risk premium. Correspondingly, if the forward risk premium is quite volatile, as many studies indicate, the analysis here shows that such volatility could significantly heighten exchange-rate volatility.

7. Volatility and Welfare

Can a fully anticipated rise in Home monetary volatility potentially be welfare-improving? What is the effect on Foreign? We have seen that an increase in Home monetary volatility not only leads to a surprising rise in the Home currency's nominal exchange value, but it can also lead to an improvement in Home's expected terms of trade. In addition, expected consumption may rise if agents are sufficiently risk averse. Given that expected global consumption is too low in the nonstochastic steady-state equilibrium (due to the existence of monopoly power), this last effect, taken by itself, would appear offer a potential improvement in global welfare. In Section 4.4 we examined how monetary shocks are transmitted between countries ex post. Now we ask about the ex ante welfare effects of different policy *rules*.

7.1. Calculating Ex Ante Utility

Answering such questions turns out to be remarkably straightforward. In comparing the systematic effects of alternative policies, the relevant measure of welfare is ex ante welfare $E_{t-1}U_t$. We will temporarily ignore the empirically small money-services component of utility, in which case the Home representative agent's *period* objective reduces to

$$E_{t-1}u_t^R \equiv E_{t-1}\left\{\frac{C_t^{1-\rho}}{1-\rho} - \frac{\kappa_t}{2}Y_t^2\right\}.$$

Observe, however, that the first-order condition for optimal price setting, Equation (16), implies that in a symmetric equilibrium,

$$E_{t-1}\{\kappa_t Y_t^2\} = \left(\frac{\theta-1}{\theta}\right)E_{t-1}\{C_t^{1-\rho}\}, \tag{36}$$

since by Equation (13), $Y = PC/P_H$ (where, recall, $C = C^w$). Therefore, suppressing time subscripts,

$$E\left\{\frac{C^{1-\rho}}{1-\rho} - \frac{\kappa}{2}Y^2\right\} = E\left\{\frac{C^{1-\rho}}{1-\rho} - \frac{\theta-1}{2\theta}C^{1-\rho}\right\}$$

$$= E\left\{\frac{2\theta - (1-\rho)(\theta-1)}{2\theta(1-\rho)}C^{1-\rho}\right\},$$

an expression we can easily evaluate given that C is lognormally distributed and that we have already solved for Ec, σ_c^2 and σ_e^2.

To simplify matters slightly and without affecting our main qualitative results, we will abstract from productivity shocks. Then, making use of Equation (19), the final term of the last equation can be solved as[27]

$$Eu^R = E\left\{\frac{2\theta - (1-\rho)(\theta-1)}{2\theta(1-\rho)}C^{1-\rho}\right\}$$

$$= \left[\frac{2\theta - (1-\rho)(\theta-1)}{2\theta(1-\rho)}\right]\left(\frac{\theta-1}{\theta\kappa}\right)^{\frac{1-\rho}{1+\rho}}$$

$$\times \exp(1-\rho)\left[-\frac{2n(1-n)}{1+\rho}\sigma_e^2 - \sigma_c^2\right]. \tag{37}$$

From this equality we deduce that

$$\frac{\partial(Eu^R)}{\partial\sigma_c^2} = -(1-\rho)Eu^R < 0$$

(since the sign of u^R is the same as that of $1-\rho$). One can similarly calculate that

$$\frac{\partial(Eu^R)}{\partial\sigma_e^2} = -\frac{(1-\rho)}{2(1+\rho)}Eu^R < 0.$$

Thus, expected welfare is unambiguously decreasing in both the variability of consumption and exchange rates.

Let us assume that the only shocks are Home monetary shocks drawn from a time-invariant distribution. In that case we can draw on the last

---

[27] The text expression makes use of the fact that the expression

$$-\frac{1-\rho}{1+\rho}\left\{\left[2 - \frac{1}{2}(1-\rho)^2\right]\sigma_e^2\right\} + \frac{(1-\rho)^2}{2}\sigma_c^2$$

simplifies to $-(1-\rho)\sigma_c^2$.

section's results. Since

$$\sigma_c^2 = \left[\frac{n(1 + \bar{i}\varepsilon)}{\rho(1 + \bar{i})}\right]^2 \sigma_\mu^2$$

[recall (34)] and $\sigma_e^2 = \sigma_\mu^2$ are both increasing in σ_μ^2, it follows that Home welfare unambiguously falls as monetary variability rises.

What is the intuition for this unambiguous result, despite the fact that higher volatility can induce greater work effort, raising world consumption closer to the first-best competitive level? In this monopolistically distorted world, why wouldn't introducing a small amount of uncertainty have a first-order welfare benefit (if it raises consumption) and only a second-order cost (starting from a position of zero volatility)? The answer, loosely speaking, is that because the consumption shift itself is induced only by the change in uncertainty, the countervailing welfare effects must be of the same order of magnitude.[28] Intuitively, the output, consumption, and terms-of-trade effects of greater money-supply variability are all side effects of individuals' imperfectly successful attempts to shield themselves from a higher level of outside risk.

7.2. Equality of Expected Home and Foreign Utilities

The ex post effects of shocks are not necessarily the same at home and abroad in this model. As we discussed in Section 4.4, macroeconomic shocks can lead to internationally asymmetric labor-supply responses even though their consumption effects are symmetric.[29] In contrast to knowing about the ex post international effects of specific shocks, however, we are often interested in seeing how alternative *regimes* affect the ex ante distribution of global welfare. For example, how does a fully anticipated increase in Home's monetary variability affect Home and Foreign welfare? This regime change entails internationally asymmetric changes in several macro variables. Remarkably, however, the overall ex ante welfare effects on Home and Foreign are identical because

$$Eu^R = Eu^{*R} \tag{38}$$

always.

Equality (38) follows directly from the Home and Foreign first-order conditions for price setting, Equations (16) and (17). Indeed, Home and Foreign expected utility will still be proportional even if output enters

---

[28] We thank Meg Mayer for this intuition.
[29] See also Appendix D.

with a different exponent into Home versus Foreign utility. Even though the ex post effects of shocks need not be symmetric, *expected* utility is still equal across the two countries because producers formulate production plans to ensure that equality.[30]

We have not taken into account the terms in M/P in the utility function, but even these are identical if money shocks are permanent. (In the period of the shock Home real balances rise by n percent since the price level rises by $1 - n$ percent. Foreign real balances also rise by n percent as the Foreign currency appreciates.) Provided the term χ in (1) is realistically small, any differences due to real balance effects are presumably third-order in any event.

The model therefore provides an intriguing example in which there is no conflict between Home and Foreign objectives in choosing the exchange-rate *regime,* despite asymmetries in both ex ante price setting behavior and ex post outcomes. Observe that if we relaxed the assumption in Equation (2) that commodity-preference weights equal population weights, Equation (38) would no longer hold, but it would still be true that ex ante Home and Foreign utilities are *proportional.* In that case, too, countries would always agree on the choice of the exchange-rate regime.

7.3. Country Size and the Cost of Currency Volatility

Equation (37) has implications for the relation between country size and the cost of exchange volatility. When one of the countries, say Home, is so big that it occupies nearly the entire world, $n \approx 1$, then exchange rate volatility obviously has only a negligible effect on its welfare (because the price level is nearly perfectly predictable in that case). Surprisingly, how-ever, exchange rate volatility also has no effect on the welfare of Foreign, which is of size $1 - n \approx 0$. Equation (38) yields the same implication: If country size shields Home from the effects of exchange-rate variability,

---

[30] Under perfectly flexible prices, with the disutility of labor in both countries of the form $\kappa Y^v / v (v > 1)$, we would have

$$\kappa Y^v = \left(\frac{\theta - 1}{\theta}\right) C^{1-\rho}$$

in every state of nature. From this relationship it follows that $u^R = u^{*R}$ ex post. With optimally preset prices, however, Eq. (36) holds instead of the preceding displayed equation, and so $u^R = u^{*R}$ holds in expectation – Eq. (38). Obviously this is a special result that depends on the power form of the utility components, but it is still an interesting and important case. Deviations from purchasing power parity can cause the equality of expected utilities to break down, as in Obstfeld and Rogoff (2000), but need not, see Obstfeld (2001).

minuscule Foreign must gain commensurately.[31] This result seems to contradict the conventional wisdom that small countries are hurt relatively
more by currency volatility, and therefore would do well to fix their exchange rates.

What explains the result? In this case, Foreign's reduction in planned
output raises its terms of trade just enough to compensate it entirely
for exchange risk; see Equation (18). And since Foreign goods make up
an infinitesimal part of Home's consumption basket, this terms of trade
change has essentially no effect on Home. Thus, a very small country may
have little or no incentive to peg its currency to that of a very large trading
partner.[32]

7.4. Quantifying the Cost of Currency Volatility

One can use expression (37) to quantify the gain from moving to a fixed exchange rate regime. Assume for this purpose that all shocks are monetary.
The experiment we consider is a monetary regime change that reduces σ_e^2
to zero by pegging the exchange rate, while maintaining the variance of
world monetary growth (and hence σ_c^2) at its prior level. The calculation
we offer is meant only as an illustration, but it suggests that welfare losses
due to monetary shocks' exchange-rate effects could be large.

We compute the percentage increase λ in output under flexible prices,
$(\frac{\theta-1}{\theta\kappa})^{\frac{1}{1+\rho}}$, that makes the consumer as well off with exchange variability as
with $\lambda = 0$ but $\sigma_e^2 = 0$. (We hold σ_c^2 constant across regimes as explained
above, and refer to the equivalent variation λ as the "cost of exchange-rate
variability.") The cost λ is the solution to

$$(1+\lambda)^{1-\rho} \exp\left[-\frac{2n(1-n)(1-\rho)}{1+\rho}\sigma_e^2\right] = 1,$$

or

$$\lambda = \exp\left[\frac{2n(1-n)}{1+\rho}\sigma_e^2\right] - 1.$$

Imagine that the time interval during which prices are set is a year,
that $n = \frac{1}{2}$, that $\rho = 1$, and that σ_e equals 0.20, or 20% per year. Then
the cost of exchange-rate variability would be a full 1% of GDP per year

---

[31] Similarly, Eq. (19) implies that σ_e^2 does not affect the expected log of consumption in
either country when Home is nearly the whole world.

[32] On the other hand, in a model with many equally-sized monetary unions, welfare would be
enhanced (given an absence of real shocks) by a reduction in the number of independently
fluctuating currencies.

($\lambda = 0.01$), a substantial number given the low degree of risk aversion that was assumed. Raising the degree of risk aversion – while holding intertemporal substitutability constant – would raise this estimated cost.

8. Summary

This paper develops an explicitly stochastic treatment of a "new open economy macroeconomics" model along the lines of the one suggested by Obstfeld and Rogoff (1995). A main contribution of the paper is to introduce powerful new tools for investigating the allocational effects of macroeconomic uncertainties. Our log–linear model allows the explicit computation of risk premia and underscores the factors that determine risk premia when monetary surprises systematically cause output to change. The model admits possibly large effects of risk premia on exchange-rate levels – even when the risk premia themselves are of moderate size. By modeling nominal price setting by monopolistic producers under uncertainty, this paper shows that there will be a risk premium in the expected terms of trade that may differ in sign from the conventional currency risk premium.

The most compelling application of the model is, however, to welfare analysis. Explicit modeling of price setting behavior under uncertainty – rather than the assumption of certainty-equivalence behavior that is common in the literature – leads to very simple and powerful welfare results. Another contribution of this paper is to provide the first exact general-equilibrium account of the welfare costs of exchange-rate volatility, an issue absolutely central to the concept of optimum currency areas, but one that has not been adequately modeled to date (Krugman 1995). Empirically, these welfare costs can be substantial. Our model also provides an intriguing case in which Home and Foreign have the same incentives in designing an optimal world exchange rate system, despite potentially large asymmetries in both ex ante price setting and ex post welfare effects. Though there are many differences in outcomes for the two countries, these wash away in ex ante welfare calculations if producers set their money prices optimally.[33]

Needless to say, while our model is highly suggestive of effects and channels that had long proven elusive to international macro-modelers, it

---

[33] Appendices explore some additional issues, including the ex post international transmission of monetary shocks and the bearing of national monopoly power in trade on the size and sign of international transmission.

is only a special case. The literature subsequent to this paper has pursued a broad range of pertinent extensions and policy applications.

Appendix A. Flexible-Price Output Levels and Government Spending Shocks

The first section of this appendix describes the flexible-price output level implied by the model. The second shows how government spending shocks could be introduced.

A.1. Equilibrium Output with Flexible Prices

Under flexible prices, the first-order condition governing aggregate supply is given by[34]

$$Y(h)^{\frac{1+\theta}{\theta}} = \left(\frac{\theta-1}{\theta\kappa}\right)\left(\frac{P_H}{P}\right)^{\frac{\theta-1}{\theta}} (C^w)^{\frac{1}{\theta}} C^{-\rho}. \tag{39}$$

We derive from Equations (39) and (13) the log-linear relations:

$$(1+\rho)y = \log\left(\frac{\theta-1}{\theta\kappa}\right) + (1-\rho)(1-n)(p_H - p_F),$$

$$(1+\rho)y^* = \log\left(\frac{\theta-1}{\theta\kappa^*}\right) - (1-\rho)n(p_H - p_F). \tag{40}$$

In logs, Equation (12) is

$$p_H - p_F = y^* - y.$$

We can use this equation, together with those in (40), to solve for $p_H - p_F$, y, and y^*. The equilibrium terms of trade under flexible prices are

$$p_H - p_F = \frac{1}{2}\log\left(\frac{\kappa}{\kappa^*}\right),$$

so that the Home and Foreign flex-price output levels are

$$y = \frac{1}{1+\rho}\log\left(\frac{\theta-1}{\theta\kappa}\right) + \frac{(1-n)(1-\rho)}{2(1+\rho)}\log\left(\frac{\kappa}{\kappa^*}\right),$$

$$y^* = \frac{1}{1+\rho}\log\left(\frac{\theta-1}{\theta\kappa^*}\right) - \frac{n(1-\rho)}{2(1+\rho)}\log\left(\frac{\kappa}{\kappa^*}\right).$$

---

[34] This is the same as Eq. (15) from Chapter 10 of Obstfeld–Rogoff (1996), except that here $\rho \neq 1$ and supply responds positively when the general price of Home goods, P_H, rises relative to the overall CPI, P. Obstfeld and Rogoff (1995) and Corsetti and Pesenti (2001) treat the case $\rho \neq 1$.

Observe that because $p = np_H + (1 - n)p_F$,

$$c = c^* = c^W = ny + (1 - n)y^*$$
$$= \frac{1}{1+\rho}\left[n\log\left(\frac{\theta-1}{\theta\kappa}\right) + (1-n)\frac{1}{1+\rho}\log\left(\frac{\theta-1}{\theta\kappa^*}\right)\right].$$

A.2. Government Spending Shocks

Introducing government spending shocks into the model is straightforward. Suppose Home government spending falls entirely on Home output and that

$$Y - G = Y\exp(-\gamma)$$

and similarly that $Y^* - G^* = Y^*\exp(-\gamma^*)$. In equilibrium $PC_H^W\exp(\gamma) = P_H Y$, or

$$\left(\frac{P_H}{P}\right)^{-1}C^W\exp(\gamma) = Y.$$

The implication is that the spending shock can be viewed as shifting the demand curve facing a country.

Thus, with flexible prices, each home producer faces a demand curve

$$Y^d(h) = \left[\frac{P(h)}{P_H}\right]^{-\theta}\left(\frac{P_H}{P}\right)^{-1}C^W\exp(\gamma).$$

Clearly the only change from the corresponding text equation is replacement of C^W by $C^W\exp(\gamma)$, so we can write the producer's first-order condition as

$$Y(h)^{\frac{1+\theta}{\theta}} = \left(\frac{\theta-1}{\theta\kappa}\right)\left(\frac{P_H}{P}\right)^{\frac{\theta-1}{\theta}}[C^W\exp(\gamma)]^{\frac{1}{\theta}}C^{-\rho},$$

from which we can derive

$$(1+\rho)y = \log\left(\frac{\theta-1}{\theta\kappa}\right) + (1-\rho)(1-n)(p_H - p_F) + \rho\gamma,$$

$$(1+\rho)y^* = \log\left(\frac{\theta-1}{\theta\kappa}\right) - (1-\rho)n(p_H - p_F) + \rho\gamma^*.$$

Because $p_H - p_F = y^* - \gamma^* - (y - \gamma)$ [by the obvious generalization of (12)], we can use the preceding two equations to derive

$$p_H - p_F = \frac{1}{2}\left[(\gamma - \gamma^*) + \log\left(\frac{\kappa}{\kappa^*}\right)\right].$$

Combining the preceding three equations (and simplifying by assuming that $\kappa = \kappa^*$) yields

$$y = \frac{1}{2}\gamma - \frac{1}{2}\left(\frac{1-\rho}{1+\rho}\right)\gamma^w + \left(\frac{1}{1+\rho}\right)\log\left(\frac{\theta-1}{\theta\kappa}\right),$$

$$y^* = \frac{1}{2}\gamma^* - \frac{1}{2}\left(\frac{1-\rho}{1+\rho}\right)\gamma^w + \left(\frac{1}{1+\rho}\right)\log\left(\frac{\theta-1}{\theta\kappa}\right).$$

One can also derive:

$$c = c^* = c^w = \left(\frac{1}{1+\rho}\right)\left[\log\left(\frac{\theta-1}{\theta\kappa}\right) - \gamma^w\right].$$

The analysis of the sticky-price case is similarly straightforward.

Appendix B. Optimal Price Setting by Producers Facing Monetary and Productivity Shocks

This appendix presents the detailed derivation of the ex ante logarithmic terms of trade and consumption solutions reported as Equations (18) and (19). In Section 3 we derived the first-order condition

$$E\{C^{1-\rho}\} = E\left\{\kappa\left(\frac{\theta}{\theta-1}\right)\left(\frac{PC}{P_H}\right)^2\right\}$$

[Equation (16)]. Because P_H is predetermined, the latter can be written as

$$P_H = \sqrt{\left(\frac{\theta}{\theta-1}\right)\frac{E\{\kappa P^2 C^2\}}{E\{C^{1-\rho}\}}}.$$

The parallel Foreign relation,

$$E\{C^{1-\rho}(\theta-1)\} = E\left\{\kappa\theta\left(\frac{P^*C}{P_F^*}\right)^2\right\},$$

[Equation (17)], can be written as

$$P_F^* = \sqrt{\left(\frac{\theta}{\theta-1}\right)\frac{E\{\kappa^* P^{*2}C^2\}}{E\{C^{1-\rho}\}}}.$$

Recall that the Home and Foreign price indices are $P = P_H^n(\mathcal{E}P_F^*)^{1-n}$, $P^* = (P_H/\mathcal{E})^n(P_F^*)^{1-n}$. Using these definitions, we infer from the two preceding price-setting equations that

$$\left(\frac{P_H}{P_F^*}\right)^{1-n} = \sqrt{\left(\frac{\theta}{\theta-1}\right) \frac{E\{\kappa \mathcal{E}^{2(1-n)} C^2\}}{E\{C^{1-\rho}\}}},$$

$$\left(\frac{P_F^*}{P_H}\right)^{n} = \sqrt{\left(\frac{\theta}{\theta-1}\right) \frac{E\{\kappa^* \mathcal{E}^{-2n} C^2\}}{E\{C^{1-\rho}\}}}.$$

We assume that C and $\mathcal{E}$ are lognormally distributed (an assumption consistent with general equilibrium, as the text shows). Note that

$$E\{\kappa \mathcal{E}^{2(1-n)} C^2\} = E\{\exp[\log \kappa + 2(1-n)e + 2c]\}.$$

Thus, under lognormality,

$$E\{\kappa \mathcal{E}^{2(1-n)} C^2\} = \exp\left[E \log \kappa + 2(1-n)Ee + 2Ec + \frac{1}{2}\sigma_\kappa^2 + 2(1-n)^2\sigma_e^2 \right.$$
$$\left. + 2\sigma_c^2 + 2(1-n)\sigma_{\kappa e} + 2\sigma_{\kappa c} + 4(1-n)\sigma_{ce}\right].$$

Similarly,

$$E\{C^{1-\rho}\} = \exp\left[(1-\rho)Ec + \frac{1}{2}(1-\rho)^2\sigma_c^2\right].$$

The equation for $(P_H/P_F^*)^{1-n}$ above therefore becomes

$$\left(\frac{P_H}{P_F^*}\right)^{1-n} = \left(\frac{\theta}{\theta-1}\right)^{\frac{1}{2}} \exp\left\{\frac{1}{2}E\log\kappa + (1-n)Ee + \frac{1}{2}(1+\rho)Ec \right.$$
$$+ \frac{1}{4}\sigma_\kappa^2 + (1-n)^2\sigma_e^2 + \left[1 - \frac{1}{4}(1-\rho)^2\right]\sigma_c^2$$
$$\left. + (1-n)\sigma_{\kappa e} + \sigma_{\kappa c} + 2(1-n)\sigma_{ce}\right\}.$$

Likewise,

$$\left(\frac{P_F^*}{P_H}\right)^{n} = \left(\frac{\theta}{\theta-1}\right)^{\frac{1}{2}} \exp\left\{\frac{1}{2}E\log\kappa^* - nEe + \frac{1}{2}(1+\rho)Ec + \frac{1}{4}\sigma_{\kappa^*}^2 \right.$$
$$\left. + n^2\sigma_e^2 + \left[1 - \frac{1}{4}(1-\rho)^2\right]\sigma_c^2 - n\sigma_{\kappa^* e} + \sigma_{\kappa^* c} - 2n\sigma_{ce}\right\}.$$

Taking logs of these two equations leads to

$$(1-n)(p_{\mathrm{H}} - p_{\mathrm{F}}^* - Ee) - \frac{1}{2}\log\left(\frac{\theta}{\theta-1}\right) = \frac{1}{2}E\log\kappa + \frac{1}{2}(1+\rho)Ec$$
$$+ \frac{1}{4}\sigma_\kappa^2 + (1-n)^2\sigma_e^2 + \left[1 - \frac{1}{4}(1-\rho)^2\right]\sigma_c^2$$
$$+ (1-n)\sigma_{\kappa e} + \sigma_{\kappa c} + 2(1-n)\sigma_{ce}$$

and

$$-n(p_{\mathrm{H}} - p_{\mathrm{F}}^* - Ee) - \frac{1}{2}\log\left(\frac{\theta}{\theta-1}\right) = \frac{1}{2}E\log\kappa^* + \frac{1}{2}(1+\rho)Ec$$
$$+ \frac{1}{4}\sigma_{\kappa^*}^2 + n^2\sigma_e^2 + \left[1 - \frac{1}{4}(1-\rho)^2\right]\sigma_c^2 - n\sigma_{\kappa^* e} + \sigma_{\kappa^* c} - 2n\sigma_{ce}.$$

As noted in the text, we make the simplifying assumptions that κ and κ^* have identical lognormal distributions and are serially uncorrelated, so that $E_{t-1}\log\kappa_t = E_{t-1}\log\kappa_t^*$. Subtracting the second from the first of the last two equations gives the expected terms of trade under the simplifying assumptions, Equation (18):

$$p_{\mathrm{H}} - p_{\mathrm{F}}^* - Ee = (1-2n)\sigma_e^2 + 2\sigma_{ce} + (1-n)\sigma_{\kappa e} + n\sigma_{\kappa^* e} + \sigma_{\kappa c} - \sigma_{\kappa^* c}.$$

Finally, the preceding equations yield the expected log of (world) consumption, Equation (19):

$$Ec = \frac{1}{1+\rho}\left\{ \log\left(\frac{\theta-1}{\theta}\right) - E\log\kappa - \frac{1}{2}\sigma_\kappa^2 - 2n(1-n)\sigma_e^2\right.$$
$$- \left[2 - \frac{1}{2}(1-\rho)^2\right]\sigma_c^2 - 2n(1-n)(\sigma_{\kappa e} - \sigma_{\kappa^* e})$$
$$\left. - 2[n\sigma_{\kappa c} + (1-n)\sigma_{\kappa^* c}]\right\}.$$

Appendix C. An Important Special Case with an Exact Solution

Because the interest rate enters the money demand equation (23), it is not possible, in general, to write that equation in logs without resorting to a linearization. There is, however, one important special case where a closed-form solution exists. This case is of some interest not only in understanding the ramifications of the model for the exchange-rate risk premium but also because this simple case may be useful in various potential applications of the model.[35]

Suppose that $\varepsilon = 1$ so that money enters in the utility function (1) as $\chi \log(\frac{M_s}{P_s})$. Then the intertemporal Euler equation for money (21) becomes

$$1 = \frac{\chi P_t C_t^\rho}{M_t} + \beta E_t \left\{ \frac{P_t}{P_{t+1}} \left(\frac{C_t}{C_{t+1}} \right)^\rho \right\}, \tag{41}$$

where $\beta \equiv 1/(1 + \delta)$.

Assume that money follows a random walk with drift,

$$\frac{M_{t+1}}{M_t} = (1 + \mu)\epsilon_t, \tag{42}$$

where ϵ_t is a positive serially uncorrelated shock with mean 1. (Lognormality is not needed for the special case.) Foreign is symmetric with trend money-growth parameter μ^*. Consumption may also be stochastic, due to sticky prices, productivity shocks, and so on. We require only weak stationarity assumptions on the consumption process, which may be correlated with money.

The basic trick to solving the model is to rewrite Equation (41) as

$$1 = \frac{\chi P_t C_t^\rho}{M_t} + \beta \frac{\chi P_t C_t^\rho}{M_t} E_t \left\{ \frac{M_t}{M_{t+1}} \cdot \frac{M_{t+1}}{\chi P_{t+1} C_{t+1}^\rho} \right\}. \tag{43}$$

Let us try a candidate solution in which

$$\frac{\chi P_t C_t^\rho}{M_t} \equiv \psi$$

is constant for all t. In this case, Equation (43) simplifies to

$$1 = \frac{\chi P_t C_t^\rho}{M_t} + \beta E_t \left\{ \frac{M_t}{M_{t+1}} \right\},$$

or, taking advantage of (42),

$$\frac{\chi P_t C_t^\rho}{M_t} = 1 - \frac{\beta E_t(1/\epsilon_{t+1})}{1 + \mu}. \tag{44}$$

Note that in deriving this expression, we only required that μ and $E_t(1/\epsilon_{t+1})$ be constant over time. (Obviously, we are implicitly imposing

---

[35] The example here is developed for the flexible-price case in Obstfeld and Rogoff (1996, Section 8.7.3).

no speculative bubbles.) Assume that $\chi = \chi^*$. If we take Equation (44) and divide it by its foreign counterpart, using the fact $P_t = \mathcal{E}_t P_t^*$, we arrive at a reduced-form expression for the exchange rate:

$$\mathcal{E}_t = \frac{M_t}{M_t^*} \left[\frac{1 - \frac{\beta E_t(1/\epsilon_{t+1})}{1+\mu}}{1 - \frac{\beta E_t(1/\epsilon_{t+1}^*)}{1+\mu^*}} \right]. \tag{45}$$

An increase in the variance of Home money growth rate raises $E_t(1/\epsilon_{t+1})$ since the inverse is a convex function; the change therefore lowers the exchange rate. Note that Equation (45) holds under either flexible or fixed prices. (One can easily check that in the log–linear model developed in the previous part of the paper, the value of $v - v^*$ is the same under sticky or flexible prices also when $\varepsilon = 1$.)

How is it possible that money-growth uncertainty can affect the exchange rate equally under either sticky or flexible prices? Recall from Equation (26) that v is the sum of two components: a term involving the covariance of prices and consumption, and a convexity term deriving from the fact that inflation enters inversely into the money Euler condition. Under flexible prices, the overall price level is more volatile. Therefore, the convexity component of v is correspondingly larger. When $\varepsilon = 1$, these two effects cancel exactly. When $\varepsilon < 1$, the convexity effect is actually larger. One can easily solve for the forward exchange rate risk premium and show that for $\varepsilon = 1$, it has the same value under fixed and flexible prices.

Appendix D. Ex Post Welfare Effects of Monetary Shocks

The first section of this appendix analyzes in detail the global ex post welfare effects of monetary disturbances. The second shows in a general setting how terms-of-trade shifts can bring about asymmetric domestic and foreign effects of domestic monetary shocks.

D.1. Calculating Ex Post Welfare Effects

The effects of a monetary innovation on the Home representative agent all occur in the initial period of the shock. For concreteness, but with no loss of generality, consider a permanent (small) percentage increase dm in Home's money supply. Let us assume temporarily that κ is nonrandom and ignore the (empirically small) money-services component of utility.

We thus focus on the period utility component

$$u^R \equiv \frac{C^{1-\rho}}{1-\rho} - \frac{\kappa}{2}Y^2;$$

see Equation (1).

Assume the shock moves the world economy away from an initial path where $C^{1-\rho}$ and Y^2 equal their expected values as of the period before. Then the utility effect of the shock dm is

$$\frac{du^R}{dm} = EC^{1-\rho}\frac{dc}{dm} - \kappa EY^2\frac{dy}{dm}.$$

Recall, however, Equation (36):

$$E\kappa Y^2 = \left(\frac{\theta-1}{\theta}\right)EC^{1-\rho}.$$

Observe further that by Equations (4), (5), and (9), in a symmetric sticky-price equilibrium,

$$dy = (1-n)de + dc.$$

Putting the last three equations together, we infer that the ex post welfare effect on Home is the sum of two separate effects:

$$\frac{du^R}{dm} = EC^{1-\rho}\left(\frac{1}{\theta}\frac{dc}{dm}\right) - EC^{1-\rho}\left(\frac{\theta-1}{\theta}\right)(1-n)\frac{de}{dm}.$$

The first term here represents the increase in welfare resulting from a rise in output when price exceeds marginal cost. This welfare gain accrues equally to Home and Foreign, as in the analysis of Obstfeld and Rogoff (1995). The second welfare term arises because the Home currency depreciation switches global demand from Foreign to Home. That term, which reduces Home's gain from its own monetary expansion and augments Foreign's, was absent from the model in Obstfeld and Rogoff (1995). [The next section of this appendix explains why, and shows that in models more general than this one, the expenditure switching exchange-rate effect on Home welfare can be negative (as here), positive, or nil (as in Obstfeld and Rogoff 1995).]

Using Equations (30) and (33) and our assumption of a permanent Home money-supply increase, we compute that

$$\frac{du^R}{dm} = \frac{EC^{1-\rho}}{\theta}\left\{\frac{(1+\bar{\imath}\varepsilon)n}{\rho(1+\bar{\imath})} - (\theta-1)(1-n)\right\}.$$

This expression shows plainly that even a small money-supply increase, despite expanding Home consumption and output, need not have a positive welfare effect on Home itself (Home residents work harder). Foreign always gains, however. If the model contained an additional distortion making Home work effort lower – such as a domestic income tax – a positive welfare effect on Home would be more likely.

D.2. The Terms of Trade and Asymmetric Transmission

What explains the asymmetric ex post international transmission of monetary shocks in the present model, as compared with the symmetric transmission in that of Obstfeld and Rogoff (1995)? The answer is clearest if we generalize the model to allow for a possibly *nonunitary* (but still constant) elasticity of substitution, ω, between Home and Foreign goods.[36] In that case the index of total consumption becomes

$$C = \left[n^{\frac{1}{\omega}} C_H^{\frac{\omega-1}{\omega}} + (1-n)^{\frac{1}{\omega}} C_F^{\frac{\omega-1}{\omega}} \right]^{\frac{\omega}{\omega-1}}, \qquad \omega > 0,$$

instead of Equation (2) (which is the $\omega = 1$ case). However, (3) still holds, and is repeated below for convenience:

$$C_H = \left[\left(\frac{1}{n} \right)^{\frac{1}{\theta}} \int_0^n C(z)^{\frac{\theta-1}{\theta}} dz \right]^{\frac{\theta}{\theta-1}},$$

$$C_F = \left[\left(\frac{1}{1-n} \right)^{\frac{1}{\theta}} \int_n^1 C(z)^{\frac{\theta-1}{\theta}} dz \right]^{\frac{\theta}{\theta-1}}, \qquad \theta > 1.$$

Consider the special case in which $\omega = \theta$, so that substitutability in consumption does not depend on production locale. In that case we have

$$C = \left[\int_0^1 C(z)^{\frac{\theta-1}{\theta}} dz \right]^{\frac{\theta}{\theta-1}},$$

as in Obstfeld and Rogoff (1995). In the general ($\theta \neq \omega$) case, we have the price indexes

$$P_H = \left[\frac{1}{n} \int_0^n P(z)^{1-\theta} dz \right]^{\frac{1}{1-\theta}}, \qquad P_F = \left[\frac{1}{1-n} \int_n^1 P(z)^{1-\theta} dz \right]^{\frac{1}{1-\theta}},$$

---

[36] Similar analyses have been developed independently by Lombardo (1999) and Tille (2000).

and the demand functions

$$C(h) = \frac{1}{n}\left[\frac{P(h)}{P_{\mathrm{H}}}\right]^{-\theta} C_{\mathrm{H}}, \qquad C(f) = \frac{1}{1-n}\left[\frac{P(f)}{P_{\mathrm{F}}}\right]^{-\theta} C_{\mathrm{F}}.$$

The demand for the aggregates C_{H} and C_{F} is given by

$$C_{\mathrm{H}} = n\left(\frac{P_{\mathrm{H}}}{P}\right)^{-\omega} C, \qquad C_{\mathrm{F}} = (1-n)\left(\frac{P_{\mathrm{F}}}{P}\right)^{-\omega} C,$$

where

$$P = [nP_{\mathrm{H}}^{1-\omega} + (1-n)P_{\mathrm{F}}^{1-\omega}]^{\frac{1}{1-\omega}}.$$

Because of these relationships, we see that individual Home and Foreign producers will face the world demand curves:

$$C(h) = \left[\frac{P(h)}{P_{\mathrm{H}}}\right]^{-\theta}\left(\frac{P_{\mathrm{H}}}{P}\right)^{-\omega} C^{\mathrm{w}}, \qquad C(f) = \left[\frac{P(f)}{P_{\mathrm{F}}}\right]^{-\theta}\left(\frac{P_{\mathrm{F}}}{P}\right)^{-\omega} C^{\mathrm{w}}.$$

$$(46)$$

The intuition behind this specification is quite important. In the model of this paper $\omega = 1 < \theta$, so the Home and Foreign output baskets are less substitutable than are different Home (or Foreign) commodities for each other. This means (as we show in a moment) that if all Home producers lower price simultaneously, the global demand response for a single producer is smaller than it would be if that producer unilaterally lowered price. From a national standpoint, therefore, producers overestimate the price elasticity of demand. (There is a pecuniary externality.) This is the key reason for asymmetric effects of small exchange-rate changes in this paper's model. When instead $\omega = \theta$ (as in Obstfeld and Rogoff 1995), each individual producer perceives a demand curve that accurately reflects the country's monopoly power in trade. This feature lies behind the symmetric effects of small exchange-rate changes in Obstfeld and Rogoff (1995).

More formally, observe that for a representative Home good (say), Equation (46) can be solved for $P(h)$ to show that real revenue is

$$\frac{P(h)Y(h)}{P} = Y(h)^{1-\frac{1}{\theta}} \left(\frac{P_H}{P}\right)^{1-\frac{\omega}{\theta}} (C^w)^{\frac{1}{\theta}}$$

$$= Y(h)^{1-\frac{1}{\theta}} \left\{ \frac{P_H}{[nP_H^{1-\omega} + (1-n)P_F^{1-\omega}]^{\frac{1}{1-\omega}}} \right\}^{1-\frac{\omega}{\theta}} (C^w)^{\frac{1}{\theta}}$$

$$= Y(h)^{1-\frac{1}{\theta}} \Phi \left(\frac{P_H}{P_F}\right)^{1-\frac{\omega}{\theta}} (C^w)^{\frac{1}{\theta}}, \tag{47}$$

where $\Phi'(P_H/P_F) > 0$.

The experiment we consider is a small increase in Home output, holding world consumption C^w constant. (This corresponds to a pure expenditure switching effect.) Notice that marginal national revenue, computed using Equation (47), is

$$NR = \left(\frac{\theta-1}{\theta}\right) \frac{P_H}{P} + \left(\frac{\theta-\omega}{\theta}\right) (\eta_\Phi)(\eta_{P_H/P_F}) \frac{P_H}{P}, \tag{48}$$

where

$$\eta_\Phi \equiv \frac{d\log\Phi(P_H/P_F)}{d\log(P_H/P_F)} > 0$$

and

$$\eta_{P_H/P_F} \equiv \frac{d\log(P_H/P_F)}{d\log Y(h)} < 0.$$

Marginal *private* revenue (as perceived by the individual producer) is just the first summand of the right-hand side of Equation (48),

$$PR = \left(\frac{\theta-1}{\theta}\right) \frac{P(h)}{P},$$

that is, PR is the derivative of total real revenue holding the aggregate terms of trade P_H/P_F constant.

In a symmetric equilibrium with $P(h) = P_H$ for all h, individual monopolistic producers produce too much (from the parochial perspective of maximizing real national revenue) when $\theta > \omega$ and $PR > NR$. Such is the case in this paper, where $\omega = 1$ is assumed. In the standard competitive model of the optimal tariff, $\theta = \infty$ and so the country overproduces absent a protective tariff. Interestingly, however, $NR > PR$ when $\theta < \omega$, so in that case national real income is raised if producers jointly expand output. In the case $\theta < \omega$ a country expanding its money supply would reap a secondary short-run gain from the depreciation of its currency, rather than the more conventional secondary terms-of-trade loss. The case analyzed in Obstfeld and Rogoff (1995) is the one in which $\theta = \omega$, so that $NR = PR$ and the expenditure switching effect of a currency depreciation has no first-order welfare consequence.

References

Abel, Andrew B. (1988). "Stock Prices under Time-Varying Dividend Risk: An Exact Solution in an Infinite-Horizon General Equilibrium Model," *Journal of Monetary Economics* 22 (November): 375–93.

Alesina, Alberto, and Lawrence H. Summers (1993). "Central Bank Independence and Macroeconomic Performance: Some Comparative Evidence," *Journal of Money, Credit and Banking* 25 (February): 151–62.

Bacchetta, Philippe, and Eric van Wincoop (2000). "Does Exchange Rate Stability Increase Trade and Welfare?" *American Economic Review* 90 (December): 1093–109.

Baxter, Marianne, and Alan C. Stockman (1989). "Business Cycles and the Exchange-Rate Regime: Some International Evidence," *Journal of Monetary Economics* 23 (May): 377–400.

Cole, Harold L., and Maurice Obstfeld (1991). "Commodity Trade and International Risk Sharing: How Much Do Financial Markets Matter?" *Journal of Monetary Economics* 28 (August): 3–24.

Corsetti, Giancarlo, and Paolo Pesenti (2001). "Welfare and Macroeconomic Interdependence," *Quarterly Journal of Economics* 116 (May): 421–45.

Devereux, Michael B., and Charles Engel (2000). "Monetary Policy in the Open Economy Revisited: Price Setting and Exchange Rate Flexibility," working paper, April.

Engel, Charles M. (1992). "On the Foreign Exchange Risk Premium in a General Equilibrium Model," *Journal of International Economics* 32 (May): 305–19.

Engel, Charles M. (1999). "On the Foreign Exchange Risk Premium in Sticky-Price General Equilibrium Models," in Peter Isard, Assaf Razin, and Andrew K. Rose (eds.), *International Finance and Financial Crises: Essays in Honor of Robert P. Flood, Jr.* (Boston: Kluwer Academic Publishers).

Fama, Eugene F. (1984). "Forward and Spot Exchange Rates," *Journal of Monetary Economics* 14 (November): 319–38.

Flood, Robert P., and Andrew K. Rose (1995). "Fixing Exchange Rates: A Virtual Quest for Fundamentals," *Journal of Monetary Economics* 36 (August): 3–37.

Frankel, Jeffrey A., and Richard A. Meese (1987). "Are Exchange Rates Excessively Volatile?" *NBER Macroeconomics Annual*, 1987: 117–53.

Goldfeld, Stephen M. (1973). "The Demand for Money Revisited," *Brookings Papers on Economic Activity* 1: 577–638.

Helpman, Elhanan, and Assaf Razin (1979). "Towards a Consistent Comparison of Alternative Exchange Rate Systems," *Canadian Journal of Economics* 12 (August 1979): 394–409.

Hodrick, Robert J. (1989). "Risk, Uncertainty, and Exchange Rates," *Journal of Monetary Economics* 23 (May): 433–60.

Kimball, Miles S. (1995). "The Quantitative Analytics of the Basic Neomonetarist Model," *Journal of Money, Credit, and Banking* 27 (November, part 2): 1241–77.

Krugman, Paul R. (1995). "What Do We Need to Know about the International Monetary System?" in Peter B. Kenen (ed.), *Understanding Interdependence: The Macroeconomics of the Open Economy*. (Princeton: Princeton University Press).

Lewis, Karen K. (1995). "Puzzles in International Financial Markets," in Gene Grossman and Kenneth Rogoff (eds.), *Handbook of International Economics*, vol. 3. (Amsterdam: Elsevier Science Publishers).

Lombardo, Giovanni (1999). "On the Trade Balance Response to Monetary Shocks: The Marshall–Lerner Conditions Reconsidered," working paper, Trinity College Dublin (October).

Lucas, Robert E., Jr. (1982). "Interest Rates and Currency Prices in a Two-Country World," *Journal of Monetary Economics* 22 (July): 3–42.

Meese, Richard A., and Kenneth Rogoff (1983). "The Out-of-Sample Failure of Empirical Exchange Rate Models: Sampling Error or Misspecification?" in Jacob A. Frenkel (ed.), *Exchange Rates and International Macroeconomics*. (Chicago: University of Chicago Press).

Miller, Merton H., and Daniel Orr (1966). "A Model of the Demand for Money by Firms," *Quarterly Journal of Economics* 80 (August): 413–35.

Mussa, Michael (1986). "Nominal Exchange Rate Regimes and the Behavior of Real Exchange Rates: Evidence and Implications," *Carnegie–Rochester Conference Series on Public Policy* 25 (Autumn): 117–214.

Obstfeld, Maurice (1998). "Open-Economy Macroeconomics: Developments in Theory and Policy," *Scandinavian Journal of Economics* 100 (March): 247–75.

Obstfeld, Maurice (2001). "International Macroeconomics: Beyond the Mundell-Fleming Model," *International Monetary Fund Staff Papers* 47 (Special Issue): 1–39.

Obstfeld, Maurice (2002). "Inflation Targeting. Exchange-Rate Pass-Through, and Volatility," *American Economic Review* 92 (May): 102–7.

Obstfeld, Maurice, and Kenneth Rogoff (1995). "Exchange Rate Dynamics Redux," *Journal of Political Economy* 103 (June): 624–60.

Obstfeld, Maurice, and Kenneth Rogoff (1996). *Foundations of International Macroeconomics*, (Cambridge, MA: MIT Press).

Obstfeld, Maurice, and Kenneth Rogoff (2000). "New Directions for Stochastic Open Economy Models," *Journal of International Economics* 50 (February): 117–53.

Obstfeld, Maurice, and Kenneth Rogoff (2002). "Global Implications of Self-Oriented National Monetary Rules." *Quarterly Journal of Economics* 117 (May): 503–35.

Rankin, Neil (1998). "Nominal Rigidity and Monetary Uncertainty in a Small Open Economy," *Journal of Economic Dynamics and Control* 22 (May): 679–702.

Svensson, Lars E. O. (1985). "Currency Prices, Terms of Trade, and Interest Rates: A General-Equilibrium Asset-Pricing Cash-in-Advance Approach," *Journal of International Economics* 18 (February): 17–41.

Svensson, Lars E. O. (1986). "Sticky Goods Prices, Flexible Asset Prices, Monopolistic Competition, and Monetary Policy," *Review of Economic Studies* 53 (July): 385–405.

Svensson, Lars E. O., and Sweder van Wijnbergen (1989). "Excess Capacity, Monopolistic Competition, and International Transmission of Monetary Disturbances," *Economic Journal* 99 (September): 785–805.

Tille, Cedric (2000). "Beggar-Thy-Neighbor' or 'Beggar-Thyself'? The Income Effect of Exchange Rate Fluctuations," working paper, Federal Reserve Bank of New York.

Whalen, Edward L. (1966). "A Rationalization of the Precautionary Demand for Cash," *Quarterly Journal of Economics* 80 (May): 314–24.

PART TWO

FINANCIAL ISSUES IN OPEN ECONOMIES: EMPIRICS

Economic Integration, Industrial Specialization, and the Asymmetry of Macroeconomic Fluctuations*

Sebnem Kalemli-Ozcan, Bent E. Sørensen, and Oved Yosha

We show empirically that regions with a more specialized production structure exhibit output fluctuations that are less correlated with those of other regions (less "symmetric" fluctuations). Combined with the causal relation running from capital market integration to regional specialization found in an earlier study, this finding supports the idea that higher capital market integration leads to less symmetric output fluctuations. This mechanism counterbalances the effect of lower trade barriers on the symmetry of fluctuations quantified by Frankel and Rose (1998). It is further argued that more asymmetric output shocks do not necessarily imply more asymmetric *income* shocks, since more cross-country ownership of productive assets may actually render income shocks more symmetric despite the greater asymmetry of output shocks. Some evidence in support of this claim is reported. Deriving a simple closed form expression for the gains from risk sharing for CRRA utility is an independent contribution of the present article.

1. Introduction

Much of the debate on the desirability of economic integration centers on the degree of synchronization (symmetry) of macroeconomic fluctuations

* The paper appears in *Journal of International Economics*, 2001, vol. 55, 107–137, and is reprinted here under permission of Elsevier Science B.V. The paper is essentially the same, but Section 7, dealing with income asymmetry, is new. (We have also incorporated changes addressing the comments of the discussant, Lars Svensson.) We thank three referees, Andy Rose, and Lars Svensson for comments as well as participants in several seminars and conferences. The paper previously circulated as "Industrial Specialization and the Asymmetry of Shocks across Regions."

121

across countries.[1] It has been noted that the process of economic integration itself will affect the symmetry of macroeconomic fluctuations. Frankel and Rose (1998) argue that removal of trade barriers will entail more correlated business cycles, because a higher level of trade will allow demand shocks to more easily spread across national borders. They further mention that economic integration will render policy shocks more correlated and that knowledge and technology spillovers will increase (Coe and Helpman 1995).[2] Krugman (1993), on the other hand, claims that lower barriers to trade will induce countries to specialize more, rendering output fluctuations less, not more, symmetric.[3] Figure 5.1 summarizes these effects visually.

Frankel and Rose (1998) provide empirical evidence for the mechanism they propose by regressing the pairwise correlation of business cycles on bilateral trade intensity instrumented by distance for a sample of OECD countries.[4] They obtain a positive and significant coefficient, which suggests that even if the effect proposed by Krugman is present in the data, it is dominated by the mechanism they describe.[5]

Our goal here is twofold. First, we want to draw attention to yet another mechanism: Economic integration will lead to better income insurance through greater capital market integration which will, ceteris paribus, induce higher specialization in production and more trade rendering fluctuations less symmetric across countries. Second, we establish empirically

---

[1] In recent years, the discussion of European monetary integration has dominated the scene. It is argued that the cost of joining a monetary union and giving up independent monetary policy will be low if countries have highly synchronized (symmetric) business cycles. See De Grauwe and Vanhaverbeke (1993) for an exposition of the main issues. Naturally, this debate builds on Mundell's (1961) classic analysis of Optimum Currency Areas.

[2] These additional mechanisms should also contribute to fluctuations becoming more symmetric following economic integration.

[3] Krugman corroborates his argument with the observation that U.S. states are more specialized in production than European countries.

[4] It is well established empirically that trade volume increases with geographical proximity; see Table 1 in Frankel and Rose (1998).

[5] The effect suggested by Krugman operates via interindustry trade while that proposed by Frankel and Rose applies mainly to intraindustry trade. In their analysis, Frankel and Rose use the total volume of trade instrumented by distance. Since distance affects both inter- and intraindustry trade, the positive relation between trade volume and business cycle correlation indicates that the effect suggested by Krugman is not the dominant one. Rose (2000) adds another empirical building block to the Frankel–Rose mechanism by providing cross-sectional country- and regional-level evidence that a common currency enhances the volume of trade. Canova and Dellas (1993) also study the relation of trade interdependencies and business cycles, focusing on the transmission across countries of business cycle fluctuations and obtain mixed results. They do not discuss the potential endogenous response of country-level business cycles to economic integration.

that higher specialization in production indeed translates into less symmetry of output fluctuations; see Fig. 5.1.

The claim that economic integration will induce higher specialization in production through better cross-country income insurance has been substantiated empirically by Kalemli-Ozcan, Sørensen, and Yosha (1999).

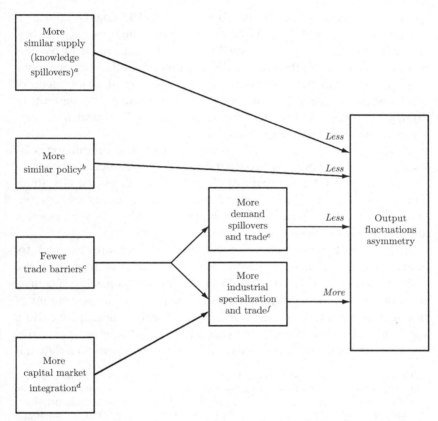

Figure 5.1. The effects of economic integration on fluctuations asymmetry.
[a] Coe and Helpman (1995).
[b] This channel is mentioned by Frankel and Rose (1998).
[c] Frankel and Rose (1998) estimate the overall effect on fluctuations asymmetry of lowering trade barriers. They instrument by distance (a trade barrier). Krugman (1993) stresses the effect of lower trade barriers on specialization.
[d] Kalemli-Ozcan, Sorensen, and Yosha (1999) estimate the effect of greater interregional income insurance on industrial specialization. In the current paper, we estimate the effect of greater industrial specialization on fluctuations asymmetry.
[e] Typically, more intraindustry trade.
[f] Typically, more interindustry trade.

They established that capital market integration leads to higher specialization in production. Here we find that higher specialization in production is associated with less symmetry of output fluctuations. Together, these findings substantiate an effect of income insurance on industrial specialization which, other things equal, results in less symmetric output fluctuations.[6]

There is no contradiction between our empirical findings and those reported by Frankel and Rose (1998) since the mechanism we suggest (better opportunities for income diversification) is independent of barriers to trade.[7] Our papers thus isolate distinct potential effects of economic integration on fluctuations asymmetry that are part of a rich menu of economic mechanisms that will jointly shape postintegration patterns of GDP fluctuations.[8] Which effect will dominate in the European Monetary Union remains an open empirical question.

To establish empirically that higher specialization in production is associated with less symmetry of output fluctuations, we calculate measures of asymmetry in GDP fluctuations for OECD countries and U.S. states and regress them on industrial specialization indices. The regressions control for relevant economic and demographic variables and yield positive and significant coefficients for the specialization indices.

In the context of economic integration, a natural measure of asymmetry is one that quantifies the potential loss of welfare due to asymmetric GDP fluctuations in the absence of risk sharing mechanisms. (Of course, we want an asymmetry measure that is independent of the amount of risk sharing actually obtained.) To construct such a measure we use a simple model of risk sharing among countries inhabited by representative agents. First, we evaluate the welfare that each country would obtain if it

[6] Our finding in this paper also serves as partial corroboration for the mechanism suggested by Krugman (1993). But to our knowledge, the positive effect of lower trade barriers on industrial specialization has not yet been established by systematic empirical analysis.

[7] In particular, the main instrument used by Frankel and Rose – geographical distance – seems to be orthogonal to the amount of income diversification across regions and countries. Sørensen and Yosha (1998) find that the amount of insurance across OECD countries (including Japan, Canada, and the United States) is very similar to the amount of insurance across European Union countries, and Sørensen and Yosha (2000) find that the amount of insurance within different regions of the United States is very similar to the amount of insurance within the U.S. as a whole. It seems that the amount of insurance among regions and countries is determined by institutional factors (for instance, the legal and financial environment); see Kalemli-Ozcan, Sørensen, and Yosha (1999).

[8] See Giannetti (1999) for yet another such mechanism. She argues that industrial composition determines who benefits from knowledge spillovers. In her model, high-productivity rich regions will become richer and even more specialized in the high-productivity sector relative to poor regions as a result of economic integration.

were constrained to consume its own GDP. Next, we evaluate the welfare that each country would obtain if output were pooled across the entire OECD. The difference represents *potential* gains from risk sharing that we here regard as a measure of fluctuations asymmetry. The logic is that the more a country can gain from sharing risk with other countries in a group, the more asymmetric are its GDP shocks relative to the group.[9] The derivation of a simple closed form expression for the gains from risk sharing is an independent contribution of the present article.[10]

Asymmetry of output (GDP) may not be important for the stability of a monetary union if there is substantial risk sharing between members of the union. Rather, the potential welfare losses from income and consumption asymmetry might be the relevant indicators of stability. We demonstrate that asymmetry of personal income across U.S. states is substantially lower than asymmetry of output. (We do not consider asymmetry of consumption since only retail sales are available at the U.S. state level and welfare gain measures are very sensitive to measurement error.)

In the next section, we review relevant conceptual issues. In Section 3, we sketch a stylized model of fluctuations in order to provide a framework for interpreting our findings. In Section 4, we present our measure of fluctuations asymmetry which is derived in detail in the Appendix. In Section 5, we define the specialization indices that we use and in Section 6, we describe our data and report the empirical results. Section 7 displays asymmetry measures for U.S. states based on personal income, and Section 8 concludes the paper.

2. Conceptual Issues

In the presence of production risk and with no markets for insuring it, countries that specialize in the production of a small number of goods may suffer a loss in economic welfare due to the high variance of GDP.[11] But if international financial markets and goods markets are integrated,

---

[9] An analogous reasoning holds for U.S. states.

[10] Cole and Obstfeld (1991) point out that changes in the terms of trade can provide insurance. In their model, countries produce different goods and consume similar baskets of goods. An (exogenous) increase in the physical amount of output of a good will lead to a decline in the price of that good, which can be considered as "automatic insurance" through the terms of trade. We utilize nominal GDP numbers (which already incorporate price responses) deflated by consumer prices. That is, the potential gains from risk sharing calculated in the present article are the potential gains from financial market integration beyond any automatic insurance from term-of-trade responses.

[11] See Brainard and Cooper (1968), Kemp and Liviatan (1973), and Ruffin (1974).

countries are able to insure against asymmetric shocks through diversification of ownership and can therefore "afford" to have a specialized production structure.[12] The central empirical implication of this idea is that better insurance among countries should be associated with higher country-level specialization in production. (An analogous logic holds for regions within countries.) This was confirmed empirically by Kalemli-Ozcan, Sørensen, and Yosha (1999) who established a causal link running from risk sharing (income insurance), facilitated by a developed and reliable financial system, to specialization in production.[13]

Financial integration will likely lead to more specialization since entrepreneurs will be less reluctant to "put more eggs in the same basket." This is because a greater fraction of their (or their investors') income will be derived from other sources, such as internationally diversified investment funds. Further, foreign investors will be buying shares in domestic firms since they themselves will be seeking to diversify their portfolios internationally. It is also likely that governments will insist less on subsidizing diversity within national borders.

What are the implications for the European Monetary Union? Today, there is little risk sharing between countries,[14] but capital market integration is bound to increase with further economic integration. First, there is some indication that a change is already taking place in Europe. Liebermann (1999) has replicated the Sørensen and Yosha (1998) study, extending the sample period to include the 1990s. She finds significantly

---

[12] See Helpman and Razin (1978a, 1978b) and Feeney (1994). Further work on this topic includes Anderson (1981), Grossman and Razin (1984, 1985), and Helpman (1988). The idea that insurance induces specialization has made an impact in the economic growth and development literature; see Greenwood and Jovanovic (1990), Saint-Paul (1992), Acemoglu and Zilibotti (1997), and Feeney (1999). Closely related to the topic of this paper is Obstfeld (1994a). In his model, countries choose the investment mix in risky (high return) projects and safe (low return) projects. International capital market integration provides insurance, inducing countries to shift investment toward high return projects promoting faster growth.

[13] To address the possibility of endogeneity bias, they used instrumental variables which are exogenous to the degree of specialization but are likely to be correlated with the extent of observed interregional risk sharing. These include quantitative indicators of the "legal environment" that are likely to have an impact on the amount of cross-regional ownership of assets, for example, the degree of protection of investor rights (La Porta et al. 1998).

[14] See French and Poterba (1991) and Tesar and Werner (1995) who document "home bias" in portfolio holdings, Backus, Kehoe, and Kydland (1992) who compare cross-country GDP correlations and consumption correlations, and Sørensen and Yosha (1998) and Arreaza (1998) who carry out cross-country variance decompositions of shocks to GDP for EC/OECD and Latin American countries respectively. All these studies point to negligible risk sharing through cross-country ownership of assets.

higher cross-country insurance via capital markets during the period 1992–97, which indicates that capital markets in Europe are integrating. Second, the high degree of cross-regional ownership in the United States, documented by Asdrubali, Sørensen, and Yosha (1996), suggests that economic and monetary unification will indeed induce a greater geographical spread of ownership across Europe.[15]

We expect the main impact on specialization to occur in manufacturing where corporate ownership is most prevalent. At the one-digit level, production patterns are determined to a large extent by exogenous circumstances, most notably the existence of natural resources such as oil, minerals, or fertile land. However, cross-border insurance should have an impact on specialization even at the one-digit level – at least at the margin. To illustrate, with insurance against asymmetric fluctuations it would be less risky for the Italian Riviera regions to further specialize in tourism and for Norway to further specialize in oil production.

If countries indeed specialize more as a result of international capital market integration, the opportunities to insure *within* countries will be reduced. Therefore, higher specialization in production should render country-level GDP fluctuations less symmetric. The point can be illustrated with the following stylized example. Suppose that all shocks are industry-specific and uncorrelated across industries. If there is full specialization, in the sense that no two countries overlap in sectors with nonzero production, then GDP across countries will have zero correlation. If there is no specialization, in the sense that all countries have an identical sectoral composition of output, then GDP will be perfectly correlated across countries. If there is partial specialization, the correlation of GDP across countries will be positive but not perfect and, in general, the greater the specialization, the closer to zero are GDP correlations. However, not all shocks need be specific to industries – we present a stylized model which allows for other sources of shocks in Section 3.

We use data for the 50 U.S. states and a sample of OECD countries to test empirically whether countries and states that are more specialized (at the one-digit level and in manufacturing) are subject to less symmetric fluctuations. We repeat the analysis for the sample of U.S. states alone – this may be more informative about conditions in an economic union – and obtain similar results.

---

[15] Interestingly, Kenen (1969) points out that well-diversified countries suffer less from asymmetric GDP fluctuations and should be more inclined to join a monetary union. He does not, however, take the further step of arguing that joining a monetary union will itself affect the degree of industrial specialization through the mechanism described above.

It is worth stressing that although the effect of capital market integration on the asymmetry of macroeconomic fluctuations is expected to happen over time, there is no compelling need to formulate and test a dynamic model using time-series data. Paraphrasing Rose (2000, p. 11), one can perfectly well exploit cross-sectional variation to trace the effects of capital market integration on the asymmetry of fluctuations.

3. A Stylized Model of Fluctuations

In order to focus the discussion, we make use of a simple stylized model. We follow Frankel and Rose (1998) and express the per capita GDP growth process of countries i and j as

$$
\begin{aligned}
\Delta \log \text{gdp}_t^i &= \sum_s \alpha_s^i u_{s,t} + \beta^i v_t^i, \\
\Delta \log \text{gdp}_t^j &= \sum_s \alpha_s^j u_{s,t} + \beta^j v_t^j.
\end{aligned}
\tag{1}
$$

The variables on the left hand side should be regarded as generic expressions for per capita GDP fluctuations in each country (whether measured as log-differences of GDP at the one year frequency or as HP-filtered GDP, etc.).[16] The variable $u_{s,t}$ represents a time t sector-specific shock to the output in sector s which is common to both countries. It reflects technological changes, sudden changes in the prices of inputs that are more heavily used in some sectors and changes in the composition of demand. The variables α_s^i and α_s^j are the weights of sector s in the total output of countries i and j – they are not indexed by t to indicate that they do not change from year to year.[17]

The variables v_t^i and v_t^j represent the time t country-specific GDP shocks that are common to all the sectors in each economy and they are best interpreted as country-wide policy shocks. The variables β^i and β^j represent the weights in each country of the country-wide (as opposed to sector-specific) shocks.

The variables $u_{s,t}$, v_t^i, and v_t^j are assumed to be identically distributed random variables with mean zero and unit variance. They are further assumed to be independently distributed over time. The sector-specific shocks, $u_{s,t}$, are assumed to be independently distributed of v_t^i and v_t^j, but

---

[16] For brevity, we will often omit the adjective "per capita."

[17] It is well known that industrial composition is not constant over time. Kim (1995), for example, documents how industrial specialization in the United States gradually changed over the past century, while Imbs and Waczairg (2000) formalize the idea that countries experience "stages of diversification" as they develop and grow. Our empirical analysis (as well as the analysis in Frankel and Rose 1998) is cross-sectional, and uses data from a relatively short time period. The formulation in Equation (1) is, therefore, appropriate for our purposes even if the constants α_s^i and α_s^j slowly change over time.

the latter variables have a time-invariant correlation coefficient denoted ρ^{ij}.

The correlation of the country-specific GDP shocks, ρ^{ij}, has two interpretations. It captures the common element in the shocks themselves, such as the extent to which major strikes are likely to occur in the same year in both countries. It also captures the common *response* of GDP in both countries to shocks that occur in only one of the countries, such as the response of aggregate demand in both countries to increased government spending in one country (a "Keynesian" demand spillover effect).

Consider the first term on the right-hand side of Equations (1), $\Sigma_s \alpha_s^i u_{s,t}$ and $\Sigma_s \alpha_s^j u_{s,t}$. Their correlation is $\Sigma_s \alpha_s^i \alpha_s^j$. We predict that the distribution of the sector shares, α_s, will become more dissimilar across countries as a result of capital market integration with various countries specializing in specific sectors. As a result, the correlation across countries of sector-specific shocks, $\Sigma_s \alpha_s^i \alpha_s^j$, will decrease.[18] Therefore, the correlation of GDP fluctuations (i.e., of $\Delta \log \text{gdp}_t^i$ and $\Delta \log \text{gdp}_t^j$) will also decrease.

The stylized model also illustrates that our analysis is complementary to that of Frankel and Rose (1998). They concentrate on the second term on the right-hand side of Equations (1), $\beta^i v_t^i$ and $\beta^j v_t^j$, representing country-specific shocks. The correlation of these terms (ρ^{ij}) will increase as a result of economic integration through lower trade barriers and increased intra-industry trade, and so will the correlation of GDP fluctuations, $\Delta \log \text{gdp}_t^i$ and $\Delta \log \text{gdp}_t^j$. Of course, lowering of trade barriers is also likely to make the distribution of sector shares more dissimilar as predicted by Krugman (1993); but according to the results of Frankel and Rose (1998) this effect is dominated by increased correlation of country-specific shocks. In order to predict the total effect of economic integration on fluctuations asymmetry one needs to know the elasticities of the sector shares, α_s, of the demand shock correlations, ρ, and of the weights, β, with respect to *all* the relevant variables that will change as a result of economic and financial integration. This should be high on the research agenda of scholars interested in the economics of monetary unification.

4. Measuring the Asymmetry of Fluctuations

Academic research on the asymmetry of economic shocks, at the regional and national levels, dates back at least to Cohen and Wyplosz (1989) and Weber (1991) who studied output growth rate correlations for European

---

[18] To illustrate, if country i produces only good s and country j produces only good s', this correlation is zero.

countries, and to Stockman (1988) who distinguished between country-specific and industry-specific shocks.[19] This literature generated a debate,[20] and there is no consensus regarding the "correct" statistical model for country-level (or regional-level) GDP. We, therefore, opt for a more "structural" approach that builds on economic theory: We calculate the increase in utility obtained from consuming a fraction of aggregate GDP rather than actual GDP for the representative consumer of each country. More precisely, in the framework of a simple model of optimization and general equilibrium, we evaluate the increase in per capita discounted expected utility that would be achieved by moving from financial autarky (each country consumes the value of its GDP) to full insurance (each country consumes a fixed fraction of aggregate GDP). The fraction of aggregate GDP that a country consumes under full insurance is the fraction that would accrue to it in a perfect risk-sharing general equilibrium.[21] We interpret this utility gain as a measure of fluctuations asymmetry. The more a country can gain from sharing country-specific risk with other countries in a group, the more asymmetric are its GDP fluctuations relative to the group.

4.1. A Utility-Based Measure of Fluctuations Asymmetry

Our proposed measure builds on the following counterfactual thought experiment. Consider a group of countries inhabited by risk averse agents (consumers) who derive utility from consumption of a homogeneous nonstorable good. This group constitutes a "stochastic endowment economy" in the sense that the GDP of these countries is regarded as exogenous and stochastic by consumers. Securities markets in this economy are complete, permitting cross-country insurance. Consumers within each country are identical ex-ante as well as ex-post: All have the same utility

[19] The latter paper inspired numerous studies including Kollman (1995), Fatas (1997), Hess and Shin (1998), and Del Negro (1999). Bayoumi and Eichengreen (1993) focused on demand versus supply shocks identified via a vector autoregressive model, whereas De Grauwe and Vanhaverbeke (1993) distinguished between region-specific and country-specific shocks. See also Canova and Dellas (1993) and the survey by Clark and Shin (2000).

[20] Some studies suggest that economic integration will result in less symmetric shocks (De Grauwe and Vanhaverbeke 1993) or that the degree of asymmetry will not change (Forni and Reichlin 1997) while others conclude that economic integration will result in more symmetric shocks (Clark and van Wincoop 1999, Frankel and Rose 1998). These studies typically attempt to identify the full stochastic process for regional output (as in Forni and Reichlin) or concentrate directly on output correlations (as in Clark and van Wincoop and Frankel and Rose).

[21] Most of the time, we will refer only to countries, but our analysis applies equally well to states within the United States.

function, the same rate of time preference, δ, and are subject to the same realization of uncertainty.[22]

It is well known that under commonly used assumptions – symmetric information, no transaction costs, CRRA utility, identical rate of time preference for all countries – perfect risk sharing among the countries in the group implies that $c_t^i = k^i$ gdp$_t$. Here c_t^i is the per capita consumption in country i, gdp$_t$ is the aggregate per capita GDP of the group of countries under consideration, and k^i is a country-specific constant that does not vary across "states of the world" or over time.[23]

For each country, we compare the expected utility of consuming k^igdp$_t$ with that of consuming the endowment, gdp$_t^i$. To quantify these gains we must make distributional assumptions. Let the natural logarithm of the per capita GDP of the group and the per capita GDP of each country be random walks with linear trend drift. Further suppose that, conditional on gdp$_0^i$ and gdp$_0$, the joint distribution of the log-differences of these processes is stationary and normal: $\Delta \log$ gdp$_t \sim N(\mu, \sigma^2)$, $\Delta \log$ gdp$_t^i \sim N(\mu^i, \sigma_i^2)$, and cov$(\Delta \log$ gdp$_t^i, \Delta \log$ gdp$_t) = $ cov^i for all t.[24] With these assumptions we obtain closed form solutions for the gains from risk sharing and, in the process, for the equilibrium shares in aggregate consumption (the k^i·s). To the best of our knowledge, this has not been accomplished before in the literature on risk sharing.[25]

In the derivation (that is presented in full detail in the Appendix), we distinguish between CRRA utility, $\frac{1}{1-\gamma}c^{1-\gamma}(\gamma \neq 1)$, and log-utility which yields simple and intuitive expressions but is, of course, more restrictive.[26]

---

[22] We, thus, focus on fluctuations asymmetry between countries, ignoring potential asymmetry within countries.

[23] Under perfect risk sharing, each country consumes a fixed fraction of the aggregate gross product every period regardless of the realization of GDP shocks. The constant k^i represents the strength of country i's claim in the risk sharing arrangement. See Huang and Litzenberger (1988) for a derivation for CRRA utility. In the literature, the perfect risk sharing condition is often expressed in terms of aggregate consumption, but since output is assumed to be nonstorable in our model, gdp$_t$ is equal to aggregate consumption.

[24] This assumption involves an approximation since the aggregate GDP cannot, in general, be strictly log-normally distributed if each country's GDP is log-normally distributed.

[25] After the final version of this article was completed we became aware of Kim, Kim, and Levin (2000). Using a quite different approach, they obtain analytical solutions for gains from risk sharing in a two-country framework that allows for more general dynamics than we do.

[26] The approximation that aggregate GDP is log-normally distributed may introduce minor bias of unknown direction. For example, the calculated shares of aggregate GDP that each state or country would consume under perfect risk sharing do not sum precisely to 1 in our calculations (see the Appendix). However, in this study the shares sum to a number very close to one (between 1.00 and 1.01), so this bias is negligible.

The utility gains from risk sharing will be substantial only if shocks have a cumulative effect over longer horizons. If gross product were not highly persistent, these gains would be small as pointed out by Obstfeld (1994b). Indeed, the random walk assumption is important for our derivation.[27] If the actual GDP growth rate of countries is stationary, this will result in overestimation of gains from risk sharing, and underestimation of the gains if the actual GDP growth rate is more persistent than a random walk.[28] Our regression results depend only on the *relative* magnitude of the gains from risk sharing, so it is not crucial for our purpose to pin down the *level* of these gains.

It is economically more meaningful to express the gains from risk sharing in terms of consumption certainty equivalence. We do so by calculating the permanent percentage increase in the level of consumption that would generate an equivalent increase in expected utility.[29] More precisely, the gain in utility (of moving from autarky to perfect risk sharing) equals the gain in utility that would be achieved by increasing consumption permanently from GDP$_{i0}$ to GDP$_{i0} * (1 + G_i)$. G_i is our country-by-country measure of fluctuations asymmetry and, for log-utility, is given by:[30]

$$G^i = \frac{1}{\delta}\left(\frac{1}{2}\sigma^2 + \frac{1}{2}\sigma_i^2 - \text{cov}^i\right), \tag{2}$$

where δ is the intertemporal discount rate.[31] The intuition for this formula is straightforward. First, the gain from sharing risk is higher for countries with a lower covariance between $\Delta \log \text{gdp}_t^i$ and $\Delta \log \text{gdp}_t$. The interpretation is that countries with "countercyclical" output are compensated

---

[27] As it is for van Wincoop's (1994) estimation of nonexploited welfare gains from risk sharing.

[28] For U.S. states, we performed state-by-state Augmented Dickey–Fuller tests for a unit root in state gross product and were never able to reject a unit root. These tests, based on relatively short samples, have low power against near unit root alternatives, and indeed the question of whether typical macroeconomic series contain unit roots is still open. Nevertheless, as shown in the appendix to Obstfeld (1992), welfare gains are substantial when shocks to gross product are persistent whether or not the process contains an exact random walk. Another issue is that our measure may underestimate gains from insurance since we do not use preferences with separate parameters for risk aversion and intertemporal elasticity of substitution. Obstfeld (1994b) shows that welfare gains estimates are typically higher with such utility functions.

[29] We follow van Wincoop (1994) in this respect.

[30] See the Appendix for a derivation for both CRRA and log-utility.

[31] And $e^{-\delta t}$ is the intertemporal discount factor.

for providing insurance to other countries by stabilizing aggregate output. Second, the higher the variance of country i's GDP the more it contributes to smoothing shocks in other countries, other things equal, and the more it receives in exchange for this service. Third, the higher the variance of the aggregate gross product of the group, keeping the variance of country i's GDP constant, the more other countries would be willing to "pay" country i for joining the risk-sharing arrangement.[32] (The interpretation of the formula for CRRA utility is similar, although less transparent.) We regard G_i as a reasonable and intuitive country-by-country measure of fluctuations asymmetry: The more a country can gain from sharing idiosyncratic risk with other countries in a group, the more asymmetric are its shocks relative to the group.

There is nothing novel in characterizing the equilibrium allocation of an Arrow–Debreu exchange economy, but to the best of our knowledge, a closed form solution for the equilibrium sharing rule and the gains from risk sharing for CRRA utility has not been explicitly worked out before.[33]

In the empirical implementation, the parameters σ^2, σ_i^2, and cov^i are estimated using country-level (or state-level) and aggregate GDP data. A natural measure of output is GDP deflated by the Consumer Price Index (CPI). We stress the logic of deflating by the CPI rather than by a GDP-deflator: Since our measure is utility based, we want measured

---

[32] Of course, σ^2, the variance of the growth rate of aggregate GDP, cannot change without *any* of the σ_i^2's changing. The distributional approximation regarding aggregate GDP allows us to treat σ^2 as a parameter (that can be estimated from aggregate GDP data) rather than as a complicated function of the country-by-country σ_i^2's.

[33] Obstfeld (1994b) provides a closed form solution for the welfare gains due to a reduction in consumption variability in a partial equilibrium setting, whereas van Wincoop (1994) computes welfare gains from risk sharing in a general equilibrium model but relies on approximation techniques. Of course, our work builds on these papers which were the first to compute and estimate welfare gains from risk sharing taking into account the persistence of shocks to GDP; see also Tesar (1995). van Wincoop (1994) calculates potential gains from risk sharing using consumption data, measuring how much further gains from risk sharing can be achieved by moving from the observed consumption allocation (in the data) to the perfect risk sharing consumption allocation. (That is, he computes non-exploited gains from risk sharing.) The potential gains from risk sharing that we calculate have a different interpretation, as they are based on a counterfactual thought experiment: moving from autarkic (rather than actual) consumption to perfect risk sharing. The calculation of this measure uses only GDP data rendering it more appropriate as a measure of GDP fluctuations asymmetry. Of course, the techniques developed here can also be used to calculate the nonexploited gains from risk sharing using consumption data as in van Wincoop (1994).

output to reflect consumption in autarky (with countries consuming the value of their GDP). Thus, we want to translate GDP to the amount of consumption that it can buy which is obtained by deflating using the CPI.[34] Note also that our fluctuations asymmetry measure focuses entirely on the value of GDP (in terms of consumption) and its volatility, not on the composition of GDP.

5. Measuring Specialization in Production

Each specialization index is computed annually (for every country) for the relevant sample years and averaged over time. The one-digit speciali-zation index for country i is

$$\text{SPEC}_1^i = \sum_{s=1}^{S} \left(\frac{\text{GDP}_i^s}{\text{GDP}_i} - \frac{1}{J-1} \sum_{j \neq i} \frac{\text{GDP}_j^s}{\text{GDP}_j} \right)^2,$$

where GDP_i^s is the gross product of (one-digit) sector s in country i, GDP_i is the total GDP of this country, S is the number of sectors, and J is the number of countries in the group. The index represents the distance between the vector of sector shares in country i's GDP, $\text{GDP}_i^s/\text{GDP}_i$, and the vector of average sector shares across the countries other than i. It measures the extent to which country i differs from the other countries in terms of industrial composition. Similarly, the manufacturing (two-digit) specialization index for country i is

$$\text{SPEC}_{1M}^i = \sum_{s=1}^{S} \left(\frac{\text{GDP}_i^s}{\text{GDP}_i^M} - \frac{1}{J-1} \sum_{j \neq i} \frac{\text{GDP}_j^s}{\text{GDP}_j^M} \right)^2,$$

where GDP_i^s is the gross product of manufacturing sector s in country i, and GDP_i^M is the total manufacturing gross product of this country.

---

[34] To illustrate, consider Alaska and suppose that it produces *only* oil. Suppose now that physical production of oil remains fixed from period t to period $t+1$ but that the price of oil doubles, whereas the CPI is unchanged. Deflating by the GDP-deflator would yield no change in the real value of Alaska's output, whereas deflating by the CPI would yield a doubling of the value of output. The latter makes more sense since Alaskans consume approximately the same basket of goods as the rest of the nation and they therefore become "richer" when oil prices increase. In sum, when using a utility based measure of fluctuations asymmetry, output must be measured in consumption-equivalent terms.

Alternatively, we use the indices

$$\text{SPEC}_2^i = \sum_{s=1}^{S} \left| \frac{\text{GDP}_i^s}{\text{GDP}_i} - \frac{1}{J-1} \sum_{j \neq i} \frac{\text{GDP}_j^s}{\text{GDP}_j} \right|,$$

$$\text{SPEC}_{2M}^i = \sum_{s=1}^{S} \left| \frac{\text{GDP}_i^s}{\text{GDP}_i^M} - \frac{1}{J-1} \sum_{j \neq i} \frac{\text{GDP}_j^s}{\text{GDP}_j^M} \right|,$$

for one-digit and manufacturing specialization, respectively.[35]

6. Empirical Analysis

6.1. Data Used

United States: Gross state product (GSP) data are from the Bureau of Economic Analysis (BEA). Washington D.C. is very atypical and is omitted. The sample period for GSP by sector (used for computing specialization indices) is 1977–94, while for total GSP (used for computing the fluctuations asymmetry measure) it is 1963–94.[36] We transform all gross product magnitudes to per capita terms using population by state, also obtained from the BEA. We use data for ISIC one-digit industries and utilize BEA data for 21 manufacturing subsectors, which we aggregate to 9 ISIC two-digit levels. High school enrollment in percent of total population (1990) and total land mass are from the 1997 Statistical Abstract of the United States. The data are transformed to constant prices using the U.S. aggregate CPI. All the data are annual.

OECD: We use data from the OECD National Accounts 1996, Volume 2. The countries in our sample are Belgium, Denmark, France, Netherlands, West Germany, Austria, Canada, Finland, New Zealand, Norway, and the United States. We restrict attention to this sample due to missing sectoral GDP data for other OECD countries, both at the one-digit level and for manufacturing subsectors. Data for Greece are available, but were omitted a priori since during the sample period Greece was at a substantially lower level of economic development than the rest of the countries, with a very high dependence on agricultural production. The sample period for sectoral GDP (used for computing specialization

---

[35] These alternative indices put less weight on very specialized sectors.
[36] The BEA official GSP series start in 1977 and we have combined these series with older series. The BEA advises against using the older data at the sectoral level.

indices) is 1977–90 for the 9 ISIC two-digit manufacturing sectors and 1980–90 for the ISIC one-digit industries. The sample period for total GDP (used for computing the fluctuations asymmetry measure) is 1963–93. GDP is transformed to per capita terms using population data from the National Accounts, and is further converted into constant dollars using the CPI for each country (from the National Accounts) and 1990 (end of year) exchange rates (from the IMF International Financial Statistics database). Land area is from the 1997 Statistical Abstract of the United States. All the data are annual.

6.2. Asymmetry Measures and Specialization Indices

Tables 5.1 and 5.2 display the variance of real per capita GDP, its covariance with aggregate GDP, the asymmetry measures for logarithmic and CRRA utility, and the specialization indices for U.S. states and OECD countries, respectively. The variance of state-level GSP (Table 5.1) is typically higher than that of country-level GDP (Table 5.2). The gross product of oil-rich states and countries typically exhibits a low covariance with aggregate gross product (Alaska, Wyoming, Norway) – even negative in the case of Alaska.[37]

The third columns of Tables 5.1 and 5.2 provide the estimated measures of fluctuations asymmetry for log-utility. These numbers represent the permanent percentage increase in initial GDP (autarkic consumption in the initial period) that would generate the same increase in discounted expected utility as moving from autarky to perfect risk sharing. The numbers are calculated using the expression in Equation (2) multiplied by 100.[38]

For log-utility, the average (population weighted) gain from sharing risk across the 50 U.S. states is 1.27, while for OECD countries it is 0.67. For CRRA utility ($\gamma = 3$), the average gains are 1.55 and 0.62, respectively, so the sensitivity of these measures to the risk aversion parameter is not

---

[37] A careful inspection of the notes to Table 5.1 reveals that the variance of U.S. real per capita GDP is about 8% but is reported as about 6% in Table 5.2. This discrepancy is due to minor differences in the underlying data. The BEA U.S. state-level data and the OECD data are internally consistent but they are obviously not quite consistent between them.

[38] They are computed as follows: $\frac{1}{100*\delta}$ times [one half the variance of $100 * \Delta \log$ GDP + one half the first column – the second column], and the discount rate is set at $\delta = 0.02$. The variance of $100 * \Delta \log$ GDP is 8.39 for the United States and 4.08 for the aggregate OECD sample.

Table 5.1. *Fluctuations Asymmetry and Industrial Specialization: U.S. States*

States	(1) Variance (GSP)	(2) Covariance (GSP, GDP)	(3) Asymmetry Index(Log)	(4) Asymmetry Index(CRRA)	(5) 1-digit Spec. index	(6) 2-digit Spec. index
Alabama	11.57	9.05	0.46	0.54	0.63	3.69
Alaska	171.19	−9.42	49.60	79.36	13.10	22.60
Arizona	16.70	9.41	1.56	1.83	0.59	7.89
Arkansas	15.97	10.37	0.91	1.07	0.81	1.11
California	8.35	7.57	0.40	0.46	0.64	3.23
Colorado	5.06	5.05	0.84	0.98	0.53	2.42
Connecticut	10.81	7.99	0.80	0.93	1.40	7.37
Delaware	18.57	8.61	2.43	2.85	3.16	21.88
Florida	11.17	8.38	0.70	0.81	1.47	1.13
Georgia	14.65	10.46	0.53	0.63	0.36	5.40
Hawaii	10.18	4.16	2.56	2.99	4.14	20.61
Idaho	18.71	8.90	2.33	2.73	0.61	9.42
Illinois	11.09	9.19	0.27	0.32	0.49	1.24
Indiana	21.54	12.58	1.19	1.45	2.26	3.08
Iowa	23.61	11.30	2.35	2.80	1.14	2.49
Kansas	10.06	7.47	0.88	1.02	0.25	1.30
Kentucky	11.43	8.80	0.55	0.64	1.12	1.54
Louisiana	23.58	3.27	6.36	7.53	3.38	19.57
Maine	13.25	8.68	1.07	1.25	0.40	9.07
Maryland	9.41	7.99	0.46	0.53	1.42	1.11
Massachusetts	12.21	8.38	0.96	1.11	1.20	7.16
Michigan	35.57	15.27	3.36	4.18	2.12	10.63
Minnesota	15.12	10.15	0.80	0.95	0.36	2.89
Mississippi	15.24	10.00	0.90	1.06	0.68	2.15
Missouri	15.75	10.54	0.76	0.90	0.44	1.46
Montana	15.66	6.69	2.67	3.11	1.91	22.61
Nebraska	18.44	9.73	1.84	2.17	1.11	3.78
Nevada	10.78	7.66	0.96	1.11	6.07	1.69
New Hampshire	17.00	9.81	1.44	1.69	1.12	5.46
New Jersey	9.77	7.77	0.65	0.75	0.76	4.61
New Mexico	9.27	1.46	3.68	4.34	3.63	4.25
New York	8.87	7.57	0.53	0.61	1.74	1.89
North Carolina	14.41	10.13	0.63	0.75	2.26	6.87
North Dakota	72.82	10.35	15.13	19.46	3.41	3.06
Ohio	15.02	10.81	0.45	0.54	1.79	2.91
Oklahoma	14.85	3.55	4.04	4.74	1.26	3.13
Oregon	17.72	10.74	1.16	1.37	0.31	12.15
Pennsylvania	9.47	8.39	0.27	0.31	0.59	1.14
Rhode Island	10.58	8.10	0.69	0.80	1.00	2.47
South Carolina	15.38	10.66	0.61	0.73	1.49	8.87
South Dakota	35.85	11.56	5.28	6.41	2.34	4.73
Tennessee	16.63	10.94	0.79	0.94	0.81	1.03
Texas	12.19	4.17	3.06	3.58	0.96	3.28
Utah	6.59	5.39	1.05	1.23	0.44	2.13
Vermont	15.10	9.55	1.10	1.28	0.40	6.29
Virginia	8.91	7.63	0.51	0.59	0.85	3.16

(continued)

Table 5.1. *(continued)*

States	(1) Variance (GSP)	(2) Covariance (GSP, GDP)	(3) Asymmetry Index(Log)	(4) Asymmetry Index(CRRA)	(5) 1-digit Spec. index	(6) 2-digit Spec. index
Washington	11.76	8.15	0.96	1.11	0.36	2.79
West Virginia	8.60	5.43	1.53	1.79	1.60	15.37
Wisconsin	11.39	9.17	0.36	0.42	1.62	3.03
Wyoming	34.70	0.82	10.36	12.50	14.35	19.32
Average	13.75	8.53	1.27	1.55	1.23	4.17

Notes: GSP is gross state product per capita. GDP is aggregate U.S. gross domestic product per capita. The first four columns are calculated for 1963–94 and the last two columns are for 1977–94. Average numbers are population weighted.

Column 1 is $10^4 * \sigma_i^2$, where $\sigma_i^2 = \text{var}(\Delta \log \text{GSP}^i)$ [in other words, it is $\text{var}(100 * \Delta \log \text{GSP}^i)$].

Column 2 is $10^4 * \text{cov}^i$, where $\text{cov}^i = \text{cov}(\Delta \log \text{GSP}^i, \Delta \log \text{GDP})$.

Column 3 is $10^2 * \frac{1}{8}(\frac{1}{2}\sigma^2 + \frac{1}{2}\sigma_i^2 - \text{cov}^i)$, where $\delta = 0.02$ (discount rate) and $10^4 * \sigma^2 = 8.39$ [$\text{var}(100 * \Delta \log \text{GDP})$].

Column 4 is $10^2 * [\log(\delta - (1-\gamma)\mu - \frac{1}{2}(1-\gamma)^2\sigma^2) - \log(\delta - (\mu - \gamma\mu + \frac{1}{2}\sigma_i^2 + \frac{1}{2}\gamma^2\sigma^2 - \gamma\text{cov}^i)) + \frac{1}{1-\gamma}\log(\delta - (1-\gamma)\mu - \frac{1}{2}(1-\gamma)^2\sigma_i^2) - \frac{1}{1-\gamma}\log(\delta - (1-\gamma)\mu - \frac{1}{2}(1-\gamma)^2\sigma^2)]$, where the risk aversion parameter is $\gamma = 3$ and the U.S. GDP growth rate is $\mu = 0.020$. Specialization indices are defined in the text. The displayed indices are multiplied by 100.

Table 5.2. *Fluctuations Asymmetry and Industrial Specialization: OECD Countries*

Countries	(1) Variance (GDP)	(2) Covariance (GDP, GDP$_T$)	(3) Asymmetry index (Log)	(4) Asymmetry index (CRRA)	(5) 1-digit Spec. index	(6) 2-digit Spec. index
Belgium	7.65	3.11	1.37	1.28	3.28	1.07
Denmark	7.62	3.58	1.13	1.05	1.05	1.14
France	4.60	3.27	0.53	0.49	0.39	2.85
Netherlands	6.60	3.64	0.85	0.79	0.64	2.59
Germany	8.38	3.83	1.20	1.12	2.51	5.85
Austria	4.86	2.64	0.92	0.85	0.75	2.00
Canada	10.60	4.69	1.33	1.24	0.41	1.69
Finland	21.67	4.36	4.26	4.05	0.90	3.89
New Zealand	13.54	4.08	2.36	2.22	0.95	26.30
Norway	7.03	0.98	2.29	2.14	2.80	31.67
United States	5.88	4.46	0.26	0.23	0.97	5.40
Average	6.75	4.07	0.67	0.62	1.20	5.04

Notes: GDP is gross domestic product per capita of each country. GDP$_T$ is the total gross domestic product per capita of the 11 OECD countries listed in Section 6.

The first four columns are calculated for 1963–93. The fifth column displays average values for 1980–90 and the sixth column displays average values for 1977–90. Average numbers are population weighted.

Column 1 is $10^4 * \sigma_i^2$, where $\sigma_i^2 = \text{var}(\Delta \log \text{GDP}^i)$ [in other words, it is $\text{var}(100 * \Delta \log \text{GDP}^i)$].

Column 2 is $10^4 * \text{cov}^i$, where $\text{cov}^i = \text{cov}(\Delta \log \text{GDP}^i, \Delta \log \text{GDP}_T)$.

Column 3 is $10^2 * \frac{1}{8}(\frac{1}{2}\sigma^2 + \frac{1}{2}\sigma_i^2 - \text{cov}^i)$, where $\delta = 0.02$ (discount rate) and $10^4 * \sigma^2 = 4.08$ [$\text{var}(100 * \Delta \log \text{GDP}_T)$].

Column 4 is $10^2 * [\log(\delta - (1-\gamma)\mu - \frac{1}{2}(1-\gamma)^2\sigma^2) - \log(\delta - (\mu - \gamma\mu + \frac{1}{2}\sigma_i^2 + \frac{1}{2}\gamma^2\sigma^2 - \gamma\text{cov}^i)) + \frac{1}{1-\gamma}\log(\delta - (1-\gamma)\mu - \frac{1}{2}(1-\gamma)^2\sigma_i^2) - \frac{1}{1-\gamma}\log(\delta - (1-\gamma)\mu - \frac{1}{2}(1-\gamma)^2\sigma^2)]$, where the risk aversion parameter is $\gamma = 3$ and the growth rate of the aggregate GDP of the OECD countries (GDP$_T$) is $\mu = 0.023$. Specialization indices are defined in the text. The displayed indices are multiplied by 100.

substantial.[39] The estimated gains from risk sharing are quite large, but we reiterate that pinning down their level is difficult because the estimation strongly depends on the persistence of GDP shocks and on the chosen discount rate. Discount rates are usually estimated very imprecisely in econometric work and empirical measures of persistence are well known to be extremely sensitive to model specification. Nevertheless, our analysis of specialization and asymmetry depends only on the *relative* value of the asymmetry measure across countries, which is unlikely to be very sensitive to the persistence of GDP shocks and the discount rate.[40]

The third columns of Tables 5.1 and 5.2 reveal that the oil-rich states and countries (e.g., Alaska, North Dakota, Wyoming, Norway) exhibit high asymmetry measures, and it appears that small states and countries have relatively high asymmetry measures. Finland has the highest asymmetry measure among the OECD countries which is most likely due to the sharp recession experienced after the collapse of the Soviet Union. The asymmetry measures calculated with CRRA utility ($\gamma = 3$) are displayed in column 4 of Tables 5.1 and 5.2. In general, the ranking of states and countries is the same as for log-utility (column 3). For the United States the asymmetry measures are higher for CRRA utility while the opposite is true for OECD countries.[41]

The specialization indices are displayed in the last two columns of Tables 5.1 and 5.2. The numerical value of the indices are not easily interpreted, although a value of zero means that the state or country has sector shares identical to the average sector shares of the remaining states or countries. In the United States, Alaska and Wyoming are very specialized

[39] To compare our estimates for OECD countries to those reported in van Wincoop (1994), consider for instance Belgium and the United States – the first and the last entries in column 3, Table 5.2. Our estimates are 1.37 and 0.26 whereas van Wincoop's are 1.1 and 0.6, respectively. The samples differ somewhat in the number of countries included and in the time period selected, and if we had used a discount rate of 0.01 like van Wincoop, our numbers would have been 2.74 for Belgium and 0.52 for the United States. A priori, the gains from risk sharing as defined in this paper should be larger since we measure potential gains (using GDP data) while vanWincoop measures nonexploited gains (using consumption data). However, risk sharing among OECD countries is quite low (Sørensen and Yosha 1998) so all in all one should expect numbers of roughly the same order of magnitude, which is what we find. It is reassuring that the estimates obtained from two very different approaches and using different data are quite similar.

[40] Moreover, the log-utility measure is proportional to $1/\delta$, which renders the *t*-statistics in the regressions fully independent of the size of δ.

[41] We verified empirically that this is due to different growth rates of OECD countries and U.S. states during the sample period. The asymmetry measure for log-utility is independent of growth rates, but for CRRA utility we cannot fully disentangle this effect from pure risk sharing (see the Appendix).

(in oil) and Nevada is quite specialized (in services) at the one-digit level. Specialization at the two-digit manufacturing level is reported in column 6. Some U.S. states have a small and highly specialized manufacturing sector; for example Alaska (food), Montana (wood), and Hawaii (food). The manufacturing sector is, however, also very specialized in Delaware, Louisiana, and West Virginia (all in chemical industry). The set of states with high asymmetry indices is extremely similar to the set of states that Del Negro (1999) identifies as asymmetric using an econometric factor model to estimate asymmetry – it seems that the identification of asymmetric states is very robust to the method used. Among OECD countries, Belgium is the most specialized at the one-digit level (in services) and Norway and New Zealand are extremely specialized at the two-digit manufacturing level (both in food processing).[42] Norway and New Zealand are both more specialized than any U.S. state.

The population-weighted one-digit and two-digit manufacturing specialization indices for U.S. states are 1.2 and 4.2 whereas for OECD countries they are 1.2 and 5.0, suggesting that U.S. states and OECD countries are approximately equally specialized.[43]

6.3. Regression Analysis

Table 5.3 reports the central results of our paper. We present ordinary least squares (OLS) and instrumental variables (IV) regressions of the asymmetry measures on the specialization indices.[44] These regressions use the pooled sample of OECD countries and U.S. states. We control for country (and state) size using population since small countries may exhibit very asymmetric GDP fluctuations due to few opportunities for within-country diversification. We choose a square root specification which produces the best fit. We control for (log-transformed) shares of mining and agriculture in GDP since the previous tables showed that oil-rich countries might be outliers. The log-transformation is chosen based on inspection of the data

---

[42] Specialization is not necessarily driven by one sector. The sectors reported in the text, in parentheses, are mentioned for illustration only and are obtained as follows. Consider Belgium, for example. It is most specialized in services relative to other OECD countries in the sense that $\frac{GDP_i^s}{GDP_i} - \frac{1}{J-1}\sum_{j\neq i}\frac{GDP_j^s}{GDP_j}$ is largest (over all sectors s) for services in Belgium (country i).

[43] If the two strong outliers, New Zealand and Norway, are removed, the population weighted one-digit and two-digit manufacturing specialization indices for OECD countries are 1.2 and 4.6. Kalemli-Ozcan, Sørensen, and Yosha (1999) found that, in general, regions within countries are more specialized than countries. Their sample includes regions of Italy and the U.K., Japanese prefectures, Canadian provinces, communities of Spain, U.S. states, OECD countries, and Latin American countries.

[44] All the regressions include a constant (not reported).

Table 5.3. *Determinants of GDP Fluctuations Asymmetry: Ordinary Least Squares and Instrumental Variables Regressions*

Dependent variable:	(1) OLS Asym. index (Log)	(2) IV Asym. index (Log)	(3) OLS Asym. index (CRRA)	(4) IV Asym. index (CRRA)
Regressors:				
log (1-digit specialization) ($SPEC_1$ index)	0.43 (4.13)	0.68 (2.48)	0.44 (4.16)	0.73 (2.57)
log (Manuf. specialization) ($SPEC_{1M}$ index)	0.30 (3.41)	0.57 (2.20)	0.30 (3.37)	0.58 (2.15)
$(Population)^{1/2}$	−0.14 (4.36)	−0.12 (2.84)	−0.14 (4.31)	−0.12 (2.70)
log (Agriculture GDP share)	0.28 (2.36)	0.40 (2.48)	0.29 (2.35)	0.42 (2.50)
log (Mining GDP share)	0.14 (2.92)	0.09 (1.50)	0.14 (2.91)	0.09 (1.41)
Country dummy	0.33 (1.46)	0.22 (0.79)	0.10 (0.42)	−0.03 (0.10)
R^2	0.68	0.56	0.68	0.54
Partial R^2	0.30	0.13	0.30	0.16

Notes: The sample consists of the 50 U.S. states and 11 OECD countries. The OECD countries are Belgium, Denmark, France, Germany, Netherlands, Austria, Finland, Canada, New Zealand, Norway, U.S. "Agriculture GDP Share" is the average over time (1977–94 for U.S. and 1980–90 for OECD) of the GDP share of this sector in each country or state. Analogously for Mining. The instruments are, for each country or state: FIRE GDP share (computed in the same manner and for the same time periods as Agriculture and Mining GDP shares), land mass, log-population density averaged over time (1977–94 for U.S. and 1977–90 for OECD), percent high school enrollment (1990), GDP per capita averaged over time (1977–94 for U.S. and 1977–90 for OECD), and an interaction variable of the Agriculture and Mining GDP shares averaged over time. The country dummy takes a value of 1 for countries and 0 for states. The specialization indices $SPEC_1$ and $SPEC_{1M}$ are defined in the text. All variables in all regressions are weighted by log-population. The dependent variable is log-transformed in all regressions. t-values in parentheses. The Partial R^2 is the R^2 reported for the full regression minus the R^2 obtained when both specialization indices are left out.

(some countries have sector shares that are extremely small relative to other countries, so the raw shares have a highly skewed distribution).[45] We further included a dummy variable for countries. The regressions are weighted by log-population, and the dependent variable is the logarithm of the fluctuations asymmetry measure.[46] Similarly, the specialization indices are log-transformed.

[45] If the mining and agriculture sector shares are dropped the results are extremely similar.
[46] The logarithmic transformation of the asymmetry measure makes it less likely to be dominated by outliers like Alaska and Wyoming.

The main result is that higher specialization induces greater asymmetry. Both one-digit and manufacturing specialization are significant (at the 5% level) in all the specifications displayed in Table 5.3. For each regression we calculate the partial R^2 as the R^2 of the full regression minus the R^2 of a regression where both specialization indices are left out.[47] It reflects the fraction of the variance of the left-hand variable explained by the two specialization indices. It appears that specialization explains a large fraction of the variation in the asymmetry index.[48]

We cannot rule out that specialization is affected by fluctuations asymmetry. As an example, imagine that the manufacturing output of a country has a particularly high variance relative to other countries for reasons that are not related to industrial structure. Because its manufacturing production is very variable, the country is likely to decrease manufacturing production, thus affecting the specialization index (downwards if the country was specialized in manufacturing to begin with, and upwards if not). We therefore also estimate the regressions using IV methods with the following instruments for the specialization indices: land mass, the logarithm of average population density, percent high school enrollment in 1990, average GDP level, share of the Finance, Insurance, Real Estate (FIRE) sector in GDP,[49] and the product of the log-agricultural and log-mining shares in GDP.[50] There is some difference in the estimated coefficients between the OLS and IV regressions, with the coefficient of specialization being higher in the IV regressions, but the important fact is that *all* the regressions in Table 5.3 have highly significant t-statistics for both specialization indices.

Table 5.4 focuses on robustness. U.S. states are not separated by national borders and might exhibit different patterns of specialization and fluctuations asymmetry. The first column of Table 5.4 shows that the results for the United States alone are qualitatively similar to those in Table 5.3.

---

[47] The R^2 is calculated as $1 - \Sigma e_i^2 / \Sigma (Y_i - \overline{Y}_i)^2$, where $e_i = Y_i - X_i \hat{b}$, X_i and Y_i are the unweighted left- and right-hand side variables, and $\hat{b}$ is the vector of parameters estimated in the weighted regression.

[48] Since the left-hand variable is log-asymmetry, the coefficients of the log-specialization indices represent elasticities, but it is difficult to interpret their magnitude.

[49] Kalemli-Ozcan, Sørensen, and Yosha (1999) show that regional-level FIRE is highly correlated with interregional risk sharing and is, therefore, an effective instrument for specialization.

[50] We assume that when the log-levels of these sector shares are included as regressors, their product does not directly affect the degree of asymmetry. Including this instrument increases the significance of one-digit specialization but not of manufacturing specialization.

Table 5.4. *Sensitivity Analysis: Specialization Measure, Oil-Rich Countries and States, U.S. States vs. Pooled Sample*

Dependent Variable:	(1) Asym. index U.S.	(2) Asym. index pooled	(3) Asym. index pooled	(4) Asym. index U.S. (no oil)	(5) Asym. index pooled (no oil)
Regressors:					
log 1-digit specialization ($SPEC_1$ index)	0.39 (3.45)	– –	0.37 (3.56)	0.31 (2.87)	0.31 (3.23)
log Manuf. specialization ($SPEC_{1M}$ index)	0.40 (3.72)	– –	0.28 (3.25)	0.30 (3.06)	0.27 (3.41)
log 1-digit specialization ($SPEC_2$ index)	– –	1.03 (4.35)	– –	– –	– –
log Manuf. specialization ($SPEC_{2M}$ index)	– –	0.58 (3.05)	– –	– –	– –
Population$^{1/2}$	−0.17 (1.90)	−0.14 (4.26)	−0.15 (4.53)	−0.23 (2.77)	−0.13 (4.74)
log Agriculture GDP share	0.26 (2.04)	0.29 (2.43)	0.35 (2.89)	0.33 (2.93)	0.36 (3.45)
log Mining GDP share	0.17 (3.36)	0.16 (3.36)	0.13 (2.67)	0.04 (0.63)	0.01 (0.23)
Country dummy	– –	0.26 (1.16)	0.41 (1.87)		0.47 (2.37)
GDP per capita	– –	– –	0.58 (2.16)	– –	– –
Human capital	– –	– –	0.01 (0.51)	– –	– –
R^2	0.72	0.69	0.73	0.65	0.63

Notes: Asym. Index is the log-utility asymmetry index. "Pooled" refers to U.S. states and OECD countries (the sample used in Table 5.3). In the last two columns, states and countries with a Mining GDP share exceeding 10 percent are excluded (Alaska, Louisiana, New Mexico, Oklahoma, Texas, Wyoming, Norway). Human Capital is the percentage of high school enrollment in the population in 1990. GDP per capita is the average over time (1977–94 for U.S. and 1977–90 for OECD). The Country Dummy and Agriculture and Mining GDP shares are defined in Table 5.3. The specialization indices $SPEC_1$, $SPEC_{1M}$, $SPEC_2$, and $SPEC_{2M}$ are defined in the text. The dependent variable is log-transformed in all regressions. All variables in all regressions are weighted by log-population. t-values in parentheses.

In column 2, Table 5.4, we report the results of regressions using alternative specialization indices based on the absolute value of the differences between sector shares (see Section 5). The signs of the estimated parameters are the same and the t-statistics are similar to those in Table 5.3. Column 3 experiments further with regression specifications. Including (real per capita) GDP and human capital as regressors has little impact on the results. Oil-rich countries and states seemed to be outliers in Tables 5.1 and 5.2 and it may not be a sufficient remedy to include the mining share as a regressor. We, therefore, show in columns 4 and 5 results of regressions that leave out countries and states for which the GDP share of mining exceeds 10%. This has little effect on the estimated coefficients of the specialization indices. (We also tried the regression in column 5 further leaving out New Zealand which has a highly specialized manufacturing sector. That only increased the t-statistics.)

As a final robustness test, we estimated a regression similar to the one reported in the first column of Table 5.3, but using specialization measures calculated for 1980 and asymmetry measures calculated for the period 1980–94 (–93 for OECD). If changes in fluctuations asymmetry feed back quickly (within a few years) into industrial specialization, this alternative regression would potentially exhibit different results than those reported in previous tables. Yet the results for this regression are very similar to those reported in Table 5.3.[51] The asymmetry measure changes little over time so this is about as far as our data allow us to go in terms of "dynamics."

Our regressions demonstrate that asymmetry as measured by the utility based measure significantly (and robustly) increases with industrial specialization and that specialization in manufacturing has an impact on fluctuations asymmetry beyond that of one-digit specialization. The instrumental variables regressions provide support for the notion that there is an effect running from industrial specialization to the asymmetry of GDP fluctuations.[52]

6.4. Regressions Using a Pairwise Correlation Measure of Fluctuations Asymmetry

Most of the empirical papers in the literature on asymmetric shocks perform the analysis using country pairs as the unit of observation. For robustness, we perform a similar analysis. Following Frankel and Rose (1998), we compute pairwise correlations of country-level GDP (or state-level GSP)

---

[51] In the order of the rows in Table 5.3, the parameters estimated from this regression are 0.43, 0.25, −0.14, 0.15, 0.14, and 0.45, respectively. The t-statistics are also extremely similar to those reported in the first column of Table 5.3, with the most notable difference being that the log-agriculture share is not significant.

[52] A referee pointed out that although the estimated degree of specialization in manufacturing for U.S. states and OECD countries is roughly the same, the fluctuations asymmetry measure is higher for U.S. states on average. This is a potential indication that U.S. states are more specialized *within* two-digit manufacturing categories.

detrended by first differencing or Hodrick–Prescott (HP) filtering. We do not calculate correlations for mixed state-country pairs. As our "pairwise specialization measure" we use the index suggested by Krugman (1993). For example, the one-digit specialization index for countries i and j is

$$\text{SPEC}_2^{ij} = \sum_{s=1}^{S} \left| \frac{\text{GDP}_i^s}{\text{GDP}_i} - \frac{\text{GDP}_j^s}{\text{GDP}_j} \right|,$$

and the manufacturing specialization index for countries i and j, SPEC_{2M}^{ij}, is defined analogously.

We regress the pairwise asymmetry measures on the pairwise specialization measures, controlling for the same variables as in previous tables (taking the average of each pairwise variable over the sample period), and including a dummy variable for country pairs (as opposed to pairs of U.S. states). The results are displayed in Table 5.5. The estimated coefficients of the specialization indices are negative, as expected (since GDP correlations measure *symmetry*), and are highly statistically significant for both detrending methods.[53]

Our results are, thus, robust to different measures of asymmetry in GDP fluctuations, which indicates that the empirical relation between specialization in production and fluctuations asymmetry holds in the data both at the short (yearly) frequency and at the (longer) business cycle frequency.

7. Income Asymmetry versus GDP Asymmetry

In monetary unions with extensive cross-country ownership of productive assets, *income* shocks are not as asymmetric as GDP shocks. In fact, an increase in the asymmetry of GDP over time may well be accompanied with *less* income asymmetry due to better income insurance. It is hard to predict whether, on net, income asymmetry will rise or fall in a future EMU but it is useful, yet again, to study the experience of U.S. states.

The amount of income insurance among U.S. states is substantial – approximately 40% of idiodyncratic fluctuations in state-level GDP are insured using the metric suggested by Asdrubali, Sørensen, and Yosha (1996)[54] and it is therefore likely (although not a direct implication) that state-level income is less asymmetric than state-level GSP. We examine

---

[53] As in Frankel and Rose (1998), the standard errors and t-statistics are approximate since correlations between the error terms are not controlled for.

[54] See also Mélitz and Zumer (1999).

Table 5.5. *Sensitivity Analysis: Regressions Using Pairs of Countries*
and Pairs of U.S. States

Dependent variable:	(1) Pairwise GDP correlation	(2) Pairwise GDP correlation
Detrending method:	Difference	HP
Regressors: log (1-digit specialization)	−0.28 (22.30)	−0.36 (17.61)
log (Manuf. specialization)	−0.08 (6.81)	−0.04 (2.31)
(Population)$^{1/2}$	0.02 (3.10)	0.01 (4.31)
log (Agriculture GDP share)	0.05 (5.64)	0.07 (4.91)
log (Mining GDP share)	−0.08 (18.68)	−0.14 (19.47)
Pairs of countries dummy	−0.32 (9.35)	−0.27 (5.02)
R^2	0.65	0.57

Notes: The sample consists of all pairs of OECD countries and pairs of U.S. states in the sample used in Table 5.3.
"Pairwise GDP Correlation" is the correlation of the log of real GDP per capita between two countries or two U.S. states. Real GDP per capita is detrended with two different methods: first-differencing or Hodrick–Prescott filtering.
The pairwise specialization indices are defined in the text.
The other regressors are averaged over time for pairs of countries or states. For example, log (Agriculture GDP Share) is the average over time (for the same period as in previous tables) of the log of the average Agriculture GDP Share of countries i and j.
The Pairs of Countries Dummy is 1 for pairs of countries and 0 for pairs of U.S. states.
t-values in parentheses.

this by measuring asymmetry of U.S. state-level personal income using the same formula as that used for GSP in Table 5.1 – substituting income for GSP. The results are displayed in Table 5.6. Most oil states (notably Alaska and Wyoming) exhibit substantially less asymmetry of income than of GSP while several agricultural states (notably North Dakota and Iowa) exhibit as much (or even slightly more) asymmetry of income. Comparing the last rows of Tables 5.1 and 5.6, it is obvious that income asymmetry

Table 5.6. *Income Fluctuations Asymmetry: U.S. States*

States	(1) Variance $(PINC_i)$	(2) Covariance $(PINC_i, PINC)$	(3) Asymmetry index(Log)	(4) Asymmetry index(CRRA)
Alabama	5.45	4.85	0.16	0.18
Alaska	29.91	−0.67	9.03	10.70
Arizona	8.96	5.28	0.82	0.94
Arkansas	10.87	6.56	0.66	0.77
California	4.88	4.45	0.22	0.25
Colorado	2.98	3.00	0.47	0.54
Connecticut	5.84	4.33	0.51	0.59
Delaware	7.98	4.83	0.80	0.92
Florida	7.39	5.03	0.55	0.63
Georgia	7.98	5.96	0.23	0.27
Hawaii	7.09	3.11	1.44	1.65
Idaho	11.62	4.56	1.84	2.12
Illinois	6.21	5.20	0.17	0.20
Indiana	10.88	6.62	0.63	0.73
Iowa	20.35	7.59	2.51	2.95
Kansas	6.46	4.69	0.49	0.56
Kentucky	7.05	5.09	0.44	0.50
Louisiana	5.34	2.87	1.12	1.28
Maine	7.39	4.99	0.57	0.66
Maryland	4.95	4.50	0.20	0.23
Massachusetts	6.06	4.45	0.51	0.58
Michigan	14.40	7.63	1.00	1.18
Minnesota	9.98	6.08	0.67	0.78
Mississippi	8.48	5.46	0.61	0.70
Missouri	6.71	5.24	0.28	0.32
Montana	12.71	4.55	2.12	2.45
Nebraska	14.85	5.96	1.95	2.26
Nevada	8.62	4.52	1.11	1.28
New Hampshire	9.88	5.65	0.86	0.99
New Jersey	6.04	4.51	0.47	0.54
New Mexico	3.40	3.29	0.42	0.49
New York	4.23	3.93	0.31	0.36
North Carolina	8.27	6.04	0.27	0.31
North Dakota	89.15	10.36	18.33	24.31
Ohio	6.95	5.49	0.21	0.25
Oklahoma	6.03	3.14	1.16	1.33
Oregon	7.34	5.14	0.48	0.55
Pennsylvania	4.00	4.20	0.12	0.14
Rhode Island	4.28	3.84	0.37	0.42
South Carolina	7.88	5.69	0.34	0.40
South Dakota	37.21	8.23	6.41	7.72
Tennessee	8.16	6.05	0.23	0.27
Texas	5.33	3.67	0.72	0.82
Utah	4.32	3.70	0.45	0.52
Vermont	8.32	5.72	0.44	0.50
Virginia	5.57	4.87	0.18	0.21

(continued)

Table 5.6. *(continued)*

States	(1) Variance (PINC$_i$)	(2) Covariance (PINC$_i$, PINC)	(3) Asymmetry index(Log)	(4) Asymmetry index(CRRA)
Washington	6.51	4.32	0.69	0.79
West Virginia	4.94	3.23	0.84	0.96
Wisconsin	6.31	5.22	0.19	0.21
Wyoming	11.44	2.80	2.68	3.09
Average	10.34	4.92	0.57	0.67

Notes: The calculations are same as for GSP (Table 5.1) but, instead, state-level personal income is used. We assume a U.S.-wide personal income growth rate of $\mu = 0.020$. Average numbers are population weighted.

is substantially smaller than GSP asymmetry on average, suggesting that income asymmetry in a future EMU will be substantially smaller than GDP asymmetry.

This insight has implications for the stability of EMU. It is often argued that GDP asymmetry may create pressure on individual member states to leave the monetary union. However, if countries care more about their income (rather than their GDP), then the concern for the stability of EMU is overstated, because income asymmetry will probably be much smaller than GDP asymmetry.

8. Summary

We demonstrated that OECD countries and U.S. states with higher industrial specialization exhibit output shocks that are less correlated on average with aggregate OECD output and U.S. output, respectively. We argued that this constitutes evidence in support of an economic mechanism that (partly or fully) offsets the one studied by Frankel and Rose (1998). The mechanism is one where countries and states choose to specialize in production after having spread the risk of specialization in the international or nationwide capital markets so that increased variability of output will not have as large an effect on the variability of income. This should not be taken as an argument against economic integration. On the contrary, it is an argument in support of integration which will lead, true, to more asymmetric output shocks, but not necessarily to more asymmetric *income* shocks.

Appendix: A Utility-Based Measure of Fluctuations Asymmetry

We derive the fluctuations asymmetry measure for CRRA utility (and log-utility as a special case). Let countries be indexed by i. Consumers within country i are identical ex-ante and ex-post: All have the same utility function and produce the same nonstorable, homogeneous, stochastic gross product. The representative consumer of country i chooses a consumption plan in period $t = 0$, solving the problem $\max_{\{c^i_{\omega_t}\}} \int_0^\infty e^{-\delta t} \Sigma_{\omega_t} \pi_{\omega_t} u(c^i_{\omega_t}) \, dt$ subject to $\int_0^\infty \Sigma_{\omega_t} p_{\omega_t} c^i_{\omega_t} \, dt \leq \int_0^\infty \Sigma_{\omega_t} p_{\omega_t} \mathrm{gdp}^i_{\omega_t} \, dt$ where $c^i_{\omega_t}$ and $\mathrm{gdp}^i_{\omega_t}$ are per capita consumption and gross product in country i in state of nature ω_t, which occurs with probability π_{ω_t}.[55] p_{ω_t} is the price in period 0 of a period t state ω_t contingent unit of consumption, and δ is the common intertemporal discount rate. Because securities markets in period 0 are complete, each country faces a single budget constraint. Let $u(c) = \frac{1}{1-\gamma} c^{1-\gamma} (\gamma \neq 1)$. (We address the log-utility case as we proceed.) The first order condition with respect to $c^i_{\omega_t}$ can be written as $\frac{p_{\omega_t}}{\pi_{\omega_t}} = e^{-\delta t} \frac{1}{\lambda^i} (c^i_{\omega_t})^{-\gamma}$ where λ^i is a Lagrange multiplier. Market clearing implies $\Sigma_i n^i c^i_{\omega_t} = \Sigma_i n^i \mathrm{gdp}^i_{\omega_t}$ for all ω_t where n^i is country i's population. Prices are normalized so that $\int_0^\infty \Sigma_{\omega_t} p_{\omega_t} \, dt = 1$. Letting $\mathrm{gdp}_t = \Sigma_i n^i \mathrm{gdp}^i_{\omega_t} / \Sigma_i n^i$, we have $c^i_{\omega_t} = k^i \mathrm{gdp}_t$.[56] From the budget constraint: $\Sigma_i (n^i/n) k^i = 1$ where $n = \Sigma_i n^i$.

To compute k^i, multiply and divide by π_{ω_t} inside the summation operator on both sides of the budget constraint (which binds at an optimum) and substitute for $p_{\omega_t}/\pi_{\omega_t}$ using the first order condition to obtain (λ_i terms cancel) $\int_0^\infty e^{-\delta t} \Sigma_{\omega_t} \pi_{\omega_t} (c^i_{\omega_t})^{1-\gamma} \, dt = \int_0^\infty e^{-\delta t} \Sigma_{\omega_t} \pi_{\omega_t} (c^i_{\omega_t})^{-\gamma} \mathrm{gdp}^i_{\omega_t} \, dt$; substituting $k^i \mathrm{gdp}_t$ for $c^i_{\omega_t}$, and rearranging, we obtain the share of aggregate consumption that would accrue to country i in a perfect risk sharing equilibrium:

$$k^i = \left[\int_0^\infty e^{-\delta t} E_0(\mathrm{gdp}_t)^{1-\gamma} \, dt \right]^{-1} \int_0^\infty e^{-\delta t} E_0 \frac{\mathrm{gdp}^i_t}{\mathrm{gdp}^\gamma_t} \, dt. \tag{3}$$

These steps hold also for log-utility yielding:

$$k^i = \delta \int_0^\infty e^{-\delta t} E_0 \frac{\mathrm{gdp}^i_t}{\mathrm{gdp}_t} \, dt. \tag{4}$$

The interpretation is simple: the strength of country i in the risk-sharing arrangement (the share of aggregate gross product that country i

---

[55] Integrals are assumed to be convergent.

[56] See Huang and Litzenberger (1988) for a derivation for CRRA utility. The derivation for log-utility is much simpler and is provided in Sørensen and Yosha (1998).

consumes) is proportional to its discounted expected share in aggregate gross product.

The analysis so far has been independent of the nature of the joint stochastic process governing the gross product of the countries sharing risk. In order to quantify gains from risk sharing we make distributional assumptions (see Section 4) that allow us to express the constant k^i in an even simpler and economically intuitive manner. Recalling that for $z \sim N(\eta, \phi^2)$, $E e^{az} = e^{a\eta + \frac{1}{2} a^2 \phi^2}$, we have[57]

$$k^i = \left[\int_0^\infty e^{-\delta t} E_0 e^{(1-\gamma) \log \text{gdp}_t} dt \right]^{-1} \int_0^\infty e^{-\delta t} E_0 e^{\log \text{gdp}_t^i - \gamma \log \text{gdp}_t} dt,$$

$$= e^{\log \text{gdp}_0^i - \gamma \log \text{gdp}_0 - (1-\gamma) \log \text{gdp}_0} \left[\int_0^\infty e^{-\delta t} e^{(1-\gamma)\mu t + \frac{1}{2}(1-\gamma)^2 \sigma^2 t} dt \right]^{-1}$$

$$\times \int_0^\infty e^{-\delta t} e^{(\mu^i - \gamma \mu + \frac{1}{2}\sigma_i^2 + \frac{1}{2}\gamma^2 \sigma^2 - \gamma \text{cov}^i) \cdot t} dt$$

$$= \left(\frac{\text{gdp}_0^i}{\text{gdp}_0} \right) \left(\frac{\delta - (1-\gamma)\mu - \frac{1}{2}(1-\gamma)^2 \sigma^2}{\delta - (\mu^i - \gamma \mu + \frac{1}{2}\sigma_i^2 + \frac{1}{2}\gamma^2 \sigma^2 - \gamma \text{cov}^i)} \right). \tag{5}$$

Setting $\gamma = 1$ yields $k^i = (\frac{\text{gdp}_0^i}{\text{gdp}_0})(\frac{\delta}{\delta - (\mu^i - \mu + \frac{1}{2}\sigma^2 + \frac{1}{2}\sigma_i^2 - \text{cov}^i)})$ for log-utility. Here the intuition is more transparent: the risk sharing arrangement allocates a higher share of aggregate output to countries with a larger initial share in aggregate output, and to countries with a lower covariance between $\Delta \log \text{gdp}_t^i$ and $\Delta \log \text{gdp}_t$, reflecting a higher insurance value of country i for the other regions. The higher the variance of country i's GDP, other things equal, the more it can contribute to smoothing shocks in other countries; the higher the variance of the aggregate gross product of the group, keeping the variance of country i's GDP constant, the more other countries would be willing to "pay" country i for joining the risk sharing arrangement.[58]

As a technical note, the population weighted k^i coefficients in Equation (5) do not sum to one due to the distributional approximation made

---

[57] Let $z_t = (1 - \gamma)(\log \text{gdp}_t - \log \text{gdp}_0)$. Then $E z_t = (1 - \gamma)\mu t$ and var $z_t = (1 - \gamma)^2 \text{var}$ $(\Delta \log \text{gdp}_t)t = (1 - \gamma)^2 \sigma^2 t$. Let $y_t = (\log \text{gdp}_t^i - \log \text{gdp}_0^i) - \gamma(\log \text{gdp}_t - \log \text{gdp}_0)$. Then, $E y_t = (\mu^i - \gamma \mu)t$ and var $y_t = \text{var}(\Delta \log \text{gdp}_t^i - \gamma \Delta \log \text{gdp}_t)t = (\sigma_i^2 + \gamma^2 \sigma^2 - 2\gamma \text{cov}^i)t$.

[58] Of course, σ^2, the variance of the growth rate of aggregate GDP, cannot change without *any* of the σ_i^2's changing. The distributional approximation regarding aggregate GDP thus allows us to treat σ^2 as a parameter (that can be estimated from aggregate GDP data) rather than as a complicated function of the country-by-country σ_i^2's.

(that aggregate GDP is log-normally distributed). The size of the bias depends on the estimated parameters $\sigma^2, \sigma_i^2, \text{cov}^i$ and on the value of δ chosen. For our chosen value of $\delta = 0.02$ and our sample of U.S. states and OECD countries, the bias is negligible with the population weighted sum deviating by less than 0.01 from one.

The term $\mu^i - \mu$, the deviation of country i's trend growth from average trend growth (see the denominator in the last line of Equation (5)), reflects intertemporal consumption smoothing considerations. A high trend growth of country i, relative to other countries, induces a high consumption share due to the high future share in aggregate output relative to the low initial share in aggregate output.[59]

We turn to the calculation of the gains from risk sharing. If there is perfect risk sharing, the discounted expected utility of country i as a function of gdp_0^i is

$$
\begin{aligned}
U^{\mathrm{F}}\left(\operatorname{gdp}_0^i\right) &= \frac{1}{1-\gamma} \int_0^{\infty} e^{-\delta t} E_0\left(k^i \operatorname{gdp}_t\right)^{1-\gamma} dt \\
&= \frac{1}{1-\gamma}\left(\operatorname{gdp}_0^i\right)^{1-\gamma} \int_0^{\infty} e^{-\delta t}\left[\left(\frac{\delta-(1-\gamma)\mu-\frac{1}{2}(1-\gamma)^2\sigma^2}{\delta-\left(\mu^i-\gamma\mu+\frac{1}{2}\sigma_i^2+\frac{1}{2}\gamma^2\sigma^2-\gamma\operatorname{cov}^i\right)}\right)^{1-\gamma}\right. \\
&\qquad \times E_0\left(\operatorname{gdp}_t/\operatorname{gdp}_0\right)^{1-\gamma}\Bigg] \\
&= \frac{1}{1-\gamma}\left(\operatorname{gdp}_0^i\right)^{1-\gamma}\left[\left(\frac{\delta-(1-\gamma)\mu-\frac{1}{2}(1-\gamma)^2\sigma^2}{\delta-\left(\mu^i-\gamma\mu+\frac{1}{2}\sigma_i^2+\frac{1}{2}\gamma^2\sigma^2-\gamma\operatorname{cov}^i\right)}\right)^{1-\gamma}\right. \\
&\qquad \times \left. \frac{1}{\delta-(1-\gamma)\mu-\frac{1}{2}(1-\gamma)^2\sigma^2}\right].
\end{aligned}
\tag{6}
$$

The discounted expected utility of country i in autarky is

$$
\begin{aligned}
U^{\mathrm{A}}\left(\operatorname{gdp}_0^i\right) &= \frac{1}{1-\gamma}\left[\int_0^{\infty} e^{-\delta t} E_0\left(\operatorname{gdp}_t^i\right)^{1-\gamma} dt\right] \\
&= \frac{1}{1-\gamma}\left(\operatorname{gdp}_0^i\right)^{1-\gamma} \frac{1}{\delta-(1-\gamma)\mu^i-\frac{1}{2}(1-\gamma)^2\sigma_i^2}.
\end{aligned}
\tag{7}
$$

We want to express the gain $U^{\mathrm{F}}(\operatorname{gdp}_0^i) - U^{\mathrm{A}}(\operatorname{gdp}_0^i)$ as the permanent percentage increase in the level of autarkic consumption that would increase

---

[59] For log-utility, we are able to fully disentangle the gains from intertemporal smoothing and the gains from insurance.

discounted expected utility by the same amount. We thus calculate G^i that satisfies: $U^A(\text{gdp}_0^i * (1 + G^i)) = U^F(\text{gdp}_0^i)$. Taking logs, using (6), (7), and the approximation $\log(1 + G^i) \approx G^i$, and setting $\mu^i = \mu$ we obtain[60]

$$
\begin{aligned}
G^i = &\log\left(\delta - (1-\gamma)\mu - \frac{1}{2}(1-\gamma)^2\sigma^2\right) - \log\left(\delta - (1-\gamma)\mu - \frac{1}{2}\sigma_i^2\right. \\
&\left. - \frac{1}{2}\gamma^2\sigma^2 + \gamma\text{cov}^i\right) + \frac{1}{1-\gamma}\log\left(\delta - (1-\gamma)\mu - \frac{1}{2}(1-\gamma)^2\sigma_i^2\right) \\
&- \frac{1}{1-\gamma}\log\left(\delta - (1-\gamma)\mu - \frac{1}{2}(1-\gamma)^2\sigma^2\right).
\end{aligned} \tag{8}
$$

For log-utility, the derivation is considerably more elegant. The discounted expected utility gain to country i of moving from autarky to perfect risk sharing is (using the approximation $\log(1 + x) \approx x$)

$$
\begin{aligned}
G^i &= \int_0^\infty e^{-\delta t} E_0 \log[k^i \text{gdp}_t]\, dt - \int_0^\infty e^{-\delta t} E_0 \log \text{gdp}_t^i\, dt \\
&= \int_0^\infty e^{-\delta t} \log \frac{\delta}{\delta - \left(\mu^i - \mu + \frac{1}{2}\sigma^2 + \frac{1}{2}\sigma_i^2 - \text{cov}^i\right)}\, dt \\
&\quad + \int_0^\infty e^{-\delta t}(\mu - \mu^i)t\, dt \\
&= -\int_0^\infty e^{-\delta t} \log\left(1 - \frac{1}{\delta}\left(\mu^i - \mu + \frac{1}{2}\sigma^2 + \frac{1}{2}\sigma_i^2 - \text{cov}^i\right)\right)dt + \frac{1}{\delta}(\mu - \mu^i) \\
&\approx \int_0^\infty e^{-\delta t} \frac{1}{\delta}\left(\mu^i - \mu + \frac{1}{2}\sigma^2 + \frac{1}{2}\sigma_i^2 - \text{cov}^i\right)dt - \frac{1}{\delta}(\mu^i - \mu) \\
&= \int_0^\infty e^{-\delta t} \frac{1}{\delta}\left(\frac{1}{2}\sigma^2 + \frac{1}{2}\sigma_i^2 - \text{cov}^i\right)dt + \frac{1}{\delta^2}(\mu^i - \mu) - \frac{1}{\delta}(\mu^i - \mu). \tag{9}
\end{aligned}
$$

The third term in the last line of (9) is the discounted expected utility gain or loss from initially being a lender or a borrower. A low trend growth of country i relative to other countries entails a utility gain reflecting the compensation for initially being a net lender to other countries. A high trend growth relative to the average entails a utility loss reflecting the

[60] To focus on gains from risk sharing, we want to disregard as much as possible gains from intertemporal substitution. We, therefore, set $\mu_i = \mu$ (van Wincoop 1994 makes the same assumption).

payment to other countries for initially being a net borrower. The second term in the last line of (9) originates from the denominator of the expression for k^i. A high trend growth of country i relative to other countries entails a high consumption share for this region due to the high future share in aggregate output relative to the low initial share in aggregate output, and therefore, a high utility gain from risk sharing. This term is an order of magnitude larger than the previous (off-setting) term discussed above. In the empirical analysis for log-utility, we ignore both terms since we want to focus on the gains from pure risk sharing, i.e., on the first term in the last line of (9). The logarithmic utility specification allows us to study (and estimate) these gains without confounding them with gains from intertemporal substitution. The first term in (9) is the discounted expected utility gain of moving from no risk sharing to perfect risk sharing. Integrating, we obtain $\frac{1}{\delta^2}(\frac{1}{2}\sigma^2 + \frac{1}{2}\sigma_i^2 - \text{cov}^i)$. We prefer, however, to express the gains from risk sharing using the term inside the integral in the last line of (9), which corresponds precisely to G^i above. Thus, for log-utility, $G^i = \frac{1}{\delta}(\frac{1}{2}\sigma^2 + \frac{1}{2}\sigma_i^2 - \text{cov}^i)$. The intuition for this expression is provided in the main text.

References

Acemoglu, D., and F. Zilibotti (1997). "Was Prometheus unbound by chance? Risk, diversification, and growth." *Journal of Political Economy* 105, 709–51.

Anderson, J. (1981). "The Heckscher–Ohlin and Travis–Vanek theorems under uncertainty." *Journal of International Economics* 11, 239–47.

Arreaza, A. (1998). "Consumption smoothing, capital flows, and fiscal policy in Latin American countries." Central Bank of Venezuela, working paper.

Asdrubali, P., B. Sørensen, and O. Yosha (1996). "Channels of interstate risk sharing: United States 1963–90." *Quarterly Journal of Economics* 111, 1081–110.

Backus, D., P. Kehoe, and F. Kydland (1992). "International real business cycles." *Journal of Political Economy* 100, 745–75.

Bayoumi, T., and B. Eichengreen (1993). "Shocking aspects of European monetary integration." In: F. Torres, and F. Giavazzi (eds.), *Adjustment and Growth in the European Monetary Union*. (New York: Cambridge University Press).

Brainard, W., and R. Cooper (1968). "Uncertainty and diversification of international trade." *Food Research Institute Studies in Agricultural Economics, Trade, and Development* 8, 257–85.

Canova, F., and H. Dellas (1993). "Trade interdependence and the international business cycle." *Journal of International Economics* 34, 23–47.

Clark, T., and K. Shin (2000). "The sources of fluctuations within and across countries." In: G-. Hess and E. van Wincoop (eds.), *Intranational Macroeconomics*. (New York: Cambridge University Press).

Clark, T., and E. van Wincoop (1999). "Borders and business cycles." Federal Reserve Bank of Kansas City and Federal Reserve Bank of New York, working paper.

Coe, D., and E. Helpman (1995). "International R&D spillovers." *European Economic Review* 39, 859–87.

Cohen, D., and C. Wyplosz (1989). "The European Monetary Union: An agnostic evaluation." In: R. Bryant, D. Currie, J. Frenkel, P. Masson, and R. Portes (eds.), *Macroeconomic Policies in an Interdependent World*. Washington D.C.: Brookings.

Cole, H., and M. Obstfeld (1991). "Commodity trade and international risk sharing: How much do financial markets matter?" *Journal of Monetary Economics* 28, 3–24.

De Grauwe, P., and W. Vanhaverbeke (1993). "Is Europe an optimum currency area? Evidence from regional data." In: P. Masson and M. Taylor (eds.), *Policy Issues in the Operation of Currency Unions*. (New York: Cambridge University Press).

Del Negro, M. (1999). "Asymmetric shocks among U.S. states." Instituto Tecnológico Autónomo de México, working paper.

Fatas, A. (1997). "EMU: countries or regions? Lessons from the EMS experience." *European Economic Review* 41, 743–51.

Feeney, J. (1994). "Goods and asset market interdependence in a risky world." *International Economic Review* 35, 551–64.

Feeney, J. (1999). "International risk sharing, learning by doing, and growth." *Journal of Development Economics* 58, 297–318.

Forni, M., and R. Reichlin (1997). "National policies and local economies: Europe and the United States." CEPR Discussion Paper No. 1632.

Frankel, J., and A. Rose (1998). "The endogeneity of the optimum currency area criterion." *Economic Journal* 108, 1009–25.

French, K., and J. Poterba (1991). "Investor diversification and international equity markets." *American Economic Review: Papers and Proceedings* 81, 222–6.

Giannetti, M. (1999). "The effect of integration on regional disparities: Convergence, divergence, or both?" Research Department, Banca d'Italia, working paper.

Greenwood, J., and B. Jovanovic (1990). "Financial development, growth, and the distribution of income." *Journal of Political Economy* 98, 1076–107.

Grossman, G., and A. Razin (1984). "The pattern of trade in a Ricardian model with country-specific uncertainty." *International Economic Review* 26, 193–202.

Grossman, G., and A. Razin (1985). "International capital movements under uncertainty." *Journal of Political Economy* 92, 286–306.

Helpman, E., and A. Razin (1978a). "Uncertainty and international trade in the presence of stock markets." *Review of Economic Studies* 45, 239–50.

Helpman, E., and A. Razin (1978b). *A Theory of International Trade under Uncertainty*. (New York: Academic Press).

Helpman, E. (1988). "Trade patterns under uncertainty with country specific shocks." *Econometrica* 56, 645–59.

Hess, G., and K. Shin (1998). "Intranational business cycles in the United States." *Journal of International Economics* 44, 289–313.

Huang, C., and R. Litzenberger (1988). *Foundations for Financial Economics.* (New York: Elsevier Publishers).

Imbs, J., and R. Waczairg (2000). "Stages of Diversification." London Business School and Stanford University, and working paper.

Kalemli-Ozcan, S., B. Sørensen, and O. Yosha (1999). "Risk sharing and industrial specialization: regional and international evidence." University of Houston, Federal Reserve Bank of Kansas City, and Tel Aviv University, working paper.

Kemp, M., and N. Liviatan (1973). "Production and trade patterns under uncertainty." *The Economic Record* 49, 215–27.

Kenen, P. (1969). "The theory of optimum currency areas: An eclectic view." In: R. Mundell and A. Swoboda (eds.), *Monetary Problems in the International Economy.* (Chicago: University of Chicago Press).

Kim, S. (1995). "Expansion of markets and the geographic distribution of economic activities: the trends in U.S. regional manufacturing structure 1860–1987." *Quarterly Journal of Economics* 110, 881–908.

Kim, J., S. Kim, and A. Levin (2000). "Patience, persistence and properties of two-country incomplete market models." University of Virginia, Brandeis University, and Federal Reserve Board, working paper.

Kollman, R. (1995). "The correlations of productivity growth across regions and industries in the United States." *Economics Letters* 47, 437–43.

Krugman, P. (1993). "Lesson of Massachusetts for EMU." In: F. Giavazzi and F. Torres, eds., *The Transition to Economic and Monetary Union in Europe.* (New York: Cambridge University Press).

La Porta, R., F. Lopez-de-Silanes, A. Shleifer, and R. Vishny (1998). "Law and finance." *Journal of Political Economy* 106, 1113–55.

Liebermann, J. (1999). "Channels of risk sharing in the European Union." M.A. thesis, ECARES, Brussels.

Mélitz, J., and F. Zumer (1999). "Interregional and international risk sharing and lessons for EMU." *Carnegie–Rochester Conference Series on Public Policy* 51, 149–88.

Mundell, R. (1961). "A theory of optimum currency areas." *American Economic Review* 51, 657–65.

Obstfeld, M. (1992). "Evaluating risky consumption paths: The role of intertemporal substitutability." NBER Technical Paper No. 120.

Obstfeld, M. (1994a). "Risk-taking, global diversification, and growth." *American Economic Review* 84, 1310–29.

Obstfeld, M. (1994b). "Evaluating risky consumption paths: The role of intertemporal substitutability." *European Economic Review* 38, 1471–86.

Rose, A. (2000). "One money, one market: Estimating the effect of common currencies on trade." *Economic Policy* 30, 9–45.

Ruffin, R. (1974). "Comparative advantage under uncertainty." *Journal of International Economics* 4, 261–73.

Saint-Paul, G. (1992). "Technological choice, financial markets and economic development." *European Economic Review* 36, 763–81.

Sørensen, B., and O. Yosha (1998). "International risk sharing and European Monetary Unification." *Journal of International Economics* 45, 211–38.

Sørensen, B., and O. Yosha (2000). "Is risk sharing in the United States a regional phenomenon?" *Federal Reserve Bank of Kansas City Economic Review*, 33–47.

Stockman, A. (1988). "Sectoral and national aggregate disturbances to industrial output in seven European countries." *Journal of Monetary Economics* 21, 387–409.

Tesar, L. (1995). "Evaluating the gains from international risksharing." *Carnegie–Rochester Conference Series on Public Policy* 42, 95–143.

Tesar, L., and I. Werner (1995). "Home bias and high turnover." *Journal of International Money and Finance* 14, 467–92.

van Wincoop, E. (1994). "Welfare gains from international risk sharing." *Journal of Monetary Economics* 34, 175–200.

Weber, A. (1991). "EMU and asymmetries and adjustment Problems in EMS – Some empirical evidence." *European Economy* 1, 187–207.

## SIX

Uncovered Interest Parity in Crisis: The Interest Rate Defense in the 1990s*

Robert P. Flood and Andrew K. Rose

This paper tests for uncovered interest parity (UIP) using daily data for twenty-three developing and developed countries through the crisis-strewn 1990s. We find that UIP works better on average in the 1990s than in previous eras in the sense that the slope coefficient from a regression of exchange rate changes on interest differentials yields a positive co-efficient (which is sometimes insignificantly different from unity). UIP works systematically worse for fixed and flexible exchange rate countries than for crisis countries, but we find no significant differences between rich and poor countries. Finally, we find evidence that varies considerably across countries and time, but is usually weakly consistent with an effective interest rate defense of the exchange rate.

1. Introduction

Uncovered interest parity (UIP) is a classic topic of international finance; a critical building block of most theoretical models and a dismal empirical failure. UIP states that the interest differential is on average equal to the ex post exchange rate change. A strong consensus has developed in the literature that UIP works poorly; it predicts that countries with high interest rates should, on average, have depreciating currencies.

* We thank Rafael Romeu for assistance with the data and Leonardo Leiderman, Rich Lyons, Torsten Persson, and participants at the Festschrift for Assaf Razin held at Tel Aviv University for comments. The data set and a current version of this paper are available at http://haas.berkeley.edu/~arose.

Instead, such currencies tend to have appreciated. Surveys are provided by Hodrick (1987), Froot and Thaler (1990), and Lewis (1995). In this short paper, we use recent data for a wide variety of countries to reexamine the performance of UIP during the 1990s. We also provide evidence on whether departures from UIP make viable an "interest rate defense" of a fixed exchange rate regime.

It is easy to motivate another look at UIP. The vast majority of literature on UIP uses data drawn from low-inflation floating exchange rate regimes (though our previous work also uses European fixed exchange rate observations; Flood and Rose, 1996). UIP may work differently for countries in crisis, where both exchange and interest rates display considerably more volatility. This volatility raises the stakes for financial markets and central banks; it also may provide a more statistically powerful test for the UIP hypothesis. UIP may also work differently over time as financial markets deepen; UIP deviations may also vary across countries for the same reason, as recently argued by Bansal and Dahlquist (2000). Finally, and as the proximate motivation for this paper, deviations from UIP are the basis for interest rate defenses of fixed exchange rates. Consider the actions of the monetary authority of a country under speculative pressure that is considering responding with an increase in interest rates – the classic interest rate defense. If UIP holds, the domestic interest rate increase is offset exactly by a larger expected currency depreciation. Investors see through the policy actions, so that no advantage is conferred to domestic securities. Policy exploitable deviations from UIP are, therefore, a necessary condition for an interest rate defense.

In this paper we test UIP using recent high-frequency data from a large number of countries. We use data from the 1990s, and include all the major currency crises. We find that the old consensual view needs updating. While UIP still does not work well, it works better than it used to, in the sense that high interest rate countries at least tend to have depreciating currencies (though not equal to the interest rate differential). There is a considerable amount of heterogeneity in our results, which differ wildly by country. Some of this is systematic; we find that UIP works worse for fixed-rate countries. However, there is less heterogeneity by forecasting horizon, and almost none by country income.

In Section 2 we lay out our methodology; the following section provides a discussion of our data set. Our main UIP results are presented in Section 4. Section 5 presents our evidence on the interest rate defense. The paper ends with a brief summary.

2. Methodology

We use standard methods (summarized in Flood and Rose, 1996). The hypothesis of uncovered interest parity can be expressed as:

$$(1 + i_t) = (1 + i^*_t)E_t(S_{t+\Delta})/S_t \tag{1}$$

where: i_t represents the return on a domestic asset at time t of maturity Δ; i^* is the return on a comparable foreign asset; S is the domestic currency price of a unit of foreign exchange; and $E_t(.)$ represents the expectations operator conditional upon information available at t.

We follow the literature by taking natural logarithms and ignoring cross terms (most of the countries we consider have only low interest rates). Assuming rational expectations and rearranging, we derive

$$
\begin{aligned}
E_t(s_{t+\Delta} - s_t) &\approx (i - i^*)_t \\
\Rightarrow (s_{t+\Delta} - s_t) &= \alpha + \beta(i - i^*)_t + \varepsilon_t
\end{aligned}
\tag{2}
$$

where: s is the natural logarithm of S; ε_t is (minus) the forecasting error realized at $t+\Delta$ from a forecast of the exchange rate made at time t; and α and β are regression coefficients. Equation (2) has been used as the workhorse for the UIP literature. The null hypothesis of UIP can be expressed as $H_0: \alpha = 0$, $\beta = 1$. Since ε_t is a forecasting error, it is assumed to be stationary and orthogonal to information available at time t (including interest rates). Thus, OLS is a consistent estimator of β; it is the standard choice in the literature, and we follow this practice. Researchers have typically estimated β to be significantly negative, and α to be nontrivial.[1]

In practice, we modify testing (2) in two slight ways. First, we pool data from a number of countries, an admissible way of increasing the sample under the null hypothesis. Second, we use data of daily frequency for exchange rate forecasts of up to one-quarter (year) horizon. The fact that Δ is greater than unity induces ε to have a moving average "overlapping observation" structure. We account for this by estimating our covariance matrices with the Newey and West (1987) estimator, with an appropriate number of off-diagonal bands.

---

[1] Many have tried to interpret deviations from UIP as risk premia; here we simply try to measure UIP deviations carefully and encourage others to link these deviations to other phenomena.

3. The Data Set

We are interested in studying how UIP performs of late in a variety of
countries, especially those suffering from the currency crises that marked
the 1990s. These crises were usually surprising events requiring quick policy responses.[2] In this spirit, we study the crises using a high-frequency
cross-country data set. High-frequency data are of special importance
to us given our focus on the interest rate defense of fixed exchange
rates.

We gathered daily data for the interest and exchange rates of twenty-
three countries during the 1990s. Our sample includes thirteen developed countries (Australia, Canada, Denmark, Finland, France, Germany,
Italy, Japan, Norway, Sweden, Switzerland, the United Kingdom, and
the United States). We choose these countries to allow us to examine
a variety of exchange rate regimes ranging from the floating Australian
and Canadian dollars to countries like Denmark and France, European
Monetary System (EMS) participants who joined European Economic
and Monetary Union (EMU). A number of these countries also experienced currency crises in the 1990s, including Finland, Italy, Sweden, and
the UK. We include also data for ten developing countries (Argentina,
Brazil, Czech Republic, Hong Kong, Indonesia, Korea, Malaysia, Mexico,
Russia, and Thailand). The crises experienced by these countries account
for most of the important action in the 1990s; we include all "the usual
suspects." Indeed, it is difficult to think of an important emerging market
that did not experience a crisis at some point during the 1990s. Nevertheless, there are considerable periods of tranquility through the period.
These, together with the many successful and unsuccessful speculative attacks, lead us to believe that our estimates will not suffer from the "peso
problem."

Our data are drawn from two sources. Whenever possible, we use the
Bank for International Settlements (BIS) data set. Our default measure
of exchange rates is QBCA, a representative dollar spot rate quoted at
2:15 P.M. Brussels time. Our default measure of interest rates is JDBA, a
one-month euro market bid rate quoted at about 10:00 A.M. Swiss time.
However, a number of our countries do not have one or both of these
series available. Accordingly, we supplement our BIS data with series
drawn from Bloomberg. To check the sensitivity of our results with respect
to the monthly forecast horizon, we include also interest rate data for three

---

[2] See, e.g., Rose and Svensson (1994) and Boorman et al. (2000).

different maturities: one day; one week; and one quarter. Further details (including mnemonics) and the data set itself are available online. The data set has been checked and corrected for errors.

We use the United States as the "center country" for all exchange rates (including Germany), except for nine European countries (Czech Republic, Denmark, Finland, France, Italy, Norway, Sweden, Switzerland, the UK), where we treat Germany as the anchor. We choose our center countries in this way to shed the maximum amount of light on the efficacy of the interest rate defense.

Figure 6.1 contains time-series plots of the exchange rates. The price of an American dollar rates are portrayed for all countries except for the nine European countries, which portray the price of a DM. (Scales vary across different plots, as they do in all the figures.) The breaks in series are usually associated with currency crises or other regime breaks. For instance, the Brazilian exchange rate shows clearly both the adoption of the real after the hyperinflation of the early 1990s, and the flotation of the real in January 1999. Similar breaks are apparent for many other countries, including: Indonesia, Italy, Korea, Malaysia, Mexico, Russia, and Thailand. The convergence of the EMS rates and the creation of the euro in 1999 are also apparent in the (non-German) EMU rates.

Figure 6.2 is an analog showing interest rates. Monthly interest rates are shown for all countries except for Russia (where weekly rates are shown since the monthly series is short), Finland and Korea (where quarterly rates are shown for the same reason).[3] Here the currency crises appear as spikes in interest rates. These spikes are particularly obvious during the EMS crisis of 1992–93 (for e.g., Denmark, France, Italy, Norway, and Sweden), the Mexico crisis of 1994–95 (for Argentina and Mexico), the Asian crisis of 1997 (for Hong Kong, Indonesia, Korea, Malaysia, and Thailand), and the Russian crisis of 1998.

Figure 6.3 combines the exchange and interest rate data into a single series, which we call "excess returns." Excess returns ("er") are defined as $[er_{t+\Delta} \equiv (s_{t+\Delta} - s_t) - (i - i^*)_t]$, annualized appropriately. Under the UIP null hypothesis (H_0: $\alpha = 0$, $\beta = 1$) $E_t er_{t+\Delta} = 0$. Again, we use a monthly horizon as our default (so that we use one-month interest rates and set? to one month); the only exceptions are Russia (we use weekly rates and horizon), Finland and Korea (quarterly rates and horizon are used).

---

[3] We define a month as 22 business days, a week as 5 business days, and a quarter as 65 business days.

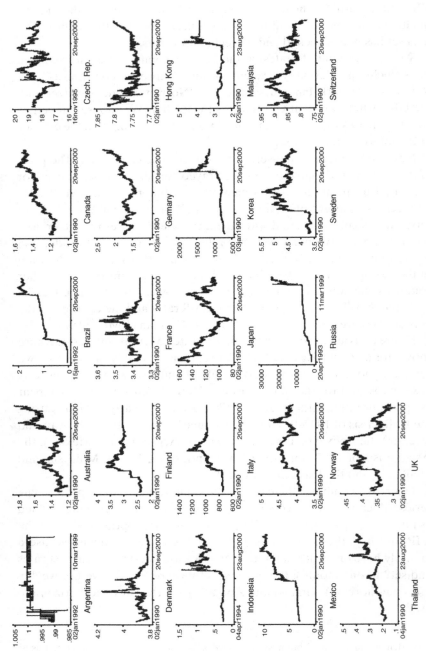

Figure 6.1. Exchange rate data

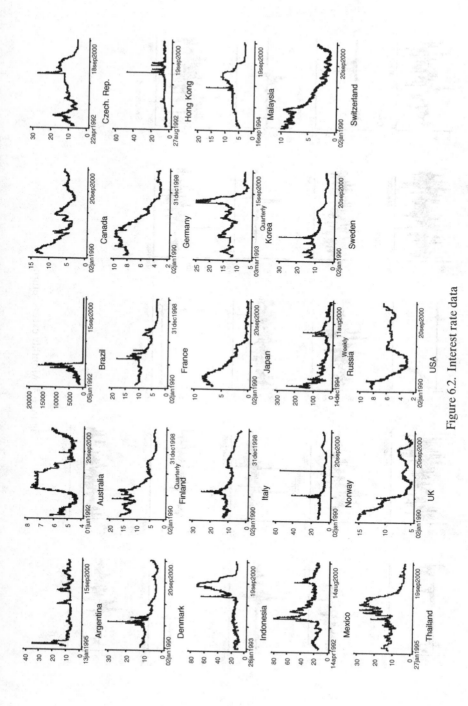

Figure 6.2. Interest rate data

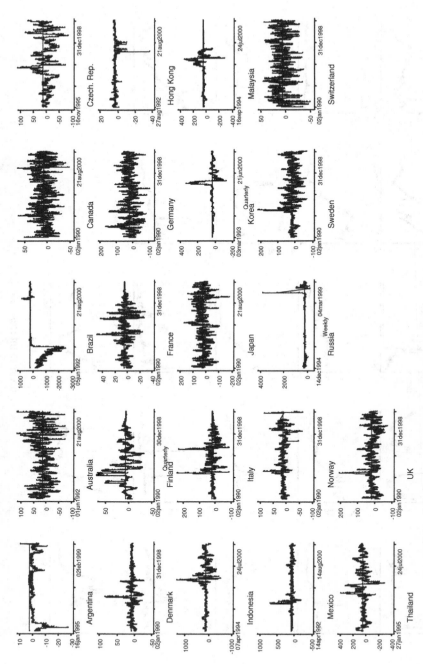

Figure 6.3. Monthly excess returns

In essence, the plots in Fig. 6.3 show the results of taking a short position in the currency. For example, since Argentina did not deviate from its peg with the U.S. dollar, the payoff from attacking the Argentine peso was consistently negative throughout the 1990s, dramatically so during the interest rate defense against the "Tequila" attacks of early 1995. The successful attacks against the Korean won, Mexican peso, and the Russian ruble show up as large positive payoffs realized at the time of the flotations.

Where Fig. 6.3 provides a look at a combination of exchange rate changes and interest differentials over time, Fig. 6.4 graphs the exchange rate changes and interest rate differentials against each other. Instead of examining the time-series patterns on a country-by-country basis as in Fig. 6.3, we pool the data across countries. Exchange rate changes (on the ordinate) are more volatile than interest rate differentials (on the abscissa) for each horizon. There is clearly no tight relationship between exchange rate changes and interest differentials. This is no surprise; interest differentials are not very useful in predicting exchange rate changes. Since the visual impression is unclear, we now proceed to more rigorous statistical analysis, which is essentially an analog to the graphs of Fig. 6.4.

4. UIP Regression Analysis

Table 6.1 provides estimates of β when Equation (2) is estimated on a country-by-country basis; that is, the regressions are estimated for an individual country over time. Newey–West standard errors that are robust to both heteroskedasticity and autocorrelation (induced by the overlapping observation problem) are recorded in parentheses below. Estimates of the intercept (a) are not reported. We focus on the monthly horizon results, but tabulate the results for the three other forecasting horizons as a sensitivity check.

The most striking thing about the estimates of β is their heterogeneity. Of the twenty-one estimates, twelve are negative and seven are positive (two are essentially zero). This in itself is interesting, since virtually all estimates in the literature are negative. Further, all but one of the negative estimates are insignificantly so, while three of the positive coefficients are significant. Finally, the point estimates vary across forecast horizon, often switching signs across horizons.

Table 6.2 pools the data across countries, so that a single β is estimated for all countries and periods of time. Here too, the results are striking. In particular, the top panel shows that the pooled estimate is positive

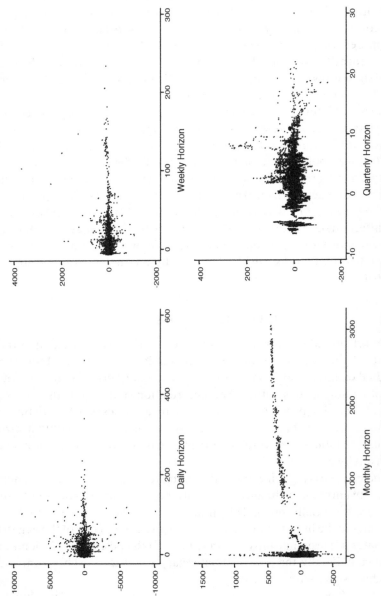

Figure 6.4. Exchange rate changes and interest rate differentials

Table 6.1. *Uncovered Interest Parity Tests by Country*

Horizon:	Daily	Weekly	Monthly	Quarterly
Argentina	.03		.00	−.003
	(.11)		(.01)	(.002)
Australia			−3.58	
			(2.55)	
Brazil	15.3		.19	
	(15.9)		(.01)	
Canada			−.58	
			(.54)	
Czech Rep.	.73		−1.27	−1.41
	(1.13)		(.85)	(1.14)
Denmark			−.03	
			(.70)	
Finland	2.50		7.06	2.56
	(2.20)		(3.80)	(1.21)
France			−1.42	
			(.62)	
Germany	−.60		.13	−.11
	(1.32)		(1.11)	(1.16)
Hong Kong	−.35	−.20	.00	−.00
	(.18)	(.06)	(.03)	(.02)
Indonesia	.22		−1.19	
	(2.05)		(1.13)	
Italy	1.66		.29	−.75
	(1.87)		(2.55)	(1.92)
Japan	−.82	−3.14	−1.71	−1.84
	(1.36)	(1.83)	(1.11)	(1.19)
Korea	3.41	1.42		−.31
	(4.12)	(2.08)		(1.57)
Malaysia			2.24	2.07
			(2.08)	(1.95)
Mexico	−.37	−.60	−.77	
	(1.00)	(.66)	(.70)	
Norway			.59	
			(.75)	
Russia	1.48	1.29	.22	
	(1.46)	(.58)	(.11)	
Sweden	.08		−.44	1.28
	(.03)		(.95)	(2.03)
Switzerland			−2.08	
			(1.40)	
Thailand	.52	−1.29	−.83	
	(1.86)	(1.57)	(1.80)	
UK	−1.15		−1.26	−1.42
	(1.06)		(.97)	(.98)

OLS Estimates of β from $(s_{t+\Delta} - s_t) = \alpha + \beta(i - i^*)_t + \varepsilon_t$ Newey–West standard errors in parentheses.

Table 6.2. *Pooled UIP Tests*

Panel A: No interactions

	β (se)	No. Obs.
Daily	.86	26,972
	(.65)	
Weekly	.87	8,033
	(.34)	
Monthly	.19	37,992
	(.01)	
Quarterly	.29	18,942
	(.39)	

Panel B: Exchange Rate Regime Interactions

	β (se)	FIX*β (se)	FLOAT*β (se)	No. Obs.	P-value: Interactions = 0
Daily	.87	−.94	−.71	26,972	.21
	(.67)	(.58)	(1.23)		
Weekly	.92	−.87	−1.26	8,033	.00
	(.37)	(.29)	(1.40)		
Monthly	.19	−.93	−.20	37,992	.01
	(.01)	(.32)	(.48)		
Quarterly	.43	−.54	−.47	18,942	.44
	(.49)	(.42)	(.94)		

Panel C: Country Income Interactions

	β (se)	OECD*β (se)
Daily	.97	−.80
	(.75)	(.48)
Weekly	.92	−1.28
	(.37)	(1.40)
Monthly	.19	−.31
	(.01)	(.36)
Quarterly	.27	.06
	(.54)	(.68)

OLS Estimates of β from $(S_{it+\Delta} - S_{it}) = \alpha + \beta(i - i^*)_{it} + \varepsilon_{it}$ Newey–West standard errors in parentheses.

at all four horizons. At the monthly horizon, β is significantly positive, though at 0.19 it is far below its theoretical value of unity. At the other horizons, β is even higher and insignificantly different from unity (and strikingly close to unity at the daily and weekly horizons).[4] Still, pooling

---

[4] Chinn and Meredith (2000) find even more positive results using long-maturity data.

is a dubious procedure given the heterogeneity manifest in Table 6.1, so we do not take these results too seriously.[5]

The other panels of Table 6.2 add interactions between dummy variables and the interest differential. Panel B includes an interaction with the exchange rate regime. We consider Argentina, Denmark, France, and Hong Kong to have fixed their exchange rates throughout the sample, while we classify Australia, Canada, Germany, Japan, Norway, and Switzerland as floaters. The other ("crisis") countries experienced at least one regime switch and are omitted as our control group.

We find that both fixers and floaters have significantly lower estimates of β, in contrast to Flood and Rose (1996) who use data from late 1970s through the early 1990s. When we interact the interest rate differential with a dummy variable that is unity for countries that were members of the OECD at the beginning of the decade, we find insignificantly different results. This result stands in contrast to the estimates provided by Bansal and Dahlquist (2000).

5. The Interest Rate Defense

In this section we develop evidence on the efficacy of the interest rate defense.

5.1. The Framework

The model upon which we base our test is the one developed by Flood and Jeanne (2000) (FJ), itself an adaptation of Krugman (1979), and Flood and Garber (1984) that allows for a policy-exploitable wedge in UIP.[6] In FJ, defense efficacy is measured in terms of prolonging the fixed exchange rate regime. In other words, the defense works if raising the domestic currency interest rate makes the fixed rate regime survive longer than it otherwise would without the rate increase. The UIP wedge in FJ is proportional to the worldwide privately held stock of domestic government issued domestic currency denominated nominal debt.[7]

The main FJ results are (a) increasing the domestic currency interest rate *prior* to a speculative attack will always *hasten* the onset of the

---

[5] This is especially true since the Hildreth–Houck random-coefficients method delivers slope coefficients which are economically and statistically insignificant on our pooled data.

[6] Other interest rate defense models include Bensaid and Jeanne (1997), Drazen (1999), and Lahiri and Végh (1999, 2000).

[7] This functional form is derived in Jeanne and Rose (1999) and is discussed more in FJ.

speculative attack for fiscal reasons; and (b) committing credibly to increase the domestic currency interest rate *after* the speculative attack may obstruct the speculative attack. The most striking result is that it is the actions to be taken *after* the attack – like promising to hit back – that may deter the attack.

The key equation in FJ is:

$$i_t^* = i_t + E_t s_{t+\Delta} - s_t + \theta B_t / S_t \tag{3}$$

where: θ is a positive constant; and B_t is worldwide private holding of domestic government issued domestic-currency bonds. The last term, $\theta B_t / S_t$, is the UIP wedge needed to analyze the interest rate defense.

FJ assume that all nominal bonds issued by the domestic government, N_t, are either held privately, B_t, or are held by the domestic monetary authority as domestic credit, D_t. FJ also assume that after the speculative attack, the exchange rate floats and domestic-monetary authority's international reserves are constant at zero. The wedge thus becomes

$$\theta[(N_t - D_t)/S_t] = \theta[(N_t - M_t)/S_t] = \theta(n_t - m_t)$$

where: $n \equiv N/S$; $m \equiv M/S$; M is high-powered money; and $D = M$ because reserves are zero.

The state variable driving FJ to the attack precipice and beyond is N. During the fixed exchange rate regime that precedes the attack, the exchange rate stabilizes goods prices, and the government fixes the interest rate on its debt. Tracking N's growth is therefore an accounting exercise. In the post-attack floating rate epoch, FJ solve their model for n, the real value of government-issued debt.[8]

5.2. The Role of Excess Returns

We study the efficacy of the interest rate defense by first using the model to find the length of the fixed rate epoch, and then examining the data to find the direction in which interest rate increases change observable determinates of efficacy.

The connection to excess returns proceeds in three steps. First, we solve for n noting that at the instant of the attack we must have $n = N/\overline{S}$, where $\overline{S}$ is the pre-attack fixed exchange rate.[9] Second, since $\overline{S}$ is fixed and N

---

[8] FJ is a perfect foresight model. The translation of their results to real-world data requires us to refer to the permanent component of disturbances.

[9] This terminal condition would be altered slightly in a stochastic setup. See, e.g., Flood and Garber (1984).

grows in lockstep with the mechanical pre-attack deficit, anything (and only those things) that increases n must increase the length of the fixed rate epoch also. Third, we have no daily data on N or, therefore, on n but we do have daily excess returns. According to the above model,

$$\text{er}_{t+\Delta} = \theta(m_t - n_t) + s_{t+\Delta} - E_t s_{t+\Delta}. \tag{4}$$

Since neither money nor debt is available at a daily frequency, our investigation of the efficacy of the interest rate defense involves regressing $\text{er}_{t+\Delta}$ on i_i. If we estimate the following OLS regression:

$$\text{er}_{t+\Delta} = \lambda + \gamma i_t + v_t, \tag{5}$$

the question then is, What can be learned?[10]

The FJ model helps but still does not allow a straightforward interpretation of the regression results. We measure $\hat{\gamma} = \theta(\Delta m/\Delta i - \Delta n/\Delta i)$; thus, even if $\theta > 0$ we do not measure the sign of $\Delta n/\Delta i$ directly. Instead, we measure it combined with $\Delta m/\Delta i$. We assume, therefore, that m is negatively related to i through substitution in money demand.

Thus if $\hat{\gamma} > 0$, we conclude $\Delta n/\Delta i < 0$, so that the interest rate defense is ineffective. If however, $\hat{\gamma} < 0$, the test is inconclusive but consistent with the efficacy of the interest rate defense. When $\hat{\gamma} = 0$, either $\theta = 0$ so that the interest rate defense is ineffective because the UIP wedge is not exploitable, or $\Delta m/\Delta i = \Delta n/\Delta I$, making the interest rate defense effective when $\Delta m/\Delta i < 0$. Our only possibility for strong results requires $\hat{\gamma} > 0$.

Model-specific considerations make our test sound narrow. But it is also possible to put a more positive spin on our evidence. What policy-makers are trying to accomplish with an active interest rate defense is to decrease the expected excess return to (short) positions against the domestic currency. That is, by increasing the domestic interest rate the authorities are trying to increase the expected excess return to holding domestic-currency debt. Our empirical work simply asks, Does this strategy usually work?

In Tables 6.3 through 6.5 we provide a number of estimates of γ. The results tabulated in Table 6.3 are analogs to those in Table 6.1 for UIP; these estimates of γ use time-series data on a country-by-country basis. Table 6.4 uses data that is pooled across countries on a year-by-year basis.

---

[10] Viewing Equation (5) as the linearization of Equation (4) turns v_t into an error composed of an exchange rate prediction error plus a linearization error. Arbitrary exclusion restrictions are required for the model-specific interpretation that follows.

Table 6.3. *Excess Return/Domestic Interest Rate Relationship by Country*

Horizon:	Daily	Weekly	Monthly	Quarterly
Argentina	−.96		−.96	−.96
	(.11)		(.01)	(.01)
Australia			−1.78	
			(2.16)	
Brazil	−65		−.81	
	(94)		(.01)	
Canada			−1.56	
			(.41)	
Czech Rep.	−.28		−2.41	−2.51
	(1.14)		(.92)	(1.15)
Denmark			−.27	
			(.25)	
Finland	1.10		2.98	1.01
	(1.22)		(1.68)	(.60)
France			−.22	
			(.16)	
Germany	−2.39		−1.56	−1.76
	(1.54)		(1.34)	(1.42)
Hong Kong	−.54	−1.14	−.71	−.69
	(.17)	(.06)	(.09)	(.10)
Indonesia	−.76		−2.17	
	(2.06)		(1.14)	
Italy	.86		1.36	1.16
	(1.04)		(1.42)	(.96)
Japan	−1.50	−8.56	−2.22	−2.49
	(1.41)	(3.54)	(1.21)	(1.29)
Korea	2.64	.41		−1.22
	(4.30)	(2.06)		(1.72)
Malaysia			1.51	1.26
			(2.25)	(2.13)
Mexico	−1.26	−1.46	−1.60	
	(.97)	(.64)	(.66)	
Norway			.25	
			(.38)	
Russia	.48	.29	−.78	
	(1.45)	(.57)	(.11)	
Sweden	−.83		.24	.80
	(.08)		(.61)	(.95)
Switzerland			−.32	
			(.47)	
Thailand	−.54	−2.51	−1.79	
	(1.93)	(1.65)	(1.81)	
UK	.31		.01	.13
	(.80)		(.71)	(.85)

OLS Estimates of γ from $er_{t+\Delta} = \lambda + \gamma i_t + v_t$ Newey–West standard errors in parentheses.

Table 6.4. *Excess Return/Domestic Interest Rate Relationship by Year*

Horizon:	Daily	Weekly	Monthly	Quarterly
1990	−.43		−.40	.52
	(.93)		(.37)	(.27)
1991	1.20		−.65	.52
	(2.72)		(.34)	(.33)
1992	−.78	−2.19	−.75	3.00
	(.14)	(.45)	(.004)	(.16)
1993	−.57	−.85	−.78	.12
	(.60)	(.54)	(.003)	(.16)
1994	.33	.80	−.84	.61
	(1.15)	(.54)	(.002)	(.19)
1995	−.58	−.49	−.73	−2.04
	(.21)	(.09)	(.02)	(.18)
1996	−.73	−.73	−.70	−1.85
	(.15)	(.09)	(.02)	(.12)
1997	.19	.37	1.10	1.03
	(1.30)	(1.05)	(.34)	(.37)
1998	1.35	3.01	−.52	−1.80
	(2.51)	(1.81)	(.36)	(.19)
1999	−1.52	−.89	−1.29	−.25
	(.88)	(.32)	(.31)	(.36)

OLS Estimates of γ from $er_{it+\Delta} = \lambda + \gamma i_{it} + v_{it}$ Newey–West standard errors in parentheses.

Finally, Table 6.5 is the analog to Table 6.2, and provides estimates of γ that use data which is pooled across both countries and time.

The estimates in Tables 6.3–6.5 show that γ is typically negative, but vary wildly. The country-specific time series evidence of Table 6.3 shows that γ varies substantially across countries and even across horizons within countries. The negative estimates for Argentina are striking but intuitive, since Argentina successfully used the interest rate defense to support the peso through the 1990s; results for Hong Kong are similar. But a number of countries such as Italy and Malaysia provide positive estimates of γ. There is also an interesting lack of strong results for Korea, Mexico, Thailand and the UK, all victims of highly visible and successful speculative attacks.

The heterogeneity of results also characterizes the results in Table 6.4 that pool data across countries within specific years. Perhaps the most striking results are the positive coefficients that characterize 1997 (the year of the Asian crisis) for all maturities. Manifestly an effective interest rate defense did not characterize that crucial year.

Table 6.5. *Pooled Excess Return/Domestic Interest*
Rate Relationship

Panel A: No interactions

	γ (se)	Num. Obs.
Daily	−.11	26,972
	(.64)	
Weekly	−.12	8,033
	(.33)	
Monthly	−.81	37,992
	(.01)	
Quarterly	−.21	18,942
	(.35)	

Panel B: Exchange Rate Regime Interactions

	γ (se)	FIX*γ (se)	FLOAT*γ (se)	P-value: Interactions = 0
Daily	−.12	−.38	−.41	.33
	(.64)	(.26)	(.62)	
Weekly	−.16	−.24	−4.17	.39
	(.35)	(.53)	(3.23)	
Monthly	−.81	−.50	−.57	.06
	(.01)	(.21)	(.28)	
Quarterly	−.25	−.37	−.76	.09
	(.35)	(.18)	(.52)	

Panel C: Country Income Interactions

	γ (se)	OECD*γ (se)
Daily	−.48	−.05
	(.47)	(.68)
Weekly	−4.02	−.16
	(3.04)	(.35)
Monthly	−.21	−.81
	(.28)	(.01)
Quarterly	.20	−.31
	(.35)	(.44)

OLS Estimates of γ from $er_{it+\Delta} = \lambda + \gamma i_{it} + v_{it}$ Newey–West standard errors in parentheses.

The results in Table 6.5 pool observations across countries and time. The typical estimate of γ is negative, significantly so at the key monthly horizon. This is consistent with the efficacy of the interest rate defense. However, the lower panels of the table show that we are unable to find a link between the efficacy of this strategy and either the exchange rate regime or income.

6. Conclusion

Uncovered interest parity works better than it used to, in the sense that interest rate differentials seem typically to be followed by subsequent exchange rate depreciation. The fact that this relationship has been positive on average during the 1990s contrasts sharply with the typically negative estimates of the past. At the daily and weekly horizons, this relationship even seems to be proportionate. Nevertheless, there are still massive departures from uncovered interest parity. There is enormous heterogeneity in the UIP relationship across countries, though we have been unable to find a close relationship between UIP departures and either the exchange rate regime and country income.

We also presented evidence on the efficacy of the interest rate defense of a fixed exchange rate. Our evidence on the interest rate defense is both model-specific and loose in the sense that data limitations prevent a direct test of the model. Nevertheless, we think it is suggestive. We cannot establish the effectiveness of this strategy; but neither has our empirical work been able to unequivocally rule it out; so far as we are concerned, the door is open. However, the evidence is murky, and we provide only slightly more evidence consistent with the interest rate defense than we do for the complete absence of any effect from the domestic interest rate on UIP deviations. We think of this as an intriguing place to pass on the baton.

References

Bansal, Ravi, and Magnus Dahlquist (2000). "The Forward Premium Puzzle: Different Tales from Developed and Emerging Economies," *Journal of International Economics* 51-1, 115–44.

Bensaid, Bernard, and Olivier Jeanne (1997). "The Instability of Fixed Exchange Rate Systems: When Raising the Interest Rate is Costly," *European Economic Review* 41, 1461–78.

Boorman, Jack, Timothy Lane, Marianne Schulze-Ghattas, Ales Bulir, Atish R. Ghosh, Javier Hamman, Alesandros Mourmouras, and Steven Phillips (2000). "Managing Financial Crises: The Experience in East Asia," IMF WP/00/107.

Chinn, Menzie, and Guy Meredith (2000). "Testing Uncovered Interest Parity at Short and Long Horizons," working paper.

Drazen, Allan (1999). "Interest Rate Defense Against Speculative Attack Under Asymmetric Information," working paper.

Flood, Robert P., and Peter M. Garber (1984). "Collapsing Exchange Rate Regimes: Some Linear Examples" *Journal of International Economics*, August, 1–13.

Flood, Robert P., and Olivier Jeanne (2000). "An Interest Rate Defense of a Fixed Exchange Rate?" IMF WP/00/158.

Flood, Robert P., and Andrew K. Rose (1996). "Fixes: Of the Forward Discount Puzzle" *Review of Economics and Statistics*.

Froot, Kenneth A., and Richard H. Thaler (1990). "Anomalies: Foreign Exchange," *Journal of Economic Perspectives* 4-3, 179–92.

Krugman, Paul (1979). "A Model of Balance of Payments Crises," *Journal of Money Credit and Banking*, August, 311–25.

Hodrick, Robert J. (1987). *The Empirical Evidence on the Efficiency of Forward and Futures Foreign Exchange Markets*. (Chur: Harwood).

Jeanne, Olivier, and Andrew K. Rose (2001). "Noise Trading and Exchange Rate Regimes," *Quarterly Journal of Economics*, in press.

Lahiri, Amartya, and Carlos A. Végh (1999). "Delaying the Inevitable: Optimal Interest Rate Policy and BOP Crises," UCLA, Dept. of Economics working paper.

Lewis, Karen K. (1995). "Puzzles in International Financial Markets" in Grossman and Rogoff (eds), *The Handbook of International Economics*.

Newey, Whitney K., and Kenneth D. West (1987). "A Simple, Positive Semi-definite, Heteroskedasticity and Autocorrelation Consistent Covariance Matrix," *Econometrica* 55-3, 703–8.

Rose, Andrew K., and Lars E.O. Svensson (1994). "European Exchange Rate Credibility Before the Fall," *European Economic Review*.

## SEVEN

When Does Capital Account Liberalization Help More than It Hurts?[1]

Carlos Arteta, Barry Eichengreen, and Charles Wyplosz

1. Introduction

The literature on the effects of capital mobility falls under two headings, reflecting the traditional divide between the two branches of international economics. While work on the effects of capital movements in models of the real economy is well advanced, due in no small part to the important contributions of Assaf Razin, the same cannot be said of research in international finance on the effects of capital account liberalization and international capital flows.

There are two explanations for the contrast, one having to do with theory, the other reflecting the limitations of existing empirics. On the theoretical side there are reasons to think that the imperfect nature of the information environment does more to complicate the effects and consequently the analysis of financial than nonfinancial transactions. Information asymmetries are endemic in financial markets. In particular, it is unrealistic to assume that agents on both sides of a financial transaction have the same information.[2] This is especially true of international

---

[1] This paper was prepared for the conference celebrating Assaf Razin's 60th birthday, held at Tel Aviv University, March 25–26, 2001. We thank Dennis Quinn and Andrew Warner for help with data and Anne Krueger and Dani Rodrik for comments.
[2] The classic illustration is that a borrower will know more than a lender about his own desire and motivation to repay, although the point is more general. This is why banks and other financial institutions play a prominent role in the modern economy: By virtue of their investments in monitoring technologies characterized by economies of scale and scope, they aspire to bridge gaps in the information environment that decentralized markets cannot. These observations are widely cited in support of the notion that information asymmetries are pervasive in financial markets.

financial transactions, in whose case information flows must travel additional physical and cultural distance. It is well understood that these imperfections in the information environment are a distortion in whose presence inward foreign financial investment can be welfare reducing. But the difficulty of characterizing the information asymmetry and therefore the incidence of the distortion means that there is no consensus on precisely when and where such immiserizing effects may take place.

In contrast, the limited conditions under which the transfer or accumulation of capital in a real trade model is immiserizing are well understood. Brecher and Diaz-Alejandro (1977) have pointed to import tariffs, while Bhagwati and Brecher (1991) have modeled the effects of rigid real wages, both of which can lead foreign capital to flow into the wrong sector with immiserizing effects. The transparency of this analysis leaves less controversy about the effects of capital mobility in models of the real economy.

The other explanation for the contrast, and the one we pursue in this paper, is that empirical studies of the effects of foreign direct investment (and, for that matter, trade in goods and services) have reached more definitive conclusions than those on portfolio capital flows. There is now a substantial body of evidence that openness to foreign direct investment (FDI) is positively associated with growth. FDI is a conduit for the transfer of technological and organizational knowledge, suggesting that countries that welcome inward FDI should have higher levels of total factor productivity and enjoy faster economic growth.[3] In contrast, studies of the effects of financial capital flows are less conclusive. In part this reflects the difficulty of measuring a multidimensional phenomenon like financial openness in an economically meaningful way. In part it reflects the sensitivity of findings to the countries and periods considered (as we document below).

This controversy is summarized by a pair of recent studies by Rodrik (1998) and Edwards (2001). Rodrik finds no correlation between capital account liberalization and growth and comes down against the presumption that opening an economy to financial capital flows has favorable effects. Substituting a more nuanced and presumably informative measure of capital account liberalization, Edwards reports in contrast a strong positive effect of capital account liberalization, one however limited mainly to high-income countries.

---

[3] While this conclusion is not uncontroversial, we think that the bulk of the evidence points in this direction. See in particular Borensztein, De Gregorio and Lee (1995), Aitken and Harrison (1999), and Bradstetter (2000).

In this paper we seek to push this literature forward another step, by scrutinizing the robustness of these results and addressing their implicit interpretation. We focus on the following questions: Is there really a positive association of capital account liberalization with growth when the former is measured in an economically meaningful way? Is it robust? Is it evident only in certain times and places? If it is limited to high-income economies, does this reflect their more advanced stage of financial and institutional development, which mitigates the domestic distortions that cause capital account liberalization to have weak or even perverse effects in the developing world? Or do the effects of capital account liberalization hinge to a greater extent on the way it is sequenced with other policy reforms?

To anticipate our conclusions, while we find some evidence of a positive association between capital account liberalization and growth, that evidence is decidedly fragile. The effects vary with time, with how capital account liberalization is measured, and with how the relationship is estimated. In our view, the evidence is insufficiently robust to support unconditional policy recommendations.

The evidence that the effects of capital account liberalization are stronger in high-income countries is similarly fragile. There is some evidence that the positive growth effects of liberalization are stronger in countries with strong institutions, as measured by standard indicators of the rule of law, but only weak evidence that the benefits grow with a country's financial depth and development.

More important than a country's stage of financial development, we find, is the sequencing of reforms. Capital account liberalization appears to have positive effects on growth only in countries that have already opened more generally. But there are significant prerequisites for opening, most obviously a consensus in favor of reducing tariff and nontariff barriers and an ability to eliminate macroeconomic imbalances in whose presence freeing up current account transactions is not possible. Which of these prerequisites turns out to matter may come as a surprise.

2. Previous Literature

The most widely-cited study of the correlation of capital account liberalization with growth is Rodrik (1998).[4] For a sample of roughly 100

---

[4] This section draws on Eichengreen (2000).

industrial and developing countries, using data for the period 1975–89, Rodrik regresses the growth of GDP per capita on the share of years when the capital account was free of restriction (as measured by the binary indicator constructed by the IMF), controlling for determinants suggested by the empirical growth literature (initial income per capita, secondary school enrolment, quality of government, and regional dummies for East Asia, Latin America, and sub-Saharan Africa).[5] He finds no association between capital account liberalization and growth and questions whether capital flows enhance economic efficiency.[6]

Given the currency of this article among economists, it is striking that the leading study of the question in political science reaches the opposite conclusion. For 66 countries, using data for the period 1960–89, Quinn (1997) reports a positive correlation between capital account liberalization (the change in capital account openness) and economic growth.[7] That correlation is statistically significant at standard confidence levels.

What accounts for the contrast is not clear. Quinn's study starts earlier (it may matter that growth in his sample period is not dominated to the same extent by the "lost decade" of the 1980s), his list of control variables is longer, and he looks at the change in capital account openness rather than the level. Edwards (2001) has emphasized that Quinn uses a more nuanced and therefore more informative measure of capital account liberalization. For 58 countries over the period 1950 to 1994 and an additional 8 countries starting in 1954, Quinn distinguishes seven categories of statutory measures. Four are current account restrictions, two are capital account restrictions, and one measures international agreements such as OECD membership constraining the ability of a country to limit exchange and capital flows. For each of these categories, Quinn codes the intensity of controls on a two-point scale (in half-point increments from 0 to 0.5, 1, 1.5, 2, with 0 denoting most intense and 2 denoting

---

[5] The capital account openness variable is taken from line E2 (restrictions on payments for capital transactions) of the table on exchange and capital controls in the IMF's *Exchange Arrangements and Exchange Restrictions* annual.

[6] The results are depicted visually, using scatter plots of the partial correlation between growth and the share of years when the capital account was liberalized over the period; the author does not report the *t*-statistic on the capital account liberalization variable. In fact precisely the same result, using the same data, was published some three years earlier by Grilli and Milesi-Ferretti (1995), who report standard errors along with their point estimates.

[7] Quinn includes a long list of ancillary variables that have been shown to explain some of the cross-country variation in growth rates, drawing on Levine and Renelt (1992).

no restriction), producing an overall index of current and capital account restrictions that ranges from 0 to 14 and a capital account restrictions measure that ranges from 0 to 4.

It also may be important that Quinn's country sample is different; in particular, he considers fewer low-income developing countries. The recent literature gives reason to think that the effects of capital account liberalization vary with financial and institutional development. Removing capital controls may be welfare and efficiency enhancing only when major imperfections in the information and contracting environment are absent; this is an implication of the theory of the second best. Portfolio capital inflows stimulate growth, the argument goes, only when markets have developed to the point where they can allocate finance efficiently and when the contracting environment is such that agents must live with the consequences of their investment decisions. The Asian crisis encouraged the belief that countries benefit from removing controls only when they first strengthen domestic markets and institutions generally; thus, we should expect a positive association with growth only when prudential supervision is first upgraded, the moral hazard created by an excessively generous implicit and explicit financial safety net is limited, corporate governance and creditor rights are strengthened, and transparent auditing and accounting standards and efficient bankruptcy and insolvency procedures are adopted. While these institutional prerequisites are difficult to measure, there is a presumption that they are most advanced in high-income countries. This is one way of understanding how Alesina, Grilli, and Milesi-Ferretti (1994) find evidence of a positive association between capital account liberalization and growth – their sample is limited to 20 high-income countries – when Grilli and Milesi-Ferretti (1995) find a negative association in a sample dominated by developing countries.[8]

Edwards (2001) addresses the hypothesis that capital account liberalization has different effects in high- and low-income countries. Using Rodrik's controls but Quinn's measure of the intensity of capital account

---

[8] The evidence is not overwhelming: Alesina, Grilli, and Milesi-Ferretti report a positive coefficient that differs significantly from zero at standard confidence levels in one of four regressions. Moreover, the specification in question does not control for initial per capita income; once it is added, the correlation in question dissolves. Bordo and Eichengreen (1998) explicitly compare industrial and developing countries, and report weak evidence that controls have a positive impact on growth in the industrial countries, and a negative impact on growth in developing countries, although the operative word is "weak."

restrictions in 1973 and 1988, he finds that liberalization boosts growth in the 1980s in high-income countries but slows it in low-income countries. (The dummy variable for capital-account openness enters negatively, in other words, while the interaction between capital account openness and per capita income enters positively.) Edwards shows further that the significance of capital controls evaporates when the IMF index used by Rodrik is substituted for Quinn's more differentiated measure. Thus, it is tempting to think that the absence of an effect in previous studies is a statistical artifact. And there is some suggestion that capital account liberalization is more beneficial in more financial and institutionally developed economies.[9]

But do these differences really reflect the level of financial and institutional development? Kraay (1998) makes the one direct attempt to test the hypothesis that the effects of capital account liberalization depend on the strength of the financial system, the effectiveness of prudential supervision and regulation, and the quality of other policies and institutions, rather than seeking to infer this from differences between industrial and developing economies.[10] The results are not encouraging: The interaction of the quality of policy and institutions with financial openness is almost never positive and significant, and it is sometimes significantly negative. But while these findings are intriguing, their generality is an open question; the other work reviewed in this section raises questions about whether they are sensitive to country sample, specification, and in particular how financial openness is measured. To the extent that capital account liberalization has different effects on growth in high- and low-income countries, the reasons for the contrast remain unclear.

---

[9] Quinn (2000) uses a very different methodology to address this question but reaches a similar conclusion. He estimates bivariate VARs using growth rates and his measures of capital account liberalization individually for a large number of middle- and low-income countries. He finds scant evidence that capital account liberalization has had a positive impact on growth in the poorest countries, but some positive evidence for middle-income countries, especially those that have other characteristics likely to render them attractive to foreign investors.

[10] Kraay uses the ratio of M2 to GDP and the ratio of domestic credit to the private sector relative to GDP as ex ante proxies for the level of financial development, and one minus the average number of banking crises per year as an ex post indicator of financial strength. As an indicator of the strength of bank regulation, he uses authorization for banks to engage in nontraditional banking activities such as securities dealing and insurance. And to capture the broader policy and institutional environment, he uses a weighted average of fiscal deficits and inflation, the black market premium, and indices of corruption and the quality of bureaucracy.

3. Basic Results

In this section we scrutinize the claim that the effects of capital account liberalization differ between high- and low-income economies – and, specifically, that they are positive in the former but not the latter.

Our point of departure is Edwards' model. Edwards regresses economic growth in the 1980s (approximately the same period considered by Rodrik) on the decennial average investment rate, years of schooling completed by 1965 (as a measure of human capital), the log of real GDP per capita in 1965 (as a measure of the scope for catch-up), and Quinn's index of capital account openness. He reports that this measure of capital account openness has a positive and generally significant effect on growth. Moreover, when capital account openness is entered both on its own and interacted with per capita incomes, the first coefficient is negative and the second positive.[11] The inflection point where the effect of capital account openness becomes positive coincides with the per capita incomes achieved by the 1980s by such relatively advanced emerging markets as Hong Kong, Israel, Mexico, Singapore, and Venezuela.

Four aspects of Edwards' data and specification are worthy of comment. First, while he uses annual data spanning the 1980s for his other variables, Edwards has Quinn's measure of capital account openness for only 1973 and 1988.[12] The 1973 value is arguably too early to have a first-order effect on growth in the 1980s, while the 1988 value is arguably too late.[13] Similarly, the difference in the level of openness in 1973 and 1988 may tell us how policies toward the capital account changed in the 1970s and 1980s, but these two snapshots are equally compatible with the possibility that the change took place before the beginning of the sample period or at its end, two scenarios that presumably imply very different effects.[14]

Second, Edwards weights his observations by GDP per capita in 1985. We worry that placing an especially heavy weight on rich countries with well-developed institutions biases the case in favor of finding a link

---

[11] In contrast, the IMF measure of capital account openness bears no association to growth, as mentioned above.

[12] Quinn has also made available his 1958 estimates to other investigators, but these are irrelevant to the current exercise.

[13] Including only the 1988 value but instrumenting it using the 1973 index, as Edwards does in some of his analysis, does not obviously solve this problem.

[14] Edwards' two sets of estimates use, alternatively, the Quinn index for 1988 and the difference between Quinn's 1973 and 1988 values.

between capital account liberalization and growth, since these are the countries in which such an effect is most plausibly present.[15]

Third, Edwards instruments his measure of capital account liberalization with a vector of concurrent and lagged economic, financial, and geographical variables. While we are sympathetic to the idea that policies toward the capital account may be affected by as well as affect growth, useful instruments – variables that are exogenous but also correlated with capital account liberalization – are hard to come by. In particular, we are skeptical that geographic variables are usefully correlated with capital account liberalization (although previous work has shown that they importantly influence the level of income and/or the rate of growth), and we would question whether the economic and financial variables invoked in this context are properly regarded as exogenous with respect to the policy.[16]

Fourth, neither Edwards nor other contributors to this literature include competing measures of economic openness and the macroeconomic policy regime. Typically, countries that open the capital account also open their economies to other transactions (for example, they will have reduced tariff and nontariff barriers to trade). In the absence of measures of these other policies, it is not obvious that the index of capital account openness is picking up the effects of financial openness as opposed to the openness of, say, the trade account. Similarly, governments may wait to open the capital account until they have first succeeded in eliminating macroeconomic imbalances that would precipitate capital flight through newly opened channels; a positive effect of capital account liberalization on growth may reflect the growth-friendly effects of macroeconomic stabilization, in other words, rather than international financial policies per se.

We show some "Edwards regressions" in Table 7.1 (single equation estimates for the 1980s, with and without weights, using the 1988 level of

---

[15] In addition, heavy weights on high-income countries, which were also the relatively fast growing countries in some of the subperiods we consider (see below), increases the danger of finding a correlation between capital account liberalization and growth because of reverse causality (insofar as the high-income countries were the ones most likely to open the capital account).

[16] In addition, Edwards derives his results from estimates of a two-equation system, where the dependent variables are GDP growth and TFP growth and the list of independent variables is the same across equations. Since the second dependent variable is derived (in part) from the first, errors in GDP growth are likely to produce (positively correlated) errors in TFP growth. When the correlation between the error terms in the two equations is taken into account via system estimation, the econometrician may therefore obtain a spuriously strong correlation with the independent variables.

Table 7.1. *Basic Regressions (Dependent Variable: Average Growth Rate of GDP Per Capita, 1980–89)*

	1	2	3	4	5	6	7	8
Investment Ratio, 1980–89 average	0.192***	0.183***	0.176***	0.182***	0.160***	0.171***	0.155***	0.167***
	(4.44)	(5.03)	(4.44)	(4.96)	(4.46)	(5.47)	(4.44)	(5.01)
Human Capital, 1965	0.720**	0.735**	0.587**	0.776**	0.500**	0.579**	0.481**	0.621**
	(2.54)	(2.15)	(2.03)	(2.26)	(2.52)	(2.24)	(2.34)	(2.35)
Log GDP per capita, 1965	−2.911***	−2.665***	−3.719***	−2.588***	−2.487***	−2.015***	−2.784***	1.888***
	(−3.41)	(3.30)	(−4.25)	(−3.14)	(−3.29)	(−3.06)	(−3.55)	(−2.88)
Level Quinn's Index, 1988	0.599	—	−0.081	—	1.005**	—	0.742	—
	(1.48)		(−0.17)		(2.35)		(1.28)	
Interaction Level Quinn 1988 * 1980 GDP per capita	—	—	0.001***	—	—	—	0.001	—
			(2.98)				(0.84)	
Difference Quinn's Index, 1973–88	—	0.600**	—	1.034**	—	0.280	—	1.204**
		(2.28)		(2.60)		(0.91)		(2.26)
Interaction Diff. Quinn 1973–88 * 1980 GDP per capita	—	—	—	−0.001	—	—	—	−0.001*
				(−1.24)				(−1.81)
Constant	15.587***	15.027***	22.790***	14.389**	13.009***	11.109***	15.723***	10.073**
	(2.87)	(2.84)	(4.01)	(2.66)	(2.77)	(2.59)	(3.03)	(2.40)
Observations	61	61	61	61	61	61	61	61
R^2	0.52	0.52	0.57	0.52	0.53	0.44	0.53	0.46

OLS regressions. *t*-statistics derived using robust standard errors in parentheses.
Columns 1–4 are unweighted. Columns 5–8 are weighted by GDP per capita in 1985.
Significance at 10, 5, and 1% denoted by * , ** , and *** respectively.

the Quinn index and, also following Edwards, the change in Quinn's index between 1973 and 1988).[17] The controls – the investment ratio, human capital, 1965 per capita GDP – are consistently significant and have their anticipated signs. In the unweighted least squares regressions, both the level of capital account openness in 1988 and its change between 1973 and 1988 enter with positive coefficients, but only the latter differs from zero at the 95% level.[18] In the weighted least squares regressions, the converse is true: the level of capital account openness differs from zero at the 95% confidence level, but the change does not. There is some evidence, then, of a positive association between capital account liberalization and growth, although it is decidedly fragile.

Following Edwards, we reestimated these equations substituting the binary measure of capital account restrictions based on information in the IMF's *Exchange Arrangements and Exchange Restrictions* annual, constructing this variable as the share of years in the sample period when the capital account was open. As in his analysis, none of the coefficients on this variable approached significance at conventional confidence levels.[19] This is support for Edwards' first point, that the growth effects of capital account liberalization are more evident when the latter is proxied by the (presumably more informative) Quinn measure.

When we interact the Quinn measure with per capita GDP in 1980 (that being the start of Edwards' sample period), we find little support for the notion that capital account liberalization has different effects in high- and low-income countries. In the unweighted least squares regressions (columns 1–4 of Table 7.1), the coefficient on the interaction of the Quinn index and 1980 per capita GDP is positive and significantly different from zero at the 95 per cent confidence level, as if the effects of liberalization are larger in high-income countries.[20] But we find no such effect in the weighted least squares regressions or when we measure capital

---

[17] Details on the data underlying this and subsequent tables can be found in the data appendix.

[18] We also augmented the list of controls to include distance from the equator, since this variable is included among the instrumental variables we experiment with below, and others (e.g., Rodrik, 2001) have argued that it has an independent impact on economic growth. While this variable often enters with a significant coefficient, adding it only reinforces our results (as we explain below).

[19] These regressions are not reported but are available from the authors on request.

[20] The coefficient on the level of the Quinn index by itself (column 3) is negative but insignificantly different from zero, lending no support to the hypothesis that liberalization damages growth in low-income countries. It is however the case that we can reject the null that both coefficients (that on the level of the Quinn index and the interaction term) are zero at the 95% confidence level.

account liberalization as the change in the Quinn index between 1973 and 1988. When we adopt this last specification, the pattern of coefficients instead suggests *smaller* growth effects of liberalization in high income countries.[21] A joint test of the significance of capital account openness measured in changes and the corresponding interaction term (not reported) allows us to reject the null that both coefficients are zero in both column 8 (the weighted least squares estimates) and in column 4 (the OLS estimates). But, to repeat, the pattern of signs is inconsistent with the notion that liberalization has negative effects in low-income countries and positive effects in high-income ones.[22]

Edwards obtains more precise coefficients on the relationship between capital account liberalization and growth, both entered linearly and interacted with per capita GDP, when using instrumental variables. Though his estimates of the nonlinear effect differ from ours not only by the use of instruments but also by being estimated as a system of two equations (where capital account liberalization affects both aggregate and TFP growth), we were led to wonder whether differences between our results and his are driven by the use of instrumental variables. We therefore reestimated the equations in Table 7.1 using two alternative sets of instruments. We first used the Hall–Jones (1999) instrument set (distance from the equator, a dummy variable for whether the country is landlocked, a dummy variable for whether it was an island, the share of the population speaking English, and the share of the population speaking a major European language). None of the measures of capital account liberalization – its level or change, entered by itself or interacted with per capital GDP – entered with a coefficient that approached significance at standard confidence levels.[23] While these instruments are plausibly exogenous, either they are not usefully correlated with capital account liberalization or the latter in fact has no independent impact on growth.

---

[21] The results are essentially the same, although a little weaker, when we use membership in the OECD in place of per capital GDP when constructing the interaction term. In the weighted least squares regressions, all interaction terms are insignificantly different from zero at conventional confidence levels.

[22] Edwards' key results – those obtaining nonlinear effects for capital account liberalization (negative at low levels of per capital income, positive at high levels) – are derived using three-stage least squares.

[23] This was true both of the individual coefficients and, when Quinn openness was entered in levels and interacted with per capital GDP, of the pair. That is, the relevant F-statistic did not lead us to reject the null that the two coefficients were effectively zero. Note that this is where the decision of whether or not to include distance from the equator as an explanatory variable for growth could matter. It is reassuring, therefore, that adding it to the list of independent variables altered none of the results reported here.

The second set of instruments is our attempt to replicate those used by Edwards: whether the capital account was open or closed in 1973, the ratio of liquid liabilities to GDP in 1970 and 1975, distance to the equator, and a dummy variable for OECD countries.[24] The results, in Table 7.2, differ sharply from before. The coefficient on the Quinn index in 1988 is still positive when entered on its own, albeit somewhat less well defined than in Table 7.1. However, when the interaction of capital account openness and per capita GDP is added, the coefficient on the level of the Quinn index turns negative (though insignificant), while the interaction term is positive and significantly different from zero at the 95% confidence level. This is very close to Edwards' result. However, this pattern obtains only when we enter capital account openness in levels (rather than changes between 1973 and 1988) and only when we estimate by unweighted least squares (as opposed to applying per capita GDP weights). And it is sensitive to the choice of instrumental variables. For example, the one coefficient on the interaction term that was previously significantly positive goes to zero when either financial depth or lagged openness (or, for that matter, both) is dropped from the instrument list but the other instrumental variables are retained.[25]

Thus, we confirm that an analysis of developing- and industrial-country experience in the 1980s yields somewhat more favorable results for the association of capital account openness and growth when capital account policies are measured using Quinn's index rather than the IMF measure. The evidence that this effect is stronger in high-income countries turns out to be extremely sensitive to specification and estimation.

4. Sensitivity Analysis

In this section we subject these results to two forms of sensitivity analysis. First, we adjust the timing of the dependent and independent variables in order to better identify the effects of capital account policies. Second, we compare the effects of capital account liberalization in different periods.

Recall that Edwards uses Quinn's measure of capital account openness in 1973 and 1988. If capital account liberalization has a significant impact

---

[24] This is our reading of the abbreviations in the instrument list at the bottom of his Table 10.

[25] In addition, we worry about the validity of the instruments, specifically whether lagged liberalization and financial depth, which move slowly and are correlated with current liberalization and financial depth, are in fact capturing the exogenous component of these international financial policies. See the discussion above.

Table 7.2. *Two-Stage Least Squares Regressions (Dependent Variable: Average Growth Rate of GDP Per Capita, 1980–89)*

	1	2	3	4	5	6	7	8
Investment Ratio, 1980–89 average	0.173***	0.179***	0.130**	0.177***	0.159***	0.176***	0.153***	0.174***
	(3.58)	(5.17)	(2.35)	(5.19)	(4.44)	(6.08)	(4.13)	(5.21)
Human Capital, 1965	0.681**	0.710*	0.379	0.674	0.453**	0.520*	0.432**	0.611*
	(2.31)	(1.84)	(1.08)	(1.61)	(2.27)	(1.84)	(2.12)	(1.85)
Log GDP per capita, 1965	−2.897***	−2.712***	−5.326***	−2.716***	−2.265**	−1.752**	−2.781	−1.643**
	(−2.83)	(−2.94)	(−2.89)	(−2.90)	(−2.63)	(−2.59)	(−1.63)	(−2.54)
Level Quinn's Index, 1988	0.802	—	−1.815	—	1.088*	—	0.465	—
	(1.48)		(−1.60)		(1.89)		(0.30)	
Interaction Level Quinn 1988 * 1980 GDP per capita	—	—	0.001**	—	—	—	0.001	—
			(2.06)				(0.41)	
Difference Quinn's Index, 1973–88	—	0.798	—	0.411	—	0.354	—	2.203
		(1.59)		(0.31)		(0.85)		(1.36)
Interaction Diff. Quinn 1973–88 * 1980 GDP per capita	—	—	—	0.001	—	—	—	−0.001
				(0.33)				(−1.14)
Constant	15.447**	15.472**	38.050**	15.605**	11.067**	8.921**	16.087	7.860**
	(2.39)	(2.58)	(2.64)	(2.58)	(2.12)	(2.13)	(1.11)	(2.04)
Observations	52	52	52	52	52	52	52	52
R^2	0.51	0.50	0.32	0.49	0.51	0.47	0.51	0.46

2SLS regressions. *t*-statistics derived using robust standard errors in parentheses.
Instruments are liquid liabilities in 1970 and 1975, distance to the equator, OECD dummy, and Quinn's index in 1973.
Columns 1–4 are unweighted. Columns 5–8 are weighted by GDP per capita in 1985.
Significance at 10, 5, and 1% denoted by *, **, and *** respectively.

on growth, this should be most evident in the immediately succeeding years. Having analyzed growth in the 1980s as a way of rendering our results as directly comparable as possible to those of Edwards and other investigators, we now focus on the effects of capital account liberalization in the years immediately following those for which we have Quinn's capital account restrictions data: 1973 and 1988. The obvious stopping point for the period starting in 1973 is 1981, the eve of the Mexican debt crisis and the "lost decade" of the 1980s, when capital flows were subdued and their growth effects were plausibly different. Our second cross section (starting in 1988) ends in 1992, since that is when our data, drawn from the Penn World Tables Mark 5.6a, end.[26] This leaves a gap in the mid-1980s. Fortunately, we were also able to obtain Quinn's measure of capital account openness for 1982.[27] Thus, we can analyze three cross sections covering the periods 1973–81, 1982–87, and 1988–92. We also pool the three cross sections. The pooled results will reassure readers worried that conditions during one or more of our periods were special ("1982–87 is unrepresentative because it is dominated by the debt crisis," for example). Aggregating across periods limits the danger that our results are being driven by period-specific effects.

The results are in the Table 7.3. In the first four columns we enter capital account openness in levels; in the second four we also interact it with per capita GDP.[28] Given the questions about instrumentation raised in the last section, we estimate the equations by ordinary least squares.

The results remain generally plausible.[29] When entered exclusively in levels, the Quinn measure of financial openness is positively associated with growth in all three periods, but only in the third of these, 1988–92,

---

[26] In principle, it would be possible to extend this sample beyond 1992 using data from other sources. But given the far-reaching changes in capital account restrictions that occurred in the 1990s, our measure of the structure of capital controls, circa 1988, would then capture little of the reality of capital account policies in the last subperiod. Since we do not have Quinn-like data on the capital account regime in the 1990s, we concluded that it makes sense to stick with a sample that ends in 1992.

[27] We thank Dennis Quinn for sharing these data with us.

[28] We report results using only the Quinn measure of openness, since when we substitute the IMF measure we obtain uniformly insignificant effects. We concentrate on unweighted regressions throughout. The use of weights and instrumental variables alters our results only slightly: The coefficients tend to be slightly less well determined, although the pattern of signs remains the same.

[29] Investment retains its consistently positive effect on growth, although the effects of human capital are somewhat weaker than before. The catch-up effect is weak in both the second and third periods, reflecting the heavy impact of the debt crisis of low- and middle-income developing countries starting in 1982 and their delayed post-1987 recovery.

Table 7.3. Growth Regressions for Alternative Periods (Dependent Variable: Average Growth Rate of GDP Per Capita during Relevant Period)

	1	2	3	4	5	6	7	8
	1973–81	1982–87	1988–92	Pooled	1973–81	1982–87	1988–92	Pooled
Investment Ratio, period average	0.207***	0.179***	0.278***	0.223***	0.209***	0.189***	0.276***	0.226***
	(4.81)	(3.27)	(4.14)	(6.46)	(4.47)	(3.44)	(4.15)	(6.40)
Human Capital, beginning of period	0.209	0.349	−0.478*	0.087	0.203	0.233	−0.420	0.059
	(1.06)	(1.60)	(−1.73)	(0.63)	(1.03)	(0.99)	(−1.50)	(0.42)
Log GDP per capita, beginning of period	−2.329***	−0.986	−1.113	−1.546***	−2.363***	−1.646*	−0.845	−1.718***
	(−3.41)	(−1.20)	(−1.09)	(−3.12)	(−3.11)	(−2.00)	(−0.63)	(−3.11)
Quinn's Index, beginning of period	0.264	0.095	1.131*	0.487**	0.246	−0.444	1.380**	0.365
	(0.94)	(0.29)	(1.98)	(2.17)	(0.66)	(−1.23)	(2.15)	(1.40)
Interaction Quinn * GDP per capita, beginning of period	—	—	—	—	0.001	0.001*	−0.001	0.001
					(0.13)	(1.99)	(−0.55)	(0.79)
Dummy for 1973–81	—	—	—	0.436	—	—	—	0.468
				(0.87)				(0.92)
Dummy for 1982–87	—	—	—	−0.739	—	—	—	−0.704
				(−1.43)				(−1.34)
Constant	15.663***	3.311	5.873	8.608***	15.932***	9.150*	3.303	10.071***
	(3.82)	(0.63)	(0.91)	(2.75)	(3.31)	(1.70)	(0.34)	(2.75)
Observations	62	62	60	184	62	62	60	184
R^2	0.34	0.29	0.27	0.26	0.34	0.33	0.27	0.27

OLS regressions. t-statistics derived using robust standard errors in parentheses.
Significance at 10, 5, and 1% denoted by *, **, and *** respectively.

is the effect significant at anything approaching conventional confidence levels. The coefficient is smallest in the period starting in 1982, when capital flows were depressed by the debt crisis, and largest in the post-1987 period, the year of the Brady Plan after which large scale portfolio capital flows resumed. But when we pool the three cross sections (adding fixed effects to differentiate the subperiods), the coefficient on capital account liberalization differs from zero at the 95% confidence level. This is the strongest evidence so far of a positive association of capital account liberalization and growth, although it is clear that this result is heavily driven by one of our cross sections.

But there is still scant evidence of a stronger growth effect in high-income countries. We obtain a significant positive coefficient on the interaction term only for the post-1982 years. Perhaps capital account liberalization worked its magic more powerfully on high-income countries in these years. Alternatively, it may simply be that high-income (OECD) countries with open capital accounts were less affected by the debt crisis of the 1980s than developing countries with open capital accounts that had grown heavily dependent on foreign borrowing. Whether this in fact tells us anything about the differential effects of capital account liberalization in different developing countries is unclear.

In the pooled sample, the coefficient on the interaction term is indistinguishable from zero. However, the coefficient on capital account liberalization in levels continues to enter positively and differs from zero at the 90% confidence level. Again, however, this result appears to be driven by the strong positive association in the post-1987 period.

Thus, more data and appropriate timing of the variables continue to provide indications a positive association of capital account liberalization with growth. However, that effect is robust only for the most recent period, that is to say, for the post–Brady Plan years. There is less evidence to this effect for earlier periods, whether these are the years of syndicated bank lending to developing countries or of the developing country debt crisis. Moreover, we find little support for the view that capital account liberalization has more favorable effects in high- and middle-income emerging markets than in poorer developing countries.

5. Do These Patterns Reflect Stages of Financial and Institutional Development?

We now ask whether the different effects of capital account liberalization in high- and low-income countries in fact reflect their different stages of financial and institutional development. To this end, we interact Quinn's index not with per capita GDP but with financial depth (proxied by the ratio of liquid liabilities to GDP) and institutional strength (the *International Country Risk Guide's* index of law and order).[30]

The results are in Table 7.4, the first four columns for financial depth (post 1973, post 1982, post 1988, and pooled, reading left to right), the last four for law and order. Those for financial depth are unpromising: none of the coefficients in question is significant individually or as a pair.[31] The results for the interaction between capital account openness and rule of law are more promising. In the first subperiod (1973–81) we obtain a negative coefficient on capital account openness in levels and a positive coefficient on the interaction term; the latter differs from zero at the 95% confidence level. The interpretation is that capital account liberalization has no effect in countries with weak contract and law enforcement but a positive effect in those with stronger ones. The results for the second subperiod (1982–87) are more striking still: both terms again enter with the expected signs, and both now differ from zero at conventional confidence levels.[32] According to this column at least, capital account liberalization hinders growth when a country rates low on the law-and-order index but helps when it rates high.[33] In comparison, the results for the most recent subperiod (1988–92) are disappointing: neither coefficient enters with its expected sign, and neither differs significantly from zero at standard confidence levels.[34]

The results for the pooled sample reflect these contrasting subsample results. The coefficient on the level of Quinn openness is zero, but the coefficient on the interaction term is positive and significant at the 90 (but not the 95%) confidence level.

Thus, we find scant support for the hypothesis that the effects of capital account liberalization reflect a country's stage of financial development. There is more support for the idea that the effects vary with the effectiveness of law and order, but the evidence is not overwhelming.

---

[30] Again, for details on this and the other variables used in the analysis, see the data appendix.

[31] Again, estimating these equations by instrumental variables changed nothing.

[32] At the 90 and 95% levels, respectively.

[33] One of the coauthors is reminded of all the money deposited in Swiss banks by depositors from countries that rate low according to the law-and-order index and with porous capital accounts.

[34] We also fail to reject the null that the two coefficients are jointly zero at conventional confidence levels.

Table 7.4. Role of Financial and Institutional Development (Dependent Variable: Average Growth Rate of GDP Per Capita during Relevant Period)

	1	2	3	4	5	6	7	8
	1973–81	1982–87	1988–92	Pooled	1973–81	1982–1987	1988–92	Pooled
Investment Ratio, period average	0.189***	0.185***	0.304***	0.225***	0.199***	0.162**	0.279***	0.214***
	(4.55)	(3.01)	(3.92)	(6.06)	(5.16)	(2.66)	(4.04)	(5.92)
Human Capital, beginning of period	0.209	0.264	−0.508*	0.049	0.112	0.250	−0.471	0.024
	(0.98)	(1.49)	(−1.69)	(0.36)	(0.62)	(1.15)	(−1.55)	(0.17)
Log GDP per capita, beginning of period	−2.488***	−0.784	−1.123	−1.594***	−2.692***	−1.569*	−1.070	−1.882***
	(−3.22)	(−1.04)	(−1.03)	(−3.19)	(−3.66)	(−1.88)	(−0.95)	(−3.73)
Quinn's Index, beginning of period	0.342	−0.285	1.142*	0.343	−0.273	−0.817**	1.194*	0.005
	(1.15)	(−0.85)	(1.75)	(1.29)	(−0.75)	(−2.04)	(1.70)	(0.02)
Interaction Quinn * Financial Depth, beginning of period	0.003	0.002	−0.002	0.002	—	—	—	—
	(0.57)	(0.56)	(−0.36)	(0.60)				
Interaction Quinn * Law and Order, beginning of period	—	—	—	—	0.171**	0.250**	−0.016	0.137**
					(2.12)	(2.44)	(−0.11)	(2.18)
Dummy for 1973–81	—	—	—	0.421	—	—	—	0.369
				(0.82)				(0.74)
Dummy for 1982–87	—	—	—	−0.690	—	—	—	−0.769
				(−1.33)				(−1.48)
Constant	16.881***	2.508	5.859	9.212***	19.053***	8.896	5.450	11.833***
	(3.49)	(0.51)	(0.83)	(2.86)	(3.94)	(1.62)	(0.68)	(3.51)
Observations	55	58	58	171	62	62	60	184
R²	0.43	0.35	0.28	0.29	0.39	0.35	0.27	0.28

OLS regressions. t-statistics derived using robust standard errors in parentheses.
Significance at 10, 5, and 1% denoted by *, **, and *** respectively.

6. Sequencing

It could be that we are not capturing the full impact of capital account liberalization on growth because we are not controlling for efforts to coordinate external financial opening with other liberalization measures. There is a large literature on sequencing that suggests that capital account liberalization initiated before the current account is opened can have strongly distortionary effects (see McKinnon 1991). If trade barriers continue to protect an uneconomical import-competing sector, foreign capital will flow there, attracted by rents and artificially inflated profits. Since the country has no comparative advantage in those activities, actually devoting more resources to import-competing production can be growth and welfare reducing. In particular, the cost of the resources that the country utilizes to service the foreign finance may exceed the cost of capital, reducing domestic incomes as well as starving other sectors of inputs to growth (Brecher and Diaz-Alejandro 1977). Similarly, the literature on the sequencing of financial liberalization measures cautions that it can be counterproductive to open the international accounts before domestic macroeconomic imbalances have been eliminated; the main effect will then be to provide avenues for capital flight.[35] If domestic financial markets are repressed, capital account liberalization allows savers to flee the local low-interest rate environment in favor of higher returns abroad. For all these reasons, capital account liberalization when macroeconomic policy is seriously out of balance is a recipe for disaster.

To capture these qualifications, we added the interaction between capital account openness, as measured by Quinn, and nonfinancial openness, as measured by Sachs and Warner (1995).[36] This is analogous to our earlier tests of the idea that the effects of capital account openness are contingent on financial depth and institutional development, but now the hypothesis is that they are contingent on the absence of trade and macroeconomic distortions. The Sachs–Warner index classifies a country as open if none of the five following criteria holds: the country had average tariff rates higher than 40%, its nontariff barriers covered on average more than 40% of imports, it had a socialist economic system, the state had a monopoly of major exports, and its black market premium exceeded 20%. The first four criteria should allow us to test the notion that capital mobility is counterproductive for an economy whose trade is

---

[35] See for example Edwards (1994) and Johnston (1998).
[36] We thank Andrew Warner for providing these data.

highly restricted and distorted.[37] The fifth is an indicative of macroeconomic policies and conditions inconsistent with a country's administered exchange rate; it should allow us to test the hypothesis that capital account liberalization is counterproductive if implemented before a country has eliminated macroeconomic imbalances.

The results are in Table 7.5, columns 1–4. The specification is analogous to that of Table 7.3 but for the addition of the interaction of the Sachs–Warner dummy with Quinn openness. We find a strong positive effect of this interaction term, almost irrespective of period.[38] In the pooled sample, it differs from zero at the 99% confidence level. This suggests that capital account openness stimulates growth when a country has eliminated major trade distortions and macroeconomic imbalances, but not otherwise.

We undertook some sensitivity analyses of this finding. We estimated the equations by weighted as well as unweighted least squares. We used Edwards' instrumental variables. We searched for and dropped outliers. We added the interaction between financial depth and financial openness and the interaction between law and order and financial openness as in Table 7.4 above. None of these changes weakened the result.

The one change that made a difference was adding Sachs–Warner openness in levels. We show the result of doing so in columns 5–8 of Table 7.5. The three openness measures (Sachs–Warner openness, Quinn capital account openness, and their interaction) are highly correlated, creating problems of multicolinearity. Only in the pooled sample is there much hope of distinguishing their effects. There, Sachs–Warner openness and Quinn openness both have (positive) coefficients that differ from zero at the 90% confidence level, while their interaction is insignificant. This points less to the importance of sequencing than to separate, noninterdependent effects on growth of both Sachs–Warner and capital account openness. But multicolinearity makes it difficult to know which interpretation is appropriate. While the relevant *F*-test allows us to reject the null that the levels of both Sachs–Warner openness and Quinn openness

---

[37] Rodriguez and Rodrik (1999) note that the state monopoly of major exports variable is derived from a World Bank index of the degree of distortions caused by export marketing boards and is positive only for sub-Saharan African countries, whose growth performance was particularly disappointing in the sample period. Since there are only two sub-Saharan African countries in our (much smaller) sample, it is not plausible in our case that this is the proper interpretation of the results we obtain when we use the Sachs–Warner openness measure.

[38] Only in the first subperiod, for 1973–81, is its coefficient not significantly greater than zero at the 95% confidence level.

Table 7.5. Role of Sequencing (Dependent Variable: Average Growth Rate of GDP Per Capita during Relevant Period)

	1	2	3	4	5	6	7	8
	1973–81	1982–87	1988–92	Pooled	1973–81	1982–87	1988–92	Pooled
Investment Ratio, period average	0.176***	0.103*	0.232***	0.173***	0.146***	0.094	0.218***	0.154***
	(4.15)	(1.68)	(3.11)	(4.53)	(3.00)	(1.49)	(2.81)	(3.74)
Human Capital, beginning of period	0.113	0.272	-0.556*	-0.002	0.123	0.260	-0.529*	-0.001
	(0.58)	(1.33)	(-1.93)	(-0.01)	(0.63)	(1.34)	(-1.97)	(-0.01)
Log GDP per capita, beginning of period	-2.382***	-1.149	-1.339	-1.759***	-2.325***	-1.156	-1.284	-1.719***
	(-3.39)	(-1.38)	(-1.34)	(-3.56)	(-3.40)	(-1.40)	(-1.24)	(-3.53)
Quinn's Index, beginning of period	0.194	-0.361	0.455	0.224	0.366	-0.128	1.049	0.509*
	(0.55)	(-1.17)	(0.61)	(0.85)	(0.93)	(-0.36)	(1.38)	(1.82)
Interaction Quinn * SW Open Index	0.458	0.919***	0.917*	0.720***	-0.134	0.469	-0.386	-0.001
	(1.67)	(3.54)	(1.81)	(3.45)	(-0.22)	(0.90)	(-0.37)	(-0.01)
SW Open Index, beginning of period	—	—	—	—	1.754	1.197	3.441	2.020*
					(1.37)	(0.78)	(1.20)	(1.83)
Dummy for 1973	—	—	—	0.690	—	—	—	0.677
				(1.40)				(1.39)
Dummy for 1982	—	—	—	-0.533	—	—	—	-0.542
				(-1.04)				(-1.07)
Constant	16.872***	6.305	9.186	11.310***	16.487***	6.115	7.614	10.679***
	(3.95)	(1.17)	(1.47)	(3.69)	(4.00)	(1.16)	(1.11)	(3.54)
Observations	60	60	59	179	60	60	59	179
R²	0.41	0.36	0.31	0.32	0.43	0.37	0.33	0.33

OLS regressions. t-statistics derived using robust standard errors in parentheses.
Significance at 10, 5, and 1% denoted by *, **, and *** respectively.

are zero, consistent with the separate, noninterdependent-effects interpretation, it also allows us to reject the null that Quinn openness and
the interaction of Sachs–Warner openness with Quinn openness are both
zero, consistent with the sequencing interpretation.

It turns out that we can get a better handle on which interpretation is
more plausible by analyzing whether absence of a favorable impact on
growth in countries that are closed according to the Sachs–Warner measure reflects distortionary trade policies or distortionary macroeconomic
policies. We do so by breaking Sachs–Warner openness up into its two
principal components, one reflecting the prevalence of tariff and nontariff barriers (distortionary trade policies), and the other reflecting the
size of the black market premium (an indicator of macroeconomic imbalances).[39] If it is the interaction term involving the black market premium
that matters, then we can say that it is the elimination of macroeconomic
imbalances that is the essential prerequisite for capital account liberalization to have positive growth effects, à la McKinnon. If, on the other hand,
it is the interaction involving tariff and nontariff barriers that is significant and important, we can say that it is the elimination of trade-related
distortions that is key, à la Brecher and Diaz–Alejandro.[40]

We measured tariff and nontariff barriers using the data of Barro and
Lee (1994), which conveniently are also utilized by Sachs and Warner.[41]
For the black market premium, we constructed three alternative measures. First, we created a dummy variable which equaled unity if the
black market premium was less than 20%.[42] While this follows Sachs and
Warner as closely as possible, it does not use all the available information.
We therefore also defined an alternative measure, 100% minus the black
market premium.[43] While this contains more information, the results obtained when using it are more likely to be dominated by a handful of

---

[39] As noted above, Sachs–Warner openness involves two additional criteria – whether a
country had a socialist economic system and the state had a monopoly of major exports –
which are likely to matter importantly for certain countries. We return to this point
below.

[40] This is similar to the approach taken by Rodriguez and Rodrik (1999), who find in growth
regressions covering a longer period that it is the black market premium in which most
of the explanatory power resides.

[41] Note that the Barro–Lee tariff and nontariff data do not vary with time. The same is true
of the Sachs–Warner index (which makes use of the Barro–Lee measures), aside from a
few selected changes imposed by its architects.

[42] We refer to this in Table 7.6 as "black market premium 1."

[43] This is "black market premium 2." We divide the premium by 100 so that the coefficients
on this variable are scaled the same as for "black market premium 1."

extreme observations. This led us to create a third version of the variable, which truncated 100% minus the black market premium at zero on the downside.[44]

It turns out that it is the interaction term between capital account openness and the black market premium that most consistently matters. Columns 1–3 of Table 7.6 display pooled regressions using the three alternative measures of the premium. The interaction with the black market premium is positive, and its coefficient is significantly greater than zero at the 90% confidence level, regardless of how that premium is defined and measured. The evidence that trade openness is a prerequisite for capital account openness to stimulate growth is less robust; while the coefficient on the interaction with Barro and Lee's trade openness measure is consistently positive, it approaches significance at conventional confidence levels in only one of the three regressions.[45]

Again, we attempted to confirm the robustness of this finding. We added interaction terms involving financial depth and law and order, as in Table 7.4. We ran regressions using weighted as well as unweighted observations. In each instance the results were essentially unchanged. The one sensitivity analysis that mattered was adding Sachs–Warner openness in levels. The results are in the last three columns of Table 7.6. Evidently, the two measures of external policy with the most robust, consistent effects on growth are (i) Sachs–Warner openness and (ii) the interaction of the black market premium with capital account openness. In other words, there is strong evidence, as before, that countries that open externally in the sense of Sachs and Warner grow faster, other things equal. In addition, however, countries that open the capital account also grow faster *but only if they first eliminate any large black market premium.* Capital account openness has favorable effects, it would appear, only when macroeconomic imbalances leading to inconsistencies between the administered exchange rate and other policies have first been eliminated.

Table 7.7 reports a selection of subperiod results.[46] These reveal that the positive effect of capital account openness on growth, *contingent on*

---

[44] Denoted "black market premium 3." Again, we divide this measure by 100 to make it as comparable as possible with "black market premium 1."

[45] We see the same pattern when we consider the individual subperiods, although the coefficients, predictably, are less well defined than when we pool the data. We discuss the subperiod results later in this section.

[46] These are discussed in the next paragraph. To conserve space, we report only the results for "black market premium 1." Those using the other measures of the black market premium are essentially identical.

Table 7.6. *Role of Trade Distortions and the Black Market Premium (Dependent Variable: Average Growth Rate of GDP Per Capita during Relevant Period)*

	1	2	3	4	5	6
	Pooled	Pooled	Pooled	Pooled	Pooled	Pooled
Investment Ratio, period average	0.235***	0.239***	0.226***	0.182***	0.189***	0.181***
	(6.30)	(6.50)	(6.17)	(3.74)	(3.96)	(3.77)
Human Capital, beginning of period	−0.059	−0.059	−0.068	−0.120	−0.119	−0.123
	(−0.35)	(−0.36)	(−0.40)	(−0.73)	(−0.72)	(−0.73)
Log GDP per capita, beginning of period	−1.884***	−1.978***	−1.819***	−1.686***	−1.775***	−1.652***
	(−3.30)	(−3.49)	(−3.12)	(−2.90)	(−3.06)	(−2.79)
Quinn's Index, beginning of period	−0.214	0.138	−0.963	−0.158	0.182	−0.777
	(−0.49)	(0.42)	(−1.40)	(−0.37)	(0.56)	(−1.12)
Interaction Quinn * Barro–Lee Trade Openness	0.324	0.522**	0.288	0.055	0.251	0.068
	(1.14)	(2.01)	(1.10)	(0.19)	(0.94)	(0.26)
Interaction Quinn * Black Market Premium 1	0.546*	—	—	0.520	—	—
	(1.69)			(1.64)		
Interaction Quinn * Black Market Premium 2	—	0.064**	—	—	0.056**	—
		(2.52)			(2.50)	
Interaction Quinn * Black Market Premium 3	—	—	1.257**	—	—	1.091*
			(1.99)			(1.71)
SW Open Index, beginning of period	—	—	—	1.644**	1.597**	1.468**
				(2.22)	(2.14)	(2.02)
Dummy for 1973	0.124	0.259	−0.003	0.268	0.397	0.159
	(0.22)	(0.46)	(−0.01)	(0.48)	(0.72)	(0.29)
Dummy for 1982	−0.773	−0.675	−0.881	−0.728	−0.640	−0.822
	(−1.30)	(−1.11)	(−1.52)	(−1.25)	(−1.08)	(−1.45)
Constant	12.159***	12.562***	12.206***	11.291***	11.637***	11.390***
	(3.41)	(3.53)	(3.37)	(3.20)	(3.28)	(3.17)
Observations	141	141	141	141	141	141
R^2	0.34	0.34	0.36	0.37	0.37	0.38

OLS regressions. *t*-statistics derived using robust standard errors in parentheses.
Significance at 10, 5, and 1% denoted by *, **, and *** respectively.

Table 7.7. *Role of Trade Distortions and the Black Market Premium, Subperiod Estimates (Dependent Variable: Average Growth Rate of GDP Per Capita during Relevant Period)*

	1	2	3	4	5	6
	1973–81	1982–87	1988–92	1973–81	1982–87	1988–92
Investment Ratio, period average	0.241***	0.193***	0.289***	0.201***	0.133*	0.249**
	(5.53)	(3.36)	(3.83)	(3.23)	(1.99)	(2.72)
Human Capital, beginning of period	0.212	0.103	−0.649*	0.161	0.018	−0.649*
	(0.96)	(0.48)	(−1.79)	(0.71)	(0.08)	(−1.86)
Log GDP per capita, beginning of period	−3.116***	−0.834	−1.429	−2.904***	−0.749	−1.255
	(−3.69)	(−1.04)	(−1.21)	(−3.20)	(−0.94)	(−1.05)
Quinn's Index, beginning of period	0.537	−1.867***	0.533	0.556	−1.614**	0.548
	(0.90)	(−3.00)	(0.73)	(0.96)	(−2.47)	(0.73)
Interaction Quinn * Barro–Lee	0.359	0.532	0.243	0.219	0.139	−0.012
	(0.89)	(1.25)	(0.41)	(0.51)	(0.27)	(−0.02)
Interaction Quinn * Black Market Premium 1	−0.284	1.016**	0.610	−0.319	1.136**	0.475
	(−0.54)	(2.46)	(1.05)	(−0.61)	(2.66)	(0.90)
SW Open Index, beginning of period	—	—	—	0.948	1.560	1.736
				(1.04)	(1.69)	(1.10)
Constant	20.889***	4.754	9.085	19.997***	4.766	8.036
	(4.03)	(0.90)	(1.24)	(3.71)	(0.91)	(1.10)
Observations	47	47	47	47	47	47
R^2	0.46	0.46	0.34	0.47	0.49	0.37

OLS regressions. *t*-statistics derived using robust standard errors in parentheses.
Significance at 10, 5, and 1% denoted by *, **, and *** respectively.

the absence of a large black market premium, is driven by the 1982–87 subperiod. In addition, previously (in Tables 7.3–7.5) the coefficient on capital account openness in levels was either positive or zero. There was no evidence, in other words, that capital account openness was *bad* for growth in countries with underdeveloped financial markets, weak institutions, severe macroeconomic imbalances, or closed current accounts. Now the coefficient on the level of Quinn's index is strongly negative in 1982–87, as if countries with significant trade distortions and large black market premia grew more slowly if they ill advisedly opened their capital accounts. That this effect is most evident in the debt-crisis years 1982–87 may be telling us that countries that poorly sequenced capital account liberalization suffered the most devastating effects of the curtailment of capital flows; they suffered a severe debt overhang and an intractable transfer problem when the debt crisis struck. It may be that improper sequencing does not actually damage growth so long as international capital markets are flush with funds, but that it can result in serious damage if lending suddenly dries up.

7. Conclusion

Economic theory creates a strong presumption that capital account liberalization has favorable effects on growth. Yet the accidents and disappointments suffered by countries liberalizing their international financial transactions remind us that reality is more complex than theory. The quest for guidance is not helped by the fact that the data do not speak loudly. Some analysts have rejected the hypothesis that there is a positive association between capital account liberalization and growth, while others have reported evidence of a favorable effect.

The idea that the effects of capital account liberalization are conditioned by a country's stage of financial and institutional development similarly has intuitive appeal. Not only are there good theoretical reasons to think that this might be the case, but it could be the failure of previous investigators to incorporate this idea that accounts for the weak and inconsistent results of their econometric studies. Yet our tests of the hypothesis are only weakly supportive. We find no evidence that the effects of capital account liberalization vary with financial depth, but somewhat more evidence that its effects vary with the rule of law.

In contrast, we find more evidence of a correlation between capital account liberalization and growth when we allow the effect to vary with other dimensions of openness. There are two interpretations of this

finding, one in terms of the sequencing of trade and financial liberalization, the other in terms of the need to eliminate major macroeconomic
imbalances before opening the capital account. By and large, our results
support the second interpretation. While trade openness has a positive
impact on growth, the effect of capital account openness is not contingent
on openness to trade. Rather, it is contingent on the absence of a large
black market premium – that is to say, on the absence of macroeconomic
imbalances. In the presence of such imbalances, capital account liberalization is as likely to hurt as to help.

If we are right, ours is the first systematic, cross-country statistical evidence that the sequencing of reforms shapes the effects of capital account
liberalization. But our analysis also suggests that this result may be period-
specific: The evidence that sequencing matters is more robust in the 1980s
than in the 1970s or 1990s. If this investigation has taught us one thing, it
is not to oversell such results. Considerable additional analysis is required
to establish the generality of such findings.

Data Appendix

Our sample includes the following 61 countries: Argentina, Australia,
Austria, Belgium, Bolivia, Brazil, Canada, Chile, Colombia, Costa Rica,
Denmark, Dominican Republic, Ecuador, Egypt, El Salvador, Finland,
France, Germany, Ghana, Greece, Guatemala, Haiti, Honduras, Hong
Kong, India, Indonesia, Iran, Iraq, Ireland, Israel, Italy, Jordan, Korea,
Liberia, Malaysia, Mexico, Myanmar, Netherlands, New Zealand,
Nicaragua, Norway, Pakistan, Panama, Paraguay, Peru, Philippines,
Portugal, Singapore, South Africa, Spain, Sri Lanka, Sweden, Switzerland,
Syrian Arab Republic, Thailand, Tunisia, Turkey, United Kingdom,
United States, Uruguay, and Venezuela.

Dependent Variable: Rate of growth of real GDP per capita, defined as
the first difference of the log of real GDP per capita in constant dollars
at 1985 international prices. Source: Penn World Tables, Mark 5.6a.

Controls:
- **Real investment share of GDP** (%) at 1985 international prices. The
  variables used in the regressions are averages of this variable over
  particular periods of time, as noted in the text and tables. Source: Penn
  World Tables, Mark 5.6a.
- **Average years of schooling** of the population over 15 years of age. This
  variable is available quinquennially for the years 1960–90. For Tables 7.1

and 7.2, the 1965 value was used. For the other tables, the values for 1970 (for the 1973 cross section), 1980 (for the 1982 cross section), and 1985 (for the 1988 cross section) were used. (Given lack of 1970 data for Egypt, the value for 1975 was used in the 1973 cross section for this country.). Source: Barro–Lee data set (see Barro and Lee 1996).

- **Log of GDP per capita** in constant dollars (chain index) at 1985 international prices. The value for 1965 is used in Tables 7.1 and 7.2. In the other tables, the value for the beginning of the corresponding period was used. Source: Penn World Tables, Mark 5.6a.

Financial and Institutional Development:
- **Financial depth**, defined as the ratio of liquid liabilities to GDP (%). Values at the beginning of the period were used. Source: Beck, Demirguc–Kunt, and Levine (1999).
- **Law and order index**, which ranges from zero to six, where a higher value represents a better institutional framework. Source: *International Country Risk Guide*. Since this index starts only in 1984, we use the 1984 value for 1973 and 1981.

Financial Openness:
- **Quinn index**, which ranges from zero to four in increments of 0.5, where a higher value represents a more open capital account. Values for 1973, 1982, and 1988 are available. The value for 1988 and the difference between the 1973 and 1988 values were used in Tables 7.1 and 7.2. In the other tables, the value for the beginning of the corresponding period was used. Source: Personal correspondence with Dennis Quinn.
- **IMF capital account openness dummy**, constructed from line E2 ("restrictions on payments for capital transactions") of the IMF *Annual Report of Exchange Arrangements and Exchange Restrictions*, various issues. The variable used was the share of years in the sample period when the capital account was open. Source: IMF.

Nonfinancial Openness:
- **Sachs–Warner openness dummy**, defined as a binary variable equal to one if *none* of the five following criteria holds: the country had average tariff rates higher than 40 per cent, its nontariff barriers covered on average more than 40% of imports, it had a socialist economic system, the state had a monopoly of major exports, and its black market premium exceeded 20%. Source: Sachs and Warner (1995), via personal correspondence with Andrew Warner.

- **Barro–Lee trade openness dummy**, defined as binary variable equal to one if a country did not have average tariff rates higher than 40% and its nontariff barriers did not cover on average more than 40% of imports. Source: Barro and Lee (1994).
- **Black market premium**, defined as percent premium over the official exchange rate. Source: Personal correspondence with Andrew Warner.

Instruments:

- **Liquid liabities to GDP** (as defined above), for 1970 and 1975. Source: Beck, Demirguc–Kunt, and Levine (1999).
- **Distance to the equator.** Source: Hall and Jones (1999).
- **OECD membership dummy.** Source: *World Development Indicators*, World Bank.
- **Language variables**, corresponding to: (a) the fraction of the population speaking English, and (b) the fraction of the population speaking one of the major languages of Western Europe: English, French, German, Portuguese, or Spanish. Source: Hall and Jones (1999).
- **Landlocked nation dummy.** Source: Andrew Rose's website.
- **Island nation dummy.** Source: Andrew Rose's website.

References

Aitken, Brian J., and Ann E. Harrison (1999). "Do Domestic Firms Benefit From Direct Foreign Investment? Evidence from Venezuela," *American Economic Review* 89, 605–18.

Alesina, Alberto, Vittorio Grilli, and Gian Maria Milesi-Ferretti (1994). "The Political Economy of Capital Controls," in Leonardo Leiderman and Assaf Razin (eds.), *Capital Mobility: The Impact on Consumption, Investment and Growth*, (Cambridge: Cambridge University Press), pp. 289–328.

Barro, Robert, and J. W. Lee (1994). "Data Set for a Panel of 138 Countries," unpublished manuscript, Harvard University.

Barro, Robert, and J. W. Lee (1996). "International Measures of Schooling Years and Schooling Quality," *American Economic Review Papers and Proceedings* 86, 218–23.

Beck, Thorsten, Asli Demirguc-Kunt, and Ross Levine (1999). "A New Database on Financial Development and Structure," Policy Research Paper No. 2146, Washington, D.C.: World Bank (July).

Bhagwati, Jagdish, and Richard Brecher (1991). "The Paradoxes of Immiserizing Growth and Donor-Enriching Recipient-Immiserizing Transfers: A Tale of Two Literatures," in Douglas Irwin (ed.), *Political Economy and International Economics: The Essays of Jagdish Bhagwati*, (Cambridge, MA: MIT Press), pp. 214–231.

Bordo, Michael and Barry Eichengreen (1998). "Implications of the Great Depression for the Evolution of the International Monetary System," in

Michael Bordo, Claudia Goldin and Eugene White (eds.). *The Defining Moment: The Great Depression and the American Economy in the Twentieth Century* (Chicago: University of Chicago Press), pp. 403–54.

Borensztein, Eduardo, Jose De Gregorio, and Jong-Wha Lee (1995). "How Does Foreign Direct Investment Affect Economic Growth?" NBER Working Paper No. 5057 (March).

Bradstetter, Lee (2000). "Is Foreign Direct Investment a Channel of Knowledge Spillovers? Evidence from Japan's FDI in the United States," NBER Working Paper No. 8015 (November).

Brecher, Richard, and Carlos Diaz-Alejandro (1977). "Tariffs, Foreign Capital and Immiserizing Growth," *Journal of International Economics* 7, 317–22.

Edwards, Sebastian (1994). "Macroeconomic Stabilization in Latin American: Recent Experience and Some Sequencing Issues," NBER Working Paper No. 4697 (April).

Edwards, Sebastian (2001). "Capital Flows and Economic Performance: Are Emerging Economies Different?" NBER Working Paper No. 8076 (January).

Eichengreen, Barry (2000). "Capital Account Liberalization: What Do Cross-Country Studies Tell Us?" *World Bank Economic Review* in press.

Grilli, Vittorio, and Gian Maria Milesi-Ferretti (1995). "Economic Effects and Structural Determinants of Capital Controls," *IMF Staff Papers* 42, 517–551.

Hall, Robert, and Charles Jones (1999). "Why Do Some Countries Produce So Much More Output Per Worker than Others?" *Quarterly Journal of Economics* 114, 83–116.

Johnston, R. Barry (1998). "Sequencing Capital Account Liberalization," *Finance and Development* 35, 20–23.

Kraay, Aart (1998). "In Search of the Macroeconomic Effects of Capital Account Liberalization," unpublished manuscript, The World Bank (October).

Levine, Ross, and David Renelt (1992). "A Sensitivity Analysis of Cross-Country Growth Regressions," *American Economic Review* 82, pp. 942–963.

McKinnon, Ronald (1991). *The Order of Economic Liberalization: Financial Control in the Transition to a Market Economy* (Baltimore: Johns Hopkins University Press).

Quinn, Dennis P. (1997). "The Correlates of Changes in International Financial Regulation," *American Political Science Review* 91, 531–551.

Quinn, Dennis P. (2000). "Democracy and International Financial Liberalization," unpublished manuscript, Georgetown University (June).

Rodriguez, Francisco, and Dani Rodrik (1999). "Trade Policy and Economic Growth: A Skeptic's Guide to the Cross-National Evidence," NBER Working Paper No. 7081 (April).

Rodrik, Dani (1998). "Who Needs Capital-Account Convertibility?" in Peter Kenen (ed.), *Should the IMF Pursue Capital Account Convertibility? Essays in International Finance* No. 207, International Finance Section, Department of Economics, Princeton University (May).

Rodrik, Dani (2001). "Comment on 'Trade, Growth and Poverty'," http:ksghome.harvard.edu/~drodrik.academic.ksg/papers.html.

Sachs, Jeffrey, and Andrew Warner (1995). "Economic Reform and the Process of Global Integration," *Brookings Papers on Economic Activity* 1, 1–118.

EIGHT

Sources of Inflation in Developing Countries*

Prakash Loungani and Phillip Swagel

1. Introduction

This paper develops stylized facts about the inflationary process in developing countries, focusing particularly on the relationship between the exchange rate regime and the sources of inflation. To this end, we examine the influences on inflation in annual data from 1964 to 1998 for 53 developing countries grouped both by region – Africa, Asia, the Mediterranean, and South America – and by exchange rate regime – fixed or floating. This broad-brush approach of pooling countries together is intended to complement the many previous analyses of inflation in developing countries that have typically focused on the experience of individual countries or small groups of them.[1]

We group sources of inflation into four categories. First, as discussed by Montiel (1989), inflation in developing countries is often linked to underlying fiscal imbalances. Such imbalances can lead to an increase in inflation either by triggering higher money growth, as in Sargent and Wallace (1981), or by triggering a balance of payments crisis and forcing an exchange rate depreciation, as in Liviatan and Piterman (1986). The interaction between inflation and the government budget constraint is also stressed in Razin and Sadka (1987) and Bruno and Fischer (1990).

---

* This paper was prepared for presentation at the conference on "Economic Policy in the International Economy," held at Tel Aviv University on March 25–26, 2001, to honor Assaf Razin's sixtieth birthday. We thank our discussant, Eran Yashiv, an anonymous referee, and other seminar participants for their helpful comments.
[1] For example, Moser (1995) provides evidence on the dominant factors influencing inflation in Nigeria, while Montiel (1989) examines inflation in Argentina, Brazil, and Israel.

Another possibility, examined by Coe and McDermott (1997) for 13 Asia economies, is that – as in the industrial countries – inflation in developing countries indicates an overheating economy and is influenced by an activity variable such as the output gap. A third source of inflation, examined by Ball and Mankiw (1995), is supply-side "cost shocks" – movements in the prices of particular goods, such as oil, that lead to persistent changes in the aggregate price level. Finally, as discussed by Chopra (1985), inflation may have a substantial inertial component arising from the sluggish adjustment of inflationary expectations or the existence of staggered wage contracts.

To provide evidence on the relative importance of these four sources for inflation, we include in our analysis the following variables:

1. money growth and exchange rates, variables suggested by the fiscal view;
2. the output gap and a measure of the world business cycle;
3. changes in the prices of oil and non-oil commodities, to capture cost shocks;
4. past realizations of inflation, to reflect the inertial component of inflation.

In examining the sources of inflation, we do not explore the underlying political and institutional features in each country which either lead to high inflation rates or provide an atmosphere conducive to achieving price stability.[2] Instead, we focus on the "proximate" sources of inflation suggested by the four views discussed above.

We find that the sources of inflation are quite diverse in African and Asian countries, which tend to have low to moderate rates of average inflation. In these countries, the most important of the four sources is the inertial component. The other three sources matter as well, but their quantitative importance is much smaller. In contrast, in economies with higher rates of average inflation, such as many in South America, the fiscal variables of money growth and exchange rate changes are predominant, with inertial inflation playing a much smaller role. We show that these differences in the relative importance of sources of inflation across regions correspond to differences in the exchange rate regime. The contribution of the fiscal component of inflation – money growth and exchange rate

---

[2] Examples of these institutional features, along with recent studies, include central bank independence, Alesina and Summers (1993); openness to trade, Romer (1993); and country size and development, Campillo and Miron (1996).

changes – is far more important in countries with floating exchange rate regimes than in those with fixed exchange rates, where inertial factors dominate the inflationary process.

The remainder of the paper is organized as follows. The next section presents our econometric method, after which Section 3 discusses data. Section 4 provides results, first for developing countries taken as a whole, and then for various groups of countries distinguished by their region and their exchange rate regime. Section 5 concludes.

2. Econometric Method

We estimate vector autoregressions (VARs) with at least the following six variables: oil price growth, non-oil commodity price growth, the output gap, money growth, inflation, and exchange rate changes. The approach is similar to that of Montiel (1989), with the exception that we pool together data across the various countries instead of estimating separate VARs for each country. We also discuss results in which we add measures of fiscal deficits and the world business cycle to this base specification.

For our cross-country panel of data, let t denote time, and i index countries. We pool the data across countries and estimate VARs of the form

$$Z_{it} = A(L)Z_{it-1} + \theta_i + \varepsilon_{it}$$

where $A(L)$ is a one-sided polynomial in the lag operator (L), θ_i denotes a set of country-specific fixed effects, and ε_{it} is a vector of normally distributed errors.[3] By pooling across countries, we impose the restriction that the estimated coefficients in each equation are the same across each country in the VAR. The fixed effects are intended to capture country-specific influences on inflation due to differences in institutional factors such as unionization rates, wage bargaining structures, or concentration ratios, all of which potentially explain the behavior of prices, but for which country- or industry-specific data are not available. In Section 4 below, we split the countries into several groups to examine the sources of inflation across regions and other groups of countries.

---

[3] It is well known that least squares estimates are biased in the presence of both fixed effects and lagged endogenous variables. However, as discussed by Nickell (1981) and Hsiao (1989, pp. 73–6), the bias is inversely proportional to the time dimension (T) of the panel; in our data set T is between 20 and 30, so that the size of the bias is likely to be small. Note that the dynamic panel data model of Holtz-Eakin, Newey, and Rosen (1988) is not appropriate for our case, since the asymptotics rely on the width of the panel (number of countries) going to infinity.

Use of a VAR allows us to look at the effect of different assumptions as to the contemporaneous interactions of the variables, notably the interactions of money growth, inflation, and exchange rates, without imposing any constraints on the particular channels through which the factors interact.[4] We present variance decompositions for inflation, as well as results on the effect of innovations ("shocks") in each of the variables on inflation. As usual, an innovation is defined as the component of each variable which is orthogonal to lags of all variables as well as contemporaneous values of variables ordered before it in the VAR. While this provides an economically meaningful definition of shocks, a pitfall of the nonstructural VAR methodology is that certain results may be sensitive to the ordering of the variables in the system. This is discussed extensively in Section 4.

3. Data

We use annual data on 53 developing countries for the years 1964 to 1998. Table 8.1 presents summary statistics, along with a list of the individual countries. Major oil-producing countries are excluded from the sample.[5] Data on money growth, inflation, and nominal exchange rates come from the IMF *International Financial Statistics*. Money growth is the difference of the log of M_2, though using base money instead does not affect our results. Inflation is the difference of the log of the CPI, while the nominal exchange rate is measured as the difference of the log of the bilateral nominal exchange rate with the U.S. dollar. The exchange rate is specified as units of domestic currency per dollar, so that an increase in the exchange rate represents a depreciation of the currency. It would be preferable to use an exchange rate which takes into account bilateral exchange rates with each country's major trading partners (such as the nominal effective exchange rate, lines nec and neu in IFS), but such a measure is not available for many of the countries in our sample. We use nominal rather than a measure of the real exchange rate; this is because real exchange rates already take into account the inflation rates we seek to explain.

Data on fiscal deficits are from the IMF's World Economic Outlook database. These are measured as the central government balance as a share of GDP, so that a negative sign indicates a deficit. A measure of the general government deficit rather than the central government deficit is

---

[4] See Clarida and Gali (1994) for a related structural model.
[5] Removing the oil-producing nation of Gabon from the sample does not change our results.

Table 8.1. *Summary Statistics for 1964–98*

Country	Obs	Inflation Average	Money Growth (M_2) Average	Money Growth (M_2) Corr. with inflation	Fiscal Balance/GDP Average	Fiscal Balance/GDP Corr. with inflation	Fiscal Balance/GDP Corr. with M_2 growth
All Countries (53 countries)	1695	16.4	22.2	0.928	−4.5	−0.019	−0.009
Inflation below 10% (24 countries)	924	6.6	12.8	0.371	−5.0	−0.017	0.018
Inflation above 10% (29 countries)	771	27.6	33.3	0.945	−3.9	−0.047	−0.039
Africa (16 countries)	494	8.8	13.0	0.481	−5.9	−0.006	0.032
Burkina Faso	15	3.5	11.6	0.455	−16.9	0.087	−0.090
Niger	35	5.4	7.5	0.419	1.9	0.200	0.383
Morocco	35	5.7	12.0	0.587	−6.0	−0.265	0.145
Ethiopia	32	6.1	11.6	0.242	−4.7	−0.220	−0.291
Gabon	34	6.2	11.6	0.574	−21.6	0.161	−0.068
Togo	31	6.4	11.2	0.419	−4.2	−0.190	0.184
Senegal	31	6.4	8.5	0.475	−1.8	−0.218	−0.009
Seychelles	27	6.8	14.7	0.280	−8.3	0.127	0.111
Cote D' Ivoire	35	7.1	11.0	0.558	−6.6	0.129	0.516
Congo	33	7.1	8.7	0.272	−5.2	−0.138	0.276
Cameroon	29	7.9	10.1	0.463	−3.1	0.089	0.567
Mauritius	35	8.2	16.1	0.391	−6.0	−0.213	0.262
Kenya	29	10.6	15.7	0.325	−5.2	−0.267	−0.099
Algeria	26	11.6	16.5	−0.003	5.1	−0.407	0.239
Madagascar	34	11.7	14.1	0.302	−4.9	−0.485	−0.185
Ghana	33	27.5	27.5	0.527	−6.2	−0.218	−0.009
Asia (11 countries)	351	9.3	17.2	0.812	−3.5	−0.018	0.086
Singapore	35	3.1	13.4	0.103	3.5	−0.117	−0.149
Malaysia	34	3.6	14.0	0.336	−3.1	−0.139	0.154
Thailand	35	5.4	16.3	0.289	−1.3	0.067	0.168
Bangladesh	12	6.0	15.6	0.365	−7.9	−0.601	−0.627
Fiji	28	7.2	10.4	0.530	−3.0	0.120	0.179
India	34	8.3	14.8	−0.310	−5.8	−0.018	−0.315
Pakistan	35	8.4	14.2	−0.132	−7.3	−0.091	−0.230
Sri Lanka	35	8.7	14.2	0.317	−10.4	0.020	−0.203
Korea	35	9.9	24.1	0.228	−1.6	−0.492	−0.564
Philippines	35	10.6	16.1	0.102	−1.9	0.186	0.188
Indonesia	33	28.2	37.1	0.969	−0.4	−0.179	−0.182
South America (19 countries)	638	27.0	32.7	0.957	−2.5	−0.081	−0.064
Panama	35	3.0	11.9	0.259	−8.2	−0.558	−0.008
Barbados	32	7.4	10.9	0.276	4.9	0.443	0.235
Trinidad	34	8.4	12.4	0.420	2.3	−0.226	0.287
Honduras	35	9.0	15.7	0.437	−6.1	0.270	0.389
Guatemala	35	9.3	14.6	0.529	−2.9	0.369	0.276
El Salvador	35	10.3	13.9	0.391	−2.3	−0.403	0.111
Dominican Rep	35	11.4	17.5	0.424	−0.3	0.064	0.152
Paraguay	35	12.6	20.7	0.552	−0.9	0.671	0.620
Costa Rica	34	13.5	21.3	0.369	−4.2	0.232	0.026
Jamaica	35	15.6	19.2	0.681	−6.5	0.298	0.439

(continued)

Table 8.1. *(continued)*

Country	Obs	Inflation Average	Money Growth (M_2) Average	Money Growth (M_2) Corr. with inflation	Fiscal Balance/GDP Average	Fiscal Balance/GDP Corr. with inflation	Fiscal Balance/GDP Corr. with M_2 growth
Colombia	31	18.2	23.4	0.514	−0.8	−0.336	−0.176
Ecuador	34	20.1	27.2	0.717	−1.7	0.462	0.514
Mexico	35	23.5	29.7	0.431	−4.6	−0.622	−0.268
Chile	35	36.6	46.8	0.920	4.3	0.010	0.041
Bolivia	35	41.9	49.4	0.982	−7.0	−0.682	−0.702
Uruguay	35	44.8	46.7	0.597	−2.0	0.103	0.064
Peru	35	60.4	62.3	0.990	−4.5	−0.090	−0.067
Argentina	35	78.4	81.1	0.980	−6.0	−0.082	−0.069
Brazil	18	142.2	95.1	0.944	−0.7	0.422	0.323
Mediterranean (7 countries)	212	14.7	21.6	0.846	−9.2	−0.163	−0.240
Malta	35	3.5	9.9	0.072	−1.9	0.349	0.176
Cyprus	35	4.7	12.7	0.146	−1.6	−0.571	−0.224
Jordan	28	7.5	13.5	0.521	−14.6	−0.451	−0.795
Egypt	35	10.2	16.5	0.539	−15.3	0.119	−0.075
Syria	33	10.7	17.3	0.086	−10.5	0.329	−0.271
Israel	34	31.8	40.9	0.813	−12.6	−0.236	−0.350
Turkey	12	32.9	40.6	0.881	−5.2	−0.367	−0.383

available for a limited subset of countries and years; the correlation between the overlapping observations of the two measures is in excess of 0.9.

The output gap is constructed as the log of potential output minus the log of actual output, so that an increase in the output gap reflects a slowdown in economic activity relative to potential. Of course, this could also indicate an increase in potential with no change in actual output. Actual output is per capita real GDP (RGDPCH) from version 5.6 of the Summers–Heston database, while potential GDP is constructed by using the filter from Coe and McDermott (1997) to smooth the log of per capita real GDP. The McDermott filter is similar to the Hodrick–Prescott filter, but with the smoothing parameter chosen by the data.[6] A measure of labor market slack such as the unemployment rate would be an obvious alternative to the output gap as a measure of real activity; unfortunately, this is not available on a consistent basis for the broad range of developing countries. We also examine the impact on inflation of the "world business cycle," measured here as the GDP-weighted growth rates of the seven largest industrial countries.

[6] Note, however, that developing countries may experience particularly large positive supply shocks by importing new technologies from the industrial countries. These large increases in potential output would tend to be averaged over by our use of a smoothing filter to construct potential output.

We construct a measure of non-oil commodity prices by matching disaggregated data on the value of imports for each country from the UN commodity trade database to commodity-specific prices of 23 commodities from IFS.[7] The prices for the 23 individual commodities are aggregated together using each country's import weights to create a country-specific measure of non-oil commodity prices. As a result, movements in the price of a particular commodity will have the largest effect on inflation in countries that most heavily import that item. The measure of oil prices is the average oil price from IFS in dollars; this is a global price and thus the same for each country. Energy prices of course vary by country due to country-specific tariffs, excise taxes, and differences in the productivity of the electrical generating and heating industries. Unfortunately, country-specific measures of energy prices are not available for our wide range of developing countries.

Table 8.1 provides a summary of the data, in total, by region, and for individual countries, with the countries sorted by average rates of inflation within each region. Average rates of inflation vary widely across regions, with moderate to low rates generally found in Africa and Asia, but quite high average rates in most South American and Mediterranean countries. Using median rather than mean rates of inflation gives similar results.

The long-run relationship implied by the quantity equation is evident in the strong correlation between money growth and inflation in the whole sample, though the strength of the relationship varies across country groupings. Most notably, there is a strong correlation between money and inflation in countries with high inflation (average inflation above 10%), but a much weaker relationship in low inflation countries (average inflation below 10%). This is true for the individual regions and countries as well.

Surprisingly, there is only weak evidence of a negative correlation between the fiscal balance and either money growth or inflation in the sample as a whole. However, the correlation is strongest (that is, most negative) in countries with high average rates of inflation, particularly in the Mediterranean region. In Africa, inflation and money growth appear to decrease with a fiscal deficit, though of course these raw correlations do not control for other factors and do not imply anything about causality. Further, 7 of the 16 African countries in the sample are members of the CFA Franc

---

[7] The commodities are cereals, vegetable oil, beef, lamb, sugar, bananas, coffee, cocoa, tea, timber, cotton, wool, rubber, tobacco, hides, copper, aluminum, iron ore, tin, nickel, zinc, lead, and fertilizer.

Zone (Cameroon, Congo, Gabon, Ivory Coast, Niger, Senegal, and Togo), and thus do not pursue independent monetary policies. Positive output growth in these countries likely leads to both fiscal surplus and to capital inflows. These inflows would be expected to expand the money supply, which is endogenous with the fixed exchange rate regime, thus providing for the positive correlations between fiscal balance, money growth, and inflation.

We next turn to results from the VARs, which allow an examination of conditional correlations between variables, issues of causality, and effects of various shocks to inflation.

4. Specifications and Results

Our method is to first find an empirical specification that best characterizes the entire sample, and then examine separate results for groupings of countries. Our base specification is a six-equation recursive VAR with the following variables:

1. Oil price growth
2. Non-oil commodity price growth
3. Output gap (as share of potential GDP)
4. Money growth
5. Exchange rate growth
6. Inflation

As discussed below, we consider two base specifications, with the difference between the two being a switch in the positions of money and exchange rate growth in the VAR. Measures of fiscal balance and the world business cycle are considered in Section 4.5, though it turns out that these variables do not affect our main results. Four lags are used in the VARs; the results do not change much if we use two, three, or five lags instead of four.

The ordering of the variables is discussed in Section 4.1, followed by variance decompositions showing the importance of each variable in accounting for inflation movements in Section 4.2, and impulse response functions showing the response of inflation to various shocks in Section 4.3. Sensitivity analysis follows in Section 4.4.

4.1. Ordering of the Variables
Table 8.2 provides two sets of results that are helpful in discussing the ordering of variables in the VAR. The top part of the table shows the

Table 8.2. *Ordering of the Variables: Regressions with Four Lags*

Significance levels for *F*-Tests
All countries, 1695 observations

Influence on Inflation	Dependent variable					
	Oil price	Non-oil price	Output gap	Money	Exchange rate	Inflation
Oil	0.00	0.02	0.15	0.15	0.23	0.18
Non-oil	0.00	0.00	0.75	0.23	0.28	0.09
Output gap	0.84	0.02	0.00	0.84	0.00	0.00
Money	0.00	0.00	0.00	0.00	0.00	0.00
Inflation	0.12	0.05	0.01	0.00	0.00	0.00
Exchange rate	0.00	0.00	0.00	0.91	0.00	0.10
R^2	0.64	0.29	0.42	0.64	0.60	0.72

A low significance level (corresponding to a large *F*-statistic, not shown) indicates that the variable in the first columns provides predictive information on the corresponding variable in the top row.

Correlations between residuals of the six equations

	Non-oil price	Output gap	Money	Exchange rate	Inflation
Oil Price	0.415	−0.098	0.081	−0.038	0.056
Non-oil price		0.003	0.058	−0.047	0.061
Output gap			0.056	0.180	0.120
Money				0.728	0.822
Exchange rate					0.825

significance level for the *F*-test of the null hypothesis that the four lags of the variable in a particular row can be excluded from the regression for the variable at the top of each of the six columns without loss of explanatory power. A small significance level (corresponding to a large *F*-statistic, not shown) indicates a rejection of the null and means instead that the variable in a given row does forecast the variable listed at the top of the column. The bottom part of the table shows the correlations between the errors of the six equations. A high correlation indicates that the ordering of the two equations in question might (but does not necessarily) matter for the results of the variance decompositions and impulse response functions. We use these results as a guide to make several assumptions as to the ordering of the base specification.

We first assume that price movements in oil and non-oil commodities are driven by exogenous developments that are not affected in the same year by the other factors. For oil prices, of course, the biggest developments in prices have resulted from OPEC-related supply disturbances. Oil and non-oil price movements are closely related, with a correlation coefficient of the errors from the two equations just over 0.4. In all specifications, however, we find that it makes little difference which of the two is ordered first. We also experimented with a single variable which combines oil and non-oil commodity prices, again with import values as weights. While this does not affect results for the other four variables, the fit of this one equation is substantially worse than the fit of either of the two separate regressions.

The other large correlations are those between money growth, inflation, and exchange rates. We assume that the contemporaneous correlation between innovations in money growth and inflation innovations reflects causation from money growth to inflation, though there is clearly some feedback from inflation to monetary aggregates within the year. A similar assumption is made with respect to the correlation between exchange rate growth and inflation, with innovations in exchange rates assumed to lead to inflation within the year.[8] While a structural model and higher frequency data are needed to disentangle the underlying relationship, the ordering of exchanges rates and inflation does not change the result that the relative importance of fiscal vs. inertial factors corresponds closely to the grouping of floating and fixed exchange rate regimes. This leaves the issue of the direction of causation between exchange rate innovations and money growth innovations; in this case, we consider both orderings.

Finally, we place the output gap before the three nominal variables (money, exchange rates, and inflation). This is because even though Table 8.2 shows that lags of money growth forecast the output gap but not vice versa, the correlation between the errors of these two equations is quite small. And it turns out that the ordering of money growth and the output gap does not matter for our results. We thus place the output gap after oil and non-oil prices and before M_2 growth in order to pair money and inflation and most cleanly isolate their interaction.

---

[8] The F-statistics in Table 8.2 indicate that lags of inflation provide information on exchange rate movements, while we cannot reject the null hypothesis that lags of exchange rates do not forecast inflation. However, block exogeneity tests indicate that inflation and exchange rates Granger cause each other, though we much more decisively reject the null that inflation has no affect on exchange rates (χ^2 statistic of 208.4) than we do the null that exchange rates have no affect on inflation (χ^2 statistic of 34.7).

Table 8.3. *Variance Decompositions for Inflation Equation: All Countries*

Money growth before exchange rate

Horizon	Oil price	Non-oil price	Output gap	Money	Exchange rate	Inflation
0	0.2	0.2	1.9	66.5	11.6	19.6
1	0.2	0.5	1.2	77.8	7.9	12.5
2	0.1	0.7	1.1	80.2	6.8	11.1
3	0.1	0.7	1.6	80.2	6.7	10.7
4	0.2	0.7	2.1	79.7	6.7	10.6
5	0.2	0.7	2.2	79.7	6.6	10.6
10	0.2	0.7	2.3	79.8	6.6	10.5

Exchange rate before money growth

Horizon	Oil price	Non-oil price	Output gap	Exchange rate	Money	Inflation
0	0.2	0.2	1.9	68.4	9.7	19.6
1	0.2	0.5	1.2	68.2	17.4	12.5
2	0.1	0.7	1.1	66.7	20.3	11.1
3	0.1	0.7	1.6	65.2	21.7	10.7
4	0.2	0.7	2.1	64.4	22.0	10.6
5	0.2	0.7	2.2	64.2	22.2	10.6
10	0.2	0.7	2.3	64.0	22.3	10.5

4.2. Importance of the Six Factors as Influences on Inflation

Table 8.3 shows the results from variance decompositions for the two specifications discussed above (exchange rates before money growth and vice versa), estimated over the entire sample (with country fixed effects). Three key findings emerge:

- Inflation is mainly a fiscal phenomenon, represented in our framework by money growth and exchange rate movements. With money (and inflation) ordered before inflation, money growth accounts for over two-thirds of the variance of inflation at both short- and long-term horizons; under the second ordering, this role is assumed by exchange rate movements. And this finding of the combined importance of money growth and inflation is not affected by putting inflation before exchange rates.
- Past realizations of inflation account for between ten and twenty percent of inflation movements. This suggests an important role for inflationary expectations and institutional features such as indexation

Table 8.4. *Variance Decompositions for Inflation Equation Africa*

Money growth before exchange rate

Horizon	Oil price	Non-oil price	Output gap	Money	Exchange rate	Inflation
0	0.3	0.8	0.8	9.2	11.1	77.8
1	0.7	2.9	0.8	10.8	12.1	72.6
2	1.4	4.0	0.8	10.2	12.5	71.0
3	2.6	4.0	1.0	10.3	12.3	69.8
4	3.2	5.2	1.1	10.0	12.3	68.2
5	3.7	6.6	1.1	9.7	13.0	65.9
10	3.7	7.9	1.2	10.1	13.8	63.3

Exchange rate before money growth

Horizon	Oil price	Non-oil price	Output gap	Exchange rate	Money	Inflation
0	0.3	0.8	0.8	17.1	3.2	77.8
1	0.7	2.9	0.8	19.0	3.9	72.6
2	1.4	4.0	0.8	18.8	3.9	71.0
3	2.6	4.0	1.0	18.4	4.2	69.8
4	3.2	5.2	1.1	18.1	4.2	68.2
5	3.7	6.6	1.1	18.4	4.4	65.9
10	3.7	7.9	1.2	18.2	5.7	63.3

schemes, both of which allow past inflation to influence current wages and price setting.

• Cost shocks and the output gap play a relatively minor role in accounting for inflation. It is possible, of course, that these influences matter more for short-term inflation movements not evident in annual data.

The next four tables split the data into four regional groups. For African countries (Table 8.4), past realizations of inflation play a predominant role, accounting for two-thirds to three-fourths of the variance of inflation – this is especially remarkable since inflation is ordered last in the VAR. The role of fiscal influences – money growth and exchange rate changes – is correspondingly lower than is the case for the entire sample. One important additional result here is that the uncertainty about the relative importance of money shocks and exchange rate shocks is reduced as well. For instance, at a ten-year horizon, money shocks account for between 6 and 10% of the variance of inflation, whereas exchange rates

Table 8.5. *Variance Decompositions for Inflation Equation Asia*

Money growth before exchange rate

Horizon	Oil price	Non-oil price	Output gap	Money	Exchange rate	Inflation
0	4.8	4.7	1.1	0.1	5.3	84.1
1	9.7	21.6	0.8	3.0	7.7	57.2
2	9.8	22.1	1.2	7.4	6.8	52.6
3	9.5	21.5	1.4	8.5	6.7	52.4
4	9.4	21.1	1.6	8.6	6.9	52.5
5	9.4	20.8	1.6	9.0	6.8	52.5
10	9.4	20.7	2.9	9.1	6.7	51.2

Exchange rate before money growth

Horizon	Oil price	Non-oil price	Output gap	Exchange rate	Money	Inflation
0	4.8	4.7	1.1	5.4	0.0	84.1
1	9.7	21.6	0.8	8.5	2.2	57.2
2	9.8	22.1	1.2	7.7	6.6	52.6
3	9.5	21.5	1.4	7.5	7.7	52.4
4	9.4	21.1	1.6	7.7	7.7	52.5
5	9.4	20.8	1.6	7.6	8.1	52.5
10	9.4	20.7	2.9	7.5	8.3	51.2

account for between 14 and 18%. In both cases, the choice of ordering does not really alter the qualitative results. Commodity shocks are somewhat more important in African countries than for developing countries as a whole, corresponding to the importance of primary commodities in these countries' economies. Even so, they are far less important influences on inflation than inertial dynamics and fiscal factors.

Results for Asian economies (Table 8.5) are broadly similar to those for Africa. The predominant factor in accounting for inflation is again past realizations of inflation, though cost shocks eclipse fiscal factors for Asia. Note that the uncertainty about the respective roles of money and exchange rate shocks is again quite small; at a ten-year horizon, money shocks account for between 8 and 9% of inflation movements, while exchange rate shocks account for between 7 and 8%.

The results for South America present a sharp contrast (Table 8.6). Inflation displays little persistence. Instead, most of the explanatory power comes from the fiscal variables, although of course our nonstructural

Table 8.6. *Variance Decompositions for Inflation Equation South America*

Money growth before exchange rate

Horizon	Oil price	Non-oil price	Output gap	Money	Exchange rate	Inflation
0	0.2	0.1	4.4	76.9	8.5	9.9
1	0.1	0.3	2.8	87.0	4.8	4.9
2	0.1	0.6	2.5	88.6	4.1	4.1
3	0.2	0.6	4.1	87.3	3.9	3.9
4	0.3	1.2	5.9	84.7	3.8	4.1
5	0.3	1.5	6.5	83.8	3.8	4.1
10	0.4	1.6	6.6	83.6	3.8	4.1

Exchange rate before money growth

Horizon	Oil price	Non-oil price	Output gap	Exchange rate	Money	Inflation
0	0.2	0.1	4.4	78.5	6.9	9.9
1	0.1	0.3	2.8	77.5	14.3	4.9
2	0.1	0.6	2.5	76.2	16.5	4.1
3	0.2	0.6	4.1	74.2	17.0	3.9
4	0.3	1.2	5.9	71.9	16.7	4.1
5	0.3	1.5	6.5	71.1	16.4	4.1
10	0.4	1.6	6.6	71.0	16.3	4.1

approach does not delineate between the roles of money and exchange rate shocks. The results for the fourth group, the Mediterranean countries (Table 8.7), fall in between those for Asia and Africa, on the one hand, and South America on the other.

What accounts for these differences across regions in the sources of inflation? While a complete investigation of this issue is not conducted in this paper, we suggest that the differences can be connected to differences in exchange rate regimes. To see this, we segment the sample into countries with exchange rate regimes that, on average over the sample period, are close to a fixed exchange rate regime and those with regimes close to a floating exchange rate regime. This segmentation relies on the work of Ghosh, Gulde, Ostry, and Wolf (1995), who classify the exchange rate regimes of a large sample of countries over the period 1960–90 into nine regimes, ranging from single currency pegs at the fixed end to floating regimes with no intervention at the floating. Using the average value for each country's exchange rate regime from 1964 to 1990, we collapse

Table 8.7. *Variance Decompositions for Inflation Equation Mediterranean*

Money growth before exchange rate

Horizon	Oil price	Non-oil price	Output gap	Money	Exchange rate	Inflation
0	2.8	0.0	3.3	27.3	12.4	54.2
1	4.9	0.7	1.5	41.0	6.5	45.6
2	4.8	0.9	1.4	43.7	5.4	43.9
3	4.4	0.8	1.1	51.7	5.8	36.2
4	4.9	0.7	1.0	55.7	5.4	32.2
5	6.3	0.7	1.0	55.3	5.1	31.5
10	7.4	1.2	1.2	54.7	5.0	30.5

Exchange rate before money growth

Horizon	Oil price	Non-oil price	Output gap	Exchange rate	Money	Inflation
0	2.8	0.0	3.3	27.3	12.3	54.2
1	4.9	0.7	1.5	21.2	26.2	45.6
2	4.8	0.9	1.4	19.4	29.7	43.9
3	4.4	0.8	1.1	16.1	41.3	36.2
4	4.9	0.7	1.0	14.6	46.5	32.2
5	6.3	0.7	1.0	14.0	46.5	31.5
10	7.4	1.2	1.2	13.8	45.9	30.5

the scheme of nine regimes into two categories, those that are relatively fixed and those that are closer to a floating exchange rate regime.

The average exchange rate regime differs substantially across regions, but there is a good deal of similarly within each region. In Africa, for example, 16 of the 19 countries in our sample countries have pegged systems and two others are close to fixed. The eleven Asian countries have regimes that are between pegged and floating regimes, but most are closer to a fixed regime than to floating. In South America, on the other hand, few countries have fixed systems, with the vast majority – 14 of the 19 countries in our sample – characterized as floating over the sample period.

Given this close relationship between regions and exchange rate regimes, it is no surprise that the results for the variance decomposition of inflation by exchange rate regime are broadly similar to those by region (Tables 8.8 and 8.9). The results for the fixed exchange rate group are quite similar to those for the African and Asian regions: inflation

Table 8.8. *Variance Decompositions for Inflation Equation: Fixed Exchange Rate Regime Countries*

Money growth before exchange rate

Horizon	Oil price	Non-oil price	Output gap	Money	Exchange rate	Inflation
0	0.2	0.9	1.8	5.1	20.6	71.4
1	2.2	5.3	1.6	7.2	22.4	61.2
2	2.7	6.6	1.6	8.1	21.3	59.7
3	3.1	6.5	1.6	9.1	21.4	58.4
4	3.2	6.5	1.6	9.7	21.1	57.8
5	3.5	6.5	1.8	10.0	21.0	57.3
10	3.7	7.0	2.2	10.4	20.6	56.1

Exchange rate before money growth

Horizon	Oil price	Non-oil price	Output gap	Exchange rate	Money	Inflation
0	0.2	0.9	1.8	24.3	1.4	71.4
1	2.2	5.3	1.6	27.2	2.4	61.2
2	2.7	6.6	1.6	26.0	3.4	59.7
3	3.1	6.5	1.6	26.4	4.1	58.4
4	3.2	6.5	1.6	26.1	4.7	57.8
5	3.5	6.5	1.8	25.9	5.1	57.3
10	3.7	7.0	2.2	25.4	5.6	56.1

has a substantial inertial component, the two fiscal variables are together the next most important influences on inflation, the range of uncertainty about the relative importance of money growth and exchange rate changes is narrow, and cost shocks and the output gap play a modest role. For the floating exchange rate group (Table 8.9), the results resemble those for South America: Fiscal variables are the predominant influence on inflation rather than inflationary inertia, while cost shocks and the output gap are relatively minor influences on inflation.

4.3. Response of Inflation to Shocks

We next assess the response of inflation to shocks to a one standard deviation shock to each of the six influences considered above (including inflation itself). The focus here is only on the response of inflation; the complete set of impulse responses – the response of all six variables to all six shocks – is available from the authors. The impulse responses for

Table 8.9. *Variance Decompositions for Inflation Equation: Flexible Exchange Rate Regime Countries*

Money growth before exchange rate

Horizon	Oil price	Non-oil price	Output gap	Money	Exchange rate	Inflation
0	0.3	0.1	5.6	71.5	8.7	13.7
1	0.2	0.3	3.7	83.3	5.1	7.5
2	0.2	0.4	3.2	85.5	4.3	6.3
3	0.2	0.5	4.9	84.2	4.2	6.0
4	0.2	0.8	7.0	81.8	4.1	6.0
5	0.2	0.9	7.7	81.1	4.1	6.0
10	0.3	0.9	7.9	80.9	4.0	6.0

Exchange rate before money growth

Horizon	Oil price	Non-oil price	Output gap	Exchange rate	Money	Inflation
0	0.3	0.1	5.6	73.2	7.1	13.7
1	0.2	0.3	3.7	73.2	15.2	7.5
2	0.2	0.4	3.2	72.3	17.6	6.3
3	0.2	0.5	4.9	69.8	18.6	6.0
4	0.2	0.8	7.0	67.5	18.5	6.0
5	0.2	0.9	7.7	66.8	18.4	6.0
10	0.3	0.9	7.9	66.6	18.3	6.0

inflation are shown in Fig. 8.1 for the sample of all countries for the two orderings of the VAR. In addition to the point estimates (the solid lines), the figures show error bands two standard deviations wide (the dashed lines).[9]

Regardless of the ordering chosen, the following conclusions hold. First, expansionary policies, whether reflected in faster money growth or exchange rate depreciation, lead to higher inflation and the impact is statistically significant. The response of inflation to money innovations is hump-shaped, with the largest impact coming a year after the monetary impulse. Second, positive oil and non-oil innovations raise inflation by

[9] The standard errors of the impulse responses are computed by the Monte Carlo method described in the manual for RATS version 4, using 1,000 draws from the estimated asymptotic distribution of the VAR coefficients and the covariance matrix of the innovations. The point estimate and standard errors are the mean and standard deviation across draws of the simulated impulse responses.

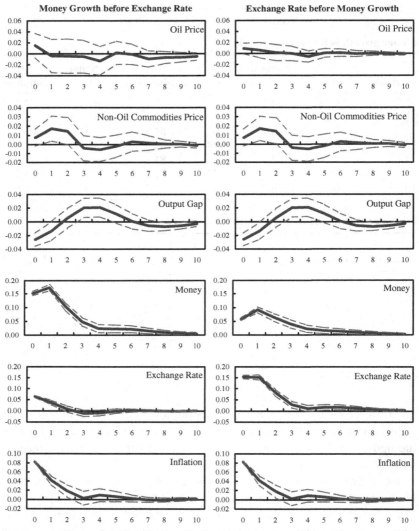

Figure 8.1. Response of inflation to shocks: all countries

only a modest amount and the impact is borderline statistically significant. Third, an increase in the output gap – that is, a weakening of the
economy – leads to a statistically significant decline in inflation, though
with a lag of one to two years and after an initial movement in the other
direction. But the magnitude of the inflation response to real activity is
generally small, so that our results provide limited support for the "gap

model" of inflation in developing countries. One explanation for the perverse initial response of inflation to a slowdown of output is that it may reflect governments' initial reliance on inflation-causing fiscal deficits in the face of falling revenues. Fourth, an exogenous increase in inflation has a persistent effect, with a statistically significant increase in inflation for two to three years following the initial impulse.

The close relationship between the variance decomposition of inflation for regions and the decomposition for exchange rate regimes holds for the impulse responses as well. The responses for Asia and Africa resemble those for pooling together economies with fixed exchange rate regimes, while those for South America are similar to those for countries with floating exchange rate regimes. In the interest of brevity, we report the impulse responses for inflation only by exchange rate regime and not by region; these are shown in Fig. 8.2 for fixed exchange rates and Fig. 8.3 for floating exchange rates. For fixed exchange rate regimes (Fig. 8.2), both oil and non-oil innovations have strong and statistically significant impacts on inflation. Even though together these account for only about 10% of the variance of inflation (as seen in Table 8.8), they matter when they happen (the impulse response is statistically significant). The response of inflation to money innovations is muted though statistically significant in countries with fixed exchange rate regimes. For floating exchange rate regimes (Fig. 8.3), oil and non-oil innovations have only small effects on inflation, while money innovations and exchange rate shocks have substantial impacts (for the latter, particularly when ordered ahead of money growth in the VAR system). This again points to the importance of fiscal factors in economies with flexible exchange rate regimes.

4.4. Sensitivity Analysis

We examined several alternative specifications beyond changes in the orderings of the variables.[10] Using base money rather than M_2 as our measure of money growth hardly affects the results. Similarly, adding the "world business cycle" (the GDP-weighted growth rates of the G7 countries) as an additional variable in the VAR has little effect on the results; this turns out to explain less than one percent of the variance of inflation in the whole sample, and no more than four percent in any of the groupings of countries.

---

[10] June Flanders suggested that another useful sensitivity test would be to see if the estimates are stable over time, particularly comparing the pre- and post-1973 periods. We intend to do this in future work.

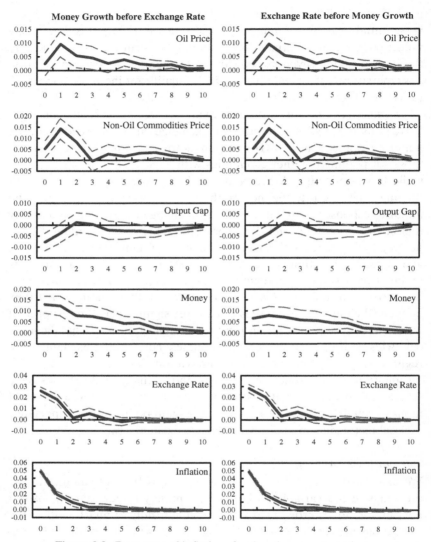

Figure 8.2. Response of inflation: fixed exchange rate regimes

We also examined the impact of shocks to the fiscal balance on inflation, money growth, and exchange rates by adding the fiscal balance to the system before money growth. This is to make fiscal effects explicit rather than implicit in the variables of money and exchange rates. The effect of a fiscal impulse on inflation depends on whether the ratio of fiscal balance to GDP exceeds a threshold value. For countries in which the average

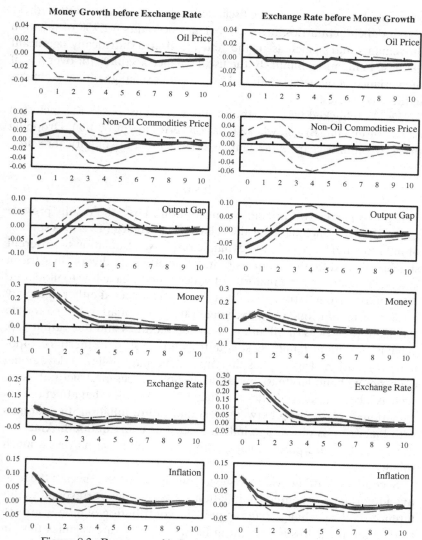

Figure 8.3. Response of inflation: flexible exchange rate regimes

deficit is smaller than 5% of GDP, the ratio of the fiscal balance to GDP accounts for little of the variance of inflation, and a one standard deviation innovation in the deficit to GDP ratio has essentially no effect on inflation. In these "small deficit" countries, the fiscal balance explains less than 1% of the variation in money growth and less than 2% of exchange rate movements. Deficits matter much more, however, when they are large;

for example, when the average fiscal deficit exceeds 5% of GDP. In these "large deficit" countries, the fiscal balance accounts for 7% of inflation movements, and an increase in the deficit leads to a statistically significant increase in inflation. Similarly, the fiscal balance accounts for over 5% of the variance of money growth and over 4% of exchange rate movements in these countries.

We also checked whether the results were sensitive to the inclusion of Argentina and Brazil, whose inflation series might be I(1). Dropping these two countries from the sample did not affect the empirical results.

5. Conclusions

This paper makes two principal contributions. First, the results provide a quantitative benchmark for the relative importance of various sources of inflation and traces out the dynamic response of inflation to different shocks. We find that the sources of inflation are quite diverse in African and Asian countries, the majority of which tend to have low to moderate rates of average inflation. Fiscal variables – as reflected either in money growth or in adjustments in exchange rate pegs – matter, but so too do shocks to the prices of oil and non-oil commodities and the output gap. What is most important in these countries, however, is the inertial component of inflation. This implies that anti-inflationary policy in developing countries with moderate to low inflation should focus on structural issues such as labor market rigidities and indexation schemes that affect the expectational relationship between past and future inflation. In countries with higher rates of average inflation, such as many in South America, fiscal variables are predominant, with inertial inflation playing a much smaller role.

Second, we present evidence suggesting that the differences in the relative importance of sources of inflation across regions correspond to differences in the exchange rate regime. The contribution of money growth to inflation is far less important in fixed exchange rate regimes than in floating exchange rate regimes. In recent years, many developing countries have departed, or are contemplating departing from, fixed exchange rate regimes. Our results suggest that this move can be inflationary unless the new monetary arrangement is able to assume some of the role that an exchange rate peg in moderating the impact of money shocks on inflation.

Several limitations of our analysis might usefully be addressed in future work. First, we impose a "common coefficient" restriction on the response of inflation to the various shocks. While we present results for various regional groups, there is still considerable heterogeneity within each regional group in the inflation experience and – quite likely – in the response of inflation to different shocks. As a result, there could be some canceling out of the effects of explanatory variables when the data for different countries are pooled. Hence, it would be useful to test the common coefficient restriction against alternatives.

Second, while the use of country-fixed effects allows for differences across countries in the average rate of inflation, there could be changes in this average over time within a country, for example from changes in institutions or other determinants of average inflation such as the degree of openness. For instance, Loungani, Razin, and Yuen (2001) provide evidence on the impact changes in restrictions on capital mobility have on macroeconomic variables.

Third, our specification does not allow for nonlinearities in the relationships between, for example, fiscal deficits and inflation or output and inflation, which have been found in some earlier work.

Fourth, since our data are annual, the effects of output gap and cost shocks may be understated, as these effects may operate at a higher frequency. One way to check this would be to use quarterly data.

Finally, future work might usefully be carried out in the context of a more structural model, such as the one presented in Gali and Gertler (1999).

References

Alesina, Alberto, and Lawrence Summers (1993). "Central Bank Independence and Macroeconomic Performance: Some Comparative Evidence," *Journal of Money, Credit, and Banking* 25, May, 1–14.

Ball, Lawrence and N. Gregory Mankiw (1995). "Relative Price Changes as Aggregate Supply Shocks," *Quarterly Journal of Economics*, February, 161–94.

Bruno, Michael and Stanley Fischer (1990). "Seignorage, Operating Rules and the High Inflation Trap," *Quarterly Journal of Economics*, 105, May, 353–74.

Campillo, Marta and Jeffrey Miron (1996). "Why Does Inflation Differ Across Countries?" NBER Working Paper No. 5540, April.

Chopra, Ajai (1985). "The Speed of Adjustment of the Inflation Rate in Developing Countries: A Study of Inertia." *IMF Staff Papers*, vol. 32, no. 4, December, 693–733.

Clarida, Richard, and Jordi Gali (1994). "Sources of Real Exchange Rate Fluctuations: How Important Are Nominal Shocks?" NBER Working Paper 4658, February.

Coe, David T., and C. John McDermott (1997). "Does the Gap Model Work in Asia?" *IMF Staff Papers*, vol. 44 no. 1, March.

Gali, Jordi and Mark Gertler (1999). "Inflation Dynamics: A Structural Econometric Analysis," *Journal of Monetary Economics* 44, October, 195–222.

Ghosh, Atish R., Anne-Marie Gulde, and Jonathan Ostry (1995). "Does the Nominal Exchange Rate Regime Matter?" IMF Working Paper No. 95/251, November 1995.

Holtz-Eakin, Douglas, Whitney Newey, and Harvey Rosen (1988). "Estimating Vector Autoregressions with Panel Data," *Econometrica* 56, November, 1371–95.

Hsiao, Cheng (1989). *Analysis of Panel Data*. (New York: Cambridge University Press).

Liviatan, Nissin, and S. Piterman (1986). "Accelerating Inflation and Balance of Payments Crises, 1973–1984," in Yoram Ben-Porath (ed.), *The Israeli Economy*, (Cambridge: Harvard University Press), pp. 320–46.

Loungani, Prakash, Assaf Razin, and Chi-wa Yuen (2001). "Capital Mobility and the Output-Inflation Tradeoff," *Journal of Development Economics*, 64, February, 255–74.

Montiel, Peter (1989). "Empirical Analysis of High-Inflation Episodes in Argentina, Brazil and Israel," *IMF Staff Papers*, vol. 36, no. 3, September, 527–49.

Moser, Gary G. (1995). "The Main Determinants of Inflation in Nigeria," *IMF Staff Papers*, vol. 42, no. 2, June, 270–89.

Nickell, Stephen (1981). "Biases in Dynamic Models with Fixed Effects," *Econometrica* 49, 1399–416.

Razin, Assaf and Efraim Sadka, eds. (1987). *Economic Policy in Theory and Practice*. (New York: St. Martin's Press).

Romer, David (1993). "Openness and Inflation: Theory and Evidence," *Quarterly Journal of Economics* 108, November, 869–903.

Sargent and Wallace (1981). "Some Unpleasant Monetarist Arithmetic," *Federal Reserve Bank of Minneapolis Quarterly Review* 5, 1–17.

PART THREE

ECONOMIC GROWTH: THEORY AND EMPIRICS

## NINE

Growth Effects and the Cost of Business Cycles*

Gadi Barlevy

In his famous monograph, Lucas (1987) put forth an argument that the welfare gains from reducing the volatility of aggregate consumption are negligible. Subsequent work that has revisited Lucas' calculation has continued to find only small benefits from reducing the volatility of consumption, further reinforcing the perception that business cycles don't matter. This paper argues instead that fluctuations could affect the growth process, which could have much larger effects than consumption volatility. I present an argument for why stabilization could increase growth without a reduction in current consumption, which could imply substantial welfare effects as Lucas (1987) already observed in his calculation. Empirical evidence and calibration exercises suggest that the welfare effects can be quite substantial, possibly as much as two orders of magnitude greater than Lucas' original estimates.

1. Introduction

Lucas (1987) argued that business cycles in the postwar United States involve only negligible welfare losses, thereby challenging the presumption that macroeconomic stabilization is highly desirable. His argument can be stated as follows. Consider a representative consumer with a conventional

* This paper is based on related work which was helped by the comments of Marco Bassetto, Larry Christiano, Elhanan Helpman, Sam Kortum, Robert Lucas, Alex Monge, Assaf Razin, Helene Rey, and various seminar participants. I wish to thank Zvi Hercowitz, who discussed the paper at the conference in honor of Assaf, the participants at the conference in which this work was presented, and the organizers of the conference who did a marvelous job arranging it.

time-separable constant-relative risk aversion (CRRA) utility function

$$\sum_{t=0}^{\infty} \beta^t \frac{C_t^{1-\gamma} - 1}{1 - \gamma}$$

where $\gamma \geq 0$. Suppose this consumer is given a consumption stream C_t defined by

$$C_t = \lambda^t (1 + \varepsilon_t) C_0. \tag{1}$$

That is, consumption is initially equal to C_0 and then on average grows at a constant rate λ, so that after t periods average consumption is equal to $\lambda^t C_0$. Actual consumption each period is allowed to deviate from this average by a random factor $1 + \varepsilon_t$, where ε_t is an i.i.d. random variable with mean 0. Using data on per-capita consumption growth from the postwar period, we can estimate λ and the volatility of ε_t. To determine the costs of aggregate fluctuations, Lucas asked how much consumption per year the consumer would be willing to sacrifice in order to avoid aggregate fluctuations, that is, to replace ε_t in each period with its mean. For reasonable estimates of risk aversion λ, the answer turns out to be astonishingly small, less than one-tenth of one percent. By contrast, Lucas calculates the consumer would be willing to sacrifice a much larger fraction of consumption per year, about 20% when $\gamma = 1$, in order to increase the average growth rate λ by one percentage point. This leads him to conclude that growth is very important for welfare, but aggregate fluctuations are not.

Despite the flurry of papers that sought to dispute Lucas' insight, his essential claim that consumption risk at business cycle frequencies is associated with minor welfare costs appears to have survived intact. Various authors have modified key assumptions that are implicit in Lucas' calculation. These include calibrating consumption to individual income streams rather than to per-capita consumption and allowing for only self-insurance, as in Imrohoroglu (1989), Atkeson and Phalen (1994), and Krusell and Smith (1999); allowing for more persistent shocks to consumption, as in Obstfeld (1994); and allowing for nonexpected utility classes of preferences that are arguably better at capturing attitude towards risk than the CRRA utility, as in Obstfeld (1994), Pemberton (1996), and Dolmas (1998). However, all of these exercises have continued to yield costs of aggregate fluctuations that rarely exceed 1% for reasonable parameterizations. In order to convincingly argue that individuals would be substantially better off if the highs and lows of postwar business cycles were eliminated, then, it would appear that we must shift attention to costs of economic fluctuations that stem from something other than consumption risk per se.[1]

While consumption risk is the most obvious cost of aggregate fluctuations, Lucas' result that changes in growth have a substantial impact on welfare suggests that another potentially important cost of fluctuations could operate through their effect on the rate of economic growth. Specifically, suppose that the level of economic activity affects the incentives for agents to undertake investment that facilitates future production, as is typical in many models of endogenous growth. Fluctuations in the level of economic activity could then conceivably affect the average rate at which consumption and income grow over time. Since Lucas demonstrated that even small changes in average growth rates have a dramatic impact on welfare, this channel could lead to a large cost of business cycles even for relatively modest growth effects. This paper seeks to formalize this intuition. That is, it examines whether eliminating fluctuations is likely to generate an increase in growth that would lead to a dramatic rise in welfare along the lines implied by Lucas' calculations. Although this question has already been tackled in Barlevy (2000), that paper focuses on a model in which R&D acts as the engine of growth. This paper shows how a similar argument arises in a model where capital accumulation serves as the engine for growth. As such, it is closer to models that have been used by others in the literature to examine endogenous growth under uncertainty, and demonstrates more clearly why they fail to generate substantial costs of business cycles. In addition, since the model allows for long-run growth without external effects, it helps clarify certain issues that are obfuscated by the presence of externalities in the R&D model. Finally, while my previous paper argued that empirical evidence on R&D is consistent with growth effects that involve substantial gains from stabilization, this paper illustrates that preliminary evidence yields similar conclusions from evidence on capital accumulation and investment.[2]

---

[1] Detractors from this view include Campbell and Cochrane (1995) and Tallarini (1999). They argue that the large premium we observe on equity illustrates individuals are willing to pay substantial amounts to avoid fluctuations in consumption. However, one has to be careful drawing this conclusion from the equity premium. First, the equity premium could be due to market frictions rather than attitude towards risk. Second, as Alvarez and Jermann (1999) point out, the equity premium and the cost of consumption fluctuations are distinct concepts. They estimate a factor model for the marginal utility of consumption using financial data and put an upper bound on the costs of fluctuations at business cycle frequencies of 0.3%.

[2] This theme has been subsequently reinforced in a revised version of Barlevy (2000) that builds on the model developed here. The revised version generalizes the model described here and carries out a more systematic quantitative analysis.

To preview my analysis, the model implies a consumption stream that is consistent with (1.1), but where the growth rate of consumption λ is no longer constant. Instead, the growth rate λ_t during each period can be expressed as a composite function of the level of economic activity, that is, $\lambda_t = \phi(i(\varepsilon_t))$, where $i(\cdot)$ denotes the investment rate for a given level of economic activity ε_t and $\phi(\cdot)$ denotes the growth rate of consumption for given level of investment. Removing fluctuations in ε_t will affect the average growth rate $E[\lambda] = E[\phi(i(\varepsilon_t))]$ in two different ways. First, depending on whether $i(\cdot)$ is concave or convex, stabilization can affect average growth by changing the average *level* of investment i. Second, depending on whether $\phi(\cdot)$ is concave or convex, stabilization can affect average growth by reducing the *volatility* of investment i.

Previous work on endogenous growth models has assumed $\phi(\cdot)$ is linear, which allows for growth effects that only operate through the average level of investment. As is now well appreciated, this relationship is inherently ambiguous, that is, $i(\cdot)$ can be either concave or convex, depending on the nature of preferences and technology. Regardless of whether stabilization leads to higher or lower investment, though, the implied welfare effects are likely to be far smaller in magnitude than those suggested by Lucas' calculation. This is because growth effects that are due to changes in average investment are inherently different from the growth effects Lucas studies. His welfare numbers correspond to increasing the growth rate of consumption starting from the same initial level of consumption, as illustrated by the solid and dashed lines in the first panel of Fig. 9.1. As long as the agent does not discount future consumption too heavily, the agent will be vastly better off with a higher growth rate. However, an increase in growth that is due to a higher average investment leaves the agent with fewer resources to consume initially, since these must be allocated to investment. Thus, the resulting consumption path begins at a lower initial level, as illustrated in the bottom panel of Fig. 9.1. Whether the agent prefers this new consumption stream depends on how the agent trades off present and future consumption, which explains why agents may voluntarily choose to lower the growth rate of consumption in response to the elimination of aggregate shocks. But more generally, since trading off present and future consumption is inherently different from increasing the growth rate of consumption from a given initial value, there is no reason to expect that the welfare gains from changing average investment in either direction will be anywhere near the magnitude of the huge gains from faster growth holding initial consumption fixed. Since previous authors focused exclusively on this type of growth effect, it is

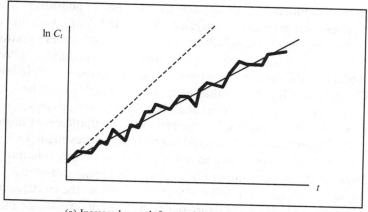

(a) Increased growth from reduced volatility of investment

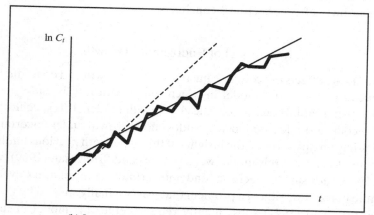

(b) Increased growth from reduced volatility of investment

Figure 9.1. Consumption paths under endogenous growth

not surprising that they find only small welfare gains from eliminating fluctuations.

By contrast, concavity in $\phi(\cdot)$ could generate an increase in growth without reducing average initial consumption. Concavity in $\phi(\cdot)$ implies diminishing returns to investment, that is, an additional unit of investment contributes less to the capital stock when investment is already high. With diminishing returns, keeping average investment unchanged but shifting resources from periods of high investment to those of low investment would lead to a faster accumulation of capital without requiring average investment to rise, and thus without requiring initial consumption to fall.

The welfare numbers Lucas computes for the value of additional growth therefore become relevant, which raises the possibility of substantial welfare costs from aggregate volatility even if growth effects are relatively modest. With sufficient concavity in the investment function $\phi(\cdot)$, a condition that is at the very least not contradicted in the data, one can obtain costs of aggregate fluctuations that are far larger than those that have been reported in previous work. As a rough benchmark, various pieces of evidence suggest that when we incorporate the growth effects of business cycles that occur because of diminishing returns to investment, individuals might be willing to sacrifice as much as 10% of their consumption to eliminate all fluctuations under reasonable specifications of utility.

The paper is organized as follows. Section 2 develops the model that can be used to distinguish between the role of the level of investment and the volatility of investment. Section 3 explores the quantitative implications of the growth effects. Section 4 concludes.

2. A Model of Endogenous Growth

To study the effects of economic fluctuations on growth and consequently on welfare, we need a model in which the growth rate is endogenous. Towards this end, I use a stochastic AK growth model. This specification has become a staple for modeling endogenous growth under uncertainty, and using it helps to relate the insights of this paper with previous findings. The first to analyze this model were Levhari and Srinivasan (1969), who used it to study savings decisions under uncertainty. They in turn solved an infinite horizon version of a problem that was originally studied by Phelps (1962). Leland (1974) subsequently reinterpreted this model in terms of long-run economic growth. Many authors have since used variations of this basic model to study environments with endogenous growth and aggregate uncertainty; recent examples include de Hek (1999) and Jones, Manuelli, and Stacchetti (1999).

The economy consists of a single representative agent who derives utility only from consumption. Time is discrete, and the agent discounts the future at a rate β. Following Lucas, I impose that the per-period utility function of the agent exhibits constant relative risk aversion, with a coefficient of risk aversion given by γ. Thus, given a consumption stream $\{C_t\}_{t=0}^{\infty}$, the utility of the agent is given by

$$\sum_{t=0}^{\infty} \beta^t U(C_t) = \sum_{t=0}^{\infty} \beta^t \frac{C_t^{1-\gamma} - 1}{1 - \gamma}.$$

Following Lucas, I will calibrate γ to equal 1. Since my analysis focuses on growth effects, the relevant interpretation for γ is as the inverse elasticity of intertemporal substitution, An estimate of 1 falls within the range of estimates for this measure in the empirical literature. For example, it falls within the confidence intervals for the estimates in Epstein and Zin (1991) using nondurable consumption data.

The agent has direct access to a production technology. Although there is an equivalent decentralized representation of this economy in which agents own inputs which they sell to producers rather than engage directly in production, it is easier expositionally to assume the agent carries out production than to introduce factor markets. The only input in the economy is capital. Moreover, production is linear in capital, where the number of units that can be produced from a given unit of capital fluctuates stochastically over time. In particular,

$$Y_t = A_t K_t,$$

where A_t is an i.i.d. random variable, and for simplicity I suppose there are only two possible realizations of A_t, namely, $A_t \in \{A_0, A_1\}$, $A_1 > A_0$.[3] Although it is somewhat contrived to assume that capital is the sole factor of production, with additional notation one can modify the model to allow for labor and human capital, as illustrated by Manuelli, Jones, and Stacchetti (1999). They show that if the production function of output is homogeneous of degree 1 in physical and human capital, there exists a unique equilibrium in which both physical and human capital are accumulated at the same rate, making the two-factor model essentially equivalent to the one-factor model considered here.

Since capital is the sole factor of production, the trend path of output (and consequently consumption) depends on the evolution of the capital stock K_t. At date 0, the agent is endowed with some initial amount of capital K_0. Beyond this date, the level of capital depends on the endogenous decisions of the agent. If an agent begins the period with K_t units, a fraction δ of the capital depreciates during the period, so that by the end of the period only $(1 - \delta)K_t$ units remain. The agent can add to the stock of capital that is left by setting aside some of the output from the current

---

[3] Thus, the only sources of fluctuations in this economy are productivity shocks. However, following Eaton (1981), we can reinterpret technology shocks in this model as government policy shocks. That is, suppose productivity were constant over time, i.e., $Y_t = AK_t$. Allowing for a government to collect an i.i.d random fraction τ_t of the income of the representative household to finance contemporaneous government purchases leaves the representative agent with an income of $Y_t = (1 - \tau_t)AK_t \equiv A_t K_t$.

period and converting it into capital. The technology for producing new capital from output is characterized by a function $\Phi(I_t, K_t)$ which depends on the existing stock of capital K_t and the amount of output set aside for producing capital I_t, where $\Phi(\cdot, \cdot)$ is assumed to be homogenous of degree 1 and increasing in its first argument. Given the homogeneity of degree 1, we can rewrite this production function as

$$\Phi(I_t, K_t) = \phi\left(\frac{I_t}{K_t}\right) K_t,$$

where $\phi'(\cdot) > 0$. The stock of capital that is available for production at the beginning of period $t + 1$ is thus given by

$$
\begin{aligned}
K_{t+1} &= \Phi(I_t, K_t) + (1 - \delta) K_t \\
&= \left[\phi\left(\frac{I_t}{K_t}\right) + 1 - \delta\right] K_t.
\end{aligned}
\tag{2}
$$

By repeated substitution of the above equation to express the capital stock at date t as a function of the initial capital stock K_0, we obtain

$$K_t = \left[\prod_{s=0}^{t} \phi\left(\frac{I_s}{K_s}\right) + 1 - \delta\right] K_0.$$

This specification corresponds to the framework originally studied by Levhari and Srinivasan (1969), except that they, and most subsequent authors who use this model, impose two additional restrictions. First, they impose full depreciation, that is, $\delta = 1$. This assumption is not very appealing when we interpret K_t as capital, but it yields a closed-form solution for the agent's maximization problem. Second, they assume $\phi(\cdot)$ is linear, and more specifically is equal to the identity function. This assumption is natural under Levhari and Srinivasan's interpretation where I_t reflects wealth that is invested at a given interest rate. However, if we interpret K_t as capital, this assumption implies output can be converted one-for-one into capital. Following Uzawa (1969), it is also quite natural to consider concave specifications for $\phi(\cdot)$, since these allow for increasing marginal installation costs. In particular, concavity in $\phi(\cdot)$ assumes that at larger levels of investment, an increasing amount of capital is required just to install the new capital (or alternatively is eaten up in the process of putting the capital in place), a condition which appears to accord well with empirical evidence on investment.

To summarize, output in period t depends on the amount of capital available for production at the beginning of the period, that is, $Y_t = A_t K_t$.

Out of this output, the agent consumes an amount C_t, and uses the remainder $I_t = Y_t - C_t$ to invest in capital for the next period. It will prove convenient to define $c_t = C_t / Y_t$ as the fraction of output the agent consumes, and $i_t = I_t / Y_t = 1 - c_t$ as the fraction of output that the agent sets aside for investment. Using this notation, we can rewrite the consumption stream the agent chooses in a form that is reminiscent of Lucas' original specification:

$$
\begin{aligned}
C_t &= c_t A_t K_t \\
&= c_t A_t \left[\prod_{s=0}^{t} \phi(i_s A_s) + 1 - \delta \right] K_0 \\
&\equiv \left[\prod_{s=0}^{t} \lambda_s \right] (1 + \varepsilon_t) C_0,
\end{aligned}
\tag{3}
$$

where $\lambda_s = \phi(i_s A_s) + 1 - \delta$ is the growth rate of the capital stock, $\varepsilon_t = \frac{c_t A_t}{c_0 A_0} - 1$ represents the level of consumption for a given level of capital, and C_0 is the initial level of consumption. Note that if the growth rate of capital λ_s were constant over time, the consumption stream the agent chooses would simplify to $\lambda^t (1 + \varepsilon_t) C_0$, which is exactly the form Lucas posited. The model instead yields a stochastic trend $[\prod_{s=0}^{t} \lambda_s] C_0$ in which the permanent component of consumption growth fluctuates over time.

Since the consumption stream above is endogenous, we can use this model to study how eliminating aggregate fluctuations should affect consumption choices and consequently the welfare of the representative agent, and thus revisit the question as to whether business cycles can involve substantial welfare losses. In the present context, the most natural notion for stabilization involves replacing the stochastic process for A_t with a constant process where productivity is equal to its average value $\overline{A} = \frac{1}{2}(A_0 + A_1)$. Before I proceed with the analysis, though, a few comments are in order. If we interpret A_t as exogenous productivity shocks, then unless government policy can directly affect technology there is no way for government intervention to avoid the cost of aggregate fluctuations. Even though the government can replicate the effects of productivity shocks through taxes, the equilibrium is Pareto optimal, and any such scheme that distorts the incentives of the agent to fool him or her into different consumption and savings choices will only result in lower welfare. Hence, the cost of business cycles represents a purely hypothetical one which cannot be avoided through active stabilization. By contrast, if we view A_t as spurious shocks to fiscal policy as per Footnote 2, we can interpret the cost of fluctuations as one that can be avoided by acting to eliminate arbitrary volatility in policy. However, it is important that the fluctuations that are eliminated are arbitrary rather than an optimal response to some other underlying shock, For example, one cannot use the logic of the model to argue that governments should avoid seasonal fluctuations in spending such as snow removal in the winter. In that case, smoothing government spending over the year would eliminate volatility, but it would also prevent resources from being allocated to address underlying weather shocks that are seasonal in and of themselves. The harm caused by the latter may offset any of the benefits from eliminating fluctuations, negating any of the benefits from stabilization, Thus, to the extent the model implies a large cost of aggregate fluctuations, it can be used to justify stabilization policies only if underlying aggregate fluctuations are arbitrary and can be eliminated through government action – such as capricious policymaking or sunspots – rather than for any underlying source of macroeconomic volatility.

The consumption stream above, is determined by the agent, who solves the maximization problem

$$V(K_0, A_0) \equiv \max_{C_t} E_0 \left[\sum_{t=0}^{\infty} \beta^t \frac{C_t^{1-\gamma}}{1-\gamma} \right] \tag{4}$$

subject to

$$K_{t+1} = \left[\phi \left(\frac{A_t K_t - C_t}{K_t} \right) + 1 - \delta \right] K_t.$$

It is easier to analyze this problem using a recursive formulation to solve for the value function $V(K_t, A_t)$, namely

$$
\begin{aligned}
V(K_t, A_t) &= \max_{C_t} \left\{ \frac{C_t^{1-\gamma}}{1-\gamma} + \beta E[V(K_{t+1}, A_{t+1})] \right\} \\
&= \max_{c_t} \left\{ \frac{(c_t A_t K_t)^{1-\gamma}}{1-\gamma} + \beta E[V([\phi(i_t A_t) + 1 - \delta] K_t, A_{t+1})] \right\}.
\end{aligned}
\tag{5}
$$

We guess that the value function $V(K_t, A_t)$ assumes the form

$$V(K_t, A_t) = \frac{a(A_t) K_t^{1-\gamma}}{1-\gamma},$$

in which case we can rewrite the above Bellman equation as

$$a(A_t) = \max_{c_t \in [0,1]} (c_t A_t)^{1-\gamma} + \beta E[a(A_{t+1})][\phi((1 - c_t)A_t) + 1 - \delta]^{1-\gamma}. \quad (6)$$

We can use this equation to solve for c_t (and thus $i_t = 1 - c_t$), allowing us to solve for the consumption stream the agent would choose when A_t fluctuates and when it is fixed. I begin analyzing this equation for the special case where $\phi(\cdot)$ is linear, that is, $\phi(x) = x$ and then turn to the case where $\phi(\cdot)$ is concave.

2.1. Growth Effects through the Level of Investment

As noted earlier, previous authors have focused on the special case where $\phi(x) = x$. To allow for a closed form solution for c_t and i_t in this environment, I need to further assume $\delta = 1$, the Bellman equation (5) above simplifies to

$$a(A_t) = \max_{c_t \in [0,1]} (c_t A_t)^{1-\gamma} + \beta E[a(A)]((1 - c_t)A_t)^{1-\gamma}.$$

From the first-order condition, we have

$$c_t^{-\gamma} = \beta E[a(A)](1 - c_t)^{-\gamma},$$

which implies c_t is independent of A_t, that is, the agent chooses to consume a constant fraction c of his income regardless of the current level of productivity. To solve for c, average the Bellman equation over the realizations of A to solve for $E[a(A)]$:

$$E[a(A)] = \frac{c^{1-\gamma} E[A^{1-\gamma}]}{1 - \beta(1 - c)^{1-\gamma} E[A^{1-\gamma}]}.$$

Substituting this back into the first order condition yields

$$c = 1 - (\beta E[A^{1-\gamma}])^{\frac{1}{\gamma}} \quad (7)$$

$$i = (\beta E[A^{1-\gamma}])^{\frac{1}{\gamma}}. \quad (8)$$

To ensure an interior solution, we need to impose that $\beta E[A^{1-\gamma}] < 1$.
The implied growth rate of the capital stock is given by

$$\lambda_t = \phi(i A_t) + 1 - \delta$$
$$= i A_t.$$

Since i is constant even when A_t fluctuates, the average growth rate is given by

$$E[\lambda_t] = E[i\,A_t]$$
$$= i\,E[A_t]$$
$$= i\,\overline{A}.$$

However, when aggregate productivity is stabilized so that $A_t = \overline{A}$ for all t, the implied growth rate is given by $i^*\overline{A}$, where i^* denotes the investment rate when aggregate productivity is constant (and equal to $\overline{A}$). Hence, the average growth rate of the capital stock $E[\lambda]$ will change if and only if $i^* \neq i$, that is, if and only if the average investment rate changes. Thus, when $\phi(\cdot)$ is linear, fluctuations will lead to changes in average growth only if the elimination of aggregate shocks induces changes in the average level of investment. From the expression for i above, the fact that $E[A^{1-\gamma}] \gtreqless \overline{A}^{1-\gamma}$ for $\gamma \lesseqgtr 1$ implies that stabilizing productivity to its average value $\overline{A}$ will increase i if $\gamma < 1$ but decrease it if $\gamma > 1$. Thus, the growth rate of capital – and consequently consumption – can either increase or decrease when aggregate shocks are stabilized, depending on the underlying preferences of the agent. The observation that whether agents save more in the absence of fluctuations depends on whether the coefficient of relative risk aversion γ is less than 1 was first established by Phelps (1962), and is by now widely appreciated.

Given the above solutions for i and c, we can now formally study how stabilization affects the path of consumption (2.2) the agent chooses. Stabilization induces three distinct changes in the consumption stream. First, setting A_t equal to its average value serves to eliminate all variation around trend consumption. Formally, since A_t is the same for all t, the deviation from trend $\varepsilon_t = \frac{c_t A_t}{c_0 A_0} - 1 = 0$. Second, for a given investment rate i, stabilizing aggregate productivity A_t replaces the stochastic trend in consumption $[\prod_{s=0}^{t} i\,A_s]C_0$ with a deterministic trend $(i\,\overline{A})^t C_0$ that has the same expectation. Thus, stabilization eliminates fluctuations *in* trend consumption as well as fluctuations *around* trend consumption. Finally, eliminating volatility affects the incentives of the agent to save, inducing a change in the investment rate from i to i^*. This will change the deterministic trend in consumption $(i\,\overline{A})^t$ and thus the average growth rate of consumption.

Each of the three effects above raises the welfare of the agent; the first two effects eliminate temporary and persistent fluctuations in consumption, while the last effect reflects the gain from allowing the agent to adjust the fraction of income consumed in response to changes in the underlying environment. However, as previous authors have shown, for reasonable specifications of utility, all three involve negligible changes in welfare when calibrated to U.S. consumption data. Lucas' original calculation showed that eliminating fluctuations in consumption around a trend will increase welfare by less than 0.1% of consumption per period even if we attribute all of the volatility in per-capita consumption to deviations from trend. Obstfeld (1994) evaluated the welfare gains of replacing a stochastic trend with a deterministic trend with the same mean. Even when he attributes all of the fluctuations in consumption to permanent shocks to trend consumption, he computes a welfare cost of no more than 0.3% when $\gamma \approx 1 - 2$. This just echoes the claim made in the Introduction that consumption risk at business cycle frequencies is of negligible importance. But growth effects associated with changes in average investment also yield only minimal welfare gains for reasonable parameter values. Epaulard and Pommeret (2000) and Matheron and Maury (2000) both compute these welfare gains, and find that for $\gamma \approx 1 - 2$, the gain from changes in the growth rate that are due to changes in average investment amounts to less than 0.1% of consumption. For $\gamma = 1$, this is not entirely surprising, since we just argued above that eliminating fluctuations has no effect on average investment and thus on growth when the coefficient of relative risk aversion is equal to unity. But even for plausible values of γ that are different from 1, the welfare gains from changes in i continue to be small.

The fact that changes in the growth rate involve only negligible welfare gains might seem at first to contradict the intuition in Lucas' original treatise in which he argued that even modest growth effects have huge welfare consequences. However, Lucas' result – that an agent would sacrifice up to 20% of his or her consumption per year to increase the growth rate by just one percentage point – pertains to an increase in growth starting from a given initial level of consumption C_0, as illustrated in the bottom panel of Fig. 9.1. By contrast, growth effects that are due to changes in the average level of investment are conceptually quite different. In particular, if the growth rate of consumption rises because average investment i rises, it must be also true that the fraction of income the agent consumes, $c = 1 - i$, will fall. Hence, a higher average growth rate will be associated with a lower expected initial consumption $C_0 = c\overline{A}K_0$, as illustrated in the bottom panel of Fig. 9.1. This fall in initial consumption wipes out most of the gains from faster growth that are inherent in Lucas' calculation. In order to generate substantial welfare gains along the magnitudes Lucas reports, one must argue that stabilization results in higher growth for a given initial consumption C_0, or alternatively, for a given level of average investment i.[4]

2.2. Growth Effects through Investment Volatility

The last remark above hints at a role for concavity in the investment function $\phi(\cdot)$ in generating large welfare costs from aggregate fluctuations. In particular, suppose that we stabilize A and force the agent to leave the average investment-to-capital ratio unchanged, that is, we force the agent to choose a savings rate i^* such that

$$i^*\overline{A} = E[iA].$$

It follows that $c^* = 1 - i^*$ satisfies

$$
\begin{aligned}
c^*\overline{A} &= (1 - i^*)\overline{A} \\
&= \overline{A} - E[iA] \\
&= E[(1 - i)A] \\
&= E[cA],
\end{aligned}
$$

which insures average initial consumption $E[C_0] = E[cA]K_0$ remains unchanged by the elimination of fluctuations. However, as long as $i_0 A_0 \neq i_1 A_1$, concavity would imply that $E[\phi(iA)] < \phi(E[iA]) = \phi(i^*\overline{A})$, so average growth is higher once shocks are eliminated even though average initial consumption remains unchanged. Intuitively, if the investment-to-capital ratio I/K fluctuates over time, diminishing returns to investment imply that resources could be reallocated to achieve a higher average growth rate of the capital stock for a given average level of I/K, shifting some investment from periods of high investment, when the return to additional investment is fairly low, to periods of low investment, when the return is fairly high, would increase the rate at which capital is accumulated. Stabilization essentially achieves this by removing the incentives for the agent to change his or her investment-to-capital ratio over time, thus

---

[4] It should be noted that welfare effects that are due to changes in the level of investment might be particularly small in the AK model, where the original growth rate (in the presence of shocks) is efficient. In a model with external effects where the equilibrium growth rate can be supoptimal, e.g., the R&D model examined in Barlevy (2000), a change in average investment may make agents significantly better or worse off by moving toward or away from the optimal growth rate. However, these welfare effects would still remain far smaller than those computed by Lucas, since shifting consumption from the present to the future or vice versa affects welfare less than changing the slope of the consumption profile holding initial consumption fixed.

allowing the agent to attain a steeper consumption path without being forced to give up initial consumption.

To establish the argument formally, I first need to argue that if A_t fluctuates over time, so will the equilibrium investment rate $I_t/K_t = i_t A_t$. However, I first need to impose some regularity conditions on $\phi(\cdot)$. Specifically, suppose $\phi(\cdot)$ is strictly concave, where $\lim_{x \to 0} \phi'(x) = \infty$ and $\lim_{x \to \infty} \phi'(x) = 0$. Under these assumptions, we can establish the following:

Proposition 1: Suppose $A_1 > A_0$. Then I/K is increasing in A, that is, the investment-to-capital ratio is strictly higher when aggregate productivity is higher.

Proof: From the first-order condition of the Bellman equation, we have

$$(c_t A_t)^{-\gamma} = \beta E[a(A_{t+1})][\phi((1 - c_t)A_t) + 1 - \delta]^{-\gamma} \phi'((1 - c_t)A_t).$$

We can rearrange this equation to obtain

$$\phi'(i_t A_t) = \frac{1}{\beta E[a(A_{t+1})]} \left(\frac{\phi(i_t A_t) + 1 - \delta}{A_t(1 - i_t)} \right)^{\gamma}. \tag{9}$$

Let $x = i A$. Then we can rewrite the first-order condition as

$$\phi'(x) = k\left(\frac{\phi(x) + 1 - \delta}{A - x} \right)^{\gamma},$$

where k is a positive constant. Since $\phi'(x)$ is decreasing in x and $(\frac{\phi(x)+1-\delta}{A-x})^{\gamma}$ is increasing in x, there exists at most one x which solves this equation. Existence then follows from the limit conditions $\lim_{x \to 0} \phi'(x) = \infty$ and $\lim_{x \to \infty} \phi'(x) = 0$. If we rewrite this equilibrium condition as $f(x, A) \equiv \phi'(x) - \frac{1}{\beta E[a(A_{t+1})]}(\frac{\phi(x)+1-\delta}{A-x})^{\gamma} = 0$, the facts that $f_x < 0$ and $f_A > 0$ imply that as A rises, x must also rise to maintain $f(x, A) = 0$, which establishes the claim. $\square$

The above Proposition establishes that if we stabilize A_t at its average value but force the agent to keep the average investment to capital ratio unchanged, the agent can attain a higher average growth starting from the same initial consumption on average. Hence, Lucas' welfare calculations' apply: If $\gamma = 1$, then for each one point increase in growth that is due to reduced volatility in investment, the agent would be willing to sacrifice approximately 20% of his consumption per year. Thus, stabilizing aggregate shocks in A_t and forcing the agent to keep the average investment-to-capital ratio constant makes the agent significantly better off. Furthermore, allowing the agent to choose a different, investment rate $i \neq i^*$ will only make him or her better off, since recall that the equilibrium of this economy is Pareto optimal. Thus, the growth effects that are due to investment volatility offer a lower bound on the welfare gains from eliminating aggregate fluctuations. More generally, if externalities imply the growth rate is inefficient, changes in average investment that are induced by the elimination of aggregate fluctuations could either increase or decrease welfare. However, as already noted above, the welfare implications of these changes are likely to be much smaller than those computed by Lucas. Thus, growth effects that stem from reduced volatility in investment have the potential to generate fairly substantial welfare gains from the elimination of aggregate volatility, much more than the estimates reported above. How large these welfare effects are likely to be depends on the extent of diminishing returns on investment, which requires looking at empirical evidence on investment.

Before turning to the relevant empirical evidence, I close with a remark about the intuition behind my results. Given the potentially large gains from smoothing the investment to capital ratio, it seems natural to ask why the agent would willingly induce volatility in investment given that it has such a dramatic impact on welfare. To obtain some insights on this, note that the first-order condition in (2.8) can be rewritten as

$$\phi'(i_t A_t) = \left[\frac{E\left[\beta V_K(K_{t+1}, A_{t+1})\right]}{U'(C_t)} \right]^{-1}.$$

This expression inside the brackets is just marginal q, that is, it is the ratio of the marginal value of a unit of capital relative to the price of investment (which is just the price of output, here normalized to 1). Thus, the first-order condition can be rewritten as

$$\phi'(i_t A_t) = \frac{1}{q_t}.$$

As long as q_t fluctuates over time, the agent will find it optimal to change the investment rate in response. From the proof of the proposition above, it follows that holding investment fixed, a positive productivity shock would tend to raise q_t, and with it the incentive to increase investment. Thus, the agent will find it optimal to increase investment in response to a positive productivity shock rather than keeping investment constant. In other words, the cost of aggregate fluctuations comes not from the fact that investment is volatile *per se,* but because the underlying environment makes it optimal for the agent to choose volatile investment. Eliminating fluctuations removes the incentives of the agents to change his or her investment rate over time, which makes the agent better off. But in the presence of aggregate fluctuations, forcing the agent to keep a constant investment to capital ratio would make him strictly worse off. Just because the agent chooses a volatile path for investment does not deny that he could be made significantly better off if the shocks that caused him to behave in this way were eliminated.

3. Quantitative Analysis

The preceding discussion demonstrates that in evaluating the effect of eliminating aggregate fluctuations on welfare, we should take into account both the reduction in consumption volatility as well as changes in the long-run average growth rate of consumption. As noted in the Introduction, previous authors have already established that consumption volatility appears to involve only negligible welfare losses. The question, then, is whether growth effects can lead to more significant welfare costs of aggregate fluctuations. One way to address this question is to adopt a reduced-form approach of estimating how the average growth rate depends on the underlying volatility present in the economy. The discussion suggests that in carrying out such an exercise, it is important to distinguish between changes in the growth rate $E[\lambda]$ holding average investment fixed and changes in $E[\lambda]$ that stem from changes in the average level of investment, since the two are associated with very different welfare implications. In particular, an increase in growth for a given level of average investment is likely to generate much larger welfare effects, since it allows for more rapid consumption growth without a drop in average initial consumption. We can gain a sense of the magnitude of this growth effect by estimating average growth as a function of the volatility of investment, holding average investment fixed:

$$E[\lambda \mid \text{average } i] = f(\sigma_i). \tag{10}$$

Using the estimated $f(\cdot)$, we can predict the level of growth that would prevail if we eliminated volatility but maintained average investment at the same level. For the model developed above, the welfare gain from moving to this new consumption stream would establish a lower bound on the welfare gains from the elimination of aggregate fluctuations, since any additional changes in the investment rate that reallocate consumption between the present and the future only make the agent better off.

Fortunately, estimates of (3.1) already exist in the literature. In particular, Ramey and Ramey (1995) estimate a similar equation using cross-country data, both for a large set of countries as well as a sample that includes only OECD countries. However, they regress average growth on the volatility of output growth σ_λ rather than the volatility of the investment σ_i, which the model above identifies as the key factor in determining average growth. This is not much of a problem, though, since stabilization would eliminate volatility in both series, and so we can use either measure of volatility to infer the implied growth rate when the volatility of the underlying shock is set to 0.[5] Ramey and Ramey find that holding the average investment share of output fixed, a one percentage point reduction in the standard deviation of output growth is associated with an increased growth rate of 0.2%. Since the standard deviation of output growth in the United States is 2.5%, eliminating aggregate shocks altogether should increase the growth rate from 2.0% to 2.5%. Applying Lucas' estimate that an agent would sacrifice 20% of consumption for a 1 point increase in growth when $\gamma = 1$, the implied welfare gain from eliminating fluctuations in A_t amounts to approximately 10% of consumption per year, two orders of magnitude greater than Lucas' original estimate. Thus, even though consumption risk represents only a minor burden of aggregate fluctuations, cross-country data seems to suggest a far more substantial burden on agents coming from the effect of aggregate fluctuations on long-run growth.

The above calculation reports the effects on growth if we forced average investment to remain unchanged. In general, though, stabilization could also affect the average level of investment, which would generate additional growth effects. In the model described above, allowing the agent to change the fraction of income allocated to investment would only make the agent better off, and so any additional changes in growth would only make the agent even better off than if we restrict average investment to remain unchanged. But in models where the growth rate is inefficient, such changes in average investment could make the agent strictly worse off, in which case the above calculation will overstate the true cost of business cycles. This issue is to some extent ameliorated by another finding documented by Ramey and Ramey, namely that the average level of i across countries appears to be uncorrelated with underlying economic volatility σ_y. Ramey and Ramey find this puzzling, relying on the intuition

---

[5] In addition, Ramey and Ramey control for average investment using the investment share of output, i.e., the ratio of investment to output, rather than the investment to capital ratio as implied by the model. Given the difficulty of assembling reliable data on capital, the output share i is much easier to measure than the investment to capital ratio $i A$. However, they do control for variables such as initial GDP per capita and measures of human capital, which could potentially capture differences in A across countries.

from previous work in which $\phi(\cdot)$ is assumed to be linear and where growth effects can only occur through changes in average investment. However, the model above delineates between growth effects that depend on the level of investment and those that depend on the volatility of investment, and the latter imply that average growth could be higher in the absence of fluctuations even if average investment remains unchanged. The fact that virtually all of the growth effects Ramey and Ramey find appear not to operate through investment is crucial for generating substantial welfare costs from aggregate fluctuations, since these alternative channels are associated with more substantial welfare gains for the agent.

Although the cross-country data yield estimates of growth effects that are associated with a large cost of business cycles, we should proceed with some caution in reading this evidence. After all, differences in growth rates across countries could be due to a variety of differences across countries, a possibility that is underscored by the fact that some of Ramey and Ramey's estimates change dramatically with the addition of certain explanatory variables. While their point estimate for the coefficient on σ_λ tends to be clustered around 0.2%, their estimates range between 0.1% and 0.9%. In addition, although the negative relationship between the volatility of growth and the average rate of growth is statistically significant, it is not estimated with great precision. This suggests looking more deeply at the source of diminishing returns to investment and gauging whether it could plausibly generate an increase in growth from 2.0% to 2.5% as suggested by the cross-country evidence. In particular, the model suggests that the key factor in generating growth effects is curvature in the production of capital. Thus, as a complement to the reduced-form approach, we can ask whether the production function for investment goods $\phi(\cdot)$ exhibits the requisite concavity to generate substantial growth effects.

To address this question, consider first the case where $\phi(\cdot)$ is isoelastic, that is,

$$\phi\left(\frac{I}{K}\right) = \left(\frac{I}{K}\right)^\phi.$$

Diminishing and positive returns to investment require a value of $\phi \in (0, 1)$. To gauge what degree of diminishing returns is necessary to generate an increase in growth along the lines suggested by the cross-country evidence, I follow Barlevy (2000) in fitting consumption data to a two-regime stochastic process that satisfies (2.2). Using postwar data, that paper estimates that the average growth rate λ is roughly equal to 2.0%, with a standard deviation of 1.8%. For the isoelastic function to generate growth fluctuations that range between 2.0% ± 1.8%, the investment rates $i_0 A_0$ and $i_1 A_1$ must satisfy

$$(i_0 A_0)^\phi + 1 - \delta = 1.002,$$
$$(i_1 A_1)^\phi + 1 - \delta = 1.038.$$

Assuming a standard depreciation rate δ of 9% per year, we can rewrite the investment rates iA as functions of ϕ, that is, $i_0 A_0 = (0.092)^{\frac{1}{\phi}}$ and $i_1 A_1 = (0.128)^{\frac{1}{\phi}}$. This allows us to compute the growth rate when investment is set equal to the average of $i_0 A_0$ and $i_1 A_1$ as a function of ϕ:

$$\phi \left(\frac{1}{2} \left((.092)^{\frac{1}{\phi}} + (.128)^{\frac{1}{\phi}} \right) \right) + 1 - \delta = \left(\frac{1}{2} \left((.092)^{\frac{1}{\phi}} + (.128)^{\frac{1}{\phi}} \right) \right)^{\phi} + .91.$$

To generate an increase in average growth from 2.0% to 2.5% as is implied by the cross-country evidence, it is necessary that $\phi = 0.21$. To check whether this degree of concavity is reasonable, we can turn to empirical evidence that relates investment rates to q. In particular, for the isoelastic functional form, the first-order condition (2.8) becomes

$$\ln \left(\frac{I}{K} \right) = \frac{1}{1 - \phi} \ln q.$$

Thus, for the isoelastic specification, an increase in growth of half a percentage requires an elasticity of investment with respect to q of $\frac{1}{1-0.21} = 1.26$. An even lower elasticity would imply even larger growth effects than those implied by the cross-country data. Turning to the literature on empirical investment equations, the estimated elasticity of investment with respect to q is typically lower than this estimate. For example, Eberly (1997) explicitly estimates an isoelastic specification using U.S. data, and obtains an elasticity of 1.22. Abel and Eberly (1995) also estimate an isoelastic specification using a different sample of firms, but obtain even smaller point estimates. Turning to other work on empirical investment equations, most researchers have tended to estimate the relationship between investment and q in levels rather than logs as would be implied by the isoelastic specification. However, we can still use these estimates to compute an elasticity at the sample mean. The reported elasticities of investment with respect to q are still lower than 1.26. For example, Abel's (1980) estimates for this the elasticity fall between 0.5 and 1.1 (p 74). More recent work on investment regressions, such as Cummins, Hassett, and Oliner (1999), who argue that their estimates find a much stronger response of investment to q than conventional studies, produce point estimates that cluster around unity. Thus, at a first pass, generating an increase in the growth rate of a half percentage point does not require implausibly large degrees of curvature in the investment function, at least when compared with available estimates of this curvature in the literature.

While the above discussion suggests modest growth effects that nonetheless yield large welfare costs of aggregate fluctuations are consistent with the empirical evidence on investment decisions, there are reasons to remain skeptical about estimates that are based on the elasticity of investment with respect to q. First, these estimates tend to be quite noisy, with some estimates well below unity. Such estimates are inconsistent with $\phi \in (0, 1)$, which is necessary for concavity for the particular specification above. However, very low estimates for this elasticity could simply be due measurement error; typically, instrumenting for q in these regressions yields higher elasticities that often exceed unity, while lower estimates are more prominent when measurement. error is not properly accounted for. But even if we treat the higher point estimates as reliable, the isoelastic specification requires fairly volatile swings in q to induce agents to alter their investment decisions in a way that would lead to fluctuations in growth between 0.2% and 3.8%. From the first-order condition above, we can compute the ratio of q_1 to q_0 that is necessary to induce the fluctuations in growth rate that we observe:

$$\frac{q_1}{q_0} = \frac{(i_0 A_0)^{\phi-1}}{(i_1 A_1)^{\phi-1}} = \left(\frac{.092}{.128}\right)^{\frac{.21-1}{.21}} = 3.46.$$

This would be associated with a standard deviation for q of roughly 55%. This is somewhat more volatile that typical series for q. For example, Summers (1981) provides time series for both q and tax-adjusted q between 1931 and 1978. The standard deviations for the series he reports are 28% and 40%, respectively. Likewise, both investment and consumption turn out to be quite volatile under the isoelastic specification, with investment in peak periods almost four times as large as investment in low periods. A natural concern, then, is whether the mechanism of diminishing returns requires volatility in both investment and incentives for investment that exceed what we observe in the data.

To address this last question, I now turn to the question of how much of an increase in growth we can anticipate if we require that q exhibit reasonable fluctuations. Formally, I ask if for a given level of $\frac{q_1}{q_0}$ there exists a concave function $\phi(\cdot)$ that is consistent with the first-order condition and which implies an increase in growth of half a percentage point. This approach essentially places an upper bound on the amount of growth that is consistent with the observed volatility in q. While this does not allow

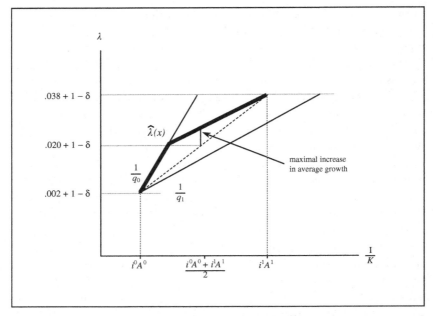

Figure 9.2. Bounds on growth effect

me to determine whether growth effects of the magnitude documented by Ramey and Ramey are *likely,* it does allow me to infer the more modest question of whether such growth effects are *possible.* A more precise assessment of the potential for cycles to affect average growth requires a better understanding of diminishing returns to investment at the aggregate level than can be gleaned from currently available literature.

The first-order condition $\phi'(iA) = q^{-1}$ establishes a natural bound on the potential increase in growth as a function of the underlying volatility in q. The reason is that for any function $\phi(\cdot)$, the first order conditions imply that

$$\frac{\phi'(i_0 A_0)}{\phi'(i_1 A_1)} = \frac{q_1}{q_0}.$$

It follows that a restriction on the standard deviation of q, which effectively restricts the ratio q_1/q_0, imposes limits on how much the first derivative $\phi'(\cdot)$ can change, and thus restricts $\phi''(\cdot)$.[6] This restriction is illustrated graphically in Fig. 9.2. As the figure illustrates, we know that the growth

---

[6] Note that this approach is not robust to the presence of constraints on investment, e.g., financing constraints. If we account for those, $\phi'(iA)$ will not equal q^{-1} but the sum of this and the multiplier on the relevant constraint.

rate $\lambda = \phi(\cdot) + 1 - \delta$ assumes a value of 1.002 when investment is low, and a value of 1.038 when investment is high. Moreover, we know that the slope of the growth rate with respect to investment at the two regimes is given by $\lambda'(i_0 A_0) = \phi'(i_0 A_0) = 1/q_0$ and $\lambda'(i_1 A_1) = \phi'(i_1 A_1) = 1/q_1$, respectively. Given particular values for the investment to capital ratio $i_0 A_0$ and $i_1 A_1$, it follows that for any concave function $\phi(\cdot)$, the growth rate $\lambda(x) = \phi(x) + 1 - \delta$ which satisfies these properties is bounded above by the function

$$\hat{\lambda}(x) = \min \left[1.002 + \frac{1}{q_0}(x - i_0 A_0), 1.038 - \frac{1}{q_1}(i_1 A_1 - x) \right] + 1 - \delta.$$

The function $\hat{\lambda}(x)$ therefore yields the maximum increase in growth that is possible given $i_0 A_0$ and $i_1 A_1$. Since $\phi(i_1 A_1) - \phi(i_0 A_0) = 0.036$ and the slope of $\phi(\cdot)$ for any concave function is confined to the interval $(\frac{1}{q_1}, \frac{1}{q_0})$, the gap $\Delta i A = i_1 A_1 - i_0 A_0$ must lie in the interval $(.036q_0, .036q_1)$ for changes in investment to account for observed fluctuations in output growth. For q equal to 1 on average, this implies fairly reasonable fluctuations in investment to match up with observed fluctuations in the growth rate over time, particularly if q_0 is well below 1. As can be inferred from Fig. 9.2, the potential increase in growth depends on the value of $\Delta i A$. Maximizing over all possible values of $\Delta i A \in (.036q_0, .036q_1)$, we obtain the following result:

Proposition 2: Stabilizing the average investment to capital ratio $i A$ to a constant $i^* \overline{A} = E[i A]$ yields an average growth rate that is bounded above by

$$\frac{1}{q_1/q_0 + 1} [\phi(i_0 A_0) + 1 - \delta] + \frac{q_1/q_0}{q_1/q_0 + 1} [\phi(i_1 A_1) + 1 - \delta]. \qquad (11)$$

Proof: The maximization problem can be expressed as

$$\max_{\Delta i A} \left[\min \left(1.002 + \frac{1}{q_0} \left(\frac{\Delta i A}{2} \right), 1.038 - \frac{1}{q_1} \left(\frac{\Delta i A}{2} \right) \right) \right].$$

At the maximum, the two expressions must be equal, since if they are not equal, it would always be possible to increase this expression either by increasing $\Delta i A$ or decreasing $\Delta i A$, depending on which expression is larger. Solving for $\Delta i A$ at the point of equality yields $\Delta i A = 0.072 \frac{q_1 q_0}{q_1 + q_0}$, and substituting back in yields the desired result. $\qquad \square$

Note that the bound in Proposition 2 is sharp, in the sense that there exists a function $\phi(\cdot)$ for which stabilization will yield the growth rate given in (3.2). This function is piecewise linear, and can be viewed as a linear approximation of the true function $\phi(\cdot)$ for a given value of $\Delta i\,A$. Using the estimates of the volatility of q based on the data from Summers (1981), we obtain

$$\phi(E[i\,A]) + 1 - \delta \le \frac{1}{2.78}1.002 + \frac{1.78}{2.78}1.038 = 1.025$$

using a standard deviation of 28% for q and

$$\frac{1}{3.33}1.002 + \frac{2.33}{3.33}1.038 = 1.027$$

for a standard deviation of 40%. Thus, the observed volatility of q does not preclude a growth rate of the magnitude suggested by the cross-country evidence. Of course, whether this growth rate is actually attained depends on the size of actual fluctuations in investment, $\Delta i\,A$, and on the degree to which $\phi(\cdot)$ is well approximated by a piecewise linear function. Without a better understanding of diminishing returns to investment, the most we can say based on the available evidence is that notwithstanding the small costs of consumption risk computed by others, there remains a scope for fairly large welfare costs of economic fluctuations due to growth effects, with some evidence suggesting such large welfare effects as being quite likely.

4. Conclusion

This paper considers the potential cost of aggregate fluctuations that stem not from consumption volatility but from the effects of aggregate fluctuations on economic growth. In a sense, it closes a circle that began with Lucas (1987), who argued that growth matters for welfare while business cycles do not. By demonstrating that business cycles can affect the rate of economic growth, this paper argues that business cycles could matter precisely because they affect growth. It demonstrates that a plausible case can be made that, for the United States, stabilizing fluctuations can lead to an increase in the growth rate of half of a percentage point without affecting average initial consumption, This produces a cost of business cycles that is over 100 times larger than what Lucas computed based on the costs of consumption risk alone.

I close with a few caveats about the conclusions of the paper. First, given the inherent weakness in the relevant data, it is probably safest to interpret the argument in this paper as demonstrating that growth effects *could* generate a substantial cost of business cycles, not that they do. Since Lucas established a small lower bound on the costs of aggregate fluctuations, his argument appeared to close the book on the notion that stabilization could somehow achieve substantial welfare gains. The most compelling argument presented here is to establish a higher upper bound by allowing for growth effects, opening the book that Lucas' calculation (as well as subsequent work) appeared to close. But without more concrete evidence on the nature of diminishing returns in the production of investment goods, it cannot offer a reliable estimate of how large these effects could be. Thus, its contribution lies in reopening the debate on whether business cycles are costly and whether stabilization is desirable, not in providing a final word in the debate.

Second, even if growth effects are as substantial as these data suggest, it is not obvious that one can recover these costs through implementation of aggregate stabilization policies. The model presented here introduces spurious volatility, and to the extent that policy is able to shut it down and allow the economy to operate on a smooth track, it can achieve a higher welfare level. However, if government policy cannot offset the source of volatlilty, as is the case with technology shocks, the cost of business cycles suggested here cannot be avoided. Thus, while the notion that stabilization can affect average long-run growth extends to other settings as well, intervention may have offsetting costs that negate the benefits described here.

References

Abel, Andrew (1980). "Empirical Investment Equations: An Integrative Framework," in *Carnegie–Rochester Conference Series on Public Policy*, 12, 39–91.

Abel, Andrew, and Janice Eberly (1995)."Investment and q with Fixed Costs; An Empirical Analysis," Wharton, working paper.

Alvarez, Fernando, and Urban Jermann (1999). "Using Asset Prices to Measure the Cost of Business Cycles," Wharton, working paper.

Atkeson, Andrew, and Christopher Phelan (1994). "Reconsidering the Costs of Business Cycles with Incomplete Markets," *NBER Macroeconomics Annual*, Stanley Fischer and Julio Rotemberg (eds.). (Cambridge, MA and London: MIT Press), pp. 187–207.

Barlevy, Gadi (2000). "Evaluating the Costs of Business Cycles in Models of Endogenous Growth," Northwestern University, working paper.

Campbell, John, and John Cochrane (1995). "By Force of Habit: A Consumption-Based Explanation of Aggregate Stock Market Behavior," NBER Working Paper No. 4995, January.

Cummins, Jason, Kevin Hassett, and Stephen Olner (1999). "Investment Behavior, Observable Expectations, and Internal Funds," Federal Reserve System Discussion Paper 99/27.

de Hek, Paul (1999). "On Endogenous Growth Under Uncertainty," *International Economic Review* 40(3), August, 727–44.

Dolmas, Jim (1998). "Risk Preferences and the Welfare Cost of Business Cycles," *Review of Economic Dynamics* 1(3), July, 646–76.

Eaton, Jonathan (1981). "Fiscal Policy, Inflation, and the Accumulation of Risky Capital," *Review of Economic Studies* 48(3), July, 435–45.

Eberly, Janice (1997). "International Evidence on Investment and Fundamentals," European Economic Review 41(6), June, 1055–78.

Epaulard, Anne, and Aude Pommeret (2000). "Recursive Utility, Growth, and the Welfare Cost of Volatility," ENSAE, working paper.

Epstein, Larry, and Stanley Zin (1991). "Substitution, Risk Aversion, and the Temporal Behavior of Consumption and Asset Returns: An Empirical Analysis," *Journal of Political Economy* 99(2), April, 263–86.

Imrohoroglu, Ayse (1989). "Cost of Business Cycles with Indivisibilities and Liquidity Constraints," *Journal of Political Economy* 97(6), December, 1364–83.

Jones, Larry, Rodolfo Manuelli, and Ennio Stacchetti (1999). "Technology (and Policy) Shocks in Models of Endogenous Growth," Northwestern University, working paper.

Krusell, Per, and Anthony Smith (1999). "On the Welfare Effects of Eliminating Business Cycles," *Review of Economic Dynamics* 2(1), January, 245–72.

Leland, Hayne (1974). "Optimal Growth in a Stochastic Environment," *Review of Economic Studies* 41(1), January, 75–86.

Levhari, David, and T. N. Srinivasan (1969). "Optimal Savings Under Uncertainty," *Review of Economic Studies.* 36(1), April, 153–63.

Lucas, Robert (1987). *Models of Business Cycles.* (Oxford: Basil Blackwell).

Matheron, Julien, and Tristan-Pierre Maury (2000). "The Welfare Cost of Fluctuations in AK Growth Models," University of Paris, working paper.

Obstfeld, Maurice (1994). "Evaluating Risky Consumption Paths: The Role of Intertemporal Substitutability," *European Economic Review* 38(7), August, 1471–86.

Pemberton, James (1996). "Growth Trends, Cyclical Fluctuations, and Welfare with Non-Expected Utility Preferences," *Economics Letters* 50(3), March, 387–92.

Phelps, Edmund (1962). "The Accumulation of Risky Capital: A Sequential Utility Analysis," *Econometrica* 30(4), October, 729–43.

Ramey, Garey, and Valerie Ramey (1995). "Cross-Country Evidence on the Link Between Volatility and Growth," *American Economic Review* 85(5), December, 1138–51.

Summers, Larry (1981). "Taxation and Corporate Investment: A *q*-Theory Approach," *Brookings Papers on Economic Activity* 1, 67–121.

Tallarini, Thomas (1999). "Risk Sensitive Business Cycles," Carnegie Mellon University, working paper.

Uzawa, Hirofumi (1969). "Time Preference and the Penrose Effect in a Two-Class Model of Economic Growth," *Journal of Political Economy* 77, 628–52.

TEN

Explaining Economic Growth*

Yair Mundlak

The discussion of economic growth has had a long history, going back to the classical economists.[1] The intensity of the discussion has varied over the years, and it has been amplified over the last two decades. This growing interest can be attributed to two main reasons: First, the concern with the persistent gap in the standard of living across countries, and second, the appearance of new insights into old problems. In this paper we take a broad overview of the field, and outline an approach that is consistent with the data. By explanation of growth we mean an explicit framework that can be confronted with the data and hopefully be validated.

To set up the background for our discussion we begin with a summary of the evidence followed by an incomplete review of the literature to illustrate the efforts of confronting the theory with the data. With this background, we review a more general framework with empirical orientation for the evaluation of the growth process. The essence of this approach is the recognition that the implemented technology and the level of inputs are jointly determined. Qualitative implications of this framework are presented and compared with the evidence. This is followed by an illustration of a cross-country analysis of the agricultural production function evaluated in terms of the given framework. Concluding remarks summarize the paper and some of the implications.

---

* The paper was read also as a Frederick Waugh Lecture at the American Agricultural Economics Association meeting, Chicago, August 8, 2001, and a similar version appeared in the *American Journal of Agricultural Economics,* December 2001.
[1] For a review of the early literature, see Hahn and Mathews 1964. For a review of contemporary literature, see Durlauf and Quah 1999.

1. Evidence

Following Chari et al. 1995, Rebelo 1995, de la Fuente 1997, and Easterly and Levine 2000 among others, we summarize some of the important empirical evidence:

1. Large disparity in per capita income or average labor productivity. The spread between countries is by far bigger than the spread over time.
2. The inequality among countries has increased due to faster growth in the richer countries.
3. At the same time, the inequality among the richer countries has declined.
4. Economic activity is highly concentrated, with factors of production flowing to the richest areas.
5. Countries with high average labor productivity have high capital–output ratio.
6. Growth rates declined in the 1980s and 1990s. The decline from 1973 was quite pervasive, suggesting a response to common shocks. However, the OECD countries suffered less than the poorer countries.[2]
7. Factor accumulation is persistent while growth rates show little persistence.

2. A Note on Technology

Growth is meant here as an increase in labor productivity, or in per capita income. Basically, economic growth is attributed to three elements: physical capital, human capital, and technical change. It is commonly agreed that there is no long-term growth without technical change. But if the technical change triggers growth in some countries, why does it fail in others? This question suggests that there are two pertinent concepts of technology: available technology (AT) and implemented technology (IT). The first concept covers the total knowledge generated everywhere up until the present, and in principle it is available to all countries. The second concept covers that part of the AT that is actually implemented.

---

[2] The European experience serves an example of changing growth rates. The average annual growth rate in the period 1830–1990 was moderate, a little above 1% with a slight positive trend from 1830–50 until World War II (a dip in the big Depression and in the war). It jumped after the war in 1950–70, but declined thereafter to a little over 2% in 1970–90 (de la Fuente 1997).

Knowledge is generated by research which involves human effort and calender time. Past experience suggests a monotonic relationship between research inputs and output. However, not much more can be said for future reference beside this qualitative empirical observation. The reason is that there is no production function that summarizes the research effort. The results of today's research are the inputs for tomorrow's research. Therefore, past experience does not offer replicas for estimating or quantifying the production structure of research (Mundlak 1993, 2000). This is unfortunate because without this information there is no purely quantitative basis for society to evaluate the consequences of resource allocation to research. For instance, in terms of the Lucas model, it is impossible to determine the productivity of resources devoted to the enhancement of human capital. For this reason, and for the fact that it is the implemented technology that generates the data, the domain for empirical discussion is the determination of the IT. This is the case whether or not it is actually recognized in the analysis. The importance of this approach cannot be overemphasized, and one of its attributes is that it introduces a channel through which economic policy affects growth. More on this below.

3. Explanations – An Overview

As the level of output–labor ratio is determined by capital–labor ratio (physical and human) and technology, it is only natural to examine the role of these factors in the explanation of growth. This is basically an exercise in the estimation of production function. To extend it to growth analysis, it is necessary to address the question of what determines the pace of resource and technology accumulation. Models vary in their emphases and specifications of the process, and also in bringing in additional considerations. This is demonstrated by the listing some of the work with a reference to some of their suggested attributes:

- Physical capital and exogenous technical change (Solow 1956, 2000; Mankiw, Romer, and Weil (MRW) 1992).
- Investment in human capital (Lucas 1998, Jones and Manuelli 1997, Rebelo 1991, and Stokey 1991)
- Externalities (Romer 1986, Caballero and Lyons 1992, and Benhabib and Jovanovic 1991).
- Externalities are not essential for growth (Jones and Manuelli 1997, Rebelo 1991, Lucas 1988, and Solow 2000)

- Research and development (Romer 1990, Grossman and Helpman 1991, and Aghion and Howitt 1992).
- Learning by doing (Arrow 1962, Romer 1986, Stokey 1988, Young 1991).
- Investment (Levine and Renelt 1992, De Long and Summers 1991, and Young 1992, 1995). It is important to note that those countries that invest heavily in physical capital also invest in education.
- Total factor productivity (TFP) is the main trigger of growth: (Prescott 1998 and Easterly and Levine 2000).
- Implementation of the available technology (Mundlak 1988, 1993, 2000). This is the main theme of this paper.

The performance is affected by public policy, and more generally by the economic environment:

- Inflation – Negative effect of inflation due to uncertainty (Fischer 1993).
- Trade policy – Openness contributes to growth (Mundlak, Cavallo and Domenech 1989, Grossman and Helpman 1991, Rivera-Batiz and Romer 1991, and Ben-David, Nordström, and Winters 2000)
- Financial intermediation – Efficient financial intermediation system helps to allocate capital in most efficient way, and to pool risk (King and Levine 1993)
- Infrastructure investment – Helps market integration (Aschauer 1989, Barro 1991, and Easterly and Rebelo 1993)
- Political process – The obsolescence of traditional techniques generates political resistence. (Persson and Tabellini 1994, Alsina and Rodrick 1991).
- Policies and growth – (Cavallo and Mundlak 1982, Mundlak, Cavallo, and Domenech 1989, Easterly and Rebelo 1993, and Knack and Keefer 1985).
- External shocks – (Easterly 2000)

Before continuing, we highlight some of the findings pertinent to our subsequent discussion. The most robust finding is the importance of physical capital as an explanatory variable. Often, the estimated elasticity of capital exceeds the factor share of capital. This finding, together with the trend of capital deepening, suggests that capital has a lot to do with growth. A question is raised on the nature of causality between capital accumulation and growth (Blomstrom, Lipsey, and Zejan 1996, pp. 275–6). This subject is related to the role of TFP. Easterly and Levine assert that the "residual" rather than factor accumulation accounts for most of the income and growth differences across nations. Prescott argues that differences in physical or human capital cannot account for the big international differences in income today. The culprit is the spread in the TFP. The suggested reason for the spread is the resistence to the adoption of new technologies and to the efficient use of currently operating technologies. The evidence on schooling as a measure of human capital is less conclusive (Pritchett 1996). Levine and Renelt conclude that many measures of economic policy are related to long-run growth. However, the relationship between long-run growth and any specific policy indicator is fragile. Thus, they propose that there is no reliable, independent statistical relationship between a wide variety of macroeconomic indicators and growth. Our subsequent discussion will deal implicitly with these views.

4. Empirics of the Solow and Related Models

Even though the growth process evolves over time, the empirical analysis commonly employed is largely cross-country analysis, which does not focus on the process itself but only on its outcome. The motivation is perhaps twofold: First, the desire to understand the reasons for the differences in growth rates across countries, a prerequisite to devising measures to improve the performance. Second, country-panel data show that most of the spread in the pertinent economic variables is between countries rather that through time.[3] The underlying assumption is that all the observations (country and time) come from the same production function. This is more than a statistical convenience. Mainstream growth theories do not allow for a heterogeneous technology, for if they did, the choice of technique would have to be part of the theory, otherwise the theory is incomplete.

The main workhorse of the empirical analysis is a Cobb–Douglas production function with constant coefficients, in line with the assumption of homogeneous technology. In many cases an exogenous technological change at a predetermined rate is imposed on the equation. A pivotal element of many studies is the empirical validity of the Solow model. In this connection, it is instructive to recognize two attributes of that model.

---

[3] For instance, in the panel discussed in the last part of the paper, the between-country spread in the inputs and outputs accounts for more than 95% of the total spread in the data. On its face, this large spread leads to more precise estimates. This does not imply, however, that the variability over time is less valuable.

The first is related to the production function. It states that without technical change the economy converges to a steady state without growth, or simply stagnation. For this it is sufficient that the capital elasticity will eventually be smaller than one as the capital–labor ratio grows. This condition is extended in a natural way if there is more than one reproducible input. This attribute is generally confirmed empirically. The second also involves the rules of resource accumulation. To make the discussion more concrete, we outline in the Appendix the structure of the MRW empirical analysis of the Solow model, with summary results, and concentrate here on the main conclusions.

In the Solow model, the variability in the *level* of labor productivity is accounted for by the variability in the saving (investment for open economies) rate and by the growth rate of the labor force. The augmented Solow model includes also a measure of schooling (MRW). At the same time, the growth *rate* should be the same for all countries, up to a stochastic term, which should be uncorrelated with the investment rate, the schooling rate, and the growth rate in the labor force. Bernanke and Gürkaynak (BG) (2001) show that, empirically, this is not the case. They assert that "The principal reason for the rejection is the strong relationship of the saving rate (I/GDP) to the long-run growth rate" (p. 13). They supplement this result by computing the TFP from national accounts and regressing it on the same regressors. The results of this analysis indicate that "[T]FP growth is cross-sectionally strongly related . . . to the saving rate and, in most cases, to the growth rate of the labor force" (p. 27). The effect of the schooling rate on TFP tends to be statistically insignificant. They conclude that "[f]uture empirical studies should focus on models that exhibit endogenous growth" (BG, abstract). In passing, it is noted that they examine the effect of endogenizing the saving rate and thus making it depend on deeper parameters which enter the intertemporal utility function and the growth rate. This extension did not help. Nor did it help to endogenize the schooling rate following the Uzawa–Lucas model (Uzawa 1965, Lucas 1988).

Basically, the empirical analysis concentrates on the estimation of the production function, with the imposition of the behavioral equations. The criteria used by MRW in judging the results are the quality of the production function fit to the data and the resemblance of the estimated capital elasticity to the factor share. There is no parallel effort to examine empirically the quality of the behavioral specification. More important, the behavioral equations are taken to be largely independent of the technology assumption. But the two may not be independent. In addition, the

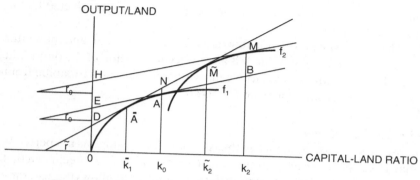

Figure 10.1. Resource constraint and the choice of technique.

analysis does not address the various issues addressed in the literature as reviewed above.

5. The Implemented Technology

Following our opening comments on technology, we turn now to examine the determination of the implemented technology and its consequences. The discussion is conducted with reference to a simple graphical illustration (Fig. 10.1).

Initially the AT consists of $\{f_1\}$, the capital–labor ratio (K/L) is given by k, and the output–labor ratio (Y/L) is given by y. The economy is at A with wage $(w) = OE$, and the return to "scarce" factor (K) is r_0. Technical change is introduced with the appearance of a new capital-intensive technique, and AT becomes $\{f_1, f_2\}$.[4] For simplicity, it is assumed that there is no setup cost involved in the implementation of the new technique. Holding L constant for simplification, the response of the economy to the technical change depends on factor supply, and this is demonstrated by two extreme possibilities: 1) The supply of K is perfectly elastic – the economy moves to M with r_0 unchanged, but w increases to OH. 2) The supply of K is perfectly inelastic – the best strategy is a convex combination of the two techniques as given by N. The resources are allocated between the two techniques. It is required that the gain from the implementation of the new technique covers the setup costs involved in the implementation. If this condition is not met, the economy remains at A and does not employ f_2. We have thus demonstrated the key proposition: The change

---

[4] See Atkinson and Stiglitz (1969) for an early discussion of technical change and the choice of techniques within the framework of activity analysis.

in the economy induced by the change in AT is strongly affected by the resource supply.

The composite production function is the locus 0, $\tilde{A}$, $\tilde{M}$, and thereafter along f_2. The output at point N is a convex combination of the outputs at $\tilde{A}$ and $\tilde{M}$. The move from A to N causes a rise in the return to capital from r_0 to $\tilde{r}$ and a decline of w from OE to OD.

5.1. Some Implications

FACTOR PRICES. A change in the AT, when factor supply is not perfectly elastic, causes a rise in the return to the scarce factor and a decline in that of the abundant factor. Once the capital accumulation allows the economy to abandon the less productive technique (pass the threshold point $\tilde{M}$), production will be carried out along a strictly concave production function and the return to capital will tend to come down from its elevated level and at the same time the wage rate will start climbing and eventually surpass the initial value. In this description, it is assumed that capital is homogeneous and can be reallocated between the two techniques. For instance, in the case of the green revolution, think of k as fertilizers–(or irrigation)–land ratio, and of the techniques as varieties. The appearance of the more productive variety results in reallocation of the land and the fertilizers between two varieties.[5]

RESOURCE FLOW. The capital–labor ratio will increase with time in response to the rise in r, and this will result in a gradual convergence to $\tilde{M}$. The green revolution serves a good example. In spite of the superior varieties of wheat and rice the process of their adoption took a long time because these varieties have been water and fertilizer intensive and the pace of the process was determined by the pace of resource mobility into agriculture (McGuirk and Mundlak 1991). To conclude, the pace of convergence to a new optimal point is largely determined by the pace of resource flow. When the new and productive techniques are capital intensive, a correlation is generated between the technology shocks and capital, as observed in empirical analysis.

TFP. The measured impact of the technical change depends on the location of the economy before and after the change, and this in turn depends on resource mobility. When factor supply is perfectly elastic, the economy moves from A to M, and the change in the TFP is given by BM.

---

[5] When capital is not homogeneous, and the two techniques require different forms of capital, the pace of the implementation of the new technique will be determined by the pace of the change in the composition of the capital goods.

When factor supply is not perfectly elastic, the TFP is given by the move from A to N. With time k rises and the economy will move along the tangent $\tilde{A}\tilde{M}$, which is associated with the new factor prices. Along this segment the technical change is fully absorbed by the change in the factor prices and the TFP remains unchanged. The upshot is that the computed TFP is path dependent. Again, this is consistent with the finding that TFP is positively correlated with the investment rate. Moreover, TFP cannot be the trigger of growth or the explanation for the income differences. TFP is endogenous and is determined within the model. The trigger is the change in the AT, and the outcome depends on the factor supply and other variables that constitute the economic environment to be discussed below.

LEARNING BY DOING. The concept of learning by doing can be applied at different levels. Following the original example presented by Arrow, the learning applies to the use of a new technique. Thus the discussion is made conditional on a change in the AT, and it is not a substitute for that change. Countries cannot simply converge to the frontier technology of the more advanced countries if they do not have the resources to implement the new technique. The speed of convergence reflects, therefore, the combined effect of the speed of learning and of resource flow.

The concept of learning by doing is also applicable to the evolution in research. As the input to today's research is the result of yesterday's research, the ones who learn are the ones who are engaged in research, and again this acts against the progress of the poor countries.

WAGE RIGIDITY. The change in factor prices is part of the transition of the economy in its response to a change in the AT. Thus, if the wage rate is fixed at the original level (or a level above AD) the transformation to the new technique may be hindered and unemployment might result. Discussions in favor of wage rigidity (e.g., Easterly, Islam, and Stiglitz 2000) assume a homogeneous technology and do not apply to the case under discussion.

INCOME DISTRIBUTION. When the new technology is intensive in a particular factor, the share of that factor in total income rises and this may augment income inequality. An example is the differences in income between the "new" and "old" economies. This change in distribution reflects two changes, the rise in the price of the scarce factor and the decline in the price of the saved factor. Such changes affect the income distribution of skilled and unskilled labor.

POLARIZATION OF GLOBAL WEALTH. A similar reasoning applies to the explanation of the international income inequality. Global factor supply is finite, and the allocation is determined by expected returns and their stability in the various areas. The richer countries are more affluent in the resources needed for the implementation of the new technology, and they benefit from the changes in the AT. Countries that do not have adequate supply of the scarce factors will lag behind. This leads to polarization. This response is particularly important for the flow of physical capital which is attracted to the high return areas. The quantities and the speed of such movements are likely to exceed those of skilled labor (brain drain).

CONVERGENCE. Total convergence of countries to the same average labor productivity requires that countries employ the same technology and have the same level of capital of all forms per unit of labor. Conditional convergence (Barro and Sala-i-Martin 1995, Ch. 1) requires that countries move to the frontier of the implemented technology for the given capital–labor ratios. The existence of conditional convergence but not total convergence places the emphasis on factor accumulation which in turn highlights the importance of having an adequate economic environment.

PRICES. For the discussion to cover more than one product, output is measured in value terms. A change in relative prices can be described graphically as a shift of the production functions. This will effect the implemented technology, and thus the implementation becomes dependent on product demand. There is, however, a difference between a change in demand and a change in AT. While the latter is not reversible, the change in demand is often transitory and does not justify a major response. The response, therefore, will depend on the perception of the nature of the change. Similarly, when the output is value added, the price of raw materials also affect the pertinent production function. This, for instance, was the case when energy prices spiked in the early 1970s. Thus the technology choice, as well the mobility of resources to durable activities with high setup cost, becomes a function of expected prices and their stability. This framework is broad in scope. For instance, in an open economy, the implemented technology is expected to be affected by the country's terms of trade and policies that determine the real exchange rate.

DEMAND AND THE EXTENT OF THE MARKET. Empirical growth analysis shows that export is an important regressor. Without rejecting other explanations for this result, the present discussion draws attention to the importance of the size of the market. National economies are open but the global economy is closed and thus tradable products face declining demand. This is well recognized in the discussion of agriculture, and it should be also applicable to other tradables, specifically manufacturing. Changes in technology that amplify the internal scale economies generate a tendency for concentration leading to a few players with overcapacity.

This generates pressure to increase export, and the more efficient producers prevail, which leads to an association between productivity and export.

6. Consequences

A formal presentation of the above approach calls for expressing the optimization problem at the firm level as a choice of the techniques to be implemented and their level of intensity, given the available technology, product demand, factor supply, and constraints (Mundlak 1988, 1993, 2000). This approach has important implications for the empirical analysis. Specifically: *Endogeneity* – The implemented technology is endogenous. *Jointness* – The implemented technology is determined jointly with the level of intensity at which the inputs are used. *Production path* – The output path is determined by the evolution of the state variables. *Identification* – In general, the aggregate production function is not identifiable. *Concavity* – When the sample is generated by more than one technique, the empirical aggregate production function is not subject to a concavity constraint, even though each of the techniques is represented by a concave production function.

With a second-degree approximation, the aggregate production function looks like a Cobb–Douglas function, but the elasticities are functions of the state variables and possibly of the inputs:

$$\ln y = \Gamma(s) + B(s, \, x) \ln x + u,$$

where y is the value added per worker, x and s are vectors of inputs per worker and state variables, respectively, $\Gamma(s)$ and $B(s, \, x)$ are the intercept and the slope of the function respectively and u is a stochastic term. At each sample point, the data consist of aggregated techniques, the composition of which changes over the sample points. To identify the aggregate production function it is necessary to break the tie between the decisions on the implemented technology from those on the level of inputs. This is achieved when deviations from the first-order conditions are more pronounced in the input decisions than in the choice of techniques.

Variations in the state variables affect the production function coefficients directly as well as indirectly, through their effect on inputs. For this reason, estimates obtained under the assumption of constant coefficients provide a distorted view. Often the estimates are not robust, and they are sensitive to the choice of the sample. This subject is discussed in detail in Mundlak (2001).

The approach was used in country growth studies using time series data. The estimation of the production function was done by imposing a stochastic equality of the factor share and the production elasticity. Those studies are too comprehensive to summarize here (see Mundlak 2001). Instead, we examine an application to pooled country data in order to highlight some of the results reviewed above.

7. Cross-Country Agricultural Production Function

The estimation of the system requires data on factor shares, which are not readily available. This makes it impossible to apply the model in the form presented above to pooled cross-country data until the needed data become available. The task is then to see what can be learned from the available data. In what follows we review the approach taken by Mundlak, Larson, and Butzer (1999) to estimate the agricultural production functions using a sample of 37 countries over the period 1970–91. The size of the sample is determined by the data availability. The pooled data are used to fit three regressions: *Between countries* (based on country means), *between time* (based on year means) and *within-time-country* (based on the deviations of the observations from country means and year means). These three regressions constitute the canonical set of pooled data in the sense that all linear estimators based on the sample can be expressed as matrix-weighted averages of these regressions.[6] Under the hypothesis, the coefficients of a Cobb–Douglas production function are affected by the economic environment, and therefore the coefficients of these regressions should differ. The *within* variables are deviations, free of the influence of country and time effects, which in part are captured by the state variables, and as such represent a more stable technology, to be referred to as the *core technology*.

The state variables consist of incentives, constraints, technology, and physical environment. The variables are:

---

[6] Often, analysis of pooled data compares within estimators (allowing for country or time effect or both) with pooled estimates. For instance, for an analysis of the MRW model using panel data see Islam (1995). Because the pooled estimates are matrix-weighted combinations of the three canonical regressions, it is insightful to estimate them. This is what we do here. In addition, we introduce explicitly the state variables. This contributes to the statistical quality of the estimates, and adds economic meaning. When computing the country or time productivity levels (effects), the inclusion of the state variables will modify the productivity measure in a meaningful way by separating the impact of the state variables from that of productivity.

OUTPUT. – agricultural GDP in 1990 U.S. dollars.

INPUTS LAND. – Hectares of arable, permanent cropland, and permanent pastures. *Labor* – Economically active population in agriculture. It is not actual employment, and as such it is a stock, rather than a flow, concept. *Fertilizers* – Total fertilizer consumption in metric tons. *Capital* – Fixed capital stock used in agriculture, plus capital in livestock and orchards. The capital variable serves the dual role of an input and a of a constraint. We return to this below.

INCENTIVES. Two measures are used to capture the direct effect of incentives on productivity, over and above their indirect effect that comes through resource allocation and accumulation: *Price* – The ratio of the prices of agriculture to manufacturing. *Price variability* – A moving standard deviation of the price, calculated from the three previous periods. The variable reflects the market risk faced by agricultural producers. *Inflation* – In addition to the sector-specific risk, there is an economy-wide market risk, that of price volatility for the economy as a whole measured by the inflation rate, calculated as the rate of change in the total GDP deflator.

Expected improvement of future profitability encourages investment and thereby augments the capital stock which appears as a variable in the analysis. The regression coefficients of the incentive variables represent only the direct effect of prices, which is the part not embedded in input changes. To obtain the full impact of the incentives on productivity, it is necessary to add their indirect effect through investment, but this is not done here.

TECHNOLOGY. The technology block consists of several variables: *Schooling* – The mean school years of the total labor force serves as a proxy for the embedded human capital. *Peak yield* – Country-specific Paasche indices (1990 = 1) of the historical peak commodity yields, weighted by land area, used to measure the level of technology in agriculture. *Development* – The state of development of the economy is measured by the per capita output in the country relative to that in the United States.

PHYSICAL ENVIRONMENT. Two variables are used to describe the physical environment for agriculture, *potential dry matter* production (PDM) and a *factor of water deficit* (FWD).[7]

---

[7] Some of the measures have to be modified for the between-country analysis: Peak yields are replaced by their average growth rates for the period. The average rate of growth in the relative price over the period replaces the level of such price. The standard deviation of the relative price over the entire period is used in place of the moving standard deviation.

The average annual growth rates (percent) of the variables in question are output 3.82, capital 4.25, land 0.12, labor −0.04, fertilizers 3.04, schooling 1.8, peak yield 1.9, development −0.29, and relative price −0.30.

8. Empirical Results

Table 10.1 presents estimates for the three canonical regressions. The three regressions display constant returns to scale. The null hypothesis that any of these regressions can be eliminated is rejected. The coefficients of the variables common to the various equations are quite different. This confirms the basic hypothesis that the regressions summarize the combined effect of changes in inputs and technology obtained under different economic environments. The interpretation of some of the results provides further insight.

INPUTS. Perhaps the most interesting result is the magnitude of the elasticity of capital, 0.37 in the *within* regression, 0.34 in the *between-country* regression, and 1.03 in the *between-time* regression. The latter represents the response common to all countries in the sample. It indicates that, on average for the sample, an increase in capital was accompanied

Table 10.1. *Cross-Country Estimates of the Production Function*

	W (country, time)		B (time)		B (country)	
Inputs						
Capital	0.37	(6.90)	1.03	(6.01)	0.34	(13.13)
Land	0.47	(3.78)			−0.03	(2.82)
Labor	0.08		−0.16	(0.16)	0.26	(13.67)
Fertilizer	0.08	(1.53)	0.14	(0.33)	0.43	(21.91)
Technology						
Schooling	0.09	(0.55)	−0.28	(0.06)	0.02	(0.52)
Peak yield	0.83	(3.80)	−0.32	(0.07)	0.06	(4.19)
Development	0.52	(3.36)	−0.21	(0.33)	0.31	(2.97)
Prices						
Relative prices	0.04	(1.78)	0.02	(0.09)	0.01	(1.95)
Price variability	−0.03	(0.97)	−0.07	(0.26)	−0.08	(2.82)
Inflation	−0.00	(0.75)	0.04	(0.71)	0.07	(4.25)
Environmental						
Potential dry matter					0.16	(2.68)
Water availability					0.44	(7.96)

Notes: In the title, W and B stand for within and between respectively. Values in parentheses are absolute values of the *t*-ratios. The R^2 for 777 observations is 0.9696.
Source: Mundlak, Larson, and Butzer 1999, p. 488.

with a proportional increase in output. This strong response is consistent with the view that physical capital has been a constraint to agricultural growth. Accordingly, the implementation of changes in the available technology were strongly affected by investment in agriculture.

The labor coefficient in the *between-time* regression is not significantly different from zero. The value of this coefficient in the *within-time-country* regression is also relatively low, whereas that of the *between-country* regression is more in line with other cross-country studies. This is no surprise because those studies are in general based on cross-country regressions. Recall that the labor is a stock variable that measures the actual employment with error. Variations over time in this variable, which on average are small, do not affect output. On the other hand, the cross-country variations of the labor variable are sizable, so that the signal-to-noise ratio is relatively large, and seem to have a substantive impact on output.

These results highlight the importance of capital in agricultural production, and indicate that agricultural technology is cost-capital intensive compared to nonagriculture. This conclusion is further reinforced by the magnitude of the land elasticity in the *core* technology. The sum of capital and land elasticities is around 0.8 in various formulations, making it clear that agriculture should be more sensitive than nonagriculture to changes in the cost of capital and less to that of labor (Mundlak, Cavallo, and Domenech 1989). This value of the sum might seem to be a bit high. In part, it may reflect the result of a somewhat low labor elasticity. It is also possible that a different choice of countries and time periods would lead to somewhat different results. In any case, a sum of 0.8 for land and capital elasticities leaves room for the conclusion on the importance of capital to remain intact.

There is a big difference in the elasticity of fertilizers in the various regressions. A value of 0.08 obtained in the within-country-time regression is considerably lower than typical values obtained in cross-country studies of the agricultural production function, which are closer to our between-country coefficient. This requires an explanation. Recall that the dependent variable is the log of value added, which is net of expenditures on fertilizers. Using the envelope theorem, under the competitive conditions, the coefficient of fertilizers should be close to zero. The difference from zero should reflect only interest charges for working capital, reflecting the time lapse between the purchase of the inputs and the time of the sale of the output. A coefficient of 0.08 indicates that about 8% of the changes in agricultural output is to be attributed to fertilizers over and above their cost. Moreover, this result is obtained for the aggregate agricultural output, whereas fertilizers are used only on plant products. It is likely that a production function for plant products alone would show a larger elasticity for fertilizers. Thus, a value of 0.08 for aggregate output may even be biased upward, which means that we have to explain why it is high rather than low. A mechanical explanation is that fertilizers capture the impact of other chemicals and more generally the modern inputs, as indicated above. Still, by the envelope theorem, the coefficient of this "extended" input should be near zero. The more substantive explanation for this deviation is that fertilizers were scarce and the elasticity reflects a high shadow price of fertilizers. This is consistent with the large increase in fertilizers supply over time. This is also consistent with the high fertilizer elasticity obtained from between-country regression, which is indicative that the new technology is fertilizer-using. Accordingly, the locus of country means represents a changing technology package where the improvement in the implemented technology is fertilizer-using. At the same time it is also capital-using but land-saving.

TECHNOLOGY. The technology variables play a dual role in the analysis. First they serve as technology shifters and as such reduce the bias caused by the correlation of inputs and technology. Second, they provide an empirical examination of how well they describe the data and thereby guide us in the search for appropriate technology indicators.

The *peak yield* serves well as a shifter of the agricultural productivity – measured by the core technology – with an elasticity of 0.83. The peak yield is a proxy for the frontier of the implemented technology. A low value for this elasticity indicates that the economic environment was not sufficiently favorable to allow the current productivity to repeat its historical records. An elasticity of 1 indicates that the current productivity is moving along with this frontier. The frontier itself progresses in response to changes in the state variables but, in the longer run, such a progress is triggered by changes in the available technology. We thus deal with a ratchet process. A jump in available technology translates itself into a change in productivity, which in turn raises the peak. The persistence of this performance depends on the economic environment. Can the elasticity take on values larger than one? The answer is yes. This can happen when initially the available technology was not fully utilized, then improvements in the economic environment allow a catchup at a fast pace.

The contribution of the level of development of the country relative to the United States is over and above that of the peak yield. It shows that the yield level is not exhaustive as a technology indicator; first, the yield variable does not represent the productivity in livestock production which accounts for about one-third of output, and second, there is a scope for improving efficiency under a given technology by coming closer to the frontier, as represented by the performance of the United States.

The between-time regression shows that, for the sample as a whole, none of the technology variables was important in accounting for the changes in agricultural productivity over time. The dominant variable is physical capital. The implication is that even though schooling and peak yields increased with time, we see no evidence that they contributed to the benefits from improvements in the available technology. It is suggested that it is the changes in the available technology that caused the increase in these variables, at least in peak yield and perhaps in schooling, but it was the availability of capital that was crucial for the countries to take full advantage of the available technology. This highlights the importance of physical capital in accounting for the changes in agricultural productivity in the study period.

The results vary for individual countries, as seen from the between-country regression, where the level of development is important in accounting for the productivity variations. This is a statement of the importance of the various attributes of the overall level of development of a country in determining the level of agricultural productivity. This may also be the reason that schooling appears to be irrelevant. To the extent that schooling matters, it may have an indirect effect through the development variable. However, to what extent schooling matters and how it can be measured using aggregate data is still an open question (Pritchett 1996).

PRICES. The test of the null hypothesis that the price block can be omitted from the analysis is rejected. On the whole, the signs of the coefficients are in line with expectations, but the precision is low. The small quantitative price effect on agricultural productivity should not be misleading; it is obtained conditional on given inputs and on technology. Thus, there is little scope for additional price effects. The fact that this effect is detected at all is of prime importance. The channels for the price effect are the level of inputs and the choice of technology, and these are represented by explanatory variables.

9. Concluding Remarks

The available technology is changing with time and a large component of this change is not predictable. The basic premise is that the implementation of the technology is endogenous within the economic system and depends on the economic environment. This is the essence of the empirical explanation of growth. Following this line of thinking, the implemented technology is determined jointly with the level of inputs. The changes in the available technology affect the demand for inputs, it increases the demand for those inputs in which the new technology is intensive. The implementation of the new technology is not necessarily immediate or pervasive. It depends largely on the supply of inputs in which the new technology is intensive. The data, and therefore their analysis, provide information on the *use* made of the changes in technology. Since the choice of inputs and the implemented technology is determined jointly, it is not always meaningful to assign causality in the relation between these two elements.

In this paper we discuss one cross-country study, interpreted in light of the presented approach. It illustrates very clearly that the coefficients of the production function depend on the economic environment and thereby support the hypothesis that the coefficients are not constant. This is only one cross-country study which uses this approach, and other samples may yield different results. Of course, nonrobustness of results is one of the attributes of the model, and therefore this will only reinforce the conclusions. This raises a question with respect to the information we get from cross-country studies which impose constant coefficients for the sample as a whole. Many of the results obtained in those studies can be interpreted in light of the present discussion.

To sum up, observations are generated in a process of convergence to changing new frontiers. The pace of this process is determined by the economic environment. This environment is largely affected by what countries do. This view suggests an important scope to the role of economic policies.

Appendix: Estimates of Growth Models

This is a summary presentation of the MRW and some results from Bernanke and Gürkaynak (BG) 2001, which can serve as a point of departure for discussions of empirical growth analyses. The empirical growth model consists of two blocks, technology and behavior. The technology is summarized by the production function, mostly a Cobb–Douglas function:

$$Y_t = A_t K_t^{\alpha} H_t^{\beta} L_t^{1-\alpha-\beta}, \tag{1}$$

where Y is output, K is the capital stock, H is a measure of schooling, L is labor, and A is the productivity level.[8] The parameters α and β are nonnegative and their sum is smaller than 1, so that the function displays constant returns to scale in the three inputs. Label variable on a per labor basis with lower case letters, and write the equation in logarithms:

$$\ln y_t = \ln A_t + \alpha \ln k_t + \beta \ln h_t. \tag{2}$$

Let g_x be $\dot{x}/x$, then as a matter of definition, the rate of growth of output is

$$g = g_A + \alpha g_k + \beta g_h. \tag{3}$$

This summarizes the specification of the technology.

The behavioral block specifies the rules for resource accumulation. The Solow model in its original form does not include schooling, and it assumes a fixed saving ratio (s_k). The rate of growth of k is

$$g_k = s_k(Y/K) - m, \tag{4}$$

where m is the sum of the depreciation rate (δ) and the rate of population growth (n), $m = \delta + n$. When schooling is added, an analogous expression can be written for the rate of growth of h, assuming for simplification the same depreciation rate for h and k:

$$g_h = s_h(Y/H) - m. \tag{5}$$

On the balanced growth path (BGP), output and inputs grow at the same rate: $g = g_k = g_h$. Thus, a constant g_k implies that Y/K is constant. Consequently

$$g = g_A/(1 - \alpha - \beta). \tag{6}$$

The balanced growth path is obtained by combining the technology and behavioral blocks. Solving Equations (4) and (5) and the production function, we obtain

$$k^* = \left(\frac{A s_h^\beta s_k^{1-\beta}}{g+m} \right)^{1/1-\alpha-\beta}, \tag{7}$$

---

[8] The productivity variable, A, is sometimes attached to labor as a labor-augmenting technical change. In the case of Cobb–Douglas function, the two possibilities are equivalent.

$$h^* = \left(\frac{A s_k^\alpha s_h^{1-\alpha}}{g+m} \right)^{1/1-\alpha-\beta}. \tag{8}$$

Substitute (7) and (8) in the production function, noting that with constant growth rate $\ln A_t = \ln A_0 + g_A t$, to obtain for the BGP

$$\ln y_t^* = \ln A_0 + g_A t + \varepsilon \left[\alpha \ln s_k + \beta \ln s_h - (\alpha + \beta) \ln(m + g) \right],$$
$$\varepsilon = 1/(1 - \alpha - \beta). \tag{9}$$

The fitting of the equation to cross-country data requires several assumptions and modifications. First, to allow for the fact that the observations need not be on the BGP, an error term is added. The error term is assumed to be uncorrelated with the regressors. This is a questionable assumption, as explained in the foregoing discussion. Second, under the assumption of homogeneous technology, the elasticities are the same for all countries. Third, it is important to be explicit about the variables used in the empirical analysis when they are not the same as those used in the theoretical construction. The Solow model was initially developed for the closed economy, so that the saving and investment rates are the same. This is different for the open economy, where foreign savings are involved, so that the investment rate replaces the domestic saving rate. Similarly, the term human capital is widely used, but its meaning is not unique. In practice, a measure of schooling is used in empirical analysis and for this reason we refer to this variable as schooling.

MRW estimated Equation (9) where the dependent variable is the actual (y), rather than the BGP, value (y^*). A numerical value is assumed for g. The regressors that change across countries are the investment and schooling rates, s_k and s_h respectively, and the population growth rate n (note that n is the only component of $m + g$ that varies across countries). They fit it to three groups of countries, for the period 1960–85 using data from Summer–Heston Penn World Tables (PWT). The samples include 98 nonoil countries, a subsample of 75 countries for which the data are more precise, and 22 OECD countries. Initially, they estimated the textbook Solow model which does not include the schooling variable. They judge the results by three criteria, the goodness of fit, the estimated value of the capital elasticity, and the acceptance of the over identifying restriction. Based on R^2 of about 0.6, MRW claim that the equation explains a great deal of country variations in y in terms of s and n. This is not a strong argument in that it amounts to testing the model against the null hypothesis that the investment rate and the population growth rate are uncorrelated with the output–labor ratio. No growth model claims this. Moreover, the R^2 for the OECD countries is rather low, 0.06. A more problematic result is that for the large samples for which the fit is reasonable the estimate of α is about 0.6, twice the factor share of capital. On the other hand, the estimate for the OECD countries, where the fit is rather poor, the value is reasonable, 0.36. Finally, α can be estimated either from the regression coefficient of s_k or from that of n. This overidentifying restriction is not rejected, which is a favorable result.

To improve the results, they augment the Solow model by adding the schooling variable, s_h. This improves the fit, the R^2 for the large samples is near 0.80, but that of the OECD countries is still low, 0.28. The estimated capital elasticity declines to a reasonable value of about 0.3 for the large samples, and to a low value of 0.14 for the OECD countries. These results suggest that the estimates are sensitive to the choice of countries. Are they also sensitive to the choice of the time period? This is one of the questions dealt with by BG. They estimate the MRW model with more recent PWT data and obtain different results, indicating that the estimates are also sensitive to the choice of the time period. Beyond this, they also conduct a strong test of the Solow model. Because the parameters are assumed constant over time, the difference of BGP output in t from that in a base period 0 is

$$\ln y_t^* - \ln y_0^* = \ln A_t - \ln A_0. \tag{10}$$

Introducing an error term to represent the difference between the actual and steady-state values, and rewriting Equation (10) for the actual values to express the growth rate yield

$$(\ln y_t - \ln y_0)/t = g_A + e_t - e_0. \tag{11}$$

Under the Solow model, the growth rate should be uncorrelated with the regressors in Equation (9). Ignoring the details of the testing procedure, BG find that it is not, neither in the textbook Solow model nor in the augmented Solow model, and thus reject the model.[9]

---

[9] To be precise, rejection is strong for the two large samples, and somewhat weaker for the OECD countries. It should however be recalled that the empirical results of the Solow model for the OECD countries is not very convincing.

References

Aghion, P., and P. Howitt (1992). "A Model of Growth Through Creative Destruction," *Econometrica*, 60 (March): 323–51.

Alsina, A., and D. Rodrick (1991). "Redistributive Politics and Economic Growth," Harvard University, working paper.

Arrow, K. J. (1962). "The Economic Implications of Learning by Doing," *Review of Economic Studies* 29 (June): 155–73.

Aschauer, D. (1989). "Is Public Expenditure Productive?" *Journal of Monetary Economics* 23 (March): 177–200.

Atkinson, A. B., and J. E. Stiglitz (1969). "A New View of Technological Change," *The Economic Journal* 79 (September): 573–8.

Barro, R. J. (1991). "Economic Growth in a Cross Section of Countries," *The Quarterly Journal of Economics* 106 (May): 407–43.

Barro, R. J., and X. Sala-i-Martin (1995). *Economic Growth*. (New York: McGraw-Hill).

Ben-David, D., H. Nordström, and A. L. Winters (2000). *Trade, Income Disparity, and Poverty*, Geneva: World Trade Organization.

Benhabib, J., and B. Jovanovic (1991). "Externalities and Growth Accounting," *American Economic Review*, 81 (March): 82–113.

Bernanke, B. S., and R. S. Gürkaynak (2001). "Is Growth Exogenous? Taking Mankiw, Romer, and Weil Seriously," Working paper 8365, NBER, Cambridge MA, July.

Blomstrom, M., R. E. Lipsey, and M. Zejan (1996). "Is fixed investment the key to economic growth?" *Quarterly Journal of Economics* 111 (February): 269–76.

Caballero, R. J. and R. K. Lyons (1992). "External Effects in U.S. Procyclical Productivity," *Journal of Monetary Economics* 29 (April): 209–25.

Cavallo, D., and Y. Mundlak (1982). *Agriculture and Economic Growth in an Open Economy: The Case of Argentina*. Washington, D.C.: International Food Policy Research Institute, Research Report No. 36.

Chari, V. V., P. J. Kehoe, and E. R. McGratten (1995). "The poverty of nations: A quantitative exploration," University of Chicago, Workshop in Growth and Development, October 4.

de la Fuente, A. (1997). "The empirics of growth and convergence: A selective review," *Journal of Econ Dynamics and Control* 21(January): 23–73.

De Long, B., and L. Summers (1991). "Equipment Investment and Economic Growth," *Quarterly Journal of Economics* 106 (May): 445–502.

Durlauf, S. N., and D. T. Quah (1999). "The New Empirics of Economic Growth," *Handbook of Macroeconomics* Vol. 1. Amsterdam: Elsevier Science, 235–308.

Easterly, W. (2000). "The Lost Decades ... and the Coming Boom? Policies, Shocks, and Developing Countries' Stagnation 1980–1998," World Bank, May.

Easterly, W., and R. Levine (2000). "It's Not Factor Accumulation: Stylized Facts and Growth Models," World Bank, March.

Easterly, W., and S. Rebelo (1993). "Fiscal Policy and Economic Growth: An Empirical Investigation," *Journal of Monetary Economics* 32 (December): 417–58.

Easterly, W., R. Islam, and J. E. Stiglitz (2000). "Shaken and Stirred: Explaining Growth Volatility," (Washington D.C.: The World Bank).

Fischer, S. (1993). "The Role of Macroeconomic Factors in Growth," *Journal of Monetary Economics* 32 (1993): 485–511.

Grossman, G., and E. Helpman (1991). *Innovation and Growth in the Global Economy,* (Cambridge, MA: MIT Press).

Hahn, F. H., and R. C. O. Mathews (1964). "The Theory of Economic Growth: A Survey," *The Economic Journal* 74 (December): 779–902.

Islam, N. (1995). "Growth Empirics: A Panel Data Approach," *Quarterly Journal of Economics* 110 (November): 1127–70.

Jones, L. E., and R. E. Manuelli (1997). "The Sources of Growth," *Journal of Economic Dynamics and Control* 21 (January): 75–114.

King, R. G., and R. Levine (1993). "Finance, Entrepreneurship, and Growth," *Journal of Monetary Economics* 32 (December): 513–42.

Knack, S., and P. Keefer (1995). "Institutions and Economic Performance: Cross-Country Tests Using Alternative Institutional Measures," *Economics and Politics* (November): 207–27.

Levine, R., and D. Renelt (1992). "Sensitivity Analysis of Cross-Country Growth Regressions," *American Economic Review* 82 (September): 942–63.

Lucas, R. E., Jr. (1988). "On the Mechanics of Economic Development," *Journal of Monetary Economics,* 22 (June): 3–43.

Mankiw, N. G., D. Romer, and D. N. Weil (1992). "A Contribution to the Empirics of Economic Growth," *Quarterly Journal of Economics* 107: (May): 407–37.

McGuirk, A., and Y. Mundlak (1991). *Incentives and Constraints in the Transformation of Punjab Agriculture,* Washington, D.C.: International Food Policy Research Institute, Research Report No. 87.

Mundlak, Y. (1988). "Endogenous Technology and the Measurement of Productivity," *Agricultural Productivity: Measurement and Explanation*, Susan M. Capalbo and John M. Antle (eds.), 316–31. Washington, D.C.: Resources for the Future.

Mundlak, Y. (1993). "On the Empirical Aspects of Economic Growth Theory," *American Economic Review* 83 (May): 415–20.

Mundlak, Y. (2000). *Agriculture and Economic Growth; Theory and Measurement,* (Cambridge, MA: Harvard University Press).

Mundlak, Y. (2001). "Production and Supply," *Handbook of Agricultural Economics,* Vol I., B. Gardner and G. Rausser (eds.), North Holland.

Mundlak, Y., D. Larson, and R. Butzer (1999). "The Determinants of Agricultural Production: A Cross-Country Analysis," *Annales de l'insee* 55–6 (September–December): 475–501.

Mundlak, Y., D. Cavallo, and R. Domenech (1989). *Agriculture and Economic Growth in Argentina, 1913–84.* Washington, D.C.: International Food Policy Research Institute, Research Report No. 76.

Prescott, E. D. (1998). "Needed: A Theory of Total Factor Productivity," *International Economic Review* 39 (August): 525–51.

Persson, T., and G. Tabellini (1994). "Is Inequality Harmful to Growth?" *American Economic Review* 84 (June): 600–621.

Pritchett, L. (1996). "Where Has All the Education Gone?" Washington, D.C.: The World Bank, Policy and Human Resources Division, Policy Research Working Paper 1581.

Rebelo, S. (1991). "Long Run Policy Analysis and Long Run Growth," *Journal of Political Economy* 99 (June): 500–21.

Rebelo, S. (1995). "On the Determinants of Economic Growth," World Congress of the IEA, Tunisia, December.

Rivera-Batiz, L., and P. Romer. (1991). "International Trade with Endogenous Technical Change," *European Economic Review* 35 (May): 971–1004.

Romer, P. M. (1986). "Increasing Returns and Long-Run Growth," *Journal of Political Economy* 94 (October): 1002–37.

Romer, P. M. (1990). "Endogenous Technological Change," *Journal of Political Economy* 98 (October) S71–S102.

Solow, R. M. (1956). "A Contribution to the Theory of Economic Growth," *Quarterly Journal of Economy* 70 (February): 65–94.

Solow, R. M. (2000). *Growth Theory: An Exposition.* (New York: Oxford University Press).

Stokey, N. (1988). "Learning by Doing and the Introduction of New Goods," *Journal of Political Economy* 96 (August): 701–17.

Stokey, N. (1991). "Human Capital, Product Quality and Growth," *Quarterly Journal of Economy* 106 (May): 587–617.

Uzawa, H. (1965). "Optimal Technical Change in an Aggregative Model of Economic Growth," *International Economic Review* 6 (January): 18–31.

Young, A. (1991). "Learning by Doing and the Dynamic Effects of International Trade," *Quarterly Journal of Economy* 106 (May): 396–405.

Young, A. (1992). "A Tale of Two Cities: Factor Accumulation and Technical Change in Hong Kong and Singapore." *NBER Macroeconomics Annual 1992.* Blanchard O. J. and S. Fischer (eds.), (Cambridge, MA: MIT Press), pp. 13–54.

Young, A. (1995). "The Tyranny of numbers: Confronting the Statistical Realities of the East Asian Growth Experience" *Quarterly Journal of Economy* 110 (August): 641–80.

PART FOUR

PUBLIC ECONOMICS

ELEVEN

Simulating Fundamental Tax Reform in the United States

David Altig, Alan J. Auerbach, Laurence J. Kotlikoff,
Kent A. Smetters, and Jan Walliser*

This paper uses a new, large-scale, dynamic life-cycle simulation model to compare the welfare and macroeconomic effects of transitions to five fundamental alternatives to the U.S. federal income tax, including a proportional consumption tax and a flat tax. The model incorporates intragenerational heterogeneity and a detailed specification of alternative tax systems. Simulation results project significant long-run increases in output for some reforms. For other reforms, namely those that seek to insulate the poor and initial older generations from adverse welfare changes, long-run output gains are modest.

Fundamental tax reform has been a hot issue, and for good reason. The U.S. tax system – a hybrid of income- and consumption-tax provisions – is complex, distortionary, and replete with tax preferences. Recent "reforms" of the tax code, including the Taxpayer Relief Act of 1997, have made the system even more complex and buttressed the argument for fundamental reform.

"Fundamental tax reform" means different things to different people. The definition adopted below is the simplification and integration of the tax code by eliminating tax preferences and taxing all sources of capital

* The views expressed here are those of the authors and do not necessarily reflect those of the Federal Reserve Bank of Cleveland, the IMF, or any other organization. We are grateful to Cristina DeNardi, Barbara Fried, Bill Gale, Jane Gravelle, participants in workshops at the University of Chicago, the NBER, the Federal Reserve Bank of Cleveland, Indiana University, and the Federal Reserve System Committee on Macroeconomics, and two anonymous referees for comments on earlier drafts. Auerbach thanks the Burch Center for Tax Policy and Public Finance and Kotlikoff thanks the National Institute of Aging and the Smith Richardson Foundation for research support.

income at the same rate. Several current tax proposals certainly deserve to be called "fundamental." They include Hall and Rabushka's (1983, 1995) flat tax, the retail sales tax, and Bradford's (1986) X tax. The flat tax and the retail sales tax are two alternative ways of taxing consumption. The X tax also taxes consumption, but places high-wage earners in higher tax brackets than low-wage earners. Another fundamental reform is to adopt a broad-based, low-rate income tax.

This paper uses a computable general equilibrium simulation model to compare the welfare and macroeconomic effects of fundamental tax reform. The model is a substantially enhanced version of the Auerbach–Kotlikoff (1987) dynamic life-cycle simulation model.[1] The new model follows the significant lead of Don Fullerton and Diane Lim Rogers (1993) in incorporating intra- as well as intergenerational inequality. Specifically, it includes 12 different groups within each cohort, each with its own earnings ability (its own endowment of human capital).

Our new model approximates U.S. fiscal institutions much more closely than does its predecessor. It includes an array of tax preferences, a progressive social security system, and a Medicare system. Including tax preferences is not only crucial for studying fundament tax reform. It also permits our use of actual tax schedules in calibrating the model.[2] Stated differently, omitting tax preferences would mean unrealistically low tax rates since the current federal income tax covers only 57% of national income.[3] The improved modeling of Social Security and Medicare is also vital, because both programs materially alter the intergenerational and intragenerational distributions of welfare and the initial set of fiscal distortions from which tax reform proceeds.

Like Auerbach and Kotlikoff (1987), we compute the economy's perfect foresight transition path. Given the magnitude of factor-price and tax-rate changes along our simulated transition paths, permitting agents to think rationally about the future is of great importance. This and other advantages vis a vis the Fullerton–Rogers (1993) model, which assumes myopic expectations, must be set against some disadvantages. Our model has a simpler production and preference structure than does the Fullerton–Rogers model, which features multiple consumption and

---

[1] A similar model, used to consider only steady states, is presented in Altig and Carlstrom (1999).

[2] The Fullerton–Rogers model, in contrast, assumes that all agents face the same marginal tax rate independent of income.

[3] See Congressional Budget Office (CBO 1997).

capital goods, intermediate inputs, and industry-specific capital income taxation. As such, it cannot measure the efficiency gains from the removal of inter-sectoral and inter-asset distortions. Nor does it incorporate the externalities present in endogenous growth models, which might provide another source of efficiency gains from tax reform (e.g., Stokey and Rebelo 1995).

Our model also omits the impact on labor supply of low-income programs such as the Earned Income Tax Credit, and several influences on saving, including earnings and lifespan uncertainty, transfer program asset tests, and liquidity constraints. The impact of these factors has been evaluated in simulation studies by Glenn Hubbard and Kenneth Judd (1987), Hubbard et al. (1995), and Eric Engen and William Gale (1996). The low intertemporal elasticity of substitution used in our simulations is, in part, a reflection of the fact that not all saving is driven by standard life-cycle concerns. However, the lack of a richer model should be borne in mind in assessing our findings.

We use our model to examine five fundamental tax reforms that span the major proposals currently under discussion. Each reform we consider replaces the federal personal and corporate income taxes in a revenue-neutral manner.[4] The reforms are a proportional income tax, a proportional consumption tax, a flat tax, a flat tax with transition relief, and the X tax.

The proportional income tax applies a single tax rate to all labor and capital income, with no exemptions or deductions. The proportional consumption tax differs from the proportional income tax by permitting 100% expensing of new investment. One may think of it as being implemented via a wage tax at the household level plus a business cash-flow tax. The flat tax differs from the proportional consumption tax by including a standard deduction against wage income and by exempting implicit rental income accruing from the ownership of housing and consumer durables. The remaining two proposals modify the flat tax to address distributional concerns. The flat tax with transition relief aids existing asset holders by permitting continued depreciation of old capital (capital in existence at the commencement of the reform). The X tax aids lower income taxpayers by substituting the flat tax's single-rate wage tax with a progressive wage tax. To recoup the lost revenue, its sets the business cash-flow tax

---

[4] To be precise, in each tax reform simulation the levels of government purchases and outstanding debt are held constant through time when measured in effective units of labor.

rate equal to the highest tax rate applied to wage income. Alternatively, one can think of the X tax as a high rate flat tax with a progressive subsidy to wages.

Each of the reforms broadens the tax base, permitting reductions in statutory marginal tax rates on labor supply and saving. And each reform imposes an implicit tax on existing wealth by introducing full expensing and, thus, shifting the tax structure toward consumption taxation. The expensing of new capital effectively eliminates the taxation of capital income at the margin. However, unlike the simple elimination of capital income taxes, this tax reduction is available to new capital only, and, consequently, reduces the value of existing capital relative to that of new capital in a manner equivalent to that of a one-time tax on their wealth. As discussed in Auerbach and Kotlikoff (1987), this capital levy is crucial to both the efficiency and long-run welfare gains from switching to consumption taxation. It permits a permanent reduction in distortionary marginal tax rates and shifts the burden of paying for government spending from young and future generations to middle-age and older initial wealth owners.

As indicated, the five reforms differ in the treatment of marginal and inframarginal capital income, the extent of base-broadening, and progressivity. These differences translate into different income and substitution effects on consumption and labor supply, which, in turn, generate the different responses to the five policies. These responses depend on our choices of parameter values. In our base case results we find the following:

The proportional income tax raises the long-run level of output by almost 5%. It also generates sizable increases in the capital stock and the supply of labor. However, the reform hurts the poor, who face low effective rates of income taxation under the current federal income tax system due to its deductions and exemptions. The proportional consumption tax raises long-run output by over 9%. The implicit wealth tax generated by this reform reduces the welfare of the initial middle aged and elderly. They respond to this and the increase in after-tax interest rates by consuming less and working more, which raises national saving and investment. The expanded capital stock and reduced fiscal burden make most of those alive in the long run significantly better off. However, eliminating tax progressivity lowers the welfare of the poorest members of society.

The flat tax's standard deduction alleviates some of the distributional concerns raised by the proportional income and proportional consumption taxes. But this deduction increases the tax rate needed to satisfy the government's intertemporal budget constraint. Consequently, long-run output rises by less than 5%. Although the flat tax's standard deduction insulates the poor from welfare losses, it hurts middle-income groups, especially in the short run but even in the long run. Its capital levy also hurts initial high-income elderly cohorts. Those welfare losses must be set against the welfare gains enjoyed by all groups in the long run.

Adding transition relief to the flat tax limits the welfare losses of initial capital owners. But this modification of the flat tax reduces aggregate income gains again, with long-run output now rising by less than 2%. Furthermore, because replacement tax rates must increase to compensate for the lost revenue associated with transition relief, all but the richest and poorest lifetime-income groups suffer welfare losses in the long run. The X tax, which raises long-term output by 6.4%, provides no transition relief. It also confronts the rich with higher effective tax rates on their labor supply. It is not surprising, then, that the X tax helps those who are poor in the long run by more than it helps those who are rich. Still, all long-run cohorts gain.

Thus, fundamental reform of the U.S. tax system offers significant long-run gains in output and general welfare, but these gains come at the expense of certain groups. Modifications that mitigate adverse transition and distributional effects also substantially reduce the long-run gains. In considering the plausibility of the results, one should bear in mind that these changes are generally much more radical than any U.S. fiscal policy change enacted in recent memory. Moreover, the structure of economic incentives and the distribution of resources are being altered in two ways – by the policies themselves and by their general equilibrium impacts on the time paths of factor prices. Hence, simple intuition about the expected magnitude of individual responses is difficult to apply to the reforms being considered.

1. The Model

1.1. Demographic Structure

The model's agents differ by their dates of birth and their lifetime labor-productivity endowments. Every cohort includes 12 lifetime-earnings groups, each with its own endowment of human capital and pattern of growth in this endowment over its lifetime. The lifetime-earnings groups also differ with respect to their bequest preferences. All agents live for 55 periods with certainty (corresponding to adult ages 21 through 75), and each j-type generation is $1 + n$ times larger than its predecessor. At age 21, each j-type cohort gives birth to a cohort of the same type. Population growth is exogenous, and each cohort is $(1+n)^{20}$ larger than its parent cohort.

1.2. Preferences and Household Budget Constraints

Each j-type agent who begins her economic life at date t chooses perfect-foresight consumption paths (c), leisure paths (l), and intergenerational transfers (b) to maximize a time-separable utility function of the form

$$U_t^j = \frac{1}{1-\frac{1}{\gamma}} \left[\sum_{s=21}^{75} \beta^{s-21} \left(c_{s,t+s-21}^{j\,1-\frac{1}{\rho}} + al_{s,t+s-21}^{j\,1-\frac{1}{\rho}} \right)^{\frac{1-\frac{1}{\gamma}}{1-\frac{1}{\rho}}} + \beta^{54} \mu^j b_{75,t+54}^{j\,1-\frac{1}{\gamma}} \right].$$

(1)

In (1), a is the utility weight on leisure, γ is the intertemporal elasticity of substitution in the leisure/consumption composite, and ρ is the intratemporal elasticity of substitution between consumption and leisure. The parameter μ^j is a j-type specific utility weight placed on bequests left to each child when the agent dies, representing a "joy of giving" bequest motive, a formulation of bequest preferences studied by Alan Blinder (1973) and others. The term $\beta = 1/(1+\delta)$, where δ is the rate of time preference, is assumed to be the same for all agents.[5]

Letting $a_{s,t}^j$ be capital holdings for type j agents, of age s, at time t, maximization of (1) is subject to a lifetime budget constraint defined by the sequence:

$$a_{s+1,t+1}^j = (1+r_t)(a_{s,t}^j + g_{s,t}^j) + w_{s,t}^j(E_{s,t}^j - l_{s,t}^j) - c_{s,t}^j$$

$$- \sum_{k=1}^K T^k(B_{s,t}^{j,k}) - Nb_{s,t}^j,$$

$$l_{s,t}^j \le E_{s,t}^j,$$

(2)

and

$$a_{75,t}^j \ge 0,$$

where r_t is the pretax return to savings, $g_{s,t}^j$ are gifts received from parents, $E_{s,t}^j$ is the time endowment, $b_{s,t}^j$ are bequests made to each of the $N = (1+n)^{20}$ children, and the functions $T^k(\cdot)$ (with tax bases $B_{s,t}^{j,k}$ as arguments) determine net tax payments from income sources $K = 1, \ldots, K$. All taxes are collected at the household level, and the tax system includes

---

[5] The relationship between γ, ρ, and the elasticity of labor supply with respect to the current wage is discussed in the Appendix.

both a personal income tax and a business profits tax. There are no liquidity constraints, so the assets in (2) can be negative, although terminal wealth – the wealth left over after final period bequests are made – must be nonnegative.

An individual's earnings ability is an exogenous function of age, type, and the level of labor-augmenting technical progress, which grows at a constant rate λ. We summarize all skill differences by age and type via an efficiency parameter ε_s^j. Thus, the wage rate for an agent of type j and age s is $w_{s,t}^j = \varepsilon_s^j w_t$, where w_t is the real wage at time t. The term ε_s^j increases with age to reflect not only the accumulation of human capital, but also the technical progress that occurs over the course of each individual's life; that is, the values of ε_s^j are set to establish a realistic longitudinal age–wage profile. To permit balanced growth without a further restriction of preferences (i.e., to keep the ratio of labor supply to labor endowment constant in the steady state), we model the growth in lifetime wages from one generation to the next as growth in time endowment rather than in the wage rate per unit of time; that is, we assume that technical progress causes the time endowment of each successive generation to grow at rate λ.[6] Thus, if $E_{s,t}^j$ is the endowment of type j at age s and time t, then $E_{s,t}^j = (1 + \lambda) E_{s,t-1}^j$, for all s, t, and j. Because E grows at rate λ from one cohort to the next, technical progress imparts no underlying trend to w_t.

Children receive transfers, with interest, at the beginning of the period after their parents make them. We restrict parental transfers to bequests, so that $b_{s,t}^j = 0$, for $s \neq 75$, and $g_{s,t}^j = 0$, for $s \neq 56$. In the steady state, therefore, $g^j = b^j$, for all j (with age subscripts dropped for convenience).

1.3. The Government
At each time t, the government collects tax revenues and issues debt (D_{t+1}) that it uses to finance government purchases of goods and services (G_t) and interest payments on the inherited stock of debt (D_t). Letting φ^j stand for the fraction of j-type agents in each generation, the government's official debt evolves according to:

$$D_{t+1} + (1+n)^t \sum_{j=1}^{12} \varphi^j \sum_{s=21}^{75} (1+n)^{-(s-21)} \sum_{k=1}^{K} T^k\left(B_{s,t}^{j,k}\right)$$
$$= G_t + (1+r_t)D_t. \tag{3}$$

---

[6] Both of these adjustments, to the slope of the wage profile and to the time endowment, are needed to incorporate the impact of technical progress on wage growth, the former because we assume that each cohort's time endowment is fixed at birth. See Auerbach et al. (1989) for a detailed discussion of this approach.

Government purchases are assumed to be either a) unproductive and generate no utility to households or b) be fixed and enter household utility functions in a separable fashion. The values of G_t and D_t are held fixed per effective worker throughout the transition path. Any reduction in government outlays resulting from a change in the government's real interest payments is passed on to households in the form of a lower tax rate.

The model also has a social security system that incorporates Old-Age and Survivors Insurance (OASI), Disability Insurance (DI), and Medicare's Hospital Insurance (HI). Old-age benefits are calculated according to the progressive statutory bend-point formula. Disability and Medicare benefits are provided as lump-sum transfers. The OASI payroll tax is set at 9.9% and applied to wage income up to a limit of $62,700. HI and DI tax rates are set at 2.9% and 1.9%, respectively. Like the OASI tax, DI contributions apply only to wages below $62,700. The HI tax, by contrast, is not subject to an earnings ceiling.

Benefits are scaled to reflect spousal and survivor benefits using distributional information provided in the 1997 OASDI Trustees Report. We set the perceived marginal link between the OASI contributions and the OASI benefits at 25%. The perceived effective OASI tax rate is, thus, 7.4% – 75% of 9.9%.[7] Lump-sum HI and DI benefits are provided on an equal basis to agents above and below age 65, respectively.

1.4. Firms and Technology

Aggregate capital (K) and labor (L) equal the respective sums of individual asset and labor supplies as indicated in Equations (4) and (5).

$$K_t = (1+n)^t \sum_{j=1}^{12} \varphi^j \sum_{s=21}^{75} (1+n)^{-(s-21)} a_{s,t}^j - D_t, \qquad (4)$$

$$L_t = (1+n)^t \sum_{j=1}^{12} \varphi^j \sum_{s=21}^{75} (1+n)^{-(s-21)} \varepsilon_s^j \left(E_{s,t}^j - l_{s,t}^j \right). \qquad (5)$$

Output (net of depreciation) is produced by identical competitive firms using a neoclassical, constant-returns-to-scale production technology. In the base case, the aggregate production technology is the standard Cobb–Douglas form:

$$Y_t = A K_t^\theta L_t^{1-\theta}, \qquad (6)$$

---

[7] See chapter 10 of Auerbach and Kotlikoff (1987) for a more detailed discussion.

where Y_t is aggregate output (national income) and θ is capital's share in production. However, in later simulations, we do consider the impact of a lower elasticity of substitution in production, σ, using a constant elasticity of substitution (CES) function.

Another important aspect of the production technology in our base case is the assumption that it is costly to adjust the capital stock. Tax reforms, particularly those that eliminate the marginal tax on capital income, can induce large increases in demand for capital. The extent to which increased demand translates into more investment, rather than higher asset values, affects both the efficiency of the tax reform and its distributional consequences. We model adjustment costs as convex, indeed as a simple quadratic function of investment:

$$C(I_t) = [1 + 0.5\psi(I_t/K_t)]I_t \tag{7}$$

with the quadratic term ψ equal to 10, a value consistent with the recent results of Cummins et al. (1994). With convex adjustment costs, investors will be induced to smooth out increases in investment, and the shadow price of new capital goods relative to their replacement cost – Tobin's q – will move in the same direction as investment.[8]

The competitive pretax, preexpensing rate of return to capital at time t is given by the marginal product of capital (defined in terms of the capital-labor ratio, κ)

$$R_t = \theta A \kappa_t^{\theta-1}. \tag{8}$$

In general, tax systems treat new and existing capital differently. Under the consumption tax, new capital is permitted immediate expensing, while existing capital receives no such deduction. Even under the existing income tax, the combined effect of accelerated depreciation and the lack of inflation indexing makes the depreciation allowances per unit of existing capital lower than those given new capital. We model provisions that treat new and existing capital differently using the mechanism of fractional expensing of new capital, at rate z. That is, we set z to account for the extent to which new capital faces a lower effective tax rate than

---

[8] The restriction of our model to a single composite capital good means that we are unable to study the differential revaluation of housing, equipment, plant, inventories, and other forms of capital arising from tax reforms. The fact that the market values of particular capital goods may change to a greater degree than those of others means that we may be under- or overstating saving and labor supply responses to tax reforms, particularly if different capital goods are disproportionately held by particular age groups and particular income classes within those age groups.

does existing capital (with $z = 1$ under the consumption tax). If τ_t^K is the time-t marginal tax rate on net capital income (i.e., the tax rate applied to capital income net of expensing) then, given (7), arbitrage between new and existing capital implies that the latter has a unit value of

$$q_t = \left(1 - z_t \tau_t^K\right) + \left(1 - \tau_t^K\right)\psi(I_t/K_t), \tag{9}$$

assuming that adjustment costs are expensed. q_t equals Tobin's q. Note that q depends not only on the strength of demand for new capital (via the second term), but also on the relative treatment of old and new capital. Tax reforms typically affect both of these terms.

The arbitrage condition arising from profit maximization implies that the posttax return is:

$$\tilde{r}_t = \frac{\left(R_t + 0.5\psi(I_t/K_t)^2\right)\left(1 - \tau_t^K\right) + q_{t+1} - q_t}{q_t}. \tag{10}$$

In (10), the total return to capital includes its after-tax marginal product[9] plus capital gains.

2. Calibration

Much of our model's parameterization is relatively standard. Exceptions include earnings-ability profiles and the fiscal structure. We turn first to these elements and then discuss more familiar preference and technology parameters. Table 11.1 summarizes our selected parameters.

2.1. Earnings Ability Profiles
The growth-adjusted earnings ability profiles in Equation (5) are of the form:

$$\varepsilon_s^j = e^{\xi_0^j + (\lambda + \xi_1^j)s + \xi_2^j s^2 + \xi_3^j s^3} \tag{11}$$

where, as discussed above, λ is the constant rate of technical progress. Values of the ξ coefficients for j-type groups 1 through 12 – in ascending order of lifetime income – are based on regressions fitted to the University of Michigan's Panel Study of Income Dynamics, using a strategy similar to that in Fullerton and Rogers (1993). The procedure involves (i) regressing the log of hourly wages on fixed-effect dummies, cubics in

---

[9] This equals R_t, as defined in (8), plus the reduction in proportional adjustment costs due the increase in the capital stock. See Auerbach (1989) for a derivation of Equations (9) and (10).

Table 11.1. *Benchmark Parameter Definitions and Values*

Symbol	Definition	Value
Preferences		
α	Utility weight on leisure	1.00
δ	Rate of time preference	0.004
γ	Intertemporal substitution elasticity	0.25
μ^j	Utility weight placed on bequests by income class j[1]	
ρ	Intratemporal substitution elasticity	0.80
Human capital		
ε_s^j	Productivity of agent in income class j at age s.	
Demographics		
n	Population growth	0.01
N	Number of children per adult, $(1+n)^{20}$	1.22
φ^j	Fraction of agents of income class j[2]	
Technology		
λ	Rate of technological change	0.01
ψ	Adjustment cost parameter	10
θ	Net capital share	0.25
σ	Constant elasticity of substitution	1.00
Values of fiscal variables in initial steady state		
—	Debt service as fraction of National Income	0.0310
—	Disability Insurance tax rate	0.0190
—	Medicare (HI) tax rate	0.0290
—	Social Security (OASI) tax rate	0.0990
—	Social Security replacement rate[3]	
—	Social Security marginal tax-benefit linkage	0.25
—	Payroll tax ceiling	$62,700
τ^C	Proportional consumption tax	0.113
τ^K	Proportional capital income tax	0.20
$\tau^W(\cdot)$	Progressive wage tax with deductions & exemptions[4]	
τ^Y	State proportional income tax less evasion adjustment	0.011
—	Reduction of wage base from itemized deductions[5]	0.0755
—	Reduction of wage base from fringe benefits[5]	0.1129
z	Expensing fraction[6]	0.20

[1] Calibrated in the initial state to match the level of bequests – as a fraction of mean national income – in Fullerton and Rogers (1993, Table 3–8), in 1996 dollars.

[2] $\varphi^1 = 0.02$, $\varphi^2 = 0.08$, $\varphi^i = 0.10$ ($3 \leq i \leq 10$), $\varphi^{11} = 0.08$, $\varphi^{12} = 0.02$.

[3] The statutory progressive bendpoint formula for 1996, scaled up by a factor of 2 to account for the fact that other non-DI benefits (mainly spousal and survivors benefits) account for 50% of all benefits paid (see 1996 OASDI Trustees Report, Table II.C7).

[4] The 1996 statutory tax function for a single individual with a deduction equal to $9,661 ($4,000 standard deduction, $2,550 personal exemption and $2,550·$N$ exemption for dependents).

[5] Total proportional base reduction above the standard deduction therefore equals 0.18845.

[6] Deductions for new investment above economic depreciation and adjustment costs.

age, and interactions between age, age-squared, and a set of demographic variables; (ii) using the estimated coefficients from step (i) to generate predicted lifetime wage profiles; (iii) sorting the data according to the present value of implied lifetime income, and dividing the sorted data into the 12 classes according to lifetime wage income; and (iv) estimating the coefficients of (11) from the simulated data profiles of each of the 12 groups.

In sorting the data for steps (iii) and (iv), we divided the population into deciles. Groups 1 and 12 comprise the bottom and top 2% of lifetime wage income earners, and groups 2 and 11 the remaining 8% of the top and bottom deciles. Each other group constitutes 10% of the population. For example, group 3 is the second decile of lifetime wage income, group four the third decile, and so on up to group 10.[10]

Figure 11.1 presents the estimated earnings ability profiles, scaled to include the effects of technical progress. Given our benchmark parameterization, peak hourly wages valued in 1996 dollars are $4.00, $14.70, and $79.50 for individuals in classes 1, 6, and 12, respectively. More generally, steady-state annual labor incomes derived from the model's assumptions and from the endogenous labor supply choices range from $9,000 to $130,000. As discussed below, these calculations include labor compensation in the form of fringe benefits.

2.2. Fiscal Structure

The model includes government purchases of goods and services, government debt, and distortionary taxes. The level of government purchases, G_t, was chosen so that the benchmark steady-state ratio of government purchases to national income equals 0.211. The level of government debt, D_t, was chosen such that the associated real interest payments equal about 3.1% of national income in the initial steady state. These values match the corresponding 1996 values for combined local, state, and federal government in the United States.

The benchmark tax system in our initial steady state is designed to approximate the salient aspects of the 1996 U.S. (federal, state, and local) tax and transfer system. It features a hybrid tax system (incorporating wage income, capital income, and consumption tax elements) and payroll taxation for the social security and Medicare programs.[11] To adjust for tax

---

[10] This procedure is described more fully in the Appendix.

[11] As the payroll tax in our model is used entirely to pay for current benefits, we set the rate slightly below its 15.3% statutory rate to account for the portion of payroll taxes devoted to trust-fund accumulation. See Table 11.2.

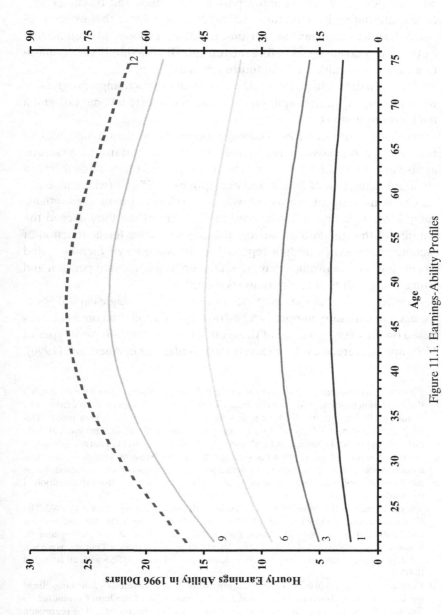

Figure 11.1. Earnings-Ability Profiles

evasion, we reduce income taxes by 2.6%. This adjustment is consistent with the degree of tax evasion reported in Slemrod and Bakija (1996). In the alternative tax structure experiments we assume that evasion reduces the postreform tax base (income net of deductions and exemptions) by the same percentage as before the reform. This is a simplifying assumption that merits exploration in future research.

We approximate the current U.S. tax system by specifying a progressive wage income tax, a flat capital income tax, a flat state income tax, and a flat consumption tax.

WAGE INCOME TAXATION. The wage income tax structure has four elements: 1) a progressive marginal rate structure derived from a quadratic approximation to the 1996 federal statutory tax rates for individuals[12]; 2) a standard deduction of $4,000 and exemptions of $5,660 (which assumes 1.2 children per agent, consistent with the model's population growth assumption); 3) itemized deductions, applied only when they exceed the amount of the standard deduction, that are a positive linear function of income estimated from data reported in the *Statistics of Income*[13]; and 4) earnings ability profiles that are scaled up to incorporate pension and fringe components of labor compensation.[14]

CAPITAL INCOME TAXATION. Since our model has a single capital good, we need to calibrate marginal and inframarginal capital income tax rates based on the average values of these rates taken across different types of U.S. capital. Here, we follow closely the calculations in Auerbach (1996),

---

[12] We use a quadratic approximation rather than the exact, discrete brackets to simplify the simulation problem. Using a differentiable tax function allows us to derive first-order conditions that do not involve kink points and shadow wages at these kink points. This simplification is particularly relevant because our household decision problem already has a kink point at the minimum taxable income level, and a potential corner solution at zero hours worked, both of which involve the calculation of shadow wage rates, as well as a nonconvexity at the point where the social security earnings ceiling is reached. These additional complications are discussed below in the section that discusses the solution of the model.

[13] The data used in this estimation were taken from all taxable returns in tax year 1993. The function was obtained by regressing deductions exclusive of mortgage interest expense on the midpoints of reported income ranges. (The deduction of interest expense on home mortgages was included in our calculation of the capital income tax rate, as we will subsequently describe.) The regression yielded a coefficient of 0.0755 with an R^2 equal to 0.99.

[14] Benefits as a function of adjusted gross income were kindly provided by Jane Gravelle of the Congressional Research Service and Judy Xanthopoulos of the Joint Committee on Taxation. Based on this information we regressed total benefits on AGI. The regression yielded a coefficient of 0.11295 with an R^2 equal to 0.99. In defining the wage-tax base, we therefore exempt roughly 11% of labor compensation from the base calculations.

who reports that income from residential capital and nonresidential capital are taxed at flat rates of 6% and 26%, respectively. Given that the U.S. capital stock is split evenly between these two forms of capital, the weighted average federal marginal tax rate on total capital income is about 16%. Because of the difference in treatment of new and existing capital, primarily in the nonresidential sector, U.S. capital faces a higher tax rate – roughly 20% for the capital stock as a whole, according to Auerbach's estimates. To incorporate these tax rates in our model, we assume that all capital income faces a 20% tax, but that 20% of new capital is expensed, thereby generating a 16% effective rate on new capital.[15] In addition to the federal taxation, both capital and wage income are subject to a proportional state income tax of 3.7%.

CONSUMPTION TAXATION. Consumption taxes in the initial steady state reflect two elements of the existing tax structure. First we impose an 8.8% tax on consumption expenditures, consistent with National Income and Product Account values for indirect business and excise revenues, a substantial component of which are state sales taxes. However, because contributions to both defined benefit and defined contribution pension plans receive consumption tax treatment, we add an additional 2.5% tax on household consumption expenditures to account for the indirect taxation of labor compensation in the form of pension benefits (Auerbach 1996). This 2.5% tax replaces the wage tax that otherwise would apply if pension contributions were taxed as income.

2.3. Preferences and Technology

Our initial choices for the remaining technology, preference, and demographic parameters are summarized in Table 11.1. The value for δ, the pure rate of time preference – about which there is little evidence – is set equal to .004 to generate a realistic value for the capital-output ratio in the initial steady state. The values of γ, ρ, and n are those in Auerbach and Kotlikoff (1987). The intertemporal elasticity, γ, is set equal to .25, representing a relatively low degree of substitution between consumption at different dates. While some studies in the literature have found higher elasticities, most have not. One possible reason is the presence of liquidity constraints and other factors that may mitigate the responsiveness of

---

[15] The absence in our model of heterogenous capital goods means that we not only fail to capture the differential revaluation of different capital goods, but we also fail to capture the additional efficiency gains that may arise from equalizing effective tax rates on different capital inputs, an issue studied by Fullerton and Rogers (1993) and others.

saving to interest rate changes. Our use of a low intertemporal elasticity of substitution serves as an imperfect proxy for such factors.

We choose α, the utility function's leisure intensity parameter, such that, on average, agents devote about 40% of their available time endowment (of 16 hours per day) to labor during their prime working years (roughly ages 21–55). As discussed in the Appendix, the combined values of γ, ρ (the intratemporal elasticity of substitution), and α generate labor supply elasticities that are well within the range of empirical estimates. Still, as this range is fairly large, we also report results for values of γ and ρ that induce smaller behavioral responses. The bequest weights in the utility function, μ^j, are chosen to match bequests as a fraction of income in the initial steady state based on estimates by Menchik and David (1982) reported in Fullerton and Rogers (1993).

2.4. Solving the Model

Following Auerbach and Kotlikoff (1987), we solve the model with a Gauss–Seidel algorithm. The calculation starts with guesses for certain key variables and then iterates on those variables until a convergence criterion is met. The model's identifying restrictions are used to compute the remaining economic variables as well as the updates for the iterations. The solution involves several steps and inner loops that solve for household-level variables before moving to an outer loop that solves for the aggregate variables including the time paths of capital stock and aggregate labor supply.

The household optimization problem is subject to the constraint that leisure not exceed the endowment of time (Equation 2). For those households who would violate the constraint, the model calculates shadow wage rates at which they exactly consume their full-time endowment. The household's budget constraint is kinked due to the tax deductions applied against wage income under the personal income tax. A household with wage income below the deduction level faces marginal and average tax rates equal to zero. A household with wage income above the deduction level faces positive marginal and average tax rates. Due to the discontinuity of the marginal tax rates, it may be optimal for some households to locate exactly at the kink. Our algorithm deals with this problem as follows. We identify a household that chooses to locate at the kink in particular periods by evaluating each period's leisure choice and corresponding wage income above and below the kink. We then calculate a set of period-specific shadow marginal tax rates from the period-specific first-order conditions that put such households exactly at kinks in each period in which being at a kink is optimal. This calculation of shadow tax rates for particular periods is simultaneous; i.e., a shadow tax rate in any particular period will influence labor supply decisions in all other periods. The payroll tax ceiling introduces additional complexity by creating a nonconvexity in the budget constraint. For those above the payroll tax ceiling, the marginal payroll tax rate on labor earnings is zero. For each period, we evaluate the utility on both sides of the nonconvex section and put households on the side that generates highest utility.

Aggregate variables of the model are solved with a forward-looking algorithm that iterates on the capital stock and labor supply over the entire transition path. Initial guesses are made for a) the time path of aggregate demands for capital and labor, b) each household's shadow wage and tax rates at each age, and c) the endogenous tax rate (for which the program is solving), the payroll tax rate, and social security and Medicare benefit levels. Given the initial guesses of the time paths of all these variables, the model calculates a) the factor prices in each period that are consistent with the use by firms of the aggregate inputs assumed to be demanded and b) the remaining lifetime consumption and leisure choices for all income classes in each current and future cohort. Shadow wages and shadow taxes are calculated to ensure that the time endowment and the tax constraints discussed above are satisfied. Households' labor supply and assets are then aggregated across cohorts and, within cohort, across lifetime income classes for each period. This aggregation generates a new guess for the time paths of the aggregate supplies of capital stock and labor supply.

In equilibrium, the factor supply time paths for capital and labor must equal their corresponding factor demand time paths. Hence, to form a new guess of the time paths of aggregate factor demands we form weighted averages of the initial guess and the supply time paths derived using the previous guess of the time path of factor demands. The time paths of the tax rate for which we are solving and the payroll tax rate are also updated to meet the revenue-neutrality requirement and to preserve the pay-as-you-go financing of Social Security and Medicare benefits.[16] The algorithm then iterates in this manner until the capital stock and labor supply time-paths converge; i.e., until the time paths of factors demanded are consistent with the time paths of factors supplied.

---

[16] Note that the social security replacement rate and absolute level of Medicare benefits are exogenous.

2.5. The Benchmark Equilibrium

Table 11.2 provides summary statistics for the initial steady state. Given our parameter choices, the model generates a pretax, preexpensing interest rate of 8.3%[17], a net national saving rate of 5.1%, and a capital/national income ratio of 2.6. Consumption accounts for 73.1% of national income, net investment for 5.1%, and government purchases of goods and services for 21.1%. These figures are close to their respective 1996 NIPA values.

The calibrated model's initial economy-wide average marginal tax rate on wage income is 21.6%, close to the figure obtained from the NBER's TAXSIM model reported in Auerbach (1996). The average wage income tax rate equals 12.2%. For all individuals in the highest lifetime income class (group 12), the average effective marginal tax rate on labor income is 29.2%. The highest realized effective marginal tax rate is 34.9%. For lifetime income class 6 – whose members have peak labor earnings of about $35,000 – the average tax rate and average marginal tax rate are 10.7% and 20.0%, respectively. For the poorest class (group 1), the corresponding rates are zero and 11.1%.[18]

In this initial steady state, bequest wealth (the accumulated value of inheritances received summed over all households) depends on the age structure of bequest receipt. Our assumption that individuals receive bequests at age 56 is made primarily for simplicity.[19] With this assumption, and our calibration of bequests themselves to the data cited earlier, bequest wealth represents 30% of the capital stock. This percentage is smaller than that reported for 1974 for overall transfer wealth by Kotlikoff and Summers (1981). The percentage would, presumably, be larger had we assumed an earlier age of bequest receipt, but still is in rough agreement

---

[17] This number is somewhat lower than the estimated 1996 return to capital relative to replacement cost of 9.3% listed in Table 11.2. In our model with nonzero adjustment costs, the before-tax interest rate determined by expressions (9) and (10) differs from the return to capital, because market value differs slightly from replacement cost (see (9)) and because the total return to capital accounted for by the interest rate also includes the reduction in adjustment costs brought about by additions to capital (see the numerator in (10)). Ignoring these two terms, the return to capital itself, equal to the term R in (8), is 9.7%.

[18] The average marginal rate for people with the lowest income exceeds zero due to positive shadow tax rates in peak earnings years.

[19] See Gale and Scholz (1994) for a discussion of the relative magnitudes of bequests and *inter vivos* transfers. While our choice of age 56 to receive inheritance seems reasonable, different ages could certainly be considered. However, each age of inheritance would alter the stock of inherited wealth and thus the economy-wide capital-output ratio. As this, in turn, would necessitate a recalibration of bequest preference parameters, the ultimate impact on our results would likely be small.

Table 11.2. *Key Variables in the Initial Steady-State and U.S. Data*

Model		Empirical Estimate and Calculation	
Concept	Value	Estimate	Calculation (using NIPA unless indicated)
Composition of National Income (fraction)			
Personal consumption	0.731	0.720	Personal consumption expenditures − housing services
Net saving rate	0.051	0.056	(National saving − capital consumption allowance)/NI
Government purchases	0.211	0.212	Consumption expenditures + gross investment for federal (defense and nondefense) and state and local − consumption of fixed capital
Tax Rates and Revenue			
Avg. marginal wage tax[1]	0.216	0.217	Auerbach (1996) based on the NBER TAXSIM model.
Government revenue	0.239	0.239	Total receipts − contributions for social insurance − property taxes (state and local)
OASDHI tax	0.146	0.147	1996 tax rate is 15.3 which includes trust fund contributions equal to about 0.6.
The Capital-Output Ratio and the Pretax Rate of Return			
Capital-Output Ratio	2.562	2.660	(1993 current-cost net stock of fixed reproducible wealth − govt. owned fixed capital) / 1993 National Income
Pretax rate of return[2]	0.083	0.093	The 1960–94 average of the sum of interest, dividends, retained earnings and all corporate taxes divided by the replacement value of capital stock (Rippe, 1995).

[1] Does not include the payroll tax.
[2] The social marginal rate of return (i.e., before corporate taxes).

with the Kotlikoff–Summers findings concerning the amount of wealth generated solely by bequests as opposed to *inter vivos* transfers, which we do not model explicitly. That said, the importance of bequests and *inter vivos* transfers for U.S. capital formation appears to have diminished through time because of the remarkable increase in recent decades in the degree of annuitization of the elderly (see Auerbach et al. 1995).

3. Initial Tax Reform Simulations

Table 11.3 summarizes the five tax reforms. Table 11.4 presents simulations for all five reforms for the base case assumptions. In each of these simulations, our initial steady state is the same, calibrated to the 1996 U.S. economy as described above. Table 11.4 also presents variables of interest for this initial steady state and for three transition years, 1997, 2010, and 2145, meant to illustrate short-run, medium-run and long-run effects. Subsequent tables, described in the next section, present the results of sensitivity analysis involving preference and technology parameters.

3.1. A Proportional Income Tax

Our first experiment replaces the progressive tax on wage income and the proportional tax on capital income with a proportional tax applied to all income. In addition, the proportional income tax eliminates the major preferences in the federal income tax, including the standard deduction, personal and dependent exemptions, itemized deductions, and the preferential tax treatment of fringe benefits. The last of these is implemented by decreasing the consumption tax rate by 0.025 and subjecting all compensation to the new proportional income tax. The investment expensing rate remains at its initial 20% level.

The first panel in Table 11.4 summarizes the aggregate results from this reform. The marginal tax rates required to satisfy the government's budget constraint stay close to 13% over the entire transition path. This value lies far below both the 21.6% average marginal rate applied to labor income and the 16% rate applied to capital income in the benchmark steady state. National income rises by 3.8% immediately and by 4.9% ultimately. In the early years of the transition, these output changes are dominated by increased work effort associated with the lower marginal tax rates. In the long run, higher wealth levels mitigate some of the increase in labor supply. However, the accumulated effects on the stock of capital from the reform more than compensate for the reduced labor supply: in the long run the capital stock increases by 5.6%. The short-run decrease in the

Table 11.3. *Key Elements of Tax Reform Experiments*

Experiment	Description

Proportional Income Tax	Eliminate all tax base reductions
	    Eliminate the standard deduction, personal exemption, exemptions for dependents, itemized deductions, preferential tax treatment of all fringe benefits (the consumption tax treatment of pension and the deductibility of nonpension benefits), and the deductibility of state income taxes at the federal level.[1]
	Flattening of tax rates
	    Replace progressive wage tax and proportional capital income tax with a proportional equal tax rate on wage and capital income. Eliminate double taxation of capital income.

Proportional Consumption Tax	Eliminate all tax base reductions Flattening of tax rates Full expensing Allow the deductibility of all new investment.

Standard Flat Tax	Eliminate all tax base reductions
	Flattening of tax rates
	Full expensing
	Protection of housing wealth
	    Housing (including consumer durables) remain untaxed.[2]
	Standard deduction
	    Allow for a deduction for a single individual equal to $9,500.

Flat Tax with Transition Relief	Eliminate all tax base reductions Flattening of tax rates Full expensing Protection of housing wealth Standard deduction Transition relief All existing assets continue to receive depreciation allowances.[3]
X Tax	Eliminate all tax base reductions Preserve current-law progressive wage tax[4] Capital income tax set at highest marginal wage tax rate Full expensing Protection of housing wealth[5]

[1] Consumption tax treatment of pensions is eliminated by decreasing the consumption tax by 0.025 and subjecting all compensation to the new proportional income tax.

[2] About 50% of the capital stock is composed of housing and consumer durables whose imputed rent is not taxed. Hence, the proportional tax rate on capital income is set to half of the tax rate on wage income.

[3] As noted in Auerbach (1996, footnote 46), under current law and with current inflation, the present value of remaining depreciation allowances per dollar of net nonresidential capital is approximately half the value of the assets. Allowing for these depreciation allowances has the same impact as forgiving half of the cash flow tax on existing assets. Hence, the cash flow tax on capital income is set to one quarter of the replacement proportional wage tax rate.

[4] General equilibrium effects and the constant government revenue constraint requires proportional shifts in the wage tax schedule (with an increase in the short run and a decrease in the long run). The average marginal tax rate is reported in Table 11.4.

[5] Since the highest marginal wage tax rate in the final steady state equals about 0.30, the capital income tax is set equal to 0.15.

Table 11.4. *Base Case Results, Five Tax Reforms*

	Year	National income[1]	Capital stock[1]	Labor supply[1]	Net saving rate	Before-tax wage[1]	Interest rate	Normalized Tobin's q	Tax rate[2]
	1996	1.000	1.000	1.000	0.051	1.000	0.083	1.000	0.216
Proportional Income Tax	1997	1.038	1.002	1.051	0.056	0.988	0.088	1.037	0.135
	2010	1.044	1.030	1.050	0.054	0.995	0.083	1.028	0.131
	2145	1.049	1.056	1.047	0.052	1.001	0.083	1.019	0.130
Proportional Consumption Tax	1997	1.044	1.010	1.063	0.073	0.987	0.079	0.960	0.142
	2010	1.063	1.108	1.054	0.067	1.013	0.076	0.934	0.138
	2145	1.094	1.254	1.046	0.059	1.046	0.073	0.906	0.127
Flat Tax (Standard)	1997	1.010	1.006	1.016	0.065	0.997	0.076	0.964	0.214
	2010	1.022	1.059	1.013	0.061	1.011	0.078	0.958	0.211
	2145	1.045	1.150	1.013	0.056	1.032	0.080	0.941	0.199
Flat Tax (Transition Relief)	1997	0.995	1.003	0.994	0.059	1.002	0.081	1.001	0.241
	2010	1.005	1.031	0.998	0.057	1.008	0.080	0.994	0.234
	2145	1.019	1.083	0.998	0.055	1.021	0.078	0.983	0.226
X Tax	1997	1.018	1.009	1.027	0.069	0.996	0.063	0.949	0.178
	2010	1.031	1.076	1.019	0.064	1.014	0.077	0.910	0.177
	2145	1.064	1.210	1.020	0.059	1.044	0.074	0.882	0.157

[1] Measured per effective labor unit and indexed with a value of 1.00 in 1996.
[2] Statutory federal rate; for 1996, this is the rate that applies to wage income.

capital–labor ratio produces a short-run increase in the before-tax interest rate and a short-run decrease in before-tax wage rate. The long-run increase in the capital–labor ratio produces the opposite effects on factor prices. This reform's initial impact on the market value of our composite capital good (measured via Tobin's q) is positive, reflecting the increase in saving and demand for capital that results from two factors: the rise in short-run disposable income (due to higher labor supply) and, to a lesser extent (because it doesn't change much), the lower marginal tax rate on capital income. The second potential effect on q, associated with changes in the relative treatment of old and new capital, is small because the level of expensing has not changed and the effective tax rate on capital income has decreased only slightly (housing capital is no longer exempt).

Figure 11.2 shows the effects of the tax reform on remaining lifetime utility for different generations by lifetime income group.[20] For ease of exposition, the figure reports the utility gains only for classes 1, 3, 6, 9 and 12. The horizontal axis of the figure lists the period the generation enters the model – reaches adulthood – relative to the period of the regime shift (period 0). For example, −1 refers to the generation that reaches adulthood just prior to the regime shift, 0 to the generation that reaches adulthood in the period of the shift, 1 in the following period, and so on.[21] The change in remaining lifetime utility is measured as the equivalent variation of remaining *full* lifetime income. In interpreting these numbers, one should keep in mind that full lifetime income includes the value of leisure. In our model, full lifetime income is more than twice the size of remaining *actual* lifetime earnings. Hence, gains or losses will tend to be larger if measured relative to either realized earnings or consumption.

In the long run, only members of lifetime income groups 8 through 12 experience increased utility from the proportional income tax reform, the rise in aggregate output notwithstanding. The main reason is that average tax rates increase for income classes 1 through 7 due to the loss of deductions and exemptions. In the short run, however, the oldest agents at the time of the reform are slightly better off since the reform increases the after-tax return to capital.

---

[20] We focus on the welfare effects of tax reforms on members of different income groups and generations, rather than on the overall efficiency change that might be calculated by aggregating such individual welfare effects. As our model's disaggregation by income class is largely secondary in the context of an efficiency analysis, it seems unnecessary to repeat the extensive analysis of efficiency already provided in Auerbach (1996), based on the original AK model.

[21] For members of the 55 transition generations, an individual's age at the time of reform equals the 21 minus the number on the horizontal axis.

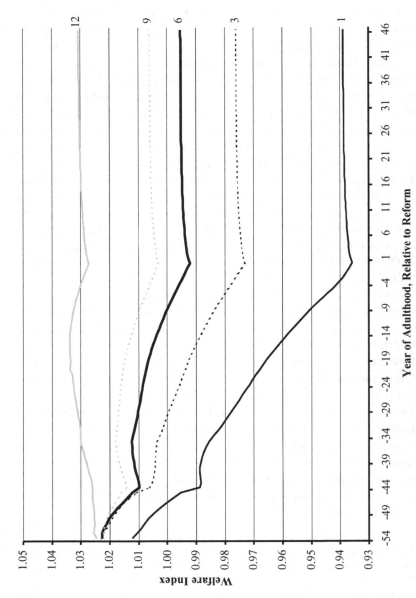

Figure 11.2. Remaining Lifetime Utility: Proportional Income Tax

3.2. A Proportional Consumption Tax

Our proportional consumption tax differs from the proportional income tax by including full expensing of investment expenditures. The government is now taxing income less domestic investment, which, in our closed economy, equals income less saving, that is, consumption. Formally, we specify the consumption tax as a combination of a labor-income tax and a business cash-flow tax. The second panel of Table 11.4 summarizes aggregate effects. The first thing to note is the 4% drop in q – the value of the existing capital stock relative to new capital. This drop occurs even though the rate of investment surges, because the impact of investment demand on q is more than offset by the sharp increase in the tax advantage of new versus old capital. This second effect constitutes the one-time effective tax on existing capital assets mentioned above.

In the period just after the tax reform, labor supply increases by 6.3%, a higher effect than was observed under the proportional income tax. This is because there are now additional factors at work beyond the reduction in marginal labor income tax rates. The rise in after-tax interest rates (because capital income is now essentially untaxed) produces substitution effects that encourage delays not only in consumption, but also in leisure, impacts reinforced by the negative wealth effect among those holding old capital.[22] These two factors also generate a substantial short-run jump in the saving rate from 5.1% to 7.3%. However, as the initial negative wealth effects diminish over time and interest rates fall with the growth in capital, the saving rate eventually recedes to 5.9%. Fourteen years into the reform (in 2010), the capital stock (per effective unit of labor) is 10.8% larger than its initial steady state value, and output is 6.3% larger. In the long run, the capital stock exceeds its initial value by 25.4%, and output exceeds its initial value by 9.4%, strong reactions that permit the consumption tax rate to fall over time, from 14.2% initially to a long-run 12.7%.

Figure 11.3 shows that, despite the large aggregate income gains, lower lifetime income groups are hurt by the reform. Although these losses are not as large as those in the proportional income tax case – indeed, several groups switch from being long-run utility losers to long-run utility winners – the regressive nature of the outcomes persists. The figure also

---

[22] There is also an income effect associated with the rise in interest rates, equal to the reduction in the present value of future consumption less the present value of future labor income. These income effects will generally be positive and discourage saving, though the effect will be much smaller than in the simple two-period life-cycle model with first-period labor supply, in which only the future-consumption term is present.

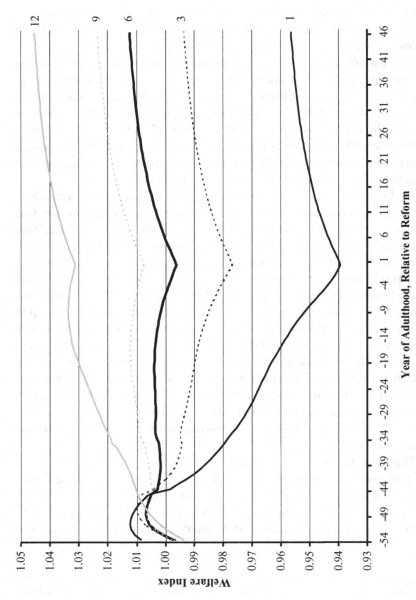

Figure 11.3. Remaining Lifetime Utility: Proportional Consumption Tax

reveals welfare losses for initial rich elderly, who own the lion's share of the existing capital stock.[23] In contrast, the initial poorest elderly gain from the tax reform. There are two reasons. First, this group consumes almost entirely out of Social Security benefits, the real value of which are unaffected by the change in asset values. Second, this group also borrows against some of their Social Security benefits prior to retirement, and their slightly negative net worth in old age shrinks in magnitude due to the policy-induced fall in the value of existing capital.

3.3. The Flat Tax

Our flat tax experiment modifies the proportional consumption tax by including a standard deduction of $9,500. In addition, it fully exempts housing wealth – about half of the capital stock – from taxation. Because policy makers are unlikely to extend the capital levy to housing, this exemption is an important step toward realism.[24]

As the third panel in Table 11.4 makes clear, the need to finance the standard deduction and tax exemption of existing housing increases the replacement tax rates well above those of the proportional consumption tax. As a result, the output effects under the flat tax are substantially reduced relative to its proportional counterpart. The long-run rise in the capital stock and level of output are, respectively, only 59% and 48% as large as those under the proportional consumption tax. The labor supply response is lower as well, reflecting the higher short- and long-run levels of marginal tax rates. The revenue-neutral flat-tax rate equals 21.4% initially and reaches 19.9% in the long run. The short-run impact on Tobin's q is quite similar to that of the proportional consumption tax, but this masks two offsetting effects. Investment demand rises less under the flat tax, moderating the positive impact of this factor on q. On the other hand, as the flat tax exempts much of existing wealth from the implicit tax old capital, it also moderates this factor's negative impact on q. In the longer run, as the first difference declines in importance (with net investment converging to zero in both instances), the second effect predominates, resulting in a higher value of q under the flat tax.

Figure 11.4 shows that the flat tax generates short-run utility effects that are similar to those of the consumption tax. The long-run utility changes

---

[23] Their welfare loss is less than the 4% capital loss they experience on their holdings of capital, because much of their welfare comes in the form of leisure.

[24] To impose the capital levy on existing housing would require taxing current owners' imputed rent and eventual sale proceeds.

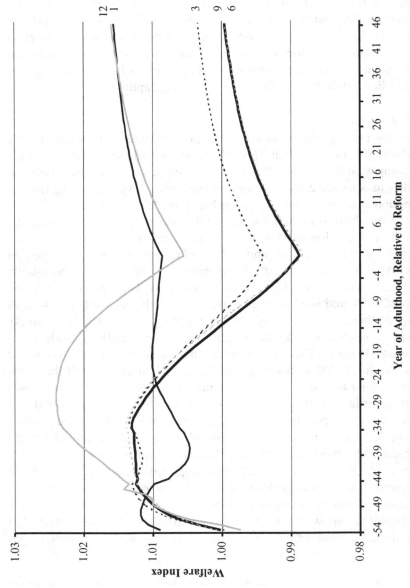

Figure 11.4. Remaining Lifetime Utility: Flat Tax (Standard)

are bunched much more closely than those of either of the proportional tax reforms. This reflects the flat tax's attention to preserving progressivity. Interestingly, the highest relative gains are for the richest and poorest lifetime income groups, with the poorest gaining from the higher standard deduction and the richest from the flattened marginal rate schedule.

The utility changes for the richest and poorest lifetime income groups also differ from those of the middle groups throughout the entire transition path. Group 12 benefits the most from reduced marginal and average tax rates. Group 1, which pays very little tax under either regime, benefits from the overall increase in wages. For those in income groups 3 through 9, the marginal and average tax rates initially change little or even rise. This stems from the revenue neutrality of the experiment, which requires a flat-tax marginal rate that initially exceeds the prereform tax rates for some agents in the middle-income classes in order to finance the lower tax rates at the top end. Those who belong to the lifetime middle-income range and enter the workforce close to the time of reform suffer utility losses along the transition path. They face relatively high tax rates of 20% to 22% on labor income for 20 to 25 years of their working life before the growth of the capital stock becomes fully effective. Once the economy grows, though, tax rates fall and wages rise, which leaves group 3 better off and raises the lifetime utility levels of groups 6 through 9 nearly to the point of indifference.

Neither the macroeconomic variables nor the welfare effects of the flat tax experiment are substantially influenced by the existence of a bequest motive. We repeated the simulation by "turning off" bequests (setting the utility bequest weight $\mu^j = 0$ for all j), simultaneously reducing the rate of time preference slightly (from .004 to .002) to maintain the same initial steady-state capital–output ratio. The resulting transition path was nearly identical to that just discussed, with the long-run increases in national income, the capital stock, and labor supply equal to 4.6% (versus 4.5%), 15.3% (versus 15.0%), and 1.4% (versus 1.3%), respectively, and no significant differences in the remaining initial steady-state computations nor in the postreform changes in output or welfare.[25] While it might seem surprising that eliminating bequests has so little impact, it should be remembered that bequests are modeled here as basically another type of future consumption. Thus, the motivations for bequest saving and life-cycle saving are essentially the same.

---

[25] Because of the extreme similarity to the simulation just presented, the results for this experiment are not shown separately in the table.

3.4. The Flat Tax with Transition Relief

One important characteristic of consumption tax reform is its treatment of existing assets and their owners. In contrast to the positive welfare gains they receive under the switch to proportional income taxation, older, higher wealth asset holders lose with the adoption of the proportional consumption tax or the flat tax. Though these losses are moderated by the surge in asset demand that limits the decline in existing asset values, the presence of such losses may make transition relief for existing assets a political necessity. Our fourth experiment adds transition relief to the flat tax by extending prereform depreciation rules for capital in place at the time of the tax reform. Since the present value of depreciation allowances equals roughly 50% of the nonresidential capital stock, transition relief is modeled by cutting the effective cash-flow tax rate in half.

As the fourth panel of Table 11.4 confirms, all of the salutary long-run aggregate effects of the standard flat tax are mitigated by the introduction of transition relief, which must be financed by permanently higher tax rates. The transition relief is, in some sense, excessive, in that the value of existing assets actually rises slightly in the short run. Still, the capital stock increases by over 8% in the long run, affording a 1.9% rise in the long-run level of output. Labor supply changes little following this tax reform, actually declining slightly below its initial steady-state level, reflecting both higher marginal tax rates (on average) and positive wealth effects.

Figure 11.5, which shows the welfare effects of the flat tax with transition relief, differs markedly from Figure 11.4, which shows the effects with no transition relief. Transition relief replaces the small short-run welfare losses of the wealthier initial elderly with sizable welfare gains, and raises the welfare gains of all income classes who are in their middle ages when the reform is begun. But these welfare gains come at the cost of smaller welfare gains for certain future generations and welfare losses for others. For example, with no transition relief, the long-run rich (members of groups 12 alive in the long run) experience more than a 1.6% gain in welfare. But with transition relief, these gains are cut nearly to zero. For middle-class households alive in the long run, the concession to initial wealth holders transforms the flat tax from having essentially no impact to a roughly 1.5% loser when measured in terms of its welfare impact. Indeed, with the exception of the very poorest and very richest members of society, transition relief transforms the flat tax into a bad deal for those alive in the medium and long runs. This is critically important to keep in mind in assessing calls for a flat tax. Many advocates of the flat tax

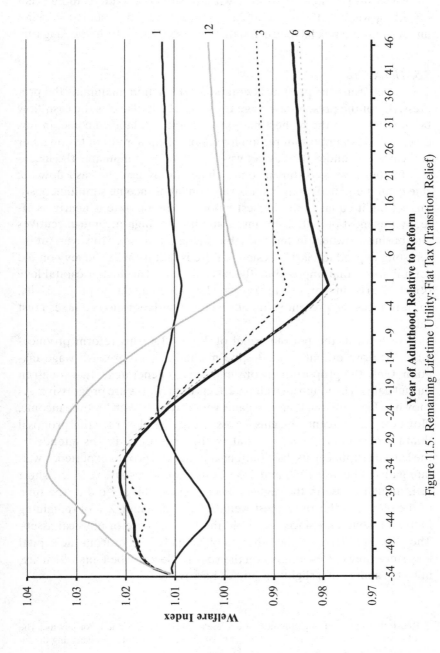

Year of Adulthood, Relative to Reform

Figure 11.5. Remaining Lifetime Utility: Flat Tax (Transition Relief)

favor transition relief, apparently without sufficient understanding that offsetting wealth effects are already present, and that short-run relief undermines the results they claim the flat tax will achieve in the long run.

3.5. The X Tax

The X tax, using the present-law standard deduction, maintains the progressivity of the present-law wage tax schedule. It also sets the cash-flow tax rate equal to the highest marginal tax rate on labor income, in this case 30%.[26] An important reason for choosing equal rates of tax on labor and cash flow under the flat tax was that doing so eliminates the incentive for businesses to shift income. Under the X tax, the cash flow tax rate cannot equal all marginal tax rates on labor income simultaneously, but setting it equal to the highest labor income tax rate is nearly as effective, as most potential shifting would involve high-income executives and business owners in the top labor income bracket. However, an interesting byproduct of this design feature is that it raises the levy on old capital above that imposed by the basic flat tax. This higher capital levy offsets the rise in marginal tax rates on labor income due to progressivity, for it reduces the present value of revenue that labor income taxes must raise.

As shown in the bottom panel of Table 11.4, this reform produces large long-run output gains despite maintaining progressive wage taxation. Only the proportional consumption tax generates larger long-run output gains. The long-run welfare effects of the X tax are progressive. As shown in Fig. 11.6, the long-run gains vary inversely with lifetime income. However, the percentage gains across groups are closer for this proposal than for any other, suggesting that, in the long run, it is – as intended – the least disruptive in its distributional impact. All groups experience welfare gains of between 1% and 2% of full lifetime resources. In the short run, though, those in the highest income class who are old at the time of the reform suffer the largest welfare loss – reaching 2% of remaining lifetime resources – since they hold the largest share of physical assets. The poorest elderly, on the other hand, actually benefit from the capital levy since they live essentially on their Social Security benefits which are, in fact, a source of a slight amount of borrowing.

---

[26] Recall that marginal wage tax rates are a linear function of taxable labor income. The adjustments required to maintain budget balance are implemented by changing the intercept of this function, while holding the slope constant.

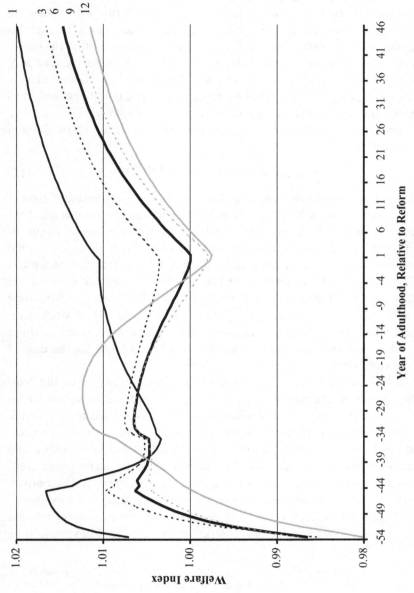

Year of Adulthood, Relative to Reform

Figure 11.6. Remaining Lifetime Utility: X Tax

4. Sensitivity Analysis

This section considers the impact of changes in assumptions regarding three key elasticity parameters for two of the tax reforms just considered, the standard flat tax and the flat tax with transition relief. In each instance, we make offsetting parameter adjustments to maintain the correspondence between our initial steady state and the benchmark economy. Table 11.5 presents the results of reductions in the production elasticity of substitution between labor and capital, *s*, and the utility function's intratemporal elasticity, ρ, and intertemporal elasticity, γ.

The first panel of the table presents simulations for the CES production function,

$$Y_t = A\big[\theta K_t^{1-1/\sigma} + (1-\theta)L_t^{1-1/\sigma}\big]^{\frac{1}{1-1/\sigma}} \tag{12}$$

in which the production elasticity of substitution, σ, is reduced from 1 (i.e., Cobb–Douglas) to 0.8, a reasonable alternative value to our base case assumption.[27] As one would expect, the lower elasticity of substitution means that the before-tax interest rate falls by more as capital accumulates, somewhat dampening the capital accumulation incentive. Thus, while the long-run interest rate is 8.0% in the base case for the standard flat tax displayed in Table 11.4, it is 7.8% in the corresponding run in Table 11.5 for $\sigma = .8$; the long-run gain in the capital stock is reduced from 15.0% to 13.6%. However, these differences, as well as those in other variables, are small. The same conclusion holds for the case of transition relief.

As discussed above, there is considerable uncertainty about the "correct" values of the parameters γ and ρ. It is therefore important to determine how sensitive the results presented thus far are to reasonable variations in these parameters. In each case, because we pose the question in terms of whether tax reform might *fail* to produce welfare and income gains, we consider *smaller* values of these elasticity parameters, which reduce the degree to which agents react to improved incentives. However, one can use these simulations to infer the effects of raising γ or ρ. The second panel of Table 11.5 presents results for each of the two flat tax variants, with the value of the intratemporal elasticity of substitution,

---

[27] As we reduce the production elasticity, we also change the capital intensity parameter, θ, from 0.25 to 0.312, and multiply the production efficiency parameter, A, by 0.962. It is a matter of simple algebra to show that these two changes ensure that the levels of capital and labor and the wage and interest rates in the initial steady state are the same as for the base case with Cobb–Douglas production.

ρ, reduced from 0.8 to 0.4. The bottom panel covers the same two reforms, this time with the intertemporal elasticity of substitution, γ, reduced from 0.25 to 0.1.[28]

The experiment with a smaller intratemporal elasticity of substitution looks quite similar to the flat-tax case under our benchmark parameterization (in Table 11.4) in the early stages of the transition path. However, in the long run, the decreased willingness to substitute higher consumption for leisure results in a decline in aggregate labor supply relative to the higher elasticity case. The smaller increase in labor supply contributes to a smaller increase in the level of saving (even though the saving *rate* is similar) and capital accumulation. As a result, capital growth is smaller as well and, although real wage growth is similar to before, the slower growth in both labor and capital makes income growth smaller as well, only 2.8% in the long run, instead of 4.5%. The relative impact is similar when transition relief is added.

The effects of the smaller intertemporal elasticity of substitution are greater, because this change reduces the responsiveness not only of labor supply, but of consumption as well. Thus, in addition to the smaller labor supply response just observed, we also see a smaller increase in the saving rate. As a result, short-run and long-run output gains are even smaller than in the upper panel of the table. Under the pure flat tax, output rises by just 1.3% in the long run; with transition relief added, long-run output actually falls by 3.1%. Thus, there is no guarantee that a realistic consumption tax reform – the flat tax with transition relief – will raise output in the long run.

5. Summary and Conclusion

Proponents and opponents of fundamental tax reform wrestle with the same question: Are the gains to the winners worth the costs to the losers? The answer involves value judgments that go beyond economic science. But forming one's judgments requires knowing what fundamental tax reform will do to the economy and to its current and future participants. This paper tries to provide a better sense of those outcomes by simulating fundamental tax reform in a much-improved version of the Auerbach–Kotlikoff model – one that considers intra- as well as intergenerational

---

[28] We adjust δ to $-.08$ to preserve the initial capital–output ratio when changing γ. However, when changing ρ, we adjust the labor intensity parameter α to 0.2, in order also to maintain the appropriate share of labor supply in total labor endowment.

Table 11.5. *Sensitivity Analysis*

	Year	National Income[1]	Capital Stock[1]	Labor Supply[1]	Net saving Rate	Before-Tax Wage[1]	Interest Rate	Normalized Tobin's q	Tax Rate[2]
				σ = 0.8					
Flat Tax (Standard)	1996	1.000	1.000	1.000	0.051	1.000	0.083	1.000	0.216
	1997	1.009	1.006	1.014	0.064	0.994	0.077	0.967	0.215
	2010	1.022	1.055	1.013	0.060	1.010	0.078	0.952	0.210
	2145	1.043	1.136	1.015	0.056	1.032	0.078	0.936	0.198
Flat Tax (Transition Relief)	1997	0.994	1.003	0.993	0.059	1.000	0.081	1.000	0.241
	2010	1.004	1.029	0.998	0.057	1.007	0.080	0.993	0.234
	2145	1.018	1.075	1.000	0.054	1.020	0.081	0.982	0.226
				ρ = 0.4					
Flat Tax (Standard)	1996	1.000	1.000	1.000	0.049	1.000	0.086	1.000	0.213
	1997	1.008	1.006	1.013	0.063	0.998	0.081	0.971	0.213
	2010	1.016	1.057	1.005	0.059	1.013	0.081	0.953	0.211
	2145	1.028	1.136	0.996	0.055	1.033	0.078	0.935	0.203
Flat Tax (Transition Relief)	1997	1.001	1.003	1.002	0.057	1.000	0.084	1.005	0.235
	2010	1.007	1.033	1.000	0.055	1.008	0.083	0.995	0.227
	2145	1.015	1.080	0.995	0.054	1.021	0.082	0.987	0.225

Year	National Income[1]	Capital Stock[1]	Labor Supply[1]	Net saving Rate	Before-Tax Wage[1]	Interest Rate	Normalized Tobin's q	Tax Rate[2]
			$\gamma = 0.1$					
1996	1.000	1.000	1.000	0.051	1.000	0.083	1.000	0.216
Flat Tax (Standard)								
1997	1.007	1.003	1.010	0.057	0.998	0.075	0.947	0.211
2010	1.007	1.019	1.004	0.054	1.004	0.082	0.932	0.217
2145	1.013	1.038	1.005	0.053	1.008	0.081	0.928	0.213
Flat Tax (Transition Relief)								
1997	0.990	1.000	0.986	0.050	1.003	0.077	0.974	0.239
2010	0.985	0.985	0.984	0.047	1.000	0.083	0.965	0.244
2145	0.969	0.920	0.983	0.049	0.983	0.088	0.975	0.256

[1] Measured per effective labor unit and indexed with a value of 1.00 in 1996.
[2] Statutory federal rate; for 1996, this is the rate that applies to wage income.

equity and one that is closely calibrated to U.S. fiscal institutions and tax policy.

The model predicts significant long-run increases in output from replacing the current U.S. federal tax system with a proportional consumption tax. For our base case, output would rise eventually by more than 9%. For middle- and upper-income classes alive in the long run, this policy is a big winner. But older transition generations suffer from the imposition of an implicit capital levy, and low-income individuals, even in the long run, suffer a significant loss as growth fails to compensate for the decline in tax progressivity.

The flat tax, which modifies the basic consumption tax by exempting housing wealth from taxation and by providing a large wage-tax deduction, improves the welfare of lower income individuals in the long run, but at a cost of more than halving the economy's long-run output rise, to 4.5% for the same economic assumptions. Even then, this reform leaves initial older generations worse off. Insulating them through transition relief, in the form of maintaining present-law depreciation allowances on existing capital, further reduces the long-run output increase – to just 1.9%.

Other reforms produce similar tradeoffs. Switching to a proportional income tax hurts current and future low lifetime earners but helps everyone else. The X tax, which combines consumption tax and progressive wage tax elements, makes everyone better off in the long run and raises output by even more than the flat tax. But this reform harms initial older generations who face an implicit tax on their wealth. Further, with smaller but still plausible labor supply and saving responses to tax changes, the potential gains and hence the scope for trading off efficiency for equity are reduced. Indeed, the last reform considered, a flat tax that offers transition relief actually reduces output in the long run for a low intertemporal elasticity of substitution. Presumably, this is not what proponents of tax reform have in mind.

Thus, our model shows that fundamental reform of the current U.S. tax structure offers the possibility of significant macroeconomic expansion and welfare gains for many, but not without true sacrifice by certain groups. Adjustments that attempt to prevent adverse distributional effects yield much more modest aggregate effects. While we have not sought to identify more complicated policies that shield all losers from sacrifice, our findings do suggest that such policies, if they exist, are likely to yield much smaller output increases than those of policies that provide no such relief.

While we have adapted our model to accommodate many of the key issues that arise when considering tax reform, there are some that we have not addressed. In treating the economy as closed, we may have overstated the depressing impact of additional capital accumulation on the rate of return and, hence, understated the potential welfare and output gains from tax reform, a conclusion consistent with the open-economy simulations presented by Auerbach (1996).

Additional gains may also accrue under any of the tax reforms considered here as a result of the more uniform treatment of different types of capital and different sectors of production. There may also be welfare gains from tax simplification arising through reduced costs of compliance and enforcement. Gains from both of these sources, though, would depend on the reformed tax system maintaining not only its reduced rates and broader base, but also its lack of special interest provisions that exist under the current tax system and could arise under at least some of the alternatives we have considered. Finally, as discussed recently by Gentry and Hubbard (1997), the distributional and efficiency effects of tax reform might change somewhat in a richer economic model incorporating variation in risk and rates of return, for one would then need to consider the risk-sharing aspects of different tax systems and the extent to which the capital levy of the consumption tax hit not only the quasi-rents of existing capital, but also true economic rents. A challenging task for future research is to determine the relative importance of these factors.

Appendix

Labor Supply Elasticities
This section of the Appendix discuss the relationship between parameters of the utility function given in expression (1) in the text and those typically estimated in the labor supply literature. Papers in this literature contain a variety of different labor supply elasticity concepts. Perhaps most useful from our perspective is that of the "λ-constant" or Frisch elasticity of labor supply (e.g., MaCurdy 1981), which measures the variation in labor supply along an optimal path with the marginal utility of income constant.[29] In some studies, elasticities estimated in this way are also referred to as intertemporal elasticities of substitution, but this equivalence does not hold for our specification of preferences, which are not separable between goods and leisure.

---

[29] Our use of the variable λ here follows the notation found in the relevant literature, and should not be confused with its use in the body of the paper, to represent the rate of technological progress.

For our time-separable utility function, a λ-constant change in the after-tax wage, w_t, affects only consumption and leisure at date t. Thus, given the optimal path for these variables (Auerbach and Kotlikoff 1987, p. 31, expressions 3.11 and 3.12), date-t leisure may be shown to satisfy

$$l_t = \left(\frac{w_t}{\alpha}\right)^{-\rho} \left(1 + \alpha^\rho w_t^{1-\rho}\right)^{\frac{\rho-\gamma}{1-\rho}} x(\lambda), \tag{A1}$$

where $x(\lambda)$ does not depend on w_t. Using (A1) we derive the following expression for the λ-constant elasticity of *labor* supply, L_t, with respect to w_t:

$$\eta = \left(\frac{l}{L}\right)(\gamma \zeta + \rho(1 - \zeta)), \tag{A2}$$

where

$$\zeta = \frac{\alpha^\rho w_t^{1-\rho}}{1 + \alpha^\rho w_t^{1-\rho}}.$$

Note that ζ corresponds to leisure's "share" in the within-period utility function. Since we calibrate the model for different values of ρ and γ so that this share is roughly .6 (and the consumption/labor share is .4), the value of η from (A2) is roughly $1.5(.6\gamma + .4\rho)$. For our base case values of $\rho = .8$ and $\gamma = .25$, this gives a value of $\eta = .7$. This elasticity is reasonable, given the range of values estimated in the literature, some of which are surveyed in Browning, Hansen, and Heckman (1998).[30] Estimates for men are in some cases higher, but typically somewhat lower, while estimates for women are generally at least as high, and in some cases much higher. Our alternative simulations that use values of $\rho = .4$ and $\gamma = .10$, yield corresponding values for η of .46 and .57, respectively.

Calculation of Earnings Ability Profiles
Our earnings ability profiles are based on the individual files of the University of Michigan's Panel Study of Income Dynamics (PSID) from 1976–88. These calculations generally follow those of Fullerton and Rogers (1993, Chapter 4), except where indicated.

The sample utilized contains 9335 observations on 891 individuals. We excluded individuals with imputed real hourly earnings less than one dollar and those with clear inconsistencies in levels of educational attainment over the time period. This sample differs from that used by Fullerton and Rogers, who aggregate individual observations into

---

[30] Other recent papers in the literature include Blundell, Meghir, and Neves (1993), Mulligan (1998), and Ziliak and Kniesner (1999).

household observations and consider only households with stable marital histories. We used the following procedure to obtain wage profiles.

(i) First-stage regressions were run on the entire data set using a common set of explanatory variables. The specification is identical to that used by Fullerton and Rogers except a birth-year variable, which is added to control for age-cohort effects. It is given by

$$\hat{w}_{it} = \pi_{0i} + \pi_1 BY_i + \pi_2 AGE_{it} + \pi_3 AGE_{it}^2 + \pi_4 AGE_{it}^3 + \pi_5 AGE_{it} EDU_{it}$$
$$+ \sum_{h=1}^{3} \pi_{h+5} AGE_{it} DUM_{it}^h + \pi_9 AGE_{it}^2 EDU_{it}$$
$$+ \sum_{h=1}^{3} \pi_{h+9} AGE_{it}^2 DUM_{it}^h + v_{it},$$

where

$\hat{w}_{it}$ = the log of the real hourly wage for person i in time t,
π_{0i} = fixed effect for person i,
BY_i = the birth year of person i,
AGE_{it} = the age of person i at time t,
EDU_{it} = the education level (in years) of person i in time t,
DUM_{it}^h = dummy variables for the marital status ($h = 1$),
race ($h = 2$), and sex ($h = 3$) of person i in time t;
potentially variable over time only for $h = 3$.

Table 11.A1 reports the resulting coefficient estimates.

(ii) The coefficient estimates obtained from step (i) were used to construct simulated life-cycle wage profiles for each individual from age 21 through 80. Unlike Fullerton and Rogers, we do not splice wage observations

Table 11.A1. *PSID Regression Results*

Variable	Coefficient	t statistic
Birth Year (BY)	−0.0005	1.47
Age (AGE)	0.0883	3.46
Age-Squared	−0.0016	3.20
Age-Cubed	6.66E − 6	2.07
Age × Education (EDU)	−0.0009	2.02
Age × Marital Status (DUM^1)	0.0081	3.37
Age × Race (DUM^2)	0.0119	2.81
Age × Sex (DUM^3)	0.0339	1.69
Age-Squared × Education	2.16E − 5	3.30
Age-Squared × Marital Status	−0.0001	2.84
Age-Squared × Race	−0.0002	2.70
Age-Squared × Sex	−0.0004	2.00
Adjusted R^2	0.9779	—

Table 11.A2. *Estimated Wage Profile Coefficients by Lifetime Income Group*

LI group	Intercept	Age	Age squared	Age cubed
1	−0.6421	0.0949	−0.00158	7E − 06
2	−0.2294	0.0941	−0.00157	7E − 06
3	0.1831	0.0929	−0.00156	7E − 06
4	0.4693	0.0907	−0.00155	7E − 06
5	0.6772	0.0882	−0.00150	7E − 06
6	0.8865	0.0853	−0.00147	7E − 06
7	0.9794	0.0884	−0.00151	7E − 06
8	1.1606	0.0864	−0.00148	7E − 06
9	1.3180	0.0855	−0.00147	7E − 06
10	1.4814	0.0862	−0.00147	7E − 06
11	1.8151	0.0856	−0.00146	7E − 06
12	2.5745	0.0853	−0.00146	7E − 06

from the PSID with predicted values in generating the profiles. Instead we simply use predicted values for all wage observations.[31] In constructing these profiles we set education to the highest reported level and assume that marital status is constant and equal to married if the individual is married at any time over the PSID sample period.

(iii) Lifetime wage income (LI) levels are imputed from the profiles generated in step (ii) according to the formula

$$\text{LI}_i = \sum_{s=21}^{80} (1+r)^{-(s-21)} (\hat{w}_{is} \cdot 4000),$$

where the discount rate r is set to 8%, $\hat{w}_{is}$ is the predicted wage of the individual at age s, and 4000 is the potential full-time endowment of work hours. This calculation follows Fullerton and Rogers, except for the choice of r.

All observations were next sorted in ascending order of lifetime wage income, and divided into the twelve groups described in the text. Following the text and letting φ^j be the fraction of the population in group j, our division yields $\varphi^j = 0.02$ for $j = 1$ and 12, $\varphi^j = 0.08$ for $j = 2$ and 11, and $\varphi^j = 0.1$ for $j = 3$ through 10.

---

[31] This difference is minor, as actual wages are observed for only a small portion of any given individual's working life. As the explanatory variables include individual fixed effects, π_{0i}, and age interacted with other individual characteristics, the use of fitted rather than actual values during the period of observed wages amounts to smoothing out high-frequency wage fluctuations.

(iv) Finally, regressions of the predicted wage observations on a common group intercept and a cubic in age were run for each group:

$$\hat{w}_{is}^{j} = \xi_0^j + \xi_1^j \text{AGE}_{is}^j + \xi_2(\text{AGE}_{is}^j)^2 + \xi_3^j(\text{AGE}_{is}^j)^3 + \nu_{is}^j.$$

The estimated coefficients appear in Table 11.A2. The profiles in Figure 1 in the paper are based on these estimates adjusted for annual efficiency growth of 1%. Taking account of the various differences in methodology, they exhibit a pattern similar to those in Fullerton and Rogers.

References

Altig, David, and Charles T. Carlstrom (1999). "Marginal Tax Rates and Income Inequality in a Life-Cycle Model." *American Economic Review*, December, 89(5), 1197–215.

Auerbach, Alan J (1989). "Tax Reform and Adjustment Costs: The Impact on Investment and Market Value." *International Economic Review*, November, 30(4), 939–62.

Auerbach, Alan J (1996). "Tax Reform, Capital Accumulation, Efficiency, and Growth," in Henry J. Aaron and William G. Gale (eds.), *Economic Effects of Fundamental Tax Reform*. Washington, D.C.: The Brookings Institution, 29–81.

Auerbach, Alan J., Jagadeesh Gokhale, Laurence J. Kotlikoff, John Sabelhaus, and David N. Weil (1995). "The Annuitization of Americans' Resources: A Cohort Analysis." NBER Working Paper No. 5089, April.

Auerbach, Alan J. and Laurence J. Kotlikoff (1987). *Dynamic Fiscal Policy*. (Cambridge, England: Cambridge University Press).

Auerbach, Alan J., Laurence J. Kotlikoff, Robert P. Hagemann, and Giuseppe Nicoletti (1989). "The Economic Dynamics of an Ageing Population: The Case of Four OECD Countries." *OECD Economic Studies*, Spring, 12, 51–96.

Blinder, Alan S (1973). "A Model of Inherited Wealth." *Quarterly Journal of Economics*, November, 87(4), 608–26.

Blundell, Richard, Costas Meghir, and Pedro Neves (1993). "Labour Supply and Intertemporal Substitution." *Journal of Econometrics*, September, 59(1–2), 137–60.

Bradford, David (1986). *Untangling the Income Tax*, (Cambridge, MA: Harvard University Press).

Browning, Martin, Lars Peter Hansen, and James J. Heckman (1998). "Micro Data and General Equilibrium Models." unpublished manuscript, September.

Congressional Budget Office (1997). *Comparing Income and Consumption Tax Bases*, CBO Paper, July.

Cummins, Jason G., Kevin A. Hassett, and R. Glenn Hubbard (1994). "A Reconsideration of Investment Behavior Using Tax Reforms as Natural Experiments." *Brookings Papers on Economic Activity*, 25(1), 1–74.

Engen, Eric M. and William G. Gale (1996). "The Effects of Fundamental Tax Reform on Saving." in Henry J. Aaron and William G. Gale (eds.), *Economic*

Effects of Fundamental Tax Reform, Washington, D.C.: The Brookings Institution, 83–121.

Fullerton, Don and Diane Lim Rogers (1993). *Who Bears the Lifetime Tax Burden?* Washington, D.C.: The Brookings Institution.

Gale, William G. and John Karl Scholz (1994). "Intergenerational Transfers and the Accumulation of Wealth." *Journal of Economic Perspectives*, Fall, *8*(4), 145–60.

Gentry, William M., and R. Glenn Hubbard (1997). "Distributional Implications of Introducing a Broad-Based Consumption Tax." in J. Poterba (ed.), *Tax Policy and the Economy*, 11, (Cambridge: MIT Press), pp. 1–47.

Hall, Robert E. and Alvin Rabushka (1983). *The Flat Tax*. (Stanford: Hoover Institution Press); (1995) 2nd ed., (Stanford: Hoover Institution Press).

Hubbard, R. Glenn and Kenneth Judd (1987). "Social Security and Individual Welfare: Precautionary Saving, Borrowing Constraints, and the Payroll Tax." *The American Economic Review*, September, *77*(4), 630–46.

Hubbard, R. Glenn, Jonathan Skinner, and Stephen P. Zeldes (1995). "Precautionary Saving and Social Insurance." *Journal of Political Economy*, April, *103*(2), 360–99.

Kotlikoff, Laurence J., and Lawrence H. Summers (1981). "The Role of Intergenerational Transfers in Aggregate Capital Accumulation." *Journal of Political Economy*, August, *89*(4), 706–32.

MaCurdy, Thomas E (1981). "An Empirical Model of Labor Supply in a Life-Cycle Setting." *Journal of Political Economy*, December, *89*(6), 1059–85.

Menchik, Paul L. and Martin David (1982). "The Incidence of a Lifetime Consumption Tax." National Tax Journal, *35*(2), 189–203.

Mulligan, Casey B (1998). "Substitution Over Time: Another Look at Life-Cycle Labor Supply," in Ben S. Bernanke and Julio J. Rotemberg (eds.), *NBER Macroeconomics Annual 1998*. (Cambridge, MA: MIT Press), pp. 75–134.

Rippe, Richard (1995). "Further Gains in Corporate Profitability." *Economic Outlook Monthly*, Prudential Securities, August 1995.

Slemrod, Joel and Jon Bakija (1996). *Taxing Ourselves: A Citizen's Guide to the Great Debate over Tax Reform*. (Cambridge, MA: MIT Press).

Stokey, Nancy L. and Sergio Rebelo (1995). "Growth Effects of Flat-Rate Taxes." *Journal of Political Economy*, June, *103*(3), 519–50.

Ziliak, James P. and Thomas J. Kniesner (1999). "Estimating Life Cycle Labor Supply Effects." *Journal of Political Economy*, April, *107*(2), 326–59.

TWELVE

The International Macroeconomics of Taxation and the Case *against* European Tax Harmonization[1]

Enrique G. Mendoza

International macroeconomic theory shows that domestic tax policy in a global economy affects foreign economic conditions via complex, dynamic interactions through relative prices, tax revenues, and wealth distribution. This paper proposes a tractable quantitative framework for assessing tax policies that is consistent with this theory. The significance of the international transmission channels of tax policy is evaluated in the context of a "workhorse" two-country dynamic general equilibrium model. The model is used to assess the potential effects of the European harmonization of capital income taxes. The results show that this policy, if enacted along the lines followed in harmonizing value-added taxes, yields large capital outflows and a significant erosion of tax revenue for Continental Europe while the opposite effects benefit the United Kingdom. Welfare in the United Kingdom rises as result, while Continental Europe may incur a substantial welfare cost.

1. Introduction

One of the main themes of Assaf Razin's extensive research program is the analysis of the policy implications of the dynamic macroeconomic

[1] This paper was written for the Economic Policy Conference in Honor of Assaf Razin organized by Elhanan Helpman and Efraim Sadka and sponsored by the Pinhas Sapir Center at Tel Aviv University. Comments and suggestions by the discussant, Michel Strawczynski, and by Jonathan Heatcote, Assaf Razin, Linda Tesar, and Hans-Werner Sinn are gratefully acknowledged. I am also grateful to Assaf for his years of mentorship and friendship. The analysis undertaken here is largely inspired by his work.

theory of international taxation. In joint work with Jacob Frenkel, with Elhanan Helpman, and with Efraim Sadka, Razin produced seminal contributions that were among the first to formalize the microfoundations of the intertemporal analysis of tax policies in open economies.[2] These studies were part of a growing literature that examined the international implications of tax policies within the context of dynamic general equilibrium models.[3]

Intertemporal models of international taxation identified weaknesses in the use of traditional static models to conduct tax policy analysis, but they also highlighted the complications involved in a theoretically consistent assessment of the open-economy implications of tax policies. The dynamic issues inherent to intertemporal closed-economy models, which involve determining whether tax changes are permanent or transitory as well as anticipated or unanticipated, are significantly compounded by the effects of three international transmission channels of tax policies. First, the price channel: A change in domestic tax policy alters the equilibrium prices of goods and financial assets that countries trade and even the foreign prices of nontraded goods. Second, the wealth channel: Depending on tax incidence and the structure of financial markets, changes in tax policy affect the cross-country distribution of physical capital and financial assets. Third, the tax–revenue-erosion channel: As a by-product of the price and wealth channels, domestic tax changes may erode foreign tax revenues and thus force distorting tax hikes or expenditure cuts. Sustainability issues also arise because international external effects on welfare resulting from these transmission channels lead to strategic behavior on the part of fiscal authorities and to international tax competition.

Early attempts to develop policy-making models based on the dynamic macroeconomic theory of international taxation were hampered by limitations of the quantitative methods available in the mid-1980s. The articles that Assaf Razin wrote with Jacob Frenkel and Steve Symansky were pioneering efforts in this regard (see Frenkel, Razin, and Symansky (1990) and (1991)). However, to make their quantitative framework tractable, the model they proposed adopted simplifying assumptions that limited its ability to deal with the three international transmission channels of

---

[2] This work includes Frenkel and Razin (1986a), (1986b), (1987), (1988) and (1989), Helpman and Razin (1987), Razin and Sadka (1989), (1990), and (1991), and Frenkel, Razin and Sadka (1991).

[3] A short list of other early contributions to this literature includes Aschauer and Greenwood (1985), Greenwood and Kimbrough (1985), Buiter (1987), and Bovenberg (1986). Frenkel and Razin (1987) and Turnovsky (1997) review the literature in detail.

tax policy.[4] In particular, their model incorporated assumptions of unitary intertemporal elasticities of substitution in consumption and linear production technologies that restricted the global interaction of tax policies through the equilibrium determination of goods and factors prices, the distribution of wealth, and the dynamics of tax bases. Moreover, their quantitative framework lacked the computation of the welfare costs associated with the transitional macroeconomic dynamics triggered by tax changes, which is now viewed as a central element of the assessment of tax policies (see Lucas (1990)). The methods required to compute these welfare costs were just being developed in a parallel literature on quantitative closed-economy studies of optimal taxation.

This paper has two main objectives. The first one is methodological: to fill some of the remaining gaps in the process of building a framework that integrates the tax policy principles derived from dynamic open-economy macroeconomics with a quantitative policymaking tool.[5] The second is to use this tool to provide an answer to a current tax-policy question. In particular, the aim is to determine the effects on macroeconomic dynamics and social welfare that are likely to result from the harmonization of capital income taxes within the European Union.

The quantitative framework proposed here is a two-country variation of the workhorse model of modern macroeconomics: the neoclassical, general-equilibrium model of exogenous balanced growth driven by labor-augmenting technological change. This model is not sophisticated in several aspects, in particular those related to distributional issues, the long-run determinants of economic growth, or the interaction between fiscal and monetary policies, but it does capture with a high degree of complexity the three channels of international transmission of tax policies identified earlier. The setup of the model is based on the model proposed by Mendoza and Tesar (1998), but the analysis differs in two important respects. First, the focus of this paper is on studying the three transmission

---

[4] Similar simplifying assumptions are also present in more recent quantitative studies of the effects of tax policy in open-economy general equilibrium models. For example, Eggert (1998) and Sorensen (1999) quantify the price and revenue-erosion effects of international tax competition in models in which dynamic effects are minimized for tractability. Eggert studies a two-period model and Sorensen examines a static multisector model similar to those used in computable general-equilibrium models of trade or public finance.

[5] Goulder and Eichengreen (1989) developed a framework with a similar objective aimed at quantifying the effects of trade liberalization in a setup with a detailed industry-level breakdown of production. One important difference with the analysis conducted here is that they abstracted from the revenue erosion effect by assuming that government budget constraints are balanced each period via lump-sum taxation.

channels of tax policy, quantifying their effects, and analyzing their key determinants. Second, this paper adopts a sharply different treatment of the revenue erosion effect by requiring countries to react to unintended changes in their ability to raise tax revenue by adjusting taxes on immobile factors of production (i.e., labor). This results in significantly more costly distortions than those that result from the adjustments in indirect taxes considered by Mendoza and Tesar. The emphasis is on proposing a framework that can easily adapt to uses in policy circles, so the model is calibrated to actual data for the four largest economies of Western Europe (France, Germany, Italy, and the United Kingdom), including estimates of their current tax structures.

The quantitative analysis shows that international transmission effects via relative prices, the world distribution of wealth, and erosion of tax revenues are very significant. A modest cut in the capital income tax in the United Kingdom results in a noticeable gain in social welfare (i.e., lifetime utility) that is equivalent to a gain of 1.1% in the trend level of consumption per capita. However, the combined effect of the three transmission channels leads to a staggering welfare loss in Continental Europe equivalent to a fall of 3.7% in the trend level of consumption per capita.

The above results are produced with the intent of showing the large magnitude of the global transmission effects of tax changes, rather than as bottom-line estimates of the final outcome of the tax cut by the United Kingdom. Given the large welfare loss for Continental Europe, one would expect that retaliation by Continental Europe would lead to tax competition or to efforts to undertake coordinated adjustments in capital income taxes. The precedent for this is the harmonization of indirect taxes already undertaken in the European Union. Hence, the analysis shifts in a second stage to consider harmonization of taxes on the income of mobile factors of production (i.e., capital) as a proxy for an ad-hoc coordinating mechanism to avoid harmful tax competition.

Tax harmonization is modeled as an agreed common tax rate on capital income that is a linear combination of the tax rates currently in place in Continental Europe and in the United Kingdom. The already-harmonized rates of indirect taxation are kept unchanged and, as a result, tax revenue erosion effects need to be offset by adjustments in the distortionary tax rate on labor income.[6] The experiment also assumes that the existing

---

[6] Tax harmonization as modeled here is not the outcome of tax competition or of "efficient" cooperation setting tax rates that represent some explicit cooperative equilibrium amongst

levels of government purchases and entitlement payments (which are lower in the United Kingdom than in Continental Europe) are kept constant at all times. At current tax rates, tax harmonization implies a capital tax cut for the United Kingdom and a tax hike for Continental Europe – the current U.K. effective capital income tax rate is about 47% while the average of effective capital income tax rates for France, Germany, and Italy is nearly 28%.[7]

The model predicts that under the above conditions harmonization of capital income taxes is not a good idea, at least not for Continental Europe. The best-case scenario is one in which Continental Europe increases its capital income tax to match the U.K.'s. Welfare in the United Kingdom increases by an amount equivalent to a 1.3% increase in trend consumption per capita, while welfare in Continental Europe increases only by 0.1%. The labor income tax is reduced by 1.1 percentage points in the United Kingdom and by 5.7 percentage points in Continental Europe. Any harmonized capital income tax set lower than the current U.K. tax rate increases the welfare gain for the United Kingdom but reduces it for Continental Europe. At harmonized tax rates set 5 percentage points or more below the U.K. tax, Continental Europe suffers a welfare loss. In the case in which the harmonized tax rate is set to the average of current U.K. and Continental Europe tax rates, the welfare gain for the U.K. is 2% but the loss for Continental Europe is 2.7%. Adjusting to the tax revenue erosion effect requires the United Kingdom to raise its labor tax by 1.8 percentage points while the labor tax in Continental Europe remains nearly unchanged.

The above results reflect the fact that, since the U.K. starts with a higher capital tax relative to Continental Europe, cutting the U.K. tax and raising the tax in Continental Europe induces important efficiency gains in favor of the United Kingdom. Cutting the U.K.'s capital income tax attracts capital into this economy, increasing its capital stock and its ability to raise tax revenue over time (so that small adjustments in the labor tax are enough to preserve intertemporal fiscal balance). The opposite occurs in Continental Europe. The higher capital income tax is not an effective means of increasing tax revenue in the face of the capital outflows that follow, and if the outflows are sufficiently large (i.e., the lower is the

---

national tax authorities. For a quantitative analysis of cooperative and noncooperative solutions to international tax competition, see Mendoza and Tesar (2001).

[7] These are the 1996 estimates of effective tax rates computed using the method proposed by Mendoza, Razin, and Tesar (1994).

harmonized tax rate relative to the current U.K. tax rate), Continental Europe may end up increasing its labor income tax as well in order to preserve intertemporal fiscal balance. If the tax rate is harmonized so that Continental Europe raises its tax to match the existing U.K. tax, the relative efficiency loss is minimized – which explains why this is the best-case scenario for Continental Europe.

The rest of the paper proceeds as follows. Section 2 presents the structure of the model and discusses the solution method and the calibration of parameter values. Section 3 uses the model to examine the implications of European capital tax harmonization. Section 4 reflects on some important caveats of the analysis and presents general conclusions.

2. A 'Workhorse' Dynamic Equilibrium Model of Taxation in Open Economies

The model is a modest variation of the two-country dynamic general equilibrium models of fiscal policy that originated in Assaf Razin's work from the 1980s, as reviewed in the Introduction. The model features two perfectly competitive, representative-agent economies with perfectly integrated goods markets and perfect mobility of financial capital. Tax policy analysis is conducted by taking as given predetermined time paths of government outlays and studying the effects of cuts in particular taxes subject to the constraint that other taxes need to be raised in order to satisfy the governments' intertemporal budget constraints.

The model differs from those in the literature of the 1980s in that the specification of preferences and technology is modified to conform to those consistent with the neoclassical general-equilibrium model of exogenous balanced growth driven by labor-augmenting technological change (see King, Plosser, and Rebelo (1988)). This framework, and variants close to it, have been widely used in quantitative closed-economy applications to study macroeconomic effects of fiscal and monetary policies (see King and Rebelo (1990); Cooley and Hansen (1992); and Chari, Christiano, and Kehoe (1994)).

The assumption that long-run growth is exogenous implies that assessments of changes in the tax structure are conducted abstracting from any effects that tax policy may have on economic growth over the long run. This is at odds with the qualitative predictions of a large class of endogenous growth models, but it is in line with their quantitative predictions and with the evidence indicating that long-run growth seems independent of the variations of tax rates observed in the data, despite significant efficiency gains on investment rates (see Lucas (1990) and Mendoza, Milesi-Ferretti, and Asea (1997)). Note, however, that despite negligible growth effects, the welfare implications of tax policies that result from efficiency gains or losses can still be very large (see Lucas (1990), Cooley and Hansen (1992), and Mendoza and Tesar (1998)).

The model examined here also differs from the early models in Frenkel and Razin (1986b) and (1987) and Helpman and Razin (1987) in that their models focused on non-Ricardian real effects of changes in lump-sum taxes by adopting the Blanchard–Yaari setup of overlapping generations. In these models, households have a shorter life horizon than governments so a cut in current taxes induces a wealth transfer from individuals born in the future (i.e., those that are alive to pay future taxes but not to enjoy current tax cuts) to those currently alive. In contrast, the model of this paper considers conventional non-Ricardian distortionary taxes on factor incomes and consumption in an infinite-horizon environment. Wealth effects are still present but in the form of cross-country wealth redistributions in the size and location of capital stocks and financial assets.

2.1. Structure of the Model

The exogenous rate of labor-augmenting technological change is the same in each country and is given by γ. The long-run rate of output growth is therefore the same in the two countries and is also equal to γ, and expenditure flows grow at that same rate in steady state in each country. This long-run balanced-growth assumption restricts the permissible set of functional forms that can be used to represent utility and production functions to those that satisfy the properties identified in King, Plosser, and Rebelo (1988). As usual, all variables in the model, except leisure and labor, are rendered stationary by expressing them as a ratio of the state of technology (the transformed variables are written in lower case), and the familiar transformations of the subjective discount rate and the asset-evolution equations apply. The paper focuses, without loss of generality, on the competitive equilibrium of the detrended model. Since these are standard procedures, the details are omitted. Also in line with standard practice, foreign variables are identified by asterisks.

Each country is inhabited by identical, infinitely lived households. They maximize a conventional isoelastic lifetime utility function over intertemporal sequences of consumption (c) and leisure (ℓ):

$$\sum_{t=0}^{\infty}[\beta(1+\gamma)^{1-\sigma}]^t \left(\frac{(c_t \ell_t^a)^{1-\sigma}}{1-\sigma} \right), \quad \sigma > 1, \quad a > 0, \quad 0 < \beta < 1. \quad (1)$$

In this expression, β is the households' subjective discount factor, $1/\sigma$ is the intertemporal elasticity of substitution in consumption, and a is a coefficient that governs the intertemporal elasticity of labor supply for a given value of σ. Note that the stationary transformation of the model implies an effective discount factor given by $\beta(1 + \gamma)^{1-\sigma}$ instead of β.

Households maximize (1) subject to the following sequence of budget constraints, taking as given all relative prices and fiscal policy variables:

$$(1 + \tau_C)c_t + (1 + \gamma)(k_{t+1} + q_t b_{t+1} + q_t^g d_{t+1}) + \left(\frac{\eta}{2} \left(\frac{x_t}{k_t} - z \right)^2 - 1 \right) k_t$$

$$= (1 - \tau_L)w_t L_t + (1 - \tau_K)(r_t - \delta)k_t + b_t + d_t + e_t \qquad (2)$$

for $t = 0, \ldots, \infty$. The left-hand side of (2) measures household expenditures. These are made of purchases of consumption goods, which include an ad valorem sales tax τ_C, new capital goods, k_{t+1}, private international bonds, b_{t+1}, and domestic government bonds d_{t+1}. The price of capital and the price of consumer goods differ because investment incurs quadratic capital-adjustment costs as a function of the ratio of net investment (x_t) to existing capital (k_t). The coefficient η determines the speed of adjustment of the capital stock, while z is set equal to the long-run investment–capital ratio to ensure that at steady state the capital adjustment cost is zero. Net investment is defined as $x_t \equiv (1 + \gamma)k_{t+1} - (1 - \delta)k_t$, where δ is the rate of depreciation of the capital stock.[8] For simplicity, international and government bonds are represented as discounted bonds. The price of private bonds is q_t, the price of public bonds is q_t^g, and their gross real rates of return are $R_t \equiv (1/q_t)$ and $R_t^g \equiv (1/q_t^g)$ respectively.

The right-hand side of (2) measures after-tax household income, which is made of factor and nonfactor incomes. Factor income is derived from supplying capital and labor (L_t) to firms at pre-tax factor prices w_t and r_t. Labor and capital income are taxed at ad valorem tax rates τ_L and τ_K respectively. The capital income tax is based on the residence principle, and the tax code provides for a depreciation allowance. Nonfactor interest income is derived from the liquidation of holdings of discounted public and private bonds. This income is assumed to be tax-free, but Mendoza and Tesar (1998) examined the implications of relaxing this assumption and found that it can have important effects on the quantitative

---

[8] Investment costs, or similar frictions like gestation lags, differentiate physical from financial assets so as to prevent the instantaneous adjustment of the domestic marginal product of capital to the world interest rate. Without these costs, the model would predict unrealistically large swings in investment and current account balances.

predictions of the model. Nonfactor income also includes lump-sum transfers from government that represent entitlement payments, these are denoted by e_t.

Equation (2) embodies an implicit assumption of "extreme home bias" in that domestic capital and public debt are owned only by domestic households. This assumption allows the model to support competitive equilibria in which free international trade in private bonds and residence-based taxation coexist, yet there can be different country-specific tax rates on domestic capital income owned by the residents of each country. As argued later, this is not possible if shares on physical capital and/or government bonds are freely traded across countries (see also Frenkel et al. (1991)). Other forms of financial-market segmentation, such as trading costs or short-selling constraints, could be introduced with the same purpose, but so far they have proven inadequate to solve the "home bias" puzzle observed in the data and they would complicate the model significantly.

Households also face a standard no–Ponzi-game restriction, which together with (2) implies that the present value of household income must equal that of expenditures plus any initial asset holdings. In addition, households face a standard normalized time constraint in choosing labor supply and leisure allocations:

$$\ell_t + L_t = 1. \tag{3}$$

Firms play a simple role in this model because they face a static optimization problem (since investment decisions are being made by households, who are assumed to own the firms). In particular, firms maximize profits subject to constant-returns-to-scale production technologies taking as given pre-tax factor prices. The detrended production function is Cobb–Douglas:

$$F(k_t, L_t) = k_t^{1-\alpha} L_t^{\alpha}, \qquad 0 < \alpha < 1, \tag{4}$$

where α is the labor income share. Without loss of generality, all corporate taxes are viewed as included in the capital income tax levied on households. Thus, at equilibrium firms demand factors of production according to standard marginal productivity rules and earn zero profits.

Fiscal policy is made of three elements. First, predetermined sequences of unproductive government expenditures and lump-sum transfer or entitlement payments, $(g_t + e_t)$ for $t = 0, \ldots, \infty$. Second, a set of time-invariant tax rates (τ_C, τ_L, τ_K). Third, a sequence of public bond issues,

d_t, for $t = 1, \ldots, \infty$. The government budget constraint is given by

$$(g_t + e_t) + d_t = \tau_c c_t + \tau_L w_t L_t + \tau_K (r_t - \delta) k_t + (1 + \gamma) q_t^g d_{t+1}. \qquad (5)$$

The left-hand side of this equation measures total government outlays (i.e., goods purchases and entitlement payments) plus debt payments. The right-hand side measures tax revenue and proceeds from sales of newly issued bonds. Government purchases, entitlements, and tax rates are viewed as the exogenous instruments of fiscal policy. Thus, any deficit or surplus in the fiscal balance (i.e., in the gap between goods purchases, entitlement payments, and tax revenue) is offset by an endogenous change in public debt net of interest and principal on existing debt. Since the government also faces a no–Ponzi-game constraint, the present value of government expenditures plus entitlement payments must equal the present value of tax revenue net of payments on initial public debt.[9] Hence, given its tax and expenditure policies and its initial bond position, the government must choose a time path of public bond issues that satisfies its intertemporal budget constraint.

Public debt is "Ricardian" in the sense that, given d_0 and the policy choices on government purchases, entitlement payments, and tax rates, the competitive equilibrium can be represented either with the path of public bonds dictated by (5) or with a sequence of lump-sum taxes (subsidies), T_t, set to an amount equal to the fiscal deficit (surplus) each period (see Mendoza and Tesar (1998) for details):

$$T_t = \tau_C c_t + \tau_L w_t L_t + \tau_K (r_t - \delta) k_t - (g_t + e_t). \qquad (6)$$

Since the object of interest for determining the competitive equilibrium of the economy and the financing needs of the government is the time path of the fiscal balance, not the path of the stock of public bonds (which at any rate depends on the exogenous initial condition d_0), the analysis is conducted using this "Ricardian" representation of the government budget constraint. This change implies also that the relevant budget constraint for households becomes:

$$(1 + \tau_C) c_t + (1 - \gamma)(k_{t+1} + q_t b_{t+1}) + \left(\frac{\eta}{2} \left(\frac{x_t}{k_t} - z \right)^2 - 1 \right) k_t$$

$$= (1 - \tau_L) w_t L_t + (1 - \tau_K)(r_t - \delta) k_t + b_t + e_t + T_t. \qquad (7)$$

---

[9] Note that (2), (5), and the no–Ponzi-game constraints on households and government imply that the present value of the trade balance equals b_0.

The market-clearing conditions for the world markets of goods and bonds are

$$k_t^{1-\alpha} L_t^{\alpha} + \left(k_t^*\right)^{1-\alpha^*} \left(L_t^*\right)^{\alpha^*} = c_t + c_t^* + x_t + \frac{\eta}{2} \left(\frac{x_t}{k_t} - z\right)^2 k_t + x_t^*$$

$$+ \frac{\eta^*}{2} \left(\frac{x_t^*}{k_t^*} - z^*\right)^2 k_t^* + g_t + g_t^*, \tag{8}$$

$$b_t + b_t^* = 0. \tag{9}$$

The competitive equilibrium of this two-country world is given by sequences of pre-tax prices $[r_t, r_t^*, q_t, w_t, w_t^*]$ and allocations $[k_{t+1}, k_{t+1}^*, b_{t+1}, b_{t+1}^*, x_t, x_t^*, L_t, L_t^*, \ell_t, \ell_t^*, c_t, c_t^*, T_t, T_t^*]$, for $t = 0, \ldots, \infty$, such that: (a) households in each country maximize utility subject to their corresponding budget constraints, time constraints and no–Ponzi-game constraints, taking as given pre-tax prices, the values of all fiscal policy variables, and date-0 holdings of capital and foreign bonds, (b) firms maximize profits subject to the Cobb–Douglas technologies taking as given pre-tax factor prices, (c) the government budget constraints hold for given tax rates and exogenous sequences of government purchases and entitlements, and (d) the global markets of goods and bonds clear.

2.2. Stationary Equilibrium, Calibration and Design of Tax Policy Experiments

Changes in tax policy are represented by changes in some or all of the elements of the domestic and/or foreign triples of time-invariant tax rates (τ_C, τ_L, τ_K) and $(\tau_C^*, \tau_L^*, \tau_K^*)$. The analysis is not aimed at solving a Ramsey optimal taxation problem but at studying the effects of once-and-for-all changes in time-invariant tax structures. This is more in line with the Harberger–Feldstein "*n*th-best economics" approach of assessing the magnitude of the distortions associated with existing policies and identifying simple, welfare-improving policy changes (see Harberger (1964)). This approach is also supported by the results of closed-economy studies by Lucas (1990) and Cooley and Hansen (1992) showing that the large welfare gains of cuts in time-invariant capital income tax rates dwarf the small effects added by time-varying taxes.[10]

---

[10] This does not alter the fact that both Ramsey optimal taxes and changes in time-invariant taxes are both time-inconsistent in standard dynamic equilibrium models like the one studied here. This problem, however, also plagues other conventional models used to assess the effects of tax changes in policy institutions.

There are two important steps to follow in the process of turning this model into a quantitative framework suitable for evaluating tax policies. First, the model must be initialized with parameter values for the functional forms that represent preferences, technology, and government policies such that the model can mimic key features of the data of the actual economies that are to be the subject of tax policy assessments. Second, the quantitative solutions of the model must be obtained using an algorithm that can solve accurately for competitive equilibria at the steady-state balanced-growth paths of alternative tax policy regimes and along the transitional dynamics between these long-run equilibria. Assessments of the welfare implications of changes in tax policy depend crucially on the latter, since tax policies that may seem welfare-improving on the basis of comparisons across long-run equilibria can be welfare-reducing once the effects of transitional dynamics are factored in (see Lucas (1990) and Mendoza and Tesar (1998)).

The calibration and simulation steps referred to above are familiar from the quantitative tax policy experiments conducted using closed-economy models as in Cooley and Hansen (1992) and Chari, Christiano, and Kehoe (1994). However, a particular complication arises in an open-economy context because international spillovers of tax policies imply changes in long-run net foreign asset positions and these positions are dependent on initial conditions. This differs sharply from the standard result in closed-economy models in which the steady-state capital stock is independent of initial conditions.

The computation of the initial "status quo" steady-state equilibrium under given current tax policies is straightforward because it is the outcome of a calibration process in which the model is parameterized so as to match basic long-run features of the data – this is the same process followed in the calibration exercises performed with closed-economy models. In contrast, the computation of the steady-state balanced-growth equilibrium under a proposed new tax policy, and the corresponding transitional dynamics, differ markedly from closed-economy studies because the dependency on initial conditions of the net foreign asset positions implies that the new long-run equilibrium and the dynamics by which it is reached must be solved simultaneously. Further details on this issue are provided in the analysis of the model's stationary equilibrium that follows below.

The long-run equilibrium of the home country along a balanced-growth path is summarized by the following system of simultaneous equations:

$$\frac{k}{y} = \frac{\beta(1+\gamma)^{1-\sigma}(1-\alpha)(1-\tau_K)}{(1+\gamma) - \beta(1+\gamma)^{1-\sigma}[1 - \delta(1-\tau_K)]}, \tag{10}$$

$$\frac{x}{y} = (\gamma + \delta)\frac{k}{y}, \tag{11}$$

$$\frac{c}{y} = 1 - \frac{x}{y} - \frac{g}{y} - \frac{nx}{y}, \tag{12}$$

$$\frac{nx}{y} = [\beta(1 + \gamma)^{1-\sigma} - 1]\frac{b}{y}, \tag{13}$$

$$L = \frac{\left(\dfrac{1 - \tau_L}{1 + \tau_C}\right)\alpha}{a\dfrac{c}{y} + \left(\dfrac{1 - \tau_L}{1 + \tau_C}\right)\alpha}. \tag{14}$$

Equation (10) follows from the steady-state Euler equation for physical capital. It expresses the capital–output ratio at steady state, k/y, as a function of preference and technology parameters, and the tax on capital income. Equation (11) is the law of motion for capital accumulation evaluated at steady state, which determines the steady-state investment rate, x/y. Equation (12) is the resource constraint of the economy, which follows from consolidating the budget constraints of households and government. This equation determines the steady-state consumption–output ratio, c/y, as a function of the investment rate, the GDP share of government purchases, g/y, and the net exports–output ratio, nx/y. Equation (13) is the foreign-asset evolution equation along a balanced-growth path. Since the parameter restrictions set in (1) imply $\beta(1 + \gamma)^{1-\sigma} < 1$, Equation (13) implies that a long-run positive (negative) foreign asset position finances a long-run trade deficit (surplus). Equation (14) represents long-run equilibrium in the labor market as given by the equality between the marginal rate of substitution between consumption and leisure and the post-tax marginal product of labor.[11]

The problem with determining the effect of tax policy changes on the long-run equilibrium of this economy is that Equations (10)–(14) form an underidentified simultaneous equation system with six unknowns (k/y, x/y, c/y, L, nx/y, and b/y) but only five equations. Equations (10)–(11) determine k/y and x/y and are identical to the equations that appear in

---

[11] Note that (14) can be used to determine the equilibrium allocation of labor at any date t along an equilibrium path, not just at steady state, if the corresponding ratio c_t/y_t is known. Note also the differences in the long-run incidence of the different taxes. The capital income tax affects k/y, x/y and, through the effect of changes in x/y on c/y, the equilibrium allocation of labor, while consumption and labor taxes affect equilibrium labor but not the investment rate and the capital output ratio.

closed-economy models. However, even given these solutions for k/y and x/y, (12)–(14) cannot determine solutions for c/y, L, nx/y, and b/y, and hence for the level of all endogenous variables.

The status quo initial calibration of the model avoids this problem by taking nx/y from the data. More precisely, the system (10)–(14) is solved for δ, β, a, c/y and b/y, given the values of other preference and technology parameters, tax rates, and long-run averages of k/y, x/y, nx/y, g/y, and L obtained from macroeconomic time series.

The initial calibration proceeds as follows. The home country is calibrated to the United Kingdom and the foreign country is calibrated to an arithmetic average of the three largest European economies (France, Germany, and Italy). The calibration is set at a quarterly frequency and uses national accounts data from the OECD's *National Accounts* and the updated estimates of effective tax rates for macroeconomic models calculated in Mendoza and Tesar (2001) using the method proposed by Mendoza, Razin, and Tesar (1994).[12] A summary of the calibration parameters is reported in Table 12.1.

The initial tax rates in the calibration were set to the 1996 estimates reported by Mendoza and Tesar (2001). Figures 12.1–12.3 plot the time series of each tax rate in the four European economies considered here. As can be observed, harmonization of indirect taxes has produced very similar consumption tax rates across the four countries, while important differences remain with regard to factor income taxes. In particular, the tax on capital income is higher in the United Kingdom than in the other countries, while the opposite is true with respect to labor income taxes. There are also upward trends in the labor income tax rates of France, Germany and Italy. The magnitude of the difference in each tax may be subject of debate, depending on the method used to estimate tax rates, but these estimates do capture the widely accepted view that the tax on capital income is higher in the United Kingdom than in Continental Europe.

The fiscal sector of the model is also calibrated to match the observed GDP shares of government purchases in the four countries considered. In this regard there is also a noticeable asymmetry between the United

---

[12] Mendoza et al. (1994) estimated tax rates for the seven largest industrialized countries (G7) over the 1968–90 period by combining tax revenue data with information from the aggregate balance sheets of households, corporations, and government from national accounts. Mendoza, Milesi-Ferretti and Asea (1997) updated these estimates through 1992 and extended them to include several OECD countries. Mendoza and Tesar (2001) updated the G7 estimates through 1996. The data are available at http://www.econ.duke.edu/~mendozae/pdfs/newtaxdata.pdf.

Table 12.1. *Calibration Parameters and the Pre–Tax-Harmonization Equilibrium*

Preference and technology parameters:
$\delta = 1.61$ $\beta = 0.99$ $a = 2.675$ $\gamma = 1.56$ $\sigma = 2$ $\alpha = 0.64$ $\eta = 10$

Fiscal policy parameters (in percent)

	United Kingdom		Continental Europe	France	Germany	Italy
τ_C^1	15.6		15.6	16.0	16.4	14.7
τ_L	24.4		47.4	50.1	42.4	49.8
τ_K	47.2		28.0	26.1	23.9	33.9
g/y	19.4		20.8	23.6	19.5	19.0

Pre–tax-harmonization balanced-growth allocations (in percent):

	United Kingdom		Continental Europe	
	Data	Model	Data	Model
c/y	64.1	64.4	57.1	57.6
x/y	17.2	17.2	20.7	20.6
nx/y	−1.0	−1.0	1.5	1.1
Tax revenue	35.3	36.1	41.1	44.7
L		20.0		15.9
k/k^*		92.9		107.6
y/y^*		111.1		90.0

Note: The data column shows averages for the period 1990–99. Continental Europe is an arithmetic average of data for France, Germany, and Italy. The data source is the OECD's National Income Accounts and Revenue Statistics. Tax rates are the 1996 estimates of effective tax rates computed using the method proposed by Mendoza, Razin, and Tesar (1994).
[1] The 1996 consumption tax in the United Kingdom is 15.2 percent but the calibration assumes an initial consumption tax that is identical across countries.

Kingdom and the other three countries. The average GDP share of government expenditures over the 1990–99 period is 0.19 in the U.K. relative to a mean of 0.21 for the other three countries (the individual country averages are 0.24 for France, 0.2 for Germany and 0.19 for Italy).

Another important aspect of the calibration relates to the initial foreign asset positions, because these together with the initial capital stocks determine the initial wealth of each economy and also determine which country experiences negative or positive income effects on account of changes in the world real interest rate triggered by tax changes. The model treats Europe as a closed economy unit, so that the sum of the bond positions of the United Kingdom and Continental Europe adds to zero. At steady state the foreign asset–GDP ratio is linearly- related to

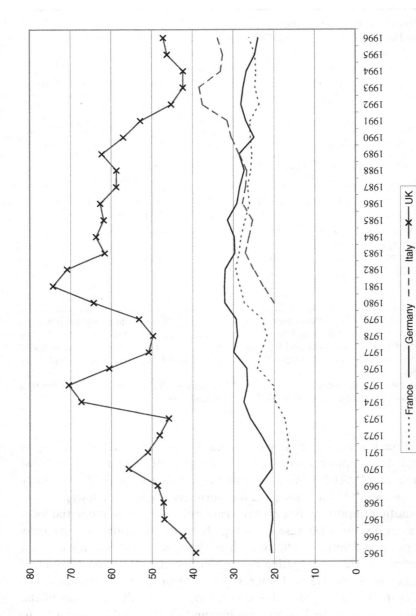

Figure 12.1. European capital income tax rates

····· France ——— Germany – – – Italy —✕— UK

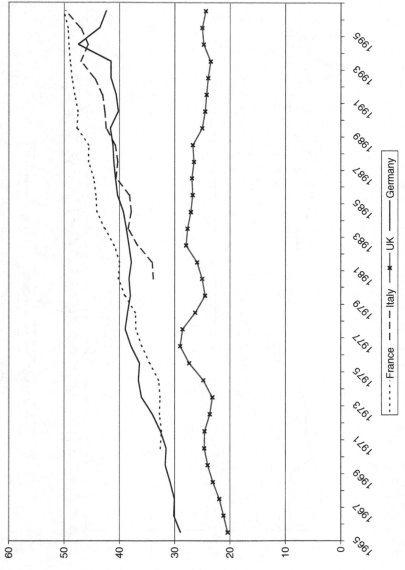

Figure 12.2. European labor income tax rates

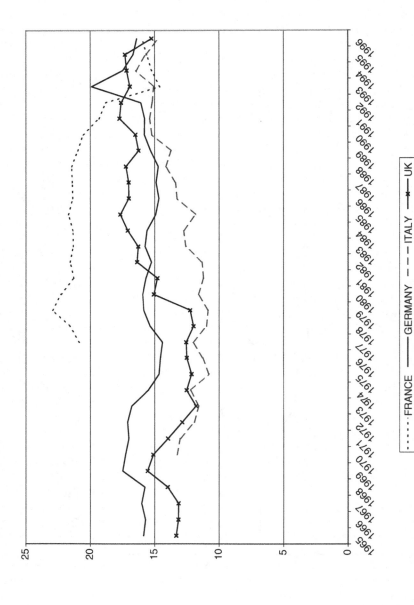

Figure 12.3. European consumption tax rates

····· FRANCE ——— GERMANY – – – ITALY —✳— UK

the net exports–GDP ratio as shown in Equation (13). Hence, the initial calibration pins down the initial foreign asset–GDP ratios by requiring the model to match the U.K.'s observed net exports–GDP ratio. The U.K. average net exports–GDP ratio for the period 1990–99 is -0.01.[13]

The rest of the calibration is similar to that proposed by Mendoza and Tesar (1998) and is completed as follows. The per capita GDP growth rate is set to $\gamma = 1.56\%$ per year (0.39% per quarter), the intertemporal elasticity of substitution is set at $1/2$ ($\sigma = 2$), and the annual investment rate is set at the 1990–99 average for the United Kingdom (0.17). The quarterly capital–output ratio is set to 2.16 (8.62 annually), the labor income share is set at 0.64, and the fraction of time spent at work is set to 20 percent. These three parameter values match estimates for the U.S. economy reported by Cooley and Hansen (1992). These three ratios are likely to differ slightly from those observed in Europe, but the aim of the analysis is to emphasize asymmetries in fiscal policy under an otherwise symmetric two-country model.

Given the above ratios, parameter values, and tax rate estimates, the solution of the system of steady-state equations (10)–(14) implies $\delta = 1.61$, $\beta = 0.99$, $a = 2.675$, $c/y = 0.64$ and $b/y = 1.044$. Preference and technology parameters are set identical across the United Kingdom and Continental Europe in order to highlight the effects of asymmetries in fiscal policy (in tax rates as well as in government expenditures and entitlements). Given identical preference and technology parameters, the foreign-country version of the system (10)–(14) is solved for k^*/y^*, x^*/y^*, nx^*/y^*, and L^* imposing the market clearing condition $b + b^* = 0$.

The above results imply a value for the long-run real interest rate of 6.1% per year. The long-run real interest rate is determined by the standard condition from balanced-growth models: $r = \rho - \gamma\sigma$, where ρ is the rate of time preference (i.e., $\rho = \beta^{-1} - 1$). It is important to note that this long-run real interest rate is invariant to tax policy changes. Hence, international transmission of tax policies via changes in the world's real interest rate can only occur during the transitional dynamics. This is an implication of the assumptions of exogenous long-run balanced growth and residence-based taxation.

Table 12.1 reports estimates of c/y, g/y, x/y, and nx/y, and the GDP ratios of tax revenue for both economies in the data and in the model, as well as the ratios of capital stock and output across the U.K. and Continental Europe. The calibration was set to mimic the U.K. ratios g/y,

---

[13] The mean next-exports GDP ratio for Continental Europe over the same period is 0.015.

x/y, and nx/y, but all the other GDP ratios in the table are endogenous solutions of the long-run equilibrium of the model. The model's ratios are roughly the same as in the data, including the tax revenue–GDP ratios, suggesting that the "status quo" calibration is a reasonable benchmark to conduct tax policy analysis.

The parameters of the capital-adjustment-cost function can be set once the long-run investment rate and capital–output ratio are known. These two determine the investment–capital ratio as $x/k = (x/y)/(k/y)$. As mentioned earlier, z is set equal to x/k so that adjustment costs are zero in the long run. The value of η is set so that the rate of convergence to the long-run, balanced-growth path matches empirical estimates of conditional growth convergence coefficients (see Mendoza and Tesar (1998)). This implies $\eta = 10$.

The solution of the transitional dynamics from the initial status quo balanced-growth path to the new long-run equilibrium associated with a proposed tax policy change is obtained using the method proposed by Mendoza and Tesar (1998). Their approach ensures that the following two critical properties of the competitive equilibrium are satisfied. First, the long-run foreign asset positions to which countries converge for a proposed tax policy scenario are consistent with foreign asset accumulation dynamics starting from initial conditions that correspond to the foreign asset positions in the status quo calibration. Second, the levels of government purchases and entitlement payments that prevailed before the tax policy change are kept constant at all times. Thus, changes in taxes under a proposed tax policy must be revenue neutral in present value (if one tax is cut and tax revenue falls as a result, the others need to increase to ensure that the present value of tax revenue matches the present value of the unchanged government outlays). The implicit assumption is that government debt adjusts to fill any gap between tax revenue and total government outlays in any given period.

The dynamic consistency of the bond positions is accomplished by solving the model combining the King–Plosser–Rebelo (KPR) linear approximation algorithm with an iterative "shooting" routine on holdings of foreign bonds. The algorithm starts with an initial guess for the long-run bond positions in the long-run equilibrium under the proposed tax policy (typically the same as the "status quo" bond positions). The long-run equilibrium conditions are then solved using the simultaneous Equations (10)–(14) and the transitional dynamics are solved by linearizing around these new balanced-growth allocations using KPR. The transitional dynamics are traced for 2,500 periods setting as initial conditions the values of k, k^*, and b in the status quo calibration. These simulations yield foreign bond positions that converge to some long-run bond positions. If the latter differ from the initial guess, the new results are adopted as a new guess and the process is repeated.

The intertemporal revenue neutrality of the proposed tax changes is ensured with a second iterative routine. Once a consistent solution for foreign asset dynamics is obtained, the algorithm checks whether the present value of the unchanged government outlays (i.e., expenditures plus entitlement payments) equals the present value of tax revenue. If this equality fails, one of the taxes is adjusted according to a rule that updates the tax rate as needed to balance the latest estimate of the government's intertemporal budget constraint. The algorithm starts again with the shooting routine on foreign bonds using the updated taxes, and the process is repeated until it converges to consistent solutions for both taxes and long-run bond positions.

Once a full solution of a tax policy experiment is obtained (i.e., long-run equilibria before and after the tax change as well as transitional dynamics), the welfare effect of the policy is computed by calculating the compensated lifetime consumption variations proposed by Lucas (1987) and (1990). Accordingly, the net welfare effect of a tax policy change is measured by the constant percentage change in consumption in all periods that leaves households indifferent between the lifetime utility obtained by remaining in the status quo equilibrium and the lifetime utility obtained by undertaking the tax policy change (inclusive of the stage of transitional dynamics in consumption and leisure).

The solution method proposed here can accommodate alternative assumptions with regard to the structure of the tax adjustments that are considered. Tax policies can be examined as unilateral changes adopted by one country, with the other country adjusting either distortionary or lump-sum taxes to preserve its revenue neutrality in the face of international spillovers of the tax changes made by the first country. Alternatively, tax policy changes can be examined as world-wide changes in some distortionary taxes met by world-wide revenue-neutral changes in other distortionary taxes.

2.3. The International Transmission Channels of Tax Policy
The model features the three main channels by which changes in country-specific tax rates have external effects on foreign countries mentioned in the introduction. First, the price channel: Changes in tax policy alter the world's real interest rate (or the price of internationally traded bonds)

and the prices of capital and labor within each country. Second, the wealth channel: Changes in tax policy have efficiency effects that affect the total capital stock of the world economy and the distribution of capital across countries. Third, the tax revenue erosion channel: The tax bases of foreign countries are affected by the price and wealth channels, forcing foreign tax authorities to implement undesired changes in their own structure of distortionary taxes in order to maintain intertemporal fiscal balance.[14]

The basic economic intuition behind the operation of these three channels can be derived from studying the optimality conditions that characterize the competitive equilibrium of the model. Consider in particular the optimal saving and investment margins in the home and foreign countries. Because of the assumptions of residence-based taxation, extreme home bias, and tax-free foreign interest income, these optimal margins imply that

(a) The intertemporal marginal rates of substitution in consumption are the same across countries and both are equal to the inverse of the price of international bonds (which is the world's gross real interest rate).

(b) The *post-tax* net marginal products of capital (including the marginal capital adjustment costs) are equalized across countries, and both are also equal to the world's gross real interest rate.

The second of these conditions implies that the home-country net marginal product of capital differs from that in the foreign country by a factor equal to $(1 - \tau_K)/(1 - \tau_K^*)$. If the home country cuts its capital income tax, arbitrage of the returns on domestic capital and foreign bonds by home agents leads them to borrow from abroad to take advantage of the increased post-tax return on domestic capital, and thus finance the attractive new investment without a costly consumption sacrifice. Foreign agents are willing to lend but at the right price (since neither country is a small open economy), and this price is reflected in the equality of intertemporal marginal rates of substitution listed in condition (a). A capital outflow from the foreign country into the home country takes place and the world's real interest rate rises. Moreover, as capital flows out of the foreign country, the foreign wage rate and price of capital (which differs in the short run from the price of consumption and the world interest

---

[14] Alternatively, this revenue-erosion effect can be modeled as forcing changes in government expenditures with production or utility benefits, which would also be distortionary.

rate because of the adjustment costs) also change. These interest rate and factor price changes represent the price channel of the international spillovers of tax policies. Note that the interest rate change can only be transitory because, as explained earlier, the long-run real interest rate is independent of tax policy and is set by the exogenous growth condition: $r = \rho - \gamma\sigma$.

The wealth channel works through the process by which the home (foreign) country increases (reduces) its debt and capital stock during the transition, as the efficiency gains of the domestic tax cut materialize. The domestic debt build-up in the early stages of transition reflects not only the borrowing incurred to expand the capital stock but also the debt acquired to distribute evenly over time the consumption benefits of the increased wealth of the economy. The home country runs a trade deficit in the short run but at steady state it services its increased long-run debt with a permanent trade surplus, while the opposite happens in the foreign country. Following Mendoza and Tesar (1998), the short-run debt build-up can be referred to as a *smoothing effect* and the servicing of the increased long-run debt can be labeled an *income redistribution effect*. The physical wealth of the world economy may increase or fall as a result of the efficiency gains of the tax cut (i.e., the world's capital stock may rise or fall), but the home country always becomes relatively wealthier than the foreign country. There is also a change in portfolio composition, the home country holds more physical capital and fewer foreign bonds at the new long-run equilibrium.

The revenue erosion channel operates via the effects of the price and wealth channels on the labor income, capital income, and consumption tax bases of the foreign country. This channel is the net result of the endogenous changes in foreign allocations and prices that determine each tax base in response to the change in home-country taxes. As the present value of foreign tax revenue changes, the foreign tax authority is faced with the choice to either adjust tax rates or cut government outlays. The model forces the latter to remain constant (although the quantitative framework can be easily altered to consider adjustments in these outlays). As a consequence, the foreign government must choose a combination of tax rate changes that yields a present value of tax revenue equal to the present value of the unchanged government outlays.[15]

---

[15] Since government outlays are constant at their pre–tax harmonization level, the present value of these outlays changes only due to changes in the time path of the world's interest rate.

The intuition developed above to account for the international transmission channels of tax policy is based on studying the effects of a cut in the domestic *capital* income tax. However, changes in the domestic labor income tax or the consumption tax induce effects on the foreign economy that operate through similar channels. The price channel is less direct because changes in domestic labor or consumption taxes do not have a direct effect on the price relevant for the investment margin in the foreign country (as is the case with the capital income tax). A cut in domestic labor or consumption taxes raises the domestic post-tax effective real wage and induces the classic income and substitution effects on the domestic supply of labor. The subsequent change in the equilibrium labor allocation has an indirect effect on the domestic marginal product of capital and this sets in motion the arbitrage effects at work in the case of changes in the domestic capital income tax. The wealth channel and the tax revenue erosion channel are also present since they reflect the effects of the price channel on the allocations of the world general equilibrium. However, it is reasonable to argue that the less-direct nature of the price channel makes all three channels of international transmission of tax policy weaker when they operate through changes in the consumption or labor taxes than through the capital income tax.[16]

One additional implication of the model's saving and investment optimality conditions is the intuition for the result that the model can support competitive equilibria in which the foreign and domestic capital income tax rates can differ despite residence-based taxation.[17] As argued earlier, this is due to the "extreme home-bias" assumption that there is no international trade in shares of ownership of the capital stock located in each country. If equity trading were allowed, and the tax system is residence-based, the home (foreign) households would pay $\tau_K(\tau_K^*)$ on their holdings of both k and $k^*(k^*$ and $k)$. Arbitrage of returns across bonds, domestic

---

[16] This can be the case even when the efficiency-driven welfare gains from cuts in the labor income tax exceed those resulting from cuts in the capital income tax. Mendoza and Tesar (1998) show an example of a U.S. labor tax cut with a larger welfare gain than a U.S. capital income tax cut even though the three channels of international spillovers are weaker.

[17] The assumptions of extreme home bias and residence-based taxation could be replaced with source-based taxation without altering the saving and investment optimality conditions (a) and (b) described earlier. Actual tax systems are a mixture of residence- and source-based systems. Frenkel, Razin, and Sadka (1991) show that personal income taxes across OECD countries are mainly residence based, while corporate income taxes are source-based in principle but supplemented by treaties that allow for credits or deductions so as to approximate residence-based taxation.

capital, and foreign capital would then require that both *post-tax* and *pre-tax* net returns on capital in each country be equalized, and this in turn would require that $\tau_K = \tau_K^*$ at equilibrium.

3. The Case Against European Tax Harmonization

This section uses the quantitative framework proposed in Section 2 to analyze the macroeconomic effects of harmonizing capital income taxes in Europe. The experiment shares the basic features of the ones conducted by Frenkel, Razin, and Symansky (1990) and (1991) and Frenkel, Razin, and Sadka (1991) for the case of the harmonization of the value-added tax (VAT). They followed the European VAT harmonization agreements and modeled VAT harmonization as a policy by which a high-VAT, low–income-tax country and a low-VAT, high–income-tax country agree to set a common VAT rate in between their existing high and low rates, adjusting income tax rates as necessary to maintain tax-revenue neutrality period by period.[18] One important difference in the analysis conducted here, however, is in that tax-revenue neutrality is not maintained period by period but in terms of the present value of tax revenue matching the present value of unchanged government outlays. Thus, the experiments below relax the assumption implicit in the VAT harmonization studies that governments cannot engage in optimal borrowing to smooth taxation.

In the capital-income-tax harmonization experiments conducted here, the U.K. starts as a high-capital, low–labor tax country while Continental Europe starts as a low-capital, high–labor tax country. The two economies agree to harmonize the capital income tax rate at a common level in between their initial tax rates. The high degree of consumption-tax harmonization already attained in Europe is preserved by assuming that the consumption tax rate is left unchanged in all countries. The initial levels of government expenditures and entitlement payments are kept constant in each period throughout the experiment, so that the assessment of the effects of tax changes is not blurred by endogenous changes in government outlays. This implies that each country must adjust its labor income tax rate so as to ensure that the present value of its total tax revenue matches the present value of its unchanged government outlays.

---

[18] VAT harmonization in Europe was achieved gradually through various agreements since 1967. Convergence of VAT rates was achieved by implementing agreements on bands for allowable general VAT rates (with a narrowing width that eventually converged to a minimum rate) and lists of products eligible for reduced and zero rates.

One important caveat is that the significance of each of the international transmission channels of tax policy is difficult to isolate in the results of the tax harmonization experiments because they reflect the combined effect of the three transmission channels resulting from changes in capital and labor tax rates in both countries in the model. To address this issue, the tax harmonization analysis is preceded by an analysis of a unilateral cut in the capital income tax by the United Kingdom that provides a clearer picture of the operation of the international spillover effects driven by relative prices, wealth distribution, and tax-revenue erosion.

3.1. Identifying the Tax Policy Transmission Channels: Unilateral Tax Cuts

The unilateral tax cut in the United Kingdom is modeled as a cut of 5 percentage points in its capital income tax from 47.2% to 42.2%. Results are reported for two scenarios. First, an ideal scenario in which Continental Europe is assumed to have access to lump-sum taxation in order to deal with the revenue-erosion effect and maintain intertemporal fiscal balance. Second, a scenario fully consistent with the assumptions of the model in which Continental Europe must use the labor tax to offset any adverse tax-revenue effects.

The first experiment is useful for gauging the magnitude of the erosion of foreign tax revenue directly induced by the U.K. tax cut free from the indirect effects of endogenous adjustments in distortionary tax rates in Continental Europe. The experiment also yields the best outcome for Continental Europe in terms of welfare because the use of lump-sum taxes to offset the tax revenue erosion effect neutralizes the distortions associated with endogenous changes in the labor or capital taxes needed to maintain intertemporal fiscal balance.[19]

Figures 12.4–12.6 plot the transitional dynamics of the variables that reflect the three channels of transmission of tax policy in this experiment. The dynamics are plotted as percent deviations from the initial "status quo," as calibrated in Section 2, for 300 quarters after the cut in the U.K. capital tax. Figure 12.4 plots the effects on prices. The world real interest

---

[19] In as much as the Ricardian representation of public debt as transfers holds, one can say that when time-invariant consumption, labor, or capital taxes are used the foreign government still has some access to lump-sum taxation. There is a clear difference, though, in that changing these tax rates is distortionary even if Ricardian transfers are used to compensate for temporary fiscal deficits or surpluses, while there are no extra distortions when the tax revenue erosion effect is offset with lump-sum taxes.

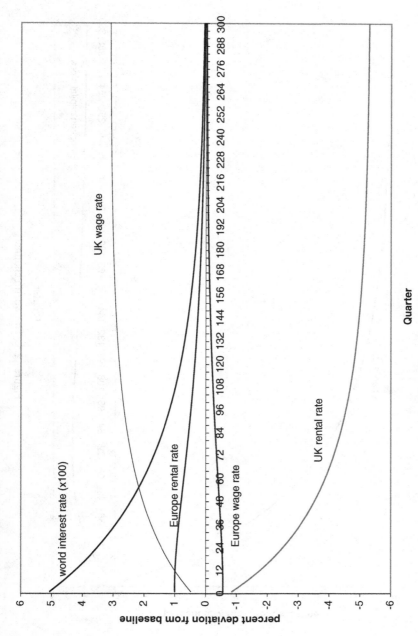

Quarter

Figure 12.4. The price channel

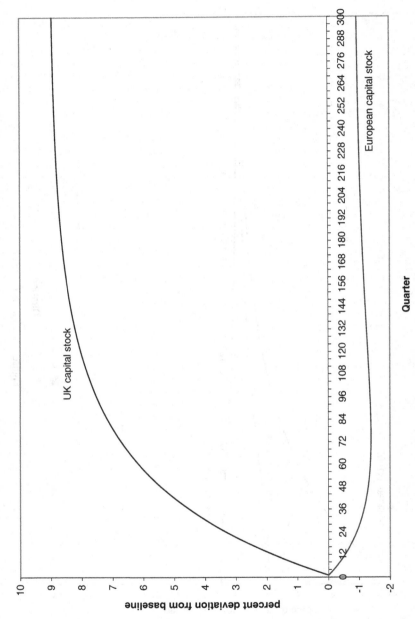

Quarter

Figure 12.5. The wealth channel

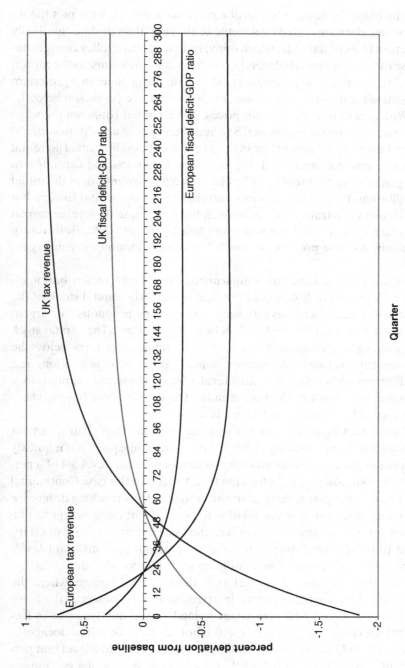

Figure 12.6. The tax revenue erosion channel

rate increases by about 5 tenths of a percentage point (in the plot the interest rate data are scaled by a factor of 100) and then declines gradually to return to its initial state, which is invariant to any tax policy changes because of the exogenous balanced-growth considerations discussed earlier. This interest rate change may seem small, but the changes in equilibrium allocations and welfare that it leads to are very large (as shown below).

With regard to pre-tax factor prices, in the United Kingdom the wage rate rises on impact by about 0.5% and then rises gradually to settle at a level nearly 3% higher than in the pre–tax-cut equilibrium. The rental rate on domestic capital falls on impact by about 1% and continues to fall gradually until it reaches a level nearly 5.5% lower than at the initial equilibrium. Pre-tax factor prices also change in Continental Europe but the changes are transitory. On impact, the rental rate on foreign capital increases by 1% while the wage rate falls by about 0.5%. Both return gradually to their pre–tax-cut levels following a monotonic convergent path.

Figure 12.5 illustrates the significance of the wealth redistribution effect with respect to holdings of physical capital. The capital stock of the United Kingdom increases following a concave, monotonous convergent sequence to a level 9% higher than before the tax cut. The capital stock in Continental Europe declines down to a minimum of 1.4% below the pre–tax-cut level and then recovers somewhat to converge to a long-run equilibrium 0.9% below the initial level. Clearly, the world's capital stock increases as a result of the tax cut in the United Kingdom but the share of it owned by Continental Europe is smaller.

Figure 12.6 illustrates the tax revenue erosion effect. European tax revenue raises on impact by about 3/4 of a percentage point but it quickly falls below the initial level and converges to a long-run level 3/4 of a percentage point lower than before the U.K. tax cut. In this case Continental Europe uses lump-sum taxes or transfers to offset any resulting difference in distortionary tax revenue relative to government outlays. Figure 12.6 shows how these lump sum taxes (i.e., the fiscal deficit as a share of GDP) need to be allocated over time so as to maintain time-invariant levels of government purchases and entitlements. The plot also shows the dynamics of tax revenue and transfers in the United Kingdom, where the labor tax is increased to restore intertemporal fiscal balance (the labor tax increases only by 1.2 percentage points). Given the dynamics of factor prices, consumption, capital and labor, there is an initial decline of almost 2% in U.K. tax revenue followed by a recovery to a level that permanently exceeds the initial level of tax revenue by 3/4 of a percentage point. The plot of the U.K. fiscal deficit reflects only adjustments in public debt (i.e., *Ricardian* lump-sum transfers) used to meet temporary tax revenue shortfalls so that the present value of distortionary tax revenue matches that of government outlays.

The U.K. tax cut sets in motion the price channel and the smoothing and income-redistribution effects of the wealth channel that lead to changes in the dynamics of macroeconomic aggregates in Continental Europe through standard income and substitution effects. In theory, some of these effects have ambiguous signs even for the functional forms used in the model. In the numerical simulation, however, Figure 12.7 shows that output and the supply of labor increase in Continental Europe on impact and then fall to permanently lower levels. Consumption does the opposite. It falls on impact and then rises gradually to a slightly higher permanent level. The trade balance–GDP ratio increases by 2 percentage points on impact, reflecting the transfer of resources going into building up the U.K.'s higher capital stock and consumption driven by the smoothing effect. In the long run, the trade balance–GDP ratio actually falls and is about 3/4 of a percentage point lower than in the initial equilibrium, reflecting the servicing of the debt that the U.K. accumulated in the process of convergence to its new steady-state equilibrium (i.e., the income-redistribution effect).

The welfare effects (i.e., the changes in lifetime utility) of this unilateral tax cut, including the transitional dynamics, are equivalent to an increase in trend consumption of 0.8% for the United Kingdom and a decline of 0.2% for Continental Europe. Given the modest unilateral tax cut that was considered, the large effects on prices, wealth distribution, and tax revenue, and the corresponding large changes in equilibrium allocations and welfare, indicate that the international transmission channels of tax policy are very strong. This is the case even in this best-case scenario in which the fall in the present value of tax revenue relative to that of government outlays in Continental Europe is made up by lump sum taxation.

Consider next the same 5-percentage-point cut in the U.K. capital income tax, but discard the assumption that Continental Europe uses lump-sum taxation to maintain fiscal balance. Continental Europe has to raise its labor tax by 3.8 percentage points, from 47.4% to 51.2% – an unintended tax hike triggered by the unilateral tax cut in the United Kingdom. The transmission channels also result in an increase in the U.K.'s labor income tax, but one that is nearly 1/4 of a percentage point smaller than in the lump-sum tax case.

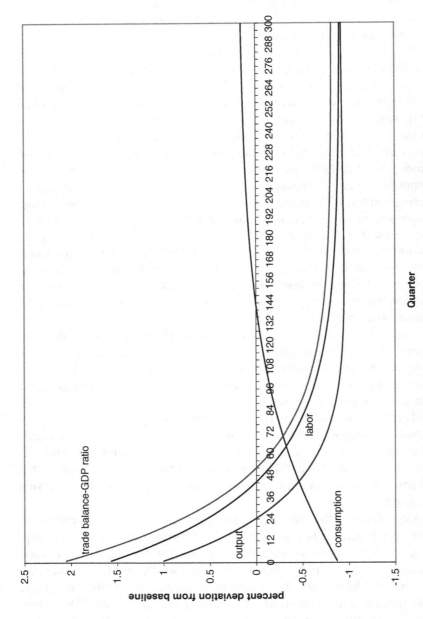

Quarter

Figure 12.7. Macroeconomic dynamics in Continental Europe

The price channel differs in that the short-lived interest rate hike is smaller, and, more importantly, factor prices in Continental Europe experience larger changes and in opposite directions compared to the lump-sum tax case. The rental rate of capital falls by 1.5% on impact and the wage rate rises by 1%. They still converge gradually following a monotonic path back to their initial levels. Pre-tax factor prices in the United Kingdom display fairly similar dynamics as before. The wealth channel is more powerful. The capital stock in the U.K. converges to a level 10% higher than in the pre–tax-cut equilibrium, while that of Continental Europe falls to a level 6% lower. The erosion of the present value of tax revenue has been prevented in boh countries by the upward adjustments in labor taxes. As a result, the initial increase in tax revenue in Continental Europe is nearly 4 times larger (3% instead of 0.75%). Interestingly, the change in Continental Europe's public deficit as a share of GDP implied by the changes in public debt consistent with keeping time-invariant government outlays is still significant. On impact, the fiscal balance improves by 1.2 percentage points of GDP.

Relative to the lump-sum tax case, the net effect of the above price, wealth, and tax erosion channels is a larger welfare gain for the United Kingdom (1.06% instead of 0.83%) and a much larger welfare loss for Continental Europe (3.7% instead of 0.21%). The difference between these welfare estimates across the lump-sum and labor-tax scenarios is a measure of the welfare implications of the tax revenue erosion channel, taking into account how the increase in the distortionary labor tax required in Continental Europe to offset the budgetary impact of the U.K. tax cut feeds back into the price and wealth transmission channels. Note that capturing these feedback effects accurately requires the model to keep track of how pre-tax factor prices, factor allocations, and consumption react in equilibrium to the tax changes. In this regard, simplifying assumptions restricting the response of these variables, such as linear production technologies, exogenous capital accumulation, or unitary intertemporal elasticity of substitution in consumption, are not innocuous.

3.2. European Tax Harmonization

The analysis turns now to the harmonization of the capital income tax across Continental Europe and the United Kingdom. The harmonized tax rate is set as the weighted average of the initial rates, $\lambda 47.2 + (1 - \lambda)27.9$, for any $\lambda \in [0, 1]$. Government outlays are kept constant in each period in both countries and labor taxes are adjusted as necessary to keep the present value of tax revenue in each country equal to the present value of the unchanged government outlays.

Table 12.2 summarizes the results of the tax harmonization experiments for $\lambda = 1, 0.75, 0.5$. For each case, the table reports the new factor income tax rates, welfare changes, and the impact and long-run effects relevant for each of the three transmission channels of tax policy. The harmonized capital income tax rates are set at 47.2%, 42.4%, and 37.6% for values of λ equal to 1, 0.75, and 0.5 respectively. Given the initial labor income tax rates of $\tau_L = 24.4\%$ and $\tau_L^* = 47.4\%$, the adjustments in labor taxes shown in Table 12.2 indicate that for high values of λ (i.e., when the harmonized capital income tax rate is closer to the existing U.K. tax) both countries cut labor income tax rates. For $\lambda = 1$ the U.K. labor tax falls to 23.3% and the labor tax in Continental Europe falls to 41.7%, while lower values of λ result in one or both countries increasing the labor tax. At $\lambda = 0.5$ the U.K. labor tax rises by almost two percentage points and the labor tax in Continental Europe increases by 0.5 percentage points.

From the perspective of welfare effects, tax harmonization does not make much sense. Welfare changes are positive for both countries the higher the value of λ, but even when the capital income tax rate is harmonized at the current U.K. rate the welfare gain for Continental Europe is very small. Lowering λ to 0.75 or 0.5 enlarges the U.K. welfare gain but it turns the gain in Continental Europe into a significant welfare loss. If the harmonized tax rate is set at the average of current tax rates welfare in the U.K. increases by 2.1% but the loss in Continental Europe is nearly 2.7%.

These results are driven by the large effects of the international transmission channels of tax policy. The transmission channels reflect in turn the fact that the options presented by tax harmonization imply a significant efficiency gain for the U.K. *relative* to Continental Europe because the capital income tax always falls in the former relative to the latter, while labor income taxes tend to move in the same direction in both countries. The logic that harmonization of capital income taxes allows the country with the initial low capital tax and high labor tax (i.e., Continental Europe) to switch to a higher capital tax and a lower labor tax, while the country in the opposite situation (i.e., the United Kingdom) switches to a lower capital tax but a lower labor tax, fails. In the best-case scenario for Continental Europe (with $\lambda = 1$), in which the harmonized tax rate is set at the level of the initial U.K. tax, both countries preserve fiscal solvency by lowering labor taxes. As λ falls, the United Kingdom lowers its capital tax and the increase in the capital tax in Continental Europe is therefore smaller. The U.K. must increase its labor tax to preserve intertemporal

Table 12.2. *Macroeconomic Effects of Capital Income Tax Harmonization in Europe*

| | Weight of current U.K. capital income tax | | | | | |
| | $\lambda = 1$ | | $\lambda = 0.75$ | | $\lambda = 0.5$ | |
	Impact effect	Long-run effect	Impact effect	Long-run effect	Impact effect	Long-run effect
New tax rates						
$\tau_K = \tau_K^*$	47.17	47.17	42.37	42.37	37.56	37.56
τ_L	23.29	23.29	24.74	24.74	26.16	26.16
τ_L^*	41.72	41.72	44.12	44.12	47.85	47.85
Welfare effects (percent compensating variation in trend consumption):						
United Kingdom		1.26		1.68		2.05
Continental Europe		0.13		−0.59		−2.68
Price channel (percent changes relative to preharmonization steady state):						
R	−0.14	0.00	−0.05	0.00	0.01	0.00
w	1.30	0.00	1.34	3.01	1.54	5.75
r	−2.26	−0.01	−2.35	−5.13	−2.69	−9.46
w^*	−3.14	−9.58	−2.48	−6.87	−1.33	−4.39
r^*	5.83	19.61	4.57	13.48	2.41	8.30
Wealth channel (percent changes relative to preharmonization steady state):						
k	0.00	3.27	0.00	11.30	0.00	19.10
k^*	0.00	−22.50	0.00	−18.03	0.00	−15.79
Tax revenue erosion channel (percent changes relative to preharmonization steady state)						
tr	−2.98	0.50	−3.83	1.16	−4.86	1.80
def/y^1	−1.10	0.18	−1.42	0.40	−1.80	0.60
tr^*	7.19	−3.06	6.55	−2.61	6.68	−2.56
def^*/y^{*1}	2.99	−1.41	2.80	−1.26	2.92	−1.26
Allocations (percent changes relative to preharmonization steady state):						
y	−2.26	3.26	−2.35	5.59	−2.69	7.83
c	3.58	0.68	1.93	1.92	0.64	2.81
x/y^1	2.78	0.00	3.73	0.93	4.86	1.80
nx/y^1	−6.88	2.23	−6.92	2.34	−7.47	2.61
L	−3.52	3.26	−3.64	2.51	1.01	−0.48
y^*	5.83	−7.30	4.57	−6.98	2.41	−8.80
c^*	6.52	−0.27	2.83	−1.02	−2.44	−4.36
x^*/y^{*1}	−5.97	−3.37	−5.13	−2.44	−4.52	−1.58
nx^*/y^{*1}	6.98	−2.63	7.11	−2.80	7.84	−3.23
L^*	9.25	2.52	7.23	−0.12	3.79	−4.62

Note: The initial tax rates are as reported in Table 12.1. The consumption tax rate remains constant and equal across countries.

[1] Difference relative to the corresponding initial GDP ratio in percentage points

fiscal balance, but this is also the case in Continental Europe despite the rise in its capital tax rate because of the adverse tax revenue implications of the price and wealth channels.

The previous argument is similar to that of a dynamic Laffer curve. Continental Europe's tax rate on capital rises but the present value of tax revenue falls relative to the present value of government outlays, requiring a higher labor income tax to make up for the difference. The effects at work to produce this Laffer-curve effect operate through the general-equilibrium dynamics of pre-tax factor prices, the interest rate, factor allocations, and consumption, which are the determinants of the time path of the tax base and the discount rate of the tax revenue stream.

The price channel data listed in Table 12.2 show that the interest rate falls on impact, but the decline is small and it becomes even smaller as λ falls. The interest rate then rises gradually to return to its invariant steady state determined by the balanced-growth condition. The impact effects on U.K. pre-tax factor prices are similar regardless of the value of λ, but the long-run effects differ sharply. If $\lambda = 1$, the harmonized tax rate equals the current U.K. tax rate and the steady-state conditions of the model imply that the long-run U.K. investment rate, rental rate of capital, and wage rate must be the same as before tax harmonization. As the capital income tax rate drops (with $\lambda = 0.75$ or 0.5), the long-run rental rate (wage rate) falls (rises) below (above) the pre–tax-harmonization level by as much as 9.5% (5.8%) for $\lambda = 0.5$. The effects on pre-tax factor prices in Continental Europe are generally larger than in the U.K.. The capital rental rate increases on impact and in the long run, while the wage rate falls, and these effects are larger the higher the value of λ. These changes in factor prices, coupled with the tax rate adjustments, could help Continental Europe to raise tax revenue but the large, gradual fall in its capital stock more than offsets the movements in factor prices and yields long-run levels of tax revenue 2.5 to 3 percentage points lower than before tax harmonization.

The large wealth redistribution reflected in the wealth channel is the main result of the increase in relative efficiency in the United Kingdom. Harmonization of the capital income tax always results in the United Kingdom owning a larger share of the world's capital. The world-wide capital stock falls for high values of λ but increases for low values of λ. Interestingly, the best welfare outcome for Continental Europe (i.e., the one with the highest λ) is obtained when its capital stock suffers the largest drop. The reason is that this is also the case in which the size of the redistribution of wealth in favor of the U.K. (as proxied by the sum of the absolute values of the changes in capital stocks) is the smallest, and this entails dynamics for pre-tax factor prices and consumption and labor allocations that allow the largest cut in the labor tax of Continental Europe. The resulting smaller distortion on the labor supply–consumption margin and the smaller redistribution of capital yield consumption and labor dynamics that support higher lifetime utility.

The model fails to produce solutions for cases in which $\lambda < 0.46$. The reason is that in this case there is no adjustment of the labor tax in Continental Europe that is consistent with maintaining a present value of tax revenue equal to the present value of government outlays. Lower λ's imply lower hikes in the capital tax in Continental Europe and larger cuts in the capital tax of the United Kingdom, which imply in turn larger efficiency losses in Continental Europe relative to the United Kingdom. Making up for the resulting larger revenue-erosion effects requires Continental Europe to increase its labor tax. However, since this tax obeys a sequence of Laffer-curve relationships each period, and since the Cobb–Douglas technology implies that these Laffer curves shift downward as Continental Europe's capital stock declines, it is possible that the present value of the sequence of tax revenue produced by the maxima of the Laffer curves falls short of what is needed to keep the present value of total tax revenue equal to that of government outlays.

4. Concluding Remarks: If Harmonization Is Undesirable, What Then?

This paper examined the quantitative significance of three key international transmission channels of tax policy: the price channel, the wealth channel, and the tax revenue erosion channel. The theoretical foundations of these transmission channels in dynamic optimizing models of the open economy have been widely studied since the 1980s, but efforts to develop quantitative applications of the theory that can be incorporated into a policymaking framework have progressed slowly due to limitations of numerical methods. This paper applied numerical solution techniques developed by Mendoza and Tesar (1998) to study the features of the transmission channels of tax policy in a two-country dynamic, general-equilibrium model based on the workhorse model of exogenous growth driven by labor-augmenting technological change. The model is calibrated to key features of the fourth largest European economies and solved with an algorithm that yields accurate solutions of short- and long-run changes in net foreign asset positions and endogenous adjustments in tax rates necessary to ensure intertemporal fiscal solvency. These have been the two main hurdles encountered in developing quantitative applications of open-economy intertemporal equilibrium models of tax policy.

The findings of this paper suggest that the macroeconomic effects reflecting the dynamic, general-equilibrium implications of the three international transmission channels of tax policy are very large. When these transmission channels are taken into account, the harmonization of capital income tax rates in Europe (as proxied by the convergence of capital tax rates to an ad hoc weighted average of existing capital income taxes) does not seem desirable – in the sense that it generally fails to yield a Pareto efficient outcome. Pareto efficiency is crucial because if one of the tax-harmonizing countries is made worse off the sustainability of the policy is called into question, and prospects for successful negotiations to implement it are poor to begin with.

What are the alternatives to capital income tax harmonization? One alternative is to explore tax harmonization in a less stringent environment, which can be viewed as an effort to undertake an Europe-wide tax reform. For instance, government outlays and harmonized indirect tax rates can be kept constant as before, but the tax authorities can jointly search for a Pareto-improving mix of capital and labor income tax rates that yields the same welfare gain to each country. Interestingly, this outcome is obtained with an agreement in which the U.K. keeps its tax on capital income unchanged and Continental Europe *increases* its capital income tax by 14.5 percentage points to 43.5%. This tax increase allows both countries to cut labor taxes and still maintain time-invariant levels of government expenditures and entitlements set at their pre–tax-harmonization levels. The labor tax falls by 0.5 and 4.9 percentage points in the U.K. and Continental Europe respectively. The welfare gain in both the U.K. and Continental Europe is equivalent to a 0.8% increase in trend consumption.

A second, more ambitious alternative is to obtain a quantitative assessment of the actual outcome that Nash or Stackelberg competition among national tax authorities can be expected to yield, and compare it with the outcome of a concerted effort for tax coordination (in the sense of adopting a tax structure fully consistent with a cooperative solution of the same tax-competition game). This is the line pursued in Mendoza and Tesar (2001). There, we use the quantitative framework used in this paper as the backbone of a more complex algorithm that solves for the reaction curves of national tax authorities taking into account the full general-equilibrium dynamics that capture the global transmission channels of tax policy. These reaction curves are then used to construct numerical solutions of Nash and Stackelberg international tax competition, the outcomes of which can be contrasted with those of cooperative equilibria. This quantitative analysis can be a useful tool for exploring the analytical results on international tax competition from studies like those by Razin and Sadka (1989, 1990). Preliminary results suggest that, in line with recent observations in the financial media and views of some Commissioners in the European Union (see *The Economist*, Feb. 10, 2001, p. 52), a good dose of tax competition might actually be welfare-improving relative to the existing tax structure, and that relative to this improvement the gains from coordinating to move to a cooperative equilibrium may be small.

It is also worth noting that the conclusion that European capital tax harmonization is undesirable is subject to important caveats that reflect some important shortcomings of the analytical model on which it is based:

1. The analysis is based solely on efficiency gains within a representative-agent framework. The model deals with large *international* redistribution effects, but ignores within-country redistribution effects which are very important in the overall assessment of alternative tax policies at a *national* level.
2. The model assumes that tax changes do not affect the rate of economic growth over the long run. Even though there is evidence that this assumption is quantitatively justifiable for a large class of models of endogenous growth (see Mendoza, Milesi-Ferretti, and Asea (1997)), there are growth effects of taxation that have yet to be explored empirically and could turn out to be important (see, for example, Peretto (1999)).
3. Tax policy in the model examined here is inherently time-inconsistent. Benevolent fiscal authorities have the incentive to reconsider previously announced tax policies if given the chance to reoptimize in the future. Economic agents take into account the entire future path of tax rates in formulating their optimal plans and these plans are time-consistent, but a government that chooses to reoptimize at some future date is oblivious to this situation. However, the European record with VAT tax harmonization suggests that the same cross-border institutions and agreements that have served as an effective commitment mechanism to make harmonized VATs sustainable could work to support broader coordinated efforts at reforming national tax systems.
4. The observed differences in tax systems currently in place in Europe (which play a crucial role in yielding the result that harmonization

is undesirable) are taken as given, so the model abstracts from explaining why tax systems differ across countries in the first place. Since the economic and political forces that drive these differences are likely to be the same as those driving harmonization efforts, it is important to develop political economy models that can tackle this issue within a quantitative framework similar to the one examined here.

5. The model assumes that government expenditures are unproductive. While the extent to which government expenditures are beneficial for private-sector production or utility is highly controversial, it is worth acknowledging that revenue-erosion effects can lead to undesirable cuts in government expenditures or entitlement programs. Still, the costly distortions due to increases in labor taxes forced by tax-revenue erosion in the model examined here may approximate similar effects as those that would result if instead productive government expenditures had to be reduced. Hence, it is unclear whether altering the model to incorporate adjustments in productive government purchases would alter the welfare outcomes reported in the paper.

6. The quantitative results can be very sensitive to the values set for some of the model's parameters. Mendoza and Tesar (1998) showed that is particularly the case with the initial net foreign asset positions, the elasticities of labor supply, and capital-adjustment costs, and the assumption of whether foreign interest income is taxed or not.

References

Aschauer, David A., and Jeremy Greenwood (1985). "Macroeconomic Effects of Fiscal Policy," *Carnegie–Rochester Conference Series on Public Policy* 23, 91–138.

Bovenberg, Lans A. (1986). "Capital Income Taxation in Growing Open Economies," *Journal of Public Economics* 31, 347–76.

Buiter, Willem H. (1987). "Fiscal Policy in Open, Interdependent Economies," in Assaf Razin and Efraim Sadka (eds.), *Economic Policy in Theory and Practice.* (London: McMillan), pp. 101–44.

Chari, V. V., Lawrence J. Christiano, and Patrick J. Kehoe (1994). "Optimal Fiscal Policy in a Business Cycle Model," *Journal of Political Economy* 102, 617–52.

Cooley, Thomas F., and Gary D. Hansen (1992). "Tax Distortions in a Neoclassical Monetary Economy," *Journal of Economic Theory* 58, 290–316.

Eggert, Wolfgang (1998), "International Repercusions of Direct Taxes," Department of Economics and Statistics, University of Konstanz, Konstanz, Germany, working paper.

Frenkel, Jacob A., and Assaf Razin (1986a). "The International Transmission and Effects of Fiscal Policies," *American Economic Review*, 76, pp. 330–335.

Frenkel, Jacob A., and Assaf Razin (1986b). "Fiscal Policies in the World Economy," *Journal of Political Economy* 94, 564–94.

Frenkel, Jacob A., and Assaf Razin (1987). *Fiscal Policies and the World Economy: An Intertemporal Approach*, 1st ed. (Cambridge, MA: MIT Press).

Frenkel, Jacob A., and Assaf Razin (1988). "Spending, Taxes and Deficits: An International-Intertemporal Approach," *Princeton Studies in International Finance No. 63*, Princeton, NJ: International Finance Section.

Frenkel, Jacob A., and Assaf Razin (1989). "International Effects of Tax Reforms," *Economic Journal* 98, 38–58.

Frenkel, Jacob A., Assaf Razin, and Steve Symansky (1990). "Simulations of International VAT Harmonization," in Horst Siebert, ed., *Reforming Capital Income Taxation*. (Tübingen: J. Mohr Publishing).

Frenkel, Jacob A., Assaf Razin, and Steve Symansky (1991). "The International Effects of VAT Harmonization," *IMF Staff Papers*.

Frenkel, Jacob A., Assaf Razin, and Efraim Sadka (1991). *International Taxation in an Integrated World*. (Cambridge, MA: MIT Press).

Goulder, Lawrence, and Barry Eichengreen (1989). "Trade Liberalization in General Equilibrium: Intertemporal and Inter-Industry Effects," NBER Working Paper No. 2965, National Bureau of Economic Research, Cambridge, MA.

Greenwood, Jeremy, and Kent P. Kimbrough (1985). "Capital Controls and Fiscal Policy in the World Economy," *Canadian Journal of Economics* 18, 743–65.

Harberger, Arnold C. (1964). "The Measurement of Waste," *American Economic Review*, LIV, 58–76.

Helpman, Elhanan, and Assaf Razin (1987). "Exchange Rate Management: Intertemporal Tradeoffs," *American Economic Review* 77, 107–23.

King, Robert G., Charles I. Plosser, and Sergio T. Rebelo (1988). "Production, Growth, and Business Cycles: I. The Basic Neoclassical Model," *Journal of Monetary Economics* 21, 195–232.

King, Robert G., and Sergio T. Rebelo (1990). "Public Policy and Economic Growth: Developing Neoclassical Implications," *Journal of Political Economy* 98, S126–50.

Lucas Jr., Robert E. (1987). *Models of Business Cycles*. (Oxford: Blackwell).

Lucas Jr., Robert E. (1990). "Supply-Side Economics: An Analytical Review," *Oxford Economic Papers* 42, 293–316.

Mendoza, Enrique G., Assaf Razin and Linda L. Tesar (1994). "Effective Tax Rates in Macroeconomics: Cross Country Estimates of Tax Rates on Factor Incomes and Consumption," *Journal of Monetary Economics* 34, 297–323.

Mendoza, Enrique G., Gian Maria Milesi-Ferretti, and Patrick Asea (1997). "On the Ineffectiveness of Tax Policy in Altering Long-Run Growth: Harberger's Superneutrality Conjecture," *Journal of Public Economics* 66, 99–126.

Mendoza, Enrique G., and Linda L. Tesar (1998). "The International Ramifications of Tax Reforms: Supply-Side Economics in a Global Economy," *American Economic Review* 88, 226–45.

Mendoza, Enrique G., and Linda L. Tesar (2001). "The Costs *and* Benefits of International Tax Competition: More on Supply-Side Economics in a

Global Economy," Department of Economics, University of Michigan, working paper.

Peretto, Pietro (1999). "Cost Reduction, Entry and the Interdependence of Market Structure and Economics Growth," *Journal of Monetary Economics*, 43, 173–195.

Razin, Assaf, and Efraim Sadka (1989). "International Tax Competition and Gains from Tax Harmonization," Foerder Institute, Working Paper No. 37–89, Tel Aviv University.

Razin, Assaf, and Efraim Sadka (1990). "Integration of the International Capital Markets: The Size of Government and Tax Coordination," in Assaf Razin and Joel Slemrod (eds.), *Taxation in the Global Economy*. (Chicago: University of Chicago Press), pp. 331–48.

Razin, Assaf, and Efraim Sadka (1991). "Efficient Incentive Investments in the Presence of Capital Flight," *Journal of International Economics*, 31, 171–181.

Sorensen, Peter Birch (1999). "The Case for International Tax Coordination Reconsidered," Institute of Economics, University of Copenhagen, working paper.

Turnovsky, Stephen (1997). *International Macroeconomic Dynamics*. (Cambridge, MA: MIT Press).

## THIRTEEN

Home Bias in Portfolios and Taxation of Asset Income

Roger H. Gordon and Vítor Gaspar

There is now extensive evidence that individual investors have a strong tendency to invest in domestic rather than foreign equity.[1] This "home bias" in portfolios can potentially have important implications for economic behavior and economic policy. For one, it suggests that extra savings in a country will be invested primarily at home, consistent with the evidence for a lack of international capital mobility reported in Feldstein and Horioka (1980). In addition, the implied lack of capital mobility may explain the observed taxation of the return to domestic capital. In particular, when capital is fully mobile internationally a tax on domestic capital in a small country does not affect the net-of-tax rate of return available to capital owners and instead would be borne by immobile factors, primarily labor. In this setting, Diamond and Mirrlees (1971) show that such a tax would be dominated by labor income taxes (or consumption taxes) even from the perspective of workers. If capital were not so mobile, however, then capital should bear part of the tax, so that the tax might well be chosen for distributional reasons.

These *presumed* implications of home bias can be judged, however, only in the context of some particular model that generates home bias. The objective of this paper is to choose a plausible explanation for the observed home bias, and then to use a formal model based on this explanation to explore whether the above two implications of home bias necessarily follow.

---

[1] See, for example, Adler and Dumas (1983) and French and Poterba (1991).

Since portfolio models conventionally forecast that investors will hold a fully diversified portfolio of equity issued worldwide,[2] some other considerations must be included in the model so that it can explain home bias. Several of the approaches that have been explored, including the one we use, presume that domestic equity helps domestic residents hedge against other risks they inevitably face.[3] For example, Hartley (1986) hypothesizes that the return on publicly traded equity will be negatively correlated with the return on nontraded domestic assets. In fact, however, Pesenti, and van Wincoop (1996) find little correlation between the returns on equity and nontraded assets in the data. Similarly, Eldor, Pines, and Schwartz (1988) hypothesize that the return to domestic equity will be negatively correlated with domestic labor income. The empirical evidence for this explanation is mixed. While Bottazzi, Pesenti, and van Wincoop (1996) report a nontrivial negative correlation between profits and the labor share of income. Baxter and Jermann (1997) document a strong positive correlation between unexpected components of employee compensation and the rest of GDP, measured at factory cost. Under these stories, however, the forecasted deviation of portfolio choice from full international diversification depends almost proportionately on the size of labor income or ownership of nontraded assets relative to total asset holdings.[4] Since the retired do not need to hedge against random future labor income, for example, they should hold portfolios that are fully diversified internationally. Yet, there is no evidence of such systematic variation in diversification across individuals in the data.

These explanations assume, however, that investors can spend their random income facing nonstochastic consumer prices. In this paper, we

[2] See Solnik (1974) for an early formal demonstration.

[3] Other explanations have also been explored. For example, Obstfeld and Rogoff (2000) argue that costs of international trade might be sufficient to explain home bias. Brennan and Cao (1997) and Kang and Stulz (1997) provide suggestive evidence that asymmetric information is the explanation. Gordon and Bovenberg (1996) explore a related model focusing on FDI rather than portfolio investment.

[4] To see this in the case of a CAPM model, assume that investors in country i earn random labor income $L\tilde{w}_i$, that the return on equity from any country j, denoted $\tilde{s}_j$, is normally distributed with mean g_j and variance σ_j^2, and that the yield on risk-free bonds equals r. For simplicity, assume that the returns on equity are independent across countries, but that the return on domestic equity is correlated with labor income, with a covariance between $\tilde{w}_i$ and $\tilde{s}_i$ equal to ρ. The individual's optimal investment, E_j, in equity from country j then satisfies $E_j = (g_j - r)/(\gamma\sigma^2) - \iota L\rho/(\sigma^2)$, where γ measures the coefficient of absolute risk aversion and where ι equals one when j is the home country and zero otherwise. If investors have constant relative risk aversion, so that γ is inversely proportional to wealth, then the claim follows exactly.

instead pursue a hypothesis proposed by Adler and Dumas (1983) that equity may help investors hedge against random domestic consumer prices.[5] The argument relies on three key assumptions. First, domestic residents are assumed to prefer to consume goods produced domestically.[6] The second key assumption is that indexed bonds are not available – if indexed bonds existed, then individuals can hedge against random consumer prices simply by buying indexed bonds.[7] Third, the prices of domestic capital and domestic consumption goods are assumed to be closely linked.[8] Given these assumptions, domestic equity provides a hedge against consumer price fluctuations.[9] The hedge is not perfect, given the inherent risk in the return to real capital, but some specialization in domestic equity is still forecast. In contrast to equity, bonds from different countries are perfect substitutes in this setting.

The resulting home bias in equity holdings should disappear, however, if monetary policy instead stabilizes domestic prices, allowing exchange rates to absorb any random variation in the relative prices of consumption goods produced in different countries.[10] Under price stability, ordinary bonds are equivalent to indexed bonds, assuring a nonstochastic level of consumption by themselves, so that domestic equity can provide no further hedging gain. Also, the exchange rate risk faced on holdings of foreign equity can be fully hedged through offsetting holdings of foreign

---

[5] For a survey of past papers exploring the implications of stochastic consumer prices for portfolio diversification, see Branson and Henderson (1985).

[6] The preference for home goods consumption is commonly referred to as the Armington assumption (following Armington (1969)).

[7] Only a few countries have some form of indexed bonds, among them Australia, Canada, Denmark, France, Ireland, New Zealand, Sweden, the United States, and the U.K. See, e.g., Bank of England (1996). However, trade in these bonds is very limited, perhaps because asymmetric information about future inflation rates causes a breakdown in trade.

[8] In equilibrium, the price of existing capital, as reflected in share values, should equal the cost of new investment, e.g., Tobin's q should equal one. Also, domestic firms will shift between the production of consumption vs. investment goods in response to any change in their relative prices. As a result, equilibrium share prices and consumer prices should move together. Whether the correlation is sufficient to explain the observed degree of home bias is unclear, however. Cooper and Kaplanis (1994) develop a closely related model, and test it empirically. While their data suggest that equity does provide some hedging benefits against domestic price fluctuations, they can explain the observed degree of home bias only with implausibly low levels of risk aversion.

[9] If labor contracts fully insure labor income against variation in consumer prices, as we will assume, then the need to hedge against consumer prices is proportional to financial wealth, implying comparable degrees of portfolio specialization across investors.

[10] The portfolio implications of exchange rate risk for portfolios have been explored frequently. See, e.g., Solnik(1974) or Adler and Dumas (1983).

bonds. While the forecast as a result is that equity portfolios will be fully diversified, it is also true that *bond* portfolios now demonstrate home bias, a point that will prove important below.

Section 1 provides a formal derivation of the effects of monetary policy on equilibrium portfolio choices, focusing on two extreme cases: (1) monetary policy stabilizes domestic prices, and (2) monetary policy stabilizes the exchange rate.[11] In our framework the explanation of the observed specialization in equity assumes that monetary policies have focused on exchange rate stability.

The bulk of the paper then uses this model to examine whether the initial intuition regarding the implications of home bias for capital mobility and tax policy in fact holds, given this particular explanation for home bias. If home bias in equity portfolios causes capital immobility and facilitates the taxation of asset income, then we should find that these outcomes arise when monetary policy stabilizes exchange rates but not when it stabilizes domestic prices.

As seen in Section 2, the model implies that any increase in domestic savings will be invested primarily in domestic capital, consistent with the empirical evidence in Feldstein and Horioka (1980).[12] But this conclusion turns out to hold regardless of the choice for monetary policy, so regardless of whether equity portfolios demonstrate home bias.

Section 3 then examines in detail the equilibrium tax rates on capital income under the two alternative monetary policies. Given the presence of uncertainty, the Diamond–Mirrlees (1971) results no longer hold, regardless of the choice of monetary policy. When domestic prices are stabilized, the model forecasts that governments would tax domestic capital, and would normally treat domestic investors more favorably than foreign investors.[13] Most countries do in fact have supplementary taxes on foreign investors in domestic shares.

---

[11] Persson and Svensson (1989) also demonstrate how portfolio choice depends on monetary policy in a similar setting. The details of their model differ in many ways, however. For example, they have indexed bonds but do not allow trade in equity. They also explore very different questions. In common with Persson and Svensson (1989), we assume that the monetary regime does not affect the economic linkages across markets and across countries. This is a restrictive assumption (see Frankel and Rose (1997) and Fratszcher (2001)).

[12] In fact, when exchange rates are stabilized the model forecasts that the fraction of portfolios invested in domestic equity will equal the fraction of extra domestic savings invested in domestic capital.

[13] These results correspond to those in Gordon–Varian (1989), Werner (1994), and Nielsen (1998), and reflect primarily an optimal tariff role for tax policy. The previous papers ignored exchange rate and domestic price uncertainty, however.

When domestic prices are stochastic, in contrast, the case for capital income taxes and for subsidies to domestic residents are both much weaker. Whether foreign holdings are taxed and domestic holdings are treated more favorably now depends on parameter values. In response to the price risk, foreign investors hold fewer domestic shares, and their demand for shares is more elastic than in the case when domestic prices are stabilized, implying less gain from taxing foreign investors. In contrast, the demand for domestic shares by domestic investors is now more inelastic, due to the hedging benefits these shares provide, making taxes on domestic investors more attractive. An important complication, though, is that capital income taxes result in an inefficient reallocation of risk from foreign to domestic shareholders.[14] Therefore, taxation of asset income is more difficult under monetary policies that lead to more specialized equity portfolios, contrary to the initial intuition.

Section 4 provides a brief summary of the key results.

1. Portfolio Specialization in an Open Economy

We examine an infinitely–lived world economy containing N countries. The key assumption of the model is that consumers prefer to consume domestically produced goods.[15] For simplicity of notation, we explore the extreme assumption that they consume *only* domestic goods.[16] Denote the rate of consumption at time t by consumers in country i by C_{it}, and the resulting flow of utility they get at time t by $U(C_{it})$. Specifically, assume that

$$U(C_{it}) = \frac{C_{it}^{1-\gamma}}{1-\gamma}, \tag{1}$$

---

[14] Risk premia are not equated across investors, since there are not separate financial securities allowing trade in both the random real return to equity and random relative consumer prices.

[15] At a minimum, services and other "nontradables" are purchased at home. Other goods, which in principle are tradable, can still have different designs and attributes in different countries, tailored to domestic tastes. As a result, they are not perfect substitutes for goods from the same industry produced elsewhere.

[16] Under this assumption, any trade occurs in intermediate goods used in production, rather than in final consumer goods. As noted below, this assumption can easily be relaxed without changing the qualitative results, at the cost of making the analysis a bit messier and reducing the quantitative size of the effects we focus on. Under the opposite extreme assumption, however, in which all individuals have the same tastes, by symmetry they will also all have the same portfolio so that there can be no home bias, regardless of monetary policy.

where $\gamma > 0$ to capture risk aversion. The present value of their expected utility equals

$$W_i = E_0 \int_0^\infty e^{-\delta t} U(C_{it}) \, dt. \tag{2}$$

Individuals in country i start with assets A_{it} at date t, and can invest these assets in bonds and stocks from each of the other countries, where B_{ijt} and S_{ijt} denote holdings by individuals from country i in bonds and stocks respectively from country j at date t. The rate of return on each bond, B_{ijt}, is assumed to be nonstochastic in units of the local currency, so that[17]

$$\frac{dB_{ijt}}{B_{ijt}} = r_j \, dt. \tag{3}$$

The return on stocks in contrast is stochastic in units of the local output, and follows the stochastic process:

$$\frac{dS_{ijt}}{S_{ijt}} g_j \, dt + \sigma_j \, dz_j. \tag{4}$$

Here dz_j is a Weiner process while dt reflects any nonstochastic time trend, together implying that the value of S_{ij} is subject to geometric Brownian motion, with drift. For simplicity, we assume that the returns from equity invested in different countries are uncorrelated.[18] For now, we will assume that the parameters in Equation (4) do not depend on the aggregate demand for equity from any country j, implying a horizontal supply curve for real capital in any country j.[19]

To express the value of an investor's portfolio in units of domestic output so as to measure its rate of return in real terms, we need to correct

---

[17] For simplicity of notation, we assume that interest rates do not change over time. However, allowing such changes would not alter the qualitative results derived below.

[18] Adler and Dumas (1983) found that the correlations in the returns to equity portfolios from different countries are in fact very low. However, evidence since then suggests that correlations have been increasing over time (Longin and Solnik(1995)), and may be higher during crises (Iwaisako (1996)). For a recent survey of this evidence, see De Bandt and Hartmann (2000). Our results on the extent of portfolio diversification are unaffected, however, by common risks and depend simply on the size of the idiosyncrasy shocks to equity returns.

[19] At this point, the model is partial equilibrium, with the rates of return on assets set exogenously. In Section III, when we undertake the comparative static analysis of tax changes, we need to flesh out the model further, to make these rates of return a function of the underlying production process. While this general-equilibrium structure is essential for tax policy analysis, it is not needed for the characterization of the equilibrium here, so is postponed.

for exchange rate movements and changes in the price of domestic output. Let e_{jt} equal the number of units of some hypothetical base currency that can be purchased by a unit of country j's currency at date t, and let p_{jt} equal the domestic price of a unit of country j's output. In general, both the exchange rate and the price, p_{jt}, can evolve stochastically over time. We assume that the price for any country j's output in units of the base currency[20] evolves according to an exogenous stochastic process,[21] so that

$$\frac{d(e_{jt} p_{jt})}{e_{jt} p_{jt}} = \eta_j \, dt + \theta_j \, dz_j^e. \tag{5}$$

For simplicity, we assume that the output prices in the various countries, measured in terms of the base currency, are statistically independent both from each other[22] and from the return to equity.[23]

By focusing on the value of a unit of each country's output in units of the *base* currency, we are focusing on real rather than nominal values, and on the values abroad rather than at home. Real prices differ across goods from different countries, for example, because the design and attributes of goods from each country differ. They can change independently over time in the international market because of randomly changing attributes, or randomly changing values abroad for given attributes.[24] Note that purely nominal inflation risk is ignored in the study. Such price risk, given flexible exchange rates, should lead to equal and offsetting changes in p_{jt} and e_{jt}, so not show up in Equation (5), nor in any of the special cases examined below. As a result, the study abstracts from purely monetary phenomena, focusing instead on real changes.

In studying the potential impact of monetary policy on the equilibrium, we will focus on two special cases. In the first, each country stabilizes

---

[20] This base currency is therefore the numeraire in the model, when measuring the values of all goods.

[21] By making this process exogenous, we intentionally eliminate the possibility that monetary or fiscal policies can be used to affect the terms of trade and therefore substitute for explicit tariffs.

[22] Under this assumption, if exchange rates but not prices are stochastic, then the implied variance–covariance matrix of conventional measures of the exchange rate for any country j, relative say to the U.S. dollar (denoted by e_{ju}), will satisfy $\text{var}(e_{ju}) = \theta_j^2 + \theta_u^2$ and $\text{cov}(e_{iu}, e_{ju}) = \theta_u^2$. Therefore, our assumptions simply imply equal off-diagonal elements in this matrix.

[23] An earlier draft allowed for a nonzero correlation with the return to equity, and few insights of interest resulted.

[24] For example, random domestic fads in each country can lead to random changes in the attributes of domestically produced goods, and collectively can lead to random changes in the value of each good in the international market.

the domestic price of its own output, so that p_{jt} is nonstochastic and all relative price movements are captured by exchange rate movements. For simplicity of notation in this case, we set $p_{jt} = 1$ for all j. Under these assumptions,

$$\frac{d(e_{jt} p_{jt})}{e_{jt} p_{jt}} = \frac{de_{jt}}{e_{jt}} = \eta_j \, dt + \theta_j \, dz_j^e. \tag{5a}$$

In the second, all exchange rates are nonstochastic so that domestic output prices instead become stochastic and evolve according to[25]

$$\frac{d(e_{jt} p_{jt})}{e_{jt} p_{jt}} = \frac{dp_{jt}}{p_{jt}} = \eta_j \, dt + \theta_j \, dz_j^e. \tag{5b}$$

In allocating their real wealth, individuals in country i face the budget constraint[26]

$$A_i = \frac{\sum_j e_j (B_{ij} + p_j S_{ij})}{e_i p_i}. \tag{6}$$

Since the numerator is measured in units of the base country currency, we need to divide by the base currency price of domestic output in order to measure *real* assets.

If we were to relax our assumption that individuals consume only domestic goods, then Equation (6) needs to be modified. In particular, we would need to divide through by an appropriate price index, rather than simply by $e_i p_i$. For example, assume that C_i, rather than being a scalar, is a Cobb–Douglas function of a vector of goods: $C_i = \Pi_j X_j^{\alpha j}$, where the (base currency) price of good X_j is P_j. Then the appropriate price index equals $\Pi_j P_j^{\alpha j}$. This expression, rather than $e_i p_i$, would belong in the denominator of Equation (6). Our special case is one in which the α_i for the domestic good equals one, while all the other α_j's equal zero. If we assume instead that consumption is divided between the domestic good and some second good with a nonstochastic price, all that changes in the results below is that price risk will get less weight in the expressions. If stochastic foreign prices enter into the price index as well, then new terms are added to the expressions below. Intuitively, some foreign equity/bonds will be held to hedge against the cost of purchasing these

---

[25] Note that we implicitly assume that domestic prices are fully flexible, eliminating any of the macro disturbances caused by sticky prices.

[26] Since the return on equity was measured in units of domestic *output*, to determine its value in units of the local currency we need to multiply by p_{jt}. For simplicity of notation, we will drop the subscript t unless it seems important for the interpretation.

foreign goods, but more domestic equity/bonds will be held if domestic goods still have more weight in consumption.

For simplicity, we proceed under the extreme assumption that individuals buy only domestic goods, so that Equation (6) is a sufficient measure of real assets. Let $b_{ij} \equiv e_j B_{ij}/(e_i p_i A_i)$ equal the fraction of these assets that individuals from country i invest in bonds from country j, let $s_{ij} \equiv e_j p_j S_{ij}/(e_i p_i A_i)$ be the fraction invested in that country's equity, and let $f_{ij} \equiv b_{ij} + s_{ij}$ denote the fraction invested in any securities issued in country j.

Individuals choose these portfolio fractions at each point in time as well as their consumption rate to maximize their expected utility as defined in Equation (2). By Ito's Lemma, a second-order Taylor series approximation to the value of the objective function (assuming bounded third derivatives) can be expressed by[27]

$$W_i = \max_{\{C,b,s\}} E_0 \{ W_i + U(C_i) - \delta W(A_i) \\ + W'(A_i)\, dA_i + .5 W''(A_i)\, dA_i^2 \}. \tag{7}$$

Here dA_i represents the change in the individual's real wealth over time. Decisions are made subject to the individual's budget constraint that $\Sigma_j (b_{ij} + s_{ij}) = 1$. In addition, we assume that the aggregate supply of bonds from each country is zero, so that $\Sigma_i B_{ij} = 0$.

1.1. Equilibrium When Domestic Prices Are Stabilized

Applying Ito's Lemma again, we find that the stochastic differential of Equation (6) under the above assumptions equals

$$\frac{dA_i}{A_i} = \sum_j f_{ij} \frac{de_j}{e_j} + \sum_j s_{ij} \frac{dS_j}{S_j} + \sum_j b_{ij} \frac{dB_j}{B_j} - \frac{de_i}{e_i} \\ + .5 \left(2(1 - f_{ii}) \left(\frac{de_i}{e_i} \right)^2 \right) - \frac{C_i}{A_i}. \tag{8}$$

Using Equations (3), (4), and (5a), the expected value of this differential equals

$$E_t \frac{dA_i}{A_i} = \sum_j (r_j + \eta_j) b_{ij} + \sum_j (g_j + \eta_j) s_{ij} - \eta_i + (1 - f_{ii})\theta_i^2 - \frac{C_i}{A_i}. \tag{8a}$$

---

[27] For a description and derivation of Ito's Lemma, see for example Merton (1990, p. 78). For an application to an equivalent problem, see Merton (1969).

The expected variance of the net change in real assets, by Ito's Lemma, satisfies

$$E_t \frac{dA^2}{A^2} = \sum_j \sigma_j^2 s_{ij}^2 + \sum_j f_{ij}^2 \theta_j^2 + (1 - 2f_{ii})\theta_i^2. \qquad (9a)$$

At the optimal portfolio, increasing s_{ij} and decreasing b_{ij} to compensate has no effect on utility at the margin, implying that[28]

$$g_j - r_j = \gamma s_{ij}\sigma_j^2 \qquad (10a)$$

for all j, implying a conventional expression for the risk premium on equity. Equation (10a) immediately implies that s_{ij} is the same for all i, implying full international diversification of equity portfolios. As seen through the derivation of this first-order condition, borrowing abroad to buy foreign equity implies no net exchange rate risk, but still allows for diversification of production risk.

Similarly, at the optimal allocation, increasing b_{ij} and decreasing b_{ii} to compensate also has no effect on utility at the margin, implying that

$$(r_i + \eta_i) = (r_j + \eta_j) - \gamma f_{ij}\theta_j^2 - \gamma(1 - f_{ii})\theta_i^2 + \theta_i^2. \qquad (11)$$

Exchange rate risk abroad enters in a standard fashion: the resulting marginal risk-bearing cost for foreign bonds, $\gamma f_{ij}\theta_j^2$, is proportion to the investor's exposure to this risk. The effects of risk in the value of the domestic currency are more complicated, however. Due to Jensen's inequality, the expected value of foreign assets (in Equation (6)) is increasing in the variability of e_i, so that this variance raises the return on investing in foreign bonds by θ_i^2, even ignoring risk aversion.[29] By purchasing more foreign bonds, the investor is also more subject to the risk in the value of the domestic currency. The cost of this risk is again proportional to the amount the investor bears already, so equals $\gamma(1 - f_{ii})\theta_i^2$. The effects of risk in the domestic and the foreign currency enter Equation (11) in the same way only if $\gamma = 1$, in which case the higher expected return arising from domestic currency risk and the higher implied risk-bearing costs exactly cancel.

What are the implications of Equation (11) for equilibrium bond holdings? Consider the simple case where countries are symmetric, so that

---

[28] Given that the utility function has constant relative risk aversion, we can make use of a standard result here that $AW''(A)/W'(A) = -\gamma$.

[29] For an early recognition of this implication of Jensen's inequality, see Siegel (1972).

$A_j = A^*, r_j = r, g_j = g, \sigma_j = \sigma, \theta_j = \theta$, and $\eta_j = \eta$. Here, after some algebra the resulting first-order conditions for bond holdings can be shown to imply that $b_{ii} = b_{ij} + (\gamma - 1)/\gamma$. If $\gamma = 1$, so that $U(C) = \log(C)$, then it is easy to see from Equation (11) that bond holdings will be the same for all investors. If $\gamma < 1$, then the higher expected return on foreign bonds implies that $b_{ii} < b_{ij}$. Empirical estimates[30] of γ suggest that $\gamma \gg 1$. In this case, the higher risk-bearing costs from holding foreign bonds implies that $b_{ii} > b_{ij}$. In the limit as γ grows without bound, $b_{ii} \approx b_{ij} + 1$ implying that $s_{ij} + b_{ij} = 0$ for $j \neq i$ – investors would be fully hedged against exchange rate fluctuations, though at the cost of not taking advantage of the higher expected return on foreign securities generated by Jensen's inequality.

Making use of the fact that $\Sigma_i B_{ij} = 0$, we obtain the following result:

Result 1: When countries are symmetric and domestic prices are stabilized, equity portfolios are fully diversified internationally: $s_{ii} = s_{ij}$. However, bond portfolios are characterized by $b_{ii} = (N - 1)(\gamma - 1)/(N\gamma)$ and $b_{ij} = -(\gamma - 1)/(N\gamma)$. Only if $\gamma = 1$ are bond holdings fully diversified.

1.2. Equilibrium When Exchange Rates Are Stabilized

How does the equilibrium portfolio change when monetary policy instead stabilizes exchange rates? Consider first what happens if indexed bonds are made available, so that the return to bonds described by Equation (3) is measured in units of domestic *output* rather than the domestic currency. Now Equation (6) becomes

$$A_i = \frac{\sum_j e_j p_j (B_{ij} + S_{ij})}{e_i p_i}. \tag{6a}$$

Given Equation (6a), the choice of a monetary rule has no effect on the equilibrium. The prior results therefore continue to hold.

Few countries have indexed bonds, however.[31] Unindexed bonds fail to provide any hedge against consumer price fluctuations – their return

---

[30] See, e.g., Engel (1994).

[31] An interesting question is why, because the model implies that indexing the return on bonds raises expected utility in a country. Certainly, existing price indices are imperfect, e.g., due to their lack of correction for quality change, but that does not seem a sufficient explanation. Perhaps a market cannot easily function due to substantial inside information about innovations to these existing price indices, for example in a large firm that has a nontrivial impact on the index through its own pricing decisions and advanced knowledge of price increases in firms it purchases from.

in fact is nonstochastic, as measured in units of the base currency. Equity, though, provides some hedge against price fluctuations, given the assumption that the value of equity changes proportionately with the value of domestic output, everything else equal. But the return to equity is still risky, so unlike indexed bonds it does not provide a perfect hedge.

Consider how the equilibrium changes if in fact no countries have indexed bonds. When all bonds earn a nonstochastic rate of return in their local currency, and all exchange rates are fixed, bonds from each country become perfect substitutes, so that $r_j = r$ for all j. Investors will therefore be indifferent about which country's bonds they hold.

The stochastic differential of Equation (6) now becomes

$$E_t \frac{dA_i}{A_i} = \sum_j r b_{ij} + \sum_j (g_j + \eta_j) s_{ij} - \eta_i + (1 - s_{ii})\theta_i^2 - \frac{C_i}{A_i}. \qquad (8b)$$

The expected variance in the net change in real assets becomes

$$E_t \frac{dA_i^2}{A_i^2} = \sum_j s_{ij}^2 (\sigma_j^2 + \theta_j^2) + (1 - 2s_{ii})\theta_i^2. \qquad (9b)$$

When investing in equity, random changes in relative price levels across countries can no longer be hedged through the purchase of local bonds – only domestic equity is affected by fluctuations in local prices. In equilibrium, the investor should remain indifferent to borrowing locally to finance an extra unit of equity of country j. Now, however, the resulting first-order condition is

$$g_j + \eta_j - r = \gamma s_{ij}(\theta_j^2 + \sigma_j^2), \qquad (10b)$$

for $j \neq i$. The costs of bearing the risk in the local price level clearly makes purchases of foreign equity less attractive. Offsetting this new cost to equity investments, however, any expected appreciation in the value of foreign goods raises the rate of return on equity but not bonds issued in the country.

The analogous first-order condition for securities of country i is

$$g_i + \eta_i - r + \gamma(1 - s_{ii})\theta_i^2 = \gamma s_{ii}\sigma_i^2 + \theta_i^2. \qquad (10c)$$

The role of risk in the domestic price level here is directly parallel to the role of exchange rate risk in Equation (11). This risk raises the expected return on all assets *except* domestic equity. However, purchasing domestic equity helps reduce the utility costs of bearing this risk – these costs are proportional to current exposure, and so equal $\gamma(1 - s_{ii})\theta_i^2$.

As in Equation (11), if $\gamma = 1$, then price risk enters symmetrically in the first-order conditions for domestic and foreign equity. More generally, under the same symmetry conditions as before, we find that

$$s_i = s_j + \left(\frac{\theta^2}{\theta^2 + \sigma^2}\right)\left(\frac{\gamma - 1}{\gamma}\right). \tag{12}$$

When $\gamma = 1$, equity holdings are fully diversified. If $\gamma > 1$, however, the utility gain from extra domestic equity providing a further hedge against the risk in the consumption price level more than outweighs the lower expected return on domestic equity. For plausible parameter values, the second term on the right–hand side of Equation (12) can imply substantial specialization of portfolios in domestic equity. Therefore, the model implies home bias as long as monetary policies focus heavily on stabilizing exchange rates. For reasonable parameter values, however, we must recognize that the implied extent of home bias will not be as large as is seen in the data. At best, this is a partial explanation for home bias.

Making use of the fact that $\Sigma_j s_{ij} = 1$, we find:

Result 2: When countries are symmetric and monetary policy stabilizes the exchange rate, all bonds are perfect substitutes. However, equity holdings are characterized by

$$s_{ii} = \frac{1}{N} + \left(\frac{N-1}{N}\right)\left(\frac{\theta^2}{\theta^2 + \sigma^2}\right)\left(\frac{\gamma - 1}{\gamma}\right),$$

and

$$s_{ij} = \frac{1}{N} - \left(\frac{1}{N}\right)\left(\frac{\theta^2}{\theta^2 + \sigma^2}\right)\left(\frac{\gamma - 1}{\gamma}\right).$$

2. Price vs. Exchange Rate Stability and International Capital Mobility

What do these models imply about the degree of international capital mobility? In particular, if savings were to rise in country k, implying an increase in A_k, what will happen to real investment in each country? Feldstein and Horioka (1980) find empirically that a dollar of extra savings undertaken in a particular country raises the capital stock in that country by around 0.6 to 0.8 dollars. What does the model forecast, and how does this forecast vary with the assumed monetary policy?

Consider the implications of an increase in A_k in country k, for simplicity starting from a symmetric equilibrium in which $A_j = A^*, r_j = r,$

$\eta_j = \eta, g_j = g, \sigma_j = \sigma, \theta_j = \theta$ and $e_j p_j = 1$ for all j. In each model, investors in country k would want to expand their existing portfolios proportionately as long as market prices do not change. If prices do not change, then the fraction of the additional assets invested in real capital in country j simply equals s_{kj}. But in general, prices will be forced to change.

Consider first the case when monetary policy stabilizes exchange rates. Assuming symmetry, investors hold no debt. When their assets increase, investors in country k would like to expand their equity holdings proportionately. Given the assumed horizontal supply curve for equity, no price adjustments are needed in equilibrium. Therefore, $\partial S_k / \partial A_k = s_{kk}$. The forecasted fraction of additional domestic savings invested in domestic capital equals the fraction of the equity portfolios of domestic residents invested in domestic equity. For example, if 80% of equity portfolios are invested in domestic equity, then 80% of additional domestic savings are invested in new domestic capital, easily rationalizing the Feldstein and Horioka (1980) estimates.

What happens if monetary policy instead stabilizes the domestic price level? Now, when A_k increases, investors will try to borrow more abroad and to invest more in bonds at home. In equilibrium, this will drive up r_j for $j \neq k$, and drive down r_k. As a result, investment will go up by less than s_{kj} in any foreign country, and by more than s_{kk} at home. Since, given symmetry, $s_{kj} = s_{kk}$, this implies some capital immobility.

To solve for the specific changes that result, we first differentiate Equations (10a) and (11) with respect to A_k:

$$\frac{\partial s_{ij}}{\partial A_k} = -\frac{1}{\gamma \sigma^2} \frac{\partial r_j}{\partial A_k}, \tag{13}$$

and

$$\frac{\partial f_{ij}}{\partial A_k} = \frac{\partial f_{ii}}{\partial A_k} + \frac{1}{\gamma \theta^2} \left[\frac{\partial r_j}{\partial A_k} - \frac{\partial r_i}{\partial A_k} \right]. \tag{14}$$

Summing Equation (14) over j, substituting Equation (13), and making use of the facts that $f_{ij} = b_{ij} + s_{ij}$ and $\Sigma_j f_{ij} = 1$, we find

$$\frac{\partial b_{ii}}{\partial A_k} + \left(1 + \frac{\sigma^2}{\theta^2}\right) \frac{\partial s_{ii}}{\partial A_k} = \frac{\sigma^2}{N\theta^2} \sum_j \frac{\partial s_{ij}}{\partial A_k}. \tag{15}$$

Equations (13) and (14) in fact imply that the left-side of Equation (15) remains unchanged if b_{ii} and s_{ii} are replaced by b_{im} and s_{im}, for any m.

Note that

$$\sum_i \frac{\partial B_{im}}{\partial A_k} = b_{km} + \sum_i A_i \frac{\partial b_{im}}{\partial A_k} = 0, \tag{16a}$$

$$\sum_i \frac{\partial S_{im}}{\partial A_k} = s_{km} + \sum_i A_i \frac{\partial s_{im}}{\partial A_k}, \quad \text{and} \tag{16b}$$

$$\sum_i \sum_j \frac{\partial S_{ij}}{\partial A_k} = \sum_j s_{kj} + \sum_i \sum_j A_i \frac{\partial s_{ij}}{\partial A_k} = 1. \tag{16c}$$

Weighting Equation (15) by A_i, summing over i, and making use of Equations (16a,b,c), we find that

$$\frac{\partial S_i}{\partial A_k} = s_{ki} + \frac{\theta^2 b_{ki} + \sigma^2 \sum_j b_{kj}/N}{\theta^2 + \sigma^2}. \tag{17}$$

The left-hand side of this equation represents the change in the real capital stock in any country i that results from additional savings in country k. The right-hand side equals the extra investment, s_{ki}, that would occur ignoring price changes plus a correction term measuring the effects of interest rate changes.

This correction term consists of two components. The first measures the direct impact of changes in demand for bonds in country i. In the symmetric case, demand would increase in country k and fall elsewhere.[32] This change in the demand for local bonds feeds through less than dollar for dollar into changes in the local capital stock; the effect is larger the larger is θ^2 relative to σ^2, so the larger the resulting change in the local interest rate and the larger the impact of this interest rate change on the demand for capital. The final term measures the effects of any change in the overall demand for bonds, due to the extra savings in country k, which if positive can lower interest rates worldwide. In the symmetric case, this term disappears.

Making use of Results 1 and 2, we find:

Result 3: When countries are symmetric,

$$\frac{\partial S_k}{\partial A_k} = \frac{1}{N} + \left(\frac{N-1}{N}\right)\left(\frac{\theta^2}{\theta^2 + \sigma^2}\right)\left(\frac{\gamma - 1}{\gamma}\right),$$

---

[32] If $\theta^2 = 0$, then all bonds are perfect substitutes, and any changes in relative demands are irrelevant.

and

$$\frac{\partial S_i}{\partial A_k} = \frac{1}{N} - \left(\frac{1}{N}\right)\left(\frac{\theta^2}{\theta^2 + \sigma^2}\right)\left(\frac{\gamma - 1}{\gamma}\right).$$

Note that the degree of capital immobility is the same for both alternative monetary policies. Apparently, home bias in bonds (when domestic prices are stabilized) is as important for capital immobility as home bias in equity (when exchange rates are stabilized).

3. Implications of Stochastic Prices for Taxes on Asset Income

Past research papers ignoring the implications of risk argue that taxes on portfolio income in an open economy are either infeasible or dominated by other available tax instruments. A residence-based tax, for example, is viewed to be infeasible because governments have no effective mechanism available to monitor the foreign-source earnings of domestic investors.[33] A source-based tax on interest payments made by domestic firms and financial intermediaries has also proven to be infeasible, given that accounts denominated in the same currency with a foreign financial intermediary would be effectively a perfect substitute yet avoid the source-based tax.[34]

While a source-based tax on the earnings accruing to capital physically located in the country should be feasible, this line of research suggests that in a small open economy it would be dominated by other available taxes.[35] In response to a source-based tax on capital, investors will shift capital abroad until after-tax returns are again equated across countries. If a country is small relative to world capital markets and all investments are

---

[33] Governments can require domestic firms and financial intermediaries to report the identity of all recipients of interest and dividend income, but cannot impose equivalent requirements on foreign firms and financial intermediaries. Bilateral information-sharing agreements are not a substitute, since individuals can simply route their funds through a third country that assures anonymity. That is, residents can avoid a residence-based tax even on their investments in domestic assets simply by routing their funds through a third country, so that the owner of the domestic equity appears to be foreign according to the available information.

[34] Germany and the Netherlands for example both attempted to impose a source-based tax on interest income accruing in domestic bank accounts, and found that a large fraction of these domestic accounts were quickly shifted abroad.

[35] This conclusion follows quickly from the arguments in Diamond–Mirrlees (1971) that there should be production efficiency under an optimal tax regime. Gordon (1986) later showed that this conclusion continues to follow as long as there are flexible taxes on labor income, regardless of the rest of the tax system, assuming the only primary inputs to production and labor and capital.

perfect substitutes, then the after-tax rate of return available to investors on the world market would not be affected when one country imposes such a source-based tax. Firms would continue to locate in that country only if domestic wage rates drop enough to compensate for the increase in the before-tax cost of capital. The incidence of the tax is therefore entirely on workers. As a result, the tax is dominated by direct taxes on wages – in both cases the tax is borne entirely by workers, discouraging their labor supply, but the capital income tax creates an extra excess burden by discouraging capital investment in the country.

3.1. Tax Policy in a Nonstochastic Setting

A simple two-period, one-good, small open economy model capturing these arguments can be described as follows, to set the context for our analysis of tax policy given uncertainty. There are two types of individuals in this economy: investors and workers.[36] Investors start out with assets A which they can either consume in the first period or invest at a rate of return r. Assume that income accruing to capital physically invested in the country is subject to a tax at rate τ_r in the second period. Since domestic assets are a perfect substitute for foreign assets which earn a rate of return r^*, and since domestic taxes on *foreign* assets by assumption are infeasible, the after-tax rate of return to domestic assets must equal r^* (i.e., $r = r^*/(1 - \tau_r)$).

Workers start out in the first period with assets A_w. In the second period, these individuals can work as much as they wish at a gross-of-tax wage rate w. Labor income is subject to a tax at rate τ_w. Assume for simplicity that A_w is small enough that the workers would want to borrow if they could against their future earnings, but that such uncollateralized loans are unavailable. The indirect utility of investors and workers can be expressed by $V^1(r^*)$ and $V^2(w(1 - \tau_w))$ respectively.

The country is small relative to the world market, so takes both output prices and r^* as given. Let the output price be the numeraire. Firms produce with a constant-returns-to-scale technology, and must break even to be willing to locate in the country. The firm's unit cost must equal the output price, so that $c(w, r^*/(1 - \tau_r)) = 1$. For firms to continue to break even when τ_r increases, we infer that $\partial w/\partial \tau_r = -(K/L)r^*/(1 - \tau_r)^2$.

---

[36] This artificial distinction is introduced to simplify the discussion, by eliminating any feedback from rates of return on different assets unto labor supply decisions. Otherwise, changes in the available after-tax rate of return can induce changes in the present value of future wage rates, causing changes in the timing as well as the level of labor supply.

We assume a conventional measure of social welfare:

$$W = V^1(r^*) + V^2(w(1 - \tau_w)) + \lambda(\tau_w w L + \tau_r r^* K/(1 - \tau_r)),$$

where λ measures the social value of the expenditures financed by tax revenue. Given the pretax incomes of investors versus workers, assume that the government would like to redistribute toward workers.

Consider the impact on social welfare of a marginal increase in τ_r and a compensating drop in τ_w chosen to leave the net-of-tax wage unchanged, starting from an initial equilibrium with $\tau_r = 0$. If welfare rises, then the optimal value of τ_r is positive.

The required compensating drop in τ_w must satisfy $\partial \tau_w / \partial \tau_r = [(1 - \tau_w)/w]\partial w/\partial \tau_r$. Since the net-of-tax wage does not change, the labor supply and utility of workers are left unaffected by these combined tax changes. Investors also face an unchanged factor price. The impact on social welfare therefore depends only on what happens to government revenue. In fact,

$$\frac{\partial W}{\partial \tau_r} = \lambda \left[-\frac{r^* K}{(1 - \tau_r)^2} + \frac{r^* K}{(1 - \tau_r)^2} + \frac{\tau_r r^*}{1 - \tau_r} \frac{\partial K}{\partial \tau_r} \right].$$

Evaluated at $\tau = 0$, we find that government revenue and therefore welfare is unaffected at the margin by this tax change. Note that the extra revenue collected from capital income (before any behavioral changes) must be paid out in full to workers if their after-tax wage is to be left unaffected by the combined policies.

We conclude that the optimal value of τ_r is zero.[37] Only labor income taxes will be used to finance government expenditures. This is true regardless of the strength of the distributional preference in favor of workers.

3.2. Tax Policy When Exchange Rates Are Stochastic

To what degree do these results change when uncertainty in relative prices is present, assuming each country remains small relative to the world capital market? Is the answer affected by the presence of home bias in equity versus bond portfolios?

Past work has looked at the effects of country-specific risks,[38] and finds with such risk that investments in different countries are no longer perfect

---

[37] In fact, this two-period argument easily generalizes to a multiperiod setting. The above model could simply be embedded into a multiperiod model. The tax change analyzed could still apply in one period only. By the same arguments, a zero capital income tax rate in any period implies no change in welfare.

[38] See, e.g., Gordon and Varian (1989), Werner (1994), and Nielsen (1998).

substitutes. As a result, taxes on capital income can be attractive both as a form of an optimal tariff, and also potentially as a way to raise revenue with at least part of the burden falling on domestic capital owners rather than domestic workers. Because these papers ignored exchange rate or price risks, however, they examined a setting without any home bias. While it would be plausible to presume that home bias makes capital-income taxation even easier, nobody to date has explored the implications of home bias for tax policy. In our setting, there is home bias in bond portfolios when monetary policy stabilizes domestic prices, or home bias in equity portfolios when monetary policy stabilizes exchange rates. Is tax policy affected by such home bias?

To examine what in fact happens to optimal tax policies, we need to add some more structure to the initial model, since a general equilibrium model is needed for the analysis of tax policy. As in the two-period model, we assume for simplicity that there are two types of individuals. The situation of investors was described previously. Workers are assumed to supply labor each period at a nonstochastic before-tax real wage rate w, so that (following the labor contracting literature) capital owners bear all the risk within the firm. Workers choose how much to work, L, given that the resulting labor income is subject to tax at rate τ_w. Their resulting utility equals $\int_0^\infty U^w(C_{it}^w, L_{it})e^{-\delta t}dt$, where $C_{it}^w = w(1 - \tau_w)L_{it}$.[39]

If firms in country i hire L_i units of labor and have K_i units of capital, then their rate of profit equals

$$\pi = p_i[f(K_i, L_i) - wL_i](1 - \tau_r)\,dt + \phi_i p_i f(K_i, L_i)(1 - \tau_r)\,dz_i$$

for some measure of the amount of uncertainty, ϕ_i, facing the firms.[40] If the market value of the shares issued by firms in country i is S_i, then Equation (4) implies that

$$g_i \equiv p_i[f(K_i, L_i) - wL_i](1 - \tau_r)/S_i \tag{18}$$

and

$$\sigma_i \equiv \phi_i p_i f(K_i, L_i)(1 - \tau_r)/S_i. \tag{19}$$

---

[39] We continue to assume that these workers do not own any financial assets, i.e., fixed costs to setting up a financial account are large per capita per worker but trivial per capita for investors.

[40] Because wage payments have been assumed to be nonstochastic, they do not appear in the measure of the uncertainty facing the firm.

Firms can buy capital domestically each period and will choose to do so until the market values the return from an extra dollar of capital at just a dollar.

Government revenue, R_i, is now stochastic. Its real value, measured relative to the domestic price level, equals

$$R_i = \left[\tau_w w L_i + \frac{\tau_r}{1 - \tau_r} g_i S_i \right] dt + \frac{\tau_r}{1 - \tau_r} \sigma_i S_i \, dz_i. \tag{20}$$

The government receives the same risk as it would from owning $\tau_r S_i / (1 - \tau_r)$ privately purchased shares. If government expenditures are also stochastic, then we face the complication of how much risk should be reallocated from private to government expenditures, and the implications of this for optimal tax rates. To avoid having this issue affect the analysis of the optimal tax structure, we assume that the government keeps a nonstochastic revenue stream by transferring the risk in its tax revenue to domestic investors while compensating them enough to make these investors indifferent to the transfer.[41] This compensated transfer is equivalent to giving domestic investors $\tau_r S_i / (1 - \tau_r)$ shares in exchange for the same value of domestic bonds. The remaining government revenue, R_i^n, is nonstochastic and equals

$$R_i^n = \left[\tau_w w L_i + \frac{\tau_r}{1 - \tau_r} r_i S_i \right].$$

The government chooses its policies to maximize the following objective function:

$$W = E_0 \int_0^\infty \left[U^w(C_{it}^w, L_{it}) + U(C_{it}) + \lambda R_{it}^n \right] e^{-\delta t} dt. \tag{21}$$

Consider the same type of policy experiment described in the context of the two-period model. In particular, consider as before the impact of a marginal increase in τ_r offset by a drop in τ_w chosen so as to leave the net-of-tax wage rate and therefore labor supply and the utility of workers unchanged. The question is whether such a tax change raises welfare, starting from $\tau_r = 0$.

In the two-period model, this policy change had no impact on the welfare of investors. The two-period model also implied that the extra

---

[41] The transfer could take the form of random government expenditures on goods that are a perfect substitute for the private consumption of investors. Alternatively, we can simply assume directly that the government uses the risk premium of domestic investors when calculating the certainty-equivalent value of government revenue.

tax revenue from capital income ignoring behavioral changes would be fully offset by the compensating drop in tax payments by workers. To see how results are affected by the introduction of uncertainty, consider first the determinants of a firm's market value. To solve for this market value, we need to aggregate the first-order conditions for s_{ji} across all purchasers of the shares issued in country i in order to derive the rate of return required by the market. Multiplying Equation (10a) by A_j and summing over j gives

$$A(g_i - r_i) = \gamma \sigma_i^2 \left(\sum_j S_{ji} + \frac{\tau_r S_i}{1 - \tau_r} \right) = \gamma \sigma_i^2 \frac{S_i}{1 - \tau_r}, \qquad (22)$$

where $A \equiv \Sigma_j A_j$ and $S_{ji} \equiv s_{ji} A_j$, and where $\tau_r S_i/(1 - \tau_r)$ represents the risk transferred to domestic investors by the government. The second equality follows from the fact that $S_i = \Sigma_j S_{ji}$. Equation (22) can then be reexpressed in a somewhat more conventional form:

$$g_i = r_i + \frac{\gamma}{A} \text{cov}\,(\sigma_i dz_i, dZ_i), \qquad (23)$$

where $dZ_i = \phi p_i f(K_i, L_i)\,dz_i$.

Firms in country i will invest until $\partial S_i / \partial K_i = 1$, since a unit of capital costs $p_i = 1$. In doing so, each firm would use Equation (23) to evaluate the impact of investment on firm value, taking as given the aggregate risks, dZ_i, faced by the economy as a whole. Given Equations (18) and (19), we then find after simplifying that investment continues until

$$f_K = \frac{r_i}{(1 - \tau_r)D}, \qquad (24)$$

where

$$D \equiv 1 - \frac{\gamma}{A}\text{cov}(\phi\, dz_i, dZ_i).$$

Equation (23) can also be used to solve for the impact of a marginal change in τ_r on the equilibrium wage rate, w. Firms will continue to break even only if the wage rate drops by enough so that firm value, S_i, still equals the setup costs of the firm, K_i. Given Equations (18), (19), and (24), the assumption of constant returns to scale, the assumption that the wage rate is nonstochastic, and the envelope condition for K_i and L_i, we find that

$$(1 - \tau_r)L\frac{\partial w}{\partial \tau_r} = -\frac{r_i S_i}{(1 - \tau_r)} - S_i \frac{\partial r_i}{\partial \tau_r} - \frac{\gamma}{A}\text{cov}(\sigma_i\, dz_i, dZ_i)\left(\frac{f_K K}{f}\right)\frac{\partial K_i}{\partial \tau_r}. \qquad (25)$$

If the net-of-tax wage is to remain unchanged, the required change in τ_w satisfies $\partial \tau_w / \partial \tau_r = [(1 - \tau_w)/w](\partial w / \partial \tau_r)$. The impact on government tax revenue of a marginal change in τ_r combined with this compensating adjustment in τ_w, evaluated at $\tau_r = 0$, then can be shown to equal

$$\frac{\partial R_i^n}{\partial \tau_r} = - \left[S_i \frac{\partial r_i}{\partial \tau_r} + \frac{\gamma}{A} \mathrm{cov}(\sigma_i \, dz_i, dZ_i) \right] \left(\frac{f_K K}{f} \right) \frac{\partial K_i}{\partial \tau_r} \, dt. \qquad (26)$$

Previously, the interest rate was fixed and there was no risk premium. Now both terms are nonzero. These terms reflect terms-of-trade effects of the tax change, arising from the impact on both the market-clearing interest rate and the risk premium charged by investors. The impact of these price changes on domestic investors will need to be taken into account as well, however.[42]

To evaluate the first term in Equation (26), we need an expression for $\partial r_i / \partial \tau_r$. To obtain this, we aggregate Equation (12) over investors from each country j, comparing their return on bonds from countries i vs. j. Weighting each first-order condition by A_j, summing over j, and taking account of the fact that $\Sigma_j A_j f_{ji} = s_i$,[43] we find that

$$r_i + \eta_i = r_j + \eta_j + \frac{\gamma}{A} \left[S_i \theta_i^2 - S_j \theta_j^2 \right] + (1 - \gamma) \frac{A_i \theta_i^2 - A_j \theta_j^2}{A}. \qquad (27)$$

Note that domestic interest rates can be affected by domestic policies even in a small open economy.[44] In particular, τ_r causes S_i to change. Since $S_i = K_i$ and investment falls in response to the tax change, r_i falls. Therefore, the first term in Equation (26) represents an increase in tax revenue.

Raising τ_r naturally also causes K_i to fall. Therefore, we conclude that tax revenue increases in response to the combined tax changes. To judge whether the desired value of τ_r is positive, however, we need to examine not only the effect on government tax revenue but also the implications for

[42] In the related analyses by Gordon and Varian (1989), Werner (994), and Nielsen (1998) in which prices were assumed to be nonstochastic, taxes did not affect interest rates but did affect the risk premium as occurs here. While the added drop in the interest rate, arising from home bias in bond portfolios, increases government revenue, it also benefits foreign investors, who borrow locally, and hurts domestic investors. The net impact of this home bias in bond portfolios on taxes therefore depends on the relative importance of these offsetting effects.

[43] Given that the net supply of bonds from country i to the world economy is zero, but $\tau_r S_i / (1 - \tau_r)$ of these bonds are held by the government in country i, we infer that $\Sigma_j A_j f_{ji} = S_i$.

[44] See Solnik (1974) for a similar result.

the utility of domestic investors. To judge the extent of fiscal spillovers, we also need to look at the impact of the tax changes on the utility of foreign investors. In the nonstochastic model, neither group of investors was affected by the proposed tax change, but this is no longer true. Now, the impact on the utility of domestic investors is proportional to

$$A_i \left[b_{ii}^* \frac{\partial r_i}{\partial \tau_r} + s_{ii}^* \frac{\partial g_i}{\partial \tau_r} - \gamma s_{ii}^{*2} \sigma_i \frac{\partial \sigma_i}{\partial \tau_r} \right], \tag{28}$$

where $s_{ii}^* \equiv s_{ii} + \tau_r S_i / (A_i (1 - \tau_r))$, $b_{ii}^* \equiv b_{ii} - \tau_r S_i / (A_i (1 - \tau_r))$, and where the derivative $\partial g_i / \partial \tau_r$ implicitly includes the effects of the compensating change in τ_w. Given Equations (10a) and (23), this expression can be rewritten as

$$A_i \left[f_{ii} \frac{\partial r_i}{\partial \tau_r} + s_{ii}^* \frac{\gamma}{S_i A} \mathrm{cov}(\sigma_i \, dz_i, dZ_i) \left(\frac{f_K K}{f} \right) \frac{\partial K_i}{\partial \tau_r} \right]. \tag{29}$$

The equivalent expression for the impact of these tax changes on the utility of investors from country j equals

$$A_j \left[f_{ji} \frac{\partial r_i}{\partial \tau_r} + s_{ji} \frac{\gamma}{S_i A} \mathrm{cov}(\sigma_i \, dz_i, dZ_i) \left(\frac{f_K K}{f} \right) \frac{\partial K_i}{\partial \tau_r} \right]. \tag{30}$$

It is straightforward to show that the sum of these effects on the utility of investors equals minus $\partial R_i^n / \partial \tau_r$ – investors as a group lose given that tax revenue increases. Since $b_{ii} > b_{ji}$ and $s_{ii} = s_{ji}$, we find that each domestic investor loses more than each foreign investor per dollar of assets.

While foreign investors fare better than domestic investors, under any reasonable parameter values they still lose from the tax change. In particular, our earlier results on optimal portfolio holdings under symmetry imply that $s_{ji} = 1/N$, while $b_{ji} = -(\gamma - 1)/((N - 1)\gamma)$, so that $f_{ji} > 0$ as long as $N > \gamma$. As a result both terms in Equation (30) are negative. That foreign investors lose implies that the gain in tax revenue to the government exceeds the losses incurred by domestic investors. Since tax revenue by assumption receives more weight in the objective function than income to domestic investors, we conclude that the optimal value of τ_r is positive.

So far we have ignored possible differences in the effective tax treatment of foreign versus domestic investors in domestic equity. While the government cannot feasibly tax domestic investors at a higher rate than foreign investors since domestic investors can hide their nationality using foreign financial intermediaries, it can feasibly treat them more leniently.[45] Would it want to do so? To judge this, start with the optimal source-based capital income tax, τ_r. Then consider introducing a marginal subsidy to domestic investors at rate α in proportion to their ownership of domestic capital, adjusting the rate τ_r so as to leave the equilibrium amount of domestic investment unchanged.

For any given τ_r and α, the observed rate of return in the market on domestic shares is still defined by Equations (18) and (19). When domestic investors own these shares, however, they receive an income flow equal to $(g_i + \alpha)\, dt + \sigma_i\, dz_i$, implying that they invest until

$$g_i + \alpha - r_i = \gamma s_{ii} \sigma_i^2. \tag{10d}$$

Government revenue is now

$$R_i = \left(\frac{\tau_r S_i}{1 - \tau_r} \right) (g_i\, dt + \sigma\, dz_i) - \alpha S_{ii}\, dt.$$

As before, the government bears risks equivalent to those received from investments in $\tau_r S_i / (1 - \tau_r)$ domestic shares. To dispose of these risks, it transfers this risk to domestic investors, compensating them by enough to leave them indifferent. As a result, net government revenue becomes nonstochastic and equals

$$R_i^n = \left[\left(\frac{\tau_r S_i}{1 - \tau_r} \right) (r_i - \alpha) - \alpha S_{ii} \right] dt. \tag{20a}$$

In order to judge what combined tax rates will leave investment incentives unchanged, we proceed as before to solve for the aggregate pricing relationship. In particular, we weight Equation (10a) for each j by A_j, add over $j \neq i$ then combine this with Equation (10d) for country i (modified to reflect the extra risks acquired from the domestic governments) weighted by A_i, to find that

$$g_i = r_i - \frac{A_i \alpha}{A} + \frac{\gamma}{A} \sigma_i^2 \left[\frac{S_i}{1 - \tau_r} \right], \tag{31}$$

where we simplified using the assumption that $A_i = S_i$. Equation (31) can be reexpressed as

$$g_i^* = \frac{r_i}{1 - \tau_r} - \frac{A_i \alpha}{A(1 - \tau_r)} + \gamma \left[(\sigma_i^*)^2 S_i \right], \tag{31a}$$

---

[45] Foreign investors cannot easily take on the guise of a domestic investor to take advantage of a more favorable treatment available to domestic investors.

where a superscript * indicates a before-tax value. If the combined tax changes are to leave investment incentives unchanged, then the sum of the first two terms on the right-hand side of Equation (31a) should remain unchanged.[46] This is true if

$$\frac{\partial \tau_r}{\partial \alpha} = \frac{A_i(1 - \tau_r)}{Ar_i}. \tag{32}$$

What then happens to government revenue and the welfare of investors due to a marginal increase in α and an associated change in τ_r, starting from $\alpha = 0$? The impact on the utility of domestic investors can be calculated from Equation (28), modified to take into account the change in α. Given Equation (32), it quickly follows that the dollar equivalent gain to domestic investors equals

$$S_{ii} \left[1 - \frac{A_i}{A} \right] dt > 0.$$

Domestic investors clearly gain from these combined tax changes.

The impact of these tax changes on government revenue, evaluated at $\alpha = 0$, equals

$$\frac{\partial R_i^n}{\partial \alpha} = \left\{ \left(\frac{S_i}{1 - \tau_r} \right) \left(\frac{A_i}{A} - \tau_r \right) - S_{ii} \right\}.$$

We find that tax revenue falls if $\tau_r > A_i/A$, as almost surely must be true in a small open economy. However, the dollar equivalent gains to domestic investors are clearly larger than the losses in tax revenue – the difference equals $A_i(S_i - S_{ii})/A > 0$.[47] Therefore a positive value of α is attractive as long as the relative weight γ on government revenue is not too large. Many governments in fact do provide a subsidy to domestic investment in domestic equity, e.g., through dividend imputation schemes.[48]

---

[46] Inspection of the equilibrium condition for r_i shows that r_i remains unchanged as long as K_i remains unchanged.

[47] Foreign investors pay for this net gain to domestic residents through the drop in their return on domestic equity due to the increase in τ_r.

[48] Under these schemes, domestic investors owe personal income tax on the pretax corporate earnings used to fund dividend payments, but receive a credit for corporate taxes already paid on this income. As long as the corporate rate exceeds the personal tax rate, domestic investors receive a cash refund on net under the personal income tax. Most countries, the U.K. being a noted exception, do not provide equivalent refunds of corporate tax payments to foreign owners.

To summarize:

Result 4: When monetary policy stabilizes domestic prices, the optimal tax rate on capital income is positive. Domestic investors will be treated more favorably than foreign investors, unless the relative weight put on government revenue compared with the welfare of investors is high enough.

3.3. Tax Policy when Domestic Prices Are Stochastic

How are the results affected if monetary policy instead stabilizes the exchange rate? Consider as before the impact of introducing a source-based capital income tax at rate τ_r, with a compensating reduction in a labor income tax rate chosen to keep the net-of-tax wage unchanged. The resulting government revenue is still described by Equation (20). As before, the government transfers the risk in this revenue to domestic residents, compensating them enough to leave them indifferent.[49] Following Equation (10b), the expected amount that domestic residents must receive to be left indifferent to the transfer of this risk is

$$\frac{\tau_r S_i}{1 - \tau_r}(g_i + \eta_i - r - [1 - \gamma(1 - s_{ii})]\theta_i^2). \tag{33}$$

After paying this amount to compensate domestic residents for absorbing the risk in tax revenue, net government revenue becomes

$$R_i^n = \left[\tau_w w L_i + \frac{\tau_r S_i}{1 - \tau_r}(r - \eta_i + [1 - \gamma(1 - s_{ii})]\theta_i^2)\right]. \tag{34}$$

The change in monetary policy also has implications for the determinants of the market value of domestic firms. The first-order condition characterizing foreign demand for equity from country i remains Equation (10a). Given the nature of the risks that the government transfers to domestic residents, the first-order condition characterizing domestic demand for this equity becomes

$$g_i + \eta_i - r = \theta_i^2[1 - \gamma(1 - s_{ii})] + \gamma\left(s_{ii} + \frac{\tau_r S_i}{A_i(1 - \tau_r)}\right)\sigma_i^2. \tag{10e}$$

Assume that $S_i = A_i$, implying no net capital flows into country i. Aggregating these first-order conditions across investors as before, we

---

[49] Since no security is already traded with this particular risk characteristic, investors from different countries would charge different amounts to accept this risk. In fact, it is straightforward to show that domestic residents would charge more to accept this risk than would foreign investors. Rather than simply marketing the "security" on the market, however, we assume that the domestic government disposes of the risk through stochastic cash transfers to domestic investors with a compensating adjustment in the mean transfer.

find that

$$g_i + \eta_i - \frac{A_i}{A}\theta_i^2 = r + \frac{\gamma}{A}\mathrm{cov}(\sigma_i\,dz_i,\,dZ_i), \tag{23a}$$

where dZ_i is defined the same as in Equation (23). As long as the capital account is balanced, the extra value of equity to domestic investors as a hedge against price fluctuations is just counterbalanced by the extra costs of equity due to exchange rate risks for foreign investors, leaving no net effect of hedging demand on equity prices.

Firms in country i will invest until $\partial S_i/\partial K_i = p_i$. In doing so, they would use Equation (23a) to forecast the market's valuation of their marginal project, taking as given the aggregate risks faced by the market. Investment therefore continues until

$$f_K = \frac{r - \eta_i + (A_i/A)\theta_i^2}{(1 - \tau_r)D_u} \equiv r_K, \tag{24a}$$

where

$$D_u = 1 - \frac{\gamma}{A}\mathrm{cov}(\phi\,dz_i,\,dZ_i).$$

Equation (23a) can also be used to solve for the impact of a marginal increase in τ_r on the market clearing wage rate. Using Equations (18), (19), and (24a), we find that

$$(1 - \tau_r)L\frac{\partial w}{\partial \tau_r} = -\frac{r - \eta_i + (A_i/A)\theta_i^2}{1 - \tau_r}S_i - \frac{\gamma}{A}\mathrm{cov}(\sigma_i dz_i,\,dZ_i)\left(\frac{f_K K}{f}\right)\frac{\partial K_i}{\partial \tau_r}. \tag{25a}$$

Given the implied compensating change in τ_w, the impact of a marginal increase in τ_r, starting from $\tau_r = 0$, equals

$$\frac{\partial R_i^n}{\partial \tau_r} = S_i[1 - \gamma(1 - s_{ii}) - A_i/A]\theta_i^2 - \frac{\gamma}{A}\mathrm{cov}(\sigma_i dz_i,\,dZ_i)\left(\frac{f_K K}{f}\right)\frac{\partial K_i}{\partial \tau_r}. \tag{26a}$$

Since $\partial K_i/\partial \tau_r < 0$, the second term on the right-hand side of Equation (26a) results in an increase in tax revenue. The sign of the first term is unclear in general. Assuming symmetry among countries, however, we can use Equation (12) and the condition that $\sum_j s_{ji} = 1$ to show that

$$[1 - \gamma(1 - s_{ii}) - A_i/A] = -(\gamma - 1)\left(\frac{N-1}{N}\right)\left(\frac{\sigma^2}{\theta^2 + \sigma^2}\right).$$

This term is therefore negative as long as $\gamma > 1$, implying an ambiguous impact in general of the tax change on revenue. Revenue could fall, for example, if investment were sufficiently inelastic.

To judge whether a tax increase is attractive, we need to examine as well the impact of the tax change on the welfare of domestic investors, which is again described by Equation (28). Evaluating this expression, given Equations (26a) and (10e), we find that the dollar-equivalent impact of the combined tax changes on the welfare of domestic residents equals

$$\frac{S_{ii}}{S_i}\left[-\frac{\partial R_i^n}{\partial \tau_r} + [1 - \gamma(1 - s_{ii}) - A_i/A]\theta_i^2\left(\frac{f_K K}{f} - 1\right)\frac{\partial K_i}{\partial \tau_r}\right]. \tag{35}$$

At least under our symmetry assumption, the second term inside the brackets is negative.

If the increase in τ_r causes a fall in tax revenue, we conclude that welfare falls as well – the gains (if any) to domestic residents cannot be sufficient to offset the revenue loss. If tax revenue does increase due to an increase in τ_r, the desired τ_r is positive unless λ is small and the second term in expression (35) is too negative. While previously, we concluded unambiguously that the optimal τ_r was positive, results are no longer clear.

The key reason for this change in results is that the process of taxation leads to a worsening of the allocation across investors of the risks from domestic production. As seen comparing Equations (10b) and (10e), in equilibrium domestic investors charge a higher risk premium than foreign investors for the risk from domestic production – for domestic investors, the higher cost for bearing the production risk is offset by the hedging gains from domestic equity. Taxation leads to a further allocation of production risk to domestic investors with no further hedging gains, worsening a preexisting misallocation that results from the lack of indexed bonds.

Consider also the effect of this alternative monetary policy on the choice whether to treat domestic owners of domestic equity more favorably than foreign owners under the tax law. In particular, we start from the optimal τ_r, and examine the effects of a marginal increase in τ_r compensated by introducing a marginal subsidy to domestic owners at rate α sufficient to leave investment incentives unchanged.

The resulting first-order condition for domestic investors, assuming $S_i = A_i$, is now

$$g_i + \alpha + \eta_i - r = \theta_i^2[1 - \gamma(1 - s_{ii})] + \gamma\left(s_{ii} + \frac{\tau_r}{(1 - \tau_r)}\right)\sigma_i^2. \tag{10f}$$

Summing these first-order conditions across investors as before, we find that the market equilibrium condition is

$$g_i + \eta_i + \frac{A_i}{A}(\alpha - \theta_i^2) = r + \frac{\gamma}{A}\text{cov}(\sigma_i \, dz_i, dZ_i).$$

Starting from $\alpha = 0$, the adjustment in α needed to leave investment incentives unchanged when τ_r rises equals

$$\frac{\partial \alpha}{\partial \tau_r} = \frac{A}{A_i(1 - \tau_r)}\left[r - \eta_i + \frac{A_i}{A}\theta_i^2\right]. \tag{32a}$$

As before, the impact on domestic investors of these combined tax changes is positive. In particular, the dollar-equivalent impact on domestic investors, evaluated at $\alpha = 0$, equals

$$\left(S_{ii} + \frac{\tau_r S_i}{1 - \tau_r}\right)\left[\frac{\partial \alpha}{\partial \tau_r} - \frac{r - \eta_i + [1 - \gamma(1 - s_{ii})]\theta_i^2}{1 - \tau_r}\right].$$

Given Equation (32a), this expression is clearly positive in a small open economy.

What happens to government revenue? Net government revenue is now

$$R_i^n = \frac{\tau_r S_i}{1 - \tau_r}(r - \alpha - \eta_i + [1 - \gamma(1 - s_{ii})]\theta_i^2) - \alpha S_{ii}. \tag{34a}$$

The impact on government revenue of these combined tax changes equals

$$\frac{\partial R_i^n}{\partial \tau_r} = S_i \frac{r - \eta_i + [1 - \gamma(1 - s_{ii})]\theta_i^2}{(1 - \tau_r)^2} - \left(\frac{\tau_r S_i}{1 - \tau_r} + S_{ii}\right)\frac{\partial \alpha}{\partial \tau_r}.$$

Given Equation (32a), we find that government revenue clearly drops due to these tax changes in a small open economy.

Unlike in the previous case, the benefits to domestic investors are not necessarily larger than the loss in government revenue. In particular, the difference equals

$$(S_i - S_{ii})\left[\frac{r - \eta_i + [1 - \gamma(1 - s_{ii})]\theta_i^2}{1 - \tau_r}\right],$$

and the expression in brackets is not necessarily positive. If this expression is in fact negative, then so is the optimal value of α. Even if the expression is positive, so that domestic investors gain more than the government loses in tax revenue, the optimal value of α is positive only if the value of λ is not too large.

These results suggest that the change in monetary policy can have important effects on the optimal tax structure. The main role of taxes previously was to act as a tariff on foreign investors. Now foreign investors own a much smaller fraction of the shares in domestic equity, so that overall taxes on capital income fall more heavily on domestic shareholders. In addition, foreign demand is more elastic than before, since the relative price risk is unaffected by tax changes, reducing the optimal tariff rate. Domestic demand, however, has become less elastic due to the hedging gains from equity, making it more attractive to tax domestic owners.

Given the additional hedging demand by domestic investors for domestic equity, they continue investing until their marginal risk premium for the production risk from equity is much higher than that of the foreign investors. As a result, a marginal reallocation of production risk from foreign to domestic investors is an efficiency loss. Yet this is just what happens when taxes are imposed on foreign owners, and the resulting randomness in tax payments is transferred to domestic shareholders. As a result, taxes on foreign owners exacerbate a preexisting misallocation of risk, resulting from an incomplete set of financial securities,[50] reducing the attractiveness of the tax.

To summarize:

Result 5: When monetary policy stabilizes the exchange rate, the optimal capital income tax rate is positive only if it collects revenue and if this revenue is valued strongly enough. Domestic investors will face a lower tax rate than foreign investors only if the hedging benefits from stocks are sufficiently small and if the welfare of domestic investors is of enough importance relative to government revenue.

4. Conclusions

Equity portfolios clearly demonstrate home bias. Why remains an unanswered question. Even without a convincing explanation, however, it is all too easy to speculate about the implications of this home bias for other economic questions. In particular, it would be natural to infer that home bias in portfolios implies that extra domestic savings lead primarily to extra domestic investment. Similarly home bias would seem to facilitate taxes on the return to domestic capital, given the suggested inelastic demand for domestic capital even in a small open economy. While papers

---

[50] If indexed bonds are added to the model, the difference in risk premia disappears.

such as Gordon and Varian (1989) find in a setting without home bias that the optimal tax policy involves positive tax rates on at least foreign owners of domestic equity, as a form of optimal tariff, the hypothesis could easily be that these optimal tax rates would be yet higher in a setting with home bias.

In this paper, we have explored a particular explanation for home bias, in which residents in different countries consume mainly locally produced goods and in which the international prices of these goods change randomly over time. When monetary authority in a country stabilizes the exchange rate, so that all of this risk shows up in domestic prices, then the only hedge local residents have against these movements in consumer prices is domestic equity.[51] In contrast, when the monetary authorities stabilize the local price level, leading instead to random exchange rates, then equity portfolios will be fully diversified internationally.[52] The past discussion of home bias has focused on equity portfolios. However, with exchange rate risk there will instead be home bias in bond portfolios.

We then explore the implications of this potential explanation for home bias for capital immobility and for domestic taxes on capital income. In particular, does home bias lead to capital immobility and to higher capital-income tax rates? Do the forecasts differ depending on whether there is home bias in equity portfolios, the traditional focus, or in bond portfolios?

We do find capital immobility, consistent with the hypothesis of Feldstein and Horioka (1980). In fact, we find exactly the same extent of capital immobility whether there is home bias in equity portfolios or in bond portfolios. It turns out that the past focus on home bias in equity portfolios is misleading.

Finally, we examine the implications of home bias for optimal tax rates on capital income. Introducing home bias in bond portfolios leaves the forecasts for tax policy largely unaffected. The optimal tax rate on the capital income accruing to foreign investors is still positive, while domestic investors would normally face a lower tax rate.[53]

While it would be plausible to presume that optimal tax rates on capital income would be higher in a setting in which equity portfolios exhibit

---

[51] While the forecasted extent of home bias in domestic equity is not as large as is seen in the data, this hypothesis is in many ways more consistent with the data than other explanations for home bias that have been explored.

[52] While this exchange rate risk would seem to inhibit purchases of foreign equity, this exchange rate risk can be perfectly hedged by borrowing abroad to buy foreign equity.

[53] The home bias in bonds does affect the size of these optimal tax rates, however, and seems to weaken the market power over foreign investors and weaken the tax advantage faced by domestic investors.

home bias, we find to the contrary that tax rates on capital income likely fall and may not even remain positive when monetary policy shifts to stabilizing exchange rates, in spite of the resulting specialization in equity portfolios. To begin with, foreign demand for domestic equity falls and becomes more elastic, reducing the optimal tariff on foreign owners of domestic capital. In addition, any tax on foreign owners leads to a reallocation of production risk from foreign to domestic residents, in itself lowering efficiency.[54] Only under restrictive parameter values will domestic holders still face a lower tax rate.

These results contrary to the conventional wisdom arise in this one particular model of home bias. It could well be that some other explanation for home bias could provide support for this conventional wisdom. However, to judge this, future work will need to explore more closely the implications of any particular explanation for home bias for economic behavior more broadly. If forecasts differ across alternative explanations for home bias, then it becomes important to pursue further empirical work as well, to identify which explanation for home bias is more consistent with the data.

Acknowledgments: The views expressed are the author's own and do not necessarily reflect those of the ECB or the Eurosystem. We would very much like to thank Aaron Edlin, Soren Bo Nielsen, Teresa Ter-Minassian, the referees, and participants in seminars at the Bank of Portugal and Hong Kong School of Science and Technology and at the conference on "Economic Policy in the International Economy" in honor of Assaf Razin for comments on an earlier draft. The first author would like to acknowledge financial support from National Science Foundation Grant No. SBR-9422589 during the writing of this paper.

References

Adler, Michael, and Bernard Dumas (1983). "International Portfolio Choice and Corporation Finance: A Synthesis," *Journal of Finance* 38(3), 925–84.
Armington, Paul (1969). "A Theory of Demand for Products Distinguished by Place of Production,"*IMF Staff Papers* 27, 488–526.
Bank of England (1996). *Index-Linked Debt*. London: Bank of England.

---

[54] Without indexed bonds, too much of this risk is borne by domestic residents, who continue buying domestic equity in spite of this risk as a hedge against random domestic consumer prices.

Baxter, Marianne, and Urban Jermann (1997). "The International Diversification Puzzle Is Worse than You Think," *American Economic Review* 87, 170–80.

Bottazzi, L., P. Pesenti, and E. van Wincoop (1996). "Wages, Profits and the International Portfolio Puzzle," *European Economic Review* 40, 219–54.

Branson, William, and Dale Henderson (1985). "The Specification and Influence of Asset Markets," in Ronald Jones and Peter Kenen (eds.), *Handbook of International Economics*, vol. 2. (Amsterdam: Elsevier Science Publishers).

Brennan, Michael J., and Henry Cao (1997). "International Portfolio Investment Flows," *Journal of Finance* 52, 1851–80.

Cooper, Ian, and Evi Kaplanis (1994). "Home Bias in Equity Portfolios, Inflation Hedging, and International Capital Market Equilibrium," *Review of Financial Studies* 7, 45–60.

De Bandt, Olivier, and Philipp Hartmann (2000). "Systemic Risk: A Survey," ECB Working Paper No. 35.

Diamond, Peter, and James Mirrlees (1971). "Optimal Taxation and Public Production, I: Production Efficiency; II: Tax Rules," *American Economic Review* 61, 8–27, 261–78.

Eldor, Rafael, David Pines, and Abba Schwartz (1988). "Home Asset Preference and Productivity Shocks," *Journal of International Economics* 25(1/2), 165–76.

Engel, Charles (1994). "Test of CAPM on an International Portfolio of Bonds and Stocks," in J. Frankel, ed., *The Internationalization of Equity Markets*. Chicago: University of Chicago Press.

Feldstein, Martin S., and Charles Horioka (1980). "Domestic Savings and International Capital Flows," *The Economic Journal* 90, 314–29.

Frankel, Jefferey, and Andrew Rose (1997). "Is EMU More Justifiable Ex Post than Ex Ante?" *European Economic Review* 41, 753–60.

Fratszcher, M (2001). "Financial Market Integration in Europe: On the Effects of EMU on Stock Market," ECB Working Paper No. 48.

French, Kenneth R., and James M. Poterba (1991). "Investor Diversification and International Equity Markets," *American Economic Review* 81(2), 222–6.

Gordon, Roger H (1986). "Taxation of Investment and Savings in a World Economy," *American Economic Review* 76(5), 1086–1102.

Gordon, Roger H., and A. Lans Bovenberg (1996). "Why Is Capital so Immobile Internationally? Possible Explanations and Implications for Capital Income Taxation," *American Economic Review* 86, 1057–75.

Gordon, Roger H., and Hal Varian (1989). "Taxation of Asset Income in the Presence of a World Securities Market," *Journal of International Economics* 26(3/4), 205–26.

Hartley, Peter (1986). "Portfolio Theory and Foreign Investment – The Role of Non-Marketed Assets," *Economic Record* 62(178), pp. 286–295.

Iwaisako, Tokuo (1996). "Does International Diversification Really Diversity Risks?" working paper.

Kang, Jun Koo, and René Stulz (1997). "Why Is There a Home Bias? An Analysis of Foreign Portfolio Equity Ownership in Japan," *Journal of Financial Economics* 46, 3–28.

Longin, Francois, and Bruno Solnik (1995). "Is the Correlation in International Equity Returns Constant: 1960–1990?" *Journal of International Money and Finance* 14, 3–26.

Merton, Robert C. (1990). *Continuous-Time Finance*. Cambridge: Blackwell.

Merton, Robert C. (1969). "Lifetime Portfolio Selection Under Uncertainty: The Continuous-Time Case," *Review of Economics and Statistics* 51, 247–57.

Nielsen, Soren Bo (1998). "On Capital Income Tax Policies Under Uncertainty," *European Economic Review* 42, 1553–80.

Obstfeld, Maurice and Kenneth Rogoff (2000). "The Six Major Puzzles in International Macroeconomics: Is There a Common Cause?" NBER Working Paper No. 7777.

Persson, Torsten and Lars E. O. Svensson (1989). "Exchange-Rate Variability and Asset Trade," *Journal of Monetary Economics* 23, 485–509.

Pesenti, Paolo and Eric van Wincoop (1996). "Do Non-Traded Goods Explain the Home-Bias Puzzle?" NBER. Working Paper No. 5784.

Siegel, Jeremy J. (1972). "Risk, Interest, and Forward Exchange," *Quarterly Journal of Economics* 86, 303–9.

Solnik, Bruno H (1974). "An Equilibrium Model of the International Capital Market," *Journal of Economic Theory* 8, 500–24.

Werner, Ingrid M (1994). "Capital Income Taxation and International Portfolio Choice," *Journal of Public Economics* 53, 205–22.

FOURTEEN

Social Dumping in the Transformation Process?*

Hans-Werner Sinn

1. The Accusation of Social Dumping

Business representatives and union leaders in highly industrialized countries often accuse the governments of less developed countries of practicing social dumping in the sense of maintaining an underdeveloped welfare state to create a competitive cost advantage for their own industries. In particular they argue that the less developed countries deliberately neglect the legislation for good social standards in terms of social fringe benefits, protection against injuries, pension schemes, codetermination rights, and the like. To stop the seemingly unfair competition resulting from social dumping they postulate an international harmonization of social conditions, and sometimes they even advocate retaliatory trade restrictions to enforce the harmonization.

International agreements like those of the International Labor Organisation (ILO) or the EU Social Charter reflect this influence in that they define a number of social minimum standards that are binding for the signing parties. The EU Social Charter prescribes a weekly maximum working time, minimum recreation periods, minimum safety standards for new and old machinery, rules for the employment of minors, equal treatment of gender, minimum times for maternity leaves, dismissal protection rules for pregnant women, and many additional workers' rights.[1] Similarly, the

---

* This paper will also be forthcoming in H.-W. Sinn (2002). *The New Systems Competition*, Basil Blackwell: Oxford and London.
[1] Social Community charter of the fundamental social rights of workers, COM (89) 248 final. See also Berié (1993) and Feldmann (1999).

ILO members have agreed to establish a system of labor standards[2] regarding minimum wages, maximum working hours per week, minimum rest time per week, a guaranteed number of holidays with pay, and the prohibition of the worst forms of child labor.

This paper will analyze the motives for low labor standards in less developed countries and examine the justification of harmonization agreements like the EU Social Charter and the ILO conventions. For this purpose it will model the transition growth path of a less developed country that joins a well-developed economic core area. The EU eastern enlargement can be taken as an example of this problem. Before joining, the less developed country has a very low labor productivity, low wages, and low social standards, but after joining it will catch up by sending guest workers to the core region and attracting capital investment. Because of the factor mobility, factor prices will change and the national government of the joining country will continuously revise its social policies. The question is whether the transition process brought about jointly by private market forces and the forces of systems competition is efficient in any meaningful sense and whether, if it is not, supranational actions such as the above-mentioned harmonization agreements are necessary to improve the allocation of resources.

2. Redistribution vs. Wages in Kind

Analyzing the accusation of social dumping is not a trivial exercise because it refers to two completely different phenomena that should not be lumped together, although this is frequently done in public debates. One refers to wages, working conditions, and wage related fringe benefits that make up the employers' labor costs. The other refers to the redistribution of resources between different types of individuals, such as tax-financed transfers to the poor.

Concerning the second type of social dumping it can be shown that income redistribution between the rich and the poor will indeed be eroded

---

[2] A comprehensive introduction to ILO's labor standards can be found in Plant (1994). ILO has issued a total of 183 conventions on labor standards to date. See, in particular, the minimum wage fixing convention (No. 131, http://ilolex.ilo.ch:1567/scripts/convde.pl?C131), the hours of work (industry) convention (No. 1, http://ilolex.ilo.ch:1567/scripts/convde.pl?C1), the weekly rest (industry) convention (No. 14, http://ilolex.ilo.ch:1567/scripts/convde.pl?C14), the holidays with pay convention (revised) (No, 132, http://ilolex.ilo.ch:1567/scripts/convde.pl?C132), and the worst forms of child labor convention (No. 182, http://ilolex.ilo.ch:1567/scripts/convde.pl?C182).

in systems competition. From the point of view of an individual country, redistribution among mobile income earners is not rational. On the one hand, redistribution cannot effectively change the distribution of net incomes when labor can migrate across the borders and wages react to this migration. On the other, redistribution creates budgetary problems for the government by attracting the people who receive government benefits and driving away those who pay for them. To avoid the budgetary problems, governments cut the taxes and reduce the benefits. Redistribution is eroded even though, from an ex ante perspective, it is in the general interest of risk averse citizens from all countries. This may be called social dumping.

However, it is doubtful whether this is the kind of social dumping to which the accusations of business and union leaders in the developed countries refer primarily, because the nexus between neglecting redistribution and a competitive advantage seems less obvious than the one between bad working conditions and a competitive advantage. From a theoretical perspective the case is also not clear. It is true that a fall in net taxes on above-average income earners may reduce the cost of capital and the wage cost for qualified labor. However, reducing the net social transfers to less qualified labor may lead to emigration and higher wage demands by the workers at the bottom end of the income scale, and this, in itself, will tend to raise the wage cost. What business and union leaders have in mind, therefore, seems to be the working conditions, wages, and wage-related fringe benefits, which all have a direct impact on the wage cost.

It is undoubtedly the case that in countries like Portugal or Spain not only the wages themselves but also the safety standards in the firms, the social insurance contributions, the number of holidays, the length of maternity leave, the payment of wages in cases of sickness, the safety regulation for work places, and similar achievements of the welfare state are well below those in the more advanced European countries like Sweden or Germany. The accusation made by business representatives and union leaders is that the low wage standards are partly the result of a conscious policy of social dumping which is carried out intentionally, or at least tolerated, by the national governments of the less developed countries. These governments, it is maintained, stick to low social standards and do not care about low wages, because they know that competitive advantages for the domestic industries result.

The social standards meant in this context can best be understood as wages in kind prescribed by the government. Surely the utility of workers increases if they receive better safety standards and other wage-related fringe benefits, just as a pecuniary wage payment increases their utility, and surely the firms' labor costs increase if they have to provide these benefits, just as they would with a pecuniary wage increase. As both the pecuniary wage and the wage in kind are to be paid from the same marginal value product of labor, public legislation on wages in kind does not involve a redistribution of resources between different groups of individuals. It is instead similar to legislation setting wages itself.

This demonstrates that the two potential reasons for social dumping should not be lumped together. They refer to completely different economic phenomena, and the similarity is purely semantic, notwithstanding the fact that they both may appear simultaneously with actual policy measures. Welfare dumping is not wage dumping.

3. Why Are the Differences in Direct and Indirect Wage Costs So High?

There are at present considerable differences in wage costs in Europe. Gross hourly wage costs differ substantially among the European countries. While the average wage cost is about eighteen euros in the EU countries, the differences between the two countries with the highest and the two countries with the lowest wage costs exceed ten euros per hour, and one-third of the countries has wage costs that are more than three times as high as those of the two countries with the lowest costs. Fig. 14.1 gives an overview of the wage differences among the European countries.

The figure breaks down the wage costs into direct and indirect costs according to the EUROSTAT definitions.[3] Direct costs are defined as gross wages per hour, basically the official annual pay divided by the number of working hours. They include the employees' social security contributions, overtime supplements, shift compensation, regularly paid premia, pay for vacation and national holidays, year-end bonuses, and similar items. Indirect costs consist of employer social insurance contributions, sick pay schemes, and other social expenses such as those for sports facilities, canteens, medical services, and vocational training. Indirect wage costs according the EUROSTAT definitions are part of what this paper considers as the costs of social standards, however they do not exhaust this category of wage costs. Codetermination rights of workers, safety

---

[3] See Schröder (2000, p. 77).

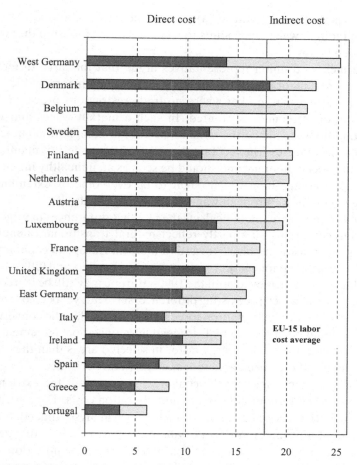

Figure 14.1. Labor cost in manufacturing in European countries 1999 (Euro per working hour)
Source: Institut der deutschen Wirtschaft, Database, 2000.
Note: Labor cost of male and female workers. The 1999 EU-15 average is a weighted average with working population (Eurostat, Eurostatistics 11/2000, p. 45) as weights.

requirements for machinery, dismissal protection rules, or constraints on working time incur additional indirect wage costs that are not included in the official definitions.

Despite these omissions the indirect wage costs shown in Fig. 14.1 are substantial, sometimes covering 40% of the total wage costs or more. They clearly are important determinants of the competitiveness of the single countries. Note that countries with a high direct wage also tend to have a high indirect wage. This points to a systematic relationship that will be explored below.

Business and union representatives argue that the large differences in wages and labor standards shown in Fig. 14.1 are incompatible with a common European market where no trade restrictions prevail and the freedom of settlement is granted. In such a market wages and working conditions should be the same to ensure fair competition among the European countries. The fact that they are not the same, it is maintained, indicates social dumping and should be seen as an unhealthy implication of systems competition which ought to be overcome by extending the scope of common European wage and working standards.

However, the argument neglects the fact that differences in wages and working conditions may partly reflect natural transitional phenomena during the adjustment phase towards a uniform European economy. After all, a truly common market without customs barriers and full economic freedom was not achieved until the 1990s. Europe may still be in a convergence phase in which preexisting differences have not yet been overcome. If this phase is driven by natural forces it is not clear that the convergence process could be improved by European harmonization agreements that force the countries to converge faster in selected areas than they would have done had they been able to make unilateral decisions.

The important aspect of the convergence process is the existence of frictions in the form of adjustment and migration costs. The abstraction from such frictions is appropriate for a long-run analysis. Indeed, the new freedom of movement in Europe will, in the long run, lead to a general convergence of economic conditions, and there can be little doubt that the mechanism of factor price equalization assumed there and described more fully by the foreign trade literature will eventually make its effect felt. With unrestricted exchange of goods, free choice of workplace and free capital movement, and the current differences in overall wage costs certainly cannot be maintained forever. Over the long term, countries like Ireland, Spain, Portugal, and Greece will find their factor prices converging towards those of the European core countries.

However, because of the frictions, factor price equalization cannot come about overnight. It may take decades for an approximate factor price equalization to take place. The main reason for the delay is the time needed for the accumulation of a modern stock of capital in the countries that are still lagging behind. It is true that financial capital is as nimble as a deer. What matters, however, is real capital, and real capital is as slow as a tortoise. Real capital faces substantial adjustment costs. Many kinds of obstacles must be overcome before it can move into low wage areas. These obstacles include management constraints, the sequential nature of building processes, the roundaboutness of multifirm production chains, learning-by-doing constraints, the initial lack of public infrastructure, and, last but not least, the time-consuming construction of the economic and political institutions that are the backbone of efficient modern market economies.

When accumulation of real capital is slow, wages, too, lag for a long time behind those in the more developed regions, and workers in the less developed areas have strong incentives to migrate to the high-wage countries as guest workers. Compared to capital, guest workers are very mobile. Many of them may come in the short term when the wage differences are large, but they return very quickly to their home countries when these differences become smaller. Nevertheless, guest workers face considerable migration costs. These show up less in migration delays than in the fact that many people prefer to stay in their own countries even when wage differentials are large. Objective and subjective costs prevent these people from simply maximizing their wages income. Looked at in this way, persistent differences in pecuniary wages between the developed and the less well developed countries of Europe seem quite natural for a long period to come despite the extension of the four basic freedoms granted in the Treaty of Rome.

Social standards are not directly explained by market forces because they are typically set by the government. Nevertheless, they may be explained indirectly, since it makes little sense for a government to prescribe in-kind benefits to workers that are out of proportion to the direct wages agreed to in private labor contracts. In the light of the empirical information given in Fig. 14.1 it seems plausible to expect governments to develop the social standards in proportion with the direct wages paid, taking the stages of their respective countries' developments into account. A sluggish adjustment of social standards may also be a natural feature of a transformation process which leads to alignment with the economic conditions in the developed regions only in the very long run.

4. A Simple Model of the Economic Catching-up Process

To analyze these issues formally, the transformation process of an initially underdeveloped country that joins a developed economic area will be modeled. The purpose of the model is to help understand the market forces and the actions of national governments in order to find an answer to the question of whether an international harmonization of labor standards and wages could improve the allocation of resources. Three levels in the hierarchy of decision problems will be considered: i) individual optimization and market equilibrium, given the national standard policy, ii) national optimization by the competitive government in terms of setting the time path of standards, and iii) supranational optimization to see whether the equilibrium in systems competition is efficient and to take counteracting harmonization if necessary. This section considers the first of these levels. The other levels are analyzed in the following sections.

Consider a small underdeveloped "joining" country that opens its borders to a large already developed "core area." Goods, financial capital, and technical knowledge are completely mobile across the country's borders. The uniform goods prices are normalized to one, and the uniform financial market interest rate is set in the core area at the level r.[4]

Real capital and labor are mobile only to a limited extent and, as discussed above, in different degrees. Real capital can only migrate slowly, but, in principle, it has no lasting location preferences for one area or another; what matters is the return that can be generated. Investments in the joining country, I, result in convex adjustment costs $\varphi(I)$ which reduce the speed of capital adjustment. It is assumed that $\varphi(0) = \varphi'(0) = 0$, $\varphi' < 0$ for $I < 0$, $\varphi' > 0$ for $I > 0$, $\varphi'' > 0$. By contrast, labor can migrate very quickly − a train journey of a few hours is often sufficient to reach a work place in the core area. Nevertheless, people typically do not want to migrate. They prefer to stay at home and migrate only if the reward in terms of a wage increase is sufficiently high. Let X stand for the number of guest workers who have migrated to the core area. Since they prefer to live at home in principle, they incur an aggregate cost $\psi(X)$, when they live and work in the core area, which measures both the subjective aversion against doing so and the objective costs involved. $\psi(X)$ does not represent one-off migration cost. Instead, it refers to the recurring costs associated with staying in the other country. Examples of the objective costs are the costs of "commuting" or of regular trips home, and of having to pay larger rents than at home. An example of the subjective cost is homesickness. Some guest workers have a low preference for their home country and do not go back there very often; for others the situation is the reverse. $\psi(X)$ describes the total costs of all guest workers staying in

---

[4] Related models can be found in Sinn (2000) and Sinn and Sinn (1991, Chapter 5).

the core country as a function of their number. Since the guest workers differ and are ranked in the order of their individual cost, it follows that $\psi'(X) > 0$. Since the first guest worker faces no cost and successive guest workers are increasingly averse to migration, it also follows that $\psi(0) = 0$ and $\psi'' > 0$.

Because free transfer of knowledge is assumed, the joining country produces its goods with the same linearly homogeneous production function $f(K, L)$ as the core area, where real capital K and labor L are the factors of production. The constant labor force potential of the joining country is L^*, and the number of guest workers is

$$X = L^* - L. \tag{1}$$

A worker can work for a fixed effective wage rate w^* in the core area or for an effective wage rate of size w at home.[5] Workers with a high home country preference, $\psi'(X) > w^* - w$, work at home because the wage differential is not sufficient to compensate them for the cost of working in the core area. The reverse holds for those workers who have some aversion against leaving home, for whom $\psi' < w^* - w$; they decide to be guest workers. The marginal worker who is just indifferent between migrating and staying at home is implicitly defined by the condition

$$\psi'(X) = w^* - w. \tag{2}$$

The effective wage rate w which drives the migration decision is the worker's subjective money equivalent of a benefit bundle consisting of the pecuniary market wage w_p and the benefit resulting from firms' expense per employee, w_s, necessary to meet the government-determined social standard,

$$w \equiv U(w_p, w_s). \tag{3}$$

It is assumed that the derivatives satisfy the assumptions $U_1, U_2 > 0$, U_{11}, $U_{22} < 0$. Similarly, w^*, the given effective wage rate in the core area, is the subjective money equivalent of the direct and indirect wage elements available there. U is linearly homogeneous and normalized in a way that

$$U(w_p, w_s) = w_p + w_s \quad \text{if } w_p \text{ and } w_s \text{ are chosen such that}$$
$$U_1 = U_2 = 1. \tag{4}$$

---

[5] The star is chosen here as the index for the labour force potential of the joining country and the wage rate of the core country, because these two values show up in the model as steady state variables of employment and the wage rate in the joining country.

To explain the empirical fact that social standards are chosen by governments rather than the firms themselves, a basic information asymmetry between workers and firms, which gives rise to a lemons problem, can be assumed. While each firm knows its expense for its own measures to improve the quality of its work places, workers have a more limited knowledge when they make their employment decisions. They know the country average, but not the efforts of their future employers at the time they sign their employment contracts. Thus, each single firm has an incentive to underinvest in the quality of its own workplaces. If it does so, it saves costs, but will not, or not immediately, be punished by not being able to attract or keep workers. To prevent an equilibrium in the labor market where the quality of work places is inefficiently low the government imposes the right social standard as a binding constraint on firms' choices. Alternatively, it can be assumed that there is no information asymmetry between workers and firms, but governments become active simply because the complicated definition of work place standards is a public good, whose production is costly so that it is cheaper having the government settings the standards than relying on each single firm doing this separately.

It is debatable whether the information asymmetry, if there is one at all, carries over to the choice between countries. However, it is much easier to acquire the information about countries than about individual firms. Thus the assumption that workers know the country-specific social standards when they make their migration decisions seems reasonable. A Pole who migrates to Germany knows under which conditions he has worked in Poland and has rather accurate expectations about the social standards prevailing in Germany.

Let t indicate calendar time. Unless otherwise indicated all equations hold for all points in time, $t > 0$, where zero is the time of joining the union. Variables like X, L, or w are time dependent magnitudes. It is assumed that no migration is possible before the time of joining and that, in the joining country, the marginal product with full employment is below the wage rate in the core area because the initial stock of capital, K_0, is sufficiently low:

$$X(t) = 0, \psi'[X(t)] = 0,$$
$$w^* - f_L(K_0, L^*) > 0 \qquad \text{for } t \leq 0. \tag{5}$$

A rational expectations equilibrium is modeled, because the national government or a supranational government like the EU cannot be assumed to have better foresight than the participants in the market. The representative firm in the joining country takes the rate of interest and the time path of the pecuniary wage as given, and in equilibrium this anticipated time path equals the actual one. The firm also knows the time path of the government-imposed social standard, and at each point in time it spends the amount of money per worker, w_s, necessary to meet the then- prevailing standard. The firm chooses the time paths of its labor use, L, and its net investment, I, such that the present value of the cash flow it generates is maximized:[6]

$$\max_{\{L,I\}_0^\infty} \int_0^\infty \{f[K(t), L(t)] - [w_p(t) + w_s(t)]L(t) - I(t) - \varphi[I(t)]\}e^{-rt}\,dt$$

$$\text{s.t.}\, K(0) = K_0 = \text{const.}, \qquad \dot{K} = I. \qquad (6)$$

The current-value Hamiltonian of this problem is

$$H = f(K, L) - (w_p + w_s)L - I - \varphi(I) + qI,$$

where q is the co-state variable of the stock of capital, namely Tobin's q. Applying Pontryagin's Maximum Principle, the first-order conditions

$$\frac{\partial H}{\partial L} = f_L - w_p - w_s = 0 \qquad (7)$$

and

$$\frac{\partial H}{\partial I} = -1 - \varphi'(I) + q = 0, \qquad (8)$$

the canonical equation

$$\dot{q} - rq = -f_K \qquad (9)$$

and the transversality condition

$$\lim_{t\to\infty} q(t)K(t)e^{-rt} = 0 \qquad (10)$$

can be derived.

---

[6] The formulation leaves open whether investment is financed by equity or loan capital. Because taxes are not discriminatory the two ways of financing are equivalent.

5. The Policy of the National Government

From the equations set up in the previous section, the government knows how migrants and private firms will react to the time path of the standard it announces and which intertemporal equilibrium will therefore emerge. Thus it effectively chooses the time path of the firms' corresponding expense per worker, w_s, so as to maximize national welfare. In the present context, national welfare, W, is the sum of the present value of the representative firm's cash flow according to (6) and the present value of the money equivalents of the direct and indirect wage benefits earned at home, $U(w_p + w_s) \cdot L$, and abroad, $w^* \cdot (L^* - L)$, minus the migration cost $\psi(L^* - L)$.[7]

$$W = \int_0^\infty \{f[K(t), L(t)] - [w_p(t) + w_s(t)]L(t) - I(t) - \varphi[I(t)]\} e^{-rt} dt$$

$$+ \int_0^\infty \{U[w_p(t), w_s(t)]L(t) + w^* \cdot [L^* - L(t)] - \psi[L^* - L(t)]\} e^{-rt} dt. \tag{11}$$

The constraints of the government's optimization include the migration rule (2) and the firms' optimality conditions (7)–(9).

Consider the effect on W of a marginal perturbation $\varepsilon(t)$ of the time path of w_s. This perturbation incurs a first-order effect and a second-order effect on national welfare. The latter results from the general equilibrium reactions of the time paths of I and L, given the time paths of the direct and indirect wage components w_p and w_s. It is zero since the marginal perturbation takes place around the private optima. None of the two integrals in (11) takes on a different value.[8]

The first-order effect results from the changes in the direct and indirect wage components, given the behavior of private agents as described by L and I. The relationship between these two wage components is given by (7), which obviously implies that $\partial w_p / \partial w_s = -1$. If the government has

---

[7] It could be argued that the return to capital earned by foreign investors that has to be financed out of the output produced in the joining area would have to be subtracted in the welfare calculation. However, if this is done, it is also necessary to add the funds flowing in at the time of investment. As the present value of the total cash flow between the joining country and its foreign investors is zero, this amendment of the equation would not affect the results. In fact, discounting with the rate of return in the core area, r, already correctly expresses the joining country's funding cost.

[8] Note, e.g., that the derivative of the integrand of the second integral with regard to L is zero because of the marginal migration condition (2).

optimized its policy, the perturbation is unable to change welfare. Thus it is a necessary condition for an optimum that

$$\Delta W|_{\{L,I\}} = \int_0^\infty \varepsilon(t)[U_2(w_p(t), w_s(t)) - U_1(w_p(t), w_s(t))]e^{-rt}dt = 0.$$

Since this condition must hold for arbitrary perturbations $\varepsilon(t)$, it is also necessary that the marginal rate of substitution between the two wage components is always one:

$$\frac{U_1(w_p, w_s)}{U_2(w_p, w_s)} = 1 \ \forall t \geq 0. \tag{12}$$

Because of the linear homogeneity of the utility function this optimality implies that the government-imposed work place standard will improve gradually in step with a rise in the market wage. Due to the normalization of the utility function assumed with (4), Equation (12) implies that the utility from having a job in the domestic economy is equal to the algebraic sum of the wage paid out to the workers and the per-capita expense involved by satisfying the government-imposed work standard. As the utility was moreover assumed in (3) to be equal to the effective wage, w, one gets:

$$w = w_p + w_s. \tag{13}$$

If the government did not satisfy Equation (12), the effective wage would be lower than this sum, because an excess burden from setting nonoptimal social standards would have to be subtracted.

Proposition 1: *Maximizing social welfare, the government of the joining country chooses a time path of the social standard such that the rate of substitution between the pecuniary wage and the firms' expenses necessary to satisfy the standard is equal to one.*

6. The Overall Welfare Optimum

After studying the optimality conditions of private agents and the national government, a supranational perspective will now be taken to check whether the accusation of social dumping is justified. Consider the optimization problem of a benevolent social planner. If the result of this optimization problem does not differ from the outcome of the previous two sections, there is no reason to intervene by harmonizing social standards or similar measures. If it does, supranational actions may be considered.

From an international perspective, the welfare goal does not differ from the national one as long as it can be assumed that the term $w^* \cdot [L^* - L(t)] - \psi[L^* - L(t)]$ correctly measures the social benefit from sending guest workers to the core country. Such an assumption is justified in the competitive small-country case considered here because w^* equals the fixed marginal product of labor in the core country minus a potential excess burden from setting suboptimal work standards. Thus the overall social optimum can be found by solving the problem

$$\max_{\{L,\, I,\, w_p,\, w_s\}_0^\infty} W, \text{ s.t. } K(0) = K_0 = \text{const. and } \dot{K} = I,$$

where W is defined as in (11). The current-value Hamiltonian for this problem is

$$H = f(K, L) - I - \varphi(I) - (w_p + w_s - U(w_p, w_s)) \cdot L + w^* \cdot (L - L^*)$$
$$- \psi(L^* - L) + qI.$$

Here, the term $(w_p + w_s - U(w_p, w_s))$ is the per capita excess burden from a nonoptimal choice of social standards and q is again the co-state variable of the stock of capital, K. The necessary conditions for a maximum of the Hamiltonian are

$$\frac{\partial H}{\partial L} = f_L - [(w_p + w_s) - U(w_p, w_s)] - w^* + \psi' = 0, \qquad (14)$$

$$\frac{\partial H}{\partial I} = -1 - \varphi'(I) + q = 0, \qquad (15)$$

$$\frac{\partial H}{\partial w_p} = -1 + U_1 = 0, \qquad (16)$$

$$\frac{\partial H}{\partial w_s} = -1 + U_2 = 0, \qquad (17)$$

and the canonical equation is

$$\dot{q} - rq = -f_K. \qquad (18)$$

The transversality condition of this problem is

$$\lim_{t \to \infty} q(t)\, K(t)\, e^{-rt} = 0. \qquad (19)$$

Equations (16) and (17) coincide with the national optimum as defined by (12) and (13) with regard to the work standard policy. Thus the term in squared brackets in (14) disappears, and obviously the marginal conditions coincide with conditions (7)–(10) which characterize a market equilibrium. This is the response to the accusation of social dumping.

Proposition 2: *The transformation process chosen by market forces and the work standard policy chosen by the joining country's government are efficient from a supranational perspective.*

If the national choices were not efficient, a supranational agency such as the EU would have to think about potential remedies including the frequently demanded harmonization of social standards. However, Proposition 2 confirms that this is not necessary. Since the decentralized solution including the decentralized choice of government actions leads to a first-best optimum, there is no social dumping and no need for centralized government actions. Systems competition with work place standards works even though systems competition with public redistribution does not.

The social optimality of the national government's choice is even warranted in a second-best sense, when the core area itself sets a nonoptimal standard, because a potential excess burden from having a wrong policy in the core area was taken into account. Nevertheless, it will be assumed in the following sections that the core area's governments have also chosen optimal social standards according to the same utility function relevant in the joining countries. In this case, there is no excess burden in the core area, and the effective wage there, w^*, equals the marginal product of labor in the core area.

7. The Properties of the Catching-Up Process

While the above analysis has clarified a number of normative policy issues, it has not yet explored the positive implications of the model setup. Suppose the government of the joining country chooses the optimal time path of social standards, firms optimize their employment and investment decisions and households optimize their migration decisions. Which transition path will be taken by a less developed country joining a well-developed core region like the EU?

Applying (8) or (15), a central differential equation for the growth of private investment over time follows from (9) or (18):

$$\dot{I} = \frac{r\,[1 + \varphi'(I)] - f_K(K, L)}{\varphi''(I)}. \tag{20}$$

It follows from Equations (1), (2), (7), and (13) that

$$w = f_L(K, L) = w^* - \psi'(L^* - L), \tag{21}$$

which implies a functional relation of the type

$$L = \phi(K) \tag{22}$$

between capital and employment, where

$$\phi'(K) = \frac{f_{LK}}{\psi'' - f_{LL}} > 0 \tag{23}$$

follows from an implicit differentiation of (21).

This indicates that if there is capital investment in the joining country, employment will increase. As assumed with (5) the joining country is undercapitalized and has a low marginal productivity of labor, and as indicated by (20) the stock of capital cannot adjust instantaneously after joining, but only gradually with the passage of time. It thus follows from (21) that there will be an immediate out-migration of guest workers and that the resulting initial wage rate will be *below* the effective wage rate in the core area by the marginal cost of staying in the host country. Since, because of the assumption of an immediate transfer of knowledge, the two countries have identical production functions, they also have the same factor price frontiers. The marginal productivity of capital in the joining country after the migration of the guest workers is thus *above* that in the core area, if it is assumed that the marginal productivity of capital in the core area is equal to the rate of interest r because the adjustment of the capital stock has already been completed there.

If capital is being accumulated after this initial adjustment, this will change the factor prices. From (21)–(23) it is possible to establish that the marginal product of labor increases,

$$\frac{d f_L[K, \phi(K)]}{dK} = \psi'' \cdot \phi' > 0,$$

and because of the negative slope of the factor price frontier the marginal product of capital declines:

$$\frac{d f_K[K, \phi(K)]}{dK} < 0.$$

Let K^* be the capital stock at which the marginal product of labor in the joining country would be equal to the wage rate in the core area: $f_L[K^*, \phi(K^*)] \equiv w^*$. The fact that the two regions have the same factor

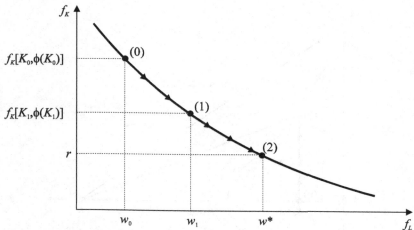

Figure 14.2. Factor price equalization between the joining region and the core region.

price frontiers then implies that the joining country's marginal productivity of capital would equal the common interest rate r if K increases to K^*:

$$f_K[K^*, \phi(K^*)] = r.$$

Figure 14.2 explains these relationships by showing the joining country's movement along the factor price frontier. Before people migrate, and before the equilibrium described above is produced, with freedom of movement capital intensity in the joining area is very low. Point (0) gives the values of the effective wage rate and the marginal productivity of capital associated with this. The spontaneous migration of guest workers that occurs immediately after joining leads to an instantaneous jump along the factor price frontier from (0) to (1). Provided that capital subsequently flows into the joining country, there will be subsequent gradual movement from Point (1) to Point (2) on the factor price frontier, where Point (2) is characterized by the critical level of capital, K^*, at which the factor prices in the core region and the joining area are equal.

The movement from (1) to (2) takes place if the stock of capital increases. How it increases can be derived from the differential Equation (20) which, by applying (22), can also be written as

$$\dot{I} = \frac{r[1 + \varphi'(I)] - f_K[K, \phi(K)]}{\varphi''(I)}. \tag{24}$$

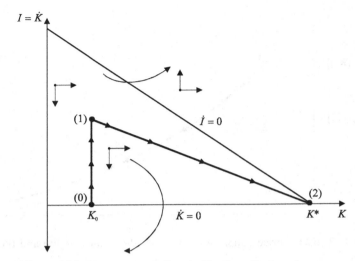

Figure 14.3. Investment and capital in the adjustment process.

The implications of this differential equation, combined with the definitional differential equation $\dot{K} = I$, are shown in Fig. 14.3. The figure includes all time paths that are compatible with (24). The $\dot{I} = 0$ curve shows those combinations of I and K for which the numerator of (24) is zero. The curve divides the figure into two areas, where movements are in different directions as shown by the arrows. Some paths cut the $\dot{I} = 0$ curve horizontally, others meet the abscissa vertically. Just one path, the stable branch, leads to the point with the coordinates $(I = 0, K = K^*)$. Only this path can characterize the market equilibrium.

Paths above the stable branch indicate positive and increasing investment up to the point where $K = K^*$. Since the marginal productivity of capital will then be equal to the market rate of interest, further investment would be unable to bear any adjustment cost. However, the positive level of investment characterizing paths above the stable branch implies such cost. This contradiction rules out the possibility that such paths could characterize a market equilibrium.

Paths below the stable branch will eventually cut the abscissa from above before the marginal product of capital is equal to the market rate of interest. After this the capital stock will shrink at an increasing speed and become zero in finite time so that the policy described by (24) becomes infeasible.

On the stable branch, the level of investment shrinks to zero as K approaches K^*. Thus K^* will not be reached in finite time, but the economy

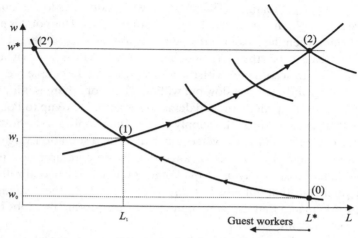

Figure 14.4. The adjustments in the labor market.

converges to this capital stock as time goes to infinity. It follows from (15) and (18) that the co-state variable, Tobin's q, is greater than one on the stable branch and converges to one as time goes to infinity. Thus it is clear that the transversality conditions (10) and (19) are met. All the necessary conditions for a welfare optimum and an optimum in the market agents' planning problem are satisfied.

The optimal adjustment strategy after integration into the common capital and labor markets is shown in Figure 14.3 by a rapid increase in investment from (0) to (1) and a gradual development from (1) to (2). In this gradual development process investment is at first very high and then becomes successively smaller. The capital stock, and with it the whole economy, thus initially grows at a very high rate and then at a gradually falling rate toward the value K^*, which characterizes complete factor price equalization.

Finally, to round off the overview, it is useful to take a look at Figure 14.4.[9] The development path of the joining country is shown there in a labor market diagram with supply and demand curves. At the time of joining, and before people and capital migrate, Point (0) on the demand

[9] The figure must be interpreted only qualitatively. For clarity of presentation the number of guest workers ($L^* - L$) is very much exaggerated in the figure. If the "joining country" can be taken to be the set of ten east European countries applying for EU membership, an emigration in the order of 5–7% or 5–7 million people can be expected. See Sinn, Flaig, Munz, and Werding (2000).

curve $f_L(K_0, L)$ is realized. The effective wage rate w_0 is low enough to ensure full employment of the labor force potential L^*. This point is not an equilibrium when the borders are open, because the wage difference with the core area exceeds the marginal migration cost, which is zero when no one migrates. In accordance with the assumptions made, people are quick but unwilling and capital is slow but willing. Therefore there is initially an instantaneous jump along the old demand for labor curve up to Point (1) where this curve is cut by the supply curve. The supply curve shows the number of workers in the reverse order of their reservation wage. The reservation wage is the effective wage rate in the core area, w^*, minus the individual cost of staying in the home country, ψ'. The realization of Point (1) means that initially $L^* - L_1$ people migrate to the core area as guest workers and that the same number of (less productive) jobs in the joining country are lost.

After Point (1) is reached capital accumulation makes itself felt in the form of a gradual rightward shift of the demand for labor curve toward position $f_L(K^*, L)$. The market equilibrium point moves out from Point (1) gradually, but with diminishing speed, along the labor supply curve toward Point (2). In the course of this gradual adjustment process, the number of guest workers falls until they all have returned home again, and the effective wage rate rises until it reaches the effective wage rate in the core area, w^*. Thus, there is only a temporary population shift from the joining country to the core area, and not a permanent one. At first, there is a rapid wave of out-migration but, over time, when wages rise as the capital stock increases, complete return migration to the home country takes place. This two-sided migration pattern is typical for guest worker migration flows from countries in transition.

Recall that this process incorporates not only private market decisions, but also the decisions of the national government in that this government gradually redefines the social standard for employment contracts. According to assumptions (3) and (4), in the national optimum as given by (12), both components of the effective wage rate w^*, the pecuniary wage w_p and the nonpecuniary wage resulting from the firms' social expenses w_s, rise in step during the adjustment from Point (1) to Point (2). As it was assumed in addition that the governments in the core area have optimized their social policies, reaching Point (2) also implies that both wage components converge toward the respective values in the core area. Eventually, the joining country's government will impose the same social standards as the governments of the core area does.

The following proposition summarizes the positive implications of the model.

Proposition 3: *Opening the borders between a less developed joining area and a well-developed core area results in a two-sided migration process. In the short term with an initially given capital stock, some of the working population of the joining country migrate as guest workers to the core area. In the joining country, this reduces the labor supply, increases wages, destroys some of the jobs, and induces the national government to raise the social standard in step with the wages. Because interest rates are the same in both regions and because the subjective and objective costs of migration mean that wage equalization cannot happen in the short run, the joining country attracts an inflow of capital from the core area. The inflow of capital increases the demand for labor in the joining country and leads to a further increase in the wage rate and the social standard, which results in a gradual return migration of the guest workers. The capital inflow dries up when the market wage and the social standard have reached the respective levels in the core area and all the guest workers have gone back home again.*

As the catching-up process described characterizes an intertemporal general equilibrium of both the market economy and systems competition and since the process represents a welfare optimal growth strategy, the hypothesis of social dumping can be – refuted. A government that acts in the national interest knows that measures to promote the use of capital would be as harmful as harmonizing the factor prices too soon, because both of these measures would involve departing from the joining country's optimal adjustment path. Wages and work-related fringe benefits must be lower than in the core area during a long transition period before an adequate capital stock has been accumulated, and in the long run, they adjust by themselves without the need for central government intervention measures. The temporary lag in wages and social standards has nothing at all to do with social dumping; it is the result of the efficient working of the Invisible Hand in systems competition.

8. Lessons from German Unification

The adjustment problem just described is extremely important for the development of the European Union, for the eastern enlargement involves the entry of countries whose economies are very backward compared to those of the core countries. Because wage costs in the new member countries are extremely low (between 10% and 15% of those in west Germany), the political pressure for a harmonization of wages and social standards is increasing in the core countries.

The practical example of German unification shows how dangerous such a policy would be. Following unification, Germany learned the painful way that the laws of the market cannot be ignored. In anticipation of a wonderful future, the policy of early equalization of wages and social standards was given the go-ahead and the economies of the new Länder were led up a blind alley. Social standards were adjusted immediately after unification, and the hourly wage costs in east German manufacturing jumped to more than 70% of the western level in only five years, although they were only 7% of this level before unification at the then prevailing exchange rate. The consequence of this explosion of the labor cost was a loss of competitiveness which destroyed nearly 80% of the jobs in manufacturing. Mass unemployment and a westward net migration of around 9% of the east German population resulted.

In terms of Fig. 14.4, the east German wage policy means that the automatic increase in wages from w_0 to w_1, which would have occurred by itself as a result of westward migration and cutbacks in the east German labor market, was not waited for. Instead, there was a movement along the labor demand curve $f_L(K_0, L)$ upward to the left toward Point $(2')$. The excess supply of labor shown in the figure is the present mass unemployment. Unemployment, at least as far as it was triggered off by too rapid an increase in wages and the immediate implementation of west German labor standards, is an obvious sign of misallocation, a waste of valuable working time, and a irrecoverable loss of national output.

Germany has had to pay for the misallocation with massive social transfers to the new Länder. In the first decade after unification, loans of € 750 net for the eastern transfers had accumulated and the government debt more than doubled. At this writing, west Germany is still transfering 4–5% of its GDP via the public budget to east Germany. The European Union cannot permit itself to make such an expensive policy mistake.

Fortunately, the German policy mistake is not likely to be repeated at the European level, because first, people can learn and second, the special policy mechanisms that were responsible for wage policies in Germany do not extend to the European level. The German problem was that the western trade unions and the western employers negotiated the east German wages among themselves – there were no east German firms in existence at the time (spring 1991) the critical wage decisions were made.

There were proxy negotiations in which both of the negotiating parties had the same interest in high east German wages because they wanted to avoid unpalatable competition in their own west German branches of industry. Similarly, western employers and union representatives helped convince the government to impose west German work standards and the west German social security system on the east Germans right from the beginning. Circumstances like these can, in principle, be ruled out for the EU accession countries because negotiations there will take place between national trade unions and national employers. This will ensure that the negotiating parties represent opposing interests with regard to wage policies. Also, it is hard to imagine that the governments of the accession countries will come under pressure from the employers' and employees' representatives of the core countries. Thus it is very likely that these countries will approximate the optimum described above more than east Germany was able to do.

9. Why Low Wages and Social Standards Do Not Indicate Social Dumping

The accusation of social dumping, which the less developed European countries seem to have engaged in because their wages and social standards are low, is not justified. Low wages, low social standards and high returns to capital are the necessary concomitants of a long-term adjustment process. Even in a common European economy without artificial barriers to factor movements there are natural barriers large enough to slow down the process of factor price equalization for a long time, and the governments of the joining countries will take this into account when they define the speed with which they adjust social standards to those in the developed core areas. In allocative terms, it is a mistake to want to overcome these barriers with counteracting policy measures. It would be particularly mistaken to attempt to enforce the equalization of factor prices and social standards appropriate for the long run by means of premature harmonization. Such an attempt would only reproduce the east German debacle in the new countries joining the European Union.

Left to themselves, decentralized choices of households, firms, and national governments will solve the adjustment problem of a relatively underdeveloped joining country in that some of the labor force potential will move to the core area as guest workers. This will then lead to spontaneous increases in wages and a parallel adjustment in social standards, which will reduce the pressure to migrate. As the effective wage level will still be well below that of the core area despite the spontaneous increase, there will be an import of capital and this will successively raise labor productivity, wages, and social standards. To the extent that the increase in effective wages results in a closure of the wage gap, it reduces the incentive for investment and thus prevents a further increase in effective wages. Wages and social standards will equalize in the long run. The mistrust of the allocative efficiency of systems competition is not justified. The lag in wages and nonwage benefits in the still-undeveloped countries is the key characteristic of an efficient transformation process.

A simple but important insight for the assessment of systems competition follows from this. Because private competition and systems competition carry out the gradual transformation of the joining country perfectly, there is no need for a supranational government like the EU to intervene by harmonizing social standards. Both the EU Social Charter and the ILO conventions are interventions of dubious use.

References

Berié, H., (1993). "Europäische Sozialpolitik. Von Messina bis Maastricht," in G. Kleinhenz, ed., *Soziale Integration in Europa* I. Schriften des Vereins für Socialpolitik NF 222/I, Berlin.

Feldmann, H., (1999). "Zehn Jahre EU-Sozialcharta," *Wirtschaftsdienst* 11, 670–76.

Plant, R., (1994). *Labour Standards and Structural Adjustment*, Geneva: International Labour Office.

Schröder, Ch., (2000). "Industrielle Arbeitskosten im internationalen Vergleich," *iw-trends* 27, No. 3, 77–91.

Sinn, G., and H.-W. Sinn (1991). *Kaltstart. Volkswirtschaftliche Probleme der deutschen Vereinigung* (Tübingen: J. C. B. Mohr (Paul Siebeck)), 1991. English translation: *Jumpstart. Economic Aspects of German Unification* (Cambridge, MA: MIT Press), 1992.

Sinn, H.-W., (2000). "EU Enlargement, Migration, and Lessons from German Unification," *German Economic Review* 1, 299–314.

Sinn, H.-W., G. Flaig, S. Munz, and M. Werding (2000). *EU-Erweiterung und Arbeitskräftemigration: Wege zu einer schrittweisen Annäherung der Arbeitsmärkte*, Munich: Study for the German Federal Ministry for Labour and Social Affairs.

PART FIVE

POLITICAL ECONOMY

FIFTEEN

Do Political Institutions Shape Economic Policy?*

Torsten Persson

Do political institutions shape economic policy? I argue that this question should naturally appeal to economists. Moreover, the answer is in the
affirmative, both in theory and in practice. In particular, recent theoretical
work predicts systematic effects of electoral rules and political regimes
on the size and composition of government spending. And results from
ongoing empirical work indicate that such effects are indeed present in
international panel data. Some empirical results are consistent with theoretical predictions: Presidential regimes have smaller governments and
countries with majoritarian elections have smaller welfare-state programs
and less corruption. Other results present puzzles for future research: the
adjustment to economic events is clearly institution-dependent, as are the
timing and nature of the electoral cycle.

1. Initial Remarks

In the last five to ten years, political economy – or "political economics," as
I prefer to call it – has been a rapidly growing field. As the label suggests,

* This paper was initially presented as the 2000 Walras–Bowley Lecture at the Eighth World
Congress of The Econometric Society, in Seattle. It is reprinted here with permission of
The Econometric Society. I am heavily indebted to Guido Tabellini, who is a coauthor of
all the work underlying this paper and provided detailed comments on a previous draft.
I would also like to thank Alan Drazen and John Moore for comments, Givanni Favara
for research assistance, and Christina Lönnblad for editorial assistance. The research
is supported by grants from the European Commission and the Swedish Council for
Research in the Humanities and Social Sciences.

431

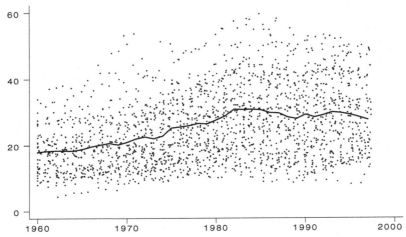

Figure 15.1. Size of government in 61 countries 1960–98 (central government expenditure in % of GDP)

this field deals with issues related to politics using the tools of modern economics. The most recent work is attractive in that it draws on several traditions: the older public-choice school, the rational-choice school in political science, and the equilibrium theory of macroeconomic policy. Collected works, monographs, and textbooks now start to appear, drawing on the contributions in the last decade. One such piece is Persson and Tabellini (2000a); others include Mueller (1997), Austen-Smith and Banks (1999), Drazen (2000), and Grossman and Helpman (2001).

An obvious motivation for this literature comes from observing economic policy outcomes. Looking across time and place, one observes large differences in policy, but also some common patterns. An example is given in Fig. 15.1, which shows a measure of the size of government in about sixty countries over the last four decades. In the figure we see that government expenditure in a typical year ranges from below 10% of GDP to well above 50%. We also see how the distribution drifts upward over time, reflecting growth in the average size of government – the curve in the graph – by about 8% of GDP from the 1960s to the mid 1990s. (I will discuss these data further in Section 3.) Such differences and similarities cry out for an explanation. An important goal in the literature has thus been to construct a positive theory of economic policy.

This brings me to the subject matter of this paper, which I will devote to current research on largely unresolved issues. As the title suggests, I will focus on attempts to identify what systematic effect political institutions might have on economic policy outcomes. This is, of course, a very broad question.[1] To narrow it down, I will confine the discussion to the institutions governing electoral rules and political regimes and their effect on fiscal policy, broadly defined. This question is not only of academic interest. For instance, reform of electoral institutions has recently taken place in Japan, Italy, and New Zealand and is a hotly debated issue in other countries. Theory and evidence on the policy consequences of alternative electoral rules would enlighten this debate.

I would like to make two main points. First, the question whether political institutions shape policy should naturally appeal to an economist. Second, the answer is yes; empirically, electoral rules and political regimes do seem to systematically influence the choice of fiscal instruments, as well as the incidence of corruption.

Next, I will outline the main ideas in a recent wave of theoretical work on this topic (Section 2). Then, I will describe some data we have just assembled, with the aforementioned theory as the main guide in sampling and measurement (Section 3). A good part of this paper will report on two ongoing empirical projects, dealing with the link from political institutions to fiscal policy and corruption (Section 4). Finally, I will sum up and discuss where research might go next (Section 5).

2. Theoretical Ideas

2.1. An Organizing Framework

Let me describe the theoretical ideas against the backdrop of a very simple framework. In particular, let us consider a bare-bones framework of fiscal policy which highlights the size of the government budget and its allocation to different purposes.[2]

The population is divided into a large number of groups, labeled by J. Membership of each group is defined by the prospective benefits of public spending. Everybody has the same preferences over policy:

$$w^J = U(c^J) + H(g)$$
$$c^J = y - \tau + f^J.$$

---

[1] Other work by economists on the broad question includes the literature on the links between budgetary institutions and budget deficits (see, for instance, the contributions in Poterba and von Hagen, 1999) and between fiscal federalism and the size of government (surveyed by Inman and Rubinfeld, 1997); see Persson and Tabellini (2000a) for further references.

[2] The core of the positive models of fiscal policy in Persson and Tabellini (2000a) is similar.

Group J has size N^J. Its members thus enjoy private consumption, c^J, given by after-tax income plus a group-specific transfer f^J. All groups pay the same tax, τ, and enjoy the same benefits of public spending on g. Government spending can thus be targeted to specific groups, as in the case of targeted transfer programs, or local public goods. But it can also take a nontargeted form benefiting all citizens, as in the case of general public goods, or broad social programs.

Policy choices are summarized by $\mathbf{q}$, a vector constrained to include nonnegative elements only:

$$\mathbf{q} = [\{f^J\}, g, \tau, r] \geq 0,$$
$$r = N\tau - g - \sum_J N^J f^J.$$

The budget constraint is standard except for one item. The variable r does not appear directly in the citizens' payoffs. Literally, it represents direct extraction of rents by politicians for private use. Less literally, it may represent – on reduced form – corrupt activities, or inefficiently designed activities that constitute a drain for the citizens but benefit politicians or their close friends.

This framework is obviously very stylized. Richer economic frameworks can certainly be studied along the same lines. Citizens would then also interact in markets, making purposeful economic choices influenced by policy. Similarly, we could replace the simplistic form of rent extraction with a structural model.

Yet, already the bare-bones framework permits a rich analysis of the politics of policymaking. To see this, note that the choice of $\mathbf{q}$ generates conflicts of interest in three different dimensions: (i) First, we have the traditional conflict among different groups of voters over the allocation of targeted spending $\{f^J\}$. (ii) The second is an agency problem: the voters at large would like higher g or lower τ, but rent-seeking politicians would instead like to spend these resources on r. (iii) A final source of conflict is that different politicians, or political parties, will compete for any available rents.

2.2. General Ideas
The basic idea in the recent literature is this: The way the three conflicts are resolved, and thus what fiscal policy we observe, hinges on the political institutions in place. This idea should appear very natural to an economist. Consider an analogy from micro theory. In a market, we have conflicts of interest between consumers and producers over price and product quality,

and among different producers over profit. How these are resolved depends on market institutions. Equilibrium prices, qualities, and profits hinge on regulation, which determines the barriers to entry and the scope for competition between producers. They also hinge on other legislation, which determines how easily consumers can hold producers accountable for bad product quality or collusive pricing behavior. The basic idea here is the same.

Political institutions certainly have many dimensions. Arguably, however, the most fundamental aspects of constitutions decide how the control rights over policy are acquired and how they can be exercised. Thus, which politicians get the power to make policy decisions is determined by voters, but is crucially influenced by rules for elections. Policy choices are made by elected politicians, but are crucially influenced by rules for rule making and legislation; that is, what political scientists call the regime type.

While economists have not paid much attention to the consequences of these institutions, political scientists certainly have. A large, mostly empirical literature has focused precisely on electoral rules and regime types. But the analysis has generally been confined to purely political phenomena, such as the number of parties, the propensity for crises, and so on. It has ignored economic policy, our topic here.[3]

This general discussion suggests a way of modeling the outcome of policymaking: q in our simple framework. In that approach, policy is the equilibrium outcome of a delegation game, where the interaction between rational voters and politicians is modeled on extensive form. Multiple principals, the voters, elect political representatives who, in turn, set policy to further their own opportunistic objectives. The principals have some leeway over their agents because they can offer them election, or reelection. But these rewards are mostly implicit, not explicit, so the constitution becomes like an incomplete contract, leaving the politicians with some power in the form of residual control rights. Alternative constitutions can now be represented by alternative rules for how this extensive-form game is being played. An exercise in comparative politics amounts to comparing the policy outcomes across the resulting equilibria.

---

[3] An exception is a recent book by Lijphart (1999), which includes cursory evidence on economic policy outcomes. Modern classics within the political science literature on comparative politics include Bingham Powell (1982), Lijphart (1984), Taagepera and Shugart (1989), Shugart and Carey (1992), and Cox (1997); see Myerson (1999) for a discussion of the theoretical literature on the consequences of different electoral rules.

2.3. Specific Predictions

Let me now describe the main ideas in a handful of recent studies that apply this comparative politics approach. I just outline the results, however, focusing on the specific predictions. Those interested can find most of the analytical details in Persson and Tabellini (2000a, Part III).

ELECTORAL RULES. I begin with the rules for electing a country's legislature. Legislative elections around the world differ in several dimensions. The political science literature emphasizes two: *district size* and the *electoral formula*. District size simply determines how many legislators acquire a seat in a voting district. The electoral formula determines how votes are translated into seats. Under plurality rule, only the winners of the highest vote shares get seats in a given district, whereas proportional representation instead awards seats in proportion to the vote share.

Anticipating already here the empirical part, we find a strong correlation in these features across real-world electoral systems. Some systems can be described as majoritarian, combining small voting districts with plurality rule. Archetypes here are elections to the U.K. parliament or the U.S. Congress, where whoever collects the most votes in a district gets the *single seat*. Some electoral systems are instead decidedly proportional, combining large electoral districts with proportional representation. Archetypes are the Dutch and Israeli elections, where parties obtain seats in proportion to their vote shares in a single national voting district. While we find some intermediate systems, most countries fall quite unambiguously into this crude classification.

Why would district size matter for government spending? One idea is that larger voting districts diffuse electoral competition, inducing parties to seek support from broad coalitions in the population. Smaller districts steer electoral competition towards narrower, geographical constituencies. Clearly, broad programs, like g in the framework above, are more effective in seeking broad support and targeted programs, like $\{f^J\}$, more effective in seeking narrow support. Proportional elections with larger districts should thus be more biased towards broad, nontargeted programs. This point has formally been made by Persson and Tabellini (1999) in a probabilistic-voting model, where policy is determined by electoral platforms before the election. Milesi-Ferretti, Perotti, and Rostagno (2000) obtain a similar result in a model of strategic delegation in voting, where policy is set after the election in bargaining among the elected politicians.

Larger districts also facilitate entry in the political process by additional candidates or parties. Myerson (1993) has used a model of electoral competition to show how a larger number of candidates under proportional elections may produce lower equilibrium rents. Essentially, with more available candidates, voters can throw out corrupt parties at a lower ideological cost.

How about the electoral formula? The winner-takes-all property of plurality rule reduces the minimal coalition of voters needed to win the election, as votes for a party not obtaining plurality are lost. With single-member districts and plurality, a party thus needs only 25% of the national vote to win: 50% in 50% of the districts. Under full proportional representation it needs 50% of the national vote. Politicians are thus induced to internalize the policy benefits for a larger segment of the population, which reinforces the previous prediction associating broader spending programs with proportional elections. Lizzeri and Persico (2001) make this point in a model with binding electoral promises, while Persson and Tabellini (2000a, Ch. 9) instead consider policy choices by an incumbent subject to reelection.

Under majoritarian elections, electoral competition often becomes concentrated to a subset of identifiable marginal districts. As these have close races with many swing voters, the perceived electoral punishments for inefficient programs become larger. The smaller expected vote losses under proportional elections induce candidates involved in electoral competition to chooses policies entailing larger rents (r in the framework above), a result derived in Persson and Tabellini, 1999.

While voters cast their ballot among individual candidates under plurality rule, they cast it among party lists under proportional representation. Such lists may dilute the incentives for *individual* incumbents to perform well. Persson and Tabellini (2000a, Ch. 9) examine the policy consequences of this difference in a model where individual politicians have career concerns in the style of Holmström (1982). They find that proportional representation (list voting) should be associated with a larger extraction of rents, as the career-concern, reelection motive becomes a weaker counterweight to the rent-extraction motive for collectively accountable politicians. A second prediction is that electoral cycles, showing up in spending or taxes, should be weaker under proportional representation. This is because the incumbents' career concerns are stronger with the individual accountability under plurality rule and because these concerns are at their strongest just before elections.

REGIME TYPES. Two especially interesting aspects of the legislative regime concern the powers over legislation: to make, amend, or veto policy proposals. The first concerns the *separation* of these powers across different politicians and offices. The second concerns the *maintenance* of these powers; in particular, whether the executive needs sustained confidence by a majority in the legislative assembly.

As in the case of electoral rules, we can make a cruder classification of real-world regimes. Presidential regimes (abbreviated *PRES*) typically have separation of powers, between the president and Congress, but also between congressional committees that hold important proposal (agenda-setting) powers in different spheres of policy (think about the U.S.). But they do not have a confidence requirement: the executive can hold on to his powers without the support of a majority in Congress. In parliamentary regimes (*PARL*), the proposal powers over legislation are instead concentrated in the hands of the government. Moreover, the government needs the continuous confidence of a majority in parliament to maintain those powers throughout an entire election period.

Why should separation of powers matter for policy? A classical argument is that checks and balances constrain politicians from abusing their powers. Persson, Roland, and Tabellini (1997, 2000) formally demonstrate this old point in models where incumbents, who decide on policy in different forms of legislative bargaining, are held accountable by retrospective voters. They show that a larger concentration of powers in parliamentary regimes makes it easier for politicians to collude with each other at the voters' expense; the weaker electoral accountability results in higher rents and taxes (r and τ in the framework above).

Another idea has to do with the confidence requirement. The parties supporting the executive hold valuable proposal powers which they risk to lose in a government crisis. Therefore, they have strong incentives to maintain a stable majority when voting on policy proposals in the legislature. Building on this idea of "legislative cohesion" due to Diermeier and Feddersen (1998), Persson, Roland, and Tabellini (2000) derive two additional predictions. First, in parliamentary regimes, a stable majority of legislators tends to pursue the joint interest of its voters. In presidential regimes, the (relative) lack of such a majority instead tends to pit the interests of different minorities against each other for different issues on the legislative agenda. Equilibrium spending in parliamentary regimes thus becomes more directed toward broad programs (g rather than f^J). Second, in parliamentary regimes, the stable majority of incumbent legislators, as well as the majority of the voters backing them, become prospective residual claimants on additional revenue. Both majorities favor high taxes and high spending. In presidential regimes, on the other hand, no such residual claimants on revenue exist and majorities

Table 15.1. *Summary of Theory*

	PRES(vs. PARL)	MAJ (vs. PR)
Size	—	?
Composition (broad vs. narrow)	—	—
Rents	—	—
Electoral Cycle	NA	+

therefore resist high spending. These forces produce larger governments (higher τ) in parliamentary regimes.

2.4. Discussion

Let me summarize the main predictions with the help of Table 15.1. According to the theory, presidential regimes should have smaller governments than parliamentary regimes, less spending on broad programs, and less rents for politicians. Under majoritarian elections, we should see less spending on broad programs than under proportional elections, and less rents. These are cross-sectional predictions; they have been derived by comparing equilibria in static models. The prediction of more pronounced electoral cycles under majoritarian elections, however, relies on a dynamic model and is thus a time-series prediction.

Is this kind of analysis convincing? Some readers may be skeptical. One critique might question whether the simple assumed game forms capture the essence of real-world political institutions. This would parallel the critique against theoretical IO that "you could prove anything by picking the right extensive form and the right informational assumptions." A related complaint would parallel the critique against incomplete-contract theory that "there are many alternative assignments of control rights and you have no strong basis for choosing this particular one."

Such criticism has some force, but may be less damaging in this case, as long as we deal with *positive* theory rather than normative constitutional engineering. A wealth of historical, political, and legal studies document how the world's democracies carry out elections and allocate political and legislative control. Thus, the rules defining a particular game need not rely on the researcher's imagination. They can and should be given a solid empirical foundation. From this perspective, comparative politics might offer a more convincing application of game theory than other examples in economics.

Defending the underlying assumptions is not the only way of convincing skeptics, however. Another criterion of success is the empirical contents of the theory. Does it help us uncover new empirical regularities? To shed some light on this question, I now turn to the empirical part of this paper.

3. Data and Specification

DATA. Let me start by briefly describing the data on political institutions and fiscal policy outcomes we have assembled for ongoing empirical research. More details can be found in Persson and Tabellini (2000b). The theory I just sketched has served as our guide in sampling and measurement. We have data for at most 61 countries. The data is yearly and runs from 1960 to 1998, a total of 39 years. This panel includes a large number of economic, social and political variables. But many observations are missing – for different reasons – which makes the panel unbalanced.

Which countries are included in the panel? The theory suggest we should study countries with democratic institutions. To assess a country's democratic status in a given year, we rely on the well-known Freedom House indexes of political rights: the so-called GASTIL indexes. We have used three selection rules. One is to include a country in the sample from the first year when it reaches a GASTIL score of less than or equal to 5, signifying that the country is "free," or "semi-free."[4] Two more demanding rules for inclusion in the sample are to require a score strictly less than or equal to 3.5 or 2, respectively, and to apply these cutoffs year by year. Unfortunately, nonavailability of data on political institutions or fiscal policy cuts down the sample size further. Here, I will only present results based on the midway sampling rule (a GASTIL score less than or equal 3.5, year by year). As the more comprehensive analysis in Persson and Tabellini (2000b) demonstrates, most results are similar in the two alternative sets of democracies.

Which political institutions do we study? Following the theory discussion in Section 2, I will report on results which are (mostly) based on two crude classifications of electoral rules and regime types. First, we code countries that relied fully on plurality (or majority) rule in their most

---

[4] There are actually two indexes: one on political rights, one on civil liberties. Each index runs from 1 to 7, where a country with scores of 1 or 2 are "free," 3 to 5 "semi-free," and 6 to 7 "not free." We take the simple average of these indexes.

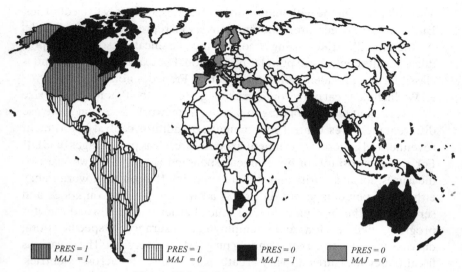

$$\boxed{\text{\small PRES} = 1} \quad \boxed{\text{\small PRES} = 1} \quad \boxed{\text{\small PRES} = 0} \quad \boxed{\text{\small PRES} = 0}$$
PRES = 1   *PRES* = 1   *PRES* = 0   *PRES* = 0
MAJ = 1   *MAJ* = 0   *MAJ* = 1   *MAJ* = 0

Figure 15.2. Political institutions 1995

recent elections to the legislature (lower chamber) as majoritarian, and the other countries as proportional. The dummy variable *MAJ* takes a value of 1 in the former case, 0 in the latter.[5] Second, countries where the survival of the executive does *not* require the confidence of the legislature are coded as presidential, the other countries as parliamentary. The resulting binary variable is called *PRES*.

These classifications change very little over time, reflecting an inertia of political institutions sometimes called an "iron law" by political scientists. The lack of time variation is unfortunate in that it provides us with almost no experiments in the form of regime changes. But it is also an indication that our key maintained assumption, namely to treat institutions as exogenous and given by history, may be correct.

Figure 15.2 illustrates the institutional variation across countries in 1995. The shaded portions of the map represent the countries in the sample. Striped areas indicate presidential regimes (*PRES* = 1), solid areas parliamentary regimes (*PRES* = 0). Darker shade indicates majoritarian elections (*MAJ* = 1), lighter shade proportional elections (*MAJ* = 0). The least common system is the U.S.- style (dark-striped) combination of

---

[5] In Persson and Tabellini (1999) electoral rules were instead classified on the basis of district magnitude. The present classification based on the electoral formula yields a similar, but not identical grouping of countries.

a presidential regime with majoritarian elections, with only five countries. But each of the other three combinations is well represented in the sample. As the map illustrates, using theory in the classification sometimes produces results contrary to popular perception. For example, Switzerland is classified as a presidential regime, whereas France is not.

We include fiscal policy outcomes suggested by the theory. For the size of government (corresponding to τ in the framework of section 2) we use different measures: central government expenditure, central government revenue, and general government expenditure, all as percentages of GDP. For the composition of government spending (g vs. $\{f^J\}$) we use two measures: social security and welfare spending (by central government), either as a percentage of GDP, or as a ratio to spending on goods and services. We thus presume that it is much harder to target broad transfer programs, like pensions and unemployment insurance, to specific voting districts than it is to target spending on goods and services. These various fiscal policy measures do vary greatly across time and across countries. Indeed, Fig. 15.1 in the introduction was a plot of our panel data for central government expenditure as a percentage of GDP.

At the end of the next section, I will also describe some results from a second ongoing project (Persson, Tabellini, and Trebbi, 2000). There, we proxy rent extraction by politicians (r in the framework of section 2) by available measures of corruption. We also characterize electoral rules by two continuous measures, rather than by a single binary measure.

SPECIFICATION. Our empirical work is certainly motivated by theory. In addition to testing specific hypotheses, we also aim at establishing empirical regularities, however. We therefore adopt a relatively eclectic empirical specification describing policy outcomes:

$$y_{it} = \alpha_i + \beta_i \mathbf{u}_t + \gamma_i s_{it} + \delta x_{it} + \eta z_{it} + \varepsilon_{it}. \tag{1}$$

Here, y_{it} denotes a policy outcome in country i and year t. We allow for a country-specific component, α_i. Policy can be affected directly by the institutions $\mathbf{z}_{it}$, concretely by the value of the two dummy variables *MAJ* and *PRES* in i at t. It also depends on (vectors of) common variables $\mathbf{u}_t$ and idiosyncratic variables $(s_{it}, \mathbf{x}_{it})$. Some slope coefficients are allowed to differ across countries.

Given (1), we pose the question of a systematic effect from institutions to policy in two different ways. One is to test the nul hypothesis

$$H_0^D : \eta = 0,$$

the absence of a *direct* effect. Strictly speaking, this is what most of the theory discussed in Section 2 was really about. The other way is to test

Table 15.2. *Size of Government: Cross Sectional Estimates*

Dep. Variable	Central Spending			Central Revenue
Sample	1960–98	1960–98	1990–95	1960–98
Estimation			WLS	
PRES	− 7.95	− 6.28	− 11.14	− 6.14
	(.005)	(.073)	(.005)	(.038)
MAJ	−2.97	− 4.62	− 3.35	− 2.80
	(.178)	(.052)	(.176)	(.151)
Controls	x_1	x_1	x_1	x_1
		Cont.&Col.	Cont.&Col.	Cont.&Col.
# Obs.	1519	1445	297	1420
# Countries	59	58	54	57
R^2	0.54	0.64	0.74	0.71

p-values in brackets. Boldface fonts denote significance at the 10% level.
x_1 includes controls for income, openness, the population between 15 and 64, and over 65
(see Persson and Tabellini, 2000b).
Cont. and Col. refer to sets of dummies for continents and colonial origin, respectively (see
Persson and Tabellini, 2000b).

for the absence of an *indirect* (non-linear) effect

$$H_0^I : \beta_i = \beta_j \qquad \text{and/or } \gamma_i = \gamma_j, \qquad \text{even if } z_{it} \neq z_{jt},$$

that is, whether different institutions make policy respond to common or idiosyncratic variables in a different way. (The rationale for this test will be given shortly.) We estimate these parameters in several different fashions, which are probably best explained in the context of a specific example.

4. Empirical Regularities?

4.1. Size of Government

CROSS-SECTIONAL RESULTS. Consider first the size of government. To arrive at a straightforward test for a direct effect on policy, take the time average of (1) to obtain

$$\bar{y}_i = (\alpha_i + \beta_i \bar{u} + \gamma_i \bar{s}_i) + \delta \bar{x}_i + \eta \bar{z}_i + \bar{\varepsilon}_i. \tag{2}$$

As (2) shows, the η parameter can be readily estimated on cross-sectional data. To take account of the unbalanced panel, we use a WLS estimator weighing each country's time average by the number of observations in its panel.

Results from such regressions are displayed in Table 15.2. The dependent variable is either central government spending (as a percentage of

GDP), or central government revenue. The control variables in x_1 include a number of socio-economic factors identified by earlier studies as empirical determinants of the size of government. Given the clustering of observations in Fig. 15.2, we use dummies for continents and colonial origin as additional controls. The table displays the estimated η parameters for the *PRES* and *MAJ* dummies. Bracketed expressions are *p*-values for false rejection of $\eta = 0$. Boldface font denotes a coefficient significantly different from zero, at the 10% level.

The two institutional dummies always enter with a negative sign. But *MAJ* is rarely statistically significant.[6] On the other hand *PRES* typically is, even though one can find specifications where it is not. This finding is clearly in line with the theoretical prediction in Section 2. According to the point estimates, governments in presidential regimes are smaller by more than 5 percent of GDP.

As column 3 shows, however, the negative effect of *PRES* is stronger, above 10% of GDP, for cross sections based on data from the 1990s rather than the whole sample. Moreover, it is statistically more robust (cf. also the empirical results in Persson and Tabellini, 1999). These results suggest that the negative estimates largely reflect faster growth of government in parliamentary regimes in the last four decades. As Fig. 15.3 illustrates, this pattern is clearly visible already in the raw data. The graph is identical to Fig. 15.1, except that the data is partitioned into presidential regimes, marked with black diamonds and a thicker curve for the average, and parliamentary regimes, marked with circles and a thinner curve.

While these cross-sectional estimates are suggestive, they are potentially subject to simultaneity (omitted variable, selection) bias. We would therefore like to exploit the time variation in the data. But the lack of institutional variation over time makes it infeasible to identify the direct effect of institutions in conventional fixed-effects estimation. For practical purposes, z_{it} is given by a constant, z_i, equal to the time average $\bar{z}_i$. Thus, we cannot separately estimate the effects on policy of a country's institutions z_i and other time-invariant, country-specific features α_i.

This is why we turn to the slightly different question embodied in the test of H_0^I, namely whether different political institutions shape different

---

[6] Milesi-Ferretti, Perotti, and Rostagno (2000) find government expenditure to be smaller in countries with majoritarian elections in their study of the OECD countries over the same period. When we use general government expenditures as our dependent variable – as did Milesi-Feretti et al. – we reach a similar conclusion. In this case, data availability cuts down our sample size considerably (to about 40 countries).

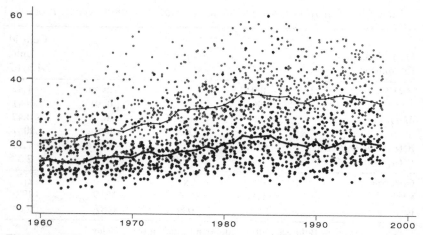

Figure 15.3. Size of government in parliamentary regimes (circles) and presidential regimes (diamonds) 1960–98 (central government expenditure in % of GDP)

policy responses to economic and political events. Even if the cross-section results might possibly be biased due to "historical omitted variables," it is less plausible to argue that the forces selecting the observed political institutions in historical times would be systematically correlated with the response to economic and political events during our recent sample period.

Recall, however, that the models in Section 2 are all static, with the exception of the career-concern model of electoral cycles. Many of our tests for indirect effects of institutions should thus be seen as a search for empirical regularities rather than tests of specific predictions.

UNOBSERVABLE COMMON EVENTS. It is plausible that a set of common economic and political events have affected fiscal policy in all countries. Think for example of the worldwide turn to the left in the late 1960s and 70s, or the productivity slowdown and oil shocks in the 1970s and 80s. But suppose we do not want to commit to, or cannot observe, all such events. Blanchard and Wolfers (2000) suggest a simple statistical method which they use to estimate how labor-market institutions might influence the adjustment of unemployment to unobservable shocks. Milesi-Ferretti, Perotti, and Rostagno (2000) indeed apply this method to study how the proportionality of electoral systems affect policy in the OECD countries.

Assume that the response to observable idiosyncratic variables is the same in all countries, $\gamma_i = \gamma_j$ in (1). Then we can lump all country-specific variables together in $\mathbf{x}_{it}$ and rewrite (1) as:

$$y_{it} = (\alpha_i + \eta \mathbf{z}_i) + [1 + \lambda(\mathbf{z}_i - \bar{\mathbf{z}})]\beta \mathbf{u}_t + \delta \mathbf{x}_{it} + \varepsilon_{it}. \qquad (3)$$

Table 15.3. *Size of Government: Unobservable Common Events 1960-98*

Dep. Variable Estimation		Central spending NLS, FE	Central revenue NLS, FE	
PRES	**− 0.91**		**− 0.99**	**− 1.42**
	(.000)		(.000)	(.000)
MAJ		**− 0.29**	**− 0.43**	**− 0.47**
		(.000)	(.000)	(.000)
$\beta^*(u_T - u_1)^*PRES$	− 12.73		− 13.46	− 7.17
$\beta^*(u_T - u_1)^*MAJ$		− 2.99	− 5.84	− 2.37
Controls	x_1	x_1	x_1	x_1
# Obs.	1519	1519	1519	1492
R^2	0.87	0.86	0.87	0.88

p-values in brackets. Boldface fonts denote significance at the 10% level.
x_1 includes the same variables as in Table 15.2; all regressions include a set of country dummies.

We can use a set of time dummies to estimate βu_t, the common effect of the common events in (3). The institution-specific effect of the common events u_t is proportional to the term $\lambda(z_i - \bar{z})$, where $\bar{z}$ denotes the cross-country average of z_i. The form of (3) suggests that we should estimate the crucial parameter λ by NLS, and include fixed effects to control for the country-specific intercept.

Table 15.3 shows some results based on annual data. (Persson and Tabellini, 2000b also report results based on five-year averages, which may better handle measurement error and allow for discretionary adjustments of policy.) The country-specific controls are the same variables as in the cross-sectional regressions. The interaction parmeters λ for both *PRES* and *MAJ* are negative and highly significant. To interpret the results, consider a common event in period t that raises government spending by 1% of GDP in an average country; that is, an event such that $\beta(u_t - u_{t-1}) = 1$. Coefficients around −1 and −0.5 mean that the effect of this event is 1% smaller in presidential (compared to parliamentary) regimes and 0.5% smaller under majoritarian (compared to proportional) elections.

Another way of gauging the results is to ask how the *cumulative* effect of the common events over the course of the sample period, $\beta(u_T - u_1)$, differs across institutions. The point estimates suggest that the cumulative difference between presidential and parliamentary regimes is above 10% of GDP. This number fits well with the estimated cross-sectional difference from the 1990s reported in Table 15.2. Thus, we can attribute much of the current size difference between these regimes to a different adjustment to a set of common shocks in the preceding decades.

OBSERVABLE ECONOMIC EVENTS. Alternatively, we can test for an effect of institutions on the adjustment to observable events. We start by economic events, then turn to electoral events. Yet another rewrite of (1) leads to the following expression:

$$y_{it} = (\alpha_i + \eta z_i) + (\beta + \phi z_i)\mathbf{u}_t + (\gamma + \mu z_i)\mathbf{s}_{it} + \delta \mathbf{x}_{it} + \varepsilon_{it}. \tag{4}$$

In (4) the parameters ϕ and μ allow for institution-dependent adjustments to common and idiosyncratic variables. As an observable common variable in $\mathbf{u}_t$ we have tried the oil price, and as idiosyncratic variables in $\mathbf{s}_{it}$ we have included lagged policy y_{it-1}, the share of the population above 65, and the deviation of income from its (Hodrick–Prescott) trend. One way of estimating the ϕ and μ parameters in (4) is to allow for the first, country-specific term by using the fixed-effects estimator. To get more efficient estimates of spending and revenue equations, we also estimate them jointly with SUR. An alternative way, is to wipe the country-specific intercept out by taking first differences. In this case, we use two different estimators. One is an IV-estimator: we include Δy_{it-1} in the regression and instrument it by y_{it-2} and ($\Delta \mathbf{u}_{t-1}$, $\Delta \mathbf{s}_{it-1}$, $\Delta \mathbf{x}_{it-1}$) (plus the corresponding interaction terms). The other is a GLS-estimator: We do not include Δy_{it-1} in the regression, but allow for panel-specific autocorrelation and heteroskedasticity in ε_{it}.[7]

The results in Table 15.4 indicate systematic indirect effects of institutions when it comes to income shocks and lagged policy. (Results for oil prices and population shares are less robust.) The fixed effects (SUR) estimates in columns 1–3 suggest that negative income shocks raise spending as a share of GDP. But this effect is absent, or even overturned, in presidential regimes and under majoritarian elections. These systems are also associated with less inertia in spending, although here the effect of majoritarian elections is weaker. The instrumental variable estimates in column 4 and the GLS estimates in column 5 show that the results for income shocks are very robust, while the results on inertia are a bit less stable.

---

[7] It is well-known that the presence of a lagged dependent variable can bias the fixed effects estimator (see e.g., Baltagi, 1995). The problem may be less serious in our panel than in the typical labor context, as the bias diminishes in T and our T is about 40. The IV estimator we use was suggested by Anderson and Hsiao (1981) and Arrellano and Bond (1991) to correct for the bias in dynamic panels.

Table 15.4. *Size of Government: Observable Economic Events 1960–98*

Dep. variable Estimation	Central Spending		Revenue	Central Spending	
	FE Levels	SUR, FE Levels	SUR, FE Levels	IV Diffs.	GLS Diffs.
LAG_SIZE	0.84	0.83	0.83	0.66	
	(.000)	(.000)	(.000)	(.002)	
P* LAG_SIZE	− 0.29	− 0.28	− 0.25	− 0.35	
	(.000)	(.000)	(.000)	(.318)	
M* LAG_SIZE	− 0.05	− 0.04	− 0.04	− 0.12	
	(.073)	(.115)	(.040)	(.804)	
YSHOCK	− 0.19	− 0.19	− 0.07	− 0.24	− 0.23
	(.000)	(.000)	(.092)	(.002)	(.000)
P*YSHOCK	0.27	0.29	0.10	0.32	0.30
	(.000)	(.000)	(.058)	(.000)	(.000)
M*YSHOCK	0.23	0.23	0.11	0.22	0.12
	(.000)	(.000)	(.020)	(.001)	(.001)
Controls	x_2	x_2	x_2	x_2	x_2
# Obs.	1475	1432	1432	1421	1472
R^2	0.81	0.95	0.96		

p-values in brackets. Boldface fonts denote significance at the 10% level.
P and *M* denote interaction with the *PRES* and *MAJ* dummies, respectively.
x_2 is equal to x_1 plus the trend corresponding to *YSHOCK* and the oil price (see Persson and Tabellini, 2000b).
R^2 in the fixed-effects regression (column 1) refers to the within estimator.

Persson and Tabellini (2000b) distinguish between positive and negative income shocks. Their preliminary results point towards an asymmetry: in parliamentary and proportional systems negative income shocks significantly raise the spending share, whereas positive income shocks do not lower the spending share. In presidential and majoritarian systems, on the other hand, positive shocks raise spending, whereas negative shocks do nothing. This suggests ratchet effects in the growth of government, but of a very different nature across political systems.

Understanding better the reasons behind the different adjustments to income shocks is an intriguing topic for future theoretical and empirical research.

ELECTORAL CYCLES. Finally, we look for an electoral cycle in total government spending or tax revenue and whether this cycle depends on political institutions. For this purpose, we expand s_{it} – the country i variables with institution-specific effects on policy – to also include dummies for

Table 15.5. *Size of Government: Electoral Cycles 1960–95*

Dep. variable Estimation	Central Spending		Central Revenue	
	FE, SUR Levels	IV Diffs.	FE, SUR Levels	IV Diffs.
$PRES*EL_t$	0.10	− 0.15	− 0.31	− 0.47
	(.784)	(.710)	(.328)	(.297)
$PRES*EL_{t-1}$	**− 0.80**	**− 1.02**	**0.52**	**0.87**
	(.031)	**(.017)**	**(.095)**	**(.013)**
$PARL*EL_t$	− 0.03	− 0.27	**− 0.31**	**− 0.45**
	(.899)	(.261)	**(.066)**	**(.026)**
$PARL*EL_{t-1}$	− 0.11	− 0.22	0.15	0.31
	(.565)	(.373)	(.366)	(.129)
Controls	x_3	x_3	x_4	x_4
# Obs.	1350	1339	1350	1316
R^2	0.95		0.96	

p-values in brackets. Boldface fonts denote significance at the 10% level.
EL_t and EL_{t-1} are dummy variables for the election and post-election years, respectively.
x_3 is equal to x_2 plus all the variables (including the interaction terms) in column 1 of Table 15.4 minus oil prices plus a set of year dummies; x_4 is constructed exactly as x_3 but with lagged central revenue taking the place of lagged central spending.

election years as well as post-election years. Otherwise, the specification, including all the economic shocks and controls, is the same as in Table 15.4 (except that the we do not include the oil shocks but instead include a set of common time dummies to allow more precise estimates of the electoral cycle). We also use the same estimation methods.

When the institutional dummies are not included, we find a significant and sizeable postelection cycle in spending, with spending cuts being postponed until after the election. For revenues, we find significant cuts in the election year and (less robust) hikes in the postelection year. These results are remarkable in their own right, as earlier studies have typically not found robust evidence fiscal electoral cycles in broad international data sets, with the exception of the recent study by Shi and Svensson (2000).[8]

As Table 15.5 reveals, however, these electoral cycles are highly institution-dependent. The postelection cycle – a cut in spending by about 1% of GDP and a gain in revenue by 0.5% to 1% of GDP – is clearly present only in presidential regimes. The preelection tax cuts, on the other hand,

---

[8] See Alesina, Roubini, and Cohen (1997) and Drazen (2000) for surveys of the earlier literature.

are visible only in parliamentary regimes. As in the case of the adjustment to income shocks, we do not have a good explanation for these differences.

We have also tried to test the prediction of the career-concern model discussed in Section 2 of a stronger preelectoral cycle under majoritarian elections. While the signs of the point estimates are consistent with this prediction, their significance is not robust across samples and estimation methods.

4.2. Composition of Government

Let me turn to the composition of government. Recall that our measures here are central government spending on social security and welfare as a percentage of GDP and the ratio of the same variable to spending on goods and services. Persson and Tabellini (2000b) carry out the same battery of tests as those for government size above. Here, I will just give a brief overview of the results.

The *cross-sectional results* show that broad, non-targeted programs are indeed smaller under majoritarian elections, as predicted by the theory. Ceteris paribus, social security and welfare spending appears to be about 2 percentage points smaller as a share of GDP, and 20–30% lower as a ratio to spending on goods and services. Statistically, these results are more fragile than the results for overall spending. Qualitatively, they are in line with findings of Milesi-Ferretti et al. (2000) for the OECD countries. In this case, however, we find no systematic effect of the regime type.

Unobservable common events are estimated to have a much smaller effect on the spending ratio under majoritarian elections. The cumulative effect on this ratio (from the early 1970s to the 90s) is on the order of 10%. Common events have a smaller effect on social security and welfare in presidential regimes, with a cumulative effect of 4–5% of GDP. But the latter result may largely capture the higher overall growth of government in parliamentary regimes.

Observable economic events again trigger institution-specific adjustments. As for aggregate spending, we find negative effects of income shocks on social security and welfare spending. But these effects are significantly smaller, or even nullified, under majoritarian elections and presidential regimes.

For electoral cycles, finally, the findings are quite intriguing. When we do not condition on political institutions, no electoral cycle is observed. But when we do, we find systematic evidence of both preelection and postelection effects. In connection with a typical election, spending on social security and welfare *rises* by about 0.2% of GDP both before and after the election in countries with proportional elections in parliamentary regimes. Under majoritarian elections in parliamentary countries *no* effects are visible, however, while in presidential regimes social spending tends to *fall* by 0.1–0.2% of GDP after elections (in consistency with the results for aggregate spending). It is perhaps plausible that we should see spending hikes in parliamentary and proportional systems if politicians in these systems indeed have stronger incentives to rely just on broad programs to get elected or reelected, as suggested by the theory surveyed in Section 2. A theory of the composition of the electoral cycle under different political institutions has not yet been worked out, however, and constitutes a further challenge for future research.

4.3. Corruption

It is not easy to find empirical counterparts to rent extraction (r in the simple model) which are comparable across countries. The best proxies are probably those international surveys that try to measure the extent of corruption. I will end by reporting on another ongoing project (Persson, Tabellini, and Trebbi, 2000) that relies on such corruption data.

Transparency International conducts a careful survey, including measures of "grand corruption" at the highest levels of government which conforms well with the theoretical models discussed in Section 2. The TPI score runs from 0 (perfectly clean) to 10 (highly corrupt). Unfortunately, these scores are only available annually from the late nineties. Therefore, we must limit our study to cross-country data.

On the other hand, this study includes finer measures of the electoral rule than the single, dichotomous *MAJ* dummy. Based on the theory, we use two continuous variables. *DISMAG* measures district size (1 minus the inverse of average district magnitude, in legislative elections). *PLIST* instead measures the electoral formula, namely the share of legislators elected via party lists (rather than individually). Both measures run between 0 and 1: a score of 0 on both of them corresponds to first past the post in one-member districts, whereas a score of 1 on both corresponds to full proportionality in very large districts.

The intersection of our corruption, electoral, and socio-economic data limits the study to at most 82 countries. Some results are shown in Table 15.6. The control vector x_b consists of a dozen economic, social, and cultural variables found to correlate closely with corruption in earlier studies (see Persson, Tabellini, and Trebbi, 2000). As the first (empty) column

Table 15.6. *Corruption: Cross Sectional Estimates*

Dep. variable Estimation	TPI-scores 1996–98 WLS				
PRES	− 0.30 (.369)				
MAJ	− 0.61 (.015)				
PLIST			1.48 (.010)	1.51 (.009)	1.40 (.021)
DISMAG			− 1.09 (.101)	− 1.47 (.034)	− 1.40 (.041)
Controls	x_b	x_b	x_b	x_b Leg.	x_b Leg. & Col.
# Obs.	82	81	80	80	80
R^2	0.88	0.90	0.91	0.92	0.93

p-values in brackets. Boldface fonts denote significance at the 10% level.
x_b includes a set of 12 socio-economic variables; Leg. and Col. denote sets of dummies for legal and colonial origin, respectively (see Persson, Tabellini and Trebbi, 2000)

shows, these variables explain close to 90% of the cross-country variance in corruption. Nevertheless, the earlier dichotomous dummies, *PRES* and *MAJ*, improve the fit (in terms of adjusted R^2). Both have the negative sign expected from theory, but only *MAJ* is statistically significant.[9]

But this crude measure turns out to mask two effects running in opposite directions. Larger districts – higher *DISMAG* – lower corruption, whereas greater use of list voting – higher *PLIST* – raises it. Both results are consistent with the theory in Section 2: lower barriers to entry (larger districts) decrease corruption, while blunter career concerns (more party list voting) increase it. As columns 3 to 5 demonstrate, these effects are robust to including other institutional variables, namely the legal and colonial origin of countries, which earlier empirical studies have found to correlate with corruption (see e.g., Treisman, 2000).

These effects are not only statistically significant, but also quantitatively important. Consider Chile, a country considerably less corrupt than

---

[9] We also use alternative, nonparametric matching estimators to allow for more flexible functional forms and correct for potential nonrandom selection (of the electoral rule) on observables (for further discussion see Persson, Tabellini, and Trebbi, 2000). The matching estimates largely accord with the regression estimates, suggesting that majoritarian elections indeed have a negative effect on corruption.

Table 15.7. *Summary of Results*

	PRES (vs. PARL)		MAJ (vs. PR)	
	Evidence	Theory	Evidence	Theory
Size	—	—	0	?
Composition	0	—	—	—
(broad vs. narrow)				
Rents	0	—	—	—
Electoral Cycle	+/−	NA	0	+
Adjustment to events	—	NA	—	NA

its South American neighbors; its residual from the regression in the first column in Table 15.6 is about − 2.5, whereas the average South American country has a residual close to 0. Our results suggest that between a quarter and a half of this difference might be due to Chile's electoral system, the only one in the region where voters cast their ballots for individual candidates under plurality rule in two-seat districts.

5. Final Remarks

Do political institutions shape economic policy? I have argued that this question is theoretically appealing and that posing it offers an opportunity for a convincing application of game theory. I have also reported on ongoing empirical work, which suggests that the answer is a resounding yes.

The results are summarized in Table 15.7. Empirically, presidential regimes are associated with smaller governments than parliamentary regimes, a smaller and less persistent response of spending to income shocks, a stronger postelection cycle in aggregate spending and revenue, but a weaker cycle in social transfers. Majoritarian elections are associated with smaller broad spending programs than proportional elections and with less corruption; they also have smaller (and perhaps less persistent) spending responses to income shocks, and a weaker election cycle in social transfers. Several of these empirical regularities, those marked with black and bold in Table 15.7, are in line with the first wave of theory. But others, marked in gray and bold, are still awaiting a theoretical explanation. This is especially so for the results indicating institution-dependent adjustments of policy to economic events and the institution-dependent electoral cycles.

These are promising first steps in a research program. Much work certainly remains, however. So, where might research go next? One direction is clearly to refine the *theory* of policy. As just noted, our empirical results on policy adjustments and electoral cycles are in search of a theory. To understand them, we need dynamic rather than static models of the relationship between institutions and policy. Dynamic models are also necessary to understand government deficits. The results in Persson and Tabellini (2000b) indeed point to systematic differences in deficit behavior across political institutions.

On the policy side, the research so far has concentrated on government spending. It would be interesting – and certainly feasible – to use similar methods in studying other policy instruments, such as the structure of taxation including trade policy. On the institutional side, one should study the effect on policy of more detailed constitutional features; for instance, different types of checks and balances, or different types of confidence requirements.

This suggests another direction, namely refined *measurement* of political institutions. In some cases this will involve a mere, but time-consuming, compilation of data from existing sources. One example is to trace detailed changes in electoral rules over time; concretely, to compile panel data for variables like *DISMAG* and *PLIST*.

In other cases, better measures will require the collection of new primary data. A concrete example is to construct empirical measures of the separations of powers in different political regimes. As this may be a labor-intensive and open-ended task, it is important to use theory as a guide.[10]

Some *econometric issues* certainly need to be explored in more detail. Even with refined measurement, considerable measurement error will remain in our data. Sharper theory would help in trading off the prospective biases due to measurement and specification errors. Sharper hypotheses, derived from dynamic models, would be especially helpful in avoiding the pitfalls of estimation in dynamic panels.

All in all, a close interplay of theory, measurement and statistical work appears essential for making progress on the broad question I have dealt with in this paper. I hope some readers will provide some help, both in posing the question more precisely, and in probing the data for an answer.

---

[10] Existing attempts to create such measures can be found in Shugart and Carey (1992) and in Beck et al. (2000).

References

Alesina, A., N. Roubini, and G. Cohen (1997). *Political Cycles and the Macroeconomy*, MIT Press.

Anderson, T., and C. Hsiao (1981). "Estimation of Dynamic Models with Error Components," *Journal of the American Statistical Association* 76: 598–606.

Arrellano, M., and S. Bond (1991). "Some Tests of Specification for Panel Data: Monte Carlo Evidence and an Application to Employment Equations," *Review of Economic Studies* 58: 277–97.

Austen-Smith, D., and J. Banks (1999). *Positive Political Theory* I, University of Michigan Press.

Baltagi, B. (1995). *Econometric Analysis of Panel Data*, Wiley.

Beck, T., G. Clarke, A. Groff, P. Keefer and P. Keefer (2000), "New Tools and Tests in Comparative Politcal Economy: The Database of Political Institutions," The World Bank, working paper.

Bingham Powell Jr., G. (1982). *Contemporary Democracies: Participation, Stability and Violence*, Cambridge University Press.

Blanchard, O., and J. Wolfers (2000). "The Role of Shocks and Institutions in the Rise of European Unemployment: The Aggregate Evidence," 1999 Harry Johnson Lecture, *Economic Journal* 100: C1-33.

Cox, G. (1997). *Making Votes Count*, Cambridge University Press.

Diermeier, D., and T. Feddersen (1998). "Cohesion in Legislatures and the Vote of Confidence Procedure," *American Political Science Review* 92: 611–621.

Drazen, A. (2000). *Political Economy in Macroeconomics*, Princeton University Press.

Grossman, G., and E. Helpman (2001). *Special-Interest Politics*, MIT Press.

Holmström, B. (1982). "Managerial Incentive Problems – A Dynamic Perspective", in *Essays in Economics and Management in Honor of Lars Wahlbeck*, Helsinki: Swedish School of Economics.

Inman, R., and D. Rubinfeld (1997). "The Political Economy of Federalism" in Mueller, D., ed., *Perspectives on Public Choice: A Handbook*, Cambridge University Press.

Lijphart, A. (1984). *Democracies*, Yale University Press.

Lijphart, A. (1999). *Patterns of Democracy: Government Forms and Performance in Thirty-Six Countries*, Yale University Press.

Lizzeri, A., and N. Persico (2001). "The Provision of Public Goods under Alternative Electoral Incentives," *American Economic Review*, 91: 225–45.

Milesi-Ferretti, G.-M., Perotti, R., and M. Rostagno (2000). "Electoral Systems and the Composition of Public Spending," Columbia University, working paper.

Mueller, D., ed. (1997). *Perspectives on Public Choice: A Handbook*, Cambridge University Press.

Myerson, R. (1993). "Effectiveness of Electoral Systems for Reducing Government Corruption: A Game Theoretic Analysis," *Games and Economic Behaviour* 5: 118–32.

Myerson, R. (1999). "Theoretical Comparison of Electoral Systems: 1998 Schumpeter Lecture," *European Economic Review* 43: 671–97.

Persson, T., G. Roland, and G. Tabellini (1997). "Separation of Powers and Political Accountability," *Quarterly Journal of Economics* 112: 310–327.

Persson, T., G. Roland, and G. Tabellini (2000). "Comparative Politics and Public Finance," *Journal of Political Economy* 108: 1121–61.

Persson, T., and G. Tabellini (1999). "The Size and Scope of Government: Comparative Politics with Rational Politicians," 1998 Alfred Marshall Lecture, *European Economic Review* 43: 699–735.

Persson, T., and G. Tabellini (2000a). *Political Economics: Explaining Economic Policy*, MIT Press.

Persson, T., and G. Tabellini (2000b). "Political Institutions and Economic Policy Outcomes: What Are the Stylized Facts?" Institute for International Economic Studies, working paper.

Persson, T., G. Tabellini, and F. Trebbi (2000). "Electoral Rules and Corruption," Institute for International Economic Studies, working paper.

Poterba, J., and J. von Hagen, eds. (1999). *Fiscal Rules and Fiscal Performance*, University of Chicago Press.

Shi, M., and J. Svensson (2000). "Conditional Political Business Cycles: Theory and Evidence," Institute for International Economic Studies, working paper.

Shugart, M., and J. Carey (1992). *Presidents and Assemblies: Constutional Design and Electoral Dynamics*, Cambridge University Press.

Taagepera, R., and M. Shugart (1989). *Seats and Votes: The Effects and Determinants of Electoral Systems*, Yale University Press.

Treisman, D. (2000). "The Causes of Corruption: A Cross-National Study," *Journal of Public Economics* 76: 399–457.

Author Index

457

Subject Index